THE SCHOLAR'S HAGGADAH

THE SCHOLAR'S HAGGADAH

Ashkenazic, Sephardic, and Oriental Versions

with a historical-literary commentary by

Heinrich Guggenheimer

JASON ARONSON INC.
Northvale, New Jersey
London

First Jason Aronson Inc. softcover edition—1998

10 9 8 7 6 5 4 3 2 1

Library of Congress Cataloging-in-Publication Data

Haggadah. English & Hebrew
The scholar's haggadah : Ashkenazic, Sephardic, and
Oriental versions : with a historical-literary
commentary / Heinrich Guggenheimer.
p. cm.
Hebrew text accompanied by English translation.
Includes index.
ISBN 1-56821-287-9 (hardcover)
ISBN 0-7657-6040-1 (softcover)
1. Haggadot—Texts. 2. Seder—Liturgy—Texts. 3. Judaism—
Liturgy—Texts. 4. Haggadah. I. Guggenheimer, Heinrich W.
(Heinrich Walter), 1924- . II. Title.
BM674.643.G83 1995
296.4'37—dc20

94-26392

Manufactured in the United States of America. Jason Aronson Inc. offers books and cassettes. For information and catalog write to Jason Aronson Inc., 230 Livingston Street, Northvale38, New Jersey 07647.

Dedicated to the memory of my teacher

Rabbi Abraham Hillel Żulicki z"l
מוהר״ר אברהם הלל בן מרדכי זאב ז״ל

Zduńska Wola 1907 - Basel 1994

Contents

Preface

This book gives the complete text of the Passover *Haggadah* following all contemporary Jewish groups and a commentary that traces the history of the text and the rituals of the Passover night based on the earliest available sources.

The *Seder*, the ceremony of Passover night, stands alone among the many Jewish rituals in that it is a family celebration, not a group celebration requiring the attendance of at least ten adult males. The text of the main part of the *Haggadah* is remarkably uniform for all Jewish groups; this can be taken as a sign of the high antiquity of the details of this family celebration.

Many commentaries have been written on the *Haggadah* during the last one thousand years. Practically all of them were written to explain either the spiritual meaning or the ritual details of the ceremonies. The few historical investigations (listed in the bibliography under "Modern Scholarship") deal mostly with the current Ashkenazic text. Even the *Complete Haggadah* of Rabbi M. Kasher, which contains an extensive list of variant readings, fails to classify these readings by groups and, therefore, cannot readily be used for historical research. The present *Haggadah* is the first to treat the texts of all Jewish groups on an equal footing and to use the divergences or concurrences of the texts as a key to the history of the text and an understanding of its development.

The text of the *Haggadah* is accompanied by an English translation. The commentary, in English, contains translations of most of the relevant texts in Hebrew and Aramaic from the *Talmud* and later rabbinic literature. Since much of talmudic literature is based on an understanding of the biblical text that cannot be found in the standard translations, a special effort has been made to introduce the reader to the talmudic understanding of the biblical text. The reader is invited to compare the translations given here of biblical verses with the standard translations; in many cases he will find a new viewpoint in the interpretation of the texts.

To the novice, the commentary offers a key to the roots of the Passover ceremonies and an introduction to the thought and practice of talmudic-rabbinic Judaism. To the reader acquainted with talmudic texts, the book offers a history of the development of text and practice of the *Seder* celebration. It is found that while Yemenite Jewry still follows text and prescriptions of Maimonides practically in their original form, unchanged for at least 800 years, European Ashkenazic and Sephardic practice has undergone many changes. This fact has a very simple explanation. While Yemenite Jews were always oppressed and their history is full of persecutions and migrations, the Moslem rulers of their country never extended their persecutions to Jewish books. One great change occurred for part of the Yemenite population when they adopted the imported printed prayer book of the "Syrian" rite, which is the standard Sephardic text. The Yemenite text given and discussed here is the "local" (בלאדי *baladī*) text of the manuscript (and recently printed Israeli) prayer books. On the other hand, the history of the Jews in Europe is not only one of almost continuous pogroms starting with the First Crusade in 1096, but also, in particular from 1242 to 1559, one of a permanent war of the Church against Jewish learning that resulted in many public burnings of the *Talmud* and rabbinic treatises. A look at the bibliography of the present book shows that the surviving older texts were all edited during the last 150 years, mostly from one or two manuscripts preserved in Christian ecclesiastical or princely libraries (i.e., stolen before the burning of less valuable books). As a consequence, the rabbinic authorities of the late Middle Ages and the Renaissance had before them only the texts of their immediate predecessors, and much of the continuity and stability of older Jewish practice was lost. The war of the inquisition against Jewish tradition was defeated only by the printing press that could reproduce standard texts at a cheap price for distribution in many countries. A study of the history of a particular set of Jewish practices, as given in the present book, is therefore also a study of the survival of Jewish thought. Since prayer books were not usually burned, the texts of the prayers themselves came through that period of persecution in better shape than the theoretical texts. The changes in Ashkenazic and Sephardic texts can be attributed either to the influence of later mystical teachings or to changes introduced by editors without access to the large medieval literature on prayer texts. This is treated in detail in the commentary.

The present work has evolved from my notes and commentaries on the *Haggadah* regularly presented at our family's

Seder table. My sincere thanks go to my wife who encouraged me to collect and organize these notes into a book.

West Hempstead, N.Y.
November 1994

Haggadah

Preliminary Notes

The translation is based on the text common to all rituals with variations indicated by *Italics*. Rituals are indicated by
A Ashkenazic (AE Eastern Ashkenazic , AW Western Ashkenazic),
S Sephardic, Y Yemenite *balādi.*

Where necessary, translations are given for the three rituals separately in 10 point Times Roman.

Instructions are printed in 10 point or 8 point Times Roman.

The Ashkenazic text follows the consensus of the seventeenth-century printed *Haggadot* from Amsterdam and the eighteenth-century printed *Haggadot* from Germany and Austria. The vocalization has been changed according to the principle (established by Eliahu of Wilna [1722–1797], Isaac Stanow [1732–1804], and Wolf Heidenheim [1737–1832] and accepted by most of Ashkenazic Jewry) that prayer texts should be punctuated by the rules of biblical Hebrew rather than rabbinic Hebrew. Heidenheim also was the first to print the *meteg* (ֽ-) when the accent is not on the last syllable. This rule is also followed in the present *Haggadah.* In Hebrew texts common to all three rituals and printed in *sans serif,* the *meteg* is omitted but the *maqqef* (־) is included in biblical quotes (the *maqqef* is ignored in Sephardic and Yemenite texts as it was ignored in older Ashkenazic texts).

The Sephardic text is that of the Benamozegh Livorno *Maḥzor,* the standard for European, North-African, and Oriental Sephardic communities. In this standard, the *meteg* (ֽ-) is used to indicate *wide qamaẓ* (*ā*).

The Yemenite text follows the printed Tiklāl, Jerusalem 1960.

Hebrew Fonts Used

Instructions and text common to all rituals:

Sans Serif אבגדהוזחטיכלמנסעפצקרשת

Ashkenazic text: Frank-Rühl אבגדהוזחטיכלמנסעפצקרשת

Sephardic text: Modern אבגדהוזחטיכלמנסעפצקרשת

Yemenite text: Vienna Siddur אבגדהוזחטיכלמנסעפצקרשת

The Removal of Ḥameẓ

After nightfall on the Eve of the Fourteenth of Nisan (or, if the Fourteenth falls on a Sabbath, on the Eve of the Thirteenth), the house is searched by candlelight and all leavened matter is collected. Before this is done, the following benediction is recited:

Praised are You o Lord, our God, King of the Universe, Who has sanctified us with His commandments and commanded us to dispose of leavened matter.

After the leavened matter has been collected, the following declaration is made:

All leavened matter [A] *and all sour dough* in my possession which I have not seen and have not removed [AE] *or of which I have no knowledge* shall be considered destroyed [AE]*and ownerless* as the dust of the earth.

The leavened matter which has been found is carefully put away and is burned on the following morning around 10 A.M. together with the remainders of leavened matter used for breakfast. Afterward the following is said:

Ashkenazic version

All leavened matter and all sour dough in my possession which I have or have not seen, which I have or have not removed [E] *or of which I have no knowledge* shall be considered destroyed [E]*and ownerless* as the dust of the earth.

סדר ביעור חמץ

אור לי״ד בניסן, וכשחל י״ד בשבת אור לי״ג, בודקים את החמץ לאור הנר מיד אחר תפילת ערבית. וקודם הבדיקה יברך:

בָּרוּךְ אַתָּה יי אֱלֹהֵינוּ מֶלֶךְ הָעוֹלָם אֲשֶׁר קִדְּשָׁנוּ בְּמִצְוֹתָיו וְצִוָּנוּ עַל בִּעוּר חָמֵץ.

מיד אחר הבדיקה יבטל כל חמץ שברשותו הבלתי ידוע לו ויאמר:

נוסח אשכנז

כָּל־חֲמִירָא וְכָל־חֲמִיעָא דְאִיכָּא בִרְשׁוּתִי, דְּלָא חֲמִיתֵיהּ וּדְלָא בִעַרְתֵּיהּ וּדְלָא יְדַעְנָא לֵיהּ לִיבָּטֵל וְלֶהֱוֵי הֶפְקֵר כְּעַפְרָא דְאַרְעָא.

נוסח אשכנז המערבי

כָּל־חֲמִירָא וַחֲמִיעָא דְאִיכָּא בִרְשׁוּתִי, דְּלָא חֲמִיתֵיהּ וּדְלָא בִעַרְתֵּיהּ לִיבָּטֵל וְלֶהֱוֵי כְעַפְרָא דְאַרְעָא.

נוסח ספרד ותימן

כָּל חֲמִרָא דְאִכָּא בִרְשׁוּתִי. דְּלָא חֲזִיתֵיהּ. וּדְלָא בִעַרְתֵּיהּ. לֶהֱוֵי בָּטִיל וְחָשִׁיב כְּעַפְרָא דְאַרְעָא.

החמץ שנמצא נוהגים לשמרו עד שעת הביעור ולשורפו בערב פסח בסוף השעה החמישית (ואם ערב פסח בשבת שורפם ביום שישי באותה שעה) ומבטלים פעם שניה קודם שעה שישית בערב פסח:

נוסח אשכנז

כָּל־חֲמִירָא וְכָל־חֲמִיעָא דְאִיכָּא בִרְשׁוּתִי, דַּחֲמִתֵּיהּ וּדְלָא חֲמִיתֵיהּ, דְּבִעַרְתֵּיהּ וּדְלָא בִעַרְתֵּיהּ וּדְלָא יְדַעְנָא לֵיהּ, לִיבָּטֵל וְלֶהֱוֵי הֶפְקֵר כְּעַפְרָא דְאַרְעָא.

נוסח אשכנז המערבי

כָּל־חֲמִירָא וַחֲמִיעָא דְאִיכָּא בִרְשׁוּתִי, דַּחֲמִתֵּיהּ וּדְלָא חֲמִיתֵיהּ, דְּבִעַרְתֵּיהּ וּדְלָא בִעַרְתֵּיהּ, לִיבָּטֵל וְלֶהֱוֵי כְעַפְרָא דְאַרְעָא.

Sephardic and Oriental version

All leavened matter in my possession which I have or have not seen, which I have or have not removed shall be considered destroyed as the dust of the earth.

In the Yemenite ritual, any person who does not understand Aramaic should say in Hebrew:

All leavened matter that is in my house shall be considered destroyed.

Sephardic prayer after the burning of the *Ḥameẓ*:

May it be Your will, Lord our God and God of our fathers, to have mercy on us and save us from the prohibition of leavened matter even in the most minute amounts, us, our family, and all of Israel, in this year and the coming years, all the days of our lives. Just as we did remove *ḥameẓ* from our homes and burned it, so we pray that we should be able to remove evil inclinations from within us always, all the days of our lives, and we should merit always to cling to good intentions, to Your Torah, to the fear and love of You: we, our children and grandchildren. May this be Your eternal pleasure. Amen Selah.

נוסח ספרד ותימן

כָּל חֲמִרָא דְאִכָּא בִרְשׁוּתִי. דִי חֲזִיתֵיהּ. דְּלָא חֲזִיתֵיהּ. דִּי בְעַרְתֵּיהּ וּדְלָא בְעַרְתֵּיהּ. לֶהֱוֵי בָטִיל וְחָשִׁיב כְּעַפְרָא דְאַרְעָא.

נוסח תימן

מי שאינו מבין לשון ארמית יאמר: **כָּל חָמֵץ שֶׁיֵּשׁ לִי בְּתוֹךְ בֵּיתִי יְהֵא בָטֵל.**

תחינה

יהי רצון מלפניך ה׳ אלהינו ואלהי אבותינו שתרחם עלינו ותצילנו מאיסור חמץ אפילו מכל שהוא לנו ולכל בני ביתינו ולכל ישראל בשנה זו ובכל שנה ושנה כל ימי חיינו וכשם שבערנו חמץ מבתינו ושרפנוהו כך תזכנו לבער היצר הרע מקרבנו תמיד כל ימי חיינו ותזכנו לדבק ביצר הטוב ובתורתך וביראתך ואהבתך תמיד אנחנו וזרענו וזרע זרענו כן יהי רצון אמן נצח סלה ועד.

The Order of the Night

Qiddush, Washing of the Hands;

Celery, Breaking of the *Maẓẓah;*

Recital, Washing of the Hands;

Blessing Bread and *Maẓẓah;*

Bitter Herbs, Hillel's Sandwich;

Festive Meal;

Hidden *Maẓẓah,* Grace;

Hallel, Conclusion.

סימני הסדר

קַדֵּשׁ וּרְחַץ
כַּרְפַּס יַחַץ
מַגִּיד רָחְצָה
מוֹצִיא מַצָּה

מָרוֹר כּוֹרֵךְ
שֻׁלְחָן עוֹרֵךְ
צָפוּן בָּרֵךְ
הַלֵּל נִרְצָה

Prayer

The following prayer may be said by the head of the household in Sephardic and Yemenite families.

Master of the Universe! We know that we are flesh and that neither we nor any creatures have the power to grasp Your majesty and greatness as it is said (*Ps.* 147:5): "Our Master is great and powerful; His understanding cannot be told," even if we could understand all sciences, the combinations of Your Holy Names, the true intentions of each and every single benediction and commandment, all the particular actions and combinations of the holy heavenly properties that might derive from them; but all the more since we are flesh, we do not have the understanding of Adam and nobody among us knows anything.

Therefore, may it be Your pleasure o Lord, our God and God of our fathers, that You may count and accept every single commandment that we shall now perform before You, the commandment of the Four Cups, the commandments regarding dippings, the commandment of discussing the Exodus from Egypt, the commandment of eating *maẓẓah*, bitter herbs, *ḥaroset*, and *afiqomen* (*Ps.* 90:17): "Let the work of our hands be sustained" as if we had grasped the intentions of all conjunctions of Holy Names generated by them and all the particular actions and combinations of holy, heavenly secrets, their consequences and secondary consequences. May it please You to join our general good intentions to our particular deeds for all the commandments that will be performed by us in this night; may they rise before You together with all performances of these commandments realized by Your children who know and concentrate on all the proper intentions for each one of these commandments.

We now perform these commandments for the Oneness of the Holy, praised be He, and His glory, in awe and love to realize the unity of the Names YH and WH in perfect unity in the name of all of Israel, to reconstitute their roots in Heaven in appropriate measure in all their details, rules, and minutiae, to fulfill the intention of our Creator Who sanctified us with His commandments and commanded us to perform these commandments to please Him, cause abundant blessing in all worlds, and turn our actions or speech into the Lord's vessels, the actions to bring our work into the inner sanctum and our speech to bring the great light to hover over them. May the efficient performance of these commandments reconstitute all the sparks that fell into the peels, reconstitute all 613 commandments contained in each one of these commandments, cause combinations of the Four Letters of the Holy Name, and purify our persons, spirits, and souls to be worthy to wake the Lower Waters through the performance of the commandments of this night; may they arise for Divine pleasure to awake the Friend's love, Amen Selah.

(*Ps.* 90:17) May the grace of the Lord, our God, be upon us! May the work of our hands be sustained upon us! May He sustain the work of our hands!

תחינה

תחינה לבעל הבית לפני הסדר

רבונו של עולם, אתה יודע כי בשר אנחנו ואין בנו ולא בשום בריה כח להשיג מעלתך וגדולתך כדבר האמור גדול אדונינו ורב כח לתבונתו אין מספר; גם אם היינו משכילים בכל חכמה ובצירוף שמותיך הקדושים וכוונת כל ברכה וברכה ומצוה בפני עצמה ובכל הייחודים וזיווגי מדות הקדושות העליונות הראויות לבוא על ידיהם וכל שכן כי בשר אנחנו ולא בינת אדם לנו ואין אתנו יודע עד מה. לכן יהי רצון מלפניך יי אלהינו ואלהי אבותינו שיהא חשוב ומרוצה לפניך כל מצוה ומצוה הנעשות על ידינו עתה לפניך הן במצות ארבע כוסות הן במצות טיבולים ובמצות סיפור יציאת מצרים הן במצות אכילת מצה ומרור וחרוסת ואפיקומן מעשה ידינו כוננה עלינו כאלו נכוין בכל צירופי שמות הקדושים העולים מתוכם ובכל הייחודים וזיווגי סודות הקדושות העליונות וגידולי גידוליהן הראויות לבוא על ידיהם ותצרף מחשבתנו לטובה דרך כלל למעשה פרטיות לכל המצוות אשר יעשו על ידינו בלילה הזה ויעלו לפניך עם שאר מעשה המצוות האלה הנעשות על ידי בניך היודעים והמכונים כל הכונות הראויות לתת לכל מצוה ומצוה מאלה. ואולם אנחנו עושים אלה המצוות לשם יחוד קודשא בריך הוא ושכינתיה בדחילו ורחימו ליחדא שם י״ה בו״ה ביחודא שלים בשם כל ישראל לתקן את שרשם במקום עליון בשיעור קומה בכל פרטיהם ותיקוניהם ודקדוקיהן לעשות את כונת יוצרנו אשר קדשנו במצותיו וצונו לעשות המצוות האלה לתת נחת רוח לפניו ולגרום שפע ברכה רבה בכל העולמות ולהביא על ידי מעשה או כלי הדיבור אשר נעשה בו המעשה כלי יי. ובמעשה עצמו להביא אל הקודש פנימה ובדיבור להביא המאור הגדול להיות חופף עליהם מלמעלה ובכח סגולת אלה המצוות יתוקנו כל הנצוצות שנפלו על ידינו תוך הקליפות ולתקן בכל תרי״ג מצוות הנכללות בכל מצוה ומצוה מאלו ולגרום זיווג בארבע אותיות השם הקדוש ולזכך נפשנו רוחנו ונשמתנו להיות ראויות לעורר מיין תתאין על ידי מעשה המצוות הנעשות בלילה הזה ותעלה לרצון לעורר אהבת דודים אמן סלה.

ויהי נועם יי אלהינו עלינו ומעשה ידינו כוננה עלינו ומעשה ידינו כוננהו:

Qiddush

The Seder starts at nightfall with *Qiddush*. The First Cup is filled and *Qiddush* is recited. On Sabbath, the words and sentences given in small print are added.

Ashkenazic Ritual

(*Gen.* 1:31–2:3) (There was evening, there was morning) The Sixth Day. Heaven and earth and all their hosts were completed. God completed His work on the Seventh Day; He rested on the Seventh Day from all His work which He had done. God blessed the Seventh Day, and sanctified it, for on it He rested from all His work, which God had created in doing.

Praised are You o Lord, our God, King of the Universe, Creator of the fruit of the vine.

Praised are You o Lord, our God, King of the Universe, Who chose us from all peoples, exalted us over all tongues, and sanctified us through His commandments. You gave us, o Lord our God, in love Sabbath days for rest, festivals for joy, holidays of pilgrimage at stated times for rejoicing, this Sabbath day and this holiday of unleavened bread, the season of our liberation, in love a holy assembly in remembrance of the Exodus from Egypt. Truly You chose us and sanctified us above all peoples and let us inherit Your sacred Sabbath and festivals in love and goodwill, in joy and rejoicing. Praised are You, o Lord, Who sanctifies the Sabbath, Israel, and the Holidays.

On Saturday night, add:

Praised are You o Lord, our God, King of the Universe, Creator of the illuminating fire.

Praised are You o Lord, our God, King of the Universe, Who separates between holy and secular, between light and darkness, between Israel and the Gentiles, between the Seventh Day and the six days of work. You made a distinction between the holiness of the Sabbath and the holiness of holidays, You sanctified the Seventh Day compared to the six days of work, You separated and sanctified Your people Israel with Your holiness. Praised are You o Lord, Who separates between sanctity and sanctity.

Praised are You o Lord, our God, King of the Universe, Who has kept us alive, maintained us, and enabled us to reach this festive time.

One drinks all or most of the cup while reclining toward the left.

קדש

עם צאת הכוכבים מוזגים את הכוס הראשון ואומרים קידוש.
בשבת מוסיפים את המילים הנדפסות באותיות קטנות.

נוסח אשכנז

(וַיְהִי עֶרֶב וַיְהִי בֹקֶר) יוֹם הַשִּׁשִּׁי. וַיְכֻלּוּ הַשָּׁמַיִם וְהָאָרֶץ וְכָל־צְבָאָם. וַיְכַל אֱלֹהִים בַּיּוֹם הַשְּׁבִיעִי מְלַאכְתּוֹ אֲשֶׁר עָשָׂה וַיִּשְׁבֹּת בַּיּוֹם הַשְּׁבִיעִי מִכָּל־מְלַאכְתּוֹ אֲשֶׁר עָשָׂה. וַיְבָרֶךְ אֱלֹהִים אֶת־יוֹם הַשְּׁבִיעִי וַיְקַדֵּשׁ אֹתוֹ, כִּי בוֹ שָׁבַת מִכָּל־מְלַאכְתּוֹ אֲשֶׁר בָּרָא אֱלֹהִים לַעֲשׂוֹת.

בָּרוּךְ אַתָּה יי אֱלֹהֵינוּ מֶלֶךְ הָעוֹלָם בּוֹרֵא פְּרִי הַגָּפֶן.

בָּרוּךְ אַתָּה יי אֱלֹהֵינוּ מֶלֶךְ הָעוֹלָם אֲשֶׁר בָּחַר בָּנוּ מִכָּל־עָם וְרוֹמְמָנוּ מִכָּל־לָשׁוֹן וְקִדְּשָׁנוּ בְּמִצְוֹתָיו. וַתִּתֶּן־לָנוּ יי אֱלֹהֵינוּ בְּאַהֲבָה (שַׁבָּתוֹת לִמְנוּחָה וּ)מוֹעֲדִים לְשִׂמְחָה, חַגִּים וּזְמַנִּים לְשָׂשׂוֹן, אֶת־יוֹם (הַשַּׁבָּת הַזֶּה וְאֶת־יוֹם) חַג הַמַּצּוֹת הַזֶּה זְמַן חֵרוּתֵנוּ (בְּאַהֲבָה) מִקְרָא קֹדֶשׁ זֵכֶר לִיצִיאַת מִצְרָיִם. כִּי בָנוּ בָחַרְתָּ וְאוֹתָנוּ קִדַּשְׁתָּ מִכָּל־הָעַמִּים (וְשַׁבָּת) וּמוֹעֲדֵי קָדְשֶׁךָ (בְּאַהֲבָה וּבְרָצוֹן) בְּשִׂמְחָה וּבְשָׂשׂוֹן הִנְחַלְתָּנוּ. בָּרוּךְ אַתָּה יי מְקַדֵּשׁ (הַשַּׁבָּת וְ)יִשְׂרָאֵל וְהַזְּמַנִּים.

במוצאי שבת מוסיפים:

בָּרוּךְ אַתָּה יי אֱלֹהֵינוּ מֶלֶךְ הָעוֹלָם בּוֹרֵא מְאוֹרֵי הָאֵשׁ.

בָּרוּךְ אַתָּה יי אֱלֹהֵינוּ מֶלֶךְ הָעוֹלָם הַמַּבְדִּיל בֵּין קֹדֶשׁ לְחוֹל, בֵּין אוֹר לְחֹשֶׁךְ, בֵּין יִשְׂרָאֵל לָעַמִּים, בֵּין יוֹם הַשְּׁבִיעִי לְשֵׁשֶׁת יְמֵי הַמַּעֲשֶׂה. בֵּין קְדֻשַּׁת שַׁבָּת לִקְדֻשַּׁת יוֹם טוֹב הִבְדַּלְתָּ וְאֶת־יוֹם הַשְּׁבִיעִי מִשֵּׁשֶׁת יְמֵי הַמַּעֲשֶׂה קִדַּשְׁתָּ, הִבְדַּלְתָּ וְקִדַּשְׁתָּ אֶת־עַמְּךָ יִשְׂרָאֵל בִּקְדֻשָּׁתֶךָ. בָּרוּךְ אַתָּה יי הַמַּבְדִּיל בֵּין קֹדֶשׁ לְקֹדֶשׁ.

בָּרוּךְ אַתָּה יי אֱלֹהֵינוּ מֶלֶךְ הָעוֹלָם שֶׁהֶחֱיָנוּ וְקִיְּמָנוּ וְהִגִּיעָנוּ לַזְּמַן הַזֶּה.

ושותים את רוב הכוס בהסבת שמאל.

Sephardic Ritual

Preparatory prayer by the head of the house:

It is my intention to perform the First Cup of the Four Cups for the Oneness of the Holy One, praise to Him, and His glory, through Him Who is hidden and secret, in the name of all of Israel.

On Sabbath, the words and sentences given in small print are added:

(*Gen.* 1:31-2:3) (There was evening, there was morning) The Sixth Day. Heaven and earth and all their hosts were completed. God completed His work on the Seventh Day; He rested on the Seventh Day from all His work. God blessed the Seventh Day and sanctified it because on it He rested from all His work which God had created in doing.

(*Lev.* 23:4) These are the festivals of the Lord, holy assemblies, that you shall call at their stated times.

Is it agreeable, gentlemen?

Praised are You o Lord, our God, King of the Universe, Creator of the fruit of the vine.

Praised are You o Lord, our God, King of the Universe, Who chose us from all peoples, exalted us over all tongues, and sanctified us through His commandments. You gave us, o Lord our God, in love Sabbath days for rest, festivals for joy, holidays of pilgrimage at stated times for rejoicing, this Sabbath day and this holiday of unleavened bread, this good day of holy assembly, the season of our liberation, in love a holy assembly in remembrance of the Exodus from Egypt. Truly You chose us and sanctified us above all peoples and let us inherit Your holy Sabbath and festive times in love and goodwill, in joy and rejoicing. Praised are You, o Lord, Who sanctifies the Sabbath, Israel, and the holidays.

On Saturday night, add:

Praised are You o Lord, our God, King of the Universe, Creator of the illuminating fire.

Praised are You o Lord, our God, King of the Universe, Who separates between holy and secular, between light and darkness, between Israel and the Gentiles, and between the Seventh Day and the six days of work. You made a distinction between the holiness of the Sabbath and the holiness of holidays, You sanctified the Seventh Day compared to the six days of work, You separated and sanctified Your people Israel in Your holiness. Praised are You o Lord, Who separates between sanctity and sanctity.

Praised are You o Lord, our God, King of the Universe, Who has kept us alive, maintained us, and enabled us to reach this festive time.

One drinks all or most of the cup while reclining toward the left.

נוסח ספרד

הריני רוצה לקיים כוס ראשון מארבעה כוסות לשם ייחוד קב״ה ושכינתיה
על ידי ההוא טמיר ונעלם בשם כל ישראל.

בשבת מוסיפים את המילים הנדפסות באותיות קטנות.

(וַיְהִי עֶרֶב וַיְהִי בוֹקֶר) יוֹם הַשִּׁשִּׁי. וַיְכֻלּוּ הַשָּׁמַיִם וְהָאָרֶץ וְכָל־צְבָאָם. וַיְכַל
אֱלֹהִים בַּיּוֹם הַשְּׁבִיעִי מְלַאכְתּוֹ אֲשֶׁר עָשָׂה וַיִּשְׁבּוֹת בַּיּוֹם הַשְּׁבִיעִי מִכָּל מְלַאכְתּוֹ
אֲשֶׁר עָשָׂה. וַיְבָרֶךְ אֱלֹהִים אֶת יוֹם הַשְּׁבִיעִי וַיְקַדֵּשׁ אוֹתוֹ, כִּי בוֹ שָׁבַת מִכָּל
מְלַאכְתּוֹ אֲשֶׁר בָּרָא אֱלֹהִים לַעֲשׂוֹת.

אֵלֶּה מוֹעֲדֵי יי מִקְרָאֵי קֹדֶשׁ אֲשֶׁר תִּקְרְאוּ אֹתָם בְּמוֹעֲדָם.
סַבְרִי מָרָנָן.
בָּרוּךְ אַתָּה יי אֱלֹהֵינוּ מֶלֶךְ הָעוֹלָם בּוֹרֵא פְּרִי הַגָּפֶן.
בָּרוּךְ אַתָּה יי אֱלֹהֵינוּ מֶלֶךְ הָעוֹלָם אֲשֶׁר בָּחַר בָּנוּ מִכָּל עָם וְרוֹמְמָנוּ מִכָּל לָשׁוֹן וְקִדְּשָׁנוּ בְּמִצְוֹתָיו. וַתִּתֶּן לָנוּ יי אֱלֹהֵינוּ בְּאַהֲבָה, (שַׁבָּתוֹת לִמְנוּחָה וּ)מוֹעֲדִים לְשִׂמְחָה, חַגִּים וּזְמַנִּים לְשָׂשׂוֹן, אֶת יוֹם (הַשַּׁבָּת הַזֶּה אֶת יוֹם) חַג הַמַּצּוֹת הַזֶּה, אֶת יוֹם טוֹב מִקְרָא קֹדֶשׁ הַזֶּה, זְמַן חֵרוּתֵינוּ בְּאַהֲבָה מִקְרָא קֹדֶשׁ זֵכֶר לִיצִיאַת מִצְרָיִם. כִּי בָנוּ בָחַרְתָּ וְאוֹתָנוּ קִדַּשְׁתָּ מִכָּל־הָעַמִּים (וְשַׁבָּתוֹת) וּמוֹעֲדֵי קָדְשְׁךָ (בְּאַהֲבָה וּבְרָצוֹן) בְּשִׂמְחָה וּבְשָׂשׂוֹן הִנְחַלְתָּנוּ. בָּרוּךְ אַתָּה יי מְקַדֵּשׁ (הַשַּׁבָּת וְ)יִשְׂרָאֵל וְהַזְּמַנִּים.

בְּמוֹצָאֵי שַׁבָּת מוֹסִיפִים:
בָּרוּךְ אַתָּה יי אֱלֹהֵינוּ מֶלֶךְ הָעוֹלָם בּוֹרֵא מְאוֹרֵי הָאֵשׁ.

בָּרוּךְ אַתָּה יי אֱלֹהֵינוּ מֶלֶךְ הָעוֹלָם הַמַּבְדִּיל בֵּין קֹדֶשׁ לְחוֹל וּבֵין אוֹר לְחֹשֶׁךְ וּבֵין יִשְׂרָאֵל לָעַמִּים וּבֵין יוֹם הַשְּׁבִיעִי לְשֵׁשֶׁת יְמֵי הַמַּעֲשֶׂה. בֵּין קְדֻשַּׁת שַׁבָּת לִקְדֻשַּׁת יוֹם טוֹב הִבְדַּלְתָּ וְאֶת יוֹם הַשְּׁבִיעִי מִשֵּׁשֶׁת יְמֵי הַמַּעֲשֶׂה קִדַּשְׁתָּ, וְהִבְדַּלְתָּ וְקִדַּשְׁתָּ אֶת עַמְּךָ יִשְׂרָאֵל בִּקְדֻשָּׁתֶךָ. בָּרוּךְ אַתָּה יי הַמַּבְדִּיל בֵּין קֹדֶשׁ לְקֹדֶשׁ.

בָּרוּךְ אַתָּה יי אֱלֹהֵינוּ מֶלֶךְ הָעוֹלָם שֶׁהֶחֱיָנוּ וְקִיְּמָנוּ וְהִגִּיעָנוּ
לַזְּמַן הַזֶּה.
ושותים את רוב הכוס בהסבת שמאל.

Ritual of Yemen and the Island of Djerba

(*Ps.* 116:13) I lift up the cup of salvation, I invoke the Name of the Lord.
(*Ps.* 117:1) Give thanks to the Lord, the truly Good One; truly His kindness is forever.
(*Ps.* 23) A Psalm of David; the Lord is my shepherd, I shall not want.
On grassy pastures He will let me rest, to quiet waters He will lead me.
He restores my soul, He leads me to paths of justice for His Name.
Walking even through a very dark valley, I fear no evil for You are with me.
Your rod and Your staff comfort me.
You prepare before me a table against my enemies, you anoint my head with oil, my cup overflows.
Surely goodness and grace shall follow me all the days of my life,
And I shall dwell in the house of the Lord forever.

On the Sabbath, the words in small print are added.

(*Gen.* 1:31–2:3) (There was evening, there was morning) The Sixth Day. Heaven and earth and all their hosts were completed. God completed His work on the Seventh Day, He rested on the Seventh Day from all His work. God blessed the Seventh Day and sanctified it because on it He rested from all His work, which God had created in doing.

Is it agreeable, gentlemen? The company answers: To life!
Praised are You o Lord, our God, King of the Universe, Creator of the fruit of the vine.

Praised are You o Lord, our God, King of the Universe, Who sanctified us from all peoples, exalted us above all tongues, chose us and made us great, wanted us and gave us splendor.

As a heave-offering He separated us from all peoples, a desirable land He let us inherit.
He sanctified His name in the world, for the sake of the Patriarchs who did His will.
Great things He did for us, His wonders are beyond description.
Assembly of Saints He called us, Desirable Vineyard and Enjoyable Plantation.
He called them Treasure for His name, as First Offering He took them from all peoples.
They are compared to the heavenly hosts, and named like the stars of heaven.
They were superior in the world, and honored by all nations.
The splendor of their faces is like the splendor of the sun, their looks like angels.
Kings will see them and rise, princes prostrate themselves
For the sake of the faithful Lord of Hosts, of the Holy of Israel Who chose them.

נוסח תימן והאי ג׳רבה

כּוֹס יְשׁוּעוֹת אֶשָּׂא וּבְשֵׁם יי אֶקְרָא. הוֹדוּ לַיי כִּי טוֹב כִּי לְעוֹלָם חַסְדּוֹ.

מִזְמוֹר לְדָוִד, יי רֹעִי לֹא אֶחְסָר.
בִּנְאוֹת דֶּשֶׁא יַרְבִּיצֵנִי, עַל מֵי מְנוּחוֹת יְנַהֲלֵנִי.
נַפְשִׁי יְשׁוֹבֵב, יַנְחֵנִי בְמַעְגְּלֵי צֶדֶק לְמַעַן שְׁמוֹ.
גַּם כִּי אֵלֵךְ בְּגֵיא צַלְמָוֶת לֹא אִירָא רָע כִּי אַתָּה עִמָּדִי,
שִׁבְטְךָ וּמִשְׁעַנְתֶּךָ הֵמָּה יְנַחֲמֻנִי.
תַּעֲרֹךְ לְפָנַי שֻׁלְחָן נֶגֶד צֹרְרָי, דִּשַּׁנְתָּ בַשֶּׁמֶן רֹאשִׁי, כּוֹסִי רְוָיָה.
אַךְ טוֹב וָחֶסֶד יִרְדְּפוּנִי כָּל יְמֵי חַיָּי, וְשַׁבְתִּי בְּבֵית יי לְאֹרֶךְ יָמִים.

בשבת מוסיפים את המילים הנדפסות באותיות קטנות.

(וַיְהִי עֶרֶב וַיְהִי בֹקֶר) יוֹם הַשִּׁשִּׁי. וַיְכֻלּוּ הַשָּׁמַיִם וְהָאָרֶץ וְכָל צְבָאָם. וַיְכַל אֱלֹהִים בַּיּוֹם הַשְּׁבִיעִי מְלַאכְתּוֹ אֲשֶׁר עָשָׂה וַיִּשְׁבֹּת בַּיּוֹם הַשְּׁבִיעִי מִכָּל מְלַאכְתּוֹ אֲשֶׁר עָשָׂה. וַיְבָרֶךְ אֱלֹהִים אֶת יוֹם הַשְּׁבִיעִי וַיְקַדֵּשׁ אֹתוֹ, כִּי בוֹ שָׁבַת מִכָּל מְלַאכְתּוֹ אֲשֶׁר בָּרָא אֱלֹהִים לַעֲשׂוֹת.

סַבְרִי מָרָנָן. והשומעים עונים לְחַיֵּי.
בָּרוּךְ אַתָּה יי אֱלֹהֵינוּ מֶלֶךְ הָעוֹלָם בּוֹרֵא פְּרִי הַגָּפֶן.
בָּרוּךְ אַתָּה יי אֱלֹהֵינוּ מֶלֶךְ הָעוֹלָם אֲשֶׁר קִדְּשָׁנוּ מִכָּל עָם וְרוֹמְמָנוּ מִכָּל לָשׁוֹן, בָּחַר בָּנוּ וַיְגַדְּלֵנוּ רָצָה בָנוּ וַיְפָאֲרֵנוּ.

תְּרוּמָה הִבְדִּילָנוּ מִכָּל עָם   אֶרֶץ חֶמְדָּה הִנְחִיל אוֹתָנוּ.
קִדֵּשׁ אֶת שְׁמוֹ בָעוֹלָם   בִּגְלַל אָבוֹת שֶׁעָשׂוּ אֶת רְצוֹנוֹ.
גְּבוּרוֹת עָשָׂה לְמַעֲנֵהוּ   וְאֵין חֵקֶר לְנִפְלְאוֹתָיו.
עֲדַת קְדוֹשִׁים אוֹתָנוּ קָרָא   כֶּרֶם חֶמְדָּה וּנְטַע שַׁעֲשׁוּעִים.
וַיִּקְרָאֵם סְגוּלָּה לִשְׁמוֹ   וְרֵאשִׁית לְקָחָם מִכָּל גּוֹיֵי הָאֲרָצוֹת.
שֶׁהֵם מְשׁוּלִים בִּצְבָא מָרוֹם   וּמְכוּנָּנִים כְּכוֹכְבֵי רָקִיעַ.
וַיִּהְיוּ עֶלְיוֹנִים בְּקֶרֶב תֵּבֵל   וְנִכְבָּדִים עַל כָּל הָאוּמּוֹת.
זִיו פְּנֵיהֶם כְּזִיו הַשֶּׁמֶשׁ   וּמַרְאֵה דְמוּתָם כְּמַלְאֲכֵי שָׁרֵת.
לָהֶם יִרְאוּ מְלָכִים וָקָמוּ   שָׂרִים וְהִשְׁתַּחֲווּ.
לְמַעַן יי צְבָאוֹת אֲשֶׁר נֶאֱמָן   קְדוֹשׁ יִשְׂרָאֵל אֲשֶׁר בָּם בָּחַר.
כָּל רוֹאֵיהֶם יַכִּירוּם   כִּי הֵם זֶרַע בֵּרַךְ יי.
וַיְקַדְּשֵׁנוּ קְדוּשַּׁת עוֹלָם   וּשְׁמוֹ הַגָּדוֹל עָלֵינוּ קָרָא.
אוֹתָנוּ קָרָא עֵדָה לִשְׁמוֹ   סְגוּלָּה וְנַחֲלָה מִימוֹת עוֹלָם.
וַיְקָרְבֵנוּ לִפְנֵי הַר סִינַי   וַיַּגִּישֵׁנוּ לִפְנֵי חוֹרֵב.

All who see them shall recognize that they are the seed blessed by the Lord.
He sanctified us by eternal holiness, His great Name He called over us.
He called us Assembly for His Name, Treasure and Possession from Creation.
He brought us before Mount Sinai, let us step before Horeb.
He let us inherit the words of life, written by the finger of His majesty.
The Lord, our God, did for us miracles and deeds of strength, He liberated us from the hand of the enemy.
The Lord, our God, gave us forthright laws, true teachings, good orders, and commandments.

You gave us, o Lord our God, in love Sabbath days for rest, festive days for joy, holidays of pilgrimage at stated times for rejoicing, this day of rest and this holiday of unleavened bread, this good day of holy assembly, the season of our liberation, in love a remembrance of the Exodus from Egypt.

He chose this day from all days, wanted it, and sanctified it from all seasons
That one should sing His praise for His miraculous works, to remember it every year
To proclaim that on this day the Lord led his servants out of Egypt, He let us escape from the crucible of iron.
To proclaim that on this day the Lord took vengeance on their enemies, and hurled their oppressors into the sea.
To proclaim that on this day they willingly took upon themselves the yoke of His kingdom, and served Him wholeheartedly.
To proclaim that on this day the Lord did miracles and strong deeds for his loved ones, and great wonders for the descendants of His beloved.

Truly You chose us and sanctified us from all peoples and let us inherit Your holy festivals in joy and rejoicing. Praised are You, o Lord, Who sanctifies the Sabbath, Israel, and the holidays.

On Saturday night, add:

Praised are You o Lord, our God, King of the Universe, Creator of the illuminating fire.

Praised are You o Lord, our God, King of the Universe, Who separates between holy and secular, between light and darkness, between Israel and the Gentiles, and between the Seventh Day and the six days of work. You made a distinction between the holiness of the Sabbath and the holiness of holidays. (You sanctified the Seventh Day compared to the six days of work.) You separated Your people Israel in Your holiness. Praised are You o Lord, Who separates between sanctity and sanctity.

Praised are You o Lord, our God, King of the Universe, Who has kept us alive, maintained us, and enabled us to reach this festive time.

One drinks all or most of the cup while reclining toward the left.

וַיּוֹרִישֵׁנוּ דִּבְרֵי חַיִּים כְּתוּבִים בְּאֶצְבַּע הֲדָרוֹ.
וַיַּעַשׂ לָנוּ יי אֱלֹהֵינוּ נִסִּים וּגְבוּרוֹת וַיִּגְאָלֵנוּ מִיַּד אוֹיֵב.
וַיִּתֵּן לָנוּ יי אֱלֹהֵינוּ מִשְׁפָּטִים יְשָׁרִים וְתוֹרוֹת אֱמֶת חוּקִים וּמִצְוֹת טוֹבִים.

וַתִּתֶּן לָנוּ יי אֱלֹהֵינוּ בְּאַהֲבָה, (שַׁבָּתוֹת לִמְנוּחָה) מוֹעֲדִים לְשִׂמְחָה, חַגִּים וּזְמַנִּים לְשָׂשׂוֹן, אֶת יוֹם (הַמָּנוֹחַ הַזֶּה אֶת יוֹם) חַג הַמַּצּוֹת הַזֶּה, אֶת יוֹם טוֹב מִקְרָא קֹדֶשׁ הַזֶּה, זְמַן חֵרוּתֵנוּ בְּאַהֲבָה זֵכֶר לִיצִיאַת מִצְרָיִם.

וַיִּבְחַר בּוֹ בַּיּוֹם הַזֶּה מִכָּל הַיָּמִים וַיִּרְצֶה בוֹ וַיְקַדְּשֵׁהוּ מִכָּל הַזְּמַנִּים.
לִהְיוֹת מְהַלְלִים בּוֹ עַל פְּלָאֵי מַעֲשָׂיו לִהְיוֹת מַזְכִּירִים אוֹתוֹ בְּכָל שָׁנָה וְשָׁנָה.
לְהוֹדִיעַ כִּי בוֹ הוֹצִיא יי אֶת עֲבָדָיו מִמִּצְרַיִם מִכּוּר הַבַּרְזֶל אוֹתָנוּ מִלֵּט.
לְהוֹדִיעַ כִּי בוֹ עָשָׂה יי נְקָמוֹת בְּאוֹיְבֵיהֶם וּבוֹ שִׁקַּע צָרֵיהֶם בַּיָּם.
לְהוֹדִיעַ כִּי בוֹ קִבְּלוּ עֲלֵיהֶם עוֹל מַלְכוּתוֹ בְּרָצוֹן וַעֲבָדוּהוּ בְּלֵבָב שָׁלֵם.
לְהוֹדִיעַ כִּי בוֹ עָשָׂה יי נִסִּים וּגְבוּרוֹת לְאוֹהֲבָיו וְנִפְלָאוֹת רַבּוֹת לִבְנֵי יְדִידָיו.

כִּי בָנוּ בָחַרְתָּ וְאוֹתָנוּ קִדַּשְׁתָּ מִכָּל הָעַמִּים וּמוֹעֲדֵי קָדְשְׁךָ בְּשִׂמְחָה וּבְשָׂשׂוֹן הִנְחַלְתָּנוּ. בָּרוּךְ אַתָּה יי מְקַדֵּשׁ (הַשַּׁבָּת וְ)יִשְׂרָאֵל וְהַזְּמַנִּים.

במוצאי שבת מוסיפים:

בָּרוּךְ אַתָּה יי אֱלֹהֵינוּ מֶלֶךְ הָעוֹלָם בּוֹרֵא מְאוֹרֵי הָאֵשׁ.
בָּרוּךְ אַתָּה יי אֱלֹהֵינוּ מֶלֶךְ הָעוֹלָם הַמַּבְדִּיל בֵּין קֹדֶשׁ לְחוֹל וּבֵין אוֹר לְחֹשֶׁךְ וּבֵין יִשְׂרָאֵל לַגּוֹיִים וּבֵין יוֹם הַשְּׁבִיעִי לְשֵׁשֶׁת יְמֵי הַמַּעֲשֶׂה. וּבֵין קְדֻשַּׁת שַׁבָּת לִקְדֻשַּׁת יוֹם טוֹב הִבְדַּלְתָּ (וְיוֹם הַשְּׁבִיעִי הַגָּדוֹל וְהַקָּדוֹשׁ מִשֵּׁשֶׁת יְמֵי הַמַּעֲשֶׂה קִדַּשְׁתָּ), וְהִבְדַּלְתָּ אֶת עַמְּךָ יִשְׂרָאֵל בִּקְדֻשָּׁתֶךָ. בָּרוּךְ אַתָּה יי הַמַּבְדִּיל בֵּין קֹדֶשׁ לְקֹדֶשׁ.

בָּרוּךְ אַתָּה יי אֱלֹהֵינוּ מֶלֶךְ הָעוֹלָם שֶׁהֶחֱיָנוּ וְקִיְּמָנוּ וְהִגִּיעָנוּ לַזְּמַן הַזֶּה.

ושותים בהסבת שמאל.

Washing of the Hands

In Ashkenazic households, the head of the house washes his hands without reciting a benediction.

In Sephardic households, everyone washes his hands without reciting a benediction.

In Yemenite households, everyone washes his hands following the rules of washing for bread. While drying the hands with a towel, one recites:

Praised are You o Lord, our God, King of the Universe, Who sanctified us through His commandments and commanded us to lift the hands (for washing).

Celery

The head of the household takes pieces of the vegetable, dips them, and distributes them to all members of his party. Ashkenazim dip in salt water or vinegar, Sephardim in vinegar, and Yemenites in *ḥaroset*.

Before eating, the head of the household recites:

Praised are You o Lord, our God, King of the Universe, Creator of the fruit of the soil.

Breaking of the Maẓẓah

In all rituals except the *baladī* Yemenite ritual, the head of the household breaks the middle *maẓẓah* and puts the larger piece away for *afiqomen*. The other piece is returned to its place.

In Djerba and most of Tunisia, one uses freshly baked soft *maẓẓah* and breaks the piece for *afiqomen* in the shape of a Hebrew *waw*. While breaking, the head of the household recites:

In this way, the Lord tore the sea into twelve pieces and the Israelites passed the sea on dry soil.

Afterward, the *afiqomen* is wrapped in a napkin; one of the participants takes it on his shoulder, walks with it at least six feet, and recites:

A remembrance of our forefathers who left Egypt with their provisions bundled in their clothes on their backs.

In some families, this is recited in Arabic; some families add other declarations to the recital.

רחץ

במנהג אשכנז, בעל הבית נוטל ידיו בלי ברכה.
במנהג ספרד, כל המסובים נוטלים לידיהם בלי ברכה.

במנהג תימן, נוטלים ידיהם כראוי לפת ומברכים:
בָּרוּךְ אַתָּה יי אֱלֹהֵינוּ מֶלֶךְ הָעוֹלָם אֲשֶׁר קִדְּשָׁנוּ בְּמִצְוֹתָיו וְצִוָּנוּ עַל נְטִילַת יָדָיִם.

כרפס

יקח כרפס או ירק אחר, יטבול ויברך:
נוסח אשכנז: בָּרוּךְ אַתָּה יי אֱלֹהֵינוּ מֶלֶךְ הָעוֹלָם בּוֹרֵא פְּרִי הָאֲדָמָה.
נוסח ספרד ותימן: בָּרוּךְ אַתָּה יי אֱלֹהֵינוּ מֶלֶךְ הָעוֹלָם בּוֹרֵא פְּרִי הָאֲדָמָה.

הספרדים מטבילים בחומץ, האשכנזים בחומץ או במי מלח, והתימנים בחרוסת.
המברך אוכל ונותן לכל המסובים.

יחץ

בכל המנהגים חוץ ממנהג בלאדי תימני מסדר הסדר לוקח את המצה האמצעית ויבצענה לשני חלקים, יתן חציה האחת בין שתי המצות השלמות וחציה האחרת יצניע לאפיקומן.

מנהג תוניסיה לאומר בשעת בציעה: כַּךְ קָרַע יי אֶת הַיָּם עַל שְׁנֵים עָשָׂר קְרָעִים. וַיֵּצְאוּ מִמֶּנּוּ בְּנֵי יִשְׂרָאֵל בַּיַּבָּשָׁה.
ואחר הבציעה שמים את האפיקומן צרור במפה ואחד מן המסובים נותן אותו על שכמו,
הולך ארבע אמות ואומר: זֵכֶר לַאֲבוֹתֵינוּ שֶׁיָּצְאוּ מִמִּצְרַיִם וּמִשְׁאֲרוֹתָם צְרוּרוֹת בְּשִׂמְלוֹתָם עַל שִׁכְמָם.

ויש מנהגים שונים בזה. וכל משפחה תתנהג לפי מנהגה.

Recital

In the Sephardic ritual, the Second Cup is filled.
In the Yemenite ritual, the cups are rinsed and filled for the Second Cup.

The *Seder* plate is lifted up and the *maẓẓot* are displayed. In the Western Ashkenazic ritual, bone and egg are removed from the *Seder* plate.

In Djerba and most of Tunisia, one lifts the plate over the heads of all participants and says three times in a loud voice:

Yesterday we were slaves, today free people.
Today we are here, next year free people in the Land of Israel.

Here starts the *Haggadah.*

[SY] We left Egypt in hurry.

[S]*It is my intention and I am prepared to fulfill the commandment to tell about the Exodus from Egypt for the Oneness of the Holy One, praise to Him and His Glory, through Him Who is hidden and secret, in the name of all of Israel.*

The *Maẓẓot* (in the Sephardic ritual, the broken piece) are shown to the participants.

This is the bread of poverty which our forefathers ate [AS]*in* [Y]who left the land of Egypt.
Everybody who is hungry should come and eat,
Everybody [AS]*in need* [Y]obliged to celebrate Passover should come and celebrate Passover.
This year we are here; next year we shall be in the land of Israel.
This year we are slaves [SY]*here;* next year we shall be free men [S]*in the land of Israel.*

מגיד

מנהג ספרד: מוזגים את הכוס השני (חוץ ממנהג דרום תוניסיה).

מנהג תימן: רוחצים את הכוסות ומוזגים כוס שני.

מגביהים את הקערה מעל השלחן [באשכנז המערבית מסירים הביצה והזרוע מן הקערה].

בתוניסיה מגביהים את הקערה ומסבבים אותה על ראשי המסובים ואומרים בקול רם שלושה פעמים:

אֶתְמוֹל הָיִינוּ עֲבָדִים, הַיּוֹם בְּנֵי חוֹרִין. הַיּוֹם כָּאן, לְשָׁנָה הַבָּאָה בְּאַרְעָא דְיִשְׂרָאֵל בְּנֵי חוֹרִין.

ואומרים ההגדה

נוסח אשכנז

(כּ)הָא לַחְמָא עַנְיָא דִּי אֲכָלוּ אַבְהָתָנָא בְּאַרְעָא דְמִצְרָיִם. כָּל־דִּכְפִין יֵיתֵי וְיֵכוּל. כָּל־דִּצְרִיךְ יֵיתֵי וְיִפְסַח. הַשַּׁתָּא הָכָא. לְשָׁנָה הַבָּאָה בְּאַרְעָא דְיִשְׂרָאֵל. הַשַּׁתָּא עַבְדֵי. לְשָׁנָה הַבָּאָה בְּנֵי חוֹרִין.

נוסח ספרד

בִּבְהִילוּ יָצָאנוּ מִמִּצְרַיִם.

הריני מוכן ומזומן לקיים המצוה לספר ביציאת מצרים לשם ייחוד קב״ה ושכינתיה על ידי ההוא טמיר ונעלם בשם כל ישראל.

באומר 'הא' יגביה הפרוסה בידו ויאומר הא לחמא בקול רם.

הָא לַחְמָא עַנְיָא. דִּי אֲכָלוּ אַבְהָתָנָא בְּאַרְעָא דְמִצְרַיִם. כָּל דִּכְפִין יֵיתֵי וְיֵכוּל. כָּל דִּצְרִיךְ יֵיתֵי וְיִפְסַח. הַשַּׁתָּא הָכָא. לְשָׁנָה הַבָּאָה בְּאַרְעָא דְיִשְׂרָאֵל. הַשַּׁתָּא הָכָא עַבְדֵי. לְשָׁנָה הַבָּאָה בְּאַרְעָא דְיִשְׂרָאֵל בְּנֵי חוֹרִין.

נוסח תימן

בִּבְהִילוּ יָצָאנוּ מִמִּצְרַיִם

הָא לַחְמָא עַנְיָא דַּאֲכַלוּ אַבָהָתַנוּ דִּנְפַקוּ מֵאַרְעָא דְּמִצְרַיִם. כָּל דִּכְפִין יֵיתֵי וְיֵיכוּל וְכָל דִּצְרִיךְ לְפַסַּח יֵיתֵי וִיפַסַּח. שַׁתָּא הָכָא. לְשָׁנָה הַבָּאָה בְּאַרְעָא דְּיִשְׂרָאֵל. שַׁתָּא הָכָא עַבְדֵי. לְשַׁתָּא דְּאָתְיָא בְּנֵי חוֹרֵי.

In the Ashkenazic and Djerba rituals one pours the Second Cup.

The *Seder* plate is removed. In Western Ashkenazic families, bone and egg are restored and the *mazzot* are covered but the plate is not removed. The youngest participant who can read asks the Four Questions:

Ashkenazic text:

How is this night different from all other nights?

On all other nights we may eat leavened bread or *mazzah*, this night only *mazzah*.

On all other nights we may eat various vegetables, this night bitter herb.

On all other nights we do not dip even once, this night two times.

On all other nights we eat both sitting on chairs and lying on couches, this night we all lie on couches.

Sephardic text:

How is this night different from all other nights?

On all other nights we do not dip even once, this night two times.

On all other nights we may eat leavened bread or *mazzah*, this night only *mazzah*.

On all other nights we may eat various vegetables, this night bitter herb.

On all other nights we eat both sitting on chairs and lying on couches, this night we all lie on couches.

באשכנז ובאי ג׳רבה מוזגים את הכוס השני.

בספרד ותימן מסירים את הקערה מעל השולחן.
באשכנז המערבית מחזירים ביצה וזרוע ומכסים את המצות.
קטן החבורה היודע לקרא שואל:

נוסח אשכנז

מַה נִּשְׁתַּנָּה הַלַּיְלָה הַזֶּה מִכָּל־הַלֵּילוֹת?
שֶׁבְּכָל־הַלֵּילוֹת אָנוּ אוֹכְלִין חָמֵץ וּמַצָּה, הַלַּיְלָה הַזֶּה כֻּלּוֹ מַצָּה.
שֶׁבְּכָל־הַלֵּילוֹת אָנוּ אוֹכְלִין שְׁאָר יְרָקוֹת, הַלַּיְלָה הַזֶּה מָרוֹר.
שֶׁבְּכָל־הַלֵּילוֹת אֵין אָנוּ מַטְבִּילִין אֲפִילוּ פַּעַם אֶחָת, הַלַּיְלָה הַזֶּה שְׁתֵּי פְעָמִים.
שֶׁבְּכָל־הַלֵּילוֹת אָנוּ אוֹכְלִין בֵּין יוֹשְׁבִין וּבֵין מְסֻבִּין, הַלַּיְלָה הַזֶּה כֻּלָּנוּ מְסֻבִּין.

נוסח ספרד

מַה נִּשְׁתַּנָּה הַלַּיְלָה הַזֶּה מִכָּל הַלֵּילוֹת?
שֶׁבְּכָל הַלֵּילוֹת, אֵין אָנוּ מַטְבִּילִין. אֲפִילוּ פַּעַם אַחַת, וְהַלַּיְלָה הַזֶּה שְׁתֵּי פְעָמִים.
שֶׁבְּכָל הַלֵּילוֹת, אָנוּ אוֹכְלִין חָמֵץ אוֹ מַצָּה, וְהַלַּיְלָה הַזֶּה כֻּלּוֹ מַצָּה.
שֶׁבְּכָל הַלֵּילוֹת, אָנוּ אוֹכְלִין שְׁאַר יְרָקוֹת, וְהַלַּיְלָה הַזֶּה מָרוֹר.
שֶׁבְּכָל הַלֵּילוֹת, אָנוּ אוֹכְלִין וְשׁוֹתִין, בֵּין יוֹשְׁבִין וּבֵין מְסֻבִּין, וְהַלַּיְלָה הַזֶּה כֻּלָּנוּ מְסֻבִּין.

Yemenite text:

How is this night different from all other nights?
On all other nights we do not dip even once, this night two times.
On all other nights we may eat leavened bread or *mazzah*, this night only *mazzah*.
On all other nights we may eat various vegetables, this night bitter herbs.
On all other nights we eat and drink both sitting on chairs and lying on couches, this night we all lie on couches.

In the Yemenite ritual, the smallest boy who knows how to read recites the following Arabic summary for the benefit of women and toddlers.

What is the difference of this night from all other nights?
When our grandfathers and fathers left Egypt, the house of slavery, where they had worked and mixed straw in bricks, for whom? For Pharaoh, the total sinner, whose head was awry with pride, and whose mouth was open like an oven; then God brought down upon the Egyptians

Blood, Frogs, Lice and Fleas, Wild Animals, Animal Disease, Scab, Hail, Locusts, Darkness, and Death of the Firstborn.

Until the oldest woman became the target of a thousand curses, her idol became dough and was eaten by the dog, and all cried in that night. There was a great wailing in Egypt to confirm what is written (*Ex.* 12:30): "There was a great wailing in Egypt since there was no house without a dead person in it." And God liberated us with strong hand and outstretched arm, great judgments, wonders, and apparitions, through Moses our teacher, may peace be upon him. And the following is the answer:

נוסח תימן

מַה נִּשְׁתַּנָּה הַלַּיְלָה הַזֶּה מִכָּל הַלֵּילוֹת?
שֶׁבְּכָל הַלֵּילוֹת אֵין אָנוּ מַטְבִּילִין אֲפִילוּ פַּעַם אַחַת, וְהַלַּיְלָה הַזֶּה שְׁתֵּי פְעָמִים.
שֶׁבְּכָל הַלֵּילוֹת אָנוּ אוֹכְלִים חָמֵץ וּמַצָּה, וְהַלַּיְלָה הַזֶּה כֻּלּוֹ מַצָּה.
שֶׁבְּכָל־הַלֵּילוֹת אָנוּ אוֹכְלִים שְׁאַר יְרָקוֹת, וְהַלַּיְלָה הַזֶּה מְרוֹרִים.
שֶׁבְּכָל־הַלֵּילוֹת אָנוּ אוֹכְלִים בֵּין יוֹשְׁבִין וּבֵין מְסֻבִּין, וְהַלַּיְלָה הַזֶּה כֻּלָּנוּ מְסֻבִּין.

ונוהגים שהקטן היודע לקרוא אומר פיסקא זו בלשון ערב כדי שיבינו הנשים והטף:

מַא כְּבַּר הַדִ'ה אַלְלַיְלַה, מִן גְמִיע אַלְלְיַאלִי?
כַּרגּוּ גְדוּדְנַא וְאַבַּאיְנַא מִן מִצר בַּית אַלְעֲבוּדִיַּה מַא כַּאנוּ יִפְעֲלוּ, אַלתִּבְּן פִי אַללִבְּן, לִמַן, לְפַרעֹה אַלרָשָׁע אַלגָמוּר, אַלדִ'י רַאסֵה סַאע אַלצִמעוּר וְפֻמֵה סַאע מִנַאק אַלתַנוּר, וְאַורַד אללה עַלַי אַלמִצרִיּוּן
אַלדַם, וְאַלצִפַאדִע, אַלקַמל וְאַלקֻמַל, וְאַלוְחוּש, וְאַלפִנַא, וְאַלגְרַב, וְאַלבְרַד, וְאַלגְרַאד, וְאַלצְלַאם, וְמוּת אַלאַבְכַּאר.
חַתַּי עֲגוּז בְּגוּז, עֲלַיהַא אַלף לַעֲנַה תְגוּז, כַּאן מַעַהַא מַעבּוּד מִן עִגְנַה, דִ'כַּל אַלכַּלבּ אֲכַלהַא, וַצְרַכַת תִלךְ אַללַיְלַה, וְכַּאן צֻרַאך עֲצִים בְּמִצר, לְקַיֵּם מַה שֶּׁנֶּאֱמַר, כִּי אֵין בַּיִת אֲשֶׁר אֵין שָׁם מֵת.
וְכַלַצְהֻם אללה בְּיַד שְׁדִידַה וְדְרַאע מַמדוּדַה וַאחכַּאם עֲצִימַה, וְאַיַאת וַבְרַאהִין עֲלַי מֹשֶׁה רַבֵּנוּ עָלָיו הַשָּׁלוֹם, וְהַדַ'א אַלגְוַאבּ:

The plate is returned. In Ashkenazic and most Sephardic families the *mazzot* are uncovered.

(*Deut.* 6:21): "We were slaves to Pharaoh in Egypt but the Lord our God led us out from there with a strong hand and an outstretched arm." If the Holy One, praise to Him, had not [AS]led [Y]*liberated* our forefathers from Egypt, [A]*then* [SY]*still* we, our children, and our grandchildren would be subservient to Pharaoh in Egypt. And even if all of us were wise, all of us understanding, [A]*all of us aged*, all of us learned in the Torah, we would still have the obligation to tell about the Exodus from Egypt and whoever tells [AS]much [Y]*at length* about the Exodus is praiseworthy.

Once Rebbi Eliezer, Rebbi Yehoshua, Rebbi Eleazar ben Azariah, [AS]*Rebbi Akiba*, and Rebbi Tarphon were reclining on couches in Bene Berak and were telling about the Exodus from Egypt during the entire night until their students came and said to them: "Our teachers, the time has come for the recitation of the *Shema*' for morning prayers."

מחזירים את הקערה. באשכנז ורוב ספרד מגלים את המצות.

נוסח אשכנז

עֲבָדִים הָיִינוּ לְפַרְעֹה בְּמִצְרָיִם וַיּוֹצִיאֵנוּ יי אֱלֹהֵינוּ מִשָּׁם בְּיָד חֲזָקָה וּבִזְרֹעַ נְטוּיָה. וְאִלּוּ לֹא הוֹצִיא הַקָּדוֹשׁ בָּרוּךְ הוּא אֶת־אֲבוֹתֵינוּ מִמִּצְרַיִם הֲרֵי אָנוּ וּבָנֵינוּ וּבְנֵי בָנֵינוּ מְשֻׁעְבָּדִים הָיִינוּ לְפַרְעֹה בְּמִצְרָיִם. וַאֲפִילוּ כֻּלָּנוּ חֲכָמִים, כֻּלָּנוּ נְבוֹנִים, כֻּלָּנוּ זְקֵנִים, כֻּלָּנוּ יוֹדְעִים אֶת־הַתּוֹרָה, מִצְוָה עָלֵינוּ לְסַפֵּר בִּיצִיאַת מִצְרָיִם, וְכָל־הַמַּרְבֶּה לְסַפֵּר בִּיצִיאַת מִצְרַיִם הֲרֵי זֶה מְשֻׁבָּח.

נוסח ספרד

עֲבָדִים הָיִינוּ לְפַרְעֹה בְּמִצְרַיִם, וַיּוֹצִיאֵנוּ יי אֱלֹהֵינוּ מִשָּׁם בְּיָד חֲזָקָה וּבִזְרוֹעַ נְטוּיָה. וְאִלּוּ לֹא הוֹצִיא הַקָּדוֹשׁ בָּרוּךְ הוּא אֶת אֲבוֹתֵינוּ מִמִּצְרַיִם, עֲדַיִן אָנוּ וּבָנֵינוּ וּבְנֵי בָנֵינוּ מְשֻׁעְבָּדִים הָיִינוּ לְפַרְעֹה בְּמִצְרַיִם. וַאֲפִילוּ כֻּלָּנוּ חֲכָמִים, כֻּלָּנוּ נְבוֹנִים, כֻּלָּנוּ זְקֵנִים, כֻּלָּנוּ יוֹדְעִים אֶת הַתּוֹרָה, מִצְוָה עָלֵינוּ לְסַפֵּר בִּיצִיאַת מִצְרַיִם, וְכָל הַמַּרְבֶּה לְסַפֵּר בִּיצִיאַת מִצְרַיִם הֲרֵי זֶה מְשֻׁבָּח.

נוסח תימן

עֲבָדִים הָיִינוּ לְפַרְעֹה בְּמִצְרַיִם, וַיּוֹצִיאֵנוּ יי אֱלֹהֵינוּ מִשָּׁם בְּיָד חֲזָקָה וּבִזְרוֹעַ נְטוּיָה. וְאִלּוּ לֹא גָאַל הַקָּדוֹשׁ בָּרוּךְ הוּא אֶת אֲבוֹתֵינוּ מִמִּצְרַיִם, עֲדַיִן אָנוּ וּבָנֵינוּ וּבְנֵי בָנֵינוּ מְשֻׁעְבָּדִים הָיִינוּ לְפַרְעֹה בְּמִצְרַיִם. וַאֲפִילוּ כֻּלָּנוּ חֲכָמִים, כֻּלָּנוּ נְבוֹנִים, כֻּלָּנוּ יוֹדְעִים אֶת הַתּוֹרָה, מִצְוָה עָלֵינוּ לְסַפֵּר בִּיצִיאַת מִצְרַיִם, וְכָל הַמַּאֲרִיךְ לְסַפֵּר בִּיצִיאַת מִצְרַיִם, הֲרֵי זֶה מְשֻׁבָּח.

מַעֲשֶׂה בְּרַבִּי אֱלִיעֶזֶר וְרַבִּי יְהוֹשֻׁעַ וְרַבִּי אֶלְעָזָר בֶּן עֲזַרְיָה וְרַבִּי עֲקִיבָא וְרַבִּי טַרְפוֹן שֶׁהָיוּ מְסֻבִּין בִּבְנֵי בְרַק, וְהָיוּ מְסַפְּרִים

מַעֲשֶׂה בְּרַבִּי אֱלִיעֶזֶר, וְרַבִּי יְהוֹשֻׁעַ, וְרַבִּי אֶלְעָזָר בֶּן עֲזַרְיָה, וְרַבִּי עֲקִיבָא, וְרַבִּי טַרְפוֹן, שֶׁהָיוּ מְסֻבִּין בִּבְנֵי בְרָק,

מַעֲשֶׂה בְּרַבִּי אֱלִיעֶזֶר, וְרַבִּי יְהוֹשֻׁעַ, וְרַבִּי אֶלְעָזָר בֶּן עֲזַרְיָה, (וְרַבִּי עֲקִיבָא,) וְרַבִּי טַרְפוֹן, שֶׁהָיוּ מְסֻבִּין בִּבְנֵי בְרָק, וְהָיוּ

(*Berakhot* I,8) Rebbi Eleazar ben Azariah said [Y]*to them*: "I am like a seventy year old man and never could succeed in proving that one has to mention the Exodus every night, until Ben Zoma derived it from the verse (*Deut.* 16:3): ". . . so that you should remember the day of your Exodus from Egypt the entire days of your life." "The days of your life" would indicate the daylight hours but "the **entire** days of your life" includes the night also. However, the Sages say "the days of your life" means the present world, "the **entire** days of your life" includes the Messianic Age.

Praised be the Omnipresent One, [AS]*praised be He. Praised be He,* Who gave the Torah to His people Israel. The Torah spoke about four children: one wise, one wicked, one simple-minded, and one who does not know how to ask.

בִּיצִיאַת מִצְרַיִם כׇּל־אוֹתוֹ הַלַּיְלָה, עַד שֶׁבָּאוּ תַלְמִידֵיהֶם וְאָמְרוּ לָהֶם רַבּוֹתֵינוּ הִגִּיעַ זְמַן קְרִיאַת שְׁמַע שֶׁל שַׁחֲרִית.

וְהָיוּ מְסַפְּרִים בִּיצִיאַת מִצְרַיִם כׇּל אוֹתוֹ הַלַּיְלָה, עַד שֶׁבָּאוּ תַלְמִידֵיהֶם, וְאָמְרוּ לָהֶם רַבּוֹתֵינוּ, הִגִּיעַ זְמַן קְרִיאַת שְׁמַע שֶׁל שַׁחֲרִית.

מְסַפְּרִים בִּיצִיאַת מִצְרַיִם כׇּל אוֹתוֹ הַלַּיְלָה, עַד שֶׁבָּאוּ תַלְמִידֵיהֶם, וְאָמְרוּ לָהֶם רַבּוֹתֵינוּ, הִגִּיעַ זְמַן קְרִיַּת שְׁמַע שֶׁל־שַׁחֲרִית.

אָמַר רַבִּי אֶלְעָזָר בֶּן עֲזַרְיָה, הֲרֵי אֲנִי כְּבֶן שִׁבְעִים שָׁנָה, וְלֹא זָכִיתִי שֶׁתֵּאָמֵר יְצִיאַת מִצְרַיִם בַּלֵּילוֹת, עַד שֶׁדְּרָשָׁהּ בֶּן זוֹמָא, שֶׁנֶּאֱמַר ׳לְמַעַן תִּזְכּוֹר אֶת־יוֹם צֵאתְךָ מֵאֶרֶץ מִצְרַיִם כֹּל יְמֵי חַיֶּיךָ׳. יְמֵי חַיֶּיךָ, הַיָּמִים; כֹּל יְמֵי חַיֶּיךָ, הַלֵּילוֹת. וַחֲכָמִים אוֹמְרִים יְמֵי חַיֶּיךָ, הָעוֹלָם הַזֶּה; כֹּל יְמֵי חַיֶּיךָ, לְהָבִיא לִימוֹת הַמָּשִׁיחַ.

אָמַר רַבִּי אֶלְעָזָר בֶּן עֲזַרְיָה, הֲרֵי אֲנִי כְּבֶן שִׁבְעִים שָׁנָה, וְלֹא זָכִיתִי שֶׁתֵּאָמֵר יְצִיאַת מִצְרַיִם בַּלֵּילוֹת, עַד שֶׁדְּרָשָׁהּ בֶּן זוֹמָא, שֶׁנֶּאֱמַר ׳לְמַעַן תִּזְכּוֹר אֶת יוֹם צֵאתְךָ מֵאֶרֶץ מִצְרַיִם כֹּל יְמֵי חַיֶּיךָ׳. יְמֵי חַיֶּיךָ הַיָּמִים, כֹּל יְמֵי חַיֶּיךָ הַלֵּילוֹת. וַחֲכָמִים אוֹמְרִים יְמֵי חַיֶּיךָ, הָעוֹלָם הַזֶּה; כֹּל יְמֵי חַיֶּיךָ, לְהָבִיא לִימוֹת הַמָּשִׁיחַ.

אָמַר לָהֶם רַבִּי אֶלְעָזָר בֶּן עֲזַרְיָה, הֲרֵי אֲנִי כְּבֶן שִׁבְעִים שָׁנָה, וְלֹא זָכִיתִי שֶׁתֵּאָמֵר יְצִיאַת מִצְרַיִם בַּלֵּילוֹת, עַד שֶׁדְּרָשָׁהּ בֶּן זוֹמָא, שֶׁנֶּאֱמַר, ׳לְמַעַן תִּזְכּוֹר אֶת יוֹם צֵאתְךָ מֵאֶרֶץ מִצְרַיִם כֹּל יְמֵי חַיֶּיךָ׳. יְמֵי חַיֶּיךָ הַיָּמִים, כֹּל יְמֵי חַיֶּיךָ הַלֵּילוֹת. וַחֲכָמִים אוֹמְרִים יְמֵי חַיֶּיךָ, הָעוֹלָם הַזֶּה; כֹּל יְמֵי חַיֶּיךָ, לְהָבִיא אֶת יְמוֹת הַמָּשִׁיחַ.

בָּרוּךְ הַמָּקוֹם בָּרוּךְ הוּא, בָּרוּךְ שֶׁנָּתַן תּוֹרָה לְעַמּוֹ יִשְׂרָאֵל בָּרוּךְ הוּא. כְּנֶגֶד

בָּרוּךְ הַמָּקוֹם בָּרוּךְ הוּא, בָּרוּךְ שֶׁנָּתַן תּוֹרָה לְעַמּוֹ יִשְׂרָאֵל, בָּרוּךְ הוּא. כְּנֶגֶד אַרְבָּעָה בָנִים

בָּרוּךְ הַמָּקוֹם שֶׁנָּתַן תּוֹרָה לְיִשְׂרָאֵל עַמּוֹ בָּרוּךְ הוּא. כְּנֶגֶד אַרְבָּעָה בָנִים דִּבְּרָה

What does the wise one say? (*Deut.* 6:20): "What are the testimonials, the ordinances, and the laws that the Lord our God has commanded us?" So you tell him: By the rules of Passover (*Pesaḥim* X,8) "there can be no revelry after the *Pesaḥ*."

What does the wicked one say? (*Ex.* 12:26): "What does this service mean to you?" "To you," not to him. Since he excluded himself from the community, [Y]*therefore* he negated the principle (of Judaism). Now you shall blunt his teeth and tell him (*Ex.* 13:8): "This is on account of what the Lord did for me when I left Egypt." "For me," but not for him. If he had been there, he would not have been redeemed.

אַרְבָּעָה בָנִים דִּבְּרָה תוֹרָה: אֶחָד חָכָם, אֶחָד רָשָׁע, אֶחָד תָּם, וְאֶחָד שֶׁאֵינוֹ יוֹדֵעַ לִשְׁאוֹל.

דִּבְּרָה תוֹרָה: אֶחָד חָכָם, אֶחָד רָשָׁע, אֶחָד תָּם, וְאֶחָד שֶׁאֵינוֹ יוֹדֵעַ לִשְׁאַל.

תּוֹרָה: אֶחָד חָכָם, אֶחָד רָשָׁע, אֶחָד תָּם, וְאֶחָד שֶׁאֵינוֹ יוֹדֵעַ לִשְׁאַל.

חָכָם מַה הוּא אוֹמֵר? 'מָה הָעֵדוֹת וְהַחֻקִּים וְהַמִּשְׁפָּטִים אֲשֶׁר צִוָּה יי אֱלֹהֵינוּ אֶתְכֶם.' וְאַף אַתָּה אֱמוֹר לוֹ: כְּהִלְכוֹת הַפֶּסַח אֵין מַפְטִירִין אַחַר הַפֶּסַח אֲפִיקוֹמָן.

חָכָם מָה הוּא אוֹמֵר? 'מָה הָעֵדוֹת וְהַחֻקִּים וְהַמִּשְׁפָּטִים אֲשֶׁר צִוָּה יי אֱלֹהֵינוּ אֶתְכֶם.' אַף אַתָּה אֱמוֹר לוֹ כְּהִלְכוֹת הַפֶּסַח: אֵין מַפְטִירִין אַחַר הַפֶּסַח אֲפִיקוֹמֶן.

חָכָם מַה הוּא אוֹמֵר? 'מָה הָעֵדוֹת וְהַחֻקִּים וְהַמִּשְׁפָּטִים אֲשֶׁר צִוָּה יי אֱלֹהֵינוּ אֶתְכֶם.' אַף אַתָּה אֱמוֹר לוֹ כְּהִלְכוֹת הַפֶּסַח: אֵין מַפְטִירִין אַחַר הַפֶּסַח אֲפִיקוֹמַן.

רָשָׁע מַה הוּא אוֹמֵר? 'מָה הָעֲבוֹדָה הַזֹּאת לָכֶם?' לָכֶם וְלֹא לוֹ! וּלְפִי שֶׁהוֹצִיא אֶת־עַצְמוֹ מִן הַכְּלָל כָּפַר בָּעִקָּר, וְאַף אַתָּה הַקְהֵה אֶת־שִׁנָּיו וֶאֱמוֹר לוֹ 'בַּעֲבוּר זֶה עָשָׂה יי לִי בְּצֵאתִי מִמִּצְרָיִם', לִי וְלֹא לוֹ; אִלּוּ הָיָה שָׁם, לֹא הָיָה נִגְאָל.

רָשָׁע מָה הוּא אוֹמֵר? 'מָה הָעֲבוֹדָה הַזֹּאת לָכֶם?' לָכֶם וְלֹא לוֹ! וּלְפִי שֶׁהוֹצִיא אֶת עַצְמוֹ מִן הַכְּלָל, כָּפַר בָּעִקָּר. אַף אַתָּה הַקְהֵה אֶת שִׁנָּיו וֶאֱמוֹר לוֹ 'בַּעֲבוּר זֶה עָשָׂה יי לִי בְּצֵאתִי מִמִּצְרָיִם', לִי וְלֹא לוֹ; וְאִלּוּ הָיָה שָׁם, לֹא הָיָה נִגְאָל.

רָשָׁע מַה הוּא אוֹמֵר? 'מָה הָעֲבוֹדָה הַזֹּאת לָכֶם?' לָכֶם וְלֹא לוֹ! וּלְפִי שֶׁהוֹצִיא אֶת עַצְמוֹ מִן הַכְּלָל וְכָפַר בָּעִיקָּר, אַף אַתָּה הַקְהֵה אֶת שִׁנָּיו וֶאֱמוֹר לוֹ 'בַּעֲבוּר זֶה עָשָׂה יי לִי בְּצֵאתִי מִמִּצְרָיִם', לִי וְלֹא לוֹ; וְאִלּוּ הָיָה שָׁם, לֹא הָיָה נִגְאָל.

What does the simple-minded one say? (*Ex.* 13:14): "What is this? Then you shall tell him: With a mighty hand did the Lord lead me out of Egypt, the house of slaves."

And you yourself should start with the child who does not know how to ask, as it is said (*Ex.* 13:8): "You must tell your child on that day as follows: This is on account of what the Lord did for me during my Exodus from Egypt."

[Y]*"You must tell your child,"* I might think that this obligation starts with the new moon (of Nisan). [AS]The verse ([Y]*You must learn from what it)* says: "On that day" (the Fourteenth of Nisan). If on that day, I might start during daylight. [AS]The verse *(*[Y]*You must learn from what it)* says: "This is on account." [AS]"**This** *is on account"* can only mean: At the time when *maẓẓah* and bitter herbs lie before you.

Originally, our forefathers were idolators but now the Omnipresent One, [Y]*praised be He*, brought us to His service as it is said (*Jos.* 24:2–4): "Joshua said to the entire people: So says the Lord, the God of Israel: Your forefathers always lived on the far side of the River (Euphrates), Teraḥ the father of Abraham and the father of Naḥor, and they worshiped other gods.

תָּם מַה הוּא אוֹמֵר? 'מַה זֹּאת?' וְאָמַרְתָּ אֵלָיו, 'בְּחֹזֶק יָד הוֹצִיאָנוּ יי מִמִּצְרַיִם מִבֵּית עֲבָדִים.'

וּשְׁאֵינוֹ יוֹדֵעַ לִשְׁאוֹל אַתְּ פְּתַח לוֹ, שֶׁנֶּאֱמַר 'וְהִגַּדְתָּ לְבִנְךָ בַּיּוֹם הַהוּא לֵאמֹר: בַּעֲבוּר זֶה עָשָׂה יי לִי בְּצֵאתִי מִמִּצְרָיִם.'

יָכוֹל מֵרֹאשׁ חֹדֶשׁ, תַּלְמוּד לוֹמַר 'בַּיּוֹם הַהוּא'. אִי בַּיּוֹם הַהוּא יָכוֹל מִבְּעוֹד יוֹם, תַּלְמוּד לוֹמַר 'בַּעֲבוּר זֶה'. 'בַּעֲבוּר זֶה' לֹא אָמַרְתִּי אֶלָּא בְּשָׁעָה שֶׁיֵּשׁ מַצָּה וּמָרוֹר מֻנָּחִים לְפָנֶיךָ.

וְשֶׁאֵינוֹ יוֹדֵעַ לִשְׁאַל אַתְּ פְּתַח לוֹ, שֶׁנֶּאֱמַר 'וְהִגַּדְתָּ לְבִנְךָ בַּיּוֹם הַהוּא לֵאמֹר: בַּעֲבוּר זֶה עָשָׂה יי לִי בְּצֵאתִי מִמִּצְרָיִם.' יָכוֹל מֵרֹאשׁ חֹדֶשׁ, תַּלְמוּד לוֹמַר 'בַּיּוֹם הַהוּא'. אִי בַּיּוֹם הַהוּא יָכוֹל מִבְּעוֹד יוֹם, תַּלְמוּד לוֹמַר 'בַּעֲבוּר זֶה'. 'בַּעֲבוּר זֶה' לֹא אָמַרְתִּי אֶלָּא בְּשָׁעָה שֶׁמַּצָּה וּמָרוֹר מוּנָּחִים לְפָנֶיךָ.

וּשְׁאֵינוֹ יוֹדֵעַ לִשְׁאַל אַתְּ פְּתַח לוֹ, שֶׁנֶּאֱמַר 'וְהִגַּדְתָּ לְבִנְךָ בַּיּוֹם הַהוּא לֵאמֹר: בַּעֲבוּר זֶה עָשָׂה יי לִי בְּצֵאתִי מִמִּצְרָיִם.' 'וְהִגַּדְתָּ לְבִנְךָ', יָכוֹל מֵרֹאשׁ הַחֹדֶשׁ, תַּלְמוּד לוֹמַר 'בַּיּוֹם הַהוּא'. אִי בַּיּוֹם הַהוּא יָכוֹל מִבְּעוֹד יוֹם, תַּלְמוּד לוֹמַר 'בַּעֲבוּר זֶה', לֹא אָמַרְתִּי אֶלָּא בְּשָׁעָה שֶׁיֵּשׁ מַצָּה וּמָרוֹר מוּנָּחִים לְפָנֶיךָ.

מִתְּחִלָּה עֹבְדֵי עֲבֹדָה זָרָה הָיוּ אֲבוֹתֵינוּ וְעַכְשָׁיו קֵרְבָנוּ הַמָּקוֹם לַעֲבֹדָתוֹ, שֶׁנֶּאֱמַר 'וַיֹּאמֶר יְהוֹשֻׁעַ אֶל־כָּל־הָעָם: כֹּה־אָמַר יי אֱלֹהֵי יִשְׂרָאֵל, בְּעֵבֶר הַנָּהָר יָשְׁבוּ אֲבוֹתֵיכֶם מֵעוֹלָם, תֶּרַח אֲבִי אַבְרָהָם וַאֲבִי נָחוֹר,

מִתְּחִלָּה עוֹבְדֵי עֲבֹדָה זָרָה הָיוּ אֲבוֹתֵינוּ, וְעַכְשָׁיו קֵרְבָנוּ הַמָּקוֹם לַעֲבֹדָתוֹ, שֶׁנֶּאֱמַר 'וַיֹּאמֶר יְהוֹשֻׁעַ אֶל כָּל הָעָם: כֹּה אָמַר יי אֱלֹהֵי יִשְׂרָאֵל, בְּעֵבֶר הַנָּהָר יָשְׁבוּ אֲבוֹתֵיכֶם מֵעוֹלָם, תֶּרַח אֲבִי אַבְרָהָם וַאֲבִי נָחוֹר, וַיַּעַבְדוּ

מִתְּחִלָּה עוֹבְדֵי עֲבֹדָה זָרָה הָיוּ אֲבוֹתֵינוּ, וְעַכְשָׁיו קֵרְבָנוּ הַמָּקוֹם בָּרוּךְ הוּא לַעֲבֹדָתוֹ, שֶׁנֶּאֱמַר 'וַיֹּאמֶר יְהוֹשֻׁעַ אֶל כָּל הָעָם: כֹּה אָמַר יי אֱלֹהֵי יִשְׂרָאֵל, בְּעֵבֶר הַנָּהָר יָשְׁבוּ אֲבוֹתֵיכֶם מֵעוֹלָם, תֶּרַח אֲבִי אַבְרָהָם

But I took your father Abraham from beyond the River, I let him walk through the entire land of Canaan, I examined him for descendants and gave him Isaac. To Isaac I gave Jacob and Esau and I gave Mount Seïr to Esau as an inheritance but Jacob and his sons descended into Egypt."

In Southern Tunisia one adds here the recital of *Utqul Djerba* or *Utqul Gafṣa*, Arabic texts that describe the recognition by Abraham of God as unique Creator and his ordeal in the fiery oven. The texts are given in the appendix to the *Haggadah*.

Praise to Him Who keeps His promise to [Y]*His people* Israel, praise to Him. The Holy One, praise to Him, [A]*computed* [SY]is computing the End to do what He said to our father Abraham in the Covenant Between the Pieces, as it is said (*Gen.* 15:13–14): "He said to Abram, you should certainly know that your descendants will be strangers in a land that is not theirs; **they** will enslave and mistreat them for four hundred years.

וַיַּעַבְדוּ אֱלֹהִים
אֲחֵרִים. וָאֶקַּח
אֶת־אֲבִיכֶם
אֶת־אַבְרָהָם מֵעֵבֶר
הַנָּהָר, וָאוֹלֵךְ אֹתוֹ
בְּכָל־אֶרֶץ כְּנָעַן
וָאַרְבֶּ(ה) אֶת־זַרְעוֹ
וָאֶתֶּן־לוֹ אֶת־יִצְחָק.
וָאֶתֵּן לְיִצְחָק
אֶת־יַעֲקֹב וְאֶת־עֵשָׂו,
וָאֶתֵּן לְעֵשָׂו אֶת־הַר
שֵׂעִיר לָרֶשֶׁת אוֹתוֹ,
וְיַעֲקֹב וּבָנָיו יָרְדוּ
מִצְרָיִם.'

אֱלֹהִים אֲחֵרִים.
וָאֶקַּח אֶת אֲבִיכֶם
אֶת אַבְרָהָם מֵעֵבֶר
הַנָּהָר, וָאוֹלֵךְ אֹתוֹ
בְּכָל אֶרֶץ כְּנָעַן,
וָאַרְבֶּה אֶת זַרְעוֹ,
וָאֶתֵּן לוֹ אֶת יִצְחָק.
וָאֶתֵּן לְיִצְחָק אֶת
יַעֲקֹב וְאֶת עֵשָׂו,
וָאֶתֵּן לְעֵשָׂו אֶת הַר
שֵׂעִיר לָרֶשֶׁת אוֹתוֹ,
וְיַעֲקֹב וּבָנָיו יָרְדוּ
מִצְרַיִם.'

וַאֲבִי נָחוֹר, וַיַּעַבְדוּ
אֱלֹהִים אֲחֵרִים.
וָאֶקַּח אֶת אֲבִיכֶם
אֶת אַבְרָהָם מֵעֵבֶר
הַנָּהָר, וָאוֹלֵךְ אֹתוֹ
בְּכָל אֶרֶץ כְּנָעַן,
וָאַרְבֶּה אֶת זַרְעוֹ,
וָאֶתֵּן לוֹ אֶת יִצְחָק.
וָאֶתֵּן לְיִצְחָק אֶת
יַעֲקֹב וְאֶת עֵשָׂו,
וָאֶתֵּן לְעֵשָׂו אֶת הַר
שֵׂעִיר לָרֶשֶׁת אוֹתוֹ,
וְיַעֲקֹב וּבָנָיו יָרְדוּ
מִצְרָיִם.'

בדרום תוניסיה מוסיפים כאן סיפור בלשון ערב 'ותקול ג'רבה' או 'ותקול גפצה' המתארים איך הכיר אברהם אבינו את בוראו והניסים שנעשו לאברהם אבינו; נוסחאות אלו מודפסות בנספח בסוף ההגדה.

בָּרוּךְ שׁוֹמֵר הַבְטָחָתוֹ
לְיִשְׂרָאֵל, בָּרוּךְ הוּא.
שֶׁהַקָּדוֹשׁ בָּרוּךְ הוּא
חִשֵּׁב אֶת־הַקֵּץ,
לַעֲשׂוֹת כְּמָה שֶׁאָמַר
לְאַבְרָהָם אָבִינוּ
בִּבְרִית בֵּין הַבְּתָרִים,
שֶׁנֶּאֱמַר 'וַיֹּאמֶר
לְאַבְרָם יָדֹעַ תֵּדַע כִּי
גֵר יִהְיֶה זַרְעֲךָ בְּאֶרֶץ
לֹא לָהֶם, וַעֲבָדוּם
וְעִנּוּ אֹתָם אַרְבַּע
מֵאוֹת שָׁנָה. וְגַם

בָּרוּךְ שׁוֹמֵר
הַבְטָחָתוֹ לְיִשְׂרָאֵל,
בָּרוּךְ הוּא.
שֶׁהַקָּדוֹשׁ בָּרוּךְ
הוּא מְחַשֵּׁב אֶת
הַקֵּץ, לַעֲשׂוֹת כְּמָה
שֶׁאָמַר לְאַבְרָהָם
אָבִינוּ בִּבְרִית בֵּין
הַבְּתָרִים, שֶׁנֶּאֱמַר
'וַיֹּאמֶר לְאַבְרָם
יָדֹעַ תֵּדַע כִּי גֵר
יִהְיֶה זַרְעֲךָ בְּאֶרֶץ
לֹא לָהֶם, וַעֲבָדוּם
וְעִנּוּ אֹתָם אַרְבַּע
מֵאוֹת שָׁנָה. וְגַם

בָּרוּךְ שׁוֹמֵר
הַבְטָחָתוֹ לְיִשְׂרָאֵל
עַמּוֹ, בָּרוּךְ הוּא.
שֶׁהַקָּדוֹשׁ בָּרוּךְ הוּא
מְחַשֵּׁב אֶת הַקֵּץ,
לַעֲשׂוֹת כְּמוֹ שֶׁאָמַר
לְאַבְרָהָם אָבִינוּ
בִּבְרִית בֵּין
הַבְּתָרִים, שֶׁנֶּאֱמַר
'וַיֹּאמֶר לְאַבְרָם יָדֹעַ
תֵּדַע כִּי גֵר יִהְיֶה
זַרְעֲךָ בְּאֶרֶץ לֹא
לָהֶם, וַעֲבָדוּם וְעִנּוּ
אֹתָם אַרְבַּע מֵאוֹת

Also every nation whom they will serve I shall judge and after that they will leave with great wealth."

In the Ashkenazic and Sephardic rituals one covers the *mazzot* and takes the cup. In the Ashkenazic ritual one lifts the cup.

This is what sustained our fathers and us. For not only once somebody rose against us AS*to annihilate us,* but in every generation they rise against us to annihilate us; but the Holy One, praise to Him, rescues us from their hands.

One puts down the cup and uncovers the *mazzot.*

Go and learn. What did Laban the Aramean want to do to our father Jacob? Pharaoh Y*the wicked one* made his ordinance only regarding males but Laban wanted to uproot everything, as it is said (*Deut.* 26:5): **"The Aramean is destroying my father but he descended into Egypt; there he dwelt temporarily with few men and there he became a great, strong, and numerous people."**

AS*"He descended into Egypt," forced by the Divine word.*

אֶת־הַגּוֹי אֲשֶׁר יַעֲבֹדוּ דָּן אָנֹכִי וְאַחֲרֵי כֵן יֵצְאוּ בִּרְכֻשׁ גָּדוֹל.׳

אֶת הַגּוֹי אֲשֶׁר יַעֲבֹדוּ דָּן אָנֹכִי, וְאַחֲרֵי כֵן יֵצְאוּ בִּרְכוּשׁ גָּדוֹל.׳

שָׁנָה. וְגַם אֶת הַגּוֹי אֲשֶׁר יַעֲבֹדוּ דָּן אָנֹכִי, וְאַחֲרֵי כֵן יֵצְאוּ בִּרְכוּשׁ גָּדוֹל.׳

באשכנז וספרד מכסים את המצות. באשכנז מגביהים את הכוס.

וְהִיא שֶׁעָמְדָה לַאֲבוֹתֵינוּ וְלָנוּ. שֶׁלֹּא אֶחָד בִּלְבַד עָמַד עָלֵינוּ לְכַלּוֹתֵינוּ, אֶלָּא שֶׁבְּכָל־דּוֹר וָדוֹר עוֹמְדִים עָלֵינוּ לְכַלּוֹתֵינוּ, וְהַקָּדוֹשׁ בָּרוּךְ הוּא מַצִּילֵנוּ מִיָּדָם.

וְהִיא שֶׁעָמְדָה לַאֲבוֹתֵינוּ וְלָנוּ. שֶׁלֹּא אֶחָד בִּלְבַד עָמַד עָלֵינוּ לְכַלּוֹתֵינוּ, אֶלָּא שֶׁבְּכָל דּוֹר וָדוֹר עוֹמְדִים עָלֵינוּ לְכַלּוֹתֵינוּ, וְהַקָּדוֹשׁ בָּרוּךְ הוּא מַצִּילֵנוּ מִיָּדָם.

הִיא שֶׁעָמְדָה לַאֲבוֹתֵינוּ וְלָנוּ. שֶׁלֹּא אֶחָד בִּלְבַד עָמַד עָלֵינוּ, אֶלָּא שֶׁבְּכָל דּוֹר וָדוֹר עוֹמְדִים עָלֵינוּ לְכַלּוֹתֵינוּ, וְהַקָּדוֹשׁ בָּרוּךְ הוּא מַצִּילֵנוּ מִיָּדָם.

מניחים את הכוס ומגלים את המצות.

צֵא וּלְמַד, מַה בִּקֵּשׁ לָבָן הָאֲרַמִּי לַעֲשׂוֹת לְיַעֲקֹב אָבִינוּ; שֶׁפַּרְעֹה לֹא גָזַר אֶלָּא עַל הַזְּכָרִים וְלָבָן בִּקֵּשׁ לַעֲקוֹר אֶת־הַכֹּל, שֶׁנֶּאֱמַר ׳אֲרַמִּי אֹבֵד אָבִי, וַיֵּרֶד מִצְרַיְמָה, וַיָּגָר שָׁם בִּמְתֵי מְעָט, וַיְהִי שָׁם לְגוֹי גָּדוֹל, עָצוּם, וָרָב.׳ וַיֵּרֶד מִצְרַיְמָה, אָנוּס

צֵא וּלְמַד, מַה בִּקֵּשׁ לָבָן הָאֲרַמִּי לַעֲשׂוֹת לְיַעֲקֹב אָבִינוּ; שֶׁפַּרְעֹה לֹא גָזַר אֶלָּא עַל הַזְּכָרִים וְלָבָן בִּקֵּשׁ לַעֲקוֹר אֶת הַכֹּל, שֶׁנֶּאֱמַר ׳אֲרַמִּי אֹבֵד אָבִי וַיֵּרֶד מִצְרַיְמָה וַיָּגָר שָׁם בִּמְתֵי מְעָט וַיְהִי שָׁם לְגוֹי גָּדוֹל עָצוּם וָרָב.׳ וַיֵּרֶד מִצְרַיְמָה,

צֵא וּלְמַד, מַה בִּקֵּשׁ לָבָן הָאֲרַמִּי לַעֲשׂוֹת לְיַעֲקֹב אָבִינוּ; שֶׁפַּרְעֹה הָרָשָׁע לֹא גָזַר אֶלָּא עַל הַזְּכָרִים, וְלָבָן בִּקֵּשׁ לַעֲקוֹר אֶת הַכֹּל, שֶׁנֶּאֱמַר ׳אֲרַמִּי אֹבֵד אָבִי וַיֵּרֶד מִצְרַיְמָה וַיָּגָר שָׁם.׳ מְלַמֵּד שֶׁלֹּא יָרַד לְהִשְׁתַּקֵּעַ, אֶלָּא לָגוּר שָׁם, שֶׁנֶּאֱמַר ׳וַיֹּאמְרוּ אֶל פַּרְעֹה

AS"*He dwelt there temporarily";* this teaches us that he (A*our father Jacob)* did not descend to be absorbed (A *in Egypt*) but for temporary dwelling, as it is said (*Gen.* 47:4): "They said to Pharaoh: We entered the country for temporary residence because there is no pasture for the sheep-flocks of your servants since the famine is heavy in the land of Canaan; now may your servants please stay in the land of Goshen."

"With few men," as it is said (*Deut.* 10:22): "Seventy souls strong did your fathers descend into Egypt but now the Lord, your God, made you numerous like the stars in the sky."

"There he became a people." This teaches us that Israel was distinguishable there.

"Great, strong," as it is said (*Ex.* 1:7): "The children of Israel were fruitful like vermin, they became numerous and very powerful, and the land became full of them."

"And numerous," as it is said:

עַל פִּי הַדִּבּוּר.

וַיָּגָר שָׁם. מְלַמֵּד שֶׁלֹּא יָרַד יַעֲקֹב אָבִינוּ לְהִשְׁתַּקֵּעַ בְּמִצְרַיִם אֶלָּא לָגוּר שָׁם, שֶׁנֶּאֱמַר 'וַיֹּאמְרוּ אֶל־פַּרְעֹה לָגוּר בָּאָרֶץ בָּאנוּ, כִּי־אֵין מִרְעֶה לַצֹּאן אֲשֶׁר לַעֲבָדֶיךָ, כִּי כָבֵד הָרָעָב בְּאֶרֶץ כְּנָעַן, וְעַתָּה יֵשְׁבוּ־נָא עֲבָדֶיךָ בְּאֶרֶץ גֹּשֶׁן.'

בִּמְתֵי מְעָט, כְּמָה שֶׁנֶּאֱמַר 'בְּשִׁבְעִים נֶפֶשׁ יָרְדוּ אֲבוֹתֶיךָ מִצְרָיְמָה, וְעַתָּה שָׂמְךָ יי אֱלֹהֶיךָ כְּכוֹכְבֵי הַשָּׁמַיִם לָרוֹב.'

וַיְהִי שָׁם לְגוֹי גָּדוֹל, מְלַמֵּד שֶׁהָיוּ יִשְׂרָאֵל מְצוּיָּנִין שָׁם.

לְגוֹי גָּדוֹל, עָצוּם, כְּמָה שֶׁנֶּאֱמַר 'וּבְנֵי יִשְׂרָאֵל פָּרוּ וַיִּשְׁרְצוּ וַיִּרְבּוּ וַיַּעַצְמוּ בִּמְאֹד מְאֹד וַתִּמָּלֵא הָאָרֶץ אוֹתָם.'

וָרָב, כְּמָה שֶׁנֶּאֱמַר 'רְבָבָה כְּצֶמַח הַשָּׂדֶה

אָנוּס עַל פִּי הַדִּבֵּר.

וַיָּגָר שָׁם. מְלַמֵּד שֶׁלֹּא יָרַד לְהִשְׁתַּקֵּעַ אֶלָּא לָגוּר שָׁם, שֶׁנֶּאֱמַר 'וַיֹּאמְרוּ אֶל פַּרְעֹה לָגוּר בָּאָרֶץ בָּאנוּ, כִּי אֵין מִרְעֶה לַצֹּאן אֲשֶׁר לַעֲבָדֶיךָ, כִּי כָבֵד הָרָעָב בְּאֶרֶץ כְּנָעַן, וְעַתָּה יֵשְׁבוּ נָא עֲבָדֶיךָ בְּאֶרֶץ גֹּשֶׁן'

בִּמְתֵי מְעָט, כְּמוֹ שֶׁנֶּאֱמַר 'בְּשִׁבְעִים נֶפֶשׁ יָרְדוּ אֲבוֹתֶיךָ מִצְרָיְמָה, וְעַתָּה שָׂמְךָ יי אֱלֹהֶיךָ כְּכוֹכְבֵי הַשָּׁמַיִם לָרוֹב.'

וַיְהִי שָׁם לְגוֹי גָּדוֹל, מְלַמֵּד שֶׁהָיוּ יִשְׂרָאֵל מְצוּיָּנִים שָׁם.

לְגוֹי גָּדוֹל, עָצוּם, כְּמוֹ שֶׁנֶּאֱמַר 'וּבְנֵי יִשְׂרָאֵל פָּרוּ וַיִּשְׁרְצוּ וַיִּרְבּוּ וַיַּעַצְמוּ בִּמְאֹד מְאֹד וַתִּמָּלֵא הָאָרֶץ אוֹתָם.' **וָרָב,** כְּמוֹ שֶׁנֶּאֱמַר ('וָאֶעֱבוֹר עָלַיִךְ וָאֶרְאֵךְ מִתְבּוֹסֶסֶת

לָגוּר בָּאָרֶץ בָּאנוּ, כִּי אֵין מִרְעֶה לַצֹּאן אֲשֶׁר לַעֲבָדֶיךָ, כִּי כָבֵד הָרָעָב בְּאֶרֶץ כְּנָעַן, וְעַתָּה יֵשְׁבוּ נָא עֲבָדֶיךָ בְּאֶרֶץ גֹּשֶׁן.'

בִּמְתֵי מְעָט, כְּמוֹ שֶׁנֶּאֱמַר 'בְּשִׁבְעִים נֶפֶשׁ יָרְדוּ אֲבוֹתֶיךָ מִצְרָיְמָה, וְעַתָּה שָׂמְךָ יי אֱלֹהֶיךָ כְּכוֹכְבֵי הַשָּׁמַיִם לָרוֹב.'

וַיְהִי שָׁם לְגוֹי, מְלַמֵּד שֶׁהָיוּ יִשְׂרָאֵל מְצוּיָּנִים שָׁם.

גָּדוֹל וְעָצוּם, כְּמוֹ שֶׁנֶּאֱמַר 'וּבְנֵי יִשְׂרָאֵל פָּרוּ וַיִּשְׁרְצוּ וַיִּרְבּוּ וַיַּעַצְמוּ בִּמְאֹד מְאֹד וַתִּמָּלֵא הָאָרֶץ אוֹתָם.'

וָרָב, כְּמוֹ שֶׁנֶּאֱמַר 'רְבָבָה כְּצֶמַח הַשָּׂדֶה נְתַתִּיךְ, וַתִּרְבִּי וַתִּגְדְּלִי וַתָּבֹאִי בַּעֲדִי עֲדָיִים, שָׁדַיִם נָכֹנוּ וּשְׂעָרֵךְ

The following verse is added by some followers of the Sephardic ritual. It is added after the next verse by the Ashkenazic (ḥasidic) followers of the *ARI*. (*Ez.* 16:6): "I passed by you and saw you wallowing in your blood and I said to you: In your blood you shall live, in your blood you shall live."

(*Ez.* 16:7): "I made you numerous like the plants of the field; you increased and grew, you were adorned with the choicest ornaments, firm breasts, and growing hair, but you were nude and naked."

AS(*Deut.* 26:6): **"The Egyptians gave us a bad name and mistreated us; they imposed hard labor on us."**

"The Egyptians gave us a bad name," as it is said (*Ex.* 1:10): "Let us outwit them so their numbers should not grow because it might be that, in case of war they also would join our enemies, make war upon us, and leave the country."

"They mistreated us," as it is said (*Ex.* 1:11): "They put officers of forced labor over the people in order to mistreat them when they were carrying heavy loads; they built storage cities for Pharaoh, Pithom, and Ra'amses."

"They put hard labor on us," as it is said (*Ex.* 1:13): "Egypt enslaved the children of Israel with back-breaking work."

נְתַתִּיךְ, וַתִּרְבִּי וַתִּגְדְּלִי וַתָּבֹאִי בַּעֲדִי עֲדָיִים, שָׁדַיִם נָכֹנוּ וּשְׂעָרֵךְ צִמֵּחַ, וְאַתְּ עֵרוֹם וְעֶרְיָה.׳

בנוסח האר״י האשכנזי מוסיפים:

׳וָאֶעֱבוֹר עָלַיִךְ וָאֶרְאֵךְ מִתְבּוֹסֶסֶת בְּדָמָיִךְ, וָאֹמַר לָךְ בְּדָמַיִךְ חֲיִי, וָאֹמַר לָךְ בְּדָמַיִךְ חֲיִי׳.

בְּדָמַיִךְ, וָאֹמַר לָךְ בְּדָמַיִךְ חֲיִי, וָאֹמַר לָךְ בְּדָמַיִךְ חֲיִי.׳) ׳רְבָבָה כְּצֶמַח הַשָּׂדֶה נְתַתִּיךְ, וַתִּרְבִּי וַתִּגְדְּלִי וַתָּבֹאִי בַּעֲדִי עֲדָיִים, שָׁדַיִם נָכֹנוּ וּשְׂעָרֵךְ צִמֵּחַ, וְאַתְּ עֵרוֹם וְעֶרְיָה.׳

צִמֵּחַ, וְאַתְּ עֵרוֹם וְעֶרְיָה.׳

וַיָּרֵעוּ אֹתָנוּ הַמִּצְרִים וַיְעַנּוּנוּ וַיִּתְּנוּ עָלֵינוּ עֲבֹדָה קָשָׁה.

וַיָּרֵעוּ אֹתָנוּ הַמִּצְרִים, כְּמָה שֶׁנֶּאֱמַר ׳הָבָה נִתְחַכְּמָה לוֹ, פֶּן יִרְבֶּה, וְהָיָה כִּי תִקְרֶאנָה מִלְחָמָה וְנוֹסַף גַּם־הוּא עַל־שֹׂנְאֵינוּ, וְנִלְחַם־בָּנוּ וְעָלָה מִן־הָאָרֶץ.׳

וַיְעַנּוּנוּ, כְּמָה שֶׁנֶּאֱמַר ׳וַיָּשִׂימוּ עָלָיו שָׂרֵי מִסִּים לְמַעַן עַנֹּתוֹ בְּסִבְלֹתָם, וַיִּבֶן עָרֵי מִסְכְּנוֹת לְפַרְעֹה, אֶת פִּתֹם וְאֶת רַעַמְסֵס.׳

וַיִּתְּנוּ עָלֵינוּ עֲבֹדָה קָשָׁה, כְּמָה שֶׁנֶּאֱמַר

וַיָּרֵעוּ אֹתָנוּ הַמִּצְרִים וַיְעַנּוּנוּ וַיִּתְּנוּ עָלֵינוּ עֲבֹדָה קָשָׁה.

וַיָּרֵעוּ אֹתָנוּ הַמִּצְרִים, כְּמוֹ שֶׁנֶּאֱמַר ׳הָבָה נִתְחַכְּמָה לוֹ, פֶּן יִרְבֶּה, וְהָיָה כִּי תִקְרֶאנָה מִלְחָמָה וְנוֹסַף גַּם הוּא עַל שֹׂנְאֵינוּ, וְנִלְחַם בָּנוּ וְעָלָה מִן הָאָרֶץ.׳

וַיְעַנּוּנוּ, כְּמוֹ שֶׁנֶּאֱמַר ׳וַיָּשִׂימוּ עָלָיו שָׂרֵי מִסִּים לְמַעַן עַנֹּתוֹ בְּסִבְלֹתָם, וַיִּבֶן עָרֵי מִסְכְּנוֹת לְפַרְעֹה, אֶת פִּתֹם וְאֶת רַעַמְסֵס.׳

וַיִּתְּנוּ עָלֵינוּ עֲבֹדָה קָשָׁה, כְּמוֹ שֶׁנֶּאֱמַר

וַיָּרֵעוּ אֹתָנוּ הַמִּצְרִים, כְּמוֹ שֶׁנֶּאֱמַר ׳הָבָה נִתְחַכְּמָה לוֹ פֶּן יִרְבֶּה, וְהָיָה כִּי תִקְרֶאנָה מִלְחָמָה וְנוֹסַף גַּם הוּא עַל שֹׂנְאֵינוּ, וְנִלְחַם בָּנוּ וְעָלָה מִן הָאָרֶץ.׳

וַיְעַנּוּנוּ, כְּמוֹ שֶׁנֶּאֱמַר ׳וַיָּשִׂימוּ עָלָיו שָׂרֵי מִסִּים לְמַעַן עַנֹּתוֹ בְּסִבְלֹתָם, וַיִּבֶן עָרֵי מִסְכְּנוֹת לְפַרְעֹה, אֶת פִּתֹם וְאֶת רַעַמְסֵס.׳

וַיִּתְּנוּ עָלֵינוּ עֲבֹדָה קָשָׁה, כְּמוֹ שֶׁנֶּאֱמַר ׳וַיַּעֲבִדוּ מִצְרַיִם אֶת

AS(*Deut*. 26:7) "**We cried to the Lord, the God of our fathers; the Lord heard our voices and He saw our deprivation, our worries, and our oppression.**"

"We cried to the Lord, the God of our fathers," as it is said (*Ex*. 2:23): "It was in those momentous days that the king of Egypt died. The children of Israel sighed because of the labor and they cried; their prayers ascended to God from their labor."

"The Lord heard our voices," as it is said (*Ex*. 2:24): "God heard their outcry and God remembered His covenant with Abraham, Isaac, and Jacob."

"He saw our deprivation," that is the separation of spouses as it is said (*Ex*. 2:25): "God saw the children of Israel and God knew."

'וַיַּעֲבִדוּ מִצְרַיִם
אֶת־בְּנֵי יִשְׂרָאֵל
בְּפָרֶךְ.'

וַנִּצְעַק אֶל־יְיָ אֱלֹהֵי
אֲבֹתֵינוּ, וַיִּשְׁמַע יְיָ
אֶת־קֹלֵנוּ, וַיַּרְא
אֶת־עָנְיֵנוּ
וְאֶת־עֲמָלֵנוּ
וְאֶת־לַחֲצֵנוּ.

וַנִּצְעַק אֶל־יְיָ אֱלֹהֵי
אֲבֹתֵינוּ, כְּמָה שֶׁנֶּאֱמַר
'וַיְהִי בַיָּמִים הָרַבִּים
הָהֵם וַיָּמָת מֶלֶךְ
מִצְרַיִם, וַיֵּאָנְחוּ
בְנֵי־יִשְׂרָאֵל
מִן־הָעֲבֹדָה וַיִּזְעָקוּ,
וַתַּעַל שַׁוְעָתָם
אֶל־הָאֱלֹהִים
מִן־הָעֲבֹדָה.'

וַיִּשְׁמַע יְיָ אֶת־קֹלֵנוּ,
כְּמָה שֶׁנֶּאֱמַר 'וַיִּשְׁמַע
אֱלֹהִים אֶת־נַאֲקָתָם,
וַיִּזְכֹּר אֱלֹהִים
אֶת־בְּרִיתוֹ
אֶת־אַבְרָהָם,
אֶת־יִצְחָק,
וְאֶת־יַעֲקֹב.'

וַיַּרְא אֶת־עָנְיֵנוּ, זוֹ
פְּרִישׁוּת דֶּרֶךְ אֶרֶץ,

'וַיַּעֲבִדוּ מִצְרַיִם
אֶת בְּנֵי יִשְׂרָאֵל
בְּפָרֶךְ.'

וַנִּצְעַק אֶל יְיָ
אֱלֹהֵי אֲבֹתֵינוּ,
וַיִּשְׁמַע יְיָ אֶת
קֹלֵנוּ, וַיַּרְא אֶת
עָנְיֵנוּ וְאֶת עֲמָלֵנוּ
וְאֶת לַחֲצֵנוּ.

וַנִּצְעַק אֶל יְיָ
אֱלֹהֵי אֲבֹתֵינוּ,
כְּמוֹ שֶׁנֶּאֱמַר 'וַיְהִי
בַיָּמִים הָרַבִּים
הָהֵם וַיָּמָת מֶלֶךְ
מִצְרַיִם, וַיֵּאָנְחוּ
בְנֵי יִשְׂרָאֵל מִן
הָעֲבֹדָה וַיִּזְעָקוּ,
וַתַּעַל שַׁוְעָתָם אֶל
הָאֱלֹהִים מִן
הָעֲבֹדָה.'

וַיִּשְׁמַע יְיָ אֶת
קֹלֵנוּ, כְּמוֹ שֶׁנֶּאֱמַר
'וַיִּשְׁמַע אֱלֹהִים
אֶת נַאֲקָתָם, וַיִּזְכֹּר
אֱלֹהִים אֶת בְּרִיתוֹ
אֶת אַבְרָהָם, אֶת
יִצְחָק, וְאֶת יַעֲקֹב.'

וַיַּרְא אֶת עָנְיֵנוּ, זוֹ
פְּרִישׁוּת דֶּרֶךְ אֶרֶץ,
כְּמוֹ שֶׁנֶּאֱמַר 'וַיַּרְא
אֱלֹהִים אֶת בְּנֵי
יִשְׂרָאֵל, וַיֵּדַע

בְּנֵי יִשְׂרָאֵל בְּפָרֶךְ.'

וַנִּצְעַק אֶל יְיָ אֱלֹהֵי
אֲבֹתֵינוּ, כְּמוֹ
שֶׁנֶּאֱמַר 'וַיְהִי בַיָּמִים
הָרַבִּים הָהֵם וַיָּמָת
מֶלֶךְ מִצְרַיִם,
וַיֵּאָנְחוּ בְנֵי יִשְׂרָאֵל
מִן הָעֲבֹדָה וַיִּזְעָקוּ,
וַתַּעַל שַׁוְעָתָם אֶל
הָאֱלֹהִים מִן
הָעֲבֹדָה.'

וַיִּשְׁמַע יְיָ אֶת קֹלֵנוּ,
כְּמוֹ שֶׁנֶּאֱמַר 'וַיִּשְׁמַע
אֱלֹהִים אֶת נַאֲקָתָם,
וַיִּזְכֹּר אֱלֹהִים אֶת
בְּרִיתוֹ אֶת אַבְרָהָם,
אֶת יִצְחָק, וְאֶת
יַעֲקֹב.'

וַיַּרְא אֶת עָנְיֵנוּ, זוֹ
פְּרִישׁוּת דֶּרֶךְ אֶרֶץ,
כְּמוֹ שֶׁנֶּאֱמַר 'וַיַּרְא
אֱלֹהִים אֶת בְּנֵי
יִשְׂרָאֵל, וַיֵּדַע
אֱלֹהִים.'

וְאֶת עֲמָלֵנוּ, אֵלּוּ
הַבָּנִים, כְּמוֹ שֶׁנֶּאֱמַר

"Our worries," these are the sons, as it is said (*Ex.* 1:22): "Every son who is born alive you shall throw into the Nile but every daughter you shall let live."

"And our oppression," this is the suffering, as it is said (*Ex.* 3:9): "Also I have seen the oppression with which the Egyptians oppress them."

[AS](*Deut.* 26:8) **"The Lord led us out of Egypt with strong hand, outstretched arm, great apparitions, signs, and miracles."**

"The Lord led us out of Egypt," not through an angel, nor through a seraph, nor through an agent, but the Holy One, praise to Him, in His splendor [AS]*by Himself*, as it is said (*Ex.* 12:12): "I shall cross the land of Egypt in that night, I shall smite every firstborn in the land of Egypt, from human to animal, and I shall execute judgments against all idols in Egypt; I am the Lord."

כְּמָה שֶׁנֶּאֱמַר 'וַיַּרְא אֱלֹהִים אֶת־בְּנֵי יִשְׂרָאֵל, וַיֵּדַע אֱלֹהִים.'

וְאֶת־עֲמָלֵנוּ, אֵלּוּ הַבָּנִים, כְּמָה שֶׁנֶּאֱמַר 'כָּל־הַבֵּן הַיִּלּוֹד הַיְאֹרָה תַּשְׁלִיכֻהוּ, וְכָל־הַבַּת תְּחַיּוּן.'

וְאֶת־לַחֲצֵנוּ, זֶה הַדְּחַק, כְּמָה שֶׁנֶּאֱמַר 'וְגַם־רָאִיתִי אֶת־הַלַּחַץ אֲשֶׁר מִצְרַיִם לֹחֲצִים אֹתָם.'

אֱלֹהִים.'

וְאֶת עֲמָלֵנוּ, אֵלּוּ הַבָּנִים, כְּמוֹ שֶׁנֶּאֱמַר 'כָּל הַבֵּן הַיִּלּוֹד הַיְאֹרָה תַּשְׁלִיכֻהוּ, וְכָל הַבַּת תְּחַיּוּן.'

וְאֶת לַחֲצֵנוּ, זֶה הַדְּחַק, כְּמוֹ שֶׁנֶּאֱמַר 'וְגַם רָאִיתִי אֶת הַלַּחַץ אֲשֶׁר מִצְרַיִם לֹחֲצִים אֹתָם.'

'כָּל הַבֵּן הַיִּלּוֹד הַיְאֹרָה תַּשְׁלִיכֻהוּ, וְכָל הַבַּת תְּחַיּוּן.'

וְאֶת לַחֲצֵנוּ, זֶה הַדְּחַק, כְּמוֹ שֶׁנֶּאֱמַר 'וְגַם רָאִיתִי אֶת הַלַּחַץ אֲשֶׁר מִצְרַיִם לֹחֲצִים אֹתָם.'

וַיּוֹצִאֵנוּ יי מִמִּצְרַיִם בְּיָד חֲזָקָה וּבִזְרֹעַ נְטוּיָה וּבְמֹרָא גָּדֹל וּבְאֹתוֹת וּבְמֹפְתִים.

וַיּוֹצִאֵנוּ יי מִמִּצְרַיִם, לֹא עַל יְדֵי מַלְאָךְ, וְלֹא עַל יְדֵי שָׂרָף, וְלֹא עַל יְדֵי שָׁלִיחַ, אֶלָּא הַקָּדוֹשׁ בָּרוּךְ הוּא בִּכְבוֹדוֹ וּבְעַצְמוֹ, שֶׁנֶּאֱמַר 'וְעָבַרְתִּי בְאֶרֶץ־מִצְרַיִם בַּלַּיְלָה הַזֶּה, וְהִכֵּיתִי כָל־בְּכוֹר בְּאֶרֶץ מִצְרַיִם מֵאָדָם וְעַד־בְּהֵמָה,

וַיּוֹצִאֵנוּ יי מִמִּצְרַיִם בְּיָד חֲזָקָה וּבִזְרֹעַ נְטוּיָה וּבְמֹרָא גָּדֹל וּבְאֹתוֹת וּבְמֹפְתִים.

וַיּוֹצִאֵנוּ יי מִמִּצְרַיִם, לֹא עַל יְדֵי מַלְאָךְ, וְלֹא עַל יְדֵי שָׂרָף, וְלֹא עַל יְדֵי שָׁלִיחַ, אֶלָּא הַקָּדוֹשׁ בָּרוּךְ הוּא בִּכְבוֹדוֹ וּבְעַצְמוֹ, שֶׁנֶּאֱמַר 'וְעָבַרְתִּי בְאֶרֶץ מִצְרַיִם בַּלַּיְלָה הַזֶּה, וְהִכֵּיתִי כָל בְּכוֹר בְּאֶרֶץ מִצְרַיִם,

וַיּוֹצִאֵנוּ יי מִמִּצְרַיִם, לֹא עַל יְדֵי מַלְאָךְ, לֹא עַל יְדֵי שָׂרָף, לֹא עַל יְדֵי שָׁלִיחַ, **אֶלָּא** הַקָּדוֹשׁ בָּרוּךְ הוּא בִּכְבוֹדוֹ, שֶׁנֶּאֱמַר 'וְעָבַרְתִּי בְאֶרֶץ מִצְרַיִם בַּלַּיְלָה הַזֶּה, וְהִכֵּיתִי כָל בְּכוֹר בְּאֶרֶץ מִצְרַיִם מֵאָדָם וְעַד בְּהֵמָה, וּבְכָל אֱלֹהֵי מִצְרַיִם אֶעֱשֶׂה שְׁפָטִים, אֲנִי יי.'

תוספת אגדה זה נמצאת בסדור חלף מהמדרש וראוי

Required insert for Ashkenazic and Sephardic rituals:

"I shall cross through the land of Egypt," I, not an angel.

"I shall smite every firstborn," I, not a seraph.

"And I shall execute judgments against all idols in Egypt," I, not A*the* S*an* agent.

"I am the Lord," I, no other.

Optional insert for Yemenites and some Oriental communities of the Sephardic ritual only:

Our teachers of blessed memory said: When the Holy One, praise to Him, descended upon the Egyptians in Egypt, nine hundred million descended with Him. Some of them were angels of fire, some angels of hail, some angels of fear, some angels of trembling, some angels of shivering; trembling and shivering seizes everyone who sees them. They said before Him: "Sovereign of the world, Highest power, Master of masters! When a king of flesh and blood goes to war, his generals and ministers surround his majesty. Now You, King over emperors, please command us, since we are your servants and they (Israel) are the children of Your covenant, to descend and wage war against them (the Egyptians)." He answered them: "I shall not be satisfied unless I shall descend myself, I in My majesty, I in My greatness, I in My holiness, I am the One and no other."

"With a strong hand," that is the animal plague, as it is said (*Ex.* 9:3): "Behold, the hand of the Lord shall be on your animals in the fields, on the donkeys, horses, camels, kine, and sheep; a very heavy murrain."

"Outstretched arm," this is the sword, as it is said (*1 Chr.* 21:16): ". . . his sword drawn in his hand, stretched out against Jerusalem."

"Great apparition," this is the revelation of the Divine

וּבְכָל־אֱלֹהֵי מִצְרַיִם אֶעֱשֶׂה שְׁפָטִים, אֲנִי יי׳.

׳וְעָבַרְתִּי בְאֶרֶץ־מִצְרַיִם׳, אֲנִי וְלֹא מַלְאָךְ. ׳וְהִכֵּיתִי כָל־בְּכוֹר׳, אֲנִי וְלֹא שָׂרָף. ׳וּבְכָל־אֱלֹהֵי מִצְרַיִם אֶעֱשֶׂה שְׁפָטִים׳, אֲנִי וְלֹא הַשָּׁלִיחַ. ׳אֲנִי יי׳, אֲנִי הוּא וְלֹא אַחֵר.

בְּיָד חֲזָקָה, זוֹ הַדֶּבֶר, כְּמָה שֶׁנֶּאֱמַר ׳הִנֵּה יַד־יי הוֹיָה בְּמִקְנְךָ אֲשֶׁר בַּשָּׂדֶה, בַּסּוּסִים, בַּחֲמֹרִים, בַּגְּמַלִּים, בַּבָּקָר וּבַצֹּאן, דֶּבֶר כָּבֵד מְאֹד׳.

וּבִזְרֹעַ נְטוּיָה, זוֹ הַחֶרֶב, כְּמָה שֶׁנֶּאֱמַר ׳וְחַרְבּוֹ שְׁלוּפָה בְּיָדוֹ, נְטוּיָה עַל יְרוּשָׁלָיִם׳.

וּבְמֹרָא גָּדֹל, זוֹ גִּלּוּי שְׁכִינָה, כְּמָה שֶׁנֶּאֱמַר ׳אוֹ הֲנִסָּה אֱלֹהִים לָבוֹא לָקַחַת לוֹ גוֹי מִקֶּרֶב גּוֹי, בְּמַסֹּת בְּאֹתֹת וּבְמוֹפְתִים, וּבְמִלְחָמָה, וּבְיָד

מֵאָדָם וְעַד בְּהֵמָה, וּבְכָל אֱלֹהֵי מִצְרַיִם אֶעֱשֶׂה שְׁפָטִים, אֲנִי יי׳.

׳וְעָבַרְתִּי בְאֶרֶץ מִצְרַיִם׳, אֲנִי וְלֹא מַלְאָךְ. ׳וְהִכֵּיתִי כָל בְּכוֹר׳, אֲנִי וְלֹא שָׂרָף. ׳וּבְכָל אֱלֹהֵי מִצְרַיִם אֶעֱשֶׂה שְׁפָטִים׳, אֲנִי וְלֹא שָׁלִיחַ. ׳אֲנִי יי׳, אֲנִי הוּא וְלֹא אַחֵר.

בכורדיסתאן מוסיפים כאן ׳אמרו רז״ל׳, נמצא בנוסח תימן.

בְּיָד חֲזָקָה, זוֹ הַדֶּבֶר, כְּמוֹ שֶׁנֶּאֱמַר ׳הִנֵּה יַד יי הוֹיָה בְּמִקְנְךָ אֲשֶׁר בַּשָּׂדֶה, בַּסּוּסִים, בַּחֲמֹרִים, בַּגְּמַלִּים, בַּבָּקָר וּבַצֹּאן, דֶּבֶר כָּבֵד מְאֹד׳.

וּבִזְרֹעַ נְטוּיָה, זוֹ הַחֶרֶב, כְּמוֹ שֶׁנֶּאֱמַר ׳וְחַרְבּוֹ שְׁלוּפָה בְּיָדוֹ, נְטוּיָה עַל יְרוּשָׁלָםִ׳.

וּבְמֹרָא גָּדֹל, זֶה גִּלּוּי שְׁכִינָה, כְּמוֹ שֶׁנֶּאֱמַר ׳אוֹ הֲנִסָּה אֱלֹהִים לָבוֹא

לאמרה להזכיר חסדי המקום ואהבתו וחבתו לעם נחלתו, לא עשה כן לכל גוי. וזה נוסחה:

אמרו רז״ל כשירד הקב״ה על המצרים במצרים ירדו עמו תשעת אלפים רבבות, מהם מלאכי אש, ומהם מלאכי ברד, ומהם מלאכי רתת, ומהם מלאכי זיע, ומהם מלאכי חלחלה, ורתת וחלחלה אוחזות למי שהוא רואה אותם. אמרו לפניו: רבש״ע, אלהי האלהים ואדוני הארונים, והלא מלך ב״ו כשהוא יורד למלחמה, שריו ועבדיו מקיפים בכבודו, ואתה מלך מלכי המלכים דיין עלינו שאנחנו עבדיך והם בני בריתך, נרד ונעשה עמהם מלחמה. אמר להם, אין דעתי מתקררת עד שארד אני בעצמי, אני בכבודי, אני בגדולתי, אני בקדושתי, אני יי, אני הוא ולא אחר.

בְּיָד חֲזָקָה, זֶה הַדֶּבֶר, כְּמוֹ שֶׁנֶּאֱמַר ׳הִנֵּה יַד יי הוֹיָה בְּמִקְנְךָ אֲשֶׁר בַּשָּׂדֶה, בַּסּוּסִים, בַּחֲמֹרִים, בַּגְּמַלִּים, בַּבָּקָר וּבַצֹּאן, דֶּבֶר

presence, as it is said (*Deut.* 4:34): "Or did any power ever try to come, to take for himself a nation from the midst of another nation with trials, with signs and miracles and war, with a strong hand and an outstretched arm, and with great apparitions, like all that the Lord, your God, performed for you in Egypt before your eyes."

"Signs," this is the staff (of Moses), as it is said (*Ex.* 4:17): "Take this staff in your hands because you shall do the signs with it."

"And miracles," that is the blood, as it is said (*Joel* 3:3): "I shall perform miracles in the sky and on the earth:"

In all rituals except Western Ashkenazic families one dips a finger into the wine glass and lifts out a drop for every one of the expressions: "blood, fire, columns of smoke," also for each one of the Ten Plagues and the three abbreviations of R. Yehudah for a total of sixteen drops. In Western Ashkenazic families one takes a drop only for the Ten Plagues and the three abbreviations for a total of thirteen drops. Some families use a small spoon instead of a finger; see the commentary. Some Oriental communities pour the wine into another cup or vessel.

"Blood, Fire, and Columns of Smoke."

חֲזָקָה, וּבִזְרוֹעַ נְטוּיָה, וּבְמוֹרָאִים גְּדֹלִים, כְּכֹל אֲשֶׁר־עָשָׂה לָכֶם יי אֱלֹהֵיכֶם בְּמִצְרַיִם, לְעֵינֶיךָ׃'

וּבְאֹתוֹת, זֶה הַמַּטֶּה, כְּמָה שֶׁנֶּאֱמַר 'וְאֶת־הַמַּטֶּה הַזֶּה תִּקַּח בְּיָדֶךָ, אֲשֶׁר תַּעֲשֶׂה־בּוֹ אֶת־הָאֹתֹת׃'

וּבְמֹפְתִים, זֶה הַדָּם, כְּמָה שֶׁנֶּאֱמַר 'וְנָתַתִּי מוֹפְתִים בַּשָּׁמַיִם וּבָאָרֶץ,

במנהג האר"י נוהגים לזרוק יין באצבע (או בכפית) מן הכוס כשאומרים **דָּם, וָאֵשׁ, וְתִימֲרוֹת עָשָׁן**, וכן בעשר מכות ובסימנים של ר' יהודה, סך הכל ט"ז פעמים.

דָּם וָאֵשׁ וְתִימֲרוֹת עָשָׁן.

לָקַחַת לוֹ גוֹי מִקֶּרֶב גּוֹי, בְּמַסֹּת בְּאֹתֹת וּבְמוֹפְתִים, וּבְמִלְחָמָה, וּבְיָד חֲזָקָה, וּבִזְרוֹעַ נְטוּיָה, וּבְמוֹרָאִים גְּדֹלִים, כְּכֹל אֲשֶׁר עָשָׂה לָכֶם יי אֱלֹהֵיכֶם בְּמִצְרַיִם, לְעֵינֶיךָ׃'

וּבְאֹתוֹת, זֶה הַמַּטֶּה, כְּמוֹ שֶׁנֶּאֱמַר 'וְאֶת הַמַּטֶּה הַזֶּה תִּקַּח בְּיָדֶךָ, אֲשֶׁר תַּעֲשֶׂה בּוֹ אֶת הָאֹתֹת׃'

וּבְמֹפְתִים, זֶה הַדָּם, כְּמוֹ שֶׁנֶּאֱמַר 'וְנָתַתִּי מוֹפְתִים בַּשָּׁמַיִם וּבָאָרֶץ,

יזה היין באצבע (או בכפית) מן הכוס כשאומרים **דָּם, וָאֵשׁ, וְתִימְרוֹת עָשָׁן**, וכן בעשר מכות ובסימנים של ר' יהודה, סך הכל ט"ז פעמים.

דָּם וָאֵשׁ וְתִימְרוֹת עָשָׁן׃'

כָּבֵד מְאֹד׃'

וּבִזְרֹעַ נְטוּיָה, זוֹ הַחֶרֶב, כְּמוֹ שֶׁנֶּאֱמַר 'וְחַרְבּוֹ שְׁלוּפָה בְּיָדוֹ, נְטוּיָה עַל יְרוּשָׁלָםִ׃'

וּבְמֹרָא גָּדֹל, זֶה גִּלּוּי שְׁכִינָה, כְּמוֹ שֶׁנֶּאֱמַר 'אוֹ הֲנִסָּה אֱלֹהִים לָבוֹא לָקַחַת לוֹ גוֹי מִקֶּרֶב גּוֹי, בְּמַסֹּת בְּאֹתֹת וּבְמוֹפְתִים וּבְמִלְחָמָה, וּבְיָד חֲזָקָה, וּבִזְרוֹעַ נְטוּיָה, וּבְמוֹרָאִים גְּדֹלִים, כְּכֹל אֲשֶׁר עָשָׂה לָכֶם יי אֱלֹהֵיכֶם בְּמִצְרַיִם לְעֵינֶיךָ׃'

וּבְאֹתוֹת, זֶה הַמַּטֶּה, כְּמוֹ שֶׁנֶּאֱמַר 'וְאֶת הַמַּטֶּה הַזֶּה תִּקַּח בְּיָדֶךָ, אֲשֶׁר תַּעֲשֶׂה בּוֹ אֶת הָאֹתֹת׃'

וּבְמֹפְתִים, זֶה הַדָּם, כְּמוֹ שֶׁנֶּאֱמַר 'וְנָתַתִּי מוֹפְתִים בַּשָּׁמַיִם וּבָאָרֶץ,

נוהגים לזרוק באצבע מן הכוס כשאומרים **דָּם, וָאֵשׁ, וְתִימְרוֹת עָשָׁן**, וכן בעשר מכות ובסימנים של ר' יהודה, סך הכל ט"ז פעמים.

Another interpretation: "With strong hand" two (words), "outstretched arm" two (words), "great apparition" two (words), "signs" two (as plural), "miracles" two (as plural): These are the Ten Plagues that the Holy One, praise to Him, brought on the Egyptians in Egypt, namely:

Blood, Frogs, Lice, Wild Beasts, Murrain, Skin Disease, Hailstorm, Locusts, Darkness, Slaying of the Firstborn.

Rebbi Yehudah used to give them acronyms:

Dĕẓakh, ʻĂdash, Bĕ'aḥav.

Rebbi Yossi the Galilean says: How can one prove that the Egyptians were hit in Egypt by ten plagues but on the sea by fifty plagues? In Egypt it says (*Ex.* 8:15): "The magicians said to Pharaoh: This is a finger of God." But on the sea it says (*Ex.* 14:31): "Israel saw the great hand that the Lord had done against the Egyptians and the people feared the Lord and believed in the Lord and Moses His servant."
How much were they hit by the finger? Ten plagues! From this you can say that in Egypt they were hit by ten plagues and on the sea by fifty plagues.
Rebbi Eliezer says: How can one prove that each single plague which the Holy One, praise to Him, brought on the Egyptians in Egypt consisted of four (separate) plagues? It is said (*Ps.* 78:49):

"He sends against them the embers of His wrath
Anger and rage and trouble
A band of messengers of disasters."

Anger — One, Rage — Two, Trouble — Three, A band of messengers of disasters — Four. Therefore, they were hit in Egypt by forty plagues and on the sea by two hundred plagues.
Rebbi Akiba says: How can one prove that each single plague which the Holy One, praise to Him, brought on the Egyptians

דָּם וָאֵשׁ וְתִימְרוֹת
עָשָׁן.

בכל העדות נוהגים לזרוק מן הכוס כשמזכירים כל מכה ומכה של עשר מכות וכן בדצ״ך, עד״ש, באח״ב

דָּבָר אַחֵר. בְּיָד חֲזָקָה שְׁתַּיִם, וּבִזְרֹעַ נְטוּיָה שְׁתַּיִם, וּבְמֹרָא גָּדֹל שְׁתַּיִם, וּבְאֹתוֹת שְׁתַּיִם, וּבְמֹפְתִים שְׁתַּיִם, אֵלּוּ עֶשֶׂר מַכּוֹת שֶׁהֵבִיא הַקָּדוֹשׁ בָּרוּךְ הוּא עַל הַמִּצְרִים בְּמִצְרַיִם, וְאֵלּוּ הֵן:

דָּם, צְפַרְדֵּעַ, כִּנִּים, עָרוֹב, דֶּבֶר, שְׁחִין, בָּרָד, אַרְבֶּה, חֹשֶׁךְ, מַכַּת בְּכוֹרוֹת.

רַבִּי יְהוּדָה הָיָה נוֹתֵן בָּהֶם סִימָנִים:
דְּצַ״ךְ, עֲדַ״שׁ, בְּאַחַ״ב.

רַבִּי יוֹסֵי הַגְּלִילִי אוֹמֵר: מִנַּיִן אַתָּה אוֹמֵר, שֶׁלָּקוּ הַמִּצְרִים בְּמִצְרַיִם עֶשֶׂר מַכּוֹת, וְעַל הַיָּם לָקוּ חֲמִשִּׁים מַכּוֹת. בְּמִצְרַיִם מַה הוּא אוֹמֵר? ׳וַיֹּאמְרוּ הַחַרְטֻמִּים אֶל פַּרְעֹה: אֶצְבַּע אֱלֹהִים הִיא׳. וְעַל הַיָּם מַה הוּא אוֹמֵר? ׳וַיַּרְא יִשְׂרָאֵל אֶת הַיָּד הַגְּדֹלָה אֲשֶׁר עָשָׂה יי בְּמִצְרַיִם, וַיִּירְאוּ הָעָם אֶת יי וַיַּאֲמִינוּ בַּיי וּבְמֹשֶׁה עַבְדּוֹ׳. כַּמָּה לָקוּ בְּאֶצְבַּע? עֶשֶׂר מַכּוֹת! אֱמוֹר מֵעַתָּה: בְּמִצְרַיִם לָקוּ עֶשֶׂר מַכּוֹת וְעַל הַיָּם לָקוּ חֲמִשִּׁים מַכּוֹת.

רַבִּי אֱלִיעֶזֶר אוֹמֵר: מִנַּיִן שֶׁכָּל מַכָּה וּמַכָּה שֶׁהֵבִיא הַקָּדוֹשׁ בָּרוּךְ הוּא עַל הַמִּצְרִים בְּמִצְרַיִם הָיְתָה שֶׁל אַרְבַּע מַכּוֹת? שֶׁנֶּאֱמַר ׳יְשַׁלַּח בָּם חֲרוֹן אַפּוֹ: עֶבְרָה וָזַעַם וְצָרָה, מִשְׁלַחַת מַלְאֲכֵי רָעִים׳. עֶבְרָה אַחַת, וָזַעַם שְׁתַּיִם, וְצָרָה שָׁלֹשׁ, מִשְׁלַחַת מַלְאֲכֵי רָעִים אַרְבַּע. אֱמוֹר מֵעַתָּה בְּמִצְרַיִם לָקוּ אַרְבָּעִים מַכּוֹת וְעַל הַיָּם לָקוּ מָאתַיִם מַכּוֹת.

רַבִּי עֲקִיבָא אוֹמֵר: מִנַּיִן שֶׁכָּל מַכָּה וּמַכָּה שֶׁהֵבִיא הַקָּדוֹשׁ בָּרוּךְ הוּא עַל הַמִּצְרִים בְּמִצְרַיִם הָיְתָה שֶׁל חָמֵשׁ מַכּוֹת? שֶׁנֶּאֱמַר ׳יְשַׁלַּח בָּם: חֲרוֹן אַפּוֹ, עֶבְרָה וָזַעַם וְצָרָה, מִשְׁלַחַת מַלְאֲכֵי

in Egypt consisted of five (separate) plagues? It is said (*Ps.* 78:49): "He sends against them: the embers of His wrath, anger and rage and trouble, a band of messengers of disasters." The embers of His wrath — One, Anger — Two, Rage — Three, Trouble — Four, A band of messengers of disasters — Five. Therefore, they were hit in Egypt by fifty plagues and on the sea by two hundred and fifty plagues.

For how many [Y]*doubled and redoubled* supernatural good things are we indebted to the Omnipresent One, [Y]*praise to Him*?

If He had led us out of Egypt but had not punished them, it would have been enough for us!

If He had punished them but not [Y]*passed judgment on* their idols, it would have been enough for us!

If He had ([AS]*punished*) [Y]*passed judgment on* their idols but had not killed their firstborn, it would have been enough for us!

If He had killed their firstborn but had not given us their money, it would have been enough for us!

Insert for Yemenites and other Oriental communities:

How can we prove that He gave us their money? It says (*Ex.* 12:36): ". . . they lent to them, so they emptied Egypt." They made Egypt like a trap without bait or the depth of the sea without fish. And why does Scripture prefer the booty of the Red Sea over the booty of Egypt? In Egypt they took the contents of private houses but on the Red Sea they took the contents of the treasuries. In this sense it is said (*Ps.* 68:14): "Wings of the dove covered with silver and her limbs with fine gold." "Wings of the dove covered with silver": that is the booty of Egypt; "and her limbs with fine gold": this is the booty of the Sea. (*Ez.* 16:7): "You did increase and grow": that is the booty of Egypt; "you were adorned with the choicest ornaments": this is the booty of the Sea. (*Cant.* 1:11): "Pillars of gold we shall make for you": that is the booty of the Sea; "with inlaid of silver": this is the booty of Egypt.

רָעִים. חֲרוֹן אַפּוֹ אַחַת, עֶבְרָה שְׁתַּיִם, וָזַעַם שָׁלֹשׁ, וְצָרָה אַרְבַּע, מִשְׁלַחַת מַלְאֲכֵי רָעִים חָמֵשׁ. אֱמוֹר מֵעַתָּה בְּמִצְרַיִם לָקוּ חֲמִשִּׁים מַכּוֹת וְעַל הַיָּם לָקוּ חֲמִשִּׁים וּמָאתַיִם מַכּוֹת.

נוסח אשכנז וספרד

כַּמָּה מַעֲלוֹת טוֹבוֹת לַמָּקוֹם עָלֵינוּ.

אִלּוּ הוֹצִיאָנוּ מִמִּצְרַיִם, וְלֹא עָשָׂה בָהֶם שְׁפָטִים דַּיֵּנוּ.
אִלּוּ עָשָׂה בָהֶם שְׁפָטִים, וְלֹא עָשָׂה בֵאלֹהֵיהֶם דַּיֵּנוּ.
אִלּוּ עָשָׂה בֵאלֹהֵיהֶם, וְלֹא הָרַג בְּכוֹרֵיהֶם דַּיֵּנוּ.
אִלּוּ הָרַג בְּכוֹרֵיהֶם, וְלֹא נָתַן לָנוּ אֶת מָמוֹנָם דַּיֵּנוּ.

בכורדיסתאן ובעדות המזרח אחרות מוסיפים כאן "ומנין" כמו במנהג תימן.

אִלּוּ נָתַן לָנוּ אֶת מָמוֹנָם, וְלֹא קָרַע לָנוּ אֶת הַיָּם דַּיֵּנוּ.
אִלּוּ קָרַע לָנוּ אֶת הַיָּם, וְלֹא הֶעֱבִירָנוּ בְתוֹכוֹ בֶּחָרָבָה דַּיֵּנוּ.
אִלּוּ הֶעֱבִירָנוּ בְתוֹכוֹ בֶּחָרָבָה, וְלֹא שִׁקַּע צָרֵינוּ בְּתוֹכוֹ דַּיֵּנוּ.
אִלּוּ שִׁקַּע צָרֵינוּ בְּתוֹכוֹ, וְלֹא סִפֵּק צָרְכֵּנוּ בַּמִּדְבָּר אַרְבָּעִים שָׁנָה דַּיֵּנוּ.
אִלּוּ סִפֵּק צָרְכֵּנוּ בַּמִּדְבָּר אַרְבָּעִים שָׁנָה, וְלֹא הֶאֱכִילָנוּ אֶת הַמָּן דַּיֵּנוּ.
אִלּוּ הֶאֱכִילָנוּ אֶת הַמָּן, וְלֹא נָתַן לָנוּ אֶת הַשַּׁבָּת דַּיֵּנוּ.
אִלּוּ נָתַן לָנוּ אֶת הַשַּׁבָּת, וְלֹא קֵרְבָנוּ לִפְנֵי הַר סִינַי דַּיֵּנוּ.
אִלּוּ קֵרְבָנוּ לִפְנֵי הַר סִינַי, וְלֹא נָתַן לָנוּ אֶת הַתּוֹרָה דַּיֵּנוּ.
אִלּוּ נָתַן לָנוּ אֶת הַתּוֹרָה, וְלֹא הִכְנִיסָנוּ לְאֶרֶץ יִשְׂרָאֵל דַּיֵּנוּ.
אִלּוּ הִכְנִיסָנוּ לְאֶרֶץ יִשְׂרָאֵל, וְלֹא בָנָה לָנוּ אֶת בֵּית הַבְּחִירָה דַּיֵּנוּ.

נוסח תימן ועדות המזרח

כַּמָּה מַעֲלוֹת טוֹבוֹת כְּפוּלוֹת וּמְכֻפָּלוֹת לַמָּקוֹם בָּרוּךְ הוּא עָלֵינוּ.

אִלּוּ הוֹצִיאָנוּ מִמִּצְרַיִם, וְלֹא עָשָׂה בָהֶם שְׁפָטִים דַּיֵּנוּ.

If He had given us their money but had not split the sea for us, it would have been enough for us!

If He had split the sea for us but had not let us pass on a dry path, it would have been enough for us!

If He had let us pass on a dry path but had not sunk our enemies in the sea, it would have been enough for us!

If He had sunk our enemies in the sea but had not provided for our needs in the desert for forty years, it would have been enough for us!

If He had provided for our needs in the desert for forty years but had not fed us on Mannah, it would have been enough for us!

If He had fed us on Mannah but had not given us the Sabbath, it would have been enough for us!

If He had given us the Sabbath but had not brought us before Mount Sinai, it would have been enough for us!

If He had brought us before Mount Sinai but had not given us the Torah, it would have been enough for us!

If He had given us the Torah but had not brought us into the Land of Israel, it would have been enough for us!

If He had brought us into the Land of Israel but had not built for us the Chosen Temple, it would have been enough for us!

All the more are we obliged to the Omnipresent One Y*praise to Him* for doubled and redoubled benefactions!

He led us out of Egypt, punished the Egyptians, judged their

אִלּוּ עָשָׂה בָהֶם שְׁפָטִים, וְלֹא עָשָׂה דִין בֵּאלֹהֵיהֶם דַּיֵּינוּ.
אִלּוּ עָשָׂה דִין בֵּאלֹהֵיהֶם, וְלֹא הָרַג אֶת בְּכוֹרֵיהֶם דַּיֵּינוּ
אִלּוּ הָרַג אֶת בְּכוֹרֵיהֶם, וְלֹא נָתַן לָנוּ אֶת מָמוֹנָם דַּיֵּינוּ.

וּמִנַּיִן שֶׁנָּתַן לָנוּ אֶת מָמוֹנָם, שֶׁנֶּאֱמַר ׳וַיַּשְׁאִלוּם וַיְנַצְּלוּ אֶת מִצְרָיִם׳, אִם עֲשָׂאוּהָ כִּמְצוּדָה זוֹ שֶׁאֵין בָּהּ דָּגָן, וְאִם עֲשָׂאוּהָ כִּמְצוּלָה זוֹ שֶׁאֵין בָּהּ דָּגָה. לָמָּה מְחַבֵּב הַכָּתוּב אֶת בִּזַּת הַיָּם יוֹתֵר מִבִּזַּת מִצְרַיִם? אֶלָּא מַה שֶּׁהָיָה בַּבָּתִּים נְטָלוּהוּ בְּמִצְרַיִם, וּמַה שֶּׁהָיָה בְּבָתֵּי סוּרָאוֹת נְטָלוּהוּ עַל הַיָּם, וְכֵן הוּא אוֹמֵר: ׳כַּנְפֵי יוֹנָה נֶחְפָּה בַכֶּסֶף׳ זוֹ בִּזַּת מִצְרַיִם, ׳וְאֶבְרוֹתֶיהָ בִּירַקְרַק חָרוּץ׳ זוֹ בִּזַּת הַיָּם; ׳וַתִּרְבִּי וַתִּגְדְּלִי׳ זוֹ בִּזַּת מִצְרַיִם, ׳תּוֹרֵי זָהָב נַעֲשֶׂה לָּךְ׳ זוֹ בִּזַּת הַיָּם, ׳עִם נְקֻדּוֹת הַכָּסֶף׳ זוֹ בִּזַּת מִצְרַיִם.

אִלּוּ נָתַן לָנוּ אֶת מָמוֹנָם, וְלֹא קָרַע לָנוּ אֶת הַיָּם דַּיֵּינוּ.
אִלּוּ קָרַע לָנוּ אֶת הַיָּם, וְלֹא הֶעֱבִירָנוּ בְתוֹכוֹ בֶּחָרָבָה דַּיֵּינוּ.
אִלּוּ הֶעֱבִירָנוּ בְתוֹכוֹ בֶּחָרָבָה, וְלֹא שִׁקַּע שׂוֹנְאֵינוּ בְּתוֹכוֹ דַּיֵּינוּ.
אִלּוּ שִׁקַּע שׂוֹנְאֵינוּ בְּתוֹכוֹ, וְלֹא סִפֵּק צָרְכֵּינוּ בַּמִּדְבָּר אַרְבָּעִים שָׁנָה דַּיֵּינוּ.
אִלּוּ סִפֵּק צָרְכֵּינוּ בַּמִּדְבָּר אַרְבָּעִים שָׁנָה, וְלֹא הֶאֱכִילָנוּ אֶת הַמָּן דַּיֵּינוּ.
אִלּוּ הֶאֱכִילָנוּ אֶת הַמָּן, וְלֹא נָתַן לָנוּ אֶת הַשַּׁבָּת דַּיֵּינוּ.
אִלּוּ נָתַן לָנוּ אֶת הַשַּׁבָּת, וְלֹא קֵרְבָנוּ לִפְנֵי הַר סִינַי דַּיֵּינוּ.
אִלּוּ קֵרְבָנוּ לִפְנֵי הַר סִינַי, וְלֹא נָתַן לָנוּ אֶת הַתּוֹרָה דַּיֵּינוּ.
אִלּוּ נָתַן לָנוּ אֶת הַתּוֹרָה, וְלֹא הִכְנִיסָנוּ לְאֶרֶץ יִשְׂרָאֵל דַּיֵּינוּ.
אִלּוּ הִכְנִיסָנוּ לְאֶרֶץ יִשְׂרָאֵל, וְלֹא בָנָה לָנוּ אֶת בֵּית הַבְּחִירָה דַּיֵּינוּ.

נוסח אשכנז

עַל אַחַת כַּמָּה וְכַמָּה טוֹבָה כְפוּלָה וּמְכֻפֶּלֶת לַמָּקוֹם עָלֵינוּ! שֶׁהוֹצִיאָנוּ מִמִּצְרַיִם, וְעָשָׂה בָהֶם שְׁפָטִים,

נוסח ספרד

עַל אַחַת כַּמָּה וְכַמָּה טוֹבָה כְּפוּלָה וּמְכֻפֶּלֶת לַמָּקוֹם עָלֵינוּ! הוֹצִיאָנוּ מִמִּצְרַיִם, עָשָׂה בָהֶם שְׁפָטִים, עָשָׂה בֵאלֹהֵיהֶם,

נוסח תימן

עַל אַחַת כַּמָּה וְכַמָּה טוֹבָה כְּפוּלָה וּמוּכְפֶּלֶת לַמָּקוֹם בָּרוּךְ הוּא עָלֵינוּ! הוֹצִיאָנוּ מִמִּצְרַיִם, עָשָׂה בָהֶם שְׁפָטִים,

idols, killed their firstborn, gave us their money, split the sea for us, let us pass on a dry path, sank our enemies in the sea, provided for our needs in the desert for forty years, fed us on Mannah, gave us the Sabbath, brought us before Mount Sinai, gave us the Torah, brought us into the Land of Israel, and built for us the Chosen Temple to atone for all our transgressions.

Rabban Gamliel [AS]used to say ([Y]*said*): Everyone who did not teach these three words on Passover did not fulfill his duty, to wit:

Pesaḥ, Maẓẓah, Maror.

What is the etymology of the *Pesaḥ* (Passover) that our forefathers ate when the Temple was standing? It is that the [AS]*Holy* [Y]*Omnipresent* One, praise to Him, passed over the houses of our forefathers in Egypt,

וְעָשָׂה בֵּאלֹהֵיהֶם, וְהָרַג בְּכוֹרֵיהֶם, וְנָתַן לָנוּ אֶת־מָמוֹנָם, וְקָרַע לָנוּ אֶת־הַיָּם, וְהֶעֱבִירָנוּ בְּתוֹכוֹ בֶּחָרָבָה, וְשִׁקַּע צָרֵינוּ בְּתוֹכוֹ, וְסִפֵּק צְרָכֵינוּ בַּמִּדְבָּר אַרְבָּעִים שָׁנָה, וְהֶאֱכִילָנוּ אֶת־הַמָּן, וְנָתַן־לָנוּ אֶת־הַשַּׁבָּת, וְקֵרְבָנוּ לִפְנֵי הַר סִינַי, וְנָתַן לָנוּ אֶת־הַתּוֹרָה, וְהִכְנִיסָנוּ לְאֶרֶץ יִשְׂרָאֵל, וּבָנָה לָנוּ אֶת־בֵּית הַבְּחִירָה לְכַפֵּר עַל כָּל־עֲוֹנוֹתֵינוּ.

הָרַג בְּכוֹרֵיהֶם, נָתַן לָנוּ אֶת מָמוֹנָם, קָרַע לָנוּ אֶת הַיָּם, הֶעֱבִירָנוּ בְּתוֹכוֹ בֶּחָרָבָה, שִׁקַּע צָרֵינוּ בְתוֹכוֹ, סִפֵּק צְרָכֵינוּ בַּמִּדְבָּר אַרְבָּעִים שָׁנָה, הֶאֱכִילָנוּ אֶת הַמָּן, נָתַן לָנוּ אֶת הַשַּׁבָּת, קֵרְבָנוּ לִפְנֵי הַר סִינַי, נָתַן לָנוּ אֶת הַתּוֹרָה, הִכְנִיסָנוּ לְאֶרֶץ יִשְׂרָאֵל, וּבָנָה לָנוּ אֶת בֵּית הַבְּחִירָה לְכַפֵּר עַל כָּל עֲוֹנוֹתֵינוּ.

עָשָׂה דִין בֵּאלֹהֵיהֶם, הָרַג אֶת בְּכוֹרֵיהֶם, נָתַן לָנוּ אֶת מָמוֹנָם, קָרַע לָנוּ אֶת הַיָּם, הֶעֱבִירָנוּ בְּתוֹכוֹ בֶּחָרָבָה, שִׁקַּע שׂוֹנְאֵינוּ בְּתוֹכוֹ, סִפֵּק צְרָכֵינוּ בַּמִּדְבָּר אַרְבָּעִים שָׁנָה, הֶאֱכִילָנוּ אֶת הַמָּן, נָתַן לָנוּ אֶת הַשַּׁבָּת, קֵרְבָנוּ לִפְנֵי הַר סִינַי, נָתַן לָנוּ אֶת הַתּוֹרָה, הִכְנִיסָנוּ לְאֶרֶץ יִשְׂרָאֵל, בָּנָה לָנוּ אֶת בֵּית הַבְּחִירָה לְכַפֵּר בּוֹ עַל כָּל עֲוֹנוֹתֵינוּ.

רַבָּן גַּמְלִיאֵל הָיָה אוֹמֵר: כָּל־שֶׁלֹּא אָמַר שְׁלֹשָׁה דְבָרִים אֵלּוּ בַּפֶּסַח לֹא יָצָא יְדֵי חוֹבָתוֹ, וְאֵלּוּ הֵן: **פֶּסַח מַצָּה וּמָרוֹר.**

רַבָּן גַּמְלִיאֵל הָיָה אוֹמֵר: כָּל מִי שֶׁלֹּא אָמַר שְׁלֹשָׁה דְבָרִים אֵלּוּ בַּפֶּסַח, לֹא יָצָא יְדֵי חוֹבָתוֹ, וְאֵלּוּ הֵן: **פֶּסַח מַצָּה וּמָרוֹר.**

רַבָּן גַּמְלִיאֵל אוֹמֵר: כָּל שֶׁלֹּא אָמַר שְׁלֹשָׁה דְבָרִים (אֵלּוּ) בַּפֶּסַח, לֹא יָצָא יְדֵי חוֹבָתוֹ, וְאֵלּוּ הֵן: **פֶּסַח מַצָּה וּמְרוֹרִים.**

פֶּסַח שֶׁהָיוּ אֲבוֹתֵינוּ אוֹכְלִים בִּזְמַן שֶׁבֵּית הַמִּקְדָּשׁ קַיָּם, עַל שׁוּם מָה? עַל שׁוּם שֶׁפָּסַח הַקָּדוֹשׁ בָּרוּךְ הוּא עַל

פֶּסַח שֶׁהָיוּ אֲבוֹתֵינוּ אוֹכְלִין בִּזְמַן שֶׁבֵּית הַמִּקְדָּשׁ קַיָּם, עַל שׁוּם מָה? עַל שׁוּם

פֶּסַח שֶׁהָיוּ אוֹכְלִים בִּזְמַן שֶׁבֵּית הַמִּקְדָּשׁ קַיָּם, עַל שֵׁם מָה? עַל שֵׁם שֶׁפָּסַח הַמָּקוֹם בָּרוּךְ הוּא עַל בָּתֵּי אֲבוֹתֵינוּ

as it is said (*Ex.* 12:27): "You shall say: This is a Passover sacrifice to the Lord Who passed over the houses of the children of Israel in Egypt when He smote the Egyptians but spared our houses; the people fell down and prostrated themselves."

In Kurdistan and Baghdad, the following poem is inserted. The author's name Aharon Cohen is given in the acrostic.

The faithful composed praise
To God and slaughtered
Say, a sacrifice
of Passover for the Lord!

Sing songs,
Be happy in the Guarded Night,
On *mazzot* and bitter herbs
Eat and drink my wine!

The First of all,
Through the faithful envoy,
From the hand of all tormentors
He saved all my throngs!

The wonders of God I remember,
His grace I recited,
Now I know
How great is the Lord!

Like the stars of the sky,
Manasse and Ephraim
Leave Egypt,
All the hosts of the Lord!

He gave His Torah
To His people and assembly,
The keepers of His commandments,
The people saved by the Lord!

בָּתֵּי אֲבוֹתֵינוּ
בְּמִצְרַיִם, שֶׁנֶּאֱמַר
'וַאֲמַרְתֶּם זֶבַח פֶּסַח
הוּא לַיי, אֲשֶׁר פָּסַח
עַל־בָּתֵּי בְנֵי־יִשְׂרָאֵל
בְּמִצְרַיִם, בְּנָגְפּוֹ
אֶת־מִצְרַיִם
וְאֶת־בָּתֵּינוּ הִצִּיל,
וַיִּקֹּד הָעָם וַיִּשְׁתַּחֲווּ.'

שֶׁפֶּסַח הַקָּדוֹשׁ
בָּרוּךְ הוּא עַל בָּתֵּי
אֲבוֹתֵינוּ בְּמִצְרַיִם,
שֶׁנֶּאֱמַר 'וַאֲמַרְתֶּם
זֶבַח פֶּסַח הוּא לַיי,
אֲשֶׁר פָּסַח עַל בָּתֵּי
בְנֵי יִשְׂרָאֵל
בְּמִצְרַיִם, בְּנָגְפּוֹ
אֶת מִצְרַיִם וְאֶת
בָּתֵּינוּ הִצִּיל, וַיִּקֹּד
הָעָם וַיִּשְׁתַּחֲווּ.'

בְּמִצְרַיִם, שֶׁנֶּאֱמַר
'וַאֲמַרְתֶּם זֶבַח פֶּסַח
הוּא לַיי, אֲשֶׁר פָּסַח
עַל בָּתֵּי
בְנֵי־יִשְׂרָאֵל
בְּמִצְרַיִם, בְּנָגְפּוֹ אֶת
מִצְרַיִם וְאֶת בָּתֵּינוּ
הִצִּיל, וַיִּקֹּד הָעָם
וַיִּשְׁתַּחֲווּ.'

בכורדיסתאן ובבל מוסיפים את הפיוט הבא:

אֱמוּנִים עִרְכוּ שֶׁבַח
לָאֵל וְטִבְחוּ טֶבַח
וַאֲמַרְתֶּם זֶבַח
פֶּסַח הוּא לַיי.

הָרִימוּ קוֹל שִׁירִים
שִׂמְחוּ בְּלֵיל שִׁמּוּרִים
עַל מַצּוֹת וּמְרוֹרִים
אִכְלוּ וּשְׁתוּ יֵינִי.

רִאשׁוֹן לְכָל רִאשׁוֹנִים
עַל יַד צִיר אֱמוּנִים
מִיַּד כָּל מְעַנִּים
הִצִּיל כָּל הֲמוֹנָי.

נִסֵּי אֵל זָכַרְתִּי
וַחֲסָדָיו סִפַּרְתִּי
עַתָּה יָדַעְתִּי
כִּי גָדוֹל יי.

כְּכֹכְבֵי הַשָּׁמַיִם
מְנַשֶּׁה וְאֶפְרַיִם
צְאוּ מִמִּצְרַיִם
כָּל צִבְאוֹת יי.

הִנְחִיל תּוֹרָתוֹ
לְעַמּוֹ וַעֲדָתוֹ
שׁוֹמְרֵי מִצְוָתוֹ
עַם נוֹשַׁע בַּיי.

Wonderful are Your deeds,
Powerful Your wonders,
They should say, all who trust in You:
It is good to trust the Lord!

One shows the *maẓẓot* (in the Sephardic ritual, the broken *maẓẓah*):

What is the etymology of this *maẓẓah* that we eat? It is that the dough of our forefathers had no time to ferment when the King of kings over kings, the Holy One, praise to Him, appeared to them and saved them SY*immediately*, as it is said (*Ex.* 12:39): "They baked the dough which they had taken out of Egypt as dry cakes (*'uggōt maẓẓōt*) because it was not fermented, for they were expelled from Egypt and could not tarry; also they had no food prepared for themselves."

One shows the *maror:*

What is the etymology of the bitter herbs (*mārōr*) that we eat? It is that the Egyptians made the life of our forefathers bitter, as it is said (*Ex.* 1:14): "They made their lives bitter with hard work, with mortar and bricks and all kinds of work on

נִפְלָאִים מַעֲשֶׂיךָ
וַעֲצוּמִים נִסֶּיךָ
יֹאמְרוּ כָּל חוֹסֶיךָ
טוֹב לַחֲסוֹת בַּיי.

מגביה את המצה ואומר:

מַצָּה זוּ שֶׁאָנוּ אוֹכְלִים, עַל שׁוּם מָה? עַל שׁוּם שֶׁלֹּא הִסְפִּיק בְּצֵקָם שֶׁל אֲבוֹתֵינוּ לְהַחֲמִיץ עַד שֶׁנִּגְלָה עֲלֵיהֶם מֶלֶךְ מַלְכֵי הַמְּלָכִים הַקָּדוֹשׁ בָּרוּךְ הוּא וּגְאָלָם, שֶׁנֶּאֱמַר 'וַיֹּאפוּ אֶת־הַבָּצֵק אֲשֶׁר הוֹצִיאוּ מִמִּצְרַיִם עֻגוֹת מַצּוֹת כִּי לֹא חָמֵץ, כִּי־גֹרְשׁוּ מִמִּצְרַיִם וְלֹא יָכְלוּ לְהִתְמַהְמֵהַּ, וְגַם־צֵדָה לֹא־עָשׂוּ לָהֶם.'

מגביה את המצה הפרוסה ואומר:

מַצָּה זוּ שֶׁאָנוּ אוֹכְלִין עַל שׁוּם מַה? עַל שׁוּם שֶׁלֹּא הִסְפִּיק בְּצֵקָם שֶׁל אֲבוֹתֵינוּ לְהַחְמִיץ עַד שֶׁנִּגְלָה עֲלֵיהֶם מֶלֶךְ מַלְכֵי הַמְּלָכִים הַקָּדוֹשׁ בָּרוּךְ הוּא וּגְאָלָם מִיַּד, שֶׁנֶּאֱמַר 'וַיֹּאפוּ אֶת הַבָּצֵק אֲשֶׁר הוֹצִיאוּ מִמִּצְרַיִם עֻגוֹת מַצּוֹת כִּי לֹא חָמֵץ, כִּי גֹרְשׁוּ מִמִּצְרַיִם וְלֹא יָכְלוּ לְהִתְמַהְמֵהַּ, וְגַם צֵדָה לֹא עָשׂוּ לָהֶם.'

מגביה את המצה ואומר:

מַצָּה זוּ שֶׁאֲנַחְנוּ אוֹכְלִים עַל שֵׁם מָה? עַל שֵׁם שֶׁלֹּא הִסְפִּיק בְּצֵקָן שֶׁל אֲבוֹתֵינוּ לְהַחְמִיץ, עַד שֶׁנִּגְלָה עֲלֵיהֶם מֶלֶךְ מַלְכֵי הַמְּלָכִים הַקָּדוֹשׁ בָּרוּךְ הוּא וּגְאָלָם מִיָּד, שֶׁנֶּאֱמָר 'וַיֹּאפוּ אֶת הַבָּצֵק אֲשֶׁר הוֹצִיאוּ מִמִּצְרַיִם עֻגוֹת מַצּוֹת כִּי לֹא חָמֵץ, כִּי גֹרְשׁוּ מִמִּצְרַיִם וְלֹא יָכְלוּ לְהִתְמַהְמֵהַּ, וְגַם צֵדָה לֹא עָשׂוּ לָהֶם.'

מגביה את המרור ואומר:

מָרוֹר זֶה שֶׁאָנוּ אוֹכְלִים, עַל שׁוּם מָה? עַל שׁוּם שֶׁמֵּרְרוּ הַמִּצְרִים אֶת־חַיֵּי אֲבוֹתֵינוּ בְּמִצְרַיִם, שֶׁנֶּאֱמַר 'וַיְמָרְרוּ אֶת־חַיֵּיהֶם בַּעֲבֹדָה

מָרוֹר זֶה שֶׁאָנוּ אוֹכְלִין, עַל שׁוּם מַה? עַל שׁוּם שֶׁמֵּרְרוּ הַמִּצְרִים אֶת חַיֵּי אֲבוֹתֵינוּ בְּמִצְרַיִם, שֶׁנֶּאֱמַר 'וַיְמָרְרוּ אֶת חַיֵּיהֶם בַּעֲבֹדָה קָשָׁה,

מְרוֹרִים אֵלּוּ שֶׁאֲנַחְנוּ אוֹכְלִים, עַל שֵׁם מַה? עַל שֵׁם שֶׁמֵּרְרוּ הַמִּצְרִים אֶת חַיֵּי אֲבוֹתֵינוּ בְּמִצְרַיִם, שֶׁנֶּאֱמָר 'וַיְמָרְרוּ אֶת חַיֵּיהֶם

the fields; all their work they were forced to perform at hard labor."

[Y]*And* in every generation, one has to [A]*view* [SY]*conduct* himself as if he himself had gone out of Egypt, [AS]*as it is said* (*Ex.* 13:8): *"You shall tell your son on that day: This is on account of what the Lord did for me when I left Egypt."* [SY]*Since* the Holy One, praise to Him, not only liberated our forefathers but He liberated us with them, as it is said (*Deut.* 6:23): "He took us out from there to bring us, to give us the Land which He had sworn unto our fathers."

One covers the *mazzot*, lifts the cup until one has recited the final benediction.

Therefore, we are obliged to

[A]*thank, sing His praise, laud, glorify, exalt, dignify, praise, elevate, and acclaim*

[S]*thank, sing His praise, laud, glorify, exalt, dignify, and acclaim*

[Y]*thank, sing His praise, laud, glorify, exalt, dignify, and declare victorious, praise*

קָשָׁה, בְּחֹמֶר וּבִלְבֵנִים
וּבְכָל־עֲבֹדָה בַּשָּׂדֶה,
אֵת כָּל־עֲבֹדָתָם אֲשֶׁר
עָבְדוּ בָהֶם בְּפָרֶךְ.׳

בְּחֹמֶר וּבִלְבֵנִים
וּבְכָל עֲבֹדָה בַּשָּׂדֶה,
אֵת כָּל עֲבֹדָתָם
אֲשֶׁר עָבְדוּ בָהֶם
בְּפָרֶךְ.׳

בַּעֲבֹדָה קָשָׁה,
בְּחֹמֶר וּבִלְבֵנִים
וּבְכָל עֲבֹדָה בַּשָּׂדֶה,
אֵת כָּל עֲבֹדָתָם
אֲשֶׁר עָבְדוּ בָהֶם
בְּפָרֶךְ.׳

בְּכָל־דּוֹר וָדוֹר חַיָּב
אָדָם לִרְאוֹת
אֶת־עַצְמוֹ כְּאִלּוּ הוּא
יָצָא מִמִּצְרָיִם, שֶׁנֶּאֱמַר
׳וְהִגַּדְתָּ לְבִנְךָ בַּיּוֹם
הַהוּא לֵאמֹר: בַּעֲבוּר
זֶה עָשָׂה יי לִי בְּצֵאתִי
מִמִּצְרָיִם.׳ לֹא
אֶת־אֲבוֹתֵינוּ בִּלְבַד
גָּאַל הַקָּדוֹשׁ בָּרוּךְ
הוּא, אֶלָּא אַף אוֹתָנוּ
גָּאַל עִמָּהֶם, שֶׁנֶּאֱמַר
׳וְאוֹתָנוּ הוֹצִיא מִשָּׁם,
לְמַעַן הָבִיא אֹתָנוּ,
לָתֶת לָנוּ אֶת־הָאָרֶץ
אֲשֶׁר נִשְׁבַּע לַאֲבֹתֵינוּ.׳

בְּכָל דּוֹר וָדוֹר
חַיָּב אָדָם
לְהַרְאוֹת אֶת עַצְמוֹ
כְּאִלּוּ הוּא יָצָא
מִמִּצְרַיִם, שֶׁנֶּאֱמַר
׳וְהִגַּדְתָּ לְבִנְךָ בַּיּוֹם
הַהוּא לֵאמֹר:
בַּעֲבוּר זֶה עָשָׂה יי
לִי בְּצֵאתִי
מִמִּצְרַיִם.׳ שֶׁלֹּא
אֶת אֲבוֹתֵינוּ בִּלְבַד
גָּאַל הַקָּדוֹשׁ בָּרוּךְ
הוּא, אֶלָּא אַף
אוֹתָנוּ גָּאַל עִמָּהֶם,
שֶׁנֶּאֱמַר ׳וְאוֹתָנוּ
הוֹצִיא מִשָּׁם, לְמַעַן
הָבִיא אֹתָנוּ, לָתֶת
לָנוּ אֶת הָאָרֶץ
אֲשֶׁר נִשְׁבַּע
לַאֲבֹתֵינוּ.׳

וּבְכָל דּוֹר וָדוֹר חַיָּב
אָדָם לְהַרְאוֹת אֶת
עַצְמוֹ כְּאִלּוּ הוּא
יָצָא מִמִּצְרַיִם שֶׁלֹּא
אֶת אֲבוֹתֵינוּ בִּלְבַד
גָּאַל, אֶלָּא אַף
אוֹתָנוּ גָּאַל, שֶׁנֶּאֱמַר
׳וְאוֹתָנוּ הוֹצִיא
מִשָּׁם, לְמַעַן הָבִיא
אֹתָנוּ, לָתֶת לָנוּ אֶת
הָאָרֶץ אֲשֶׁר נִשְׁבַּע
לַאֲבֹתֵינוּ.׳

יכסה את המצות, וכל אחד יגביה כוסו ביד ימינו עד שחותם ׳גאל ישראל׳.

לְפִיכָךְ אֲנַחְנוּ חַיָּבִים
לְהוֹדוֹת, לְהַלֵּל,
לְשַׁבֵּחַ, לְפָאֵר, לְרוֹמֵם,
לְהַדֵּר, לְבָרֵךְ, לְעַלֵּה,

לְפִיכָךְ אֲנַחְנוּ
חַיָּבִים לְהוֹדוֹת,
לְהַלֵּל, לְשַׁבֵּחַ,
לְפָאֵר, לְרוֹמֵם,
לְהַדֵּר, וּלְקַלֵּס, לְמִי

לְפִיכָךְ אֲנַחְנוּ
חַיָּבִים לְהוֹדוֹת,
לְהַלֵּל, לְשַׁבֵּחַ,
לְפָאֵר, לְרוֹמֵם,

Him, Who did all these miracles for our fathers and for us.
He led us from slavery to freedom,
[A]*from agony to joy, from mourning to festival, from darkness to great light, from servitude to salvation!*
[S]*from agony to joy, from mourning to festival, from darkness to great light!*
[Y]*from servitude to salvation, from mourning to festival, from darkness to great light!*
Therefore, we shall say before Him ([A]*a new song*)
Hallelujah!

In Yemen, the celebrant recites the *Hallel* and the company answers each half verse by "Hallelujah."

Psalm 113

Hallelujah!

Sing praise, o servants of the Lord,
Sing the praise of the Name of the Lord!
The Name of the Lord shall be praised,
From now to eternity!
From sunrise to its setting,
The name of the Lord is praised!
High over all peoples is the Lord,
Higher than the heavens is His glory!
Who is like the Lord our God?
He Who resides very high,
He Who looks down very low,
In heaven and on earth.
He lifts up the poor from the dust,
From dunghills He elevates the downtrodden,
To seat him with the nobles,
With the nobles of his people!

וּלְקַלֵּס, לְמִי שֶׁעָשָׂה
לַאֲבוֹתֵינוּ וְלָנוּ אֶת־כָּל
הַנִּסִּים הָאֵלּוּ.
הוֹצִיאָנוּ מֵעַבְדוּת
לְחֵירוּת, מִיָּגוֹן
לְשִׂמְחָה, וּמֵאֵבֶל לְיוֹם
טוֹב, וּמֵאֲפֵלָה לְאוֹרָה,
וּמִשִּׁעְבּוּד לִגְאֻלָּה,
וְנֹאמַר לְפָנָיו (שִׁירָה
חֲדָשָׁה) הַלְלוּיָהּ.

שֶׁעָשָׂה לַאֲבוֹתֵינוּ
וְלָנוּ אֶת כָּל
הַנִּסִּים הָאֵלּוּ.
הוֹצִיאָנוּ מֵעַבְדוּת
לְחֵרוּת, וּמִיָּגוֹן
לְשִׂמְחָה, וּמֵאֵבֶל
לְיוֹם טוֹב,
וּמֵאֲפֵלָה לְאוֹר
גָּדוֹל, וְנֹאמַר לְפָנָיו
הַלְלוּיָהּ.

לְהַדֵּר, לְנַצֵּחַ,
וּלְבָרֵךְ, לְמִי שֶׁעָשָׂה
לַאֲבוֹתֵינוּ וְלָנוּ אֶת
כָּל הַנִּסִּים הָאֵלּוּ,
וְהוֹצִיאָנוּ מֵעַבְדוּת
לְחֵירוּת, וּמִשִּׁעְבּוּד
לִגְאֻלָּה, וּמִיָּגוֹן
לְשִׂמְחָה, וּמֵאֵבֶל
לְיוֹם טוֹב, וּמֵאֲפֵלָה
לְאוֹר גָּדוֹל, וְנֹאמַר
לְפָנָיו הַלְלוּיָהּ.

בתימן ראש המשפחה קורא את ההלל וכל המסובים עונים ׳הללויה׳ על כל פיסקא ופיסקא.

הַלְלוּיָהּ
הַלְלוּ עַבְדֵי יי
הַלְלוּ אֶת־שֵׁם יי.
יְהִי שֵׁם יי מְבֹרָךְ
מֵעַתָּה וְעַד־עוֹלָם.
מִמִּזְרַח־שֶׁמֶשׁ עַד־מְבוֹאוֹ
מְהֻלָּל שֵׁם יי.
רָם עַל־כָּל־גּוֹיִם יי
עַל־הַשָּׁמַיִם כְּבוֹדוֹ.
מִי כַּיי אֱלֹהֵינוּ
הַמַּגְבִּיהִי לָשָׁבֶת.
הַמַּשְׁפִּילִי לִרְאוֹת
בַּשָּׁמַיִם וּבָאָרֶץ.
מְקִימִי מֵעָפָר דָּל
מֵאַשְׁפּוֹת יָרִים אֶבְיוֹן.
לְהוֹשִׁיבִי עִם־נְדִיבִים
עִם נְדִיבֵי עַמּוֹ.

He installs the barren of the family
As happy mother of children!
Hallelujah!

Psalm 114

When Israel went out of Egypt,
The House of Jacob from a barbarous people,
Then Judah became His sanctuary,
Israel His dominions.
The sea saw, and fled,
The Jordan turned backward.
The mountains danced like rams,
The hills like young sheep.
What ails you, o sea, that you flee,
O Jordan, that you turn backward,
O mountains, that you dance like rams,
Hills like young sheep?
Before the Master, Creator of the Earth,
Before the God of Jacob,
He who turns the rock into a water pond,
The pebble into a spring of water!

Ashkenazic and Sephardic Rituals

In Kurdish and some other Oriental communities one follows the Yemenite text but without the benediction over wine.

S*I am ready and prepared to observe the commandment of the Second Cup for the Oneness of the Holy One, praise to Him, and His Glory, through Him Who is hidden and secret, in the name of all of Israel.*

Praised are You o Lord, our God, King of the Universe, Who has redeemed us and has redeemed our forefathers from

מוֹשִׁיבִי עֲקֶרֶת הַבַּיִת
אֵם־הַבָּנִים שְׂמֵחָה
הַלְלוּיָהּ.

בְּצֵאת יִשְׂרָאֵל מִמִּצְרָיִם
בֵּית יַעֲקֹב מֵעַם לֹעֵז.
הָיְתָה יְהוּדָה לְקָדְשׁוֹ
יִשְׂרָאֵל מַמְשְׁלוֹתָיו.
הַיָּם רָאָה וַיָּנֹס
הַיַּרְדֵּן יִסֹּב לְאָחוֹר.
הֶהָרִים רָקְדוּ כְאֵילִים
גְּבָעוֹת כִּבְנֵי־צֹאן.
מַה־לְּךָ הַיָּם כִּי תָנוּס
הַיַּרְדֵּן תִּסֹּב לְאָחוֹר.
הֶהָרִים תִּרְקְדוּ כְאֵילִים
גְּבָעוֹת כִּבְנֵי־צֹאן.
מִלִּפְנֵי אָדוֹן חוּלִי אָרֶץ
מִלִּפְנֵי אֱלוֹהַּ יַעֲקֹב.
הַהֹפְכִי הַצּוּר אֲגַם־מָיִם
חַלָּמִישׁ לְמַעְיְנוֹ־מָיִם.

נוסח אשכנז

בָּרוּךְ אַתָּה יי אֱלֹהֵינוּ מֶלֶךְ הָעוֹלָם אֲשֶׁר גְּאָלָנוּ וְגָאַל אֶת־אֲבוֹתֵינוּ מִמִּצְרַיִם וְהִגִּיעָנוּ הַלַּיְלָה הַזֶּה לֶאֱכוֹל בּוֹ מַצָּה וּמָרוֹר. כֵּן יי אֱלֹהֵינוּ וֵאלֹהֵי אֲבוֹתֵינוּ יַגִּיעֵנוּ לְמוֹעֲדִים וְלִרְגָלִים אֲחֵרִים הַבָּאִים לִקְרָאתֵנוּ לְשָׁלוֹם, שְׂמֵחִים בְּבִנְיַן עִירֶךָ וְשָׂשִׂים בַּעֲבוֹדָתֶךָ. וְנֹאכַל שָׁם מִן הַזְּבָחִים וּמִן הַפְּסָחִים אֲשֶׁר יַגִּיעַ דָּמָם עַל קִיר מִזְבַּחֲךָ לְרָצוֹן, וְנוֹדֶה לְךָ שִׁיר חָדָשׁ עַל גְּאֻלָּתֵנוּ וְעַל פְּדוּת נַפְשֵׁנוּ. בָּרוּךְ אַתָּה יי גָּאַל יִשְׂרָאֵל.

Egypt and let us attain to this night to eat *mazzah* and bitter herbs. May it please You, o Lord, our God and God of our fathers, to let us attain in peace more festive seasons and holidays, when we shall rejoice in the rebuilding of Your city and enjoy Your service. There we shall eat from the family offerings and the *pesah* sacrifices whose blood shall reach the wall of Your altar for goodwill; then we shall thank You with a new song for our redemption and the liberation of our persons. Praised be You o Lord, Who did save Israel.

Ashkenazic Ritual

Praised are You o Lord, our God, King of the Universe,

Creator of the fruit of the vine.

Ashkenazic and Sephardic rituals: One drinks the larger part of the cup reclining on one's left side.

Yemenite Ritual

Praised are You o Lord, our God, King of the Universe, Who has redeemed us and has redeemed our forefathers from Egypt and let us attain this night to eat *mazzah* and bitter herbs.

א You saved our fathers from Egypt with strong hand and outstretched arm.

ב During the stay of our fathers in the land of Egypt they were deprived and enslaved under the hand of Pharaoh, king of Egypt.

ג Even there they were fruitful and increased like the dust of the earth; they grew in stature like the cedars of Lebanon.

ד Pharaoh talked about eradicating their name and planned to extinguish any memory of them from the world.

ה He and his people had a common plan; their council tried to outwit the seed of Israel.

ו They made their lives bitter with forced labor; they lost their spirit in a great strangulation.

ז The seed of Yeshurun were clothed in sighs because the hand of the enemy grew strong over them.

ח The Eternally Existing heard their voice, the King of kings over kings listened to them.

ט The Good and Equitable One raised Moses from among them; God's beloved (Aaron) was sent by his vision.

בָּרוּךְ אַתָּה יי אֱלֹהֵינוּ מֶלֶךְ הָעוֹלָם בּוֹרֵא פְּרִי הַגָּפֶן.

שותים את הכוס בהסבת שמאל.

נוסח ספרד

בכורדיסתאן אומרים הברכה אם ההוספה לפי נוסח תימן אבל בלי הברכה ״בורא פרי הגפן״.

הריני מוכן ומזומן לקיים מצות כוס שני של ארבעה כוסות לשם יחוד קב״ה ושכינתיה ע״י ההוא טמיר ונעלם בשם כל ישראל

בָּרוּךְ אַתָּה יי אֱלֹהֵינוּ מֶלֶךְ הָעוֹלָם, אֲשֶׁר גְּאָלָנוּ וְגָאַל אֶת אֲבוֹתֵינוּ מִמִּצְרַיִם, וְהִגִּיעָנוּ הַלַּיְלָה הַזֶּה לֶאֱכוֹל בּוֹ מַצָּה וּמָרוֹר. כֵּן יי אֱלֹהֵינוּ וֵאלֹהֵי אֲבוֹתֵינוּ, הַגִּיעֵנוּ לְמוֹעֲדִים וְלִרְגָלִים אֲחֵרִים, הַבָּאִים לִקְרָאתֵינוּ לְשָׁלוֹם, שְׂמֵחִים בְּבִנְיַן עִירָךְ וְשָׂשִׂים בַּעֲבוֹדָתָךְ. וְנֹאכַל שָׁם מִן הַזְּבָחִים וּמִן הַפְּסָחִים, אֲשֶׁר יַגִּיעַ דָּמָם עַל קִיר מִזְבַּחְךָ לְרָצוֹן, וְנוֹדֶה לְךָ שִׁיר חָדָשׁ, עַל גְּאוּלָּתֵנוּ וְעַל פְּדוּת נַפְשֵׁנוּ. בָּרוּךְ אַתָּה יי גָּאַל יִשְׂרָאֵל.

שותים את הכוס בהסבת שמאל.

נוסח תימן

בָּרוּךְ אַתָּה יי אֱלֹהֵינוּ מֶלֶךְ הָעוֹלָם, אֲשֶׁר גְּאָלָנוּ וְגָאַל אֶת אֲבוֹתֵינוּ מִמִּצְרַיִם, וְהִגִּיעָנוּ לַלַּיְלָה הַזֶּה לֶאֱכוֹל בּוֹ מַצָּה וּמְרוֹרִים.

אַתָּה גָּאַלְתָּ אֶת אֲבוֹתֵינוּ מִמִּצְרַיִם, בְּיָד חֲזָקָה וּבִזְרוֹעַ נְטוּיָה.
בִּהְיוֹת אֲבוֹתֵינוּ בְּתוֹךְ אֶרֶץ מִצְרַיִם, הָיוּ מְעוּנִּים וּמְשׁוּעְבָּדִים תַּחַת יַד פַּרְעֹה מֶלֶךְ מִצְרַיִם.
גַּם שָׁם פָּרוּ וְרָבוּ כַּעֲפַר הָאָרֶץ, וּכְאַרְזֵי הַלְּבָנוֹן גָּבְהוּ בְקוֹמָה.
דִּבֵּר פַּרְעֹה לִמְחוֹת אֶת שְׁמָם, וּלְאַבֵּד זִכְרָם מִקֶּרֶב תֵּבֵל.
הוּא וְעַמּוֹ בְּעֵצָה אַחַת הָיוּ, וַיִּתְחַכְּמוּ סוֹד עַל זֶרַע יִשְׂרָאֵל.
וַיְמָרְרוּ אֶת חַיֵּיהֶם בְּפֶרֶךְ, וּבְתַשְׁנִיק גָּדוֹל קָצְרָה רוּחָם.
זֶרַע יְשׁוּרוּן אֲנָחָה לָבָשׁוּ, כִּי יַד אוֹיֵב גָּבְרָה עֲלֵיהֶם.
חַי וְקַיָּם שָׁמַע בְּקוֹלָם, מֶלֶךְ מַלְכֵי הַמְּלָכִים הֶאֱזִין לָהֶם.
טוֹב וְיָשָׁר מֵהֶם גִּדֵּל מֹשֶׁה, יְדִיד בְּחָזוֹן הַשְׁלָח.
יַחַד הֶרְאָם בְּאוֹתוֹת שַׁדַּי, וּבְמִינֵי נְגָעִים שֶׁנִּשְׁפְּטוּ בְּנֵי חָם.
כָּל בְּכוֹרֵיהֶם לַטֶּבַח מָסַר, וְרֵאשִׁית בִּטְנָם לְדֶבֶר גָּדוֹל הִסְגִּיר.
לָכֵן נָפְלָה צְעָקָה גְדוֹלָה בְּמִצְרַיִם, בְּכִי וּמִסְפֵּד בְּכָל חוּצוֹתֶיהָ.
מֵעַבְדוּת לְחֵירוּת יָצְאוּ יְדִידִים, וְאֵין כּוֹשֵׁל בְּמִסְפַּר שְׁבָטִים.
נְהָגָם בְּטוּבוֹ צוּר עוֹלָמִים, וְהִגִּיעָם לְיַם סוּף בְּרַחֲמִים רַבִּים.

י Together, they showed them the signs of the Almighty and the different plagues with which the sons of Ham were visited.

כ He delivered all their firstborn to slaughter; He handed over the first of their bodies to a big plague.

ל This caused a great outcry in Egypt, wailing and dirges in all its streets.

מ The beloved ones went from slavery to freedom; no one stumbled among all tribes.

נ The Rock of Ages led them in His Goodness; He let them reach the Red Sea in great mercy.

ס He closed the Sea with the crowd of its waves; the hater pursued with the crowd of his army.

ע They lifted their eyes upward; they asked for mercy from the Strong of Israel.

פ Those saved by the Lord opened their mouths to laud their King for His many miracles.

צ He submerged the chariots of the enemies of His people and threw their haters into the waters of the deep.

ק The Lord split the waters of the Red Sea to keep the oath He had sworn to our father Abraham.

ר The beloved ones saw the corpses of their haters as they were lying on the seashore.

ש Song and chant and words of praise said Moses before his Creator.

ת Praise, splendor, and words of glorification did the redeemed sing to their Savior.

May it please You o Lord, our God and God of our fathers, to let us attain in peace more festive seasons and holidays, when we shall rejoice in the rebuilding of Your city and enjoy Your service. There we shall eat from the family offerings and the *pesaḥ* sacrifices whose blood shall reach the wall of Your altar for goodwill; then we shall thank You with a new song for our redemption and the liberation of our persons. Praised are You o Lord, Savior of Israel.

Praised are You o Lord, our God, King of the Universe,
Creator of the fruit of the vine.

One drinks the larger part of the cup reclining on one's left side.

סָגַר הַיָּם בַּהֲמוֹן גַּלָּיו, וְשׂוֹנֵא רוֹדֵף בַּהֲמוֹן חֵילוֹ.
עֵינֵיהֶם נָשְׂאוּ לַמָּרוֹם, לְבַקֵּשׁ רַחֲמִים מֵאֲבִיר יַעֲקֹב.
פִּיהֶם פָּתְחוּ גְאוּלֵי יי, לְשַׁבֵּחַ לְמַלְכָּם עַל רוֹב נִפְלְאוֹתָיו.
צָלֲלוּ רִכְבּוֹ בְּאוֹיְבֵי עַמּוֹ, וְהִשְׁלִיךְ שׂוֹנְאֵיהֶם לְתוֹךְ מֵי מְצוּלָה.
קָרַע יי אֶת מֵי יַם סוּף, לְקַיֵּם שְׁבוּעָה שֶׁנִּשְׁבַּע לְאַבְרָהָם אָבִינוּ.
רָאוּ יְדִידִים בְּפִגְרֵי שׂוֹנְאֵיהֶם, שֶׁהֵם מוּטָלִים עַל שְׂפַת הַיָּם.
שִׁירָה וְזִמְרָה וְדִבְרֵי הַלֵּל, אָמַר מֹשֶׁה לִפְנֵי קוֹנֵהוּ.
תְּהִלָּה וְתִפְאֶרֶת וְדִבְרֵי תוּשְׁבָּחוֹת, אָמְרוּ פְּדוּיִם לִפְנֵי גוֹאֲלָם.

כֵּן יי אֱלֹהֵינוּ יַגִּיעֵנוּ לְמוֹעֲדִים וְלִרְגָלִים אֲחֵרִים, הַבָּאִים לִקְרָאתֵינוּ לְשָׁלוֹם, שְׂמֵחִים בְּבִנְיַן עִירָךְ וְשָׂשִׂים בַּעֲבוֹדָתָךְ. וְנֹאכַל שָׁם מִן הַזְּבָחִים וּמִן הַפְּסָחִים, שֶׁיַּגִּיעַ דָּמָם עַל קִיר מִזְבַּחֲךָ לְרָצוֹן, וְנוֹדֶה לְךָ שִׁיר חָדָשׁ, עַל גְּאוּלָּתֵנוּ וְעַל פְּדוּת נַפְשֵׁנוּ. בָּרוּךְ אַתָּה יי גּוֹאֵל (נ״א גָּאַל) יִשְׂרָאֵל.

בָּרוּךְ אַתָּה יי אֱלֹהֵינוּ מֶלֶךְ הָעוֹלָם בּוֹרֵא פְּרִי הַגָּפֶן.

ויסב על צד שמאל וישתה.

Washing of the Hands

One washes one's hands and recites the benediction while drying one's hands.

Praised are You o Lord, our God, King of the Universe, Who sanctified us through His commandments and commanded us to lift the hands (for washing).

Blessing Bread and Maẓẓah

In the Ashkenazic ritual, the celebrant now takes the three *maẓẓot*, one on top of the other.

In the Sephardic ritual, the celebrant takes only the uppermost *maẓẓah*.

In the Yemenite ritual, the celebrant breaks the middle *maẓẓah* into two, puts one half away for *afiqomen*, and takes the entire top and broken middle *maẓẓot*.

The *maẓẓot* are held in both hands while the benediction is recited.

Praised are You o Lord, our God, King of the Universe, Who brings forth bread from the earth.

In the Eastern European Ashkenazic and Sephardic rituals, the following benediction is recited while the celebrant holds the top two *maẓẓot* in his hands.

In the Western European ritual, the celebrant still holds all three *maẓẓot*.

In the Yemenite ritual, each of the participants receives a piece of the *maẓẓah* (*kĕzayit;* see commentary) and keeps it in his hand until the celebrant has pronounced the benediction:

Praised are You o Lord, our God, King of the Universe, Who sanctified us through His commandments and commanded us about the eating of *maẓẓah.*

In the Ashkenazic and Sephardic rituals each participant now receives a piece (minimum size *kĕzayit*) of the two top *maẓẓot*. Ashkenazic Jews do not dip the *maẓẓah*. Some Sephardic communities dip the *maẓẓah* in salt following the instructions of R. Isaac Luria. Yemenites dip the *maẓẓah* in *ḥaroset*.

The *maẓẓah* is eaten while reclining on one's left side.

Bitter Herbs

Each participant receives a piece (minimum size *kĕzayit*) of bitter herbs (in the tradition of R. Isaac Luria romaine lettuce) dipped in *ḥaroset*. The *maror* is eaten without reclining after the recitation of the benediction by the celebrant:

Praised are You o Lord, our God, King of the Universe, Who sanctified us through His commandments and commanded us about the eating of bitter herbs.

רחצה

נוטלים לידים בברכה

בָּרוּךְ אַתָּה יי אֱלֹהֵינוּ מֶלֶךְ הָעוֹלָם אֲשֶׁר קִדְּשָׁנוּ בְּמִצְוֹתָיו
וְצִוָּנוּ עַל נְטִילַת יָדָיִם.

מוֹצִיא מַצָּה

במנהג אשכנז ובאי ג'רבה נוטל את שלושת המצות כסדרן בשתי ידיו ומברך.
במנהג ספרד נוטל רק המצה העליונה השלמה.
במנהג תימן בוצע מצה אחת לשנים, יניח החצי לאפיקומן, ולוקח מצה וחצי בידו
ומברך:

בָּרוּךְ אַתָּה יי אֱלֹהֵינוּ מֶלֶךְ הָעוֹלָם הַמּוֹצִיא לֶחֶם מִן הָאָרֶץ.
במנהג אשכנז (אבל לא במנהג אשכנז המערבי) ובאי ג'רבה מניח המצה התחתונה ואוחז במצה העליונה
והאמצעית ומברך.

במנהג ספרד מוסיף המצה הפרוסה למצה שבידו ומברך.
במנהג תימן יחלק למסובין לכל אחד כזית ולא יאכלו אותה עד שיברך על המצה:

בָּרוּךְ אַתָּה יי אֱלֹהֵינוּ מֶלֶךְ הָעוֹלָם אֲשֶׁר קִדְּשָׁנוּ בְּמִצְוֹתָיו
וְצִוָּנוּ עַל אֲכִילַת מַצָּה.
במנהגי אשכנז וספרד נותן לכל אחד כזית המוציא מן המצה העליונה וכזית המצוה מן
המצה הפרוסה ואוכלים ביחד, בהסבת שמאל.
במנהג ספרד יש שמטבילים המצה במלח כדעת האר"י והמחבר.
במנהג תימן מטבילים את המצה בחרוסת ואוכלים בהסבה.

מָרוֹר

יקח מרור (חסה במנהג האר"י) ומטבלו בחרוסת ומברך (ובתימן מחלק לכל המסובין
לפני הברכה):

בָּרוּךְ אַתָּה יי אֱלֹהֵינוּ מֶלֶךְ הָעוֹלָם אֲשֶׁר קִדְּשָׁנוּ בְּמִצְוֹתָיו
וְצִוָּנוּ עַל אֲכִילַת מָרוֹר.
במנהגי אשכנז וספרד מחלק כזית מרור לכל אחד מן המסובין, מטבלים בחרוסת
ואוכלים בלי הסבה. במנהג תימן כל אחד מטבל בחרוסת ואוכל.

Hillel's Sandwich

Every participant receives a piece of *maror* (in the tradition of R. Isaac Luria, horseradish) placed between two pieces of the bottom *maẓẓah*. In the Sephardic and Yemenite rituals and many Eastern European Ashkenaziç families, the entire sandwich is dipped in *ḥaroset*. It is eaten while reclining after the celebrant has read the declaration:

Ashkenazic text:

The words in parentheses may be added in families that do not dip the sandwich.

(Without dipping and without benediction) a remembrance of the Temple following Hillel.

Hillel, in the time of the Temple, did the following: He made a sandwich of *pesaḥ, maẓẓah,* and bitter herbs and ate them together to perform what has been prescribed (*Num.* 9:11): "On *maẓẓot* and bitter herbs they shall eat it."

Sephardic text:

A remembrance of the Temple following Hillel who made a sandwich (of *pesaḥ, maẓẓah,* and bitter herbs) and ate them together to perform what has been prescribed (*Num.* 9:11): "On *maẓẓot* and bitter herbs they shall eat it."

Yemenite text:

Without a benediction, according to Hillel the elder who said (*Num.* 9:11): "On *maẓẓot* and bitter herbs they shall eat it."

Festive Meal

In most Oriental communities, the eggs and meats from the *Seder* plate are distributed. The festive meal follows.

Hidden Maẓẓah

After the meal, a piece (minimum amount *kĕzayit*) of the piece of *maẓẓah* kept for *afiqomen* is distributed to each participant and is eaten while reclining. This is the last piece of solid food consumed this night.

Sephardic text:

I am ready and prepared to observe the commandment of afiqomen for the Onenessof the Holy, praise to Him, and His Glory, through Him Who is hidden and secret, in the name of all of Israel.

A remembrance of the *pesaḥ* sacrifice that was eaten when satiated.

כורך

נוסח אשכנז

מחלק לכל אחד כזית מצה מן המצה התחתונה וכזית מרור (במנהג האר"י חזרת) וכורכן ביחד. יש משפחות המטבלים בחרוסת. ברוב אשכנז לא אומרים את המילים בסוגריים:

(בְּלֹא טִבּוּל וּבְלֹא בְרָכָה)

זֵכֶר לְמִקְדָּשׁ כְּהִלֵּל. כֵּן עָשָׂה הִלֵּל בִּזְמַן שֶׁבֵּית הַמִּקְדָּשׁ קַיָּם, הָיָה כּוֹרֵךְ מַצָּה וּמָרוֹר וְאוֹכֵל בְּיַחַד, לְקַיֵּם מַה שֶּׁנֶּאֱמַר 'עַל מַצּוֹת וּמְרֹרִים יֹאכְלֻהוּ'.

נוסח ספרד

מחלק לכל אחד כזית מצה מן המצה התחתונה וכזית וחזרת ומטבילה בחרוסת ואומר

זֵכֶר לַמִּקְדָּשׁ כְּהִלֵּל הַזָּקֵן שֶׁהָיָה כּוֹרְכָן וְאוֹכְלָן בְּבַת אַחַת (פֶּסַח מַצָּה וּמָרוֹר) לְקַיֵּם מַה שֶּׁנֶּאֱמַר 'עַל מַצּוֹת וּמְרוֹרִים יֹאכְלוּהוּ'.

נוסח תימן

כורכין מצה ומרור יחד כזית מכל אחד ומטבלו בחרוסת ואומר

בְּלֹא בְרָכָה זֵכֶר לְמִקְדָּשׁ כְּהִלֵּל הַזָּקֵן שֶׁאָמַר 'עַל מַצּוֹת וּמְרוֹרִים יֹאכְלוּהוּ'.

שלחן עורך

ואוכלים את הכריכה בהסבה. ברוב עדות המזרח מחלקים את הבשר ואת הביצים שבקערה. אחר כך אוכלים ושותים כרצונם.

צפון

אחר הסעודה בעל הבית מחלק לכל אחד כזית מן המצה השמורה לאפיקומן ואוכלים אותו בהסיבה ואין אוכלים אחריו כלום.

מנהג ספרד

הנני מוכן ומזומן לקיים מצות אכילת אפיקומן לשם יחוד קב"ה ושכינתיה ע"י ההוא טמיר ונעלם בשם כל ישראל.

זֵכֶר לְקָרְבַּן פֶּסַח הַנֶּאֱכַל עַל הַשָּׂבָע.

Grace

Ashkenazic Ritual

One fills the Third Cup.

In many families one sings *Ps.* 126 before saying Grace.

If the company includes at least three males over 13 years of age, one starts with *zimmun*. If there are at least ten males over 13, one adds the words in parentheses. If the participants are *all* female, the rule of *zimmun* applies to persons over the age of 12. Without *zimmun* one starts with the second paragraph.

The celebrant: Gentlemen, let us give praise!

Company: May the Name of the Lord be praised from now to eternity!

The celebrant: With your permission, let us praise (our God) Whose food we ate!

Company: Praised be (our God) Whose food we ate and by Whose goodness we live!

The celebrant: Praised be (our God) Whose food we ate and by Whose goodness we live, praise to Him and to His Name!

Praised are You o Lord, our God, King of the Universe, Who feeds the entire world in His goodness; in grace, kindness, and mercy He gives bread to all flesh because His kindness is eternal. Through His great kindness we never lacked food; may we never lack food forever and ever for the sake of His great Name. Truly He feeds and provides for all, is good to everyone, and has food prepared for all His creatures whom He created [followers of the Lurianic rite add: as it is said (*Ps.* 145:16): "You Who open Your hand and graciously satisfy all living beings"]. Praised are You o Lord, Who provides food to all.

We thank You o Lord, our God, that You let our fathers inherit a desirable, good, and spacious land, and that You o Lord, our God, did lead us out of Egypt and redeemed us from the house of slaves, and for Your Covenant which You have sealed in our flesh, and for Your Torah which You have taught us, and for Your laws which You have made known to us, and the life, grace, and kindness, which You have graciously bestowed upon us, and the food with which You feed and You provide for us always, every day, every time, and every hour. For all this we thank You, o Lord, our God, and we praise You; may Your name be praised by every living being, always, for ever and ever, as it is written (*Deut.* 8:10): "You will eat and be satisfied; then you must

ברך

נוסח אשכנז

מוזגים את הכוס השלישי.
יש נוהגים לאמר מזמור קכו, 'שיר המעלות בשוב יי', לפני ברכת המזון.
אם בין המסובין לפחות שלושה גברים בגיל המצות חייבים בזימון:

בעל הבית: רַבּוֹתַי נְבָרֵךְ, אוֹ בלשון אידיש: רַבּוֹתַי, מִיר ווֶעלֶן בֶּענְשֶׁן.

המסובים: יְהִי שֵׁם יי מְבֹרָךְ מֵעַתָּה וְעַד עוֹלָם.

בעל הבית: (בִּרְשׁוּת ...) נְבָרֵךְ (בעשרה: אֱלֹהֵינוּ) שֶׁאָכַלְנוּ מִשֶּׁלּוֹ.

המסובים: בָּרוּךְ (בעשרה: אֱלֹהֵינוּ) שֶׁאָכַלְנוּ מִשֶּׁלּוֹ וּבְטוּבוֹ חָיִינוּ.

בעל הבית: בָּרוּךְ (בעשרה: אֱלֹהֵינוּ) שֶׁאָכַלְנוּ מִשֶּׁלּוֹ וּבְטוּבוֹ חָיִינוּ. בָּרוּךְ הוּא
וּבָרוּךְ שְׁמוֹ.

ביחידות מתחילים כאן

בָּרוּךְ אַתָּה יי אֱלֹהֵינוּ מֶלֶךְ הָעוֹלָם הַזָּן אֶת־הָעוֹלָם כֻּלּוֹ בְּטוּבוֹ, בְּחֵן, בְּחֶסֶד
וּבְרַחֲמִים, הוּא נוֹתֵן לֶחֶם לְכָל־בָּשָׂר כִּי לְעוֹלָם חַסְדּוֹ. וּבְטוּבוֹ הַגָּדוֹל
תָּמִיד לֹא חָסַר לָנוּ, וְעַל יֶחְסַר לָנוּ, מָזוֹן לְעוֹלָם וָעֶד בַּעֲבוּר שְׁמוֹ הַגָּדוֹל,
כִּי הוּא (אֵל) זָן וּמְפַרְנֵס לַכֹּל, וּמֵטִיב לַכֹּל, וּמֵכִין מָזוֹן לְכָל־בְּרִיּוֹתָיו אֲשֶׁר
בָּרָא. (יש מוסיפים: כָּאָמוּר 'פּוֹתֵחַ אֶת־יָדֶךָ וּמַשְׂבִּיעַ לְכָל־חַי רָצוֹן'.) בָּרוּךְ אַתָּה
יי, הַזָּן אֶת־הַכֹּל.

נוֹדֶה לְךָ יי אֱלֹהֵינוּ עַל שֶׁהִנְחַלְתָּ לַאֲבוֹתֵינוּ אֶרֶץ חֶמְדָּה טוֹבָה וּרְחָבָה, וְעַל
שֶׁהוֹצֵאתָנוּ יי אֱלֹהֵינוּ מֵאֶרֶץ מִצְרַיִם וּפְדִיתָנוּ מִבֵּית עֲבָדִים, וְעַל בְּרִיתְךָ
שֶׁחָתַמְתָּ בִּבְשָׂרֵנוּ, וְעַל תּוֹרָתְךָ שֶׁלִּמַּדְתָּנוּ, וְעַל חֻקֶּיךָ שֶׁהוֹדַעְתָּנוּ, וְעַל חַיִּים
חֵן וָחֶסֶד שֶׁחוֹנַנְתָּנוּ, וְעַל אֲכִילַת מָזוֹן שָׁאַתָּה זָן וּמְפַרְנֵס אוֹתָנוּ תָּמִיד,
בְּכָל־יוֹם וּבְכָל־עֵת וּבְכָל־שָׁעָה. וְעַל הַכֹּל יי אֱלֹהֵינוּ אֲנַחְנוּ מוֹדִים לָךְ
וּמְבָרְכִים אוֹתָךְ, יִתְבָּרַךְ שִׁמְךָ בְּפִי (נוסח האר״י: בְּפֶה) כָּל־חַי תָּמִיד לְעוֹלָם
וָעֶד, כַּכָּתוּב וְאָכַלְתָּ וְשָׂבָעְתָּ, וּבֵרַכְתָּ אֶת־יי אֱלֹהֶיךָ עַל־הָאָרֶץ הַטּוֹבָה
אֲשֶׁר נָתַן־לָךְ. בָּרוּךְ אַתָּה יי, עַל הָאָרֶץ וְעַל הַמָּזוֹן.

praise the Lord, your God, for the good land that He gave you." Praised are You o Lord, for the Land and for the food.

Have mercy, o Lord, our God, on Israel Your people, on Jerusalem Your city, on Zion the dwelling place of Your glory, on the kingdom of David Your anointed, and on the great and holy House upon which Your Name is mentioned. Our God, our Father, be our shepherd, feed us, provide for us, sustain us, let us earn a living, and relieve us soon, o Lord, our God, from all our worries. May it please You o Lord, our God, not to make us need the charities of flesh and blood or their loans, but only the gift of Your full, open, holy, and abundant hand so that we shall never become ashamed or disgraced.

On Sabbath add:

May You be pleased to give us ease of mind, o Lord, our God, through Your commandments and the commandment of this great and holy Sabbath day. Truly this is a great and holy day before You to refrain from work and to rest, in love, conforming to the commandments of Your pleasure. May it be Your pleasure, o Lord our God, to give us rest so we should experience neither worry nor sorrow nor sigh on the day of our rest. Let us see, o Lord, our God, the consolation of Zion, Your city, and the rebuilding of Jerusalem, the city of Your sanctuary, because You are the Master of all salvations and consolations.

Our God and God of our fathers! May there arise, come, arrive, be accepted, received with pleasure, heard, taken notice of, and be remembered before You the remembrance and notice of ourselves and the remembrance of our fathers, the remembrance of the Messiah the son of David Your servant, the remembrance of Jerusalem the city of Your sanctuary, and the remembrance of your entire people, the house of Israel, for survival, good, grace, goodwill, mercy, life, and peace on this day of the festival of unleavened bread. Remember us on it, o Lord, our God, in a good way; take notice of us on it for blessing, and help us on it to life! Spare us with a word of help and mercy and let us find grace! Have mercy on us and help us because our eyes are on You since You are a gracious and merciful God (and King).
And do build Jerusalem, the holy city, soon in our days. Praised are You o Lord, Who in His mercy builds Jerusalem. Amen.

Praised are You o Lord, our God, King of the Universe, Almighty, our Father, our King, our Pride, our Creator, our Savior, Who formed us, our Holy One, the Holy of Jacob, our Shepherd, the Shepherd of Israel, the good King Who every single day does good to all, He treated us well, He is treating us well, He will treat us well, He was kind to us, He is being kind to us, He will be kind to us forever in grace, kindness, mercy, relief, success, blessing, help, consolation, provision, sustenance,

רַחֵם יי אֱלֹהֵינוּ עַל יִשְׂרָאֵל עַמֶּךָ, וְעַל יְרוּשָׁלַיִם עִירֶךָ, וְעַל צִיּוֹן מִשְׁכַּן כְּבוֹדֶךָ, וְעַל מַלְכוּת בֵּית דָּוִד מְשִׁיחֶךָ וְעַל הַבַּיִת הַגָּדוֹל וְהַקָּדוֹשׁ שֶׁנִּקְרָא שִׁמְךָ עָלָיו. אֱלֹהֵינוּ אָבִינוּ, רְעֵנוּ, זוּנֵנוּ, פַּרְנְסֵנוּ וְכַלְכְּלֵנוּ וְהַרְוִיחֵנוּ, וְהַרְוַח־לָנוּ יי אֱלֹהֵינוּ מְהֵרָה מִכָּל־צָרוֹתֵינוּ. וְנָא אַל־תַּצְרִיכֵנוּ יי אֱלֹהֵינוּ לֹא לִידֵי מַתְּנַת בָּשָׂר וָדָם, וְלֹא לִידֵי הַלְוָאָתָם, כִּי אִם לְיָדְךָ הַמְּלֵאָה הַפְּתוּחָה הַקְּדוֹשָׁה וְהָרְחָבָה, שֶׁלֹּא נֵבוֹשׁ וְלֹא נִכָּלֵם לְעוֹלָם וָעֶד.

בשבת מוסיפים

רְצֵה וְהַחֲלִיצֵנוּ יי אֱלֹהֵינוּ בְּמִצְוֹתֶיךָ וּבְמִצְוַת יוֹם הַשְּׁבִיעִי הַגָּדוֹל וְהַקָּדוֹשׁ הַזֶּה, כִּי יוֹם זֶה גָּדוֹל וְקָדוֹשׁ הוּא לְפָנֶיךָ, לִשְׁבָּת בּוֹ וְלָנוּחַ בּוֹ בְּאַהֲבָה כְּמִצְוַת רְצוֹנֶךָ. בִּרְצוֹנְךָ הָנִיחַ לָנוּ יי אֱלֹהֵינוּ שֶׁלֹּא תְהִי צָרָה וְיָגוֹן וַאֲנָחָה בְּיוֹם מְנוּחָתֵנוּ. וְהַרְאֵנוּ יי אֱלֹהֵינוּ בְּנֶחָמַת צִיּוֹן עִירֶךָ וּבְבִנְיַן יְרוּשָׁלַיִם עִיר קָדְשֶׁךָ, כִּי אַתָּה הוּא בַּעַל הַיְשׁוּעוֹת וּבַעַל הַנֶּחָמוֹת.

אֱלֹהֵינוּ וֵאלֹהֵי אֲבוֹתֵינוּ. יַעֲלֶה וְיָבוֹא וְיַגִּיעַ וְיֵרָאֶה וְיֵרָצֶה וְיִשָּׁמַע וְיִפָּקֵד וְיִזָּכֵר זִכְרוֹנֵנוּ וּפִקְדוֹנֵנוּ, וְזִכְרוֹן אֲבוֹתֵינוּ, וְזִכְרוֹן מָשִׁיחַ בֶּן־דָּוִד עַבְדֶּךָ, וְזִכְרוֹן יְרוּשָׁלַיִם עִיר קָדְשֶׁךָ, וְזִכְרוֹן כָּל־עַמְּךָ בֵּית יִשְׂרָאֵל לְפָנֶיךָ, לִפְלֵיטָה, וּלְטוֹבָה, וּלְחֵן, וּלְחֶסֶד וּלְרַחֲמִים, וּלְחַיִּים וּלְשָׁלוֹם בְּיוֹם חַג הַמַּצּוֹת הַזֶּה. זָכְרֵנוּ יי אֱלֹהֵינוּ בּוֹ לְטוֹבָה, וּפָקְדֵנוּ בוֹ לִבְרָכָה, וְהוֹשִׁיעֵנוּ בוֹ לְחַיִּים, וּבִדְבַר יְשׁוּעָה וְרַחֲמִים חוּס וְחָנֵּנוּ, וְרַחֵם עָלֵינוּ וְהוֹשִׁיעֵנוּ, כִּי אֵלֶיךָ עֵינֵינוּ, כִּי אֵל (מֶלֶךְ) חַנּוּן וְרַחוּם אָתָּה.

וּבְנֵה יְרוּשָׁלַיִם עִיר הַקֹּדֶשׁ בִּמְהֵרָה בְיָמֵינוּ. בָּרוּךְ אַתָּה יי בּוֹנֵה בְרַחֲמָיו יְרוּשָׁלָיִם, אָמֵן.

בָּרוּךְ אַתָּה יי אֱלֹהֵינוּ מֶלֶךְ הָעוֹלָם, הָאֵל אָבִינוּ, מַלְכֵּנוּ, אַדִּירֵנוּ, בּוֹרְאֵנוּ, גֹּאֲלֵנוּ, יוֹצְרֵנוּ, קְדוֹשֵׁנוּ קְדוֹשׁ יַעֲקֹב, רוֹעֵנוּ רוֹעֵה יִשְׂרָאֵל, הַמֶּלֶךְ הַטּוֹב וְהַמֵּטִיב לַכֹּל, שֶׁבְּכָל־יוֹם וָיוֹם הוּא הֵטִיב, הוּא מֵטִיב, הוּא יֵטִיב לָנוּ, הוּא גְמָלָנוּ, הוּא גוֹמְלֵנוּ, הוּא יִגְמְלֵנוּ לָעַד, לְחֵן לְחֶסֶד וּלְרַחֲמִים, וּלְרֶוַח הַצָּלָה וְהַצְלָחָה, בְּרָכָה וִישׁוּעָה, נֶחָמָה פַּרְנָסָה וְכַלְכָּלָה, וְרַחֲמִים וְחַיִּים וְשָׁלוֹם וְכָל־טוֹב, וּמִכָּל־טוּב עַל יְחַסְּרֵנוּ.

mercy, life, peace, and all good; He will not let us want any good thing.
The Merciful One, He shall reign over us for ever and ever.
The Merciful One, He shall be praised in Heaven and on earth.
The Merciful One, He shall be lauded in every generation, and may He glorify Himself in us for all eternity, and may He show His majesty over us forever in all worlds.
The Merciful One, may He provide for us an honorable living.
The Merciful One, may He break the yoke from off our necks and lead us upright into our Land.
The Merciful One, may He send ample blessing over this house and this table at which we have eaten.
The Merciful One, may He send us the prophet Elijah of blessed memory to announce to us good news, help, and consolations.
The Merciful One, may He bless

guest: the head of this house and the mistress of this house,

child: my father and teacher, the head of this house, and my mother and teacher, the mistress of this house,

guest and child: them, their house, their children, and all that is theirs,

husband: me and my wife wife: me and my husband

husband and wife: and my children and all that is ours,

all: and all that are assembled here, us and all our belongings, the way our fathers Abraham, Isaac, and Jacob were blessed in everything, of everything, everything, so may He bless us all together in a perfect blessing. Amen.

In Heaven may they credit them and us with keeping the peace; may we be deemed worthy of blessing from the Lord and justice from the God Who helps us; may we find grace and goodwill in the eyes of God and man.

On Sabbath: The Merciful One, may He let us inherit the day which is all Sabbath and rest, the eternal life.
The Merciful One, may He let us inherit the day which is totally good (some families add: the day which is never ending, the day when the Just sit with crowns on their heads, enjoying the splendor of the Divine Presence; may our lot be with them!).
The Merciful One, may He let us take part in the days of the Messiah and the life of the World to Come.
(*2 Sam.* 22:51) He is a tower of help for His king, and is kind to His anointed, to David and his descendants forever. He who makes peace in His heights, may He make peace for us and all Israel. Amen.

הָרַחֲמָן הוּא יִמְלוֹךְ עָלֵינוּ לְעוֹלָם וָעֶד.

הָרַחֲמָן הוּא יִתְבָּרַךְ בַּשָּׁמַיִם וּבָאָרֶץ.

הָרַחֲמָן הוּא יִשְׁתַּבַּח לְדוֹר דּוֹרִים, וְיִתְפָּאַר בָּנוּ לָנֶצַח נְצָחִים, וְיִתְהַדַּר בָּנוּ לָעַד וּלְעוֹלְמֵי עוֹלָמִים.

הָרַחֲמָן הוּא יְפַרְנְסֵנוּ בְּכָבוֹד.

הָרַחֲמָן הוּא יִשְׁבּוֹר עֻלֵּנוּ מֵעַל צַוָּארֵנוּ וְהוּא יוֹלִיכֵנוּ קוֹמְמִיּוּת לְאַרְצֵנוּ.

הָרַחֲמָן הוּא יִשְׁלַח בְּרָכָה מְרֻבָּה בַּבַּיִת הַזֶּה וְעַל שֻׁלְחָן זֶה שֶׁאָכַלְנוּ עָלָיו.

הָרַחֲמָן הוּא יִשְׁלַח לָנוּ אֶת־אֵלִיָּה הַנָּבִיא זָכוּר לַטּוֹב, וִיבַשֶּׂר לָנוּ בְּשׂוֹרוֹת טוֹבוֹת יְשׁוּעוֹת וְנֶחָמוֹת.

הָרַחֲמָן הוּא יְבָרֵךְ

ברכת האורח: אֶת־בַּעַל הַבַּיִת הַזֶּה וְאֶת־בַּעֲלַת הַבַּיִת הַזֶּה

ברכת הבנים: אֶת־אָבִי מוֹרִי בַּעַל הַבַּיִת הַזֶּה וְאֶת־אִמִּי מוֹרָתִי בַּעֲלַת הַבַּיִת הַזֶּה

אורח ובנים: אוֹתָם וְאֶת־בֵּיתָם וְאֶת־זַרְעָם וְאֶת־כָּל־אֲשֶׁר לָהֶם

בעל הבית: אוֹתִי וְאֶת־אִשְׁתִּי וְאֶת־זַרְעִי וְאֶת־כָּל־אֲשֶׁר לִי

בעלת הבית: אוֹתִי וְאֶת־בַּעֲלִי וְאֶת־זַרְעִי וְאֶת־כָּל־אֲשֶׁר לִי

וְאֶת כָּל־הַמְּסוּבִּין כָּאן, אוֹתָם וְאֶת־זַרְעָם וְאֶת־כָּל־אֲשֶׁר לָהֶם, אוֹתָנוּ וְאֶת־כָּל־אֲשֶׁר לָנוּ, כְּמוֹ שֶׁנִּתְבָּרְכוּ אֲבוֹתֵינוּ אַבְרָהָם יִצְחָק וְיַעֲקֹב בַּכֹּל, מִכֹּל, כֹּל, כֵּן יְבָרֵךְ אוֹתָנוּ כֻּלָּנוּ יַחַד בִּבְרָכָה שְׁלֵמָה, וְנֹאמַר אָמֵן.

בַּמָּרוֹם יְלַמְּדוּ עֲלֵיהֶם (עָלָיו) וְעָלֵינוּ זְכוּת שֶׁתְּהִי לְמִשְׁמֶרֶת שָׁלוֹם, וְנִשָּׂא בְרָכָה מֵאֵת יי וּצְדָקָה מֵאֱלֹהֵי יִשְׁעֵנוּ, וְנִמְצָא־חֵן וְשֵׂכֶל טוֹב בְּעֵינֵי אֱלֹהִים וְאָדָם.

בשבת: הָרַחֲמָן הוּא יַנְחִילֵנוּ יוֹם שֶׁכֻּלּוֹ שַׁבָּת וּמְנוּחָה לְחַיֵּי הָעוֹלָמִים.

הָרַחֲמָן הוּא יַנְחִילֵנוּ יוֹם שֶׁכֻּלּוֹ טוֹב (ויש מוסיפים: יוֹם שֶׁכֻּלּוֹ אָרוּךְ, יוֹם שֶׁצַּדִּיקִים יוֹשְׁבִים וְעַטְרוֹתֵיהֶם בְּרָאשֵׁיהֶם וְנֶהֱנִים מִזִּיו הַשְּׁכִינָה וִיהִיֶה חֶלְקֵנוּ עִמָּהֶם.)

הָרַחֲמָן הוּא יְזַכֵּנוּ לִימוֹת הַמָּשִׁיחַ וּלְחַיֵּי הָעוֹלָם הַבָּא.

מִגְדּוֹל יְשׁוּעוֹת מַלְכּוֹ, וְעוֹשֶׂה חֶסֶד לִמְשִׁיחוֹ, לְדָוִד וּלְזַרְעוֹ עַד עוֹלָם.

עֹשֶׂה שָׁלוֹם בִּמְרוֹמָיו, הוּא יַעֲשֶׂה שָׁלוֹם עָלֵינוּ וְעַל כָּל־יִשְׂרָאֵל, וְאִמְרוּ אָמֵן.

(*Ps*. 34:10) Fear the Lord, His saints, because those who fear Him will not want.
(*Ps*. 34:11) The lion cubs may be poor and hungry, but those who fear the Lord will not lack any good thing.
(*Ps*. 118:1) Give thanks to the Lord, the truly Good One; truly His kindness is forever.
(*Ps*. 145:16) You open Your hand and graciously satisfy all living beings.
(*Jer*. 17:7) Praised be the man who trusts in the Lord; may the Lord be his succor.
(*Ps*. 37:25) I was young, now I am old, but I never could accept that a just man should be abandoned and his children beg for bread.
(*Ps*. 29:10) The Lord will empower His people, the Lord will bless His people with peace.

Praised are You o Lord, our God, King of the Universe,
Creator of the fruit of the Vine.

One drinks the Third Cup reclining.

יְראוּ אֶת־יי קְדֹשָׁיו
כִּי אֵין מַחְסוֹר לִירֵאָיו.
כְּפִירִים רָשׁוּ וְרָעֵבוּ
וְדֹרְשֵׁי יי לֹא־יַחְסְרוּ כָל־טוֹב.
הוֹדוּ לַיי כִּי־טוֹב
כִּי לְעוֹלָם חַסְדּוֹ.
פּוֹתֵחַ אֶת־יָדֶךָ
וּמַשְׂבִּיעַ לְכָל־חַי רָצוֹן.
בָּרוּךְ הַגֶּבֶר
אֲשֶׁר יִבְטַח בַּיי
וְהָיָה יי מִבְטַחוֹ.
נַעַר הָיִיתִי גַּם־זָקַנְתִּי
וְלֹא רָאִיתִי צַדִּיק נֶעֱזָב
וְזַרְעוֹ מְבַקֶּשׁ לָחֶם.
יי עֹז לְעַמּוֹ יִתֵּן
יי יְבָרֵךְ אֶת־עַמּוֹ בַשָּׁלוֹם.

בָּרוּךְ אַתָּה יי אֱלֹהֵינוּ מֶלֶךְ הָעוֹלָם בּוֹרֵא פְּרִי הַגָּפֶן.

ושותים בהסבת שמאל.

Sephardic Ritual

One fills the Third Cup but not completely.

If the company includes at least three males over 13 years of age, one starts with *zimmun*. If there are at least ten males over 13, one adds the words in parentheses. If the participants are all female, the rules of *zimmun* apply to persons over the age of 12. Without *zimmun* one starts with the second paragraph.

I am ready and prepared to fulfill the commandment to say Grace for the Unity of the Holy, praise to Him, and His Glory, through Him Who is hidden and secret, in the name of all of Israel.

The celebrant: Let us praise (our God) Whose food we ate!

Company: Praised be (our God) Whose food we ate and by Whose goodness we live!

The celebrant: Praised be (our God) Whose food we ate and by Whose goodness we live, praise to Him and to His Name and to His remembrance for ever and ever!

Djerba/Amsterdam text

Praised are You o Lord, our God, King of the Universe, Who feeds the entire world in His goodness; in grace, kindness, and mercy giving bread to all flesh because His kindness is eternal. Through His great kindness He never made us lack food and shall never make us lack food for ever and ever. Truly He is the God Who feeds and provides for all, His table is set for all, He has food prepared for all His creatures whom He created in His mercy and abundant grace, as it is said (*Ps.* 145:16): "You Who open Your hand and satisfy all living beings in favor." Praised are You, o Lord, Who feeds all.

Livorno text

Praised are You o Lord, our God, King of the Universe, Who feeds us even when our deeds do not warrant it, Who provides for us even when our righteousness does not warrant it, Who multiplies His goodness over us, Who feeds us and the entire world in His goodness; in grace, kindness, consolation, and mercy, He gives bread to all flesh because His kindness is eternal. Through His great kindness we never lacked food; may we never lack food for ever and ever for the sake of His great Name. Truly He feeds and provides for all, His table is set for all, and He ordered sustenance and food prepared for all His creatures whom He created in His mercy and His great kindness, as it is said (*Ps.* 145:16): "You Who open Your hand and graciously satisfy all living beings." Praised are You o Lord, Who feeds all (in His mercy).

נוסח סְפָרַד.

ממלאים את הכוס השלישי אבל לא מוזגים.
אם בין המסובין לפחות שלושה גברים בגיל המצוות חייבים בזימון.

הריני מוכן ומזומן לקיים מצות עשה של ברכת המזון ולברך על הכוס, לשם יחוד קב״ה ושכינתיה אל ידי ההוא טמיר ונעלם בשם כל ישראל.

נוסח ליוורנו

בעל הבית: נְבָרֵךְ שֶׁאָכַלְנוּ מִשֶּׁלּוֹ.

המסובים: בָּרוּךְ שֶׁאָכַלְנוּ מִשֶּׁלּוֹ וּבְטוּבוֹ הַגָּדוֹל חָיִינוּ.

בעל הבית: בָּרוּךְ שֶׁאָכַלְנוּ מִשֶּׁלּוֹ וּבְטוּבוֹ הַגָּדוֹל חָיִינוּ.

בָּרוּךְ הוּא וּבָרוּךְ שְׁמוֹ וּבָרוּךְ זִכְרוֹ לְעוֹלְמֵי עַד.

ביחידות מתחילים כאן

בָּרוּךְ אַתָּה יי אֱלֹהֵינוּ מֶלֶךְ הָעוֹלָם, הַזָּנֵנוּ וְלֹא מִמַּעֲשֵׂנוּ, הַמְפַרְנְסֵנוּ וְלֹא מִצִּדְקוֹתֵינוּ, הַמַּעֲדִיף טוּבוֹ עָלֵינוּ, הַזָּן אוֹתָנוּ וְאֶת הָעוֹלָם כֻּלּוֹ בְּטוּבוֹ, בְּחֵן, בְּחֶסֶד, בְּרֵיוַח וּבְרַחֲמִים, נוֹתֵן לֶחֶם לְכָל בָּשָׂר כִּי לְעוֹלָם חַסְדּוֹ. וּבְטוּבוֹ הַגָּדוֹל תָּמִיד לֹא חָסֵר לָנוּ, וְעַל יֶחְסַר לָנוּ מָזוֹן תָּמִיד לְעוֹלָם וָעֶד, כִּי הוּא זָן וּמְפַרְנֵס לַכֹּל, וְשֻׁלְחָנוֹ עָרוּךְ לַכֹּל, וְהִתְקִין מִחְיָה וּמָזוֹן לְכָל בְּרִיּוֹתָיו, אֲשֶׁר בָּרָא בְּרַחֲמָיו וּבְרוֹב חֲסָדָיו. כָּאָמוּר 'פּוֹתֵחַ אֶת יָדֶיךָ וּמַשְׂבִּיעַ לְכָל חַי רָצוֹן'. בָּרוּךְ אַתָּה יי, הַזָּן אֶת־הַכֹּל.

נוסח אמשטרדם והאי ג׳רבה

אם בין המסובין לפחות שלושה גברים בגיל המצוות יאמר המברך:

נְבָרֵךְ (בעשרה: אֱלֹהֵינוּ) שֶׁאָכַלְנוּ מִשֶּׁלּוֹ

המסובים: בָּרוּךְ (בעשרה: אֱלֹהֵינוּ) שֶׁאָכַלְנוּ מִשֶּׁלּוֹ וּבְטוּבוֹ חָיִינוּ.

המברך: בָּרוּךְ (בעשרה: אֱלֹהֵינוּ) שֶׁאָכַלְנוּ מִשֶּׁלּוֹ וּבְטוּבוֹ חָיִינוּ.

ביחידות מתחילים כאן

בָּרוּךְ אַתָּה יי אֱלֹהֵינוּ מֶלֶךְ הָעוֹלָם הָאֵל הַזָּן אֶת הָעוֹלָם כֻּלּוֹ בְּטוּבוֹ, בְּחֵן, בְּחֶסֶד וּבְרַחֲמִים, נוֹתֵן לֶחֶם לְכָל בָּשָׂר כִּי לְעוֹלָם חַסְדּוֹ. וּבְטוּבוֹ הַגָּדוֹל תָּמִיד לֹא חָסֵר לָנוּ, וְעַל יֶחְסַר לָנוּ, מָזוֹן תָּמִיד לְעוֹלָם וָעֶד, כִּי הוּא אֵל זָן וּמְפַרְנֵס לַכֹּל, וְשֻׁלְחָנוֹ עָרוּךְ לַכֹּל וְהִתְקִין מִחְיָה וּמָזוֹן לְכָל בְּרִיּוֹתָיו אֲשֶׁר בָּרָא בְּרַחֲמָיו וּבְרוֹב חֲסָדָיו כָּאָמוּר 'פּוֹתֵחַ אֶת־יָדֶךָ וּמַשְׂבִּיעַ לְכָל־חַי רָצוֹן'. בָּרוּךְ אַתָּה יי, הַזָּן אֶת הַכֹּל.

We thank You o Lord, our God, that You let our fathers inherit a desirable, good, and spacious land, Covenant, and Torah, that You did lead us out of Egypt and did redeem us from the house of slaves, for the Covenant which You have sealed in our flesh, for Your Torah which You have taught us, for the laws of Your pleasure which You have made known to us, and for the life and food You have fed and provided us. For all this we thank You o Lord, our God, and praise Your name, as it is said (*Deut.* 8:10): "You will eat and be satisfied, then you must praise the Lord, your God, for the good land (here one mixes the Third Cup with fresh water) that He gave you." Praised are You o Lord, for the Land and for the food.

For our Land and the inheritance of our fathers we thank You o Lord, our God, that You let our fathers inherit a desirable, good, and spacious land (Women omit: Covenant, Torah), life, and food, that You did lead our fathers out of Egypt and did redeem us from the house of slaves (Women omit: for Your Covenant which You have sealed in our flesh, for Your Torah which You have taught us), for the laws of Your pleasure which You have made known to us, and for the life and food with which You feed and You provide for us. For all this we thank You o Lord, our God, and we praise You, may Your name be praised by every living being, always, for ever and ever, as it is written (*Deut.* 8:10): "You will eat and be satisfied, then you must praise the Lord, your God (here one mixes the Third Cup with fresh water), for the good land that He gave you." Praised are You, o Lord, for the Land and for the food.

Have mercy o Lord, our God, on Israel Your people, on Jerusalem Your city, on Mount Zion the dwelling place of Your glory, on Your Temple, Your abode, Your holy hall, on the great and holy house over which Your Name is mentioned. Our Father, be our shepherd, feed us, provide for us, sustain us, let us earn a living, and relieve us soon from all our worries. May it please You o Lord, our God, to make us need neither the charities of flesh and blood nor their loans, their gifts being scanty and paid by great shame, but only the gift of Your full, abundant, rich, and open hand so that we shall never become ashamed in this world nor disgraced in the future world. And return the kingdom of David Your anointed to its place soon.

On Sabbath add:

O Lord, our God, may You be pleased and give us ease of mind through Your commandments and the commandment of this Seventh Day, this great and holy Sabbath. Truly this is a great and holy day before You. We shall refrain from work and to rest on it in love, conforming to the commandments of Your pleasure. May there be neither worry nor sorrow on the day of our rest. Let us see the

עַל אַרְצֵנוּ וְעַל נַחֲלַת אֲבוֹתֵינוּ
נוֹדֶה לְּךָ יי אֱלֹהֵינוּ, עַל
שֶׁהִנְחַלְתָּ לַאֲבוֹתֵינוּ אֶרֶץ
חֶמְדָּה טוֹבָה וּרְחָבָה, (הנשים לא
תאמרנה בְּרִית וְתוֹרָה) חַיִּים
וּמָזוֹן, עַל שֶׁהוֹצֵאתָנוּ מֵאֶרֶץ
מִצְרַיִם וּפְדִיתָנוּ מִבֵּית
עֲבָדִים, (הנשים לא תאמרנה וְעַל
בְּרִיתְךָ שֶׁחָתַמְתָּ בִּבְשָׂרֵנוּ, וְעַל
תּוֹרָתְךָ שֶׁלִּמַּדְתָּנוּ,) וְעַל חֻקֵּי
רְצוֹנְךָ שֶׁהוֹדַעְתָּנוּ, וְעַל חַיִּים
וּמָזוֹן שָׁאַתָּה זָן וּמְפַרְנֵס
אוֹתָנוּ. וְעַל הַכֹּל יי אֱלֹהֵינוּ
אָנוּ מוֹדִים לָךְ, וּמְבָרְכִים אֶת
שְׁמָךְ, כָּאָמוּר 'וְאָכַלְתָּ וְשָׂבָעְתָּ
וּבֵרַכְתָּ אֶת יי אֱלֹהֶיךָ עַל
הָאָרֶץ הַטּוֹבָה (ומוזגים את הכוס
כשאומרים על הארץ הטובה) אֲשֶׁר
נָתַן לָךְ.' בָּרוּךְ אַתָּה יי, עַל
הָאָרֶץ וְעַל הַמָּזוֹן.

נוֹדֶה לְּךָ יי אֱלֹהֵינוּ עַל
שֶׁהִנְחַלְתָּ לַאֲבוֹתֵינוּ אֶרֶץ
חֶמְדָּה טוֹבָה וּרְחָבָה, בְּרִית
וְתוֹרָה, חַיִּים וּמָזוֹן, עַל
שֶׁהוֹצֵאתָנוּ מֵאֶרֶץ מִצְרַיִם
וּפְדִיתָנוּ מִבֵּית עֲבָדִים, עַל
בְּרִיתְךָ שֶׁחָתַמְתָּ בִּבְשָׂרֵנוּ, וְעַל
תּוֹרָתְךָ שֶׁלִּמַּדְתָּנוּ, וְעַל חֻקֵּי
רְצוֹנְךָ שֶׁהוֹדַעְתָּנוּ, וְעַל חַיִּים
וּמָזוֹן שָׁאַתָּה זָן וּמְפַרְנֵס
אוֹתָנוּ. עַל הַכֹּל יי אֱלֹהֵינוּ
אָנוּ מוֹדִים לָךְ וּמְבָרְכִים אֶת
שְׁמָךְ, כָּאָמוּר 'וְאָכַלְתָּ וְשָׂבָעְתָּ,
וּבֵרַכְתָּ אֶת יי אֱלֹהֶיךָ עַל
הָאָרֶץ הַטּוֹבָה אֲשֶׁר נָתַן לָךְ.'
בָּרוּךְ אַתָּה יי, עַל הָאָרֶץ וְעַל
הַמָּזוֹן.

רַחֵם יי אֱלֹהֵינוּ עָלֵינוּ וְעַל יִשְׂרָאֵל עַמָּךְ, וְעַל יְרוּשָׁלַיִם עִירָךְ, וְעַל צִיּוֹן מִשְׁכַּן כְּבוֹדָךְ, וְעַל הֵיכָלָךְ, וְעַל מְעוֹנָךְ, וְעַל דְּבִירָךְ, וְעַל הַבַּיִת הַגָּדוֹל וְהַקָּדוֹשׁ שֶׁנִּקְרָא שִׁמְךָ עָלָיו. אָבִינוּ, רְעֵנוּ, זוּנֵנוּ, פַּרְנְסֵנוּ כַּלְכְּלֵנוּ, הַרְוִיחֵנוּ, הַרְוַח לָנוּ מְהֵרָה מִכָּל צָרוֹתֵינוּ. וְאַל תַּצְרִיכֵנוּ יי אֱלֹהֵינוּ לֹא לִידֵי מַתְּנוֹת בָּשָׂר וָדָם, וְלֹא לִידֵי הַלְוָאָתָם, שֶׁמַּתְּנָתָם מְעוּטָה וְחֶרְפָּתָם מְרוּבָּה, אֶלָּא לְיָדְךָ הַמְּלֵאָה הַפְּתוּחָה הַקְּדוֹשָׁה וְהָרְחָבָה הָעֲשִׁירָה וְהַפְּתוּחָה, שֶׁלֹּא נֵבוֹשׁ בָּעוֹלָם הַזֶּה וְלֹא נִכָּלֵם בָּעוֹלָם הַבָּא. וּמַלְכוּת בֵּית דָּוִד מְשִׁיחָךְ תַּחֲזִירֶנָּה לִמְקוֹמָהּ בִּמְהֵרָה בְיָמֵינוּ.

בשבת מוסיפים

רְצֵה וְהַחֲלִיצֵנוּ יי אֱלֹהֵינוּ בְּמִצְוֹתֶיךָ, וּבְמִצְוַת יוֹם הַשְּׁבִיעִי, הַשַּׁבָּת הַגָּדוֹל וְהַקָּדוֹשׁ הַזֶּה, כִּי יוֹם גָּדוֹל וְקָדוֹשׁ הוּא מִלְּפָנֶיךָ, נִשְׁבּוֹת בּוֹ וְנָנוּחַ בּוֹ בְּאַהֲבָה כְּמִצְוַת חֻקֵּי רְצוֹנֶךָ. וְעַל תְּהִי צָרָה וְיָגוֹן וַאֲנָחָה

consolation of Zion soon, in our days, because You are the Master of consolations. Even though we ate and drank, we did not forget the destruction of Your great and holy house. Do not forget us forever and do not neglect us eternally because You are a great and holy God.

Our God and God of our fathers! May there arise, come, arrive, be accepted, received with pleasure, heard, taken notice of, and be remembered before You the remembrance and notice of ourselves and the remembrance of our fathers, the remembrance of the Messiah, the son of David Your servant, the remembrance of Jerusalem, the city of Your sanctuary, and the remembrance of your entire people, the house of Israel, for survival, good, grace, goodwill, mercy, life, and peace on this day of the festival of unleavened bread, this holiday of holy assembly, to have mercy upon us on it and to help us. Remember us on it, o Lord, our God, in a good way; take notice of us on it for blessing; and help us on it for good life! Spare us with a word of help and mercy and let us find grace! Have compassion and mercy on us, help us because our eyes are on You since You are a gracious and merciful God and King.

And do build Your city of Jerusalem soon in our days. Praised are You o Lord, Who in His mercy builds reconstructed Jerusalem (silently: Amen).

May the city of Zion be built with song during our lifetime and the life of the entire congregation, the house of Israel. May the holy service be founded in Jerusalem and may the Palace be lawfully restituted soon as in the days of old.

Praised are You o Lord, our God, King of the Universe, Eternal God, our Father, our King, our Pride, our Creator, our Savior, our Holy One, the Holy One of Jacob, our Shepherd, the Shepherd of Israel, the good King Who does good to all, every day He treated us well, He is treating us well, He will treat us well, He was kind to us, He is being kind to us, He will be kind to us forever in grace, goodwill, mercy, helping relief, and all good.

The Merciful One, He shall be praised on the throne of His splendor.
The Merciful One, He shall be praised in Heaven and on earth.
The Merciful One, He shall be praised by us in all generations.
The Merciful One, may He lift the fortunes of His people.
The Merciful One, may He glorify Himself in us for all eternity.
The Merciful One, may He provide for us in honor and not in shame, in legal and not in illegal ways, in comfort and not in hurt.
The Merciful One, may He make peace among us.

בְּיוֹם מְנוּחָתֵנוּ. וְהַרְאֵנוּ בְּנֶחָמַת צִיּוֹן בִּמְהֵרָה בְיָמֵינוּ, כִּי אַתָּה הוּא בַּעַל הַנֶּחָמוֹת. וְאַף עַל פִּי שֶׁאָכַלְנוּ וְשָׁתִינוּ, חָרְבַּן בֵּיתְךָ הַגָּדוֹל וְהַקָּדוֹשׁ לֹא שָׁכַחְנוּ, אַל תִּשְׁכָּחֵנוּ לָנֶצַח וְאַל תִּזְנָחֵנוּ לָעַד כִּי אֵל גָּדוֹל וְקָדוֹשׁ אָתָּה.

אֱלֹהֵינוּ וֵאלֹהֵי אֲבוֹתֵינוּ. יַעֲלֶה וְיָבוֹא יַגִּיעַ יֵרָאֶה וְיֵרָצֶה, יִשָּׁמַע יִפָּקֵד וְיִזָּכֵר זִכְרוֹנֵנוּ, וְזִכְרוֹן אֲבוֹתֵנוּ, זִכְרוֹן יְרוּשָׁלַיִם עִירָךְ, וְזִכְרוֹן מָשִׁיחַ בֶּן דָּוִד עַבְדָּךְ, וְזִכְרוֹן כָּל עַמְּךָ בֵּית יִשְׂרָאֵל לְפָנֶיךָ, לִפְלֵטָה לְטוֹבָה לְחֵן וּלְחֶסֶד וּלְרַחֲמִים (לְחַיִּים טוֹבִים וּלְשָׁלוֹם) בְּיוֹם חַג הַמַּצּוֹת הַזֶּה, בְּיוֹם טוֹב מִקְרָא קֹדֶשׁ הַזֶּה, לְרַחֵם בּוֹ עָלֵינוּ וּלְהוֹשִׁיעֵנוּ. זָכְרֵנוּ יי אֱלֹהֵינוּ בּוֹ לְטוֹבָה, וּפָקְדֵנוּ בוֹ לִבְרָכָה, וְהוֹשִׁיעֵנוּ בוֹ לְחַיִּים טוֹבִים, בִּדְבַר יְשׁוּעָה וְרַחֲמִים חוּס וְחָנֵּנוּ, וַחֲמוֹל וְרַחֵם עָלֵינוּ, וְהוֹשִׁיעֵנוּ כִּי אֵלֶיךָ עֵינֵינוּ, כִּי אֵל מֶלֶךְ חַנּוּן וְרַחוּם אָתָּה.

וּתִבְנֶה יְרוּשָׁלַיִם עִירָךְ בִּמְהֵרָה בְיָמֵינוּ. בָּרוּךְ אַתָּה יי בּוֹנֶה בְרַחֲמָיו יְרוּשָׁלָיִם, (בלחש אָמֵן).

בְּחַיֵּינוּ וּבְחַיֵּי כָּל קְהַל בֵּית יִשְׂרָאֵל תִּבָּנֶה עִיר צִיּוֹן בְּרִנָּה, וְתִכּוֹן עֲבוֹדַת הַקֹּדֶשׁ בִּירוּשָׁלַיִם, וְאַרְמוֹן עַל מִשְׁפָּטוֹ יֵשֵׁב בְּקָרוֹב כְּבָרִאשׁוֹנָה. בָּרוּךְ אַתָּה יי אֱלֹהֵינוּ מֶלֶךְ הָעוֹלָם לָעַד, הָאֵל אָבִינוּ, מַלְכֵּנוּ, אַדִּירֵנוּ, בּוֹרְאֵנוּ, גֹּאֲלֵנוּ, קְדוֹשֵׁנוּ קְדוֹשׁ יַעֲקֹב, רוֹעֵנוּ רוֹעֵה יִשְׂרָאֵל, הַמֶּלֶךְ הַטּוֹב וְהַמֵּטִיב לַכֹּל, שֶׁבְּכָל יוֹם וָיוֹם הוּא הֵטִיב לָנוּ, הוּא מֵטִיב לָנוּ, הוּא יֵטִיב לָנוּ, הוּא גְמָלָנוּ, הוּא גוֹמְלֵנוּ, הוּא יִגְמְלֵנוּ לָעַד, חֵן וְחֶסֶד וְרַחֲמִים, וְרֶוַח וְהַצָּלָה וְכָל טוֹב.

הָרַחֲמָן הוּא יִשְׁתַּבַּח עַל כִּסֵּא כְבוֹדוֹ.
הָרַחֲמָן הוּא יִשְׁתַּבַּח בַּשָּׁמַיִם וּבָאָרֶץ.
הָרַחֲמָן הוּא יִשְׁתַּבַּח בָּנוּ לְדוֹר דּוֹרִים.
הָרַחֲמָן הוּא קֶרֶן לְעַמּוֹ יָרִים.
הָרַחֲמָן הוּא יִתְפָּאַר בָּנוּ לָנֶצַח נְצָחִים.
הָרַחֲמָן הוּא יְפַרְנְסֵנוּ בְּכָבוֹד וְלֹא בְּבִזּוּי, בְּהֶתֵּר וְלֹא בְאִסּוּר, בְּנַחַת וְלֹא בְּצַעַר.
הָרַחֲמָן הוּא יִתֵּן שָׁלוֹם בֵּינֵינוּ.

The Merciful One, may He send blessing, gain, and success in all our work.

The Merciful One, may He make our way succeed.

The Merciful One, may He soon break the yoke of the Diaspora from our neck.

The Merciful One, may He soon lead us upright to our Land.

The Merciful One, may He heal us in complete healing, healing of the soul and healing of the body.

The Merciful One, may He open His ample hand for us.

The Merciful One, may He bless every single one of us by His great Name just like our fathers Abraham, Isaac, and Jacob were blessed in everything, from everything, everything, so may He bless us together in a perfect blessing. May this be His pleasure; let us say Amen.

The Merciful One, may He spread over us the tabernacle of His peace.

On Sabbath: The Merciful One, may He let us inherit the world which is all Sabbath and rest, the eternal life.

The Merciful One, may He let us reach other festive seasons and holidays that may come to us in peace.

The Merciful One, may He plant His Torah and His love in our hearts and may the fear of Him be on our faces so that we should not sin (*Ex.* 20:20).

Prayer of the guest:

The Merciful One, may He bless this table at which we ate, bring to it all the delicacies of the world, and may it be like the table of our father Abraham: Every hungry person shall eat at it, every thirsty person shall drink at it. The Merciful One, may He bless the master of this house, the giver of this meal, him, his children, his wife, and all his possessions; may He bless him with children that will not die and with property that will not come to an end. (*Deut.* 33:11): "May the Lord bless his strength and have pleasure in the work of his hands." May his properties be successful and close to the city. May there never be any sin nor thought of transgression near him from now to eternity. May he be happy and enjoy riches and property and honor from now to eternity. May he not be ashamed in this world nor disgraced in the World to Come. Amen, may this be God's pleasure.

The Merciful One, may He let us live, give us merit, and bring us close to the days of the Messiah, the building of the Temple, and the life of the Future World.

(*2 Sam.* 22:51) He is a tower of help for His king, and is kind to His anointed, to David and his descendants forever.

(*Ps.* 34:11) The lion cubs may be poor and hungry, but those who fear the Lord will not lack any good.

(*Ps.* 37:25–26) I was young, now I am old, but I never could accept that

הָרַחֲמָן הוּא יִשְׁלַח בְּרָכָה רְוָחָה וְהַצְלָחָה בְּכָל מַעֲשֵׂה יָדֵינוּ.
הָרַחֲמָן הוּא יַצְלִיחַ אֶת דְּרָכֵינוּ.
הָרַחֲמָן הוּא יִשְׁבּוֹר עוֹל הַגָּלוּת מְהֵרָה מֵעַל צַוָּרֵנוּ.
הָרַחֲמָן הוּא יוֹלִיכֵנוּ מְהֵרָה קוֹמְמִיוּת לְאַרְצֵנוּ.
הָרַחֲמָן הוּא יִרְפָּאֵנוּ רְפוּאָה שְׁלֵמָה רְפוּאַת הַנֶּפֶשׁ וּרְפוּאַת הַגּוּף.
הָרַחֲמָן הוּא יִפְתַּח לָנוּ אֶת יָדוֹ הָרְחָבָה.
הָרַחֲמָן הוּא יְבָרֵךְ כָּל אֶחָד וְאֶחָד מִמֶּנּוּ בִּשְׁמוֹ הַגָּדוֹל כְּמוֹ שֶׁנִּתְבָּרְכוּ אֲבוֹתֵינוּ אַבְרָהָם יִצְחָק וְיַעֲקֹב בַּכֹּל מִכֹּל כֹּל, כֵּן יְבָרֵךְ אוֹתָנוּ יַחַד בִּבְרָכָה שְׁלֵמָה, וְכֵן יְהִי רָצוֹן וְנֹאמַר אָמֵן.
הָרַחֲמָן הוּא יִפְרוֹשׂ עָלֵינוּ סֻכַּת שְׁלוֹמוֹ.
הָרַחֲמָן הוּא יִטַּע תּוֹרָתוֹ וְאַהֲבָתוֹ בְּלִבֵּנוּ וְתִהְיֶה יִרְאָתוֹ עַל פָּנֵינוּ לְבִלְתִּי נֶחֱטָא.

ברכת האורח

הָרַחֲמָן הוּא יְבָרֵךְ אֶת הַשֻּׁלְחָן הַזֶּה שֶׁאָכַלְנוּ עָלָיו, וִיסַדֵּר בּוֹ כָּל מַעֲדַנֵּי עוֹלָם, וְיִהְיֶה כְּשֻׁלְחָנוֹ שֶׁל אַבְרָהָם אָבִינוּ, כָּל רָעֵב מִמֶּנּוּ יֹאכַל, וְכָל צָמֵא מִמֶּנּוּ יִשְׁתֶּה.
הָרַחֲמָן הוּא יְבָרֵךְ בַּעַל הַבַּיִת הַזֶּה וּבַעַל הַסְּעוּדָה הַזֹּאת, הוּא וּבָנָיו וְאִשְׁתּוֹ וְכָל אֲשֶׁר לוֹ, בְּבָנִים שֶׁלֹּא יָמוּתוּ, וּבִנְכָסִים שֶׁלֹּא יִתַּמּוּ, לֹא יֵבוֹשׁ בָּעוֹלָם הַזֶּה וְלֹא יִכָּלֵם לָעוֹלָם הַבָּא, וְיִהְיוּ נְכָסָיו מֻצְלָחִים וּקְרוֹבִים לָעִיר, וְלֹא יִשְׁלוֹט שָׂטָן בְּמַעֲשֵׂה יָדָיו, וְאַל יִזְדַּקֵּק לְפָנָיו שׁוּם דְּבַר חֵטְא וְהִרְהוּר עָוֹן, מֵעַתָּה וְעַד עוֹלָם.

הָרַחֲמָן הוּא יְחַיֵּינוּ וִיזַכֵּנוּ וִיקָרְבֵנוּ לִימוֹת הַמָּשִׁיחַ וּלְחַיֵּי הָעוֹלָם הַבָּא.
מִגְדּוֹל יְשׁוּעוֹת מַלְכּוֹ, וְעֹשֶׂה חֶסֶד לִמְשִׁיחוֹ, לְדָוִד וּלְזַרְעוֹ עַד עוֹלָם.
כְּפִירִים רָשׁוּ וְרָעֵבוּ, וְדוֹרְשֵׁי יי לֹא יַחְסְרוּ כָל טוֹב.
נַעַר הָיִיתִי גַּם זָקַנְתִּי, וְלֹא רָאִיתִי צַדִּיק נֶעֱזָב, וְזַרְעוֹ מְבַקֶּשׁ לָחֶם.
כָּל הַיּוֹם חוֹנֵן וּמַלְוֶה, וְזַרְעוֹ לִבְרָכָה.

a just man be abandoned and his children should beg for bread. All day long he loves and lends, and his seed is a blessing.

What we ate shall be satisfying, what we drank shall be healthy, what we left over shall be for a blessing, as it is written (2 *Kings* 4:44): "He put before them, they ate and left over according to the word of the Lord."

(*Ps.* 11:15) May you be blessed for the Lord, the Creator of Heaven and earth.

(*Jer.* 17:7) Praised be the man who trusts in the Lord; may the Lord be his succor.

(*Ps.* 29:10) The Lord will empower His people, the Lord will bless His people with peace.

He who makes peace in His heights, may He make peace for us and all Israel, Amen.

The following benediction refers both to this and to the last cup of wine

(*Ps.* 116:13) I shall lift up the cup of salvations and invoke the name of the Lord.

Praised are You o Lord, our God, King of the Universe, Creator of the fruit of the vine.

One drinks the Third Cup reclining.

מַה שֶּׁאָכַלְנוּ יִהְיֶה לְשָׂבְעָה, וּמַה שֶּׁשָּׁתִינוּ יִהְיֶה לִרְפוּאָה, וּמַה שֶּׁהוֹתַרְנוּ יִהְיֶה לִבְרָכָה, כְּדִכְתִיב 'וַיִּתֵּן לִפְנֵיהֶם וַיֹּאכְלוּ וַיּוֹתִירוּ כִּדְבַר יי.'

בְּרוּכִים אַתֶּם לַיי עֹשֵׂה שָׁמַיִם וָאָרֶץ.

בָּרוּךְ הַגֶּבֶר אֲשֶׁר יִבְטַח בַּיי וְהָיָה יי מִבְטַחוֹ.

יי עֹז לְעַמּוֹ יִתֵּן יי יְבָרֵךְ אֶת עַמּוֹ בַשָּׁלוֹם.

עוֹשֶׂה שָׁלוֹם בִּמְרוֹמָיו הוּא יַעֲשֶׂה שָׁלוֹם עָלֵינוּ וְעַל כָּל יִשְׂרָאֵל וְאִמְרוּ אָמֵן.

וצריך לכוין בברכת בורא פרי הגפן על כוס שלישי זה לפטור בברכה זו גם הכוס הרביעי.

כּוֹס יְשׁוּעוֹת אֶשָּׂא וּבְשֵׁם יי אֶקְרָא

סַבְרִי מָרָנָן. בָּרוּךְ אַתָּה יי אֱלֹהֵינוּ מֶלֶךְ הָעוֹלָם בּוֹרֵא פְּרִי הַגֶּפֶן.

ושותים כל אחד כוסו בהיסיבה.

Yemenite Ritual

The cups are rinsed, dried, and filled for the third time.
If the company includes at least three males over 13 years of age, one starts with *zimmun*. If there are at least ten males over 13, one adds the words in parentheses. Without *zimmun* one starts with the second paragraph.

The celebrant: Let us praise (our God) Whose food we ate!

Company: Praised be (our God) Whose food we ate and by Whose goodness we live!

The celebrant: Praised be (our God) Whose food we ate and by Whose goodness we live!

Praised are You o Lord, our God, King of the Universe, Who feeds the entire world in goodness, grace, kindness, and mercy. Through His great kindness we never did lack food and never shall lack food for ever and ever because He feeds, nurtures, and provides for all, as it is said (*Ps.* 145:16): "You open Your hand and graciously satisfy all living beings." Praised are You, o Lord, Who in His mercy feeds all.

We thank You o Lord, our God, and we praise You, our King, that You let our fathers inherit a desirable, good, and spacious land, Covenant, and Torah, and that You have led us out of Egypt and redeemed us from the house of slaves, and for Your Torah which You have taught us, and for the laws of Your pleasure which You have made known to us. For all this we thank You o Lord, our God, and we praise You; may Your name be praised by every living being, always, for ever and ever, as it is written (*Deut.* 8:10): "You will eat and be satisfied, then you must praise the Lord, your God, for the good land that He gave you." Praised are You, o Lord, for the Land and for the food.

Have mercy o Lord, our God, on Israel Your people, on Jerusalem Your city, on Zion the abode of Your glory, and on the great and holy house upon which Your Name is mentioned. And return the kingdom of David, Your anointed, to its place in our days.

On Sabbath add:

Our God and God of our fathers, may You be pleased and give us ease of mind through Your commandments and the commandment of this great and holy Sabbath day. We shall refrain from work and rest on it, conforming to the commandments of Your pleasure. May there be neither worry nor sorrow on the day of our rest.

Our God and God of our fathers! May there arise, come, arrive, be accepted, received with pleasure, heard, taken notice of, and be remembered before You the remembrance and notice of ourselves and

בִּרְכַּת הַמָּזוֹן נוּסַח תֵּימָן.

רוחצים את הכוסות ומוזגים כוס שלישי.

אם בין המסובין לפחות שלושה גברים בגיל המצוות יאמר המברך: נְבָרֵךְ (בעשרה: אֱלֹהֵינוּ) שֶׁאָכַלְנוּ מִשֶּׁלּוֹ.

המסובים: בָּרוּךְ (בעשרה: אֱלֹהֵינוּ) שֶׁאָכַלְנוּ מִשֶּׁלּוֹ וּבְטוּבוֹ חָיִינוּ.

המברך: בָּרוּךְ (בעשרה: אֱלֹהֵינוּ) שֶׁאָכַלְנוּ מִשֶּׁלּוֹ וּבְטוּבוֹ חָיִינוּ.

ביחידות מתחילים כאן

בָּרוּךְ אַתָּה יי אֱלֹהֵינוּ מֶלֶךְ הָעוֹלָם הַזָּן אֶת־הָעוֹלָם כֻּלּוֹ בְּטוּב, בְּחֵן, בְּחֶסֶד, בְּרַחֲמִים. וְטוּבוֹ הַגָּדוֹל לֹא חָסַר לָנוּ, וְעַל יֶחְסַר לָנוּ לְעוֹלָם וָעֶד, כִּי הוּא זָן וּמֵזִין וּמְפַרְנֵס לַכֹּל כָּאָמוּר ׳פּוֹתֵחַ אֶת יָדֶךָ וּמַשְׂבִּיעַ לְכָל חַי רָצוֹן׳. בָּרוּךְ אַתָּה יי, הַזָּן בְּרַחֲמָיו אֶת הַכֹּל.

נוֹדֶה לְךָ יי אֱלֹהֵינוּ, וּנְבָרֶכְךָ מַלְכֵּנוּ, כִּי הִנְחַלְתָּ אֶת אֲבוֹתֵינוּ אֶרֶץ חֶמְדָּה טוֹבָה וּרְחָבָה, בְּרִית וְתוֹרָה, וְעַל שֶׁהוֹצֵאתָנוּ מֵאֶרֶץ מִצְרַיִם וּפְדִיתָנוּ מִבֵּית עֲבָדִים, וְעַל תּוֹרָתְךָ שֶׁלִּמַּדְתָּנוּ, וְעַל חֻקֵּי רְצוֹנָךְ שֶׁהוֹדַעְתָּנוּ. עַל כּוּלָּם יי אֱלֹהֵינוּ אֲנַחְנוּ מוֹדִים לָךְ וּמְבָרְכִים אֶת שְׁמָךְ, כָּאָמוּר ׳וְאָכַלְתָּ וְשָׂבָעְתָּ, וּבֵרַכְתָּ אֶת יי אֱלֹהֶיךָ עַל הָאָרֶץ הַטּוֹבָה אֲשֶׁר נָתַן לָךְ׳. בָּרוּךְ אַתָּה יי, עַל הָאָרֶץ וְעַל הַמָּזוֹן.

רַחֵם יי אֱלֹהֵינוּ עָלֵינוּ וְעַל יִשְׂרָאֵל עַמָּךְ וְעַל יְרוּשָׁלַיִם עִירָךְ וְעַל צִיּוֹן מִשְׁכַּן כְּבוֹדָךְ וְעַל הַבַּיִת הַגָּדוֹל וְהַקָּדוֹשׁ שֶׁנִּקְרָא שִׁמְךָ עָלָיו, וּמַלְכוּת בֵּית דָּוִד מְשִׁיחָךְ תַּחֲזִיר לִמְקוֹמָהּ בְּיָמֵינוּ.

בשבת מוסיפים

אֱלֹהֵינוּ וֵאלֹהֵי אֲבוֹתֵינוּ. רְצֵה וְהַחֲלִיצֵנוּ בְּמִצְוֹתֶךָ וּבְמִצְוַת יוֹם הַמָּנוֹחַ הַשְּׁבִיעִי הַזֶּה. נִשְׁבּוֹת בּוֹ וְנָנוּחַ בּוֹ כְּמִצְוַת רְצוֹנֶךָ וְאַל תְּהִי צָרָה וְיָגוֹן בְּיוֹם מְנוּחָתֵנוּ.

אֱלֹהֵינוּ וֵאלֹהֵי אֲבוֹתֵינוּ. יַעֲלֶה וְיָבֹא יַגִּיעַ יֵרָאֶה יֵרָצֶה יִשָּׁמַע יִפָּקֵד יִזָּכֵר זִכְרוֹנֵנוּ, זִכְרוֹן אֲבוֹתֵנוּ, זִכְרוֹן יְרוּשָׁלַיִם עִירָךְ, זִכְרוֹן

the remembrance of our fathers, the remembrance of the Messiah, the son of David Your servant, the remembrance of Jerusalem, the city of Your sanctuary, and the remembrance of your entire people, the house of Israel, for survival, good, grace, goodwill, mercy, life, and peace on this holiday, this festive time of the festival of unleavened bread. Remember us on it, o Lord, our God, in a good way; take notice of us on it for blessing; and help us on it to life! Spare us with a word of help and mercy and let us escape on it all worry and sorrow and let us enjoy on it complete happiness since You are a gracious and merciful God and King.
Build Your city of Jerusalem as You have said. Praised are You o Lord, Who in His mercy builds Jerusalem; Amen.

Praised are You o Lord, our God, King of the Universe, Almighty, our Father, our King, our Pride, our Creator, our Holy One, the Holy of Jacob, the good and beneficial King Who every single day in His goodness gives us grace, kindness, mercy, and all good things.

The Merciful One, He shall be lauded in all generations.
The Merciful One, He shall be glorified in all eternity.
The Merciful One, may He provide for us in honor.
The Merciful One, may He find us worthy for the days of the Messiah, the building of the Temple, and the life of the Future World.

Prayer of the guest; in parentheses, answer of the company to his prayer.
The Merciful One, may He bless each single one of us by His Name. Further, may God bless, conserve, help, make fruitful, plant, make rich, put in order, refresh, let live, and prolong the days of our master and teacher, the head of this house, the master of this meal. May God bless him, also her who is his helpmate, his brothers, children, and relatives; may those be blessed who look out for his good and peace (Amen, and may you be blessed). May all be much blessed with property, riches, extraordinary wisdom, bodily strength, sons, and daughters (Amen), with sons studying Torah and keeping the Commandments in Israel, daughters that shall not die, numerous properties that shall not come to an end, riches and honor that shall not disappear (Amen) and may all good things never end for you! May this table from which we ate and the cup from which we drank be full of delicacies, enriched with blessed portions and full of all good things like the table of our father Abraham which was blessed by the Omnipresent with everything, from everything, everything; may this be the Divine pleasure (may it be Divine pleasure). May it please the Omnipresent, praise to Him, that you, our master and teacher, head of this house and master of this meal, that you should not be ashamed of us nor we be ashamed of you, that you should not be ashamed of your beginning nor disgraced at your end; your future shall extend to generations to come; may your properties be safe, successful, increasing, close to the city; may Satan never rule over nor be close to your work, nor to the work of anyone of the people of the house of Israel; may there never be put, neither before you nor before us nor before any of the people of the house of Israel, any bad thing or thought of transgression, sin or offense, from now to eternity. But

מָשִׁיחַ בֶּן דָּוִד עַבְדֶּךָ, וְזִכְרוֹן כָּל עַמְּךָ בֵּית יִשְׂרָאֵל לְפָנֶיךָ, לִפְלֵטָה לְטוֹבָה לְחֵן וּלְחֶסֶד וּלְרַחֲמִים, בְּיוֹם מִקְרָא קֹדֶשׁ הַזֶּה בְּיוֹם חַג הַמַּצּוֹת הַזֶּה, לְרַחֵם בּוֹ עָלֵינוּ וּלְהוֹשִׁיעֵנוּ. זָכְרֵנוּ יי אֱלֹהֵינוּ בּוֹ לְטוֹבָה, פָּקְדֵנוּ בוֹ לִבְרָכָה, הוֹשִׁיעֵנוּ בוֹ לְחַיִּים, בִּדְבַר יְשׁוּעָה וְרַחֲמִים חוּס וְחָנֵּנוּ וְרַחֵם עָלֵינוּ, וּמַלְּטֵנוּ בוֹ מִכָּל צָרָה וְיָגוֹן וְשַׂמְּחֵנוּ בוֹ שִׂמְחָה שְׁלֵמָה כִּי אֵל מֶלֶךְ חַנּוּן וְרַחוּם אָתָּה.

וּבְנֵה אֶת יְרוּשָׁלַיִם עִירְךָ כַּאֲשֶׁר דִּבַּרְתָּ. בָּרוּךְ אַתָּה יי בּוֹנֶה בְּרַחֲמָיו אֶת יְרוּשָׁלָיִם אָמֵן.

בָּרוּךְ אַתָּה יי אֱלֹהֵינוּ מֶלֶךְ הָעוֹלָם הָאֵל אָבִינוּ מַלְכֵּנוּ אַדִּירֵנוּ בּוֹרְאֵנוּ קְדוֹשֵׁנוּ קְדוֹשׁ יַעֲקֹב הַמֶּלֶךְ הַטּוֹב וְהַמֵּטִיב שֶׁבְּכָל יוֹם וָיוֹם הוּא גוֹמְלֵנוּ חֵן וְחֶסֶד וְרַחֲמִים וְכָל טוֹב.

הָרַחֲמָן יִשְׁתַּבַּח לְדוֹרֵי דוֹרִים
הָרַחֲמָן יִתְפָּאַר לְנֵצַח נְצָחִים.
הָרַחֲמָן יְפַרְנְסֵנוּ בְּכָבוֹד.
הָרַחֲמָן יְזַכֵּנוּ לִימוֹת הַמָּשִׁיחַ וּלְבִנְיַן בֵּית הַמִּקְדָּשׁ וּלְחַיֵּי הָעוֹלָם הַבָּא.

ברכת האורח, והמסובים עונים את המילים בסוגריים:

הָרַחֲמָן יְבָרְכֵנוּ כֻּלָּנוּ כָּל אֶחָד וְאֶחָד אִישׁ בִּשְׁמוֹ. וְעוֹד אֱלֹהִים יְבָרֵךְ וְיִשְׁמוֹר וְיִסְעוֹד וְיַפְרֶה וְיַרְבֶּה וְיַשְׁתִּיל וְיַעְשִׁיר וִיתַקֵּן וִיחַלֵּץ וִיחַיֶּה וְיַאֲרִיךְ אֶת יְמֵי מָרֵנוּ וְרַבֵּנוּ בַּעַל הַבַּיִת הַזֶּה וּבַעַל הַסְּעוּדָה הַזֹּאת, אֱלֹהִים יְבָרֵךְ אוֹתוֹ וְעֶזְרוֹ וְאֶחָיו וּבָנָיו וּקְרוֹבָיו וְדוֹרְשֵׁי טוֹבָתוֹ וְדוֹרְשֵׁי שְׁלוֹמוֹ יִתְבָּרְכוּ (אמן, וְאַתָּה תִּתְבָּרֵךְ). גַּם יִתְבָּרְכוּ הַכֹּל בִּמְאֹד מְאֹד, בְּהוֹן בְּעוֹשֶׁר בְּחָכְמָה מוּפְלָאָה בְּחִלּוּץ עֲצָמוֹת בְּבָנִים, וּבָנוֹת (אמן), בְּבָנִים שֶׁיִּהְיוּ עוֹסְקֵי בַּתּוֹרָה וּמְקַיְּמֵי מִצְוֹת בְּיִשְׂרָאֵל, וּבְבָנוֹת שֶׁלֹּא יָמוּתוּ, וּבִנְכָסִים מְרוּבִּים שֶׁלֹּא יִתַּמּוּ, וּבְעוֹשֶׁר וּבְכָבוֹד שֶׁלֹּא יִכְלֶה (אמן, וְאַתָּה לֹא תִכְלֶה מִכָּל טוּב). וְהַשֻּׁלְחָן הַזֶּה שֶׁאָכַלְנוּ עָלָיו, וְכוֹס שֶׁשָּׁתִינוּ בּוֹ יְהֵא מְעוּדָּן מְדוּשָּׁן מְפוּתְבָּג מְבוֹרָךְ מָלֵא כָּל טוֹבָה כְּשֻׁלְחָנוֹ שֶׁל אַבְרָהָם אָבִינוּ אֲשֶׁר בֵּרְכוֹ הַמָּקוֹם בַּכֹּל מִכֹּל כֹּל וְכֵן יְהִי רָצוֹן (יהי רצון). יְהִי רָצוֹן לִפְנֵי הַמָּקוֹם בָּרוּךְ הוּא שֶׁאַתָּה מָרֵנוּ וְרַבֵּנוּ בַּעַל הַבַּיִת הַזֶּה וּבַעַל הַסְּעוּדָה הַזֹּאת שֶׁלֹּא תֵבוֹשׁ בָּנוּ וְלֹא נֵבוֹשׁ בָּךְ, לֹא תֵבוֹשׁ בְּרֵאשִׁיתְךָ וְלֹא תִכָּלֵם בְּאַחֲרִיתְךָ, אַחֲרִיתְךָ תִּהְיֶה לְדוֹרֵי דוֹרִים, נְכָסֶיךָ יִהְיוּ מוּצָלִים מַצְלִיחִים

you should be worthy (Amen, and may you be worthy), may all of you be worthy and may I, the unimportant and young one, also be worthy with you to see the building of Jerusalem, as saved and successful comrades as of old. In Heaven on high may they grant you this (may they grant you this). May God from on High send blessing to your stores, may He bless your bread and water, as it is written (*Ex.* 23:25): "If you serve the Lord, your God, He will bless your bread and your water; I shall remove sickness from your midst." And it is said (*Ex.* 23:26): "There will be neither a miscarrying nor a barren woman in your land; I shall make the number of your days complete." May the Lord fill your (*i.e., the host's*) desires to good purpose. May the Lord fill your (*i.e., the company's*) desires to good purpose. May all of you, gentlemen who are assembled here, be blessed by my God, Amen. May you be helped. May you be redeemed. May you be saved. May you get rich. May you be protected. May you be sustained. May you succeed. May you understand. Please recite with me and I shall recite with you a praise for the Creator of the World (*Ps.* 89:53): "Praised be the Lord forever, Amen and Amen."

(2 *Sam.* 22:51) He is a tower of help for His king, and is kind to His anointed, to David and his descendants forever.
(*Ps.* 34:11) The lion cubs may be poor and hungry but those who seek the Lord will not miss any good thing.
(*Ps.* 118:1) Give thanks to the Lord, the truly good; truly His kindness is forever.

Praised are You o Lord, our God, King of the Universe, Creator of the fruit of the vine.

The Third Cup is consumed reclining.

מַשְׂבִּיחִים, קְרוֹבִים לָעִיר, וְאַל יִמְשׁוֹל הַשָּׂטָן, (וּבְךָ לֹא יִמְשׁוֹל), וְאַל יִזְדַּקֵּק לֹא
בְּמַעֲשֶׂיךָ וְלֹא בְּמַעֲשֵׂה עַמּוֹ בֵּית יִשְׂרָאֵל, וְאַל יוּשַּׂם לֹא לְפָנֶיךָ וְלֹא לְפָנֵינוּ
וְלֹא לִפְנֵי כָּל עַמּוֹ בֵּית יִשְׂרָאֵל שׁוּם דָּבָר רַע וְהִרְהוּר עֲבֵירָה וְחֵטְא וְעָוֹן
מֵעַתָּה וְעַד עוֹלָם, אֲבָל תִּזְכּוּ (אמן ואתה תזכה) תִּזְכּוּ כֻּלְּכֶם וְגַם אֲנִי הַקַּל
וְהַצָּעִיר אֶזְכֶּה עִמָּכֶם לִרְאוֹת בְּבִנְיָנָהּ שֶׁל יְרוּשָׁלַיִם, חֲבֵרִים מוּצָּלִים מוּצְלָחִים
בִּבְתְחִלָּה. מִמָּרוֹם יְלַמְּדוּ עָלֶיךָ וְעָלֵינוּ זְכוּת (ועליך ילמדו זכות). מִמָּרוֹם יְשַׁלַּח
הָאֵל אֶת הַבְּרָכָה בַּאֲסָמֶיךָ וִיבָרֵךְ אֶת לַחְמְךָ וְאֶת מֵימֶיךָ כִּדְכְתִיב ׳וַעֲבַדְתֶּם
אֶת יי אֱלֹהֵיכֶם וּבֵרַךְ אֶת לַחְמְךָ וְאֶת מֵימֶיךָ וַהֲסִירוֹתִי מַחֲלָה מִקִּרְבֶּךָ׳.
וְנֶאֱמָר ׳לֹא תִהְיֶה מְשַׁכֵּלָה וַעֲקָרָה בְּאַרְצֶךָ אֶת מִסְפַּר יָמֶיךָ אֲמַלֵּא׳. יְמַלֵּא יי
כָּל מִשְׁאֲלוֹתֶיךָ לְטוֹבָה. יְמַלֵּא יי כָּל מִשְׁאֲלוֹתֵיכֶם לְטוֹבָה. וְעוֹד כְּלַלְּכֶם
רַבּוֹתַי הַמְּסוּבִּין כַּאן יִתְבָּרְכוּ בֵּאלֹהֵי אָמֵן. תִּוָּשְׁעוּ, תִּפָּדוּ, תּוּצָּלוּ, תְּעוּטְּרוּ,
תְּמוּגָּנוּ, תְּכוּלְכָּלוּ, תַּצְלִיחוּ, תַּשְׂכִּילוּ, תֵּעָנוּ וְיַעַן עִמָּכֶם שֶׁבַח לְבוֹרֵא עוֹלָם:
בָּרוּךְ יי לְעוֹלָם אָמֵן וְאָמֵן.

מִגְדּוֹל יְשׁוּעוֹת מַלְכּוֹ וְעוֹשֶׂה חֶסֶד לִמְשִׁיחוֹ לְדָוִד וּלְזַרְעוֹ עַד עוֹלָם.
כְּפִירִים רָשׁוּ וְרָעֵבוּ וְדוֹרְשֵׁי יי לֹא יַחְסְרוּ כָל טוֹב.
הוֹדוּ לַיי כִּי טוֹב כִּי לְעוֹלָם חַסְדּוֹ.

בָּרוּךְ אַתָּה יי אֱלֹהֵינוּ מֶלֶךְ הָעוֹלָם בּוֹרֵא פְּרִי הַגָּפֶן.

ושותים בהסיבת שמאל.

Hallel

In Sephardic and Yemenite families, the Fourth Cup is filled (Yemenites first rinse and dry the cups). In most Eastern European Ashkenazic families, the cups are filled and, in addition, the cup of Elijah is filled. All Ashkenazic families open the door at this moment.

(*Ps*. 79:6–7) Pour out Your wrath over the Gentiles who do not know You,
and over the kingdoms that do not invoke Your name.
Because they devoured Jacob and laid waste his dwelling place.

In the Ashkenazic ritual one adds:

(*Ps*. 69:25) Pour out Your fury over them, may Your rage catch them.
(*Thr*. 3:66) Pursue them with rage and destroy them from under the skies of the Lord.

The door is closed and the Fourth Cup poured if the glasses are still empty.

Psalm 115

Not to us, not to us,
 But to Your Name give honor,
 For Your kindness, for Your truth.
Why should the Gentiles say:
 Where is their God?
But our God is in Heaven
 He does whatever He desires.
Their idols are silver and gold,
 Crafted by the hands of men.
They have a mouth but cannot talk,
 They have eyes but cannot see.
They have ears but cannot hear,
 They have a nose but cannot smell.
With their hands they cannot feel,
 With their feet they cannot walk,
 No voice is in their throats.
May those who make them be like them,

הלל

במנהג אשכנז פותחים את הדלת וממלאים כוסו של אליהו (במנהג אשכנז המערבי ממלאים כוסו של אליהו לפני הקידוש). במנהגי ספרד ותימן מוזגים את הכוס הרביעי.

שְׁפֹךְ חֲמָתְךָ אֶל הַגּוֹיִם אֲשֶׁר לֹא יְדָעוּךָ
וְעַל־הַמַּמְלָכוֹת אֲשֶׁר בְּשִׁמְךָ לֹא קָרָאוּ.
כִּי אָכַל אֶת־יַעֲקֹב וְאֶת־נָוֵהוּ הֵשַׁמּוּ.

במנהג אשכנז מוסיפים

שְׁפָךְ־עֲלֵיהֶם זַעְמֶךָ וַחֲרוֹן אַפְּךָ יַשִּׂיגֵם.
תִּרְדֹּף בְּאַף וְתַשְׁמִידֵם מִתַּחַת שְׁמֵי יי.

במנהג אשכנז סוגרים את הדלת ומוזגים את הכוס הרביעי.

לֹא לָנוּ, יי, לֹא־לָנוּ
כִּי־לְשִׁמְךָ, תֵּן כָּבוֹד
עַל־חַסְדְּךָ, עַל־אֲמִתֶּךָ.
לָמָּה, יֹאמְרוּ הַגּוֹיִם
אַיֵּה־נָא, אֱלֹהֵיהֶם.
וֵאלֹהֵינוּ בַשָּׁמָיִם
כֹּל, אֲשֶׁר־חָפֵץ עָשָׂה.
עֲצַבֵּיהֶם, כֶּסֶף וְזָהָב
מַעֲשֵׂה, יְדֵי אָדָם.
פֶּה־לָהֶם, וְלֹא יְדַבֵּרוּ
עֵינַיִם לָהֶם, וְלֹא יִרְאוּ.
אָזְנַיִם לָהֶם, וְלֹא יִשְׁמָעוּ
אַף לָהֶם, וְלֹא יְרִיחוּן.
יְדֵיהֶם, וְלֹא יְמִישׁוּן
רַגְלֵיהֶם, וְלֹא יְהַלֵּכוּ
לֹא־יֶהְגּוּ, בִּגְרוֹנָם.
כְּמוֹהֶם, יִהְיוּ עֹשֵׂיהֶם

All who trust in them!
Israel, trust in the Lord!
He is their help and shield.
House of Aaron, trust in the Lord!
He is their help and shield.
Those who fear the Lord, trust in the Lord!
He is their help and shield!

The Lord will bless those who remember us,
Will bless the house of Israel,
Will bless the house of Aaron.
He will bless those who fear the Lord,
The small ones with the great ones!
May the Lord give increase to you,
To you and your sons!
You are blessed before the Lord,
The Maker of Heaven and Earth.
The Heavens are Heavens for the Lord,
But the earth He gave to mankind.
The dead do not sing praise to the Lord,
Nor do all those descending into silence.
But we shall praise the Lord,
From now to eternity,
Hallelujah!

Psalm 116

I am loving; truly the Lord listened,
To my voice, my supplications.
Truly He turned His ear to me
When I would call Him in my days.
Fetters of Death surrounded me,

כֹּל, אֲשֶׁר בֹּטֵחַ בָּהֶם.
יִשְׂרָאֵל, בְּטַח בַּיי
עֶזְרָם וּמָגִנָּם הוּא.
בֵּית אַהֲרֹן, בִּטְחוּ בַיי
עֶזְרָם וּמָגִנָּם הוּא.
יִרְאֵי יי, בִּטְחוּ בַיי
עֶזְרָם וּמָגִנָּם הוּא.

יי, זְכָרָנוּ יְבָרֵךְ
יְבָרֵךְ, אֶת־בֵּית יִשְׂרָאֵל
יְבָרֵךְ, אֶת־בֵּית אַהֲרֹן.
יְבָרֵךְ, יִרְאֵי יי
הַקְּטַנִּים, עִם־הַגְּדֹלִים.
יֹסֵף יי עֲלֵיכֶם
עֲלֵיכֶם, וְעַל בְּנֵיכֶם.
בְּרוּכִים אַתֶּם, לַיי
עֹשֵׂה, שָׁמַיִם וָאָרֶץ.
הַשָּׁמַיִם שָׁמַיִם, לַיי
וְהָאָרֶץ, נָתַן לִבְנֵי־אָדָם.
לֹא הַמֵּתִים, יְהַלְלוּ־יָהּ
וְלֹא, כָּל־יֹרְדֵי דוּמָה.
וַאֲנַחְנוּ, נְבָרֵךְ יָהּ
מֵעַתָּה וְעַד־עוֹלָם
הַלְלוּיָהּ.

אָהַבְתִּי, כִּי־יִשְׁמַע יי
אֶת־קוֹלִי, תַּחֲנוּנָי.
כִּי־הִטָּה אָזְנוֹ לִי
וּבְיָמַי אֶקְרָא.
אֲפָפוּנִי חֶבְלֵי־מָוֶת

Netherworld's boundaries found me,
Sorrow and trouble I did find.
But to the Name of the Lord I would appeal,
Please, o Lord, let my soul escape!
The Lord is kind and just,
Our God is merciful.
The Lord watches over the simple-minded;
I am poor and He will help me.
Return, my soul, to your rest,
Because the Lord favored you.
Since You rescued my soul from Death,
My eye from tears,
My foot from being pushed,
I shall walk before the Lord,
In the Lands of the Living.
I did believe it when I said,
"I am very poor,"
I said rashly,
"All men are false."

How shall I give back to the Lord,
All His bounties toward me?
I shall lift up a cup of salvations,
And invoke the Name of the Lord.
I shall pay my vows to the Lord,
In the presence of His entire people.
Hard in the eyes of the Lord
Is the death sent to His pious ones.
O Lord, because I am Your slave,
I am Your slave, son of Your bondsmaid,

וּמְצָרֵי שְׁאוֹל מְצָאוּנִי
צָרָה וְיָגוֹן אֶמְצָא.
וּבְשֵׁם־יי אֶקְרָא
אָנָּה יי, מַלְּטָה נַפְשִׁי.
חַנּוּן יי וְצַדִּיק
וֵאלֹהֵינוּ מְרַחֵם.
שֹׁמֵר פְּתָאיִם יי
דַּלֹּתִי, וְלִי יְהוֹשִׁיעַ.
שׁוּבִי נַפְשִׁי, לִמְנוּחָיְכִי
כִּי־יי, גָּמַל עָלָיְכִי.
כִּי חִלַּצְתָּ נַפְשִׁי, מִמָּוֶת
אֶת־עֵינִי מִן־דִּמְעָה
אֶת־רַגְלִי מִדֶּחִי.
אֶתְהַלֵּךְ, לִפְנֵי יי
בְּאַרְצוֹת, הַחַיִּים.
הֶאֱמַנְתִּי, כִּי אֲדַבֵּר
אֲנִי, עָנִיתִי מְאֹד.
אֲנִי, אָמַרְתִּי בְחָפְזִי
כָּל־הָאָדָם כֹּזֵב.

מָה־אָשִׁיב לַיי
כָּל־תַּגְמוּלוֹהִי עָלָי.
כּוֹס־יְשׁוּעוֹת אֶשָּׂא
וּבְשֵׁם יי אֶקְרָא.
נְדָרַי, לַיי אֲשַׁלֵּם
נֶגְדָה־נָּא, לְכָל־עַמּוֹ.
יָקָר, בְּעֵינֵי יי
הַמָּוְתָה, לַחֲסִידָיו.
אָנָּה יי, כִּי־אֲנִי עַבְדֶּךָ
אֲנִי עַבְדְּךָ, בֶּן־אֲמָתֶךָ

You opened my fetters!
To You I shall bring a sacrifice of thanks,
I shall invoke the Name of the Lord.
I shall pay my vows to the Lord
In the presence of His entire people,
In the courtyards of the Lord's house,
In the center of Jerusalem, Hallelujah!

Psalm 117

Sing the praise of the Lord, all Gentiles,
Laud Him all nations!
Truly His kindness to us is overpowering,
And the Lord is true forever,
Hallelujah!

Psalm 118

The verses indicated by an asterisk are repeated.

Give thanks to the Lord, the truly Good One,
Truly, His kindness is forever!
Let Israel say:
Truly, His kindness is forever!
Let the house of Aaron say:
Truly, His kindness is forever!
Let those who fear the Lord say:
Truly, His kindness is forever!
From distress I called the Lord;
He answered me in the Lord's wideness.
The Lord is with me, I shall not fear.
What can man do to me?
The Lord is with me, He is among my helpers,
Then I shall look down on my enemies.
It is better to seek shelter in the Lord
Than to trust in man;
It is better to seek shelter in the Lord

פִּתַּחְתָּ, לְמוֹסֵרָי.
לְךָ אֶזְבַּח, זֶבַח תּוֹדָה
וּבְשֵׁם יי אֶקְרָא.
נְדָרַי, לַיי אֲשַׁלֵּם
נֶגְדָה־נָּא, לְכָל־עַמּוֹ.
בְּחַצְרוֹת בֵּית יי
בְּתוֹכֵכִי יְרוּשָׁלָ‍ִם
הַלְלוּיָהּ.

הַלְלוּ אֶת־יי, כָּל־גּוֹיִם
שַׁבְּחוּהוּ, כָּל־הָאֻמִּים.
כִּי גָבַר עָלֵינוּ חַסְדּוֹ
וֶאֱמֶת־יי לְעוֹלָם
הַלְלוּיָהּ.

הוֹדוּ לַיי כִּי־טוֹב
כִּי לְעוֹלָם חַסְדּוֹ.
יֹאמַר־נָא יִשְׂרָאֵל
כִּי לְעוֹלָם חַסְדּוֹ.
יֹאמְרוּ־נָא בֵית־אַהֲרֹן
כִּי לְעוֹלָם חַסְדּוֹ.
יֹאמְרוּ־נָא יִרְאֵי יי
כִּי לְעוֹלָם חַסְדּוֹ.
מִן־הַמֵּצַר, קָרָאתִי יָּהּ
עָנָנִי בַמֶּרְחָב יָהּ.
יי לִי, לֹא אִירָא
מַה־יַּעֲשֶׂה לִי אָדָם.
יי לִי, בְּעֹזְרָי
וַאֲנִי, אֶרְאֶה בְשֹׂנְאָי.
טוֹב, לַחֲסוֹת בַּיי

Than to trust in princes.
All Gentiles surround me,
But in the Name of the Lord I shall cut them down.
They encircle and surround me,
But in the Name of the Lord I shall cut them down.
They encircle me like bees,
They are destructive like fire of thorns,
But in the Name of the Lord I shall cut them down.
You pushed me until I was falling,
But the Lord helped me.
My strength and song is the Lord,
He was my salvation.
A sound of song and salvation
Is in the tents of the just,
The Lord's right hand does powerful deeds.
The Lord's right hand is lifted up;
The Lord's right hand does powerful deeds.
I shall not die, truly I shall live,
And I shall tell the works of the Lord.
The Lord certainly has made me suffer,
But He did not give me over to Death.
Open for me the gates of equity;
I shall enter them and thank the Lord.
This is the gate of the Lord;
The just will enter thereby.
*I thank You, since You answered me,
And You were my salvation.*

מִבְּטֹחַ, בָּאָדָם.
טוֹב, לַחֲסוֹת בַּיי
מִבְּטֹחַ, בִּנְדִיבִים.
כָּל־גּוֹיִם סְבָבוּנִי
בְּשֵׁם יי, כִּי אֲמִילַם.
סַבּוּנִי גַם־סְבָבוּנִי
בְּשֵׁם יי, כִּי אֲמִילַם.
סַבּוּנִי כִדְבֹרִים
דֹּעֲכוּ, כְּאֵשׁ קוֹצִים
בְּשֵׁם יי, כִּי אֲמִילַם.
דָּחֹה דְחִיתַנִי לִנְפֹּל
וַיי עֲזָרָנִי.
עָזִּי וְזִמְרָת יָהּ
וַיְהִי־לִי, לִישׁוּעָה.
קוֹל רִנָּה וִישׁוּעָה
בְּאָהֳלֵי צַדִּיקִים
יְמִין יי, עֹשָׂה חָיִל.
יְמִין יי, רוֹמֵמָה
יְמִין יי, עֹשָׂה חָיִל.
לֹא־אָמוּת כִּי־אֶחְיֶה
וַאֲסַפֵּר, מַעֲשֵׂי יָהּ.
יַסֹּר יִסְּרַנִּי יָּהּ
וְלַמָּוֶת, לֹא נְתָנָנִי.
פִּתְחוּ־לִי שַׁעֲרֵי־צֶדֶק
אָבֹא־בָם, אוֹדֶה יָהּ.
זֶה־הַשַּׁעַר לַיי
צַדִּיקִים, יָבֹאוּ בוֹ.
אוֹדְךָ, כִּי עֲנִיתָנִי
וַתְּהִי־לִי, לִישׁוּעָה.

אוֹדְךָ, כִּי עֲנִיתָנִי   וַתְּהִי־לִי, לִישׁוּעָה.

*The stone rejected by the builders
Became the cornerstone.*
*This was from the Lord;
It is wonderful in our eyes.*
*This is the day the Lord made;
Let us enjoy and be happy on it.*
Please, o Lord, please save!
Please, o Lord, please make succeed!
*Blessed is he who comes in the name of the Lord,
We bless you from the House of the Lord.*
*The Lord is God, He enlightens us;
Bind the festival sacrifice with braided cord,
Reaching to the corners of the altar.*
*You are my God, I shall thank You;
My God, I shall exalt You.*
*Give thanks to the Lord, the truly Good One;
Truly, His kindness is forever!*

The following is recited by non-ḥasidic Ashkenazic families.

A*O Lord, our God, may all Your creatures sing Your praise and may all Your pious, the righteous who do Your will, and all Your people, the house of Israel, thank You in song. May they praise, laud, glorify, extol, proclaim Your power, sanctify and crown Your Name, our King, because it is good to thank You, and it is beautiful to chant to Your Name because You are God from eternity to eternity.*

אֶבֶן, מָאֲסוּ הַבּוֹנִים
הָיְתָה, לְרֹאשׁ פִּנָּה.

אֶבֶן, מָאֲסוּ הַבּוֹנִים   הָיְתָה, לְרֹאשׁ פִּנָּה.

מֵאֵת יְיָ, הָיְתָה זֹּאת
הִיא נִפְלָאת בְּעֵינֵינוּ.

מֵאֵת יְיָ, הָיְתָה זֹּאת   הִיא נִפְלָאת בְּעֵינֵינוּ.

זֶה־הַיּוֹם, עָשָׂה יְיָ
נָגִילָה וְנִשְׂמְחָה בוֹ.

זֶה־הַיּוֹם, עָשָׂה יְיָ   נָגִילָה וְנִשְׂמְחָה בוֹ.

אָנָּא יְיָ, הוֹשִׁיעָה נָּא

אָנָּא יְיָ, הוֹשִׁיעָה נָּא.

אָנָּא יְיָ, הַצְלִיחָה נָּא.

אָנָּא יְיָ, הַצְלִיחָה נָּא.

בָּרוּךְ הַבָּא, בְּשֵׁם יְיָ
בֵּרַכְנוּכֶם, מִבֵּית יְיָ.

בָּרוּךְ הַבָּא, בְּשֵׁם יְיָ   בֵּרַכְנוּכֶם, מִבֵּית יְיָ.

אֵל יְיָ, וַיָּאֶר לָנוּ
אִסְרוּ־חַג בַּעֲבֹתִים
עַד־קַרְנוֹת, הַמִּזְבֵּחַ.

אֵל יְיָ, וַיָּאֶר לָנוּ   אִסְרוּ־חַג בַּעֲבֹתִים   עַד־קַרְנוֹת, הַמִּזְבֵּחַ.

אֵלִי אַתָּה וְאוֹדֶךָּ
אֱלֹהַי, אֲרוֹמְמֶךָּ.

אֵלִי אַתָּה וְאוֹדֶךָּ   אֱלֹהַי, אֲרוֹמְמֶךָּ.

הוֹדוּ לַיְיָ כִּי־טוֹב
כִּי לְעוֹלָם חַסְדּוֹ.

הוֹדוּ לַיְיָ כִּי־טוֹב   כִּי לְעוֹלָם חַסְדּוֹ.

במנהג אשכנז (להוציא נוסח האר״י האשכנזי) אומרים כאן יהללוך בלי חתימה

יְהַלְלוּךָ יְיָ אֱלֹהֵינוּ עַל כָּל־מַעֲשֶׂיךָ, וַחֲסִידֶיךָ עוֹשֵׂי רְצוֹנֶךָ וְכָל־עַמְּךָ בֵּית
יִשְׂרָאֵל בְּרִנָּה יוֹדוּ, וִיבָרְכוּ, וִישַׁבְּחוּ, וִיפָאֲרוּ, וִירוֹמְמוּ, וְיַעֲרִיצוּ, וְיַקְדִּישׁוּ,
וְיַמְלִיכוּ אֶת־שִׁמְךָ מַלְכֵּנוּ, כִּי לְךָ טוֹב לְהוֹדוֹת וּלְשִׁמְךָ נָאֶה לְזַמֵּר, כִּי
מֵעוֹלָם וְעַד עוֹלָם אַתָּה אֵל.

Give thanks to the Lord, the truly Good One, Truly, His kindness is forever!
Give thanks to Almighty God, Truly, His kindness is forever!
Give thanks to the Master of masters, Truly, His kindness is forever!
Who alone performs great miracles, Truly, His kindness is forever!
Who creates the Heavens in wisdom, Truly, His kindness is forever!
Who extends the earth over the waters, Truly, His kindness is forever!
Who creates great stars, Truly, His kindness is forever!
The sun, to reign during the day, Truly, His kindness is forever!
The moon and the stars to reign in the night, Truly, His kindness is forever!
Who smites Egypt through their firstborn, Truly, His kindness is forever!
And leads Israel out from their midst, Truly, His kindness is forever!
With strong hand and outstretched arm, Truly, His kindness is forever!
Who cuts clefts into the Red Sea, Truly, His kindness is forever!
And made Israel pass through it, Truly, His kindness is forever!
And hurled Pharaoh and his army into the Red Sea, Truly, His kindness is forever!
Who let His people walk through the desert, Truly, His kindness is forever!
And smote great kings, Truly, His kindness is forever!
And killed noble kings, Truly, His kindness is forever!
Siḥon, the king of the Emorite, Truly, His kindness is forever!
And Og, the king of Bashan, Truly, His kindness is forever!
And gave their land as inheritance, Truly, His kindness is forever!
An inheritance for His servant Israel, Truly, His kindness is forever!
Who remembered us when we were downtrodden, Truly, His kindness is forever!
And liberated us from our oppressors, Truly, His kindness is forever!
He gives bread to all creatures, Truly, His kindness is forever!
Give thanks to the God of Heaven, Truly, His kindness is forever!

הוֹדוּ לַיי כִּי־טוֹב	כִּי לְעוֹלָם חַסְדּוֹ.
הוֹדוּ, לֵאלֹהֵי הָאֱלֹהִים	כִּי לְעוֹלָם חַסְדּוֹ.
הוֹדוּ, לַאֲדֹנֵי הָאֲדֹנִים	כִּי לְעוֹלָם חַסְדּוֹ.
לְעֹשֵׂה נִפְלָאוֹת גְּדֹלוֹת לְבַדּוֹ	כִּי לְעוֹלָם חַסְדּוֹ.
לְעֹשֵׂה הַשָּׁמַיִם, בִּתְבוּנָה	כִּי לְעוֹלָם חַסְדּוֹ.
לְרוֹקַע הָאָרֶץ, עַל־הַמָּיִם	כִּי לְעוֹלָם חַסְדּוֹ.
לְעֹשֵׂה, אוֹרִים גְּדֹלִים	כִּי לְעוֹלָם חַסְדּוֹ.
אֶת־הַשֶּׁמֶשׁ, לְמֶמְשֶׁלֶת בַּיּוֹם	כִּי לְעוֹלָם חַסְדּוֹ.
אֶת־הַיָּרֵחַ וְכוֹכָבִים, לְמֶמְשְׁלוֹת בַּלָּיְלָה	כִּי לְעוֹלָם חַסְדּוֹ.
לְמַכֵּה מִצְרַיִם, בִּבְכוֹרֵיהֶם	כִּי לְעוֹלָם חַסְדּוֹ.
וַיּוֹצֵא יִשְׂרָאֵל, מִתּוֹכָם	כִּי לְעוֹלָם חַסְדּוֹ.
בְּיָד חֲזָקָה, וּבִזְרוֹעַ נְטוּיָה	כִּי לְעוֹלָם חַסְדּוֹ.
לְגֹזֵר יַם־סוּף, לִגְזָרִים	כִּי לְעוֹלָם חַסְדּוֹ.
וְהֶעֱבִיר יִשְׂרָאֵל בְּתוֹכוֹ	כִּי לְעוֹלָם חַסְדּוֹ.
וְנִעֵר פַּרְעֹה וְחֵילוֹ בְיַם־סוּף	כִּי לְעוֹלָם חַסְדּוֹ.
לְמוֹלִיךְ עַמּוֹ, בַּמִּדְבָּר	כִּי לְעוֹלָם חַסְדּוֹ.
לְמַכֵּה, מְלָכִים גְּדֹלִים	כִּי לְעוֹלָם חַסְדּוֹ.
וַיַּהֲרֹג, מְלָכִים אַדִּירִים	כִּי לְעוֹלָם חַסְדּוֹ.
לְסִיחוֹן, מֶלֶךְ הָאֱמֹרִי	כִּי לְעוֹלָם חַסְדּוֹ.
וּלְעוֹג, מֶלֶךְ הַבָּשָׁן	כִּי לְעוֹלָם חַסְדּוֹ.
וְנָתַן אַרְצָם לְנַחֲלָה	כִּי לְעוֹלָם חַסְדּוֹ.
נַחֲלָה, לְיִשְׂרָאֵל עַבְדּוֹ	כִּי לְעוֹלָם חַסְדּוֹ.
שֶׁבְּשִׁפְלֵנוּ, זָכַר לָנוּ	כִּי לְעוֹלָם חַסְדּוֹ.
וַיִּפְרְקֵנוּ מִצָּרֵינוּ	כִּי לְעוֹלָם חַסְדּוֹ.
נֹתֵן לֶחֶם, לְכָל־בָּשָׂר	כִּי לְעוֹלָם חַסְדּוֹ.
הוֹדוּ, לְאֵל הַשָּׁמָיִם	כִּי לְעוֹלָם חַסְדּוֹ.

The souls of all living shall praise Your Name, o Lord, our God, and the spirit of all flesh shall always glorify and extol Your remembrance, our King. Y*From generation to generation,*

from eternity to eternity You are Almighty and apart from You

A*we do not have any king, liberator and savior, redeemer and rescuer and provider and merciful.*

S*we do not have any king, liberator and savior, redeemer and rescuer, respondent and merciful.*

Y*There is no god,*

In any time of need and distress, we have no king,

S*helping and supporting*

Y*liberator and savior*

except You

Y*Redeemer and Rescuer, Provider and Merciful.*

AS*God of our forefathers and of ourselves,*

God of all creatures, Master of all that are born, Whose praise is song in A*many,* S*all* hymns, Who manages His world in kindness and His creatures in Y*great* mercy. And the Lord

S*is awake,*

Y*is the true God, He*

does neither slumber nor sleep. He awakens the sleeping, He rouses those who are fast asleep (*i.e.*, the dead),

A*He makes the dumb talk, frees the bound, supports the falling, straightens the bent,*

S*raises the dead, heals the sick, makes the blind see, straightens the bent, makes the dumb talk, and deciphers what is hidden,*

Y*supports the falling, heals the sick, frees the bound,*

only You we thank.

נוסח אשכנז

נִשְׁמַת כָּל־חַי תְּבָרֵךְ אֶת־שִׁמְךָ יי אֱלֹהֵינוּ וְרוּחַ כָּל־בָּשָׂר תְּפָאֵר וּתְרוֹמֵם זִכְרְךָ מַלְכֵּנוּ תָּמִיד. מִן הָעוֹלָם וְעַד הָעוֹלָם אַתָּה אֵל, וּמִבַּלְעָדֶיךָ אֵין לָנוּ מֶלֶךְ גּוֹאֵל וּמוֹשִׁיעַ, פּוֹדֶה וּמַצִּיל וּמְפַרְנֵס וּמְרַחֵם. בְּכָל־עֵת צָרָה וְצוּקָה, אֵין לָנוּ מֶלֶךְ אֶלָּא אָתָּה.

אֱלֹהֵי הָרִאשׁוֹנִים וְהָאַחֲרוֹנִים, אֱלוֹהַּ כָּל־בְּרִיּוֹת, אֲדוֹן כָּל־הַתּוֹלָדוֹת, הַמְהֻלָּל בְּרֹב הַתִּשְׁבָּחוֹת, הַמְנַהֵג עוֹלָמוֹ בְּחֶסֶד וּבְרִיּוֹתָיו בְּרַחֲמִים. וַיי לֹא־יָנוּם וְלֹא־יִישָׁן, הַמְעוֹרֵר יְשֵׁנִים, וְהַמֵּקִיץ נִרְדָּמִים, וְהַמֵּשִׂיחַ אִלְּמִים, וְהַמַּתִּיר אֲסוּרִים, וְהַסּוֹמֵךְ נוֹפְלִים, וְהַזּוֹקֵף כְּפוּפִים, לְךָ לְבַדְּךָ אֲנַחְנוּ מוֹדִים.

אִלּוּ פִינוּ מָלֵא שִׁירָה

נוסח ספרד

נִשְׁמַת כָּל חַי תְּבָרֵךְ אֶת שִׁמְךָ יי אֱלֹהֵינוּ וְרוּחַ כָּל בָּשָׂר תְּפָאֵר וּתְרוֹמֵם זִכְרְךָ מַלְכֵּנוּ תָמִיד. מִן הָעוֹלָם עַד הָעוֹלָם אַתָּה אֵל, וּמִבַּלְעָדֶיךָ אֵין לָנוּ מֶלֶךְ גּוֹאֵל וּמוֹשִׁיעַ פּוֹדֶה וּמַצִּיל, וְעוֹנֶה וּמְרַחֵם, בְּכָל עֵת צָרָה וְצוּקָה, אֵין לָנוּ מֶלֶךְ עוֹזֵר וְסוֹמֵךְ אֶלָּא אַתָּה.

אֱלֹהֵי הָרִאשׁוֹנִים וְהָאַחֲרוֹנִים, אֱלוֹהַּ כָּל בְּרִיּוֹת, אֲדוֹן כָּל תּוֹלָדוֹת, הַמְהֻלָּל בְּכָל הַתִּשְׁבָּחוֹת, הַמְנַהֵג עוֹלָמוֹ בְּחֶסֶד וּבְרִיּוֹתָיו בְּרַחֲמִים. וַיי עֵר, לֹא יָנוּם וְלֹא יִישָׁן, הַמְעוֹרֵר יְשֵׁנִים, וְהַמֵּקִיץ נִרְדָּמִים, מְחַיֵּה מֵתִים וְרוֹפֵא חוֹלִים, פּוֹקֵחַ עִוְרִים וְזוֹקֵף כְּפוּפִים, הַמֵּשִׂיחַ אִלְּמִים, וְהַמְפַעֲנֵחַ נֶעֱלָמִים, וּלְךָ לְבַדְּךָ

נוסח תימן

נִשְׁמַת כָּל חַי תְּבָרֵךְ אֶת שִׁמְךָ יי אֱלֹהֵינוּ וְרוּחַ כָּל בָּשָׂר תְּפָאֵר וּתְרוֹמֵם אֶת זִכְרְךָ מַלְכֵּנוּ תָּמִיד. לְדוֹר וָדוֹר, מֵעוֹלָם וְעַד עוֹלָם, אַתָּה הוּא הָאֵל, וּמִבַּלְעָדֶיךָ אֵין אֱלֹהִים, וְאֵין לָנוּ מֶלֶךְ, גּוֹאֵל וּמוֹשִׁיעַ בְּכָל עֵת צָרָה וְצוּקָה, אֶלָּא אָתָּה, פּוֹדֶה וּמַצִּיל, מְפַרְנֵס וּמְרַחֵם.

אֱלוֹהַּ כָּל הַבְּרִיּוֹת, אֲדוֹן הַתּוֹלָדוֹת, הַמְהֻלָּל בַּתִּשְׁבָּחוֹת, הַמַּנְהִיג עוֹלָמוֹ בְּחֶסֶד וּבְרִיּוֹתָיו בְּרַחֲמִים רַבִּים. וַיי אֱלֹהִים אֱמֶת, לֹא יָנוּם וְלֹא יִישָׁן, הַמְעוֹרֵר יְשֵׁנִים, וְהַמֵּקִיץ רְדוּמִים, וְסוֹמֵךְ נוֹפְלִים, וְרוֹפֵא חוֹלִים, וּמַתִּיר אֲסוּרִים, וּלְךָ אֲנַחְנוּ מוֹדִים.

וְאִלּוּ פִינוּ מָלֵא שִׁירָה כַּיָּם, וּלְשׁוֹנֵנוּ

If our mouths were full of song like the sea, our tongues full of melodies like the mass of its waves, our lips full of praise like the vastness of the sky; if our eyes were radiant like sun and moon, our hands spread out like eagles of the sky, and our feet light like those of the deer, still we could never sufficiently thank you, o Lord, our God [A]*and God of our fathers,* and praise Your name for one of the [A]*thousand* thousand thousands myriad of myriads times that You did good things to our fathers [SY]*of old.* You, o Lord, our God, did deliver us from Egypt, did redeem us from the house of slaves, fed us during famine, provided for us in times of plenty, saved us from the sword, let us escape the plague, and freed us from serious and [A]*chronic* [SY]*frequent* illnesses, Your mercy has helped us until now, Your kindness has not deserted us,

[A]*please, o Lord, our God, do not forever abandon us.*

כַּיָּם, וּלְשׁוֹנֵנוּ רִנָּה כַּהֲמוֹן גַּלָּיו, וְשִׂפְתוֹתֵינוּ שֶׁבַח כְּמֶרְחֲבֵי רָקִיעַ, וְעֵינֵינוּ מְאִירוֹת כַּשֶּׁמֶשׁ וְכַיָּרֵחַ, וְיָדֵינוּ פְרוּשׂוֹת כְּנִשְׁרֵי שָׁמָיִם, וְרַגְלֵינוּ קַלּוֹת כָּאַיָּלוֹת, אֵין אֲנַחְנוּ מַסְפִּיקִים לְהוֹדוֹת לְךָ יי אֱלֹהֵינוּ וֵאלֹהֵי אֲבוֹתֵינוּ וּלְבָרֵךְ אֶת־שְׁמֶךָ, עַל אַחַת מֵאָלֶף אֶלֶף אַלְפֵי אֲלָפִים וְרִבֵּי רְבָבוֹת פְּעָמִים הַטּוֹבוֹת שֶׁעָשִׂיתָ עִם אֲבוֹתֵינוּ וְעִמָּנוּ. מִמִּצְרַיִם גְּאַלְתָּנוּ יי אֱלֹהֵינוּ וּמִבֵּית עֲבָדִים פְּדִיתָנוּ, בְּרָעָב זַנְתָּנוּ וּבְשָׂבָע כִּלְכַּלְתָּנוּ, מֵחֶרֶב הִצַּלְתָּנוּ וּמִדֶּבֶר מִלַּטְתָּנוּ וּמֵחֳלָיִם רָעִים וְנֶאֱמָנִים דִּלִּיתָנוּ. עַד הֵנָּה עֲזָרוּנוּ רַחֲמֶיךָ וְלֹא עֲזָבוּנוּ חֲסָדֶיךָ, וְאַל תִּטְּשֵׁנוּ יי אֱלֹהֵינוּ לָנֶצַח.

אֲנַחְנוּ מוֹדִים.

וְאִלּוּ פִינוּ מָלֵא שִׁירָה כַּיָּם, וּלְשׁוֹנֵנוּ רִנָּה כַּהֲמוֹן גַּלָּיו, וְשִׂפְתוֹתֵינוּ שֶׁבַח כְּמֶרְחֲבֵי רָקִיעַ, וְעֵינֵינוּ מְאִירוֹת כַּשֶּׁמֶשׁ וְכַיָּרֵחַ, וְיָדֵינוּ פְרוּשׂוֹת כְּנִשְׁרֵי שָׁמַיִם, וְרַגְלֵינוּ קַלּוֹת כָּאַיָּלוֹת, אֵין אָנוּ מַסְפִּיקִין לְהוֹדוֹת לְךָ יי אֱלֹהֵינוּ, וּלְבָרֵךְ אֶת שִׁמְךָ מַלְכֵּנוּ, עַל אַחַת מֵאֶלֶף אַלְפֵי אֲלָפִים, וְרוֹב רִבֵּי רְבָבוֹת, פְּעָמִים הַטּוֹבוֹת, נִסִּים וְנִפְלָאוֹת שֶׁעָשִׂיתָ עִמָּנוּ וְעִם אֲבוֹתֵינוּ מִלְּפָנִים. מִמִּצְרַיִם גְּאַלְתָּנוּ יי אֱלֹהֵינוּ, מִבֵּית עֲבָדִים פְּדִיתָנוּ, בְּרָעָב זַנְתָּנוּ וּבְשָׂבָע כִּלְכַּלְתָּנוּ, מֵחֶרֶב הִצַּלְתָּנוּ וּמִדֶּבֶר מִלַּטְתָּנוּ וּמֵחֳלָאִים רָעִים וְרַבִּים דִּלִּיתָנוּ. עַד הֵנָּה עֲזָרוּנוּ רַחֲמֶךָ וְלֹא עֲזָבוּנוּ חֲסָדֶךָ.

רִנָּה כַּהֲמוֹן גַּלָּיו, וְשִׂפְתוֹתֵינוּ שֶׁבַח כְּמֶרְחֲבֵי רָקִיעַ, וְעֵינֵינוּ מְאִירוֹת כַּשֶּׁמֶשׁ וְכַיָּרֵחַ, וְיָדֵינוּ פְרוּשׂוֹת כְּנִשְׁרֵי שָׁמָיִם, וְרַגְלֵינוּ קַלּוֹת כָּאַיָּלוֹת, אֵין אָנוּ מַסְפִּיקִין לְהוֹדוֹת לְךָ יי אֱלֹהֵינוּ, וּלְבָרֵךְ אֶת שִׁמְךָ מַלְכֵּנוּ, עַל אַחַת מֵאֶלֶף אַלְפֵי אֲלָפִים וְרוֹב רִבֵּי רְבָבוֹת פְּעָמִים הַטּוֹבוֹת, שֶׁעָשִׂיתָ עִמָּנוּ וְעִם אֲבוֹתֵינוּ. מִלְּפָנִים, מִמִּצְרַיִם גְּאַלְתָּנוּ יי אֱלֹהֵינוּ, מִבֵּית עֲבָדִים פְּדִיתָנוּ, בְּרָעָב זַנְתָּנוּ וּבְשָׂבָע כִּלְכַּלְתָּנוּ, וּמֵחֶרֶב הִצַּלְתָּנוּ, וּמִדֶּבֶר מִלַּטְתָּנוּ, וּמֵחֳלָאִים רָעִים רַבִּים דִּלִּיתָנוּ מַלְכֵּנוּ. וְעַד הֵנָּה עֲזָרוּנוּ רַחֲמֶךָ יי אֱלֹהֵינוּ וְלֹא עֲזָבוּנוּ חֲסָדֶךָ.

עַל כֵּן, אֵבָרִים שֶׁפִּלַּגְתָּ בָּנוּ, וְרוּחַ

Therefore, the limbs which You gave us, spirit and soul which You breathed into us, and the tongue which You put into our mouths, all of them shall

[A]*thank, praise, laud, glorify, extol, proclaim the power of, sanctify, crown,*

[S]*thank, praise, laud, glorify, sing to*

[Y]*thank You and praise*

Your Name, our King

[S]*always* [Y]*for Your many extraordinary miracles.*

Certainly, every mouth shall thank You,

[A]*every tongue shall swear by You,*

[SY]*every tongue shall laud You and every eye expect You,* every knee shall bow to You, every erect man shall prostrate himself before You. All hearts shall fear You, the innards and kidneys shall sing to Your Name, as it is [A]*written* [SY]*said* (*Ps.* 35:10): "All my bones shall say: O Lord, who is like You, Who saves the poor from one stronger than himself, and the poor and downtrodden from his despoiler?"

[S]*You hear the supplication of the poor; You are mindful of the oppressed and You save.*

[A]*Who can be compared to You, who may be equal to You, who can be valued like You* (cf. *Deut.* 10:17), *the great, strong, awesome God, the Highest Power, Owner of Heaven and earth?*

עַל כֵּן אֵבָרִים שֶׁפִּלַּגְתָּ בָּנוּ, וְרוּחַ וּנְשָׁמָה שֶׁנָּפַחְתָּ בְּאַפֵּינוּ, וְלָשׁוֹן אֲשֶׁר שַׂמְתָּ בְּפִינוּ, הֵן הֵם יוֹדוּ, וִיבָרְכוּ, וִישַׁבְּחוּ, וִיפָאֲרוּ, וִירוֹמְמוּ, וְיַעֲרִיצוּ, וְיַקְדִּישׁוּ, וְיַמְלִיכוּ אֶת־שִׁמְךָ מַלְכֵּנוּ. כִּי כָל־פֶּה לְךָ יוֹדֶה, וְכָל־לָשׁוֹן לְךָ תִשָּׁבַע, וְכָל־בֶּרֶךְ לְךָ תִכְרַע, וְכָל־קוֹמָה לְפָנֶיךָ תִשְׁתַּחֲוֶה, וְכָל־לְבָבוֹת יִירָאוּךָ, וְכָל־קֶרֶב וּכְלָיוֹת יְזַמְּרוּ לִשְׁמֶךָ, כַּדָּבָר שֶׁכָּתוּב ׳כָּל עַצְמֹתַי תֹּאמַרְנָה יי מִי כָמוֹךָ, מַצִּיל עָנִי מֵחָזָק מִמֶּנּוּ, וְעָנִי וְאֶבְיוֹן מִגֹּזְלוֹ.׳

עַל כֵּן אֵבָרִים שֶׁפִּלַּגְתָּ בָּנוּ, וְרוּחַ וּנְשָׁמָה שֶׁנָּפַחְתָּ בְּאַפֵּנוּ, וְלָשׁוֹן אֲשֶׁר שַׂמְתָּ בְּפִינוּ, הֵן הֵם יוֹדוּ, וִיבָרְכוּ, וִישַׁבְּחוּ, וִיפָאֲרוּ, וִישׁוֹרְרוּ אֶת שִׁמְךָ מַלְכֵּנוּ תָּמִיד. כִּי כָל פֶּה לְךָ יוֹדֶה, וְכָל לָשׁוֹן לְךָ תְשַׁבֵּחַ, וְכָל עַיִן לְךָ תְצַפֶּה, וְכָל בֶּרֶךְ לְךָ תִכְרַע, וְכָל קוֹמָה לְפָנֶיךָ תִשְׁתַּחֲוֶה, וְהַלְּבָבוֹת יִירָאוּךָ, וְכָל קֶרֶב וּכְלָיוֹת יְזַמְּרוּ לִשְׁמֶךָ, כַּדָּבָר שֶׁנֶּאֱמַר ׳כָּל עַצְמֹתַי תֹּאמַרְנָה יי מִי כָמוֹךָ, מַצִּיל עָנִי מֵחָזָק מִמֶּנּוּ, וְעָנִי וְאֶבְיוֹן מִגֹּזְלוֹ.׳

וּנְשָׁמָה שֶׁנָּפַחְתָּ בְּאַפֵּנוּ, וְלָשׁוֹן אֲשֶׁר שַׂמְתָּ בְּתוֹךְ פִּינוּ, הֵן הֵן יוֹדוּ לְךָ, וִיבָרְכוּ אֶת שִׁמְךָ יי אֱלֹהֵינוּ עַל רוֹב נִסֵּי פְלָאֶיךָ. כִּי כָל פֶּה לְךָ יוֹדֶה, וְכָל לָשׁוֹן לְךָ תְשַׁבֵּחַ, וְכָל עַיִן אֵלֶיךָ תְצַפֶּה, וְכָל בֶּרֶךְ לְךָ תִכְרַע, וְכָל קוֹמָה לְפָנֶיךָ תִשְׁתַּחֲוֶה, וְהַלְּבָבוֹת יִירָאוּךָ, וְהַקְּרָבִים וְהַכְּלָיוֹת יְזַמְּרוּ לִשְׁמֶךָ, כַּדָּבָר שֶׁנֶּאֱמַר ׳כָּל עַצְמֹתַי תֹּאמַרְנָה יי מִי כָמוֹךָ, מַצִּיל עָנִי מֵחָזָק מִמֶּנּוּ, וְעָנִי וְאֶבְיוֹן מִגֹּזְלוֹ.׳

מִי יִדְמֶה־לָּךְ וּמִי יִשְׁוֶה־לָּךְ וּמִי יַעֲרָךְ־לָךְ, הָאֵל הַגָּדוֹל הַגִּבּוֹר וְהַנּוֹרָא, אֵל עֶלְיוֹן, קֹנֵה שָׁמַיִם וָאָרֶץ. נְהַלֶּלְךָ וּנְשַׁבֵּחֲךָ וּנְפָאֶרְךָ

שַׁוְעַת עֲנִיִּים אַתָּה תִשְׁמַע, צַעֲקַת הַדַּל תַּקְשִׁיב וְתוֹשִׁיעַ.

We shall sing Your praise, laud and glorify You, and praise Your holy Name, as it is said (*Ps.* 103:1): *"For David. My soul, praise the Lord, and all my innards His holy Name."*

God in the power of Your strength,
Great in the glory of Your name,
Eternal Power and Awesome in Your awesomeness,
He Who reigns forever, Exalted One and Holy One is His Name!

And it is [AS]*written* [Y]*said* (*Ps.* 33:1): "Sing, o just, in the Lord; praise becomes the straightforward."

In the mouth of the straightforward You shall be [A]*praised in song* [SY]*extolled*
And by the [A]*words* [SY]*lips* of the just You shall be praised
And by the tongues of [Y]*all* pious You shall be [A]*extolled* [SY]*declared holy*
And in the midst of the holy You shall be [A]*declared holy* [SY]*praised in song.*

And in the choirs of the myriads of Your people Israel

וּנְבָרֵךְ אֶת־שֵׁם
קָדְשֶׁךָ, כָּאָמוּר ’לְדָוִד,
בָּרְכִי נַפְשִׁי אֶת־יי,
וְכָל־קְרָבַי אֶת־שֵׁם
קָדְשׁוֹ.‘

הָאֵל בְּתַעֲצוּמוֹת עֻזֶּךָ,
הַגָּדוֹל בִּכְבוֹד שְׁמֶךָ
הַגִּבּוֹר לָנֶצַח וְהַנּוֹרָא
בְּנוֹרְאוֹתֶיךָ,
הַמֶּלֶךְ הַיּוֹשֵׁב עַל כִּסֵּא
רָם וְנִשָּׂא.
שׁוֹכֵן עַד, מָרוֹם
וְקָדוֹשׁ שְׁמוֹ.

וְכָתוּב ’רַנְּנוּ צַדִּיקִים
בַּיי, לַיְשָׁרִים נָאוָה
תְהִלָּה.‘

בְּפִי יְשָׁרִים תִּתְהַלָּל
וּבְדִבְרֵי צַדִּיקִים
תִּתְבָּרַךְ
וּבִלְשׁוֹן חֲסִידִים
תִּתְרוֹמָם
וּבְקֶרֶב קְדוֹשִׁים
תִּתְקַדָּשׁ.

וּבְמַקְהֲלוֹת רִבְבוֹת
עַמְּךָ בֵּית יִשְׂרָאֵל
בְּרִנָּה יִתְפָּאַר שִׁמְךָ

וְכָתוּב ’רַנְּנוּ
צַדִּיקִים בַּיי,
לַיְשָׁרִים נָאוָה
תְהִלָּה‘

בְּפִי יְשָׁרִים
תִּתְרוֹמָם
וּבְשִׂפְתֵי צַדִּיקִים
תִּתְבָּרֵךְ
וּבִלְשׁוֹן חֲסִידִים
תִּתְקַדָּשׁ
וּבְקֶרֶב קְדוֹשִׁים
תִּתְהַלָּל

וּבְמִקְהֲלוֹת רִבְבוֹת
עַמְּךָ בֵּית יִשְׂרָאֵל,
שֶׁכֵּן חוֹבַת כָּל

נוסח תימן

וְנֶאֱמָר ’רַנְּנוּ
צַדִּיקִים בַּיי,
לַיְשָׁרִים נָאוָה
תְהִלָּה.‘

בְּפִי יְשָׁרִים
תִּתְרוֹמָם
וּבְשִׂפְתֵי צַדִּיקִים
תִּתְבָּרַךְ
וּבִלְשׁוֹן חֲסִידִים
תִּתְקַדָּשׁ
וּבְקֶרֶב קְדוֹשִׁים
תִּתְהַלָּל

וּבְמִקְהֲלוֹת רִבְבוֹת
עַמְּךָ כָּל בֵּית

[A]*may Your name be glorified in a joyful song, our King, for all generations,*
[Y]*may Your name be glorified, o Lord, our God,*
because it is the duty of all creatures before You, o Lord our God
[AS]*and God of our fathers,*
to give thanks, sing in praise, laud, glorify, extol
[A]*dignify, praise, exalt, and declare beautiful*
[S]*dignify and declare victorious*
[Y]*declare great and dignify*
by all the words of the songs, [Y]*poems,* and praises of David the son of Jesse, Your servant, Your anointed.

[S]*Therefore,* may Your Name, our King, be lauded forever, Almighty, Great and Holy King in Heaven and on earth. Truly [S]*forever* appropriate for You, o Lord, our God, [AS]*and God of our fathers,* are song and praise, laud in song and melody,
[AS]*power and rule,* [S]*eternity,* [AS]*greatness and force, praise, splendor, holiness and kingdom, blessing and thanksgiving,* [Y]*song and praise, laud in song, blessing and thanksgiving, eternity and power, praise and splendor, power, kingdom and rule,*
[AY]*from now to eternity.*
[S]*and You are Almighty from now to eternity.*

For Ashkenazic non-ḥasidic families:

Praised are You, o Lord, Almighty King, Great in praises, God to Whom thanks are due, Master of miracles, Who elected the melodious Psalms, Eternally living King.

מַלְכֵּנוּ בְּכָל־דּוֹר וָדוֹר, שֶׁכֵּן חוֹבַת כָּל־הַיְצוּרִים לְפָנֶיךָ יי אֱלֹהֵינוּ וֵאלֹהֵי אֲבוֹתֵינוּ, לְהוֹדוֹת, לְהַלֵּל, לְשַׁבֵּחַ, לְפָאֵר, לְרוֹמֵם, לְהַדֵּר, לְבָרֵךְ, לְעַלֵּה, וּלְקַלֵּס, עַל כָּל־דִּבְרֵי שִׁירוֹת וְתִשְׁבְּחוֹת דָּוִד בֶּן־יִשַׁי עַבְדְּךָ מְשִׁיחֶךָ.

הַיְצוּרִים לְפָנֶיךָ יי אֱלֹהֵינוּ וֵאלֹהֵי אֲבוֹתֵינוּ, לְהוֹדוֹת, לְהַלֵּל, לְשַׁבֵּחַ, לְפָאֵר, לְרוֹמֵם, לְהַדֵּר, וּלְנַצֵּחַ עַל כָּל דִּבְרֵי שִׁירוֹת וְתִשְׁבָּחוֹת דָּוִד בֶּן יִשַׁי עַבְדְּךָ מְשִׁיחֶךָ.

יִשְׂרָאֵל יִתְפָּאַר שִׁמְךָ יי אֱלֹהֵינוּ, שֶׁכֵּן חוֹבַת כָּל הַיְצוּרִים לְהוֹדוֹת לְךָ יי אֱלֹהֵינוּ, לְהַלֵּל, לְשַׁבֵּחַ, לְפָאַר, לְרוֹמֵם, לְגַדֵּל, וּלְהַדֵּר, עַל כָּל דִּבְרֵי שִׁירוֹת זְמִירוֹת תִּשְׁבְּחוֹת דָּוִד בֶּן יִשַׁי, עַבְדְּךָ מְשִׁיחֶךָ.

מתפללי נוסח האר״י האשכנזי אומרים 'ישתבח' כנוסח ספרד אבל אינם מסיימים ב'אמן'.

יִשְׁתַּבַּח שִׁמְךָ לָעַד מַלְכֵּנוּ, הָאֵל, הַמֶּלֶךְ הַגָּדוֹל וְהַקָּדוֹשׁ בַּשָּׁמַיִם וּבָאָרֶץ. כִּי לְךָ נָאֶה, יי אֱלֹהֵינוּ וֵאלֹהֵי אֲבוֹתֵינוּ, שִׁיר וּשְׁבָחָה הַלֵּל וְזִמְרָה עֹז וּמֶמְשָׁלָה נֶצַח גְּדֻלָּה וּגְבוּרָה תְּהִלָּה וְתִפְאֶרֶת קְדֻשָּׁה וּמַלְכוּת, בְּרָכוֹת וְהוֹדָאוֹת מֵעַתָּה וְעַד עוֹלָם. בָּרוּךְ אַתָּה יי, אֵל מֶלֶךְ, גָּדוֹל בַּתִּשְׁבָּחוֹת, אֵל

וּבְכֵן יִשְׁתַּבַּח שִׁמְךָ לָעַד מַלְכֵּנוּ, הָאֵל, הַמֶּלֶךְ הַגָּדוֹל וְהַקָּדוֹשׁ בַּשָּׁמַיִם וּבָאָרֶץ. כִּי לְךָ נָאֶה, יי אֱלֹהֵינוּ וֵאלֹהֵי אֲבוֹתֵינוּ לְעוֹלָם וָעֶד, שִׁיר וּשְׁבָחָה הַלֵּל וְזִמְרָה עוֹז וּמֶמְשָׁלָה נֶצַח גְּדֻלָּה וּגְבוּרָה תְּהִלָּה וְתִפְאֶרֶת קְדֻשָּׁה וּמַלְכוּת, בְּרָכוֹת וְהוֹדָאוֹת לְשִׁמְךָ הַגָּדוֹל וְהַקָּדוֹשׁ, וּמֵעוֹלָם וְעַד עוֹלָם אַתָּה אֵל.

יִשְׁתַּבַּח שִׁמְךָ לָעַד מַלְכֵּנוּ, הַמֶּלֶךְ הַגָּדוֹל וְהַקָּדוֹשׁ בַּשָּׁמַיִם וּבָאָרֶץ. כִּי לְךָ נָאֶה, יי אֱלֹהֵינוּ, שִׁיר וּשְׁבָח, הַלֵּל וְזִמְרָה, בְּרָכוֹת וְהוֹדָאוֹת, נֶצַח וּגְבוּרָה, גְּדֻלָּה, תְּהִלָּה וְתִפְאֶרֶת, עוֹז וּמַלְכוּת וּמֶמְשָׁלָה, מֵעַתָּה וְעַד עוֹלָם.

יְהַלְלוּךָ יי אֱלֹהֵינוּ כָּל מַעֲשֶׂיךָ, וַחֲסִידֶיךָ וְצַדִּיקִים עוֹשֵׂי רְצוֹנֶךָ, וְכָל עַמְּךָ בֵּית יִשְׂרָאֵל כֻּלָּם בְּרִנָּה יוֹדוּ

For all others:

O Lord, our God, may all Your creatures sing Your praise and may all Your pious, the righteous who do Your will, and all Your people, the house of Israel, thank You in song. [AS]May they praise, laud, glorify, extol, proclaim Your power, sanctify and crown Your name, our King, ([Yold]majesty and glory are the hallmark of Your Kingdom) because it is good to thank You, and it is beautiful to chant to Your Name because You are God from eternity to eternity.

[S(A)]*Praised are You, o Lord, King Who is glorified by Psalms.*

[Y]*Praised are You, o Lord, Almighty, King praised by song, lauded, glorified, Eternal; may He reign over us for ever and ever!*

Western Ashkenazic Jews, following R. Meir of Rothenburg, continue here with "It happened in the Middle of the Night" or, outside of Israel during the second *Seder* night, "And you shall say, a sacrifice of *Pesaḥ*." All others continue here with the Fourth Cup.

[S]*I am ready and prepared to fulfill the commandment of the Fourth Cup for the Oneness of the Holy, praise to Him, and His Glory, through Him Who is hidden and secret, in the name of all of Israel.*

[AY] Praised are You o Lord, our God, King of the Universe, Creator of the fruit of the vine.

Reclining, one drinks the Fourth Cup. This is followed by the short form of grace:

Praised are You o Lord, our God, King of the Universe, for the vine and the fruit of the vine, for the produce of the field

הַהוֹדָאוֹת, אֲדוֹן הַנִּפְלָאוֹת, הַבּוֹחֵר בְּשִׁירֵי זִמְרָה, מֶלֶךְ אֵל, חֵי הָעוֹלָמִים.

יְהַלְלוּךָ יי אֱלֹהֵינוּ כָּל מַעֲשֶׂיךָ, וַחֲסִידֶיךָ וְצַדִּיקִים עוֹשֵׂי רְצוֹנֶךָ, וְעַמְּךָ בֵּית יִשְׂרָאֵל כֻּלָּם בְּרִנָּה יוֹדוּ, וִיבָרְכוּ, וִישַׁבְּחוּ, וִיפָאֲרוּ אֶת שֵׁם כְּבוֹדֶךָ, כִּי לְךָ טוֹב לְהוֹדוֹת וּלְשִׁמְךָ נָעִים לְזַמֵּר, וּמֵעוֹלָם וְעַד עוֹלָם אַתָּה אֵל. בָּרוּךְ אַתָּה יי, מֶלֶךְ מְהֻלָּל בַּתִּשְׁבָּחוֹת אָמֵן.

לְשִׁמְךָ, (הוֹד וְהָדָר לְזֵכֶר מַלְכוּתֶךָ) כִּי (אַתָּה יי,) לְךָ טוֹב לְהוֹדוֹת וּלְשִׁמְךָ נָעִים לְזַמֵּר, וּמֵעוֹלָם וְעַד עוֹלָם אַתָּה הוּא הָאֵל. בָּרוּךְ אַתָּה יי, הָאֵל, הַמֶּלֶךְ הַמְּהֻלָּל הַמְּשֻׁבָּח הַמְּפֹאָר חַי וְקַיָּם תָּמִיד יִמְלוֹךְ לְעוֹלָם וָעֶד.

במנהג אשכנז המערבי (מנהג מהר״ם רוטנבורג) מדלגים כאן ומתחילים מיד ״ובכן ויהי בחצי הלילה״, וביום שני בחו״ל ״ובכן ואמרתם זבח פסח״.

בכל המנהגים האחרים שותים כאן את הכוס הרביעי.

מנהג ספרד

הריני מוכן ומזומן לקיים מצות כוס רביעי מארבע כוסות לשם ייחוד קב״ה ושכינתיה על ידי ההוא טמיר ונעלם בשם כל ישראל.

מנהגי אשכנז ותימן

נוסח אשכנז

בָּרוּךְ אַתָּה יי אֱלֹהֵינוּ מֶלֶךְ הָעוֹלָם בּוֹרֵא פְּרִי הַגָּפֶן.

נוסח תימן

בָּרוּךְ אַתָּה יי אֱלֹהֵינוּ מֶלֶךְ הָעוֹלָם בּוֹרֵא פְּרִי הַגָּפֶן.

שותים את הכוס בהסיבת שמאל. ואח״כ מברכים ברכה אחת מעין שלוש:

נוסח אשכנז

בָּרוּךְ אַתָּה יי אֱלֹהֵינוּ מֶלֶךְ הָעוֹלָם, עַל הַגֶּפֶן וְעַל פְּרִי הַגֶּפֶן, וְעַל תְּנוּבַת הַשָּׂדֶה, וְעַל

נוסח ספרד

בָּרוּךְ אַתָּה יי אֱלֹהֵינוּ מֶלֶךְ הָעוֹלָם, עַל הַגֶּפֶן וְעַל פְּרִי הַגֶּפֶן, וְעַל תְּנוּבַת הַשָּׂדֶה, וְעַל

נוסח תימן

בָּרוּךְ אַתָּה יי אֱלֹהֵינוּ מֶלֶךְ הָעוֹלָם, עַל הַגֶּפֶן וְעַל פְּרִי הַגֶּפֶן, וְעַל

and the desirable, good, and spacious Land which it was Your pleasure to let our fathers inherit

AS *to eat from its fruit and be satiated from its goodness.* Have mercy, o Lord, our God, on us and Your people Israel, on Your city of Jerusalem, on S*Mount* Zion the dwelling place of Your glory,

AS *on Your altar and Your Temple. Build the holy city of Jerusalem soon, in our days,*

lead us up into her midst, make us happy with her reconstruction, let us eat

AS *from the fruit of the Land*

and be satiated from its goodness; and we shall praise You for it in holiness and purity.

On Sabbath, add:

A*And may You be pleased and give us respite on this Sabbath Day,*

S*And console us on this Sabbath Day,*

Y*And let us rest, our Father, on this day of rest,*

and make us enjoy

A*this festival of unleavened bread,*

S*o Lord, our God, this festival of unleavened bread, this good day of holy assembly,*

Y*o Lord, our God, this good day of holy assembly, this festival of unleavened bread,*

because You are good and beneficent for all,

AS*and we thank You for the Land,* S*the vine,* AS*and the fruit of the vine* (for Israel wine: *the fruit of its vine). Praised are You, o Lord, for the Land and the fruit of the vine* (for Israel wine: *the fruit of its vine*).

Y*Praised are You, o Lord, for the Land and the fruits* (for Israel wine: its *fruits*).

אֶרֶץ חֶמְדָּה טוֹבָה וּרְחָבָה שֶׁרָצִיתָ וְהִנְחַלְתָּ לַאֲבוֹתֵינוּ לֶאֱכוֹל מִפִּרְיָהּ וְלִשְׂבּוֹעַ מִטּוּבָהּ. רַחֵם יי אֱלֹהֵינוּ עַל יִשְׂרָאֵל עַמֶּךָ, וְעַל יְרוּשָׁלַיִם עִירֶךָ, וְעַל צִיּוֹן מִשְׁכַּן כְּבוֹדֶךָ, וְעַל מִזְבַּחֲךָ וְעַל הֵיכָלֶךָ, וּבְנֵה יְרוּשָׁלַיִם עִיר הַקֹּדֶשׁ בִּמְהֵרָה בְיָמֵינוּ, וְהַעֲלֵנוּ לְתוֹכָהּ וְשַׂמְּחֵנוּ בְּבִנְיָנָהּ, וְנֹאכַל מִפִּרְיָהּ וְנִשְׂבַּע מִטּוּבָהּ, וּנְבָרֶכְךָ עָלֶיהָ בִּקְדֻשָּׁה וּבְטָהֳרָה. בשבת: וּרְצֵה וְהַחֲלִיצֵנוּ בְּיוֹם הַשַּׁבָּת הַזֶּה. וְשַׂמְּחֵנוּ בְּיוֹם חַג הַמַּצּוֹת הַזֶּה, כִּי אַתָּה יי טוֹב וּמֵטִיב לַכֹּל, וְנוֹדֶה לְךָ עַל הָאָרֶץ וְעַל פְּרִי הַגָּפֶן (בא״י: וְעַל פְּרִי גַפְנָהּ). בָּרוּךְ אַתָּה יי, עַל הָאָרֶץ וְעַל פְּרִי הַגָּפֶן (בא״י: וְעַל פְּרִי גַפְנָהּ).

אֶרֶץ חֶמְדָּה טוֹבָה וּרְחָבָה שֶׁרָצִיתָ וְהִנְחַלְתָּ לַאֲבוֹתֵינוּ לֶאֱכוֹל מִפִּרְיָהּ וְלִשְׂבּוֹעַ מִטּוּבָהּ. רַחֵם יי אֱלֹהֵינוּ עָלֵינוּ וְעַל יִשְׂרָאֵל עַמָּךְ, וְעַל יְרוּשָׁלַיִם עִירָךְ, וְעַל הַר צִיּוֹן מִשְׁכַּן כְּבוֹדָךְ, וְעַל מִזְבְּחָךְ וְעַל הֵיכָלָךְ, וּבְנֵה יְרוּשָׁלַיִם עִיר הַקּוֹדֶשׁ בִּמְהֵרָה בְיָמֵינוּ, וְהַעֲלֵנוּ לְתוֹכָהּ וְשַׂמְּחֵנוּ בְּבִנְיָנָהּ, וּנְבָרֶכְךָ עָלֶיהָ בִּקְדֻשָּׁה וּבְטָהֳרָה. בשבת: וְנַחְמֵנוּ בְּיוֹם הַשַּׁבָּת הַזֶּה. וְשַׂמְּחֵנוּ יי אֱלֹהֵינוּ בְּיוֹם חַג הַמַּצּוֹת הַזֶּה, בְּיוֹם טוֹב מִקְרָא קֹדֶשׁ הַזֶּה, כִּי אַתָּה טוֹב וּמֵטִיב לַכֹּל, וְנוֹדֶה לְךָ עַל הָאָרֶץ וְעַל הַגֶּפֶן וְעַל פְּרִי הַגֶּפֶן (בא״י: וְעַל פְּרִי גַּפְנָהּ). בָּרוּךְ אַתָּה יי, עַל הָאָרֶץ וְעַל פְּרִי הַגֶּפֶן (בא״י: וְעַל פְּרִי גַּפְנָהּ).

תְּנוּבַת הַשָּׂדֶה, וְעַל אֶרֶץ חֶמְדָּה, טוֹבָה וּרְחָבָה, שֶׁרָצִיתָ וְהִנְחַלְתָּ אֶת אֲבוֹתֵינוּ. רַחֵם יי אֱלֹהֵינוּ, עָלֵינוּ וְעַל יִשְׂרָאֵל עַמֶּךָ, וְעַל יְרוּשָׁלַיִם עִירֶךָ, וְעַל הַר צִיּוֹן מִשְׁכַּן כְּבוֹדֶךָ, וְהַעֲלֵנוּ לְתוֹכָהּ וְשַׂמְּחֵנוּ בְּבִנְיָנָהּ, וְנֹאכַל וְנִשְׂבַּע מִטּוּבָהּ, וּנְבָרֶכְךָ עָלֶיהָ בִּקְדֻשָּׁה וּבְטָהֳרָה. בשבת: וְהָנַח לָנוּ אָבִינוּ בְּיוֹם הַמָּנוֹחַ הַזֶּה. וְשַׂמְּחֵנוּ יי אֱלֹהֵינוּ, בְּיוֹם טוֹב מִקְרָא קֹדֶשׁ הַזֶּה, יוֹם חַג הַמַּצּוֹת הַזֶּה, כִּי אֵל טוֹב וּמֵטִיב אָתָּה. בָּרוּךְ אַתָּה יי, עַל הָאָרֶץ וְעַל הַפֵּירוֹת (בא״י: וְעַל פֵּרוֹתֶיהָ).

Conclusion

This concludes the *Seder* service for Sephardic (excluding Italian) and Oriental rites. In some communities it is the custom to recite the Song of Songs after the conclusion of the *Seder*. In some Yemenite families, poems in honor of the festival are sung; these are found on p. 151. In a number of Oriental communities, one or both of the concluding Ashkenazic songs, "Who knows One" and "A kid, a kid" are sung, the latter usually in its Arabic version.

Ashkenazic and Italian families continue:

This is the end of the order of *Pesaḥ* by its rules,
All its laws and institutions,
Since we were found worthy to prepare for it
May we be found worthy to execute it.
Pure One, Who dwells in His Heavenly Temple,
Lift up the assembly that cannot be counted;
Soon lead the firm saplings
Delivered, to Zion in song.

Next year in Jerusalem! (In Israel: Next year in the rebuilt Jerusalem!)

For the first *Seder* night (in the Diaspora)

Let us say: It happened at midnight!

א In old times, most of Your wonders were worked in the Night
ב At the first watch of this Night
ג To the pious wanderer You gave victory when You split for him the Night

It happened at midnight!

ד You did judge the king of Gerar in the dream of Night
ה You scared the Aramean in the preceding Night
ו And Israel fought with the superior being and won in the Night

It happened at midnight!

ז The firstborn seed of Patros You smote in the middle of the Night

נִרְצָה

בהרבה משפחות ספרדיות ומעדות המזרח נוהגים לקרא מגילת שיר השירים.

בהרבה קבוצות מעדות המזרח נוהגים לשיר את השירים ״אחד מי יודע״ ו״חד גדיא״ או בעברית או בלשון ערב.

במנהג תימן נוהגים כמה משפחות לזמר שירי מרי סלים אלשבזי, נמצאים בסוף ההגדה אחרי שיר ׳חד גדיא׳.

במנהג איטליה, איטליאני וספרדי, ממשיכים כמו במנהג אשכנז.

מנהג אשכנז

חֲסַל סִדּוּר פֶּסַח כְּהִלְכָתוֹ כְּכָל־מִשְׁפָּטוֹ וְחֻקָּתוֹ
כַּאֲשֶׁר זָכִינוּ לְסַדֵּר אוֹתוֹ כֵּן נִזְכֶּה לַעֲשׂוֹתוֹ
זָךְ שׁוֹכֵן מְעוֹנָה קוֹמֵם קְהַל מִי מָנָה
קָרֵב נַהֵל נִטְעֵי כַנָּה פְּדוּיִם לְצִיּוֹן בְּרִנָּה.

לַשָּׁנָה הַבָּאָה בִּירוּשָׁלָיִם (בא״י: הַבְּנוּיָה).

בלילה ראשון של סדר

וּבְכֵן וַיְהִי בַּחֲצִי הַלַּיְלָה.

אָז רֹב נִסִּים הִפְלֵאתָ בַּלַּיְלָה
בְּרֹאשׁ אַשְׁמוּרוֹת זֶה הַלַּיְלָה
גֵּר צֶדֶק נִצַּחְתּוֹ כְּנֶחֱלַק לוֹ לַיְלָה
וַיְהִי בַּחֲצִי הַלַּיְלָה.

דַּנְתָּ מֶלֶךְ גְּרָר בַּחֲלוֹם הַלַּיְלָה
הִפְחַדְתָּ אֲרַמִּי בְּאֶמֶשׁ לַיְלָה
וַיָּשַׂר יִשְׂרָאֵל לָאֵל וַיּוּכַל לוֹ לַיְלָה
וַיְהִי בַּחֲצִי הַלַּיְלָה.

זֶרַע בְּכוֹרֵי פַתְרוֹס מָחַצְתָּ בַּחֲצִי הַלַּיְלָה

ח They did not find their force when they tried to get up in the Night
ט The flight of the chief of Ḥaroshet You flattened by the stars of Night

It happened at midnight!

י The blasphemer wanted to wave his hand over the desirable place but You left his army as rotten corpses in the Night
כ Bel's statue and its base fell down during the sleep of Night
ל The mystery was revealed to the desirable man by a vision in the Night

It happened at midnight!

מ The one who intoxicated himself from Temple vessels was slain the same Night
נ The one saved from the lions' den did explain in the time of Night
ס The Agagite kept his hatred and wrote books in the Night

It happened at midnight!

ע You began Your victory over him when sleep was fleeing in the Night
פ You will work the winepress for him who watches in the Night
צ He called out like a watchman and said, Morning is coming and also Night

It happened at midnight!

ק Bring us the day that will be neither day nor Night
ר O Sublime One, make known that Yours is day and Night
ש Put up guards for Your city, all day and all Night
ת Light up like daylight the darkness of Night

It happened at midnight!

Most families continue with "For Him it is right."

For the second *Seder* night (in the Diaspora)

Let us say: And you shall say: A sacrifice of *Pesaḥ*!

א The strength of Your power You showed wonderfully on *Pesaḥ*
ב As first of all holidays You did elevate *Pesaḥ*
ג To the native born You appeared at midnight of *Pesaḥ*

חֵילָם לֹא מָצְאוּ בְּקוּמָם   בַּלַּיְלָה
טִסַּת נְגִיד חֲרוֹשֶׁת סִלִּיתָ בְכוֹכְבֵי   לַיְלָה
וַיְהִי בַּחֲצִי הַלַּיְלָה.

יָעַץ מְחָרֵף לְנוֹפֵף אִוּוּי, הוֹבַשְׁתָּ פְגָרָיו   בַּלַּיְלָה
כָּרַע בֵּל וּמַצָּבוֹ בְּאִישׁוֹן   לַיְלָה
לְאִישׁ חֲמוּדוֹת נִגְלָה רָז חֲזוֹת   לַיְלָה
וַיְהִי בַּחֲצִי הַלַּיְלָה.

מִשְׁתַּכֵּר בִּכְלֵי קֹדֶשׁ נֶהֱרַג בּוֹ   בַּלַּיְלָה
נוֹשַׁע מִבּוֹר אֲרָיוֹת פּוֹתֵר בִּעֲתוּתֵי   לַיְלָה
שִׂנְאָה נָטַר אֲגָגִי וְכָתַב סְפָרִים   בַּלַּיְלָה.
וַיְהִי בַּחֲצִי הַלַּיְלָה

עוֹרַרְתָּ נִצְחֲךָ עָלָיו בְּנֶדֶד שְׁנַת   לַיְלָה
פּוּרָה תִדְרוֹךְ לְשׁוֹמֵר מַה   מִּלַּיְלָה
צָרַח כַּשּׁוֹמֵר וְשָׂח אָתָא בֹקֶר וְגַם   לַיְלָה
וַיְהִי בַּחֲצִי הַלַּיְלָה

קָרֵב יוֹם אֲשֶׁר הוּא לֹא יוֹם וְלֹא   לַיְלָה
רָם הוֹדַע כִּי לְךָ יוֹם אַף לְךָ   לַיְלָה
שׁוֹמְרִים הַפְקֵד לְעִירְךָ כָּל־הַיּוֹם וְכָל־   הַלַּיְלָה
תָּאִיר כְּאוֹר יוֹם חֶשְׁכַּת   לַיְלָה
וַיְהִי בַּחֲצִי הַלַּיְלָה.

ממשיכים בשיר 'כי לו נאה'.

בליל שני של הסדר בחו״ל

וּבְכֵן וַאֲמַרְתֶּם זֶבַח פֶּסַח

אֹמֶץ גְּבוּרוֹתֶיךָ הִפְלֵאתָ   בַּפֶּסַח
בְּרֹאשׁ כָּל־מוֹעֲדוֹת נִשֵּׂאתָ   פֶּסַח
גִּלִּיתָ לְאֶזְרָחִי חֲצוֹת לֵיל   פֶּסַח

And you shall say: A sacrifice of *Pesaḥ*!

ד You knocked at his door in the heat of the day on *Pesaḥ*
ה He fed the fiery beings *maẓẓot* on *Pesaḥ*
ו And to the cattle he ran as a symbol for the bull of the order of *Pesaḥ*

And you shall say: A sacrifice of *Pesaḥ*!

ז The Sodomites caused wrath and they went up in fire on *Pesaḥ*
ח Lot was rescued from among them when he baked *maẓẓot* at the time of *Pesaḥ*
ט You swept out the land of Moph and Noph when You passed over on *Pesaḥ*

And you shall say: A sacrifice of *Pesaḥ*!

י O Lord, You smote every firstborn in the Night of Preservation of *Pesaḥ*
כ O Powerful One, You passed over Your firstborn with the blood of *Pesaḥ*
ל Not to let the destroyer enter my doors on *Pesaḥ*

And you shall say: A sacrifice of *Pesaḥ*!

מ The encircled city was surrounded at the time of *Pesaḥ*
נ Midyan was destroyed by the roasted barley of the *'Omer* on *Pesaḥ*
ס The best of Pul and Lud were burned in the conflagration of *Pesaḥ*

And you shall say: A sacrifice of *Pesaḥ*!

ע Still today, he wanted to get to Nob, before the time of *Pesaḥ*
פ A hand wrote to break up the watery country on *Pesaḥ*
צ The candelabrum was lit, the table was set on *Pesaḥ*

And you shall say: A sacrifice of *Pesaḥ*!

ק Hadassah assembled the congregation for a triple fast on *Pesaḥ*
ר You smashed the head of the criminal house on a pole fifty [cubits] high on *Pesaḥ*
ש These two You will bring in a moment upon the people of Uẓit on *Pesaḥ*
ת Show Your strong left hand, lift Your right hand when we celebrate in the night at the beginning of the holiday of *Pesaḥ*

And you shall say: A sacrifice of *Pesaḥ*!

וַאֲמַרְתֶּם זֶבַח פֶּסַח

דְּלָתָיו דָּפַקְתָּ כְּחוֹם הַיּוֹם בַּפֶּסַח
הִסְעִיד נוֹצְצִים עֻגוֹת מַצּוֹת בַּפֶּסַח
וְאֶל הַבָּקָר רָץ זֵכֶר לְשׁוֹר עֵרֶךְ פֶּסַח
וַאֲמַרְתֶּם זֶבַח פֶּסַח

זֹעֲמוּ סְדוֹמִים וְלֹהֲטוּ בָּאֵשׁ פֶּסַח
חֻלַּץ לוֹט מֵהֶם וּמַצּוֹת אָפָה בְּקֵץ פֶּסַח
טִאטֵאתָ אַדְמַת מוֹף וְנוֹף בְּעָבְרְךָ בַּפֶּסַח
וַאֲמַרְתֶּם זֶבַח פֶּסַח

יָהּ רֹאשׁ כָּל־אוֹן מָחַצְתָּ בְּלֵיל שִׁמּוּר פֶּסַח
כַּבִּיר, עַל בֵּן בְּכוֹר פָּסַחְתָּ בְּדַם פֶּסַח
לְבִלְתִּי תֵּת מַשְׁחִית לָבֹא בִּפְתָחַי בַּפֶּסַח
וַאֲמַרְתֶּם זֶבַח פֶּסַח

מְסֻגֶּרֶת סֻגָּרָה בְּעִתּוֹתֵי פֶּסַח
נִשְׁמְדָה מִדְיָן בִּצְלִיל שְׂעוֹרֵי עוֹמֶר פֶּסַח
שׂוֹרְפוּ מַשְׁמַנֵּי פּוּל וְלוּד בִּיקַד יְקוֹד פֶּסַח
וַאֲמַרְתֶּם זֶבַח פֶּסַח

עוֹד הַיּוֹם בְּנוֹב לַעֲמוֹד עַד גָּעָה עוֹנַת פֶּסַח
פַּס יָד כָּתְבָה לְקַעֲקֵעַ צוּל בַּפֶּסַח
צָפֹה הַצָּפִית, עָרוֹךְ הַשֻּׁלְחָן בַּפֶּסַח
וַאֲמַרְתֶּם זֶבַח פֶּסַח

קָהָל כִּנְּסָה הֲדַסָּה לְשַׁלֵּשׁ צוֹם בַּפֶּסַח
רֹאשׁ מִבֵּית רָשָׁע מָחַצְתָּ בְּעֵץ חֲמִשִּׁים בַּפֶּסַח
שְׁתֵּי אֵלֶּה רֶגַע תָּבִיא לְעוּצִית בַּפֶּסַח
תָּעוֹז יָדְךָ תָּרוּם יְמִינְךָ כְּלֵיל הִתְקַדֵּשׁ חַג פֶּסַח
וַאֲמַרְתֶּם זֶבַח פֶּסַח.

Both nights of *Seder:*

For Him it is right, it is His due!

Noble in Kingdom, Select of right, His armies say to Him:
Yours, only Yours, Yours, truly Yours, Yours, surely Yours, Yours, o Lord, is the Kingdom
For Him it is right, it is His due!

Excellent in Kingdom, In splendor of right, His trusted servants say to Him:
Yours, only Yours, Yours, truly Yours, Yours, surely Yours, Yours, o Lord, is the Kingdom
For Him it is right, it is His due!

Pure in Kingdom, Powerful of right, His officers say to Him:
Yours, only Yours, Yours, truly Yours, Yours, surely Yours, Yours, o Lord, is the Kingdom
For Him it is right, it is His due!

Unique in Kingdom, Strong of right, His attendants say to Him:
Yours, only Yours, Yours, truly Yours, Yours, surely Yours, Yours, o Lord, is the Kingdom
For Him it is right, it is His due!

Exalted in Kingdom, Awful of right, Those around Him say to Him:
Yours, only Yours, Yours, truly Yours, Yours, surely Yours, Yours, o Lord, is the Kingdom
For Him it is right, it is His due!

Humble in Kingdom, Redeemer of right, His just ones say to Him:
Yours, only Yours, Yours, truly Yours, Yours, surely Yours, Yours, o Lord, is the Kingdom
For Him it is right, it is His due!

Holy in Kingdom, Merciful of right, His angels say to Him:
Yours, only Yours, Yours, truly Yours, Yours, surely Yours, Yours, o Lord, is the Kingdom
For Him it is right, it is His due!

Strong in Kingdom, Support of right, His perfect beings say to Him:
Yours, only Yours, Yours, truly Yours, Yours, surely Yours, Yours, o Lord, is the Kingdom
For Him it is right, it is His due!

In the Western Ashkenazic ritual one adds here "Next year in Jerusalem" followed by the benediction of the Fourth Cup; the Fourth Cup is then consumed while reclining; the short form of Grace is recited afterwards followed by "This is the end. . ."

בשני לילות הסדר

כִּי לוֹ נָאֶה, כִּי לוֹ יָאֶה

אַדִּיר בִּמְלוּכָה, בָּחוּר כַּהֲלָכָה, גְּדוּדָיו יֹאמְרוּ לוֹ
לְךָ וּלְךָ, לְךָ כִּי לְךָ, לְךָ אַף לְךָ, לְךָ יי הַמַּמְלָכָה
כִּי לוֹ נָאֶה, כִּי לוֹ יָאֶה

דָּגוּל בִּמְלוּכָה, הָדוּר כַּהֲלָכָה, וָתִיקָיו יֹאמְרוּ לוֹ
לְךָ וּלְךָ, לְךָ כִּי לְךָ, לְךָ אַף לְךָ, לְךָ יי הַמַּמְלָכָה
כִּי לוֹ נָאֶה, כִּי לוֹ יָאֶה

זַכַּאי בִּמְלוּכָה, חָסִין כַּהֲלָכָה, טַפְסְרָיו יֹאמְרוּ לוֹ
לְךָ וּלְךָ, לְךָ כִּי לְךָ, לְךָ אַף לְךָ, לְךָ יי הַמַּמְלָכָה
כִּי לוֹ נָאֶה, כִּי לוֹ יָאֶה

יָחִיד בִּמְלוּכָה, כַּבִּיר כַּהֲלָכָה, לִמּוּדָיו יֹאמְרוּ לוֹ
לְךָ וּלְךָ, לְךָ כִּי לְךָ, לְךָ אַף לְךָ, לְךָ יי הַמַּמְלָכָה
כִּי לוֹ נָאֶה, כִּי לוֹ יָאֶה

מָרוֹם בִּמְלוּכָה, נוֹרָא כַּהֲלָכָה, סְבִיבָיו יֹאמְרוּ לוֹ
לְךָ וּלְךָ, לְךָ כִּי לְךָ, לְךָ אַף לְךָ, לְךָ יי הַמַּמְלָכָה
כִּי לוֹ נָאֶה, כִּי לוֹ יָאֶה

עָנָיו בִּמְלוּכָה, פּוֹדֶה כַּהֲלָכָה, צַדִּיקָיו יֹאמְרוּ לוֹ
לְךָ וּלְךָ, לְךָ כִּי לְךָ, לְךָ אַף לְךָ, לְךָ יי הַמַּמְלָכָה
כִּי לוֹ נָאֶה, כִּי לוֹ יָאֶה

קָדוֹשׁ בִּמְלוּכָה, רַחוּם כַּהֲלָכָה, שִׁנְאַנָּיו יֹאמְרוּ לוֹ
לְךָ וּלְךָ, לְךָ כִּי לְךָ, לְךָ אַף לְךָ, לְךָ יי הַמַּמְלָכָה
כִּי לוֹ נָאֶה, כִּי לוֹ יָאֶה

תַּקִּיף בִּמְלוּכָה, תּוֹמֵךְ כַּהֲלָכָה, תְּמִימָיו יֹאמְרוּ לוֹ
לְךָ וּלְךָ, לְךָ כִּי לְךָ, לְךָ אַף לְךָ, לְךָ יי הַמַּמְלָכָה
כִּי לוֹ נָאֶה, כִּי לוֹ יָאֶה.

במנהג אשכנז המערבי אומרים כאן ״לשנה הבאה בירושלים״, בורא פרי הגפן, שותים כוס רביעי בהסיבה,
ברכה אחת מעין שבע, חסל סידור פסח.

In most families, the refrain "May He build . . ." is sung after each line of three attributes.

He is Noble
May He build His Temple soon, quickly, quickly, soon in our days.
Build, o God, build, o God, build Your Temple soon!

He is Select, He is Great, He is Outstanding
He is Majestic, He is Dependable, He is Pure
He is Giving Grace, He is Pure, He is One
He is Powerful, He is All-knowing, He is King
He is Illuminating, He is Protecting, He is Strong
He is Redeemer, He is Just, He is Forceful
May He build His Temple soon, quickly, quickly, soon in our days.
Build, o God, build, o God, build Your Temple soon!

In some, mostly German, families the song is repeated in a Yiddish version:

א Almighty God
Now build Your Temple quickly, really quick and really soon, in our days quickly, yes, quickly
Now build, now build, now build Your Temple quickly!

ב Merciful God
Now build Your Temple quickly, really quick and really soon, in our days quickly, yes, quickly
Now build, now build, now build Your Temple quickly!

ג Great God, ד Humble God
Now build Your Temple quickly, really quick and really soon, in our days quickly, yes, quickly
Now build, now build, now build Your Temple quickly!

ה High God, ו Fine God, ז Sweet God, ח Graceful God
Now build Your Temple quickly, really quick and really soon, in our days quickly, yes, quickly
Now build, now build, now build Your Temple quickly!

ט Virtuous God, י Jewish God
Now build Your Temple quickly, really quick and really soon, in our days quickly, yes, quickly
Now build, now build, now build Your Temple quickly!

כ Strong God, ל Living God, מ Powerful God, נ Renowned God, ס Mild God, ע Eternal God
Now build Your Temple quickly, really quick and really soon, in our days quickly, yes, quickly
Now build, now build, now build Your Temple quickly!

פ Awesome God, צ Seemly God, ק Royal God, ר Rich God
Now build Your Temple quickly, really quick and really soon, in our days quickly, yes, quickly
Now build, now build, now build Your Temple quickly!

ש Beautiful God, ת Beloved God
Now build Your Temple quickly, really quick and really soon, in our days

בהרבה משפחות שרים את החרוז ״יבנה ביתו ... בנה ביתך בקרוב״ אחרי כל שלושה תארים

אַדִּיר הוּא

יִבְנֶה בֵיתוֹ בְּקָרוֹב, בִּמְהֵרָה, בִּמְהֵרָה, בְּיָמֵינוּ בְּקָרוֹב;
אֵל בְּנֵה, אֵל בְּנֵה, בְּנֵה בֵיתְךָ בְּקָרוֹב.

בָּחוּר הוּא, גָּדוֹל הוּא, דָּגוּל הוּא
הָדוּר הוּא, וָתִיק הוּא, זַכַּאי הוּא
חָסִיד הוּא, טָהוֹר הוּא, יָחִיד הוּא
כַּבִּיר הוּא, לָמוּד הוּא, מֶלֶךְ הוּא
נָאוֹר הוּא, סַגִּיב הוּא, עִזּוּז הוּא
פּוֹדֶה הוּא, צַדִּיק הוּא, קָדוֹשׁ הוּא
רַחוּם הוּא, שַׁדַּי הוּא, תַּקִּיף הוּא
יִבְנֶה בֵיתוֹ בְּקָרוֹב, בִּמְהֵרָה, בִּמְהֵרָה, בְּיָמֵינוּ בְּקָרוֹב;
אֵל בְּנֵה, אֵל בְּנֵה, בְּנֵה בֵיתְךָ בְּקָרוֹב.

בכמה משפחות, בעיקר במנהג אשכנז המערבי, שרים את השיר ״אדיר הוא״ גם בלשון יידיש:

אַלמעכטיגר גאָט,
נון בויא דיין טעמפיל שירָה, אַלזוֹ שיר, אונ' אַלזוֹ באַלד, אין אונזירן טאַגין שירה, יאַ שירה,
נון בויא, נון בויא, נון בויא דיין טעמפיל שירה.

באַרמהאַרציגר גאָט
נון בויא דיין טעמפיל שירָה, אַלזוֹ שיר, אונ' אַלזוֹ באַלד, אין אונזירן טאַגין שירה, יאַ שירה,
נון בויא, נון בויא, נון בויא דיין טעמפיל שירה.

גראָסר גאָט, דעמוּטיגר גאָט
נון בויא דיין טעמפיל שירָה, אַלזוֹ שיר, אונ' אַלזוֹ באַלד, אין אונזירן טאַגין שירה, יאַ שירה,
נון בויא, נון בויא, נון בויא דיין טעמפיל שירה.

הוֹכיר גאָט, וויינר גאָט, זיסר גאָט, חינטר גאָט,
נון בויא דיין טעמפיל שירָה, אַלזוֹ שיר, אונ' אַלזוֹ באַלד, אין אונזירן טאַגין שירה, יאַ שירה,
נון בויא, נון בויא, נון בויא דיין טעמפיל שירה.

טוּגליכר גאָט, יוּדישר גאָט,
נון בויא דיין טעמפיל שירָה, אַלזוֹ שיר, אונ' אַלזוֹ באַלד, אין אונזירן טאַגין שירה, יאַ שירה,
נון בויא, נון בויא, נון בויא דיין טעמפיל שירה.

כרעפטיגר גאָט, לעבענדיגר גאָט, מעכטיגר גאָט, נאַמהאַפטיגר גאָט, סענפטיגר גאָט, עיביגר גאָט,
נון בויא דיין טעמפיל שירָה, אַלזוֹ שיר, אונ' אַלזוֹ באַלד, אין אונזירן טאַגין שירה, יאַ שירה,
נון בויא, נון בויא, נון בויא דיין טעמפיל שירה.

פוֹרכטצוּמר גאָט, צימליכר גאָט, קעניגליכר גאָט, רייכר גאָט,
נון בויא דיין טעמפיל שירָה, אַלזוֹ שיר, אונ' אַלזוֹ באַלד, אין אונזירן טאַגין שירה, יאַ שירה,
נון בויא, נון בויא, נון בויא דיין טעמפיל שירה.

שיינר גאָט, תרויטר גאָט
נון בויא דיין טעמפיל שירָה, אַלזוֹ שיר, אונ' אַלזוֹ באַלד, אין אונזירן טאַגין שירה, יאַ שירה,
נון בויא, נון בויא, נון בויא דיין טעמפיל שירה.

quickly, yes, quickly
Now build, now build, now build Your Temple quickly!

You are God and no one else
Now build Your Temple quickly, really quick and really soon, in our days
quickly, yes, quickly
Now build, now build, now build Your Temple quickly!

On the second *Seder* night, some Ashkenazic families start here the Counting of the *'Omer*:

Praised are You o Lord, our God, King of the Universe, Who sanctified us by His commandments and commanded us about the counting of the *'Omer*.

Today is Day One of the *'Omer*.

May it be Your will, o Lord, our God and God of our fathers, that the Temple may be rebuilt soon, in our days, and give us a part in Your Torah.

Who knows One?
I know One! One is our God Who is in Heaven and on earth.

Who knows Two?
I know Two! Two are the tablets of the Covenant, One is our God Who is in Heaven and on earth.

Who knows Three?
I know Three! Three are the patriarchs, Two are the tablets of the Covenant, One is our God Who is in Heaven and on earth.

Who knows Four?
I know Four! Four are the matriarchs, Three are the patriarchs, Two are the tablets of the Covenant, One is our God Who is in Heaven and on earth.

Who knows Five?
I know Five! Five are the books of the Torah, Four are the matriarchs, Three are the patriarchs, Two are the tablets of the Covenant, One is our God Who is in Heaven and on earth.

Who knows Six?
I know Six! Six are the orders of the Mishnah, Five are the books of the Torah, Four are the matriarchs, Three are the patriarchs, Two are the tablets of the Covenant, One is our God Who is in Heaven and on earth.

Who knows Seven?
I know Seven! Seven are the days of the week, Six are the orders of the Mishnah, Five are the books of the Torah, Four are the matriarchs,

דוּא בִּישט גאָט אוּנ' קֵיינֶר מֶער
נוּן בּוּיא דַיין טֶעמְפֶּיל שִׁירָה, אַלזוֹ שִׁיר, אוּנ' אַלזוֹ בַּאלד, אִין אוּנזירן טאַגִין שִׁירָה, יאַ שִׁירָה,
נוּן בּוּיא, נוּן בּוּיא, נוּן בּוּיא דַיין טֶעמְפֶּיל שִׁירָה.

במנהג אשכנז יש שמתחילים כאן ספירת העומר בליל שני של פסח:

בָּרוּךְ אַתָּה יי אֱלֹהֵינוּ מֶלֶךְ הָעוֹלָם אֲשֶׁר קִדְּשָׁנוּ בְּמִצְוֹתָיו וְצִוָּנוּ עַל סְפִירַת הָעוֹמֶר.

הַיּוֹם יוֹם אֶחָד לָעוֹמֶר.

יְהִי רָצוֹן מִלְּפָנֶיךָ יי אֱלֹהֵינוּ וֵאלֹהֵי אֲבוֹתֵינוּ שֶׁיִּבָּנֶה בֵּית הַמִּקְדָּשׁ בִּמְהֵרָה בְיָמֵינוּ וְתֵן חֶלְקֵנוּ בְּתוֹרָתֶךָ.

אֶחָד מִי יוֹדֵעַ?
אֶחָד אֲנִי יוֹדֵעַ. אֶחָד אֱלֹהֵינוּ שֶׁבַּשָּׁמַיִם וּבָאָרֶץ.

שְׁנַיִם מִי יוֹדֵעַ?
שְׁנַיִם אֲנִי יוֹדֵעַ. שְׁנֵי לוּחוֹת הַבְּרִית, אֶחָד אֱלֹהֵינוּ שֶׁבַּשָּׁמַיִם וּבָאָרֶץ.

שְׁלוֹשָׁה מִי יוֹדֵעַ?
שְׁלוֹשָׁה אֲנִי יוֹדֵעַ. שְׁלוֹשָׁה אָבוֹת, שְׁנֵי לוּחוֹת הַבְּרִית, אֶחָד אֱלֹהֵינוּ שֶׁבַּשָּׁמַיִם וּבָאָרֶץ.

אַרְבַּע מִי יוֹדֵעַ?
אַרְבַּע אֲנִי יוֹדֵעַ. אַרְבַּע אִמָּהוֹת, שְׁלוֹשָׁה אָבוֹת, שְׁנֵי לוּחוֹת הַבְּרִית, אֶחָד אֱלֹהֵינוּ שֶׁבַּשָּׁמַיִם וּבָאָרֶץ.

חֲמִשָּׁה מִי יוֹדֵעַ?
חֲמִשָּׁה אֲנִי יוֹדֵעַ. חֲמִשָּׁה חוּמְשֵׁי תוֹרָה, אַרְבַּע אִמָּהוֹת, שְׁלוֹשָׁה אָבוֹת, שְׁנֵי לוּחוֹת הַבְּרִית, אֶחָד אֱלֹהֵינוּ שֶׁבַּשָּׁמַיִם וּבָאָרֶץ.

שִׁשָּׁה מִי יוֹדֵעַ?
שִׁשָּׁה אֲנִי יוֹדֵעַ. שִׁשָּׁה סִדְרֵי מִשְׁנָה, חֲמִשָּׁה חוּמְשֵׁי תוֹרָה, אַרְבַּע אִמָּהוֹת, שְׁלוֹשָׁה אָבוֹת, שְׁנֵי לוּחוֹת הַבְּרִית, אֶחָד אֱלֹהֵינוּ שֶׁבַּשָּׁמַיִם וּבָאָרֶץ.

שִׁבְעָה מִי יוֹדֵעַ?
שִׁבְעָה אֲנִי יוֹדֵעַ. שִׁבְעָה יְמֵי שַׁבַּתָּא, שִׁשָּׁה סִדְרֵי מִשְׁנָה, חֲמִשָּׁה חוּמְשֵׁי

Three are the patriarchs, Two are the tablets of the Covenant, One is our God Who is in Heaven and on earth.

Who knows Eight?
I know Eight! Eight are the days of circumcision, Seven are the days of the week, Six are the orders of the Mishnah, Five are the books of the Torah, Four are the matriarchs, Three are the patriarchs, Two are the tablets of the Covenant, One is our God Who is in Heaven and on earth.

Who knows Nine?
I know Nine! Nine are the months of birth, Eight are the days of circumcision, Seven are the days of the week, Six are the orders of the Mishnah, Five are the books of the Torah, Four are the matriarchs, Three are the patriarchs, Two are the tablets of the Covenant, One is our God Who is in Heaven and on earth.

Who knows Ten?
I know Ten! Ten are the commandments, Nine are the months of birth, Eight are the days of circumcision, Seven are the days of the week, Six are the orders of the Mishnah, Five are the books of the Torah, Four are the matriarchs, Three are the patriarchs, Two are the tablets of the Covenant, One is our God Who is in Heaven and on earth.

Who knows Eleven?
I know Eleven! Eleven are the stars, Ten are the commandments, Nine are the months of birth, Eight are the days of circumcision, Seven are the days of the week, Six are the orders of the Mishnah, Five are the books of the Torah, Four are the matriarchs, Three are the patriarchs, Two are the tablets of the Covenant, One is our God Who is in Heaven and on earth.

Who knows Twelve?
I know Twelve! Twelve are the tribes, Eleven are the stars, Ten are the commandments, Nine are the months of birth, Eight are the days of circumcision, Seven are the days of the week, Six are the orders of the Mishnah, Five are the books of the Torah, Four are the matriarchs, Three are the patriarchs, Two are the tablets of the Covenant, One is our God Who is in Heaven and on earth.

Who knows Thirteen?
I know Thirteen! Thirteen are the attributes, Twelve are the tribes, Eleven are the stars, Ten are the commandments, Nine are the months of birth, Eight are the days of circumcision, Seven are the days of the week, Six are the orders of the Mishnah, Five are the books of the

תוֹרָה, אַרְבַּע אִמָּהוֹת, שְׁלוֹשָׁה אָבוֹת, שְׁנֵי לוּחוֹת הַבְּרִית, אֶחָד אֱלֹהֵינוּ שֶׁבַּשָּׁמַיִם וּבָאָרֶץ.

שְׁמוֹנָה מִי יוֹדֵעַ?

שְׁמוֹנָה אֲנִי יוֹדֵעַ. שְׁמוֹנָה יְמֵי מִילָה, שִׁבְעָה יְמֵי שַׁבַּתָּא, שִׁשָּׁה סִדְרֵי מִשְׁנָה, חֲמִשָּׁה חוּמְשֵׁי תוֹרָה, אַרְבַּע אִמָּהוֹת, שְׁלוֹשָׁה אָבוֹת, שְׁנֵי לוּחוֹת הַבְּרִית, אֶחָד אֱלֹהֵינוּ שֶׁבַּשָּׁמַיִם וּבָאָרֶץ.

תִּשְׁעָה מִי יוֹדֵעַ?

תִּשְׁעָה אֲנִי יוֹדֵעַ. תִּשְׁעָה יַרְחֵי לֵידָה, שְׁמוֹנָה יְמֵי מִילָה, שִׁבְעָה יְמֵי שַׁבַּתָּא, שִׁשָּׁה סִדְרֵי מִשְׁנָה, חֲמִשָּׁה חוּמְשֵׁי תוֹרָה, אַרְבַּע אִמָּהוֹת, שְׁלוֹשָׁה אָבוֹת, שְׁנֵי לוּחוֹת הַבְּרִית, אֶחָד אֱלֹהֵינוּ שֶׁבַּשָּׁמַיִם וּבָאָרֶץ.

עֲשָׂרָה מִי יוֹדֵעַ?

עֲשָׂרָה אֲנִי יוֹדֵעַ. עֲשָׂרָה דִבְּרַיָּא, תִּשְׁעָה יַרְחֵי לֵידָה, שְׁמוֹנָה יְמֵי מִילָה, שִׁבְעָה יְמֵי שַׁבַּתָּא, שִׁשָּׁה סִדְרֵי מִשְׁנָה, חֲמִשָּׁה חוּמְשֵׁי תוֹרָה, אַרְבַּע אִמָּהוֹת, שְׁלוֹשָׁה אָבוֹת, שְׁנֵי לוּחוֹת הַבְּרִית, אֶחָד אֱלֹהֵינוּ שֶׁבַּשָּׁמַיִם וּבָאָרֶץ.

אַחַד עָשָׂר מִי יוֹדֵעַ?

אַחַד עָשָׂר אֲנִי יוֹדֵעַ. אַחַד עָשָׂר כּוֹכְבַיָּא, עֲשָׂרָה דִבְּרַיָּא, תִּשְׁעָה יַרְחֵי לֵידָה, שְׁמוֹנָה יְמֵי מִילָה, שִׁבְעָה יְמֵי שַׁבַּתָּא, שִׁשָּׁה סִדְרֵי מִשְׁנָה, חֲמִשָּׁה חוּמְשֵׁי תוֹרָה, אַרְבַּע אִמָּהוֹת, שְׁלוֹשָׁה אָבוֹת, שְׁנֵי לוּחוֹת הַבְּרִית, אֶחָד אֱלֹהֵינוּ שֶׁבַּשָּׁמַיִם וּבָאָרֶץ.

שְׁנֵים עָשָׂר מִי יוֹדֵעַ?

שְׁנֵים עָשָׂר אֲנִי יוֹדֵעַ. שְׁנֵים עָשָׂר שִׁבְטַיָּא, אַחַד עָשָׂר כּוֹכְבַיָּא, עֲשָׂרָה דִבְּרַיָּא, תִּשְׁעָה יַרְחֵי לֵידָה, שְׁמוֹנָה יְמֵי מִילָה, שִׁבְעָה יְמֵי שַׁבַּתָּא, שִׁשָּׁה סִדְרֵי מִשְׁנָה, חֲמִשָּׁה חוּמְשֵׁי תוֹרָה, אַרְבַּע אִמָּהוֹת, שְׁלוֹשָׁה אָבוֹת, שְׁנֵי לוּחוֹת הַבְּרִית, אֶחָד אֱלֹהֵינוּ שֶׁבַּשָּׁמַיִם וּבָאָרֶץ.

שְׁלוֹשָׁה עָשָׂר מִי יוֹדֵעַ?

שְׁלוֹשָׁה עָשָׂר אֲנִי יוֹדֵעַ. שְׁלוֹשָׁה עָשָׂר מִדַּיָּא, שְׁנֵים עָשָׂר שִׁבְטַיָּא, אַחַד עָשָׂר כּוֹכְבַיָּא, עֲשָׂרָה דִבְּרַיָּא, תִּשְׁעָה יַרְחֵי לֵידָה, שְׁמוֹנָה יְמֵי מִילָה,

Torah, Four are the matriarchs, Three are the patriarchs, Two are the tablets of the Covenant, One is our God Who is in Heaven and on earth.

In some, mostly Western Ashkenazic, families, the preceding is also sung in Yiddish.

I know One! One is our God, Who lives and Who hovers over Heaven and earth.

Two and that is really more, but that one I know! Two are the Tablets of Moses, One is our God, Who lives and Who hovers over Heaven and earth.

Three and that is really more, but that one I know! Three are the Fathers, Two are the Tablets of Moses, One is our God, Who lives and Who hovers over Heaven and earth.

Four and that is really more, but that one I know! Four are the Mothers, Three are the Fathers, Two are the Tablets of Moses, One is our God, Who lives and Who hovers over Heaven and earth.

Five and that is really more, but that one I know! Five are the Books, Four are the Mothers, Three are the Fathers, Two are the Tablets of Moses, One is our God, Who lives and Who hovers over Heaven and earth.

Six and that is really more, but that one I know! Six is the Study, Five are the Books, Four are the Mothers, Three are the Fathers, Two are the Tablets of Moses, One is our God, Who lives and Who hovers over Heaven and earth

Seven and that is really more, but that one I know! Seven is the Rest, Six is the Study, Five are the Books, Four are the Mothers, Three are the Fathers, Two are the Tablets of Moses, One is our God, Who lives and Who hovers over Heaven and earth.

Eight and that is really more, but that one I know! Eight is the Circumcision, Seven is the Rest, Six is the Study, Five are the Books, Four are the Mothers, Three are the Fathers, Two are the Tablets of Moses, One is our God, Who lives and Who hovers over Heaven and earth.

Nine and that is really more, but that one I know! Nine are the Months of Birth, Eight is the Circumcision, Seven is the Rest, Six is the Study, Five are the Books, Four are the Mothers, Three are the Fathers, Two are the Tablets of Moses, One is our God, Who lives and Who hovers over Heaven and earth.

Ten and that is really more, but that one I know! Ten are the Ten Commandments, Nine are the Months of Birth, Eight is the Circumcision, Seven is the Rest, Six is the Study, Five are the Books, Four are the Mothers, Three are the Fathers, Two are the Tablets of Moses, One is our God, Who lives and Who hovers over Heaven and earth.

Eleven and that is really more, but that one I know! Eleven are the Stars, Ten are the Ten Commandments, Nine are the Months of Birth, Eight is the Circumcision, Seven is the Rest, Six is the Study, Five are the Books, Four are the Mothers, Three are the Fathers, Two are the Tablets of Moses, One is our God, Who lives and Who hovers over Heaven and earth.

Twelve and that is really more, but that one I know! Twelve are the Tribes, Eleven are the Stars, Ten are the Ten Commandments, Nine are the Months of Birth, Eight is the Circumcision, Seven is the Rest, Six is the Study, Five are the Books, Four are the Mothers, Three are the Fathers, Two are the Tablets of Moses, One is our God, Who lives and Who hovers over Heaven and earth.

Thirteen and that is really more, but that one I know! Thirteen are the Rules of

שִׁבְעָה יְמֵי שַׁבַּתָּא, שִׁשָּׁה סִדְרֵי מִשְׁנָה, חֲמִשָּׁה חוּמְשֵׁי תוֹרָה, אַרְבַּע אִמָּהוֹת, שְׁלוֹשָׁה אָבוֹת, שְׁנֵי לוּחוֹת הַבְּרִית, אֶחָד אֱלֹהֵינוּ שֶׁבַּשָּׁמַיִם וּבָאָרֶץ.

בכמה משפחות, בעיקר במנהג אשכנז המערבי, שרים את השיר ״אחד מי יודע״ גם בלשון יידיש:

איינס דאַס ווייס איך. איינִיג דאַס איז אונזר גאָט, דער דא לעבט, אונ׳ דער דא שוועבט, אין דעם הימל אונ׳ אויף דער ערד.

צווייא אונ׳ דאַס איז אָבער מער, אונ׳ דאַס זעלביג ווייס איך. צווייא טאַפֿיל מאָזיס, איינִיג דאַס איז אונזר גאָט, דער דא לעבט, אונ׳ דער דא שוועבט, אין דעם הימל אונ׳ אויף דער ערד.

דריי אונ׳ דאַס איז אָבער מער, אונ׳ דאַס זעלביג ווייס איך. דריי זיין די פֿעטר, צווייא טאַפֿיל מאָזיס, איינִיג דאַס איז אונזר גאָט, דער דא לעבט, אונ׳ דער דא שוועבט, אין דעם הימל אונ׳ אויף דער ערד.

פֿיר אונ׳ דאַס איז אָבער מער, אונ׳ דאַס זעלביג ווייס איך. פֿיר זיין די מיטר, דריי זיין די פֿעטר, צווייא טאַפֿיל מאָזיס, איינִיג דאַס איז אונזר גאָט, דער דא לעבט, אונ׳ דער דא שוועבט, אין דעם הימל אונ׳ אויף דער ערד.

פֿינף אונ׳ דאַס איז אָבער מער, אונ׳ דאַס זעלביג ווייס איך. פֿינף זיין די ביכר, פֿיר זיין די מיטר, דריי זיין די פֿעטר, צווייא טאַפֿיל מאָזיס, איינִיג דאַס איז אונזר גאָט, דער דא לעבט, אונ׳ דער דא שוועבט, אין דעם הימל אונ׳ אויף דער ערד.

זעקש אונ׳ דאַס איז אָבער מער, אונ׳ דאַס זעלביג ווייס איך. זעקש זיין די לערנונג, פֿינף זיין די ביכר, פֿיר זיין די מיטר, דריי זיין די פֿעטר, צווייא טאַפֿיל מאָזיס, איינִיג דאַס איז אונזר גאָט, דער דא לעבט, אונ׳ דער דא שוועבט, אין דעם הימל אונ׳ אויף דער ערד.

זיבן אונ׳ דאַס איז אָבער מער, אונ׳ דאַס זעלביג ווייס איך. זיבן זיין די פֿייערונג, זעקש זיין די לערנונג, פֿינף זיין די ביכר, פֿיר זיין די מיטר, דריי זיין די פֿעטר, צווייא טאַפֿיל מאָזיס, איינִיג דאַס איז אונזר גאָט, דער דא לעבט, אונ׳ דער דא שוועבט, אין דעם הימל אונ׳ אויף דער ערד.

אַכט אונ׳ דאַס איז אָבער מער, אונ׳ דאַס זעלביג ווייס איך. אַכט זיין די בעשניידונג, זיבן זיין די פֿייערונג, זעקש זיין די לערנונג, פֿינף זיין די ביכר, פֿיר זיין די מיטר, דריי זיין די פֿעטר, צווייא טאַפֿיל מאָזיס, איינִיג דאַס איז אונזר גאָט, דער דא לעבט, אונ׳ דער דא שוועבט, אין דעם הימל אונ׳ אויף דער ערד.

ניין אונ׳ דאַס איז אָבער מער, אונ׳ דאַס זעלביג ווייס איך. ניין זיין די געווינונ, אַכט זיין די בעשניידונג, זיבן זיין די פֿייערונג, זעקש זיין די לערנונג, פֿינף זיין די ביכר, פֿיר זיין די מיטר, דריי זיין די פֿעטר, צווייא טאַפֿיל מאָזיס, איינִיג דאַס איז אונזר גאָט, דער דא לעבט, אונ׳ דער דא שוועבט, אין דעם הימל אונ׳ אויף דער ערד.

צעהן אונ׳ דאַס איז אָבער מער, אונ׳ דאַס זעלביג ווייס איך. צעהן זיין די צעהן גיבאָט, ניין זיין די געווינונ, אַכט זיין די בעשניידונג, זיבן זיין די פֿייערונג, זעקש זיין די לערנונג, פֿינף זיין די ביכר, פֿיר זיין די מיטר, דריי זיין די פֿעטר, צווייא טאַפֿיל מאָזיס, איינִיג דאַס איז אונזר גאָט, דער דא לעבט, אונ׳ דער דא שוועבט, אין דעם הימל אונ׳ אויף דער ערד.

איילף אונ׳ דאַס איז אָבער מער, אונ׳ דאַס זעלביג ווייס איך. איילף זיין די שטערן, צעהן זיין די צעהן גיבאָט, ניין זיין די געווינונ, אַכט זיין די בעשניידונג, זיבן זיין די פֿייערונג, זעקש זיין די לערנונג, פֿינף זיין די ביכר, פֿיר זיין די מיטר, דריי זיין די פֿעטר, צווייא טאַפֿיל מאָזיס, איינִיג דאַס איז אונזר גאָט, דער דא לעבט, אונ׳ דער דא שוועבט, אין דעם הימל אונ׳ אויף דער ערד.

צוועלף אונ׳ דאַס איז אָבער מער, אונ׳ דאַס זעלביג ווייס איך. צוועלף זיין די געשלעכט, איילף זיין די שטערן, צעהן זיין די צעהן גיבאָט, ניין זיין די געווינונג, אַכט זיין די בעשניידנג, זיבן זיין די פֿייערונג, זעקש זיין די לערנונג, פֿינף זיין די ביכר, פֿיר זיין די מיטר, דריי זיין די פֿעטר, צווייא טאַפֿיל מאָזיס, איינִיג דאַס איז אונזר גאָט, דער דא לעבט, אונ׳ דער דא שוועבט, אין דעם הימל אונ׳ אויף דער ערד.

דרייצעהן אונ׳ דאַס איז אָבער מער, אונ׳ דאַס זעלביג ווייס איך. דרייצעהן זיין די זיטן, צוועלף זיין די געשלעכט, איילף זיין די שטערן, צעהן זיין די צעהן גיבאָט, ניין זיין די געווינונ, אַכט זיין די בעשניידונג, זיבן זיין די פֿייערונג, זעקש זיין די לערנונג, פֿינף זיין די ביכר, פֿיר זיין די מיטר, דריי זיין די פֿעטר, צווייא טאַפֿיל מאָזיס, איינִיג דאַס איז אונזר גאָט, דער דא לעבט, אונ׳ דער דא שוועבט, אין דעם הימל אונ׳ אויף דער ערד.

Conduct, Twelve are the Tribes, Eleven are the Stars, Ten are the Ten Commandments, Nine are the Months of Birth, Eight is the Circumcision, Seven is the Rest, Six is the Study, Five are the Books, Four are the Mothers, Three are the Fathers, Two are the Tablets of Moses, One is our God, Who lives and Who hovers over Heaven and earth.

In the following song, most families of Eastern European Ashkenazic origin, as well as all Italian and Oriental families that customarily sing the song, retain the original *dĕzabbīn* (really meaning "that he sold") instead of the grammatically correct *dizvan* ("that he bought") used in Western European Ashkenazic families.

The Arabic (Syrian-Baghdadi) and Yiddish versions are faithful translations of the Aramaic (with "bought") except that *zuz* "tetradrachma" is translated as *Abbaside coin* in the Arabic and as *penny* in the Yiddish.

A kid, a kid, that my father bought for two *zuz*, a kid, a kid.

There came the cat and ate the kid that my father bought for two *zuz*, a kid, a kid.

There came the dog and bit the cat that ate the kid that my father bought for two *zuz*, a kid, a kid.

There came the stick and hit the dog that bit the cat that ate the kid that my father bought for two *zuz*, a kid, a kid.

There came the fire and burned the stick that hit the dog that bit the cat that ate the kid that my father bought for two *zuz*, a kid, a kid.

There came the water and put out the fire that burned the stick that hit the dog that bit the cat that ate the kid that my father bought for two *zuz*, a kid, a kid.

There came the ox and drank the water that put out the fire that burned the stick that hit the dog that bit the cat that ate the kid that my father bought for two *zuz*, a kid, a kid.

There came the butcher and slaughtered the ox that drank the water that put out the fire that burned the stick that hit the dog that bit the cat that ate the kid that my father bought for two *zuz*, a kid, a kid.

There came the Angel of Death and slaughtered the butcher who slaughtered the ox that drank the water that put out the fire that burned the stick that hit the dog that bit the cat that ate the kid that my father bought for two *zuz*, a kid, a kid.

The Holy, praise to Him, is coming and slaughtering the Angel of Death who slaughtered the ox that drank the water that put out the fire that burned the stick that hit the dog that bit the cat that ate the

חַד גַּדְיָא, חַד גַּדְיָא.

דְּזַבִּין (דִּזְבַן) אַבָּא בִּתְרֵי זוּזֵי, חַד גַּדְיָא, חַד גַּדְיָא.

וְאָתָא שׁוּנְרָא וְאָכְלָה (וְאָכַל) לְגַדְיָא, דְּזַבִּין (דִּזְבַן) אַבָּא בִּתְרֵי זוּזֵי, חַד גַּדְיָא, חַד גַּדְיָא.

וְאָתָא כַּלְבָּא וְנָשַׁךְ לְשׁוּנְרָא, דְּאָכְלָה (דְּאָכַל) לְגַדְיָא, דְּזַבִּין (דִּזְבַן) אַבָּא בִּתְרֵי זוּזֵי, חַד גַּדְיָא, חַד גַּדְיָא.

וְאָתָא חוּטְרָא וְהִכָּה לְכַלְבָּא, דְּנָשַׁךְ לְשׁוּנְרָא, דְּאָכְלָה (דְּאָכַל) לְגַדְיָא, דְּזַבִּין (דִּזְבַן) אַבָּא בִּתְרֵי זוּזֵי, חַד גַּדְיָא, חַד גַּדְיָא.

וְאָתָא נוּרָא וְשָׂרַף לְחוּטְרָא, דְּהִכָּה לְכַלְבָּא, דְּנָשַׁךְ לְשׁוּנְרָא, דְּאָכְלָה (דְּאָכַל) לְגַדְיָא, דְּזַבִּין (דִּזְבַן) אַבָּא בִּתְרֵי זוּזֵי, חַד גַּדְיָא, חַד גַּדְיָא.

וְאָתָא מַיָּא וְכָבָה לְנוּרָא, דְּשָׂרַף לְחוּטְרָא, דְּהִכָּה לְכַלְבָּא, דְּנָשַׁךְ לְשׁוּנְרָא, דְּאָכְלָה (דְּאָכַל) לְגַדְיָא, דְּזַבִּין (דִּזְבַן) אַבָּא בִּתְרֵי זוּזֵי, חַד גַּדְיָא, חַד גַּדְיָא.

וְאָתָא תוּרָא וְשָׁתָא לְמַיָּא, דְּכָבָה לְנוּרָא, דְּשָׂרַף לְחוּטְרָא, דְּהִכָּה לְכַלְבָּא, דְּנָשַׁךְ לְשׁוּנְרָא, דְּאָכְלָה (דְּאָכַל) לְגַדְיָא, דְּזַבִּין (דִּזְבַן) אַבָּא בִּתְרֵי זוּזֵי, חַד גַּדְיָא, חַד גַּדְיָא.

וְאָתָא הַשּׁוֹחֵט וְשָׁחַט לְתוּרָא, דְּשָׁתָא לְמַיָּא, דְּכָבָה לְנוּרָא, דְּשָׂרַף לְחוּטְרָא, דְּהִכָּה לְכַלְבָּא, דְּנָשַׁךְ לְשׁוּנְרָא, דְּאָכְלָה (דְּאָכַל) לְגַדְיָא, דְּזַבִּין (דִּזְבַן) אַבָּא בִּתְרֵי זוּזֵי, חַד גַּדְיָא, חַד גַּדְיָא.

וְאָתָא מַלְאַךְ הַמָּוֶת וְשָׁחַט לְשׁוֹחֵט, דְּשָׁחַט לְתוּרָא, דְּשָׁתָא לְמַיָּא, דְּכָבָה לְנוּרָא, דְּשָׂרַף לְחוּטְרָא, דְּהִכָּה לְכַלְבָּא, דְּנָשַׁךְ לְשׁוּנְרָא, דְּאָכְלָה (דְּאָכַל) לְגַדְיָא, דְּזַבִּין (דִּזְבַן) אַבָּא בִּתְרֵי זוּזֵי, חַד גַּדְיָא, חַד גַּדְיָא.

וְאָתָא הַקָּדוֹשׁ בָּרוּךְ הוּא וְשָׁחַט לְמַלְאַךְ הַמָּוֶת, דְּשָׁחַט לְשׁוֹחֵט, דְּשָׁחַט לְתוּרָא, דְּשָׁתָא לְמַיָּא, דְּכָבָה לְנוּרָא, דְּשָׂרַף לְחוּטְרָא, דְּהִכָּה לְכַלְבָּא, דְּנָשַׁךְ לְשׁוּנְרָא, דְּאָכְלָה (דְּאָכַל) לְגַדְיָא, דְּזַבִּין (דִּזְבַן) אַבָּא בִּתְרֵי זוּזֵי, חַד גַּדְיָא, חַד גַּדְיָא.

kid that my father bought for two *zuz*, a kid, a kid.

בכמה משפחות, בעיקר במנהג אשכנז המערבי, שרים את השיר "חד גדיא" גם בלשון יידיש:

איין ציקליין, איין ציקליין, דאַס דאָ האָט געקויפט דאָס פֿעטערליין אום צווייא פפֿענונג, איין ציקליין, איין ציקליין.

דא קאם דאס קעצליין אונ' עסט דאס ציקליין, דאַס דאָ האָט געקויפט דאָס פֿעטערליין אום צווייא פפֿענונג, איין ציקליין, איין ציקליין.

דא קאם דאס הינטליין אונ' ביס דאס קעצליין, דאס דא האט גיגעסן דאס ציקליין, דאַס דאָ האָט געקויפט דאָס פֿעטערליין אום צווייא פפֿענונג, איין ציקליין, איין ציקליין.

דא קאם דאס שטעקליין אונ' שלוג דאס הינטליין, דאס דא האט גיביסן דאס קעצליין, דאס דא האט גיגעסן דאס ציקליין, דאַס דאָ האָט געקויפט דאָס פֿעטערליין אום צווייא פפֿענונג, איין ציקליין, איין ציקליין.

דא קאם דאס פֿייערליין אונ' פֿארברענט דאס שטעקליין, דאס דא האט גישלאגן דאס הינטליין, דאס דא האט גיביסן דאס קעצליין, דאס דא האט גיגעסן דאס ציקליין, דאַס דאָ האָט געקויפט דאָס פֿעטערליין אום צווייא פפֿענונג, איין ציקליין, איין ציקליין.

דא קאם דאס וואסערליין אונ' פֿארלעשט דאס פֿייערליין, דאס דא האט פֿארברענט דאס שטעקליין, דאס דא האט גישלאגן דאס הינטליין, דאס דא האט גיביסן דאס קעצליין, דאס דא האט גיגעסן דאס ציקליין, דאַס דאָ האָט געקויפט דאָס פֿעטערליין אום צווייא פפֿענונג, איין ציקליין, איין ציקליין.

דא קאם דיר אָקס אונ' טרונק דאס וואסערליין, דאס דא האט פֿארלעשט. דאס פֿייערליין, דאס דא האט פֿארברענט דאס שטעקליין, דאס דא האט גישלאגן דאס הינטליין, דאס דא האט גיביסן דאס קעצליין, דאס דא האט גיגעסן דאס ציקליין, דאַס דאָ האָט געקויפט דאָס פֿעטערליין אום צווייא פפֿענונג, איין ציקליין, איין ציקליין.

דא קאם דער שוחט אונ' שעחט דען אָקסן, דער דא האט אויס געטרונקן דאס וואסערליין, דאס דא האט פֿארלעשט דאס פֿייערליין, דאס דא האט פֿארברענט דאס שטעקליין, דאס דא האט גישלאגן דאס הינטליין, דאס דא האט גיביסן דאס קעצליין, דאס דא האט גיגעסן דאס ציקליין, דאַס דאָ האָט געקויפט דאָס פֿעטערליין אום צווייא פפֿענונג, איין ציקליין, איין ציקליין.

דא קאם דער מלאך המות אונ' שעחט דעם שוחט, דער דא האט גישעחט דען אָקסן, דער דא האט אויס געטרונקן דאס וואסערליין, דאס דא האט פֿארלעשט דאס פֿייערליין, דאס דא האט פֿארברענט דאס שטעקליין, דאס דא האט גישלאגן דאס הינטליין, דאס דא האט גיביסן דאס קעצליין, דאס דא האט גיגעסן דאס ציקליין, דאַס דאָ האָט געקויפט דאָס פֿעטערליין אום צווייא פפֿענונג, איין ציקליין, איין ציקליין.

דא קאם אונזר ליבר הער גאָט אונ' שעחט דען מלאך המות, דער דא האט גישעחט דעם שוחט, דער דא האט גישעחט דען אָקסן, דער דא האט אויס געטרונקן דאס וואסערליין, דאס דא האט פֿארלעשט דאס פֿייערליין, דאס דא האט פֿארברענט דאס שטעקליין, דאס דא האט גישלאגן דאס הינטליין, דאס דא האט גיביסן דאס קעצליין, דאס דא האט גיגעסן דאס ציקליין, דאַס דאָ האָט געקויפט דאָס פֿעטערליין אום צווייא פפֿענונג, איין ציקליין, איין ציקליי.

המנהג בסוריה וברוב בבל לשיר את שיר "חד גדיא" בלשון ערב:

ואחד גֹדי, ואחד גֹדי, אלדי אשתרא לי אבוי פֿי עבסייתין, ואחד גֹדי, ואחד גֹדי.

וגֹא אלבזונה ואכלת אלגֹדי, אלדי אשתרא לי אבוי פֿי עבסייתין, ואחד גֹדי, ואחד גֹדי.

וגֹא אלכלב ועץֿ אלבזונה, אלדי אכלת אלגֹדי, אלדי אשתרא לי אבוי פֿי עבסייתין, ואחד גֹדי, ואחד גֹדי.

וגֹא אלעצאייא וצֹרבת אלכלב, אלדי עץֿ אלבזונה, אלדי אכלת אלגֹדי, אלדי אשתרא לי אבוי פֿי עבסייתין, ואחד גֹדי, ואחד גֹדי.

וגֹא אלנאר וחרק אלעצאייא, אלדי צֹרבת אלכלב, אלדי עץֿ אלבזונה, אלדי אכלת אלגֹדי, אלדי אשתרא לי אבוי פֿי עבסייתין, ואחד גֹדי, ואחד גֹדי.

וגֹא אלמא וטפֿא ללנאר, אלדי חרק אלעצאייא, אלדי צֹרבת אלכלב, אלדי עץֿ אלבזונה, אלדי אכלת אלגֹדי, אלדי אשתרא לי אבוי פֿי עבסייתין, ואחד גֹדי, ואחד גֹדי.

וגֹא אלתור וסקא ללמא, אלדי טפֿא ללנאר, אלדי חרק אלעצאייא, אלדי צֹרבת אלכלב, אלדי עץֿ אלבזונה, אלדי אכלת אלגֹדי, אלדי אשתרא לי אבוי פֿי עבסייתין, ואחד גֹדי, ואחד גֹדי.

וגֹא אלדבאח ודבח ללתור, אלדי סקא ללמא, אלדי טפֿא ללנאר, אלדי חרק אלעצאייא, אלדי צֹרבת אלכלב, אלדי עץֿ אלבזונה, אלדי אכלת אלגֹדי, אלדי אשתרא לי אבוי פֿי עבסייתין, ואחד גֹדי, ואחד גֹדי.

וגֹא מלך אלמות ודבח ללדבאח, אלדי דבח ללתור, אלדי סקא ללמא, אלדי טפֿא ללנאר, אלדי חרק אלעצאייא, אלדי צֹרבת אלכלב, אלדי עץֿ אלבזונה, אלדי אכלת אלגֹדי, אלדי אשתרא לי אבוי פֿי עבסייתין, ואחד גֹדי, ואחד גֹדי.

וגֹא אלמקדס תבארך הוא ודבח למלך אלמות, אלדי דבח ללדבאח, אלדי דבח ללתור, אלדי סקא ללמא, אלדי טפֿא ללנאר, אלדי חרק אלעצאייא, אלדי צֹרבת אלכלב, אלדי עץֿ אלבזונה, אלדי אכלת אלגֹדי, אלדי אשתרא לי אבוי פֿי עבסייתין, ואחד גֹדי, ואחד גֹדי.

Yemenite Passover Songs of Mori Salim Shabazi

Instruction for the *Seder*

Take the cup into your hand to start the praise,
  And give praise for the fruit of the planted vine.
But when the glory of the feast is on Sabbath,
  You should start first reciting *wayĕkhullu.*
After that read and tell,
  The praise of God and the wonders of the All-knowing.
So you shall finish and perform the institution,
  Of our sages and the great Synhedrion.
But if you fail to mention three,
  You will not have done your duty for the redemption.
These are *Pesaḥ*, also *maẓẓah* and *maror,*
  Around the table you shall form a circle.
In addition, on the table you should have greens,
  And *ḥazeret*, all well ordered.
Also, Four you should drink in joy,
  And pray to God.
Then you may eat, reclining on your left side,
  And give praise to God for delivery and redemption!

Song for Passover Night

Give praise to God who saves His beloved,
  On this day of good news for the Jews!
A new song to God sing on this day,
  When the royal people left the house of slaves.
On this day the fathers of God's assembly were saved,
  And the day is still destined to save the bound.
In this night the Egyptians were delivered to Death,
  And the captured took their captors.
In this night the firstborn were slain,
  And the armies left with their booty.
On this day the happy ones put on mourning dress,
  And the downtrodden had joy in their hearts.

שירי מרי שלום שבזי לחג הפסח

אזהרה לפסח

בְּיָדְךָ כּוֹס קְחָה רֵאשִׁית תְּהִלָּה
וּבָרֵךְ עַל פְּרִי גֶּפֶן שְׁתוּלָה
וְאִם יָבוֹא כְּבוֹד מוֹעֵד בְּשַׁבָּת
תְּהִי מַתְחִיל בְּוַיְכוּלּוּ תְחִלָּה
וְאַחַר כֵּן תְּהִי קוֹרֵא וּמַגִּיד
שְׁבָח הָאֵל וּמוֹפֵת רַב עֲלִילָה
וְכָךְ תַּשְׁלִים וְתַסְדִּירָה בְּתִיקּוּן
חֲכָמֵינוּ וְסַנְהַדְרֵי גְדוֹלָה
וְאִם לֹא תְהֶיֶה זוֹכֵר שְׁלוֹשָׁה
כְּלֹא תֵצֵא יְדֵי חוֹבַת גְּאוּלָה
וְהֵם פֶּסַח וְגַם מַצָּה וּמָרוֹר
סְבִיב שֻׁלְחָן יְהִי לָךְ כַּעֲגוּלָה
בְּעוֹד יֵשׁ לָךְ בְּתוֹךְ שֻׁלְחָן יְרָקוֹת
וַחֲזֶרֶת עֲרוֹךְ כּוּלָּה בְּלוּלָה
וְעוֹד אַרְבַּע תְּהִי שׁוֹתֶה בְשִׂמְחָה
וַאֲפִילוּ לְאֵל תִּשְׁאַל שְׁאֵלָה
וְאָז תֹּאכַל בְּמֵסַב עַל שְׂמֹאלָךְ
וְתוֹדֶה אֵל עֲלֵי פוּרְקַן גְּאוּלָּה.

שיר לליל פסח

תְּנוּ תוֹדָה לְאֵל גּוֹאֵל יְדִידִים
בְּיוֹם זֶה יוֹם בְּשׂוֹרָה לַיְהוּדִים
וְשִׁיר חָדָשׁ לְאֵל הָבוּ בְּיוֹם בּוֹ
מְלָכִים יָצְאוּ מִבֵּית עֲבָדִים
בְּיוֹם זֶה נִגְאֲלוּ אָבוֹת עֲדַת אֵל
וּבוֹ תִהְיֶה לְהִגָּאֵל עֲגִידִים
בְּלֵיל זֶה נִמְסְרוּ מִצְרִים לְמָוֶת
וּבוֹ הַלּוֹכְדִים שָׁבוּ לְכוּדִים
בְּלֵיל זֶה הָיְתָה מַכַּת בְּכוֹרוֹת
וּבוֹ עִם הַשְּׁבִי יָצְאוּ גְּדוּדִים
בְּיוֹם זֶה הַשְּׂמֵחִים חָגְרוּ שַׂק
וּבוֹ גִּיל חָגְרוּ לְבּוֹת מְרוּדִים

In that night they ate *mazzah* and roast,
  Assembled for the help of God.
In that night their ears heard good news,
  But noises of terror were in the ears of the oppressor.
He who redeemed on this Passover His prisoners,
  And quieted the much-displaced people.
May He lift a second time His right arm for the poor,
  Who are robbed and in every oppressor's hand.
May He make the noble daughter wear embroideries,
  For her may He bind fat sacrifices at the Place!
May He build His city for His people,
  And make them dwell in joy, He Who houses unmarrieds!

Song for Passover

I shall sing and rejoice, give praise to God, and prepare offering on Passover Day!
Praised be God, Master of masters, Who saved sons on Passover Day!
He bared His secret to the seed of His friend through His servant on Passover Day!
He instructed Moses to perform the sign; wonders He did on Passover Day!
He smote Pharaoh, broke his arm, cut off his seed on Passover Day!
He led out His people from among that nation, for His name's sake on Passover Day!
He remembered His grace for His servants and led out His dear ones on Passover Day!
He had mercy on them and their children and chose them on Passover Day!
He purified the meritorious, to give to the straightforward three crowns on Passover Day!
The beloved left the house of slaves and offered unblemished gifts on Passover Day!
Peace be on you and all your sons from your God on Passover Day!

בְּלֵיל זֶה אָכְלוּ מַצָּה וְצָלִי
הֲיוֹתָם עַל יְשׁוּעוֹת אֵל וְעוֹדִים
בְּלֵיל זֶה שָׁמְעָה אָזְנָם בְּשׂוֹרוֹת
וְאָזְנֵי צָר מְלֵאוֹת קוֹל פְּחָדִים
אֲשֶׁר גָּאַל בְּפֶסַח זֶה אֲסִירָיו
וְהִשְׁקִט עַם אֲשֶׁר שָׂבְעוּ נְדוּדִים
יְמִינוֹ יַחֲשׂוֹף שֵׁנִית לְדַלִּים
אֲשֶׁר הֵמָּה בְּיַד כָּל צָר שְׁדוּדִים
וּבַת נָדִיב יְהִי מַלְבִּישׁ רְקָמוֹת
וִיִקְשׁוֹר לָהּ מְקוֹם עוֹלָה רְבִיבִים
וְיִבְנֶה עִיר תְּהִלָּתוֹ לְעַמּוֹ
וְיוֹשִׁיבֵם בְּגִיל מוֹשִׁיב יְחִידִים.

שיר ליום הפסח

אָגִיל וְאֶשְׂמַח וְלָאֵל אֲשַׁבֵּחַ וְאֶזְבַּח זֶבַח בְּיוֹם הַפֶּסַח
בָּרוּךְ אֱלֹהִים אֲדוֹן הָאֲדוֹנִים שֶׁהִצִּיל בָּנִים בְּיוֹם הַפֶּסַח
גִּלָּה סוֹדוֹ לְזֶרַע יְדִידוֹ עַל יַד עַבְדּוֹ בְּיוֹם הַפֶּסַח
דִּבֵּר לְמֹשֶׁה הָאוֹת תַּעֲשֶׂה וְנִסִּים עָשָׂה בְּיוֹם הַפֶּסַח
הִכָּה פַּרְעֹה וְשִׁבֵּר זְרֹעוֹ וְהִכְרִית זַרְעוֹ בְּיוֹם הַפֶּסַח
וְהוֹצִיא לְעַמּוֹ מִבֵּין לְאוּמּוֹ וְעָשָׂה לִשְׁמוֹ בְּיוֹם הַפֶּסַח
זָכַר חֲסָדָיו לְמַעַן עֲבָדָיו וְהוֹצִיא יְדִידָיו בְּיוֹם הַפֶּסַח
חָמַל עֲלֵיהֶם וְעַל בְּנֵיהֶם וּבָחַר בָּהֶם בְּיוֹם הַפֶּסַח
טִהֵר כְּשֵׁרִים לְהַנְחִיל יְשָׁרִים שְׁלוֹשָׁה כְּתָרִים בְּיוֹם הַפֶּסַח
יָצְאוּ יְדִידִים מִבֵּית עֲבָדִים וְשָׁחֲטוּ תְּמִימִים בְּיוֹם הַפֶּסַח
וְשָׁלוֹם עֲלֵיכֶם וְעַל כָּל בְּנֵיכֶם מֵאֱלֹהֵיכֶם בְּיוֹם הַפֶּסַח

Utqul Djerba

In Djerba and nearby communities, the following Arabic *Utqul Djerba* or *Utqul Gafṣa* is inserted after "Originally, our forefathers were idolators" to tell the story of Abraham's recognition of the Unity of God.

And you should tell him: My son, in the beginning our forefathers worshiped idols and signs beginning, as pronounced by the Sages, may their memory be a blessing, in the days of Enosh by the error of the common people and of the nobles. They began a false worship; they worshiped stars and spheres and they made temples and images of wood, stone, silver, and gold, until they included all of mankind. They came, assembled, and arranged this perversity to be worshiped. They asserted that the images could cause good or evil. This continued for a long time and so the name of God was forgotten from being mentioned and there did not remain one who knew God, the Most High, until there came Abraham, may peace be on him, and taught people the worship of God and His Oneness; so said the sages, may their memory be a blessing. At the time when Abraham, may peace be on him, was born, the astrologers saw a star arise which swallowed three stars. They marched to sultan Nimrod and said to him: "Our master, at this moment Teraḥ is raising a son, and see what a significant wonder happened concerning heaven, concerning stars: there arose one star and swallowed three stars and we know, our master, he is that child, who will destroy the king and pervert religion." Nimrod sent for Teraḥ and said to him: "Teraḥ, I want your child for a thousand pieces of gold; bring him for us to kill him." Teraḥ said to him: "Master, I will give you a simile for this case. A simile of a horse to whom people said, 'We shall give you a *cafiz* (a Tunisian dry measure, about 131 gallons) of oats and come, we shall cut off your head.' The horse answered them: 'How stupid! If you cut off my head, who will eat the oats?' So it is here. If you kill my child, how can the thousand pieces of gold be useful for me?" They said to him: "Blessed to old age, this one shall die and you will have another child in his stead." He said to them: "How can I know that I will have a child instead of him or what I will have as a child?" Then, when he saw strength in his child, he locked him up and kept him alone. There, our father Abraham, may peace be on him, grew up and became a child of three years. He became distinguished for his knowledge of the heavens and the stars. He saw the sun rising in the East and setting in the West. He reasoned

ותקול ג׳רבה

שנוהגים לאומרו במנהג האי גרבה אחרי הפיסקא ״מתחלה עובדי עבודה זרה היו אבותינו״.

וּתְקוּל לוֹ יָא בְנִי. מִן אַוְּולָא כַּאנוּ אַבַּאתְנָא. עָאבְדִין לְאַצְנָאם וּלְאוֹתָן. לְאָן קָאלוּ לַחְכָמִים זִכְרָם לַבְרָכָה. פִּי אִיָּיאם אֱנוֹשׁ. גַּלְטוֹ אַנָּאס גַּלְט אָן עְצִים. וְצָארוֹ יְעַבְדוֹ עֲבוֹדָה זָרָה. וִיְעַבְדוֹ לַכְּוָאכֶּב וּלְפְלוּךְ. וַעְמְלוֹ לְהוֹם בְיוּת. וַעְמַלוֹ פִיהוֹם תַצְוִירָת מִן לַכְשַׁב וּמִן לַחְגַר וּמִן פַּצָּא וּדְהָב. חַתָּא צָארַת גְמִיע אַנָּאס. תְגִי וּתְתְגַמָּאע וִישַׁסְדוֹ לְדוּךְ לַמְעָאבַד. וִיקוּלוֹ הָאד הַצוֹרָה תַפְעַל לְכִיר וְשַׁר. פַלְמַאן טָאלַת לְמַדָּא וּטָאלַת לְאַיָּיאם. וּתְנַסָּא אֱסַם אַלְלָה מִן פְּמָאמהוֹם. וְלָא בְקָא חַד יָעְרַף אַלְלָה תוֹעֲאלָא. חַתָּא גָא אַבְרָהָם אָבִינוּ עְלֵיהּ אַסְלָאם. וְעַלַּם אַנָּאס עְבָאדַת אַלְלָה וּתוֹחִידוֹ. בְּאַן קָאלוֹ לַחְכָמִים זִכְרָם לַבְרָכָה. וַקְתְ אַן תְוָואלֶד אַבְרָהָם אָבִינוּ עְלֵיהּ אַסְלָאם. רָאיוּ לְמַסְתַנְגְמִין חַתָּא קָאם כּוֹכָב וָאחַד. וּבְלַע תַלְתְ כְּוָואכֶּב. מְשָׁאיוּ לְעַנְד נִמְרוֹד הַצֶּלְטָאן. וְקָאלוֹ לוֹ יָא מוֹלָאנָא. זְדָאד הַסָּאעָא וַלְד עַנְד תֶרַח. וּרִינָא עְגַב אַן עְצִים פִּי אַסְמָא. וּפִי אַנְגוּם. חַתָּא קָאם כּוֹכָב וָאחַד וּבְלַע תַלְתְ כְּוָואכַּב. וּאוֹחְנָא עָארְפִין יָא מוֹלָאנָא. אַנְהוּ הָאד לְוַלְד יַכְרַב לְמַלְךְ וִיפַסַּד הַדִּין. בְעַת נִמְרוֹד אוֹרָא תֶרַח. וְקָאל לוֹ יָא תֶרַח אַיָּיאךְ תְבִיע לִי וַלְדַךְ בְאָלַף דְהַב וְהָאת נְקַטְלוֹה. קָאל לוֹ תֶרַח יָא מוֹלָאִי. נְמְתַּל לַךְ פִּי הָאדָא. מְתַל לַחְצָאן אַלְדִי קָאלוּ לוֹ הַנָּאס. נַעְטִיווּךְ קְפִיז שְׁעִיר. וְהָאת נְקַטְעוֹ רָאצַךְ. קָאל לְהוֹם לַחְצָאן. יָא חַמָּק אִידָא קְטַעְתוֹ רָאצִי מִן יָאכֶּל אַשְׁעִיר. כְּדָאלַךְ הָאנָא. אִידָא קְטַלְתוֹ וַלְדִי הָאשׁ יְנְפַעְנִי אָלֶף דְהָב. קָאלוֹ לוֹ יָא מְבָארַךְ לְחָאל. הָאדָא יְמוּת וְתוֹלֶד וַלְד אָכוֹר גֵירוֹ. קָאל לְהוֹם אָנָא מָא נַעְרַף נוֹלֶד גֵירוֹ אָוו מָא נוֹלֶד. פַלְמַן רָאווֹה שַׁד עְלָא וָלְדוֹ. סַכְּתוֹ וְכַלָּאווֹה. חַתָּא כְּבַר אַבְרָהָם אָבִינוּ עְלֵיהּ אַלסְלָאם. וְצָאר וַלְד תַלְתְ סְנִין. וּצָאר יַתְמֵיֶּיז פִּי עַלְמוֹ פִּי אַסְמָא. וּפִי אַנְגוּם, וּרָא אַסֶמְס תִזְרַק מִן הַשַּׁרְק. וּתְגִב פַלְגַרְבְ. צָן פִּי כָּאטְרוֹ. אַן אַסָמְס הוֹ לְאֵילָהּ. פַלְמַן מְשָׁא אַנְהָאר. וּזַרְקֶת לִקְמַר וְלִכְּוָואכֶּב. צָן פִּי כָּאטרוֹ. אָן הוֹם אַלְדִי כַּלְקוֹ אַדַּנְיָיא. פַלְמַן

that, if the sun were a god, why would the light go away and become dark [blue] for moonlight and the stars? He reasoned that, if they [the stars] were the masters who created all earthly things, why does daybreak shine and the sun rise? He, may peace be on him, said that an intelligent person must confirm the truth by one's own mind that they [sun and stars] are created of the same kind, and a superior power makes them go according to His will. Then, when he had grasped this by his intelligence, God appeared to him in His radiance and said to him: "Abraham, how you do excel in your knowledge of heavens and stars! I am He Who created you, created them, and created all heavens and earths." At that moment, Abraham proceeded to oppose his father and said to him: "My father, please inform me who is the master who created the world." He said to him: "My son, the idols in the house, they are the masters who created the world." He said to him: "My father, noble is their law for me; let us offer a sacrifice to them so they shall be satisfied before me." Thereupon his father entered the house of the gods of wood, stone, silver, and gold, but he went to his mother and said to her: "My mother! Come and prepare a good meal for me to offer it to those idols so that they will be satisfied." Thereupon his mother went and prepared what he was asking for. He set it before them and not one of them extended his hand to eat. He, peace be on him, said: "An intelligent person must confirm that they do not see and do not hear; like them are those who make them!" and he courageously burned them. Then his father came up to him and saw them burned. He said to him: "My son! What kind of evil deed did you do!" He said to him: "My father! I had nothing to do with this! Rather they were quarreling about their food and they burned each other!" He said to him: "How stupid! Can they talk or move, or can they do good or bad? How can you say these words?" He said to him: "My father! May your ear hear what your mouth says. Why do you worship those whose mouth has no voice and no power? And you forsake the eternal God who created me and created you and created all heavens and lands!" When his father heard his speech, he ran up to Sultan Nimrod and said to him: "My lord! Examine what my son did today!" Nimrod said to Abraham: "What is the evil deed that you did?" He said to him: "My master! I did not do anything but they quarreled about their food and burned each other." He said to him: "What nonsense! Can they talk or move or do good or bad? How can you say such words?" He said to him: "My lord! May your ear hear what your mouth says! Those whose mouth has no voice and no power, why do you worship them? And you forsake the eternal God who created me and created you and created all heavens and lands!" Then Nimrod said

צְבַח אַצְבָאח. וּזְרַקְת אַסָמְסְ קָאל עְלֵיהּ אַסְלָאם. דְלְחִין תְחַקַּק
עַנְדִי אַן הוֹם מַכְלוֹקִין מִתְלִי. וּלְהוֹם אֵילָהּ יְמַשֵּׁיהוֹם כִּיף יְרִיד.
פַּלְמַן הוֹא יַתְחַדֶּת מְעָא עַקְלוֹ. תְגַלָּא עְלֵיהּ הַרַב צֶבְחָאנוּ. וְקָאל לוֹ
יָא אַבְרָהָם מָאלַךְ תָתְמֵיֶּז פִּי עַלְמֶךְ. פִּי אַסְמָא. וּפִי אַנְגוֹם. אָנָא
הוּוָא אַלְדִי כְלַקְתַךְ וּכְלַקְתְהוֹם. וּכְלַקְתְ גְמִיע אַסְמָאוָאת וּלַאְרָאצִי.
פִּי דִיךְ אָסָאעָא. מְשָׁא אַבְרָהָם לַעְנְד אוּבוּהּ. וְקָאל לוֹ יָא אֵיבֵי.
נְחַב תְכַבַּרְנִי הָאשְׁכוֹן אַלְדִי כְלַק אַדִּנְיָיא. קָאל לוֹ יָא בְנִי. תַמָּא
מְעָאבַד עַנְדִי פַלְבִית. הוֹם אַלְדִי כַלְקוֹ אַדִנְיָיא. קָאל לוֹ יָא אֵיבִי.
נְחַב תְוָורִיהוֹם לִי. בָּאש נְקַרַב לְהוֹם קָרְבָן. אַיָיאךְ יְרְצָאוו עַנְדִי.
תַם דַכְּלוֹ אוּבוּה לְבִית מַלְיָיאנָא שִׁי כְשַׁב שִׁי חְגַר וּשִׁי פַצָּא וּדְהַב
תַם מְשָׁא לְעַנְדְ אַמּוֹ. וְקָאל לְהָא יָא אַמִּי. קוּמִי צַנְעִי לִי מְעִישָׁא
טַייְבָא. נְקַרְבְּהָא לְדוּךְ לַמְעָאבַד. אַיָיאךְ יְרְצָאיו עַנְדִי. תַם קָאמַת
אַמּוֹ וּצְנְעַת לוֹ מַא רָאד. וַקְדַּם לְהוֹם לְיָאכְּלוֹ וְלָא חַד מִנְהוֹם מַד
יַדּוֹ לְיָאכַּל. קָאל עְלֵיהּ אַסְלָאם. דַלְחִין תְחַקַּק עַנְדִי. אָן הוֹם מָא
יְרָאיוֹ וְלָא יְסַמְעוֹ. כַּמְתַלְהוֹם יְכוֹן פָּאעְלְהוֹם. כַּדָא וָחְרְקְהוֹם. חַתָּא
גָא אוּבוּה. וּצָאבְהוֹם מַחְרוּקִין. קָאל לוֹ יָא בְנִי. הָאשׁ הָאד לְעַמְלָא
אָלְדִי עְמַלְתְ. קָאל יָא אִיבִי. אָנָא מָא עְמַלְתְ שָׁיְ מִן הָאדָא. אַלָּא
הוֹם יִתְכָאצְמוֹ עְלָא הֵטְעָאם. וּחַרְקוֹ בַעְצְהוֹם בָאעְץָ. קָאל לוֹ יָא
חַמָּק וָאשׁ הוֹם יִתְכַּלְמוֹ. אָו יִתְחַרְכּוּ אָו יִפַעְלוֹ כִּיר אָו שַׁר. חַתָּא
תְקוּל הָאד לְקוּל. קָאל לוֹ יָא אֵיבִי. תַסְמַע וַדְנַךְ מָה פוּמַךְ יְקוּל.
אִידָא מָא פִיהוֹם לַא קַוָּוא וְלָא גְבְרָוָּוא. עַלָאשׁ תְעַבְדוּהוֹם.
וּתְתַרְכּוּ לְאֵילָא לְאַזְלִי אַלְדִי כְלַקְנִי וּכַלְקַךְ וּכְלַק גְמִיע הַסְמָאוָואת
וּלַאְרָאצִי. כִּיף סְמָאע אוּבוּהּ כְלָאמוֹ. רַפְעוֹ לְעַנְדְ נַמְרוּד הַצֻּלְטָאן.
קָאל לוֹ יַא מוּלָאִי. נְצַר מָא עְמַל בְנִי לְיוֹם. קָאל נַמְרוּד לְאָבְרָהָם.
הָאשׁ הָאד לְעַמְלָא אַלְדִי עְמַלְתְ. קָאל לוֹ יָא סִידִי. אָנָא מָא עְמַלְתְ
שַׁי מִן הָאדָה אַלָּא הוֹם תְכַאצְמוּ עְלָא הַטְעָאם וּחַרְקוֹ בַעְצְהוּם
בָאעְץְ. קָאל לוֹ יָא חַמָּק. וָאשׁ הוּם יִתְכַּלְמוּ אָו יִתְחַרְכּוּ אָו יִפָעְלוֹ
כִּיר אָו שַׁר. חַתָּא תְקוּל הָאד לְקוּל. קָאל לוֹ יָא מוּלָאִי. תִסְמָע
וַדְנָךְ מָה פוּמָךְ יְקוּל. אִידָא מָא פִיהוֹם לַא קַוָּוא וְלָא גְבְרָוָּוא.
עַלָאשׁ תְעַבְדוּהוֹם. וּתְתַרְכּוּ לְאֵילָא לְאַזְלִי אַלְדִי כְלַקְנִי וּכַלְקַךְ
וּכְלַק גְמִיע הַסְמָאוָואת וּלַאְרָאצִי. קָאל נַמְרוּד לְאַבְרָהָם. אָנָא
הוּוָא אַלְדִי כְלַקְתַךְ וּכְלַקְתְהוֹם. וּכְלַקְתְ גְמִיע הַסְמָאוָאת וּלַאְרָאצִי.

to Abraham: "I am he who created you and created them and created all heavens and earths!" He said to him: "My master! If you are truly correct, command the sun to rise in the West and set in the East. Can you really do such things? The eternal God who ordered me to burn your idols, He will decree for me against you and He will burn you!" At this time, Nimrod said to his agents: "This one, if we let him go free and alive from judgment, he will destroy the king and pervert religion. There is no choice but to burn him." As soon as the burning could be arranged, they took our father Abraham, may peace be upon him, and threw him into a burning fiery oven. Then God appeared to him in His splendor and liberated him in his magnanimity and His glory and he walked out from there unharmed. Then all the people saw the miracle and he, may peace be upon him, gave abundantly and taught people the worship of God and His Oneness. The sages, may their memory be a blessing, added this precious note: From the devotion that Abraham our father, may peace be upon him, observed, and from his being attached alone from all the world to His side, and his perspicacity in recognizing the Oneness of the Eternal One, this deed freed him from his calamity, and he taught people the worship of God and the belief in His Oneness. And that is the proof: ויאמר יהושע אל כל העם , its translation: And Joshua said to the entire people: So says Allah, the God of Israel: On the other side of the River lived your fathers, from the beginning, Teraḥ the father of Abraham and the father of Naḥor, and they practiced foreign kinds of worships. And I took Abraham from the other side of the River and led him through the entire land of Syria and made plentiful his progeny and gave him Isaac, and to Isaac I gave Jacob and Esau and gave the mountain of Seir to Esau as inheritance but Jacob and his sons descended into Egypt.

קָאל לוֹ יָא סִידִי. אַנְכָּאן אַנְתִין עְלָא לְחַק. אְמַר לְסַמְס תַזְרַק מְן לְגַרְבְ וּתְגִיב פְּשַׁרְק. וּכָּאן מָא עְמַלְתְ שַׁיְ מְן הָאדָא. לְאִילָהּ אַלְדִי קַצַּרְנִי עְלָא מְעַבְדַךְ וַחְרַקתְהוֹם. יְקַצַּרְנִי חַתָּא עְלִיךְ וּנְחַרְקַךְ. פִּי דַאלַךְ הַסָּאעָא. קָאל נַמְרוֹד לַעְמָאלְתוֹ. הָאדָא אַנְכָּאן כַּלִּינָאהּ חַי פַּדִּנְיָיא יְכַרַב לְמַלְךְ וִיפַסַּד הַדִּין. מָא אִילְנָא אַלָּא נְחַרְקוֹהּ. כִּיף מָא חְרַק לְמְעָאבַד. תַם כְּדָאוו אַבְרָהָם אָבִינוּ עְלֵיהּ אַסְלָאם. וּרְמָאווֹהּ פִּי אָתוֹן נָאר מוֹקְדָא. פְּתְגַלָּא עְלֵיהּ הַרַב צוֹבְחָאנוֹ. וּכַלְצוֹ בַּכְרָאמָאתוֹ וּבְגְלָאלָתוֹ. וּכְרַג מְן תַם סָאלַם. חַתָּא רָאת גְמִיע הַנָּאס עְגֶב. וּבְקָא עְלֵיהּ הַסְלָאם. יְעַלַּם הַנָּאס עְבָאדַת אַלְלָהּ וּתוֹחִידוֹ. בְּאָן קָאלוֹ לַחְכָמִים זִכְרָם לַבְרָכָה. כָּאנָת יָאקוֹתָא. מְעַלְּקָא פִּי רַקְבַת אַבְרָהָם אוֹבוֹנָא עְלֵיהּ אַסְלָאם. וּכָּאנַת תַצְוֵי מְן טָרְףְ הַדִּנְיָיא. לְטַרְפְהָא. וְהָאד לְיָאקוֹתָא הִיָּיא הַתּוֹחִיד אַלְדִי כָּאן יְכַרַג מְן חַלְקוֹ. וִיעַלַּם אַנָּאס עְבָאדַת אַלְלָהּ וְתוֹחִידוֹ. וְהִיָּיא דְלִיל 'וַיֹּאמֶר יְהוֹשֻׁעַ אֶל כָּל הָעָם.' שְׁרַח דָאלַךְ. וְקָאל יְהוֹשֻׁעַ לַגְמִיע לְקוֹם. הָאיְדָא קָאל אַלְלָהּ אֵילָה יִשְׂרָאֵל. פִּי מְזָאז לְוָאד זְלְסוֹ אַבָּאתְכּוֹם מְן אַוְולָא. תֶּרַח אֵיבִי אַבְרָהָם וְאֵיבִי נָחוֹר. וְעַבְדוֹ מְעָאבֶד אוֹכְרִין. וּצְטְפִית לְאַבְרָהָם מְן מְזָאז לְוָאד וּמַשִּׁיתוֹ פִּי גְמִיע אַרְץְ הַשָּׁאם. וּכַּתַּרְתְ נַסְלוֹ. וַעְטִית לוֹ יִצְחָק. וַעְטִית לְיִצְחָק יַעְקֹב וְעֵשָׂו. וַעְטִית לְעֵשָׂיו גְבֶל שְׂעִיר יְרָאתָא. וְיַעְקֹב וּולַאדוֹ הַבְטוֹ לַמָּצֶר.

Utqul Gafṣa

And say to them: My sons, before anything there was only God, praised be He, in His radiance and His splendor!
He is One in the light of His *Shekhinah*,
And the foundation of Heaven is His dwelling.
And there was nothing with Him to serve as His instrument,
At the time when He created His earth and His Heaven.
He is the Ruler; there is no limit to His power!
The Ruler Who is crowned above His people,
That is all of Israel, into their midst He came in His love.
And before all Creation there arose His magnitude,
And by it descended the light of His *Shekhinah*,
At the time when He gave them His Torah.
The Ruler, who appointed Himself so that they should walk in obedience to Him,
And He is pleased to give them Good that no eye has yet seen,
The Ruler, Who is crowned above all praise,
And He is pleased to exact His vengeance for them;
The Ruler Whom none preceded and none will succeed,
In the beginning He created Heaven and earth.
And the Creation was void except for One,
No evening and no morning,
No space and no time,
No holidays and no Sabbath,
No days and no months,
No rivers and no oceans,
No gardens and no vegetation,
No darkness and no light,
No birds and no beasts,
No personages and no men,
Only God, praised be He, desired living things.
Then said the Holy One, praised be His Name forever:
"I am the one Who created earth and Heaven.
Let us distinguish between brightness and darkness,
To separate permanently between night and day.
I am pleased to exact vengeance upon the evildoers,
And the Day of Judgment will render them powerless;
But if they return to me in perfect repentance, We shall extend mercy to them."
At that time He assigned the moon
To distinguish between night and day,
Between dusk and dawn, between the Sabbath and the New Moon.
And He created a pair of mountains in the midst of the ocean,
And from them emerged darkness in the midst of the land;
And he who sees them will know the strength of Almighty God.
So said God, praised be He, "I am He Who created brightness and darkness,
I shall create the Water,
And by Me will be created judgment and wisdom;
By Me will be created inventiveness and intelligence.
I am He Who made a separation between water and water,

ותקול גפצה

לפיסקא ״מתחלה עוֹבדי עבוֹדה היוּ אבוֹתינוּ״.

ותקול להו יא אבני מן קבל כל שי מא כאן גיר אללה ברוך הוא בכראמאתו ובג̇לאלתו
מתואחד בנור שכינתו
ומלאיכת הסמא דאירתו
וליס כאן מעאה שריך̇ פ̇י מעאונתו
חין כ̇לק ארצ̇ו וסמאואתו
הווא הצלטאן אלדי ליס חדאדה לקוותו
הצלטאן למתווכל עלא אומתו
הייא ג̇מאעת ישראל אלדי ג̇א פ̇יהא מחבתו
וקבל מה כ̇לק הדנייא טלעת תכמימתו
ועליהא נזזל נור שכינתו
חין עטה להום תורתו
הצלטאן למתווכל עלא אלדי מאשיין פ̇י טאעתו
ומסתעד ליעטי להום כ̇יר אלדי עין ליס ראתו
הצלטאן למתווכל עלא ג̇מיע מכ̇אלפ̇ין תנייתו
והווא מסתעד ליסתנקם מנהם נקמתו
צלטאן אלדי לא קבלו חד ולא בעדו חד
אוול מא בדא כ̇לק הסמא ולארצ̇
וכאנת הדיינא כ̇אליא מה פ̇יהא חד
לא עשיי ולא צבוחאת
לא פ̇צאל ולא וקאת
לא עיאד ולא שבאת
לא אייאם ולא שהוראת
לא וידאן ולא בחוראת
לא גרסאן ולא עשובאת
לא צ̇לאם ולא צ̇ואיאת
לא טיור ולא וחשאת
לא זואיל ולא אנסאנאת
מא תמא גיר אללה ברוך הוא לחי התאבת
קאל למקדס יתבארך̇ אסמו דימא
אנא אלדי כ̇לקת לארצ̇ והסמא
נחב נכ̇ררג̇ מנהם הצ̇וו והצ̇למא
ליפ̇רז בין הליל ובין הנהאר דימא
אנא מסתעד לנאכ̇ד מן הרשעים נקמה
ויום הדין נעמל פ̇יהם חכומה
ואידא ירגעו לי בקלב כאמל נמתלא עליהם רחמה
פ̇י דיך̇ הסאעה טלעת לקמר
וצאר יפ̇רז בין הליל ובין הנהאר
בין אלעשיי ובין לפ̇ג̇ר
בין השבת ובין השהר
וכ̇לק זוג̇ גבאל פ̇י וצט לבחר
ומנהם יכרג̇ הצ̇לאם לווצט לבר
ואלדי יראהם יערף̇ קוות לאילה הג̇באר
קאל אללה ברוך הוא אנא אלדי כ̇לקת הצ̇וו וצ̇למא
אנא נכ̇לק למא
ומנני יכ̇רג̇ לעקל ולחכמה
מנני תכ̇רג̇ הצ̇בארה ולפ̇האמה
אנא אלדי נפ̇רז בין מא ללמא

Between the water of the earth and the water of the sky.
And from the water of the sky I shall produce rain,
And from it I shall water all vegetation and trees.
And from them I shall give life to all bodies and make people famous;
And from the waters of the light rain they will be hardy and notable,
And the remainder of the water the fields will absorb and be fertile."
At that moment the Ocean was collected into the sea,
And all the world was formed,
And all the springs and rivers started to emerge and pour forth,
Just as God had commanded and ordained it.
God, praised be He, said: "I am He Who created water for the sea and all rivers,
I shall create in the world fields and vegetation,
In order to nourish by them all creatures and animals,
And I shall create in them trees and plants,
In order to nourish by them all mankind.
And they shall eat and be satisfied, all the hungry,
In order to bless and thank God the merciful.
God, praised be He, said: "I am He Who created all wild animals and beasts,
They shall spread out and fill all land and waters,
And I shall create all birds of wings,
And I shall create in the sea Okeanos the Leviathan."
At that moment they came into existence and spread out over all seas and rivers,
As the Ruler had commanded concerning them.
God, praised be He, said: "I created all that is on my earth and my heavens,
I shall create man in my image,
I order him to come to take possession of the world.
And I shall make his mouth a mouth of intelligence and reasoning to understand My power!"
At that moment man was created armed with the power of thought,
And he prevailed over the world perfectly.
Heaven and earth and all that is in them,
He completed them on the Sixth Day among the Days,
And He rested on the Seventh Day from all His creating.
And God sanctified the Sabbath and fixed its blessing,
In the way all of Israel will preserve His Sabbath.
But anyone who does work on it, his prayer will not be received,
And his portion will not be with Israel
And there is no end nor limit to his punishment,
And anyone who does not observe it is as if he destroyed all His Torah.
And it is the portion that God, praised be He, gave to Adam and his wife,
And set them down at the holy place of His House.
And as his portion God, the Lord, planted a garden East of Eden,
And placed in its middle a tree; he who eats from it will know good and evil,
And He created in its middle a river to go out from Eden to irrigate the garden,
And from there it divides into four rivers.
The name of the first one is Pishon, from which comes all linen,
And it runs by the land of Ḥawila where there is the best gold,
And there is the pearl, and the crystal stone, and the roots of coral.
And the name of the second river is Giḥon, where the land of Kush lies,
And its waves are high like the sound of dangerous armies,
And its excessive power seals like a strong lock,
In the power of God, the King

ובין מא לארץ ובין מא הסמא

ומן מא הסמא נבבבט למטר

ומנהא נסקי גמיע לעשב והשגר

וביהא נעייש גמיע הזואיל ולאנסאן למשתחר

וביהא הדנייא תכלא ותעמר

ובקא למא פֿדנייא יגרי ויכתר

וחב ליכלי גמיע לבלדאן ולקטאר

פֿי דיך הסאעה גמעו פֿי אוקיינוס לבחר

וצאר עלה גמיע הדנייא מצֿור

וגמיע לעיון ולוידאן תכרג ותמהר

כיף מא אמרהו הרב וקצֿר

קאל אללה ברוך הוא אנא אלדי כלקת מא לבחר וגמיע לוידאן

אנא נכֿלק פֿדנייא רביע ועשבאן

באש נקוות מנו גמיע הזואיל ולחיואן

ונכֿלק פֿיה שגר וגרסאן

באש נקוות מנו גמיע לאנסאן

ויאכל וישבע גמיע הגֿיעאן

באש יבארך וישכר לאילה הרחמאן

קאל אללה ברוך הוא אלדי כלקת גמיע לוחוש ולחיואן

לידבבו ויכתכרו פֿי גמיע לארץ ולמיואן

ונכֿלק גמיע טיור הגֿנהאן

ונכֿלק פֿי בחר אוקיינוס לויתן

פֿי דיך הסאעא צארו ידבבו פֿי גמיע לבחור ולודאן

כמא אמר עליהם השולטאן

קאל אללה ברוך הוא אלדי כלקת גמיע מא פֿי ארצֿי וסמאואתי

נחב נכֿלק אדם בציפֿתי

באש יוגֿד כל שי פֿדניא ואתי

ונגֿעל פֿיה פֿיה פֿהאמא ועקל באש יערף קוותי

פֿי דיך הסאעא כֿלק אדם כמא כממם

ובקאת גמיע הדניא כאמלא בתמאם

הסמא ולארץֿ וגמיע מא פֿיהם

כממלהם יום סתא פֿלאייאם

ורתאח פֿי נהאר הסאבע מן גמיע צנעאתו

וקדדס אללה יום השבת וחצֿרת בראכתו

עלא האכדא יחפֿצֿו גמיע ישראל שבתו

ומן יצנע פֿיהא הצֿנעא ליס תנקבל צלאתו

וגמעא ישראל ליס תכון חצתו

וליס טרף וחדאדא לעקובתו

וגמיע מן יחפֿצֿו כיף אלדי תבבת גמיע תורתו

וכאן באעד האד השי באדֿ אללה ברוך הוא אדם וזוגֿתו

וחטהם פֿי מקאם ביתו

באש יתבתו וצֿאיאתו

ובאעדו גרס אללה הרב מן שרקי עדן גֿנאן מכֿייר

וחט פֿי וצטו שגֿרא ומן יאכל מנהא יכון יערף לכֿיר והשר

וכֿלק פֿי וצטו ואד ליכֿרגֿ מן עדן ליסקי הגֿנאן

ומן תם יפֿתרז ויכון לרבע וידאן

אסם לואחד פישון אלדי מנו יוכֿרגֿ גמיע אלכתֿאן

ומצֿור עלה ארץֿ חוילה אלדי תם כֿיאר הדהבאן

ותם הגֿוהר וחגֿאר לבלאר וערוק אלמרגֿאן

ואסם לואד אלתֿאני גיחון ומצֿור עלה ארץֿ כוש

ומוגֿו עאלי כיף חס כֿאטר הגֿיוס

ומן קוות גלוה כל מן יכֿתם עליה יכון מתרוס

בקוות לאילה לקדוש

And the name of the third river is Ḥideqel,
There it is hot, hot like pepper,
And everyone who drinks from it will have his flesh changed;
And the name of the fourth one is Furat and it is the best of rivers,
And he who drinks from it will be dry and fat.
And all these exist by the power of the merciful God.
And God, praised be He, took him [Adam] to work the garden,
And ordered him to follow this one commandment:
From all the trees of the garden you shall eat and be satisfied,
But of the tree of knowledge of good and evil: do not eat from it lest you get a black mark.
And if you transgress and do not obey you will certainly be marked for death,
And you will make darkness descend upon you and you will not be able to see.
God, praised be He, said: "We shall create for him a wife,
In order that they shall work and be able to pray and read."
At that moment He cast on him deep sleep,
And created him a wife for a helpmate,
And Adam and his consort were naked but they were not ashamed.
At that moment the snake came to stand before them,
And so he spoke to the wife.
He said to her: hear this patiently,
It will be of good use to you and in it there is no possibility of loss!
Get up, eat from the abundance of this tree,
And you will be superb like the angels of Heaven,
And you will know all in consequence of that courage.
The wife answered, girding herself,
She said to him: "I shall hand you over to the law,
God the Creator exhorted me,
Do not believe speech that will negate the preceding,
And if you sin and follow such you will certainly die."
At this moment, the snake passed by the wife, and in his fine appearance
He climbed the tree of knowledge and bent it toward him.
He spoke: "That is what I said, this is the confirmation of its truth,
And if you eat from the tree of knowledge you will certainly not die,
But like the angels of heaven you will be, knowing and understanding."
When the wife saw that the tree was spicy to eat and appetizing to the eyes,
She took some dates and ate, she and her man as a couple,
And after that they knew that they were naked
And they sewed themselves leaves of the fig-tree and wore skirts.
At that moment he heard the sound of speaking in the middle of the garden; hiding and running;
God swayed him and spoke to him: "Aren't you Adam traveling from places west?"
He spoke to Him: "I heard Your voice in the middle of the garden,
I was afraid of You that You would find me naked,
And because of that I hid!"
God, praised be He, responded: "Did you eat from the tree concerning which I commanded you?"
He spoke to Him: "The wife You gave me, from her I ate and was seduced."
God, praised be He, spoke to the wife: "What is that evil deed that you did?
And the tree I commanded you about it, from it you ate!
And you and your husband joined up together and defiled yourselves!"
The wife spoke: "The snake tempted me and I ate, turn on him!"
God spoke to the snake: "You are cursed among all wild animals,
And on your belly you shall walk in clinging and rumbling,
And your food shall be dirt and stone.
And enmity I shall put between the wife and you,

ואסם לואד התאלת חדקל
ומא סכ̇ון וחר כיף אלפ̇לפ̇ל
וכל מן ישרב מנו לחמו יתבדדל
ואסם לואד הראבע פרת והווא כ̇יאר לוידאן
ומן ישרב מנו יצח ויסמן
וג̇מיע האד השי בקוות לאילה הרחמאן
וכ̇דא אללה ברוך הוא וחטו ליכ̇דם פ̇גנאן
ווצא לו האד לכלאם לקאיילן
מן ג̇מיע שג̇ר אלג̇נאן תאכל ותכון שבעאן
ומן שג̇רת לערף̇ לכ̇יר ושר ליס תאכל מנהא חתא ברוקאן
ואידא תג̇אוזת עלא וצאייתי מות תמות בלקצ̇רה
ותצ̇לאם עליך̇ הדנייא וליס תכון תרא
קאל אללה ברוך הוא נכ̇לק לו מרא
באש תכון תכ̇דמו והווא יכון יצללי ויקרא
פ̇י דיך̇ הסאעה רמא עליה גמרא
וכ̇לק לו מרא כיף מא טלאע פ̇י תכ̇מימו
וכאן אדם וזוג̇תו עריאנין וליס יתחשמו
פ̇י דיך̇ הסאעה ג̇א לחנש וקף קודאמו
ובדא יתכללם מעא למרא
קאל להא אסמעי האד הצ̇בארה
והייא תצלח ביך̇ וליס פ̇יהא כ̇צארה
קומי דלחין כולי מן האד השג̇רא
ותכוני כיף̇ מלאיכת הסמא מתכברא
ותערפי ג̇מיע מא פ̇דנייא יג̇רא
ג̇אובת למרא בלמנטק
קאלת להו אנא נקוללך̇ לחק
אנא וצאני לאילה לכ̇אלק
ליס תדנאי פ̇יהא תכללם מעאנא מן הצאבק
ואידא תג̇אוזתו עלא וצאייתי מות תמותו
פ̇י דיך̇ הסאעה דז לחנש למרא בצחחתו
עלא שג̇רת לערף̇ וקפ̇ת קבאלתו
קאל להא אנא כלאמי מעאך̇ חקקתו
ואידא תאכלו מן שג̇רת לערף̇ ליס מות תמותו
אלא כיף̇ מלאיכת הסמא תכונו עארפ̇ין ופ̇אהמין
כיף̇ ראת אלמרא מליחה השג̇רא ללמאכלה ושאהוא לעינין
כ̇דאת מן תמארו וכלאת הייא וראג̇להא בתנין
ובאעדו ערפ̇ו אן הומאן עריאנין
וכ̇ייטו עליהם ורק לכרם ובקאו מתחג̇מין
פ̇י דיך̇ הסאעה סמע חס תכללם פ̇י וצט הג̇נאן תכ̇בבא והרב
נאדה לו אללה וקאל לו וינך̇ ג̇אובו אדם מן ג̇יהת לג̇רב
וקאל לו חסך̇ סמאעת פ̇י וצט הג̇נאן
כ̇פ̇ת מנך̇ אידא תנצ̇רני עריאן
ועליהא תכ̇בית
ג̇אובו אללה ברוך הוא ואש מן השג̇רה אלדי וציתך̇ עליה מנהא כלית
קאל לו למרא אלדי ג̇אבת לי מנו וכלית ונג̇וית
קאל אללה ברוך הוא ללמרא האש האד לעמלא אלדי עמלתי
והשג̇רא אלדי וציתך̇ עליהא מנהא כליתי
ואנתי וראג̇לך̇ תג̇אוזתו עלא וצאיאתי
קאלת למרא לחנש אלדי ג̇ואני וכלית ועלייא צ̇בבר
קאל אללה לחנש מנעול אנתי מן ג̇מיע וחשת אלבר
ועלא בטנך̇ תמשי פ̇לוטה ותכרכר
וטעאמך̇ יכון תראב וחג̇ר
ועדאוה נג̇על בין אלמרא ובינך̇

And between her offspring and your offspring,
For the length of your life and your years,
And that will recall the evil of your deed,
And you will take from it your punishment."
And to the wife he spoke: "I shall increase your suffering with your young and your pregnancy
When you give birth to your children,
And your husband will be your master for the wickedness of your evil deed
Which causes death for you and your tribe after you!"
And to Man He spoke: "Because you listened to the word of your spouse,
And you ate from the tree about which I enjoined you,
You shall be cursed for your vice;
In suffering you shall feed yourself all days of your life,
Thorns and stones will rise for you,
And in the sweat of your face shall you eat your food.
And you shall die and return to the dust from which I created you."
At that moment, God, praised be He, chased away Adam and Eve, his spouse,
Out of His garden, and she produced a child, Cain was his name.
And she added another child, his name was Abel,
And there was added to him another, Seth was his name; but Abel was killed.
There was born to Seth a child, his name was Enosh,
And from him all persons began to know God, praised be He.
And God, praised be He, spoke: "Adam shall go and die
Because he teamed up on me, sinned, but repented."
At that moment, He produced darkness around him and spoke to him: "This is to die."
Onto him came from Heaven an idea;
Because of the intensity of his distress he took a couple of stones,
And one on the other he beat and smashed,
At that moment the light was let loose from them;
So he raised on it the voice,
And made the benediction: "Creator of the illuminating fire."
This happened at the end of the Sabbath.
And then did Adam die
And it became clear to the created that all will be born and die.
It was just as the children of mankind increased,
It became clear that they became depraved and walked in the way of darkness,
And God, the Lord, repented that He had created them.
And He spoke: "By moisture-laden clouds I shall wipe them
From the earth that I gave to them,
From man to animal, to birds, all of them,
Unless they repent of the evil of their deeds."
And after that He spoke: "I shall be merciful to them,
On the earth that I gave to them,
To mankind by the merit of their father Noaḥ."
Because Noaḥ was a man, straight and perfect,
Fearing God and perfect above all men.
Then there were born to him three sons,
And when the sins increased in the world,
God, praised be He, spoke to Noaḥ: "I will inform you of the end;
One among all men is fit to rise up at
The time of their destruction, and the earth will be desolate,
Since they are beyond consolation.
Arise and make yourself an ark and stay in it,
And inside and out cover it with pitch,
And I shall enlighten you about the building:

ובין נסלהא ובין נסלך
טול עמרך וסנינך
והווא יכון מפ̇תכר שר פ̇עאיילך
ואנת תאכ̇ד מנו נקמתך
ולמרא קאל להא אנא נכתתר עדאבך פ̇י צג̇רך ופ̇י כברך
חין תולדי ולאדך
וראג̇לך יכון חכימך מן סבת שר פ̇עאילך
אלדי סבבתי למות ליך ולג̇יאלך באעדך
ולאדם קאל אן סמעת כלאם ג̇וזתך
וכלית מן השג̇רה אלדי וציתך
תכון מנעולה לוטא בסבתך
בלעדאב תתקוות ג̇מיע אייאם חיאתך
השוך ולג̇נדול ננבת לך
ובערק וג̇הך תאכל טעאמך
ותמות ותרג̇ע טראב אן מנו כ̇לקתך
פ̇י דיך הסאעה טרדד אללה ברוך הוא אדם וחוה זוג̇תו
מן עדן ג̇נאנו וג̇אבת ולד וקין סמאתו
וזאדת ולד אכ̇ר וסמאתו הבל
ונזאד לו ושת אסמו אן הבל נקתל
וסתאלד ולד לשת ואסמו אנוש
ומנו בדאו ליערפ̇ו אללה ברוך הוא ג̇מיע הנפ̇וס
וקאל אללה ברוך הוא יחב ימות אדם
אלדי תג̇אוז עלא וצאיתי ונדם
פ̇י דיך הסאעה ג̇אב עליה הצ̇לאם וקאל לו האדי למות
אלדי עליה ג̇א מן הסמא מבעות
מן קוות חרג̇ו כ̇דא זוג̇ חג̇אר
וחדא עלא וחדא יכ̇בבט ויכצצר
פ̇י דיך הסאעה נטלק מנהם הנאר
וצ̇ואת עליה הצ̇אר
ובארך עליהא בורא מאורי האש
וכאן האד השי פ̇י מוצאי שבת קדש
ובאעדו מאת בונא אדם
ובדאו למכ̇לוקין יסתאלדו וימותו פ̇י כל עאם
וכאן כמא כתתרו ולאד בנאדם
בדאו ליפ̇סדו וימשיו פ̇י טריק הצ̇לאם
ונדם עליהם אללה הרב אן כ̇לקהם
וקאל דלחין נמחיהם
מן עלא לארצ̇ אלדי עטית להם
מן בנאדם חתא לג̇איילה חתא לידב כלהם
חתא ירג̇עו מן שר פ̇עאילהם
ובעדו קאל אנא נרחמהם
מן עלא לארצ̇ אלדי עטית להם
מן בנאדם חתא לג̇איילה בזכות נח אובוהם
וכאן נח ראג̇ל מסתקים וג̇ייד
כ̇אייף מן אללה וכאמל מן ג̇מיע לעאבד
ובאעדו סתאלדו לו תלת ולאד
ובדא הדנוב ליכתר פ̇דנייא
קאל אללה ברוך הוא לנח איג̇י נכ̇ברך בלקצ̇ייא
ראו חד ג̇מיע לאנסאן טלאע חדאייא
נחב נהלכהם ותכון לארצ̇ כ̇אלייא
עלא מא כתר פ̇יהם מן מעצייא
קום אצנאע לך תיבה ואקעד פ̇יהא
ומן דאכ̇ל ומן ברא בלקטראן ג̇שיהא
ואנא נורריך ג̇מיע מצאנעהא

Make three hundred cubits its length,
And fifty cubits its width and thirty cubits its height,
And illuminate it by a narrow brilliant light,
And on its side make its door,
So that the water cannot enter.
But of all living creatures I will send you,
Male and female I shall make them enter before you,
And that shall be a sign between Me and you,
Everyone who will kneel down before the ark,
He shall enter into your care.
And you prepare food and drink,
For everyone to put before him."
And Noaḥ did all that God, the Lord, had commanded him.
And it was after seven days, the deluge started with rain,
And all the wells of the earth were opened,
And all the world began to shake,
The deep was cut open and the mountains trembled,
And all the wells of the depth were mixed strongly.
And they stagnated, forty days and forty nights by the count,
And the world was dark and black.
Then all mountains on earth were covered,
And the ark was lifted and went over the mountains of the Kurdsa;
Then all living things died and not one remained.
And God thought of Noaḥ and all that were with him in the ark and had mercy on them,
And God brought a wind blowing on the water and closing all wells and windows of heaven.
And they all left the ark into daylight from the midst of darkness,
And God blessed Noaḥ and his children,
And spoke to them: "Bear fruit and grow and go and increase!"
And He gave Noaḥ a promise that He would no more bring a deluge over the land,
"And for the promise between Me and you I shall raise the rainbow in the white clouds,
And that will be the remembrance of the promise to continue."
And the children of Noaḥ were Shem, Yefet, and Ḥam.
And it was after all that was told here,
That people were born and began tc walk on the road of darkness,
And they forget what God, praised be He, the Living and Existing, had done for them,
And they continued to worship idols, symbols, and heavenly bodies,
And they worshiped the crescent and the stars,
And idols of silver and gold,
And added idols of stone and wood,
And followed the fetishes and lied about God, the Lord,
And they built themselves all kinds of images,
And they proclaimed that the image could cause good or bad,
And their power was over everything in the world.
That it can make you rich or poor,
That it has power on dry land and the sea,
That it will assemble high to shoot or it will hide,
And to it one is obliged to give praise and thanks.
Then was forgotten the name of God from their mouths,
And they did not think of Him Who favored them,
Who had led them from darkness to light,
And had saved them from the deluge,
And from His grace and generosity had fed them;
So they continued to walk in their blindness,
And not one of them knew God, the Lord.

אעמל תלת מייאת דראע טולהא
וכ̇מסין דראע ערצ̇הא ותלאתין דראע עלוהא
ואצנע פ̇הא שמאסי לצ̇ווהא
ופ̇י ג̇נבהא תצנע פ̇ומהא
באש מא ישבצי אלמא עליהא
ואנא מן ג̇מיע לחיי תנין נזיב לך̇
דכר ונתא נדכ̇להם קודאמך̇
והאדי להמארא אלדי ביני ובינך̇
ג̇מיע אלדי קודאם התיבה יברך̇
הווא אלדי תדכ̇לו בחדאך̇
וכ̇וד לך̇ מן אלמאכלא ושראב
אן לן לחד קודאמי תקררב
וצנאע נח כמא וצצאה אללה הרב
וכאן באעד סבע אייאם בדא מא הטופ̇אן יצב
ונחללו ג̇מיע עיון אלארצ̇
ובקאת ג̇מיע הדניא תרעד
לוטא תנשק והג̇באל תנהד
וג̇מיע עיון לג̇מוק ישייבו פ̇למא בג̇הד
וקאעדת רבעין יום ורבעין לילא בלעדד
והדניא תצ̇לאם ותסואד
חתא תג̇טטאו ג̇מיע ג̇באל אלארצ̇
וסתעלאת התיבה ונזלת עלא ג̇בל אלקרוד
חתא מאת ג̇מיע לחיי ולא בקא פ̇דניא חד
ופ̇תכר אללה נח וג̇מיע אלדי מעאה פ̇תיבה ומתלא עליהם רחמא
וג̇אב אללה ריח והפ̇ת אלמא ושד ג̇מיע עיון וטואקי הסמא
וכ̇רג̇ו ג̇מיע אלדי פ̇תיבה לצ̇ו מן וצט הצ̇למא
ובארך̇ אללה נח וולאדו
וקאל להם תמרו וכתרו ומשיו ונזאדו
ועטא לנח עאהד אלדי ליס יזיד יג̇יב מא הטופ̇אן לבלאדו
ולעאהד אלדי ביני ובינך̇ נטללאע קוצי פ̇י סחאב לג̇מאם
והייא תכון תפ̇כרא לעאהד הדואם
וכאנו ולאד נח שם ויפת וחם
וכאן באעד ג̇מיע האד לכלאם
סתאלדו ג̇יאל ובדאו לימשיו פ̇י טריק הצ̇לאם
ונסאו מא פ̇על מעאהם אללה ברוך הוא חי וקיים
ובקאו יעבדו פ̇י מעאבד לאותן ואלצנאם
ויעבדו פ̇לקמר ולכואכב
ופ̇י מעאבד לפ̇צ̇ה והדהב
וזאדו חתא מעאבד לחג̇ר ולכ̇שב
ותבעו הצלבאן וכדבו אללה הרב
וצנעו להם ג̇מיע התצאוור
ויקולו להם האד התצוירא תפ̇על אלכ̇יר והשר
ועלא כל שי פ̇דניא תקצ̇ר
הייא אלדי תג̇ני ותפ̇קר
הייא אלדי תכון מעאנא פ̇לבר ופ̇לבחר
הייא תכאלנא עליה נרמיו והייא תסתר
וליהא ואג̇ב למדח והשכר
חתא נסאו אסם אללה מן פ̇מאמהם
וליס תפ̇כרו מא פ̇על מן כ̇יר מעאהם
אלדי מן הצ̇לאם לצ̇וו כ̇רג̇הם
ומן מא הטופ̇אן כ̇ללצהם
ומן פ̇צלו וחסאנו קוותהם
ובקאו מאשיין פ̇י עמאהם
ולא בקא חד פ̇יהם יערף אללה הרב

They transmitted the untruth and followed the worship of lies.
Then the astrologers saw one star running from East to West,
And on its way it swallowed three stars,
They were all astonished and remained surprised.
At that moment they went to sultan Nimrod,
And spoke to him: This is the beginning, this is to be,
We know, our lord, that at this time,
A child is born to Teraḥ who will destroy the king and ruin religion,
And he will cancel all worship of fetishes,
And he will turn all sons into Jews.
At that moment Nimrod sent for Teraḥ,
And spoke to him: "We shall make you well and let you become rich,
And it will make you thrive,
And we shall be good to you evening and morning!"
And when Teraḥ heard this speech he was happy;
Teraḥ said to Nimrod: "May you speak everything truthfully!"
Nimrod answered Teraḥ: "The child that is born to you, we desire that you cut its neck,
And for that you shall profit and be able to take it easy,
And if you do my desire I shall make you my deputy,
And you will be master over all my lands."
Teraḥ answered him and said to him: "O, my master,
What is more useful for me than my child?"
And it was after these speeches,
Abraham, our father, may peace be on him, grew
And became a child of three years exactly,
And became discerning with intelligence and he thought
And spoke: "Who created light and shadow?
And created nights and days?
And created all heavens and worlds?
Let us worship Him and pray to Him in perpetuity!"
He saw the sun rise for the day,
And said: "The sun is the creator,
It is whom we shall worship in truth,
And to him are due thanks and in songs of praise we shall enjoy,
It is he who painted the world."
Then the sun went down and the world became dark.
He said: "That one is no god but one of the servants,
And is serving during the day constantly to illuminate the world!"
At that moment he lifted his eyes to the sky
Where moon and stars were coming up.
He believed that the stars were servants but the moon was lord.
He said: "This is the god whom we shall serve with faithful heart,
And to him we shall pray and get closer.
He is the god in reality and all the idols are a lie."
Then the night passed and stars and moon set,
Daytime came up and the sun turned it to blue.
He spoke: "This can certainly be verified and confirmed,
That the Lord is not them, not what one thinks,
But they are replaceable servants and forms,
And forever this shall be intelligently transmitted."
There appeared to him the Lord in His splendor and excellence
And spoke: "Abraham, discerning you shine in my world,
I am He Who created you and formed you by my hand,

וסללמו פ̇י אילה אלחק ותבעו מעאבד לכדב
חתא ראוו אלמסתנגמין ואחד לכוכב יגרי מן השרק ללגרב
ובעד מא ג̇רא קאם ובלע תלאת כואכב
דהשו כלהם ובקא ענדהם עג̇ב
פ̇י דיך הסאעה משאו לאנד נמרוד הצלטאן
וקאלו לו האדא מא צאר והאדא מא כאן
אחנאן עארפ̇ין יא סידנא אלדי פ̇י האד הזמאן
יסתאלד ולד לתרח והווא יבדא ליכ̇רב אלמלך ויפ̇סד לדיאן
והווא יבטטל ג̇מיע מעאבד הצלבאן
והווא יהד ג̇מיע לבניאן
פ̇י דיך הסאעה בעת נמרוד עלא תרח
וקאל לו נצ̇בבר עליך צ̇בארה וביהא תרבאח
והייא אלדי תצלאח
ונכונו מתהניין עשייא וצבאח
וכיף סמאע תרח האד לכלאם פ̇ראח
קאל תרח לנמרוד תכללם מעאיא בצאח
ג̇וב נמרוד לתרח לולד אלדי יזדאד לך נחב רקבתו תנדבאח
ומנו תתהנא ותרתאח
ואידא עמלת כיף גרצ̇י אנא נעטיך מאל כתיר מן ענדי
ותכון חאכם עלא ג̇מיע בלאדי
ג̇ובו תרח וקאל לו יא סידי
האש ינפ̇עני למאל פ̇י ולדי
וכאן בעד ג̇מיע האד לכלאם
כבר אברהם אבינו עליה אסלאם
ובקא ולד תלת סנין בתמאם
ובקא יתמייז מעא עקלו ויכ̇מם
ויקול אשכון אלדי כ̇לק הצ̇ו והצ̇לאם
וכ̇לק הליאלי ולאייאם
וכ̇לק ג̇מיע הסמאואת ולעלאם
נעבד לו ונצללי לו ג̇מיע הדואם
רא השמש פ̇נהאר תזרק
קאל האדא הווא לכ̇אלק
הווא אלדי נעבד לו בלחק
ולילו השכר ולמדח יצטחק
הווא אלדי פ̇דנייא צאבק
פ̇למן ג̇אבת השמס ובקאת הדניא צ̇למה
קאל האדא ליסו אילה אלא ואחד מן לכ̇ודאמה
והווא יכ̇דם פ̇נהאר ליצ̇ווי הדניא דימא
פ̇י דיך הסאעה קאם עינו לסמא
לקא טלעו לקמר ולכואכב
צ̇ן פ̇י כאטרו אן לכואכב כ̇ודאמה ולקמר הווא הרב
קאל האדא הווא אילה אלדי נעבדו בניית אלקלב
ולילו נצלילו ונקררב
הווא לאילה לחקאני וג̇מיע למעאבד כדב
חתא משא הליל ולכואכב ולקמר ג̇אבת
טלאע הנהאר והשמס זרקת
קאל דלחין תחקק ענדי ותבת
אן האדון ליסהם אילאהאת כיף מא כ̇ממת
אלא מכ̇לוקין מתלי ומצווראת
ומאזאל מעא עקלו יתחדת
אתגללא עליה הרב צבחאנו בכראמתו ובגלאלתו
קאל לו יא אברהם מאלך תתמייז פ̇י עלמי
אנא אלדי כ̇לקתך וצוורתך בידי

I am He, the God and Lord, be My servant,
I am He Who created you and I shall raise you over all my people,
I am He Who created all the heavens and the earth,
I am alone the Ruler, there is no god before me and no god after me!
O, my beloved Abraham, I am your God and you are my worshiper,
I am He Who created you and formed you by my hand!"
At that moment, Abraham went to his father Teraḥ
And said to him: "My father, please inform me in truth,
Who created the world in six days and on the seventh he rested?
Who is the God to Whom we should be thankful and sing praise?
Who is the God to Whom we must pray evening and morning?"
And our master Abraham attached himsef to his father.
At that moment, his father laughed and was glad;
He spoke: "My son Abraham, the idols that are planted in the house,
They are who created earth and the heavens,
And all the world by their hands was built from small pieces."
Our lord Abraham answered him and spoke: "My father
I heard your speech, you brought love to my heart,
Let us go to your pleasant idols and look at them,
So that every day we may worship them,
And three prayers a day we shall pray to them,
And in addition to prayer, we shall sacrifice and offer to them,
So they shall accept what is before them!"
At that moment he went before his mother and happily said to her: "My mother,
Arise on this way, share my goal, and hear my speech,
I am going to my father's idols, a delay would burn my blood,
Please, let us worship them, that is all I think about!
Arise! and prepare good food for me,
Let us offer it to father's idols,
My heart is burning, supply me with my want!"
At that moment, his mother rose and prepared for him what he desired,
She worked excellently to give him what he had requested
So he went before them and offered
What any one of them might want to eat and drink.
He, peace be on him, said: "O Lord, how can they be useful or hurtful to me,
Not to others and not to me,
They have a mouth but do not talk, they don't compose nor do they think,
They have eyes but do not see, they do cause neither good nor destruction,
They have ears but do not hear, they do not hurt nor do they good,
They have a nose but they do not breathe, they do not get angry nor do they have mercy,
They have feet but they do not walk, they do not run nor do they get tired,
Like them should be those who made them, and everyone who relies on them!"
He brought the pickax and broke them,
He brought firewood and surrounded them,
He took fire and burned them,
And he put the pickax in the hand of the largest one
And darkened the house on them.
Then Abraham hastened to his father,
He said to him: "My father, I just tried
To please your seven idols.
But they opposed the largest one among them,
And he got angry at them!
I did not know how to worship them,
I was afraid of their dangerous power,

אנא הווא לאילה והאדון כ̇ודמי
אנא הווא אלדי כ̇לקתך ונחב נעלליך עלא ג̇מיע קומי
אנא אלדי כ̇לקת ג̇מיע הסמאואת ולארצ̇י
אנא הצלטאן לוחיד לא אילה קבלי ולא אילה בעדי
יא חביבי אברהם אנא אילאהך ואנתי עבדי
אנא אלדי כ̇לקתך וצוורתך בידי
פ̇י דיך הסאעה משא אברהם לענד אובוה תרח
וקאל לו יא איבי נחבך תכ̇ברני בצאח
האשכון אלדי כ̇לק הדינא פ̇י סת אייאם ופ̇סאבע רתאח
האשכון הווא לאילה אלדי לילו נשכר ונמדח
האשכון הווא לאילה אלדי נצללי לו עשייא וצבאח
וסידנא אברהם פ̇י אובוה יזלבאח
פ̇י דיך הסאעה אובוה צ̇הך ופ̇ראח
קאל לו יא ולדי יא אברהם מעאבד ענדי פ̇לבית מג̇רוסאת
הומאן אלדי כ̇לקו לאראצ̇י והסמאואת
וג̇מיע הדניא בידהם תהססת ותבנאת
ג̇אובו סידנא אברהם קאל לו יא אבי
סמאעת כלאמך ג̇אתני מחבבה פ̇י קלבי
עלא מעאבדך לעזאז נחב נדכ̇ל וננצ̇רהם
באש ג̇מיע אייאמי נכון נעבדהם
ותלת צלאואת פ̇נהאר נכון וצללי להם
ובאעד הצלא נכון נדבח ונקררב להם
הייאך יקבלוני ענדהם
פ̇י דיך הסאעה משא לענד אמו והווא פ̇רחאן קאל להא יא אמי
קומי פ̇י האד הדרג̇ צנעי ג̇רצ̇י ותבתי כלאמי
משית למעאבד אבי ריתהם נחרק דממי
נחב נעבדהם עלא קד תכ̇מימי
קומי דלחין צנעי מעישא טייבא
נקררבהם למעאבד באבא
ריתהם פ̇י קלבי נזאדת לי מחבבה
פ̇י דיך הסאעה קאמת אמו וצנעת לו מא חב
והדייא מליחא עמלת כמא טלב
וג̇אב קודאמהם וקררב
ומא חב חד מנהם ליאכל ולישרב
קאל עליה אסלאם האדון מא ינפ̇עו לי ולא יצ̇ררו לי
לא לג̇ירי ולא לילי
פ̇ום להם וליס יתכללמו. לא יצ̇בברו ולא יכ̇ממו
עינין להם וליס ינצ̇רו. לא יכ̇יירו ולא ישררו
ודנין להם וליס יסמעו. לא יצ̇ררו ולא ינפ̇עו
אנפ̇ להם וליס ישממו. לא יכפ̇רו ולא ירחמו
רג̇לין להם וליס יתמשאו. לא ירתאחו ולא ישקאו
מתלהם יכון פ̇אעלהם. וכל מן יתכל עליהם
ג̇אב אלפ̇אס וכצרהם
ג̇אב לחטב וצ̇וור ביהם
כ̇אד הנאר וחרקהם
וחט אלפ̇אס פ̇י יד כבירהם
וג̇לק הצ̇אר עליהם
ומשא אברהם לענד אובו בסרעא
קאל לו יא איבי רית הסאעא
עג̇ב פ̇י מעאבדך הסבעה
והומאן יתכ̇אצמו ענד כבירהם
והווא יחמק עליהם
ומא ערפ̇ת מא הווא נעבדהם
כ̇איף יעז בכ̇אטרהם

Because of the food I gave them,
I did not know how to divide it before them,
Whether to break the food into pieces; so I spoke to them:
Why their quarrel and what their litigation?"
When his father heard this speech he was full of wonder,
And went running and came near,
And clapped his hands,
And said: "My son, you are wise in lies!"
When he arrived at the opening of the gate,
He did find the fire lit on the firewood
That Abraham had used to sacrifice and offer.
He opened the doors to them,
The fire was kindled on them,
And the entire room was full of smoke;
No one could be found except the biggest one.
Teraḥ went to his son with intense seriousness,
He spoke to him: "Abraham, about this sacrifice
That you offered these idols as an evening prayer
And you did greatly lie about it
And you said: Immobile they all fought!"
He spoke to him: "My father, I did not lower my hand on them,
Therefore, I shall tell you of their quarrels.
First, I did not go to all of them in the house,
But I stopped by the largest one,
And my mother's sacrifice I offered to them.
There came the smallest among them,
And as you saw this one ran around and destroyed them!
And if you hold me for a liar, ask the largest one to tell you!"
His father answered and spoke to him: "Can he talk or burn?
I know that all this is from you!"
He spoke to him: "My father, may your ear hear what your mouth speaks!
If he cannot speak nor cause to burn,
Why do you worship them and believe in them rather than in God Who created you,
And from darkness to light has delivered you,
And with profit and benefit strengthened you!
Let us extol God Who will hear your speech and your entreaty,
And if you honestly invoke Him, He is your God in truth,
How you will be judged in fire and burned,
And people He will not allow to pronounce His name.
Let us elevate God over them, high above the curse of their mouths from baptism!"
When his father heard this speech
He ran to Nimrod the sultan.
He said to him: "My lord, let me inform you what happened to my fetishes,
What my son perpetrated today; he said, 'Let us make them an offering,
He went to offer food but set fire to them,
They were all burned and became ashes and smoke!'"
Nimrod answered and said: "Bring the destroyer to court!"

ג̇יר הטעאם חטית להם
ומא ערפ̇ת כיף צאר פ̇יהם
לאזם תמשי דלחין וקול להם
כ̇צומתהם עלאש והאש קצ̇ייתהם
כיף סמאע אובוה האד לכלאם אסתעג̇ב
ובקא ימשי יג̇רי ויתקררב
ובקא יד עלא יד יצ̇רב
ויקול ולדי תעללם לכדב
כיף וצל לפ̇ום לבאב
ילקא הנאר תשעל פ̇לחטב
פ̇י באלו אברהם דבח וקררב
חל עליהם לביבאן
ילקא להם וקררב ג̇מיע הצלבאן
שעלת פ̇יהם הניראן
וג̇מיע לבית כולהא דוכ̇כ̇אן
מה לקא ג̇יר כבירהם כיף כאן
משא תרח לענד ולדו בחרג̇א קוייא
קאל לו יא אברהם מאלה הדייא
אלדי קררבת ללמעאבד האד לעשייא
ותזיד תכדב עלייא
ותקול קאעדין יתכ̇אצמו כלהם
קאל לו יא אבי אנא מא מדיתש ידי פ̇יהם
לאכן נכ̇ברך בקצ̇ייתהם
אוול מא דכ̇לת ללבית עליהם
ג̇ית קעדת בחדא כבירהם
והדיית אמי קררבת להם
ג̇א הצג̇יר אלדי פ̇יהם
מד ידו ליאכל קבל מנהם
קאם לכביר מתאעהם ונגר עליהם
ג̇אב פ̇אס וכצרהם
ג̇אב לחטב וצ̇וור ביהם
כ̇אר הנאר וחרקהם
וכיף רית האד השי הרבת וכ̇ליתהם
ואידא כדבתני אנשד כבירהם יכ̇ברך
ג̇אובו אובוה וקאל לו ואש הווא יתכללם או יתחררך
אנא עארף האד השי לכל מנך
קאל לו יא אבי תסמע ודנך מא יתכללם פ̇מך
אידא מא יתכללם ולא יתחררך
עלאש תעבדו ותסללמו פ̇לאילה אלדי כ̇לקך
ומן הצ̇לאם לצ̇וו כ̇רג̇ך
ומן פ̇צ̇לו וחסאנו קוותך
נעלת אללה עלא מן יסמע כלאמתך ויתבעך
ואידא כאן תקול הווא אילאהך פ̇לחק
כיף תכון תחכם פ̇יה הנאר וחתרק
וענדו פ̇ום וליס ינטק
נעלת אללה עליהם ועלא מן סבב פ̇יהם מן הצאבק
חין סמאע אובוה האד לכלאם
משא לענד נמרוד הצלטאן
קאל לו יא סידי נכ̇ברך מא ג̇רא לי פ̇צלבאן
ג̇אני ולדי ליום קאל נחב נקררב להם קרבן
כיף ג̇ית לקית שעלת פ̇יהם הניראן
ונחרקו כלהם ובקאו רמאץ̇ ודוכ̇אן
ג̇אוב נמרוד וקאל ג̇יבו כ̇ראב לדיאן

Abraham came before the sultan.
Nimrod spoke to him: "What did you do to the fetishes?"
He spoke to him: "My master! I did not do anything except that
I said to my mother, my soul desires the same worship as Father's.
Please prepare me a good dish that I will take
To Father's idol house and offer them!
But when I entered, I came and rested before the biggest one,
And my mother's sacrifice I offered them.
There came the smallest from among them,
He extended his hand to eat before them,
The largest one among them rose and hit them over the head,
He brought the pickax and broke them,
He brought firewood and surrounded them,
He took fire and burned them,
He got up, ran around, and destroyed them,
And locked the room before them,
And I do not know how he broke them.
And if I lied, I will ask the biggest one to tell you!"
Nimrod spoke to Abraham: "Do they speak with their mouths?
Or do they hear with their ears, or walk with their feet, or burn any of their prey?
We are those who ordered the goldsmith to fashion them,
And the carpenter to turn them,
And use the remainder as firewood to cook breakfast.
And one day I will have better ones than these,
And how can you speak about any harm from them!"
Our lord Abraham answered and said to him: "The curse of God is on you and them
And on their worshipers!
If one day you will have a better one, why do you worship them?
But God Who commanded me concerning them and made me burn them,
He ordered me not to worship them,
He instructed me to leave the region.
You institutionalize the lie and cancel the truth;
Those that cannot salivate are for burning,
And you say that to your Creator!"
Nimrod answered Abraham and spoke to him: "I call you to judgment,
Look, I am the Creator!"
He spoke to him: "If all your speech is true
Order the sun to rise in the west and descend in the east;
And if you cannot, then God Who ordered me concerning your idols to burn them,
He will decree for me concerning you and I shall burn you like them,
And all the worship of fetishes we shall abolish,
And there will not remain one in the world who will worship them,
And it will fade from the lands and we shall civilize your state and their state,
But we shall bury you under pebbles and you will be cut off!
And over all peoples there will be a victorious ruler,
Who shall worship God, the forgiving,
And will be strong in this world and meritorious in intention,
And the God Whom he worships will free him from being slaughtered into the grave."
At that moment, evil Nimrod became an apostate
And all his army and soldiers he called together.
And spoke to them: "If we leave this one alive on the earth, he will rule over all the world,
And destroy the king and ruin religion,
Let us look no further but let us burn him in intense fires!"

ג̇א אברהם קודאם הצלטאן
קאל לו נמרוד האש פ̇עלת פ̇צלבאן
קאל לו יא סידי אנא מא פ̇עלת חאג̇א מן האד השי
ג̇יר קולת לאמו פ̇י מעאבד באבא חבבת נפ̇סי
קומי צנעי מעישה טייבא באש נחב נמשי
לבית מעאבד באבא ונקררב להם
כיף דכ̇לת ג̇ית קעדת חדא כבירהם
והדיית אומי קררבת להם
ג̇א הצג̇יר אלדי פ̇יהם
מד ידו ליאכל קבל מנהם
קאם לכביר ונגר עליהם
ג̇אב פ̇אס וכצרהם
ג̇אב לחטב וצ̇וור ביהם
כ̇אר הנאר וחרקהם
קמת הרבת וכ̇ליתהם
וגלקת לבית עליהם
ומא ערפ̇ת כיף צאר פ̇יהם
ואידא כדבתני אנשד יכ̇ברך כבירהם
קאל נמרוד לאברהם ואש הומאן יתכללמו בפ̇אמהם
או יסמעו בודניהם. או ימשיו ברג̇ליהם. או יתחררכו בג̇מיע פ̇ריסתהם
אחנאן אלדי אמרנא עלא הסייג̇א וסייג̇והם
ועלא הנג̇ג̇ארא ונג̇רוהם
ועקאב לחטב טייבנא לפ̇טור ביהם
וחתא בהאיים אפ̇צ̇ל מנהם
וכיף אנתי תקול מצ̇ררתהם מנהם
ג̇אוב סידנא אברהם וקאל לו נעלת אללה עליך ועליהם
ועלא מן יעבדהם
אידא כאן בהאיים אפ̇צ̇ל מנהם עלאש תעבדוהם
לאכן לאילה אלדי קצ̇צ̇רני עליהם וחרקתהם
יקצ̇צ̇רני חתא עלא מן יעבדהם
אפ̇המו האש תכ̇ררג̇ו מן למנטק
אתבתו לכדב ותבטלו לחק
האדא מא ילג̇מהם כאן לחרק
ותקולו האדא לכ̇אלק
ג̇אוב נמרוד לאברהם קאל לו אנא נקוללך לחק
ראהו אנא הווא לכ̇אלק
קאל לו אידא ג̇מיע כלאמך חק
האמר על השמס תכון תשרק מן לגרב ותג̇יב מן השרק
ואידא מא פ̇עלת שי מן האדה לאילה אלדי קדרני עלא מעאבדתך וחרקתהם
יקדרני חתא עליך ונחרקך כיפ̇הם
וג̇מיע מעאבד הצלבאן נבטלהם
ולא יבקא חד פ̇דניא יעבדהם
ונכשף פ̇לבלדאן ונמדן חאלך וחאלהם
לאכן נצ̇בבר עליך צ̇בארה ותכון משתור
ותכון עלא ג̇מיע לאומה צלטאן מנצור
אידא תעבד רב לג̇אפ̇ור
ותכון קוי פ̇י האד הדניא ופ̇ג̇איא משכור
ולאילה אלדי תעבדו יפ̇כך מן ג̇צרת לקבור
פ̇י דיך הסאעה כפ̇ר נמרוד הרשע

וג̇מיע ג̇יושו ועסאכרו ג̇ממע
קאל להם אידא כ̇ללינא האדא חיי פ̇דניא יכון יחכם פ̇י ג̇מיע הדניא
ויכ̇רב אלמלך ויפ̇סד הדין
מא ילנא באן נחרקוה בניראן ואקדין

And all the people together joined Nimrod
And immediately threw him into the fiery oven,
But at that moment God appeared for him, praised be He, Who had ordained all this,
And made a tree grow from all the firewood in the kiln,
Filled with crops and dates;
He stayed and ate and drank,
And in song praised and gave thanks
To the God Who had extricated him from the hand of all infidels.
And the Lord of the world called,
He spoke to him: "Abraham, My beloved, I rescued you from the heat,
I shall be with you and liberate you,
From all your enemies and those who hate you;
I shall help to bring forth rulers from you,
Therefore, from the midst of the River I am taking you."
Abraham rose from the midst of the River by decree of God, the Lord.
And all the people were astonished
And spoke: "Abraham and his God are true, but Nimrod is a liar!"
And then Nimrod could only grind his teeth.
Then our lord Abraham became the teacher of men in the worship of God the Lord,
And all those idols were burned in the fire.
And he spoke: "These are the deserts of the infidels,
But His handiwork will civilize itself,
And they will worship God, praised be He, night and day."
And so our lord Abraham walked before God,
And from him came the people of Israel, to worship God the Mighty One.

And the proof at this moment: **כה אמר יי אלהי ישראל בעבר הנהר ישבו אבותיכם מעולם.** Its translation: And Joshua said to the entire people: So says Allah, on the other side of the River dwelt your fathers from the beginning, Teraḥ the father of Abraham and the father of Naḥor, and they practiced strange worships. And I took Abraham from the other side of the River and led him through the entire land of Syria and made plentiful his progeny and gave him Isaac, and to Isaac I gave Jacob and Esau and gave the mountain of Seir to Esau as inheritance but Jacob and his sons descended into Egypt.

וגׄמיע אלאומה בחדא נמרוד מתגׄמעין

ורמאווה פֿיסע פֿי אתון הנאר

פֿסע תגׄללא עליה אללה ברוך הוא אלדׄי עלא כול שׁיי יקדר

ובקא גׄמיע חטב אלכושׁא נבבת שׁגׄר

מעביין בלגׄללא והתמאר

ובקא יאכל וישׁרב וימדדח וישׁכר

לאילה אלדׄי כׄללצו מן יד גׄמיע אלכופֿאר

וסׄייד הדׄניא עליה נגׄר

קאל לו יא אברהם יא חביבי אשׁביך מחׄייר

אנא נכון מעאך ונכׄלללצׄך

מן גׄמיע עדאך ומכׄארהינך

אנא מסתעד לנכׄררגׄ צׄלטאן מננך

דלחין מן וצׄט נהאר נכׄרגׄך

וטלאע אברהם מן וצׄט הנאר בקצׄרת אללה הרב

ובקא ענד גׄמיע הנאס עגׄב

וקאלו אברהם ואילאהו חק ונמרוד מעה כדׄב

ובקא נמרוד ידו עלא ראצׄו יצׄרב

חתא צׄאר סׄידׄנא אברהם יעללם פֿנאס עבאדת אללה הרב

וגׄמיע מן ענדו מעבוד חרקו בנאר

ויקול האדׄה מצׄאנע אלכופֿאר

וליד אלדׄי צׄנעתו תתכצׄר

ובקאו יעבדו פֿי אללה ברוך הוא ליל ונהאר

והאד השׁי מן סׄידׄנא אברהם אלדׄי פֿי אללה כׄטאר

וכׄרגׄת מנו אומת ישׂראל אלדׄי תעבד לאילאה הגׄבאר

ודליל פֿי דאלך הסׄאעה ויאמר יהושע אל כל העם כה אמר ה' אלׄהי ישׂראל בעבר הנהר
ישׁבו אבותיכם מעולם. שׁרח דאלך וקאל יהושע לגׄמיע לקום האכדׄה קאל אללה פֿי מגׄאז
לואד גׄלסו אבאתכום מן הדׄניא תרח אבי אברהם ואבי נחור ועבדו מעאבד אוכׄרין
וצטפֿית לאברהם אובוכם ומשׁיתו פֿי גׄמיע ארצׄ השׁאם. וכׄתרת נסׄלו ורזקת לו יצחק ורזקת
ליצחק יעקב ועשׂו ועטית לעשׂו גׄבל שׂעיר יראתא ויעקב וולאדו הבטו למצר.

Commentary

The Seder

The institutions of rabbinic Judaism go back to Ezra and the Men of the Great Assembly whose activities extend from the fourth century B.C.E. through Maccabean times. The Men of the Great Assembly established the general rules and the outlines of the contents of prayers and benedictions and formulated the doxologies that conclude the benedictions. The following basic statement is reported in the Babylonian *Talmud* (*b. Berakhot* 33a):[1] "R. Ḥiyya bar Abba said in the name of R. Yoḥanan: The Men of the Great Assembly instituted for Israel benedictions and prayers, *Qiddush* and *Havdalah*." (A documentation of the surviving material on prayers and benedictions from the time of the Great Assembly is contained in the notes [pp. 34-35] of I. Elbogen, התפילה בישראל בהתפתחותה ההיסטורית; see bibliography, under Modern Scholarship.) The texts of most prayers remained a personal or communal matter all through talmudic times and into the early Middle Ages. This resulted in a bewildering array of different liturgies. Even today under the pressure of many forces working toward the uniformity of worship, particularly the influence of the printing press and the *Shulḥan 'Arukh* and its commentaries, there exist a number of distinct prayer rituals. But one liturgy is practically identical for all major Jewish groups, from Western Europe to Yemen, and that is the Passover *Haggadah*. The most natural explanation for this uniformity is that the text of the *Haggadah* was fixed during the time of the Second Temple or shortly thereafter. There is both internal and external evidence to show that the *Haggadah* is one of the oldest texts of rabbinic literature available to us. The standard text of the *Haggadah* is already taken for granted in the Babylonian *Talmud;* the text of the *Haggadah* is quoted in an argument about the meaning of Hebrew עני "deprivation," in *b. Yoma* 74b (this will be discussed later in the commentary). The Babylonian *Talmud* always presumes that its students are familiar with the text of prayers and rituals; in contrast to the Jerusalem *Talmud*, in its Ashkenazic and Sephardic manuscripts it is not a source of prayer

---

1 אמר ר' חייא בר אבא אמר רבי יוחנן אנשי כנסת הגדולה תקנו להם לישראל ברכות ותפלות קדושות והבדלות.

texts or legal formularies, and no argument *e silentio* can apply to this source.

Certain features of the *Seder*, the celebration of the first night of Passover, need a preliminary discussion. The Torah (*Ex.* 13:8) instructs every head of household to tell his children of the Exodus when *mazzot* are first eaten during the Passover festival. The story of the Exodus is presented in the fashion of a Greco-Roman symposium dinner: at least during the "Night of Deliverance" the Jews behave as if they were their own masters taking their rightful place in world history. According to the *Talmudim*, the guiding precept in formulating the rules of the *Seder* is that the meal is eaten "in the way of free people," that is, of Roman citizens. In the words of the Jerusalem *Talmud* (*y. Pesaḥim* X,1 37b):[2] "R. Lewy said: Since slaves usually eat while standing, it is required that this meal be taken reclining [on couches] to demonstrate that they went from servitude to freedom." Similarly, the Babylonian *Talmud* (*b. Pesaḥim* 108a) states that the *mazzah* must be eaten and the wine drunk while reclining on couches[3] "because now is the time of the beginning of freedom." The opinion of the early Medieval authority R. Eliezer ben Natan (*RAVaN*, p. 74a) and his grandson R. Eliezer ben Joel Halevi (*RAVIA* §525) is that today one should not recline on a couch, but conduct the *Seder* in the way of a festive dinner held by the upper classes of contemporary Gentile society. This opinion was not popularly accepted and is therefore invalid but it is generally accepted for Eastern European women (*R. Moshe Isserles, Shulḥan 'Arukh Oraḥ Ḥayyim* §472 #4) and even men today do not lie on couches but recline toward their left on chairs, preferably on armchairs with leg rests. German and Sephardic wives are considered aristocratic and continue to recline in the way men do (*Kaf Haḥayyim ad loc.*, notes 27,28).

According to all talmudic sources, the participants eat and talk while reclining on couches. This custom is condemned as a foreign luxury by Amos (6:4), who castigates those "who recline on couches of ivory" since in old times participants at formal dinners were sitting on individual chairs along the wall as shown by *1 Sam.* 20:35: "The king sat, as always, on his seat, the seat at the wall." The Mesopotamian

---

2 אמר ר׳ לוי ולפי שדרך עבדים להיות אוכלין מעומד וכאן להיות מסובין להודיע שיצאו מעבדות לחירות.

3 דהשתא הוא דקא מתחלא לה חירות.

custom of reclining on couches was later adopted by Persians (*Esth.* 1:6, 7:8), Greeks, and Romans.

Dinners in Gentile antiquity always included libations to the gods. This custom is identified by the Rabbis (*Midrash Esth. rabbah* 1:8) in the description of Ahasverus's feast in the scroll of Esther (1:8): "The drinking was according to law; nobody was forced":[4] "Rav said: Nobody was forced to participate in the libations." These libations were not in general accompanied by some spilling of wine; rather they were done by a gentle shaking of the cup. This is how Rashi, the standard commentary on the Babylonian *Talmud*, sums up the discussion on Gentile libations (*b. 'Avodah Zarah* 59b):[5] ". . . because libations are always performed by shaking." Parallel to Gentile libations, one of the main features of the *Seder* is the drinking of four consecrated cups of wine in praise of God. The emphasis on the praise of God is already noted by the Sadducee author Philo of Alexandria (*De spec. leg.* II, sec. xxvii, 148):[6] "[The guests] are there not as in other festive gatherings, to indulge the belly with wine and viands, but to fulfill with prayers and hymns the custom handed down by their fathers." Similarly, the Babylonian author R. Saadia Gaon translates the Hebrew root הגד of the word *Haggadah* by Arabic שכר "to praise" (*Deut.* 26:3). It may be significant that the institution of the Four Cups is left without any basis or justification in the Babylonian *Talmud*, although one may argue that the Babylonian, as a later source, in all discussions presupposes a knowledge of the relevant passages of the *Talmud* of Jerusalem. The Jerusalem *Talmud* gives many reasons (*y. Pesaḥim* X,1 37b–c):[7] "From where are the Four Cups derived? R. Yoḥanan [said] in the name of R. Banaya: they correspond to the four verbs of deliverance (*Ex.* 6:7–8): 'Hence, say to the children of Israel: I

---

4 רב אמר אין אונס ביין נסך.

5 שאין מנסכים אלא על ידי שכשוך.

6 οἵ παραγεγόνασιν οὐχ ὡς εἰς τὰ ἄλλα συμπόσια χαριούμενοι γαστρὶ δι' οἴνου καὶ ἐδεσμάτων, ἀλλὰ πατρίον ἔθος ἐκπληρώσοντες μετ' εὐχῶν τε καὶ ὕμνων.

7 מניין לארבעה כוסות. רבי יוחנן בשם ר' בנייה כנגד ארבע גאולות לכן אמור לבני ישראל אני ה' והוצאתי אתכם וגו'. ולקחתי אתכם לי לעם וגו'. והוצאתי והצלתי וגאלתי ולקחתי. ר' יהושע בן לוי אמר כנגד ארבע כוסות של פרעה. וכוס פרעה בידי. ואשחט אותם אל כוס פרעה. ואתן את הכוס על יד פרעה. ונתת כוס פרעה בידו וגו'. ר' לוי אמר כנגד ארבע מלכיות. ורבנן אמרי כנגד ארבעה כוסות של פורענות שהקב"ה עתיד להשקות את אומות העולם. כי כה אמר ה' אלהי ישראל אלי קח את כוס היין החימה וגו'. כוס זהב בבל ביד ה'. כי כוס ביד ה'. ימטר על רשעים פחים אש וגפרית ורוח זלעפות מנת כוסם. מהו מנת כוסם. ר' אבון אמר דיפלי פוטרין כדיפלי פוטרין אחר המרחץ. וכנגדן עתיד הקב"ה להשקות את ישראל ארבע כוסות של נחמות. ה' מנת חלקי וכוסי. דשנת בשמן ראשי כוסי רוייה. והדין כוס ישועות אשא תריין.

am the Lord, I shall *take* you *out* from under the pressure of work in Egypt, I shall *save* you from their service, I shall *redeem* you with an outstretched arm and great judgments. I shall *take* you as a people for me.' R. Yehoshua ben Lewy said that they correspond to the four cups of Pharaoh (*Gen.* 40:11): 'The *cup* of Pharaoh was in my hand; I took the grapes and squeezed them into the *cup* of Pharaoh and gave the *cup* in Pharaoh's hand.' (*Gen.* 40.13): 'You will give the *cup* in the hand of Pharaoh.' R. Lewy said that they correspond to the Four Kingdoms (*Dan.* 7). Our teachers say that they correspond to the four cups of doom that the Holy One, praised be He, will make the Gentiles drink at the end of days (*Jer.* 25:15): 'Truly, so said the Lord, the God of Israel, to me: take this *cup* of the wine of wrath from my hand and make drink from it all the peoples to whom I am sending you.' (*Jer.* 51:7) 'The golden *cup* of Babylon is in the hand of the Lord, intoxicating all the land.' (*Ps.* 75:9) 'Truly a *cup* is in the hand of the Lord, intoxicating wine, fully to be mixed; He shall sprinkle from it but its dregs shall be drunk, squeezed to the last, by all the wicked of the earth.' (*Ps.* 11:6) 'He shall let rain coals on the wicked; fire, sulphur, and burning wind is the portion of their *cup*.' [What does "the portion of their cup" mean? R. Abun said: a double cup like the double cup taken after a thermal bath.] And in accordance with this correspondingly the Holy One, praised be He, will let Israel drink four cups of consolation at the End of Days (*Ps.* 16:5): 'The Lord is the portion of my part and my *cup*.' (*Ps* 23:5) 'You anointed my head with oil; my *cup* is overflowing.' (*Ps.* 116:13) 'I shall lift up the *cup* of salvations' counts for two."

The tradition of R. Yoḥanan is self-explanatory but rather unconvincing. The tradition of R. Lewy is similar to that of "our teachers" since for him the Four Cups are symbols of the doom of the four reigns of oppression. The tradition of R. Yehoshua ben Lewy seems to be far-fetched and irrelevant at first sight, but it is really the closest to a direct connection with Passover. R. Yehoshua alludes to the tradition contained in the paraphrase of Joseph's interpretation of the cup-bearer's dream in the medieval *Targum Yerushalmi (Pseudo-Jonathan)* to *Gen.* 40:12:[8] "Joseph said to him: 'The deep meaning of

---

8 ואמר ליה יוסף דין סוף פושרנא דחלמא תלתי מצוניא תלתי אבהת עלמא אינון אברהם יצחק ויעקב דמן בני בניהון עתידין למישתעבדא למצרים בטינא ובליבנא ובכל פולחנא באנפי ברא ומן בתר כדון מתפרקין על ידי תלת רעיין ודי אמרת נסיבית ית עינבייא ועצרית יתהום לכסא דפרעה ויהבית ית כסא לידא דפרעה היא פיילא דרוגזא דעתיד פרעה שתי בעקבא ואת רב מזוגייא תקבל אגר טב על חלמך טב דחלמתא ופושרני דין הוא לך תלתא מצונייא תלתא יומין הינון לפורקנך.

the dream is as follows. The three vines are the three fathers of the world, Abraham, Isaac, and Jacob, whose descendants will be enslaved in Egypt with mortar and bricks and all kinds of servitude in the open air but who afterward will be saved by three shepherds. And your words, "I took the grapes and squeezed them into the cup of Pharaoh and gave the cup in Pharaoh's hand" refer to the phial of wrath that Pharaoh will have to drink in the end. Now you, head mixer, will receive your reward for dreaming such a good dream, and the explanation of the dream for you is that the three vines signify three days to your freedom.'"

In any case, four distinct reasons for one action are an overdetermination. One may therefore assume that the Four Cups represent a traditional feature for which an explanation had to be found later, when Jews no longer were familiar with or sympathetic to Roman or Persian customs. The physical setting of the *Seder* shows that its rules are derived either from Mesopotamian usage common to Persians and Jews, or from Roman examples. In the first case, the rules would belong to the original institutions of the Men of the Great Assembly. Otherwise, the imitation of Roman styles would presuppose a friendly atmosphere between Jews and Romans, as it existed during most of the Hasmonean kingdom, which from the start was a dependent ally of Rome. The text of the Roman declaration incorporating the Jewish Commonwealth as dependent ally is reported in *1 Macc.* 15:15-21. The relations between Jews and the surrounding Hellenized peoples were never so friendly as to invite an imitation of Greek customs by Jews. The only friendly relations between Hasmoneans and Greeks were with the far-off state of Sparta (*1 Macc.* 14:20-23). Therefore, the setting of the *Seder* meal indicates that its rules must have been formulated either under Persian rule before 332 B.C.E. or under the Hasmonean dynasty between 150 and 70 B.C.E.

Eliezer ben Iehuda in his *Thesaurus* (*s.v.* כוס) points out that the Hebrew word for "cup" is feminine in biblical Hebrew, but masculine in rabbinical Hebrew. Now the detailed ritual instructions relative to the different cups are given for the First, Second, etc., Cup, with the numerals in the masculine; but the totality of cups is always referred to as אַרְבַּע כּוֹסוֹת, "four (f.) cups." This proves that the Four Cups were already an integral part of the celebration when biblical Hebrew changed into rabbinical Hebrew. Unfortunately, our knowledge of early Hasmonean Hebrew is too fragmentary to rule out completely an early Hasmonean date, but a Persian date is more likely.

Four is an even number and doing anything an even number of times is frowned upon in Jewish tradition since it is considered unlucky. In the words of the *Talmud* (*b. Pesaḥim* 109b):[9] "One may not provide less than four [cups to the poor man on welfare]: How can our teachers institute something that may bring on danger? Did we not learn: No man should eat an even number of dishes nor drink an even number of glasses nor cleanse himself an even number of times nor be satisfied [sexually] an even number of times."[10] The *Talmud* (*loc. cit.*)[11] solves the problem of even numbers in several ways: "Rav Naḥman said: Scripture says (*Ex.* 12:42), 'A night of protection,' [the night of the Fifteenth of Nisan is] a night protected from damaging influences. Rava said: The cup of wine for Grace [which is required at all dinners, not only for the *Seder* meal] can be joined to the other [three] only for good, not for evil influences. Ravina said: Our teachers instituted Four Cups in the manner of free men; each of them is a separate obligation." The last opinion is the authoritative one since its author, Ravina, was the last general editor of the Babylonian *Talmud*. This is the explicit decision of Alfassi (*Pesaḥim* §784):[12] "The rabbis said that, since each cup represents a separate obligation, we make a separate benediction for each one." Alfassi's decision is based on the Gaonic compendium *Halakhot Gedolot* (ed. E. Hildesheimer, p. 290). A dissenting decision, namely to pronounce the benediction over the first and third cups only, is attributed by the Provençal *Sefer Ha'iṭṭur* (vol. 2, p. קלג) to Rav Cohen-Tsedeq Gaon of Sura (active around 840 C.E., the first Gaon from whom a considerable body of work has come down to us) and other early authorities. Today the ruling of Alfassi is followed by Ashkenazic Jews on the authority of Rashi (1040–1105, *Sefer Ha'orah*, p. 100), who quotes a responsum of R. Sherira Gaon of Pumbeditha (died 1000 C.E.)[13] and by Yemenite

---

9 ולא יפחתו לו מארבעה: היכי מתקני רבנן מידי דאתי בה לידי סכנה ותניא לא יאכל אדם תרי ולא ישתי תרי ולא יקנח תרי ולא יעשה צרכיו תרי.

10 In Roman religious practice even numbers were also shunned (Vergil, *Eclogue* VIII,75: *Numero deus impare gaudet*, God enjoys odd numbers). This may have Pythagorean roots. [Note supplied by Dr. Eva Guggenheimer.]

11 אמר רב נחמן אמר קרא ליל שמורים ליל המשומר ובא מן המזיקין. רבא אמר כוס של ברכה מצרף לטובה ואינו מצרף לרעה. רבינא אמ ארבעה כסי תקינו רבנן דרך חירות כל חד וחד מצוה באפי נפשא הוא.

12 הוֹאיל וכל אחד ואחד מצוה בפני עצמוֹ הוּא ברכינן בורא פרי הגפן אכל כסא וכסא.

13 וארבע כוסות הללו כל אחד ואחד טעון ברכה לפניו משום דבתר קדושא אסור ליה למשתי עד שדורש מארמי אובד אבי וחותם בגאולה ומברך בורא פרי הגפן ומדאמרינן הב ונברך ברכת המזון איתסר ליה למשתי עד דמברך ומן כד דמברך בין שלישי לרביעי לא ישתה ואתסר ליה עד דאמר הלל הגדול וברכת השיר.

Each one of these Four Cups needs a separate benediction before it is consumed

Jews on the authority of Maimonides (*Hilkhot Ḥameẓ Umaẓẓah* VIII 5,10). Sephardic Jews follow the contrary decision of R. Asher ben Yeḥiel (*Rosh Pesaḥim* §24)[14] based on a long line of Spanish and Provençal authorities going back to R. Izḥaq ibn Ghiat. Their reason is that a benediction involves an invocation of the Divine Name; an unnecessary proliferation of benedictions means taking God's name in vain and violates the Third Commandment (*Ex.* 20:7). On the other hand, one may not partake of food for which one did not thank God by a benediction during that meal proper. Some older Ashkenazic authorities (*RAVIA Pesaḥim* §525, p. 156) even require a benediction of thanksgiving ("short Grace") after the first and third cups to make clear that different benedictions belong to different meals. This ruling seems to contradict the statement of Ravina in the talmudic text quoted above and it was not accepted by any Jewish group. (The conceptual details of the rules of benedictions will be discussed in detail in the section on the *Qiddush*.) It seems that the standard talmudic text quoted above is that of the Academy of Pumbeditha headed by R. Sherira Gaon. The argument of the *Sefer Ha'iṭṭur* is based on a different text:[15] "R. Naḥman bar Izḥaq said, 'It is a night of protection,' and Rava said, 'Each single cup is a separate obligation.'" These quotes probably are from R. Cohen-Tsedeq Gaon's Academy of Sura. The main implication of this text is that R. Naḥman bar Izḥaq disagrees with Rava on the thesis that in the "night of protection" one does not have to be afraid of evil forces. It is a general principle that in talmudic decisions of the later generations of talmudic sages, preference must be given to the latest authority (cf. R. Samuel

---

since one may not drink after *Qiddush* until one has explained the *Haggadah* starting from "The Aramean is destroying my father" and ending with the doxology for the liberation; after that one must praise "Him Who created the fruit of the vine." After one has exhorted the guests to say Grace, one may not drink until one has finished Grace and then one may not drink between the Third and Fourth Cups until one has completed the Great *Hallel* and its benedictions.

14 בין כוס ראשון לכוס שני שאם ירצה לשתות דשותה לא הוי היסח הדעת וכן בין שלישי לרביעי אע״ג דאסור לשתות כיון שהכוס לפניו ודעתו לשתות לא הויא הלילא הפסק והיסח הדעת הלכך נראה שאין לברך כי אם על כוס ראשון ושלישי.

One may drink between the First and Second Cups; therefore, one does not become oblivious of the fact that one has recited the benediction over wine. Between the Third and Fourth Cups one may not drink, but since the cup is in one's hand and one knows that one has to drink another cup, *Hallel* is not an interruption nor does it make oblivious [of one's obligation to drink afterward]. It seems therefore that one should make the benediction only on the First and Third Cups.

15 אר״נ בר יצחק ליל שמורים הוא ורבא אמר כל חד וחד מצוה באפה נפשה.

HaNagid, *Mevo HaTalmud*, p. 47a). The succession in time of the sages mentioned in the two versions is R. Naḥman (bar Ya'aqov) - Rava - R. Naḥman bar Izḥaq - Ravina. In the first version, the decision has to follow Ravina, but in the second we follow R. Naḥman bar Izḥaq. The *Talmud* of Jerusalem does not discuss either the number of benedictions or the problem of the even number of cups. In general, that *Talmud* is not taking evil influences into account, and since it even has a rule[16] applicable to illiterate Galilean congregations that after a recital of the basic *Haggadah* by the cantor in the synagogue the private persons (who are unable to conduct their own *Seder*) may fulfill their remaining obligation by drinking four cups in one batch, it follows that the Academy of Sura agrees with the practice of the *Yerushalmi*. In many cases the Academy of Sura, founded in the third century C.E. by Rav, who was trained in Galilee, preserved Israeli traditions, where the Academy of Pumbeditha, successor of the autochthonous Academy of Nahardea, preserved old Babylonian traditions. For example, the Academy of Sura was the home in Babylonia of the *piuṭim*, poetic enlargements, embellishments, or substitutes of prayers that were the rule in Galilee; the Academy of Pumbeditha frowned on the insertion of *piuṭim*, and some of its leaders forbade their recitation (cf. L. Ginzberg, *Ginze Schechter* II, pp. 511–516). (An example of a Galilean substitute of a prayer is given in the section on Grace.)

A general principle of Jewish law states (*Mishnah Qiddushin* I,7):[17] "All commandments requiring specific actions at specific times only apply to men but not to women" because in many cases they would interfere with the duties of the woman as a mother and supervisor of a household. The Four Cups clearly require a specific action (drinking) at a fixed time (the *Seder* night) and therefore as a commandment cannot apply to women. However, the *Talmud* states (*b. Pesaḥim* 108a),[18] "R. Yehoshua ben Lewy said in addition that women are obliged to drink these Four Cups since they also were saved by the

---

16 דא״ר יוחנן הלל אם שמען בבית הכנסת יצא. הדא אמרה אפי' שתאן בכרך אחד יצא.
Since R. Yoḥanan says that if he heard *Hallel* in the synagogue, he fulfilled his obligation. This implies that if one drinks (the Four Cups) in one batch, one has fulfilled his obligation.

17 וכל מצות עשה שהזמן גרמא אנשים הייבין ונשים פטורות.

18 ואמר ר' יהושע בן לוי נשים חייבות בארבע כוסות הללו שאף הן היו באותו הנס.

same miracle." It is noted by *Tosafot* (*ad loc., s.v.* שאף),[19] "Without that specific reason [i.e., that women were saved together with the men in Egypt], women could not be required [to drink the Four Cups] since women are free from commandments requiring an action at a fixed time, and even though the Four Cups are a rabbinic institution [whereas the principle refers to biblical commandments], their institutions follow the rules of biblical commandments." Probably the drinking of the Four Cups, like the custom of reclining, was an ancient general practice predating talmudic times and is not derived from any biblical commandment.

---

19 ואי לאו האי טעמא לא היו חייבות משום דנשים פטורות ממצות עשה שהזמן גרמא אף על גב דארבע כוסות דרבנן כעין דאורייתא תיקון.

Removal of Ḥameẓ

The holiday of Passover is called the Feast of Unleavened Bread in the Pentateuch (*Ex.* 23:15, 34:18; *Lev.* 23:6; *Num.* 28:17). The Hebrew name of Passover, *Pesaḥ*, is reserved specifically for the sacrifice that was offered in the afternoon of the Fourteenth of Nisan and eaten in the night of the Fifteenth, and for the ceremony of the Temple service in the afternoon and the *Seder* in the night. The first meaning of *Pesaḥ* appears, for example, in *Deut.* 16:2: "You shall sacrifice a *Pesaḥ* to the Lord your God . . ." and the second in *Lev.* 23:5: "In the First month, on the Fourteenth of the month in the evening, there is a *Pesaḥ* for the Lord. And on the Fifteenth day of this month there is the Feast of Unleavened Bread for the Lord. . . . "

Three biblical commandments involve leavened matter (*ḥameẓ*). One is forbidden to eat leavened food (*Ex.* 12:19–20): ". . . If anyone should eat leavened matter, that person will be excised from the congregation of Israel, be he a proselyte or indigenous to the Land. Do not eat any leavened matter. . . ." No leavened matter nor leavening nor yeast may be found in a Jewish household (*Ex.* 12:9): "For seven days, no leavening shall be found in your houses"; (*Ex.* 13:7): "There shall not be seen for you either leavend matter or leavening in your domain." All leavened matter must be removed before the afternoon of the Fourteenth of Nisan since "you may not offer the blood of My sacrifice while you still have leavened matter" (*Ex.* 23:18). Even leavened matter belonging to a third person and deposited with a Jew as a fiduciary has to be removed. This follows from the particular expression (*Ex.* 13:7), "there shall not be seen *for you*" since (*b. Pesaḥim* 5b; *y. Pesaḥim* II,2 29a)[20] "this means that you are not allowed to see your own leavened matter but you may see that of other people and of the Temple." The definition of "belonging to other people" is that the Jew has neither monetary interests nor any kind of financial obligation connected with the matter (*b. Pesaḥim* 5b)[21] "as Rava said to the people of Meḥoza: Remove the leavened

---

20 לא יראה לך שאור שלך אי אתה רואה אבל אתה רואה של אחרים ושל גבוה.

21 כי הא דאמר להו רבא לבני מחוזה בעירו חמירא דבני חילא מבתייכו כיון דאילו

matter of the soldiers [quartered with you] from your houses; since you would be held responsible and would have to pay if it is stolen or lost, the *ḥameẓ* must be considered your property." *Ḥameẓ* can be disposed of in any way one wants since (*Mishnah Pesaḥim* II,1)[22] "as long as one may eat [*ḥameẓ*], one may feed it to domestic animals, wild animals, or birds, or one may sell it to a Gentile and benefit from it." It is clear that leavened matter for which one has a fiduciary responsibility must be sold and not destroyed. Only the *ḥameẓ* left after the morning of the Fourteenth of Nisan must be destroyed.

The prohibition of *ḥameẓ* during Passover is absolute and applies even to the most minute quantities. It is therefore customary in all Jewish households to clean the house thoroughly before Passover. This informal cleaning is ended formally during the night of the Fourteenth of Nisan and the following morning. The house is searched at night by candlelight (*Tosefta Pesaḥim* I,1; *b. Pesaḥim* 7b/8a; *y. Pesaḥim* I,1 27a):[23] "One does not search by sunlight nor by the light of the moon (*b.*: nor by the light of a torch; *y.*: nor by starlight) but only by candlelight since checking with a candle is good and thorough. Even though there is no proof [of this in Scripture] there is an allusion (*Zeph.* 1:12): 'On that day, I shall search Jerusalem with candles,' and it says (*Prov.* 20:27), 'A Divine candle is the human soul.'" The reason given is that only the light of a candle can be used to search nooks and crannies; natural light always leaves parts of a room in the shadow and the light of a torch is diffuse and unsteady. It is also implied that if anybody was prevented from searching in the evening, he may search the next morning since otherwise sunlight would not be mentioned. This seems to imply that it is not necessary to turn off any electric lights while searching since the candle is still needed to search in nooks and crannies.

Since the search is a religious obligation based on the biblical

---

מיגנב ואילו מיתביד ברשותייכו קאי ובעיתו לשלומי כדילכון דמי ואסור.

22 כל שעה שמותר לאכול מאכיל לבהמה לחיה ולעופות ומוכר לנכרי ומותר בהנאתו.

23 Text of b. תנו רבנן אין בודקין לא לאור החמה ולא לאור הלבנה ולא לאור האבוקה אלא לאור הנר מפני שאור הנר יפה לבדיקה ואע״פ שאין ראיה לדבר זכר לדבר שנאמר שבעת ימים שאור לא ימצא בבתיכם ואומר ויחפש בגדול החל ואומר בעת ההיא אחפש את ירושלים בנרות.

Text of y. אין בודקין לא לאור החמה ולא לאור הלבנה ולא לאור הכוכבים אלא לאור הנר.

Text of Tosefta (*Pesaḥim* I,1): אין בודקין לאור החמה ולא לאור הלבנה אלא לאור הנר לפי שבדיקת הנר יפה מרובה. אע״פ שאין ראיה לדבר זכר לדבר והיה בעת ההיא אחפש את ירושלם בנרות ואומר נר אלהים נשמת אדם.

commandment to remove leavened matter, it is preceded by a benediction. The universal formula introducing any benediction, "Praise to You o Lord, our God, King of the Universe," is not found in the few related texts, mostly Sadducee, extant from the time of the Second Commonwealth. In the *Talmudim*, the third-century authorities Rav and R. Yoḥanan insist that this is the only admissible formula for a benediction. (*b. Berakhot* 40b):[24] "Rav said: Any benediction that does not contain an invocation of the Name is not a benediction; and R. Yoḥanan said that any benediction that does not mention the Kingdom is not a benediction." The statement of R. Yoḥanan is quoted in the Jerusalem *Talmud* in the name of the older authority Rav (*y. Berakhot* IX,1 12d).[25] It seems that this particular form of a benediction was fixed by the rabbinic authorities of the time as a demonstration against Christian ideas. A benediction must contain the Name, "Lord," the *Tetragrammaton* prominent in the declaration of faith of the *Shema'* (*Deut.* 6:4) as a symbol of the unitary nature of God: "Hear, o Israel, the Lord is our God, *the Lord* means One." The benediction also must contain the Kingdom, the invocation of God as the King of the Universe, to emphasize that God's Kingdom is here and now and of this world also.

The benediction does not refer to the search of the house but to its ultimate reason, the removal of leavened matter. The exact text is "Praised be You o Lord, our God, King of the Universe, Who has sanctified us by His commandments and commanded us about the removal of leavened matter." This text is confirmed by both *Talmudim* (*b. Pesaḥim* 7b; *y. Pesaḥim* II,2 28d). Some benedictions prescribed by the *Talmud* have this nonpersonal and nontemporal form, such as "about the circumcision," "about ritual slaughter," "about the taking of the *lulav*," while others are directed toward an action, "to wrap oneself in *ẓiẓit*," "to read the *Hallel*." In the absence of talmudic statements, the discussions cannot be conclusive, but there seems to be a fairly general agreement (*Pisqe RYD Pesaḥim*, p. 210; *Sefer Hamakhria'* #61; *Meïri Bet Habeḥirah Pesaḥim*, p. 33) that the formulation "to do . . ." is a narrow one that can be applied only to special situations. The formula "about . . ." can be applied to almost all cases and certainly to those for which the actual performance of the required action can be

---

24 אמר רב כל ברכה שאין בה הזכרת השם אינה ברכה ורבי יוחנן אמר כל ברכה שאין בה מלכות אינה ברכה.

25 רבי זעירא ורבי יהודה בשם רב כל ברכה שאין עמה מלכות אינה ברכה.

delegated to other persons, as in the search for *ḥameẓ* and the circumcision of one's son. For practical purposes, there should be no doubt that the text quoted by the *Talmud* is the one to be used. This is the conclusion of Meïri (*Pesaḥim*, p. 36) after six pages of textual, historical, and logical arguments:[26] "To conclude: the formulation of the benedictions cannot be explained smoothly except by my proposed solution, but even so, since it is not very clear that the same principles should apply in all cases, I would never agree to change the [talmudic] formula of a benediction [for logical reasons]. It is best to leave them in their ancient formulations and nobody has the right to change anything now."

Any remaining pieces of *ḥameẓ* that have not been used up or sold by noon of the Fourteenth of Nisan must be destroyed as prescribed in *Ex.* 12:15: "Seven days you shall eat *mazzot* but on the first day you must eliminate sour matter from your houses. . . ." The "first day" here is the day of *Pesaḥ*, the Fourteenth of Nisan, not the first day of the Feast of Unleavened Bread, the Fifteenth of Nisan. It is not spelled out in the Torah how unleavened matter should be eliminated. The *Mishnah* states (*Pesaḥim* II,1),[27] "R. Yehuda says *ḥameẓ* should not be removed except by fire but the Sages say one may [also] either crumble it and scatter it into the wind or throw it into the ocean." "R. Yehuda" here is R. Yehuda bar 'Illay, one of the foremost students of R. Akiba; "the Sages" are the collective of the other surviving students of R. Akiba. The general rule is that the opinion of the collective prevails over that of an individual. In any case, the *Mishnah* deals with *ḥameẓ* that has to be eliminated after its use is forbidden, that is, after noontime of the Fourteenth of Nisan; under normal circumstances one removes the *ḥameẓ* two hours earlier, when it may still be used, and therefore can be disposed of at will. Nevertheless, it is the Ashkenazic custom to burn the remaining pieces of bread products in the morning of the Fourteenth of Nisan. A suggestion of this can be found in the language of the benediction for the removal of unleavened matter. The word used, בִּעוּר, means "removal" (*RAVIA Pesaḥim* §431)[28] (cf. *Deut.* 26:13), a frequent word

---

26 וסוף דבר אין נוסח הברכות מתישב יפה אלא לפי מה שכתבנו ואע״פ כן מאחר שאין הדברים מתבררים כל כך להשוות את המדה ביניהם איני רואה לשנות במטבע הברכות וראוי להניחם על טופסיהם הישנים ואין אדם רשאי לחדש דבר מעתה.

27 ר' יהודה אומר אין ביעור אלא שריפה וחכמים אומרים (אף) מפרר וזורה לרוח או מטיל לים.

28 פירוש ביעור פינוי.

in rabbinic Hebrew and Aramaic, possibly related to Arabic בער "to excrete" (said of animals), but there is a second biblical root בער "to destroy by fire," connected by J. Barth with Arabic בעׂר "to have unquenchable thirst." The Ashkenazic custom also forces one to actually have some *ḥameẓ* to burn. This guarantees that the benediction about the removal of leavened matter is not void. The medieval Ashkenazic custom was to pronounce the benediction not at the outset of the search but at the moment one sees the first piece of *ḥameẓ* to be collected for burning (Rashi *Maḥzor Vitry Pesaḥ* §1, *Siddur Pesaḥ* §1; *RAVIA* §431, p. 62 line 10); today all groups follow the ruling of Alfassi, accepted for Ashkenazim by R. Meir of Rothenburg, to recite the benediction at the start of the search (*Hagahot Maimuniot Ḥameẓ Umaẓẓah* III, #5).

The possession of any amount of leavened matter is forbidden during Passover (*b. Pesaḥim* 30a):[29] "Rava said: Leavened matter during Passover, by itself or mixed with other matter, is forbidden in any quantity." Since nobody can be sure that he has found every last molecule of leavened matter, one declares the possible remainder of any leavened matter for which one has responsibility or of which one is the beneficial owner to be nonexistent so that one is no longer responsible, since (*b. Pesaḥim* 4b)[30] "the Torah requires only the declaration of nonexistence" (which is a form of elimination). Even without that argument, the formal declaration would be necessary (*b. Pesaḥim* 6b)[31] "since one may find a piece of *ḥameẓ* during Passover which cannot be declared nonexistent since it is no longer his property [all usufruct from it being forbidden], as R. Elazar said: Two things are not one's property but the Torah made him responsible as if they were his property, *viz.*, a pit which he dug in the public domain and *ḥameẓ* after noontime [of the Fourteenth of Nisan]." The original form of the declaration was introduced by Rav (*b. Pesaḥim* 6b; *y. Pesaḥim* II,2 28d), one of the leaders of Babylonian Jewry in the second quarter of the third century C.E. The original Hebrew form given in the Jerusalem *Talmud* is retained in the Yemenite rite for the uneducated who do not understand Aramaic; see the text of the *Haggadah*. That declaration concerns "*ḥameẓ* in my house"; it was changed to "*ḥameẓ* in my

---

29 אמר רבא הלכתא חמץ בזמנו בין במינו בין שלא במינו אסור במשהוא.

30 מדאורייתא בביטול בעלמא סגי ליה.

31 דילמא משכחת ליה לבתר איסורא ולאו ברשותיה קיימא ולא מצי מבטיל דא״ר אלעזר שני דברים אינן ברשותו של אדם ועשאן הכתוב כאילו ברשותו ואלו הן בור ברשות הרבים וחמץ משש שעות ומעלה.

possession" by an early Gaonic authority (*Halakhot Gedolot Pesaḥ*, chap. 1). The Sephardic and Oriental text is that of Maimonides, the final authority for Yemenites. This text (*Mishneh Torah Ḥameẓ Umaẓẓah* III,7) is close also to an old Ashkenazic version (*RAVIA* §431, p. 63) accepted by R. Asher ben Yeḥiel, a German scholar and a student of R. Meir of Rothenburg, who fled Germany after R. Meir's death in captivity in the tower of Ensisheim and settled in Toledo, Spain, where he became the foremost rabbinic authority (*Rosh Pesaḥim* I, #19). The Western Ashkenazic text is from the school of Rashi (*Maḥzor Vitry Pesaḥ* §1). The standard Ashkenazic text is that of the seventeenth-century authority R. Joel Sirkes (*Baḥ Ṭur Oraḥ Ḥayyim* §434); it is a combination of an old Ashkenazic text (*RAVaN Pesaḥim*):[32] "All sour matter in this house that I did not see and did not remove shall be considered void and without owner like dust" and the text of *Halakhot Gedolot*:[33] "All sour matter under my control of which I have no knowledge shall be considered void and like dust." The clause "without owner" was added by Rashi's grandson R. Jacob Tam, although it cannot possibly refer to a formal renunciation of ownership, which is valid only if made public so that others may acquire ownership of the abandoned property. This informal renunciation ("without owner like dust of the earth" rather than just "without owner") is discussed at length by the medieval authors R. Eliezer ben Joel Halevi (*RAVIA* §417, pp. 25-32) and R. Menaḥem Meïri (*Magen Avot*, chap. 18), and in a few lines by R. Joel Sirkes (*loc. cit.*). The conclusion of the thorough investigation by Meïri is that there are three kinds of legal abandonment of property. Real estate can be abandoned legally only by a declaration before three adult, unrelated males. Movables of value can be abandoned by a declaration before at least one adult. Things that are intrinsically worthless, such as bread crumbs, can be abandoned by private declaration. As a consequence, it seems that the text of R. Tam presupposes a thorough search by which all valuable leavened matter was removed; the other texts refer to all *ḥameẓ*, valuable or not.

All Ashkenazic medieval manuscripts and all early printed *Haggadot* mention in the text of the declaration only כל חמירא "all leavened matter," as in today's Sephardic text. The longer version כל

---

32 כל חמירא דאיכא בביתא הדין דלא חמיתיה ודלא ביערתיה ליבטל וליהוי הפקר כעפרא.

33 כל חמירא דאיכא ברשותי ולא ידענא ביה ליבטל וליהוי עפרא.

חמירא וכל חמיעא "all leavened matter and sour dough," occurs in legal texts from the thirteenth century (*RAVIA* §431) but in *Haggadot* only appears in the eighteenth century. The longer version was generally accepted through the editions of R. Jacob Emden, Wolf Heidenheim, and R. Eliahu of Wilna.

The declaration is repeated in the morning to include all leavened matter, even the remainders of what was intentionally left over for breakfast and for the burning ceremony. This doubling is ascribed by *Hagahot Maimuniot* (*Ḥameẓ Umaẓẓah* III #7) to the Tosafist R. Isaac ben Abraham (*RIẒBA*), the brother of R. Simson of Sens. If the Fourteenth of Nisan falls on a Sabbath, the search and the burning have to be advanced to the Thirteenth but the final declaration is still said on the Fourteenth. The Aramaic translation of the verb "to see" as חמי (Ashkenazic) is Palestinian, חזי (Sephardic) is Babylonian talmudic Aramaic.

The second declaration has to be made after the burning of leavened matter but before the time when leavened matter will be forbidden. Since the *Pesaḥ* sacrifice cannot be slaughtered before the afternoon (*Deut.* 16:6), leavened matter is not forbidden before noon. However, in order to avoid inadvertent transgressions, rabbinic tradition prescribes (*Mishnah Pesaḥim* I,4)[34] that "one may eat leavened matter the first four hours [of the Fourteenth]; one leaves it at the fifth hour and one burns it at the start of the sixth." If this referred to standard hours, one could eat till 10 A.M. and would have to burn the leavened matter at 11 A.M. However, standard hours are a modern adaptation of an astronomic convention to general use. Talmudic hours, like all hour-reckoning in antiquity except that of professional astronomers, are one-twelfth of the length of the actual day; it is not well defined whether one counts from sunrise to sunset or from the start of dawn to nightfall. In moderate latitudes, the second interpretation usually is the more restrictive one. On this basis, in most years one may eat bread in New York City till about 9:15 A.M. and has to burn the leavened matter at about 10:45 A.M. standard time.

Sephardic *Haggadot* after each declaration add a prayer composed by the eighteenth-century scholar R. Ḥayyim Josef David Azulay for redemption from evil inclinations since in talmudic

---

34 אוכלין כל ארבע ותולין כל חמש ושורפין בתחילת שש.

homiletics sour dough is a symbol of man's evil inclinations. One may compare the prayer of R. Alexander (*b. Berakhot* 17a; *y. Berakhot* IV,2 7d):[35] "Master of the Worlds! It is manifest and known before You that it is our wish to do Your will but what hinders us? The sour matter in the dough and our enslavement by governments! May it please You to save us from them so that we may return to fulfill the Laws of Your will wholeheartedly."

---

35 רבון העולמים גלוי וידוע לפניך שרצוננו לעשות רצונך ומי מעכב שאור שבעיסה ושעבוד מלכיות יהי רצון מלפניך שתצילנו מידם ונשוב לעשות חוקי רצונך בלבב שלם.

The Seder Plate

The *Seder* is celebrated by the family at the table. Each participant has a cup before him and also a plate for the vegetables and the drops of wine to be spilled during the recital of the *Haggadah*. The celebration centers around a large plate, arranged in front of the celebrant, that contains the foods needed for the ritual and, in addition, some foods representing the sacrifices of the Fourteenth of Nisan. Ashkenazic families also have an additional cup on the table that is filled with wine either at the outset or after Grace; this is discussed in the section on *Hallel*.

The arrangement of the *Seder* plate follows different rules for different Jewish groups. Those who follow talmudic principles exclusively, i.e., Western European and Yemenite Jews, place the foods so that (*b. Yoma* 33a)[36] "one does not bypass an obligation," i.e., all foods placed closer to the celebrant must be used up before foods placed farther away can be used. To the right-hand side of the celebrant are placed the basic needs of the *Seder* ritual in the order of their use: the celery or other vegetable and behind it the bitter herbs (often chicory lettuce for the *maror* itself and horseradish for the "bundle according to Hillel"). On the left-hand side are the accessories: salt water or vinegar for the vegetables and behind it *ḥaroset*, a mixture that may consist of apples, figs, dates, nuts, and spices (all foods mentioned in the Song of Songs) prepared with wine, for dipping the bitter herbs; details are given in the section *Maẓẓah and Maror*. Yemenites do not use salt water but only *ḥaroset* for all dippings, since only *ḥaroset* is mentioned in the *Talmud* and in the code of Maimonides.

Both *Talmudim* agree (*b. Pesaḥim* 116a; *y. Pesaḥim* X,3 37d)[37] that *ḥaroset* as a brownish paste symbolizes the mortar the Israelites had to use in their labors in Egypt. The Babylonian *Talmud* in addition introduces the motive that the Song of Songs is a poetic description of

36 אין מעבירים על המצוות.

37 רבי לוי אומר זכר לתפוח ור' יוחנן אומר זכר לטיט.

the Exodus by requiring apples in the *ḥaroset* as an allusion to *Cant.* 8:5: ". . . I waked you up under the apple tree. . . ." The talmudic passage (*b. Soṭah* 13b) explaining this interpretation is translated and discussed later in the commentary on the *Midrash* in the *Haggadah.* The Aramaic *Targum* of the Song of Songs is based on this interpretation; it is now available to the English reader in Marvin H. Pope's commentary on the Song of Songs.

In the center of the *Seder* plate there are three *mazzot* especially baked for the occasion from flour that was guarded from all moisture and prepared explicitly for Passover use to fulfill the commandment (*Ex.* 12:17): "You must guard the *mazzot.*" Formerly, these guarded *mazzot* were baked in order (first, second, third) and specially marked with holes by Ashkenazic and Indian Jews to be used in correct sequence. Eastern European Ashkenazim discontinued this custom following R. Joel Sirkes (*Baḥ Ṭur Oraḥ Ḥayyim* §460), since the *Talmud* frowns upon making *mazzot* in special shapes (*b. Pesaḥim* 37a).[38] These three *mazzot* were taken by Gaonic and medieval authors to symbolize the three measures of flour Abraham offered to the angels (*Gen.* 18:6) or the three Patriarchs (R. Sherira Gaon, *Oẓar Hageonim Pesaḥim,* p. 117), also the three classes of Jews (Priests, Levites, and Israelites) and the three kinds of *mazzah* required for a sacrifice of thanksgiving (*Lev.* 7:12) (*Maharil Hilkhot Haggadah*), and the three chests that were used in the Temple for contributions (*Mishnah Sheqalim* III,2) (*Roqeaḥ* §279). Since modern high-speed mills grind wheat that is wetted and therefore potentially sour, wheat for *mazzot* must be dry-milled specially for Passover. In the nineteenth century, machine-made *mazzot* were introduced with the blessing of the leaders of German Orthodoxy since they guaranteed better supervision and cleanliness. The use of machine *mazzot* was vigorously opposed by the leaders of Galician Jewry, mainly because it threatened to eliminate the livelihood of poor people occupied in the baking. Both kinds of *mazzot* are now generally available. Today, all Jewish groups use three *mazzot* for the *Seder* celebration. Maimonides (*Ḥameẓ Umazzah* VIII,6) requires only two *mazzot* for the celebration, but in this he is not followed even by Yemenites. (The reasons for the deviation of Yemenite custom from Maimonides are discussed at length by R. J. Ṣubairi in *Agadeta dePisḥa.*) It seems that Maimonides'

---

38 ת״ר יוצאין בפת נקיה ובהרדאה ובסריקין המצויירין בפסח אע״פ שאמרו אין עושין סריקין המצויירין בפסח.

decision goes back to a Palestinian custom (*RAVaN* 166a; cf. p. 239). In Gaonic Babylonia, the custom was (as it is the general custom of all Jewish groups today) to make the benediction over bread (or *mazzah*) on Friday evenings on two complete loaves as a remembrance of the double portion of Mannah that was given to every person on Fridays (*Ex.* 16:5). In Gaonic Israel, only one whole bread was used since the first part of the Mannah was already consumed on Friday. For the *Seder*, an additional whole *mazzah* is required for the "bundle according to Hillel."

Behind all the foods needed for the *Seder* observations are placed the roasted bone with meat and the egg (or eggs); these are in remembrance of the two sacrifices eaten in Jerusalem during that night, the *Pesaḥ* and the holiday offering (חגיגה, the "cattle" in *Deut.* 16:2: "You shall sacrifice a *Pesaḥ* to the Lord your God, sheep and cattle . . .") (*b. Pesaḥim* 114b; *y. Pesaḥim* X,3 37d), following the opinion of the final authority, Ravina, that "even a bone and a cooked dish will do." The bone is the symbol of the *Pesaḥ* sacrifice that had to be roasted; it is also chosen because the Hebrew name (זרוע) also means "arm" and therefore is a symbol of God's "outstretched arm." The egg is used as "cooked dish" for its symbolic value as a sign of future redemption. It is cooked because the additional sacrifice could also be cooked according to the majority opinion (R. Ḥananel *ad loc.*; cf. the section on the Four Questions). R. Moshe Isserles reports (*Oraḥ Ḥayyim* §473) that in Cracow the egg used to be roasted. Since roasted meat would be too close in appearance to the required sacrifice that can be offered in the Temple only, roasted meat cannot be eaten during the *Seder* night (*Kaf Haḥayyim* §473, note 61). In many Jewish groups the egg, together with other boiled eggs, is distributed to the participants at the dinner.

The Jewish groups who follow the Lurianic kabbalistic system explained in the next section, i.e., Sephardic and most Eastern European Ashkenazic Jews, consider the ten items [(1,2,3) *mazzot*, (4) bone, (5) egg, (6) *maror*, (7) *ḥaroset*, (8) celery, (9) horseradish, (10) the plate] as symbols for the ten emanations that created the world and therefore put the three *mazzot*, as representatives of the most sublime emanations, on the far side of the plate and then the more corporeal emanations in front of the *mazzot* in the following order: bone (right), egg (left), *maror* (center), *ḥaroset* (right), celery (left), horseradish (front center). This results in the following arrangement:

כתר חכמה בינה
Mazzot 1,2,3

גבורה Egg	חסד Bone

תפארת
Maror

הוד Celery	נצח *Haroset*

יסוד
Horseradish

The plate represents *Malkhut*; saltwater is placed separately, not on the plate, since the Lurianic *Seder* only used *haroset* following the old Oriental tradition. The accessories to the *mazzot* are arranged in two triangles; the star of David appearing on most contemporary *Seder* plates is a modern reinterpretation.

The Western European plate is arranged as follows:

Bone		Egg
Haroset	3 *Mazzot*	*Maror*
Saltwater		Celery

and the Yemenite

Bone		Egg
	Maror	
	Mazzot	
	Haroset	
	Celery	

In these diagrams, the head of the household faces the bottom of the arrangement.

In all *Haggadah* texts currently in use, the text is preceded by a rhymed "order of the night." This is found also in the Yemenite *tiqlāl*, even though Yemenites do not follow the order indicated there but break the *maẓẓah* only after the recital of the *midrash*, following Maimonides. The author of the rhymes probably is Rashi, the greatest European rabbinical authority (*Maḥzor Vitry*, p. 281). In all sources, the rhyme of the third line reads רחצה *roḥẓáh*. The correction by W. Heidenheim to רחץ *ráḥaẓ* gives the appearance of a *pizmon* rhyme AAAB CCCB but is without any historical justification; the rhyme structure of the poem is AA BB CCCB. In some groups, Ashkenazic and Sephardic, the "order of the night" is sung before every new section of the *Seder*.

The Prayer

Sephardic and Yemenite *Haggadot* present a prayer intended for the head of the household before the start of the *Seder* services. This prayer is always printed without vowels since it is based on the Lurianic mystical interpretation of Judaism and, therefore, should not be recited by the ignorant and uninitiated.

The Lurianic theory, ostensibly based on the principal kabbalistic text, the *Zohar*, is in the main an extremely literal elaboration of some talmudic statements, relying on the old kabbalistic texts, *Sefer Yeẓirah* and *Sefer Habahir*. It is generally accepted in talmudic literature that the Torah is the law of nature, the basis for the creation of the world, in two ways. First, the Torah *is* the law of nature and the tool of the creation of the world. This is the interpretation given by *Midrash Bereshit rabbah* to the verses in *Proverbs* 8 where the personified Torah speaks: (22) "The Lord acquired me at the beginning of His way, before all of His creations . . . ," (30) "I was His tool. . . ." In the words of the *Midrash*,[39] "So the Holy One, praise to Him, consulted the Torah and created the world. It is written in the Torah (*Gen.* 1:1): 'Using the beginning, God created the heavens and the earth'; but *beginnining* can mean only the Torah, as it is written (*Prov.* 8:22): 'The Lord acquired me as the *beginning* of His way.'" The second interpretation is that the world can only exist through the concrete existence of the Torah in the acts of the Jewish people. This is best expressed by the *Talmud* (*b. 'Avodah Zarah* 3a):[40] "It is said (*Jer.* 33:25), 'So says the Lord: If My covenant were not kept day and night, I would not have continued the laws of heaven and earth.' R. Shim'on ben Laqish said: What is the meaning of the verse (*Gen.* 1:31), 'It was evening, it was morning, *the* Sixth Day'? [Only in this verse do we find the definite article, the other days of creation

39 כך היה הקדוש ברוך הוא מביט בתורה ובורא את העולם. והתורה אמרה בראשית ברא אלהים. ואין ראשית אלא תורה. האי מה דאמר ה' קנני ראשית דרכו.

40 אם לא בראתי יומם ולילה חוקות שמים וארץ לא שמתי ואמר רבי שמעון בן לקיש מאי דכתיב ויהי ערב ויהי בוקר יום השׁשי מלמד שהתנה הקדוש ברוך הוא עם מעשה בראשית ואמר אם ישראל מקבלין את התורה מוטב ואם לאו אני מחזיר אתכם לתוהו ובוהו. והיינו דאמר חזקיה מאי דכתיב משמים השמעת דין ארץ יראה ושקטה אם יראה למה שקטה ואם שקטה למה יראה אלא בתחלה יראה ולבסוף שקטה.

being described as One Day, a Second Day, a Third Day, a Fourth Day, a Fifth Day.] This teaches us that the Holy One, praise to Him, put a condition on the work of Creation and said: 'If Israel will accept My Torah, all will be fine; but if not, I shall return you to *tohu wabohu* [and the day Israel accepted the Torah at Mount Sinai was *the Sixth* of Sivan].' Similarly, Ḥizqia said: What is the meaning of the verse (*Ps.* 76:9) '. . . the earth was afraid and quiet.' If afraid, why quiet? And if quiet, why afraid? At the beginning [before Israel accepted the Torah] it was afraid, and at the end it was quiet."

The kabbalistic theory of creation is also based on the expression "The Place" that appears in the *Talmud* and in the *Haggadah* as a name of God. Like most of Jewish mysticism, this theory seems to appear first in the writings of the Alexandrian Sadducee author Philo (*De Somniis* I,62-63)[41] on the verse (*Gen.* 28:11) **ויפגע במקום** "He prayed to the Place" (cf. *Jer.* 7:16, **אל תפגע בי** "do not pray to Me"): "'Place' has a threefold meaning: first, that of a space filled by a material form; secondly, that of the turn of God's word. . . . There is a third signification, in keeping with which God Himself is called a Place, by reason of His containing things and being contained in nothing whatever. . . ." The "turn of God's word" is in talmudic literature the Temple, the residence of God's presence. The possibly earliest talmudic source that spells out the same idea is *Pesiqta Rabbati* 21 (p. 104b):[42] "R. Huna in the name of R. Ami said: Why do we use a secondary designation for the Name of the Holy, praise to Him, and call Him 'The Place'? Because He is the place of the world. But we do not yet know whether He is the place of the world or the world is His place; since it is said, however (*Ex.* 33:21), 'the Lord said, there is a place with Me,' we know that He is the place of the world but the world is not His place." The last argument is illustrated by another early *Midrash* (*Tanḥuma Ki Tissa* 27, *ed. Buber* 16):[43] "R. Yosi ben Ḥalafta [a leading student of R. Akiba] said, the passage does not

---

41 τριχῶς δὲ ἐπινοεῖται τόπος, ἅπαξ μὲν χώρα ὑπὸ σώματος πεπληρωμένη, κατὰ δεύτερον δὲ τρόπον ὁ θεῖος λόγος, . . . κατὰ δὲ τρίτον σημαινόμενον αὐτὸς ὁ θεός καλεῖται τόπος τῷ περιέχειν μὲν τὰ ὅλα, περιέχεσται δὲ πρὸς μηδενὸς ἁπλῶς. . . .

42 רבי הונא בשם רבי אמי אמר מפני מה מכנים שמו של הקדוש ברוך הוא וקוראים אותו מקום. מפני שהוא מקומו של עולם. ואין אנו יודעים אם הוא מקומו של עולם ואם עולמו הוא מקומו. אלא מן מה דכתיב ויאמר ה' הנה מקום אתי ונצבת על הצור אנו יודעים שהוא מקומו של עולם ואין עולמו מקומו.

43 אמר רבי יוסי בר חלפתא הנה אני במקום הזה אינו אומר אלא הנה מקום אתי, מקומי טפילה לי ואין אני טפל למקומי.

read 'I am at that place' but 'there is a place with Me,' meaning that space is secondary to Me but I am not an attribute of space."

The old (talmudic or Gaonic) Book of the Creation (*Sefer Yeẓirah* I,2) followed up the identification of Torah and laws of nature by having the world created by a combination of[44] "10 abstract digits and 22 letters." The Hebrew word ספירה (*sĕfirah*) for "digit" was taken by later kabbalists as the *spheres* of creation, the emanations, of which the first three (represented on the Lurianic *Seder* plate by the *maẓẓot*) are represented only in spiritual Heaven (the unspatial world) while the other seven lead to the creation of the corporeal world in *Malkhut*, the Kingdom. [The names of all ten spheres are indicated on the Lurianic *Seder* plate.] The *Zohar* (I, 19b) sees in the corporeal world the nut into which the Divine Majesty has descended, as it says (*Cant.* 6:11): "I descended into the nut-garden"; without sin even the corporeal world would be spiritual, but our sins create the antispiritual "peels" or "broken shells."

The Lurianic Kabbalah transforms these homiletic statements into a practical system. The world exists only by Israel's compliance with the laws of the Torah. If all Jews were to stop observing the Torah, the world could no longer exist since it would be all "peel" without life-giving spirituality. On the other hand, if all Jews did observe all laws of the Torah, all Divine sparks that have fallen into "peels" would be redeemed and the world would be transformed into the spiritual, eternal, and unchangeable World-to-Come. Therefore, every Jew personally carries the responsibility for the redemption of the world or its eventual destruction. This idea also can be traced back to Philo, who says in connection with the counting of the *'Omer* (*De specialibus legibus* II,163),[45] "The reason of this [presentation of the first sheaf of grain] is that the Jewish nation is to the whole inhabited world what the priest is to the City." Since the particular action induced in the world by the performance of a specific commandment is God's secret, at most communicated to a few select souls, all we can do is to perform a commandment and pray for its

---

44 עשר ספירות בלי מה ועשרים ושתים אותיות.
The translation follows the authoritative commentary of R. Saadia Gaon.

45 τὸ δ'αἴτιον, ὅτι ὅν λόγον ἔχει πρὸς πόλιν ἱερεύς, τοῦτον πρὸς ἅπασαν τὴν οἰκουμένην τὸ Ἰουδαίων ἔθνος. [The editor of the Loeb edition of Philo did not realize that this interpretation of the *'Omer* ritual is the standard kabbalistic-ḥasidic one.]

beneficial effects. It is a characteristic of prayer texts of Jewish groups that follow the teachings of R. Isaac Luria (*ARI*) and his disciple Ḥayyim Viṭal (Calabrese), that whenever possible the performance of a commandment is preceded by a declaration:[46] "For the Unity of the Holy One, praise to Him, and His glory, in fear and love, to realize the unity of the names YH in WH in perfect unity in the name of all of Israel, I am ready and prepared to keep the commandment . . ." or a similar text. This declaration insures that the action is done with an intent that guarantees its usefulness for the salvation of the world and that it is done as part of general Jewish responsibility. Except for the declaration preceding the recitation of Grace, these declarations are not usually found in *Haggadot* even of kabbalistically inclined circles, except for some North African and Oriental groups otherwise adhering to the standard Sephardic ritual. The texts of these declarations vary from group to group. In the present *Haggadah*, the declarations are given following the Syrian ritual for the Sephardic text.

The declaration of intent and the connected prayer for the *Seder* is one of Ḥayyim Viṭal's own compositions. The text is mostly straightforward. The "copulations of the holy heavenly properties" are the actions in the spheres of Creation necessary to sustain the world. The need for continuous Divine intervention to sustain the existence of the world is asserted in the daily morning prayer when we address God as He "Who renews the work of Creation every day, continuously." The "understanding of Adam" (*Prov.* 30:2) was so great that he wrote a book on all future generations (*b. Bava Meẓi'a* 85b; *Gen.* 5:1); the "lower waters" are the souls who by their sins are caught in the corporeal "peels" and without help cannot be reborn to try for their final salvation.

---

46 לשם יחוד קב״ה ושכינתיה בדחילו ורחימו ליחד שם י״ה בו״ה ביחודא שלים על ידי ההוא טמיר ונעלם בשם כל ישראל הנני מוכן ומזומן לקיים מצות עשה . . .

The Qiddush

The *Qiddush* or Sanctification of the Holiday is a derivative of the same ceremony for the Sabbath. The *Qiddush* for Sabbath is the form instituted by the Men of the Great Assembly (cf. note [1]) for the execution of the commandment of the Decalogue (*Ex.* 20:8) "Remember the day of Sabbath and declare it to be holy." By analogy, the same form is used on holidays since one is also required to declare these days as holy; the biblical list of holidays is introduced by the verse (*Lev.* 23:4), "These are the festive days of the Lord, holy declarations that you have to declare . . ." and one interpretation of this is (*b. Rosh Hashanah* 32a; *Sifra Emor parashah* 11[1]):[47] "'holy declarations' means the sanctification of the day" (in prayer and/or *Qiddush*). However, according to most ancient and modern interpretations, the verse speaks of the obligation of the religious authorities to fix the calendar of the religious year; the obligation of reciting *Qiddush* on any day other than the Sabbath has no biblical foundation. This is disputed, however, by the Gaonic compendium *Halakhot Gedolot* (24b; *RAVIA Pesaḥim* §508, p. 129), which finds the obligation for a *Qiddush* on Passover, Pentecost, and Tabernacles in the biblical requirement (*Deut.* 16:1,12; 15:15) to remember the Exodus on these days. The original institution of the *Qiddush* does allow it to be pronounced over bread instead of wine. This does not apply to Passover when Four Cups of wine are required.

A day cannot be sanctified before it arrives. All Jewish reckoning of days is from evening to evening, in imitation of the Days of Creation. Since nightfall is a gradual process, Sabbath and holidays must be observed from sundown of the preceding day until it is certainly night the following day. For the fast of Yom Kippur, the Tenth of Tishrei, it is an explicit biblical command (*Lev.* 23:32) to start the fast and stop working on the Ninth. One similarly is required to "add time to any holiday from profane days" (*b. Yoma* 81b).[48] From the sources, it is not clear whether this has be taken as a biblical or as

---

47 מקרא קדש זה קדושת היום.

48 הא למדת כל מקום שנאמר שבות מוסיפין מחול על הקדש.

a rabbinic obligation. In any case, it is generally accepted that on the Sabbath one may take upon oneself the obligations of the Sabbath some time before sundown and recite *Qiddush* at that early hour. But on Passover, the cup of wine for *Qiddush* is also the first of the Four Cups required for the *Seder* night. Therefore, if the addition to the holiday from the preceding day is only sanctified by rabbinic usage, not by biblical decree, the *Qiddush* cannot be started before actual nightfall. This argument is a medieval Ashkenazic one; it originates in the circles of the French Tosafists and cannot be found in earlier sources. The details of the arguments pro and con are given in *Mordokhai Pesaḥim* (Wilna edition, 33c). The final decision not to start the Passover *Qiddush* before nightfall is found in R. Israel Isserlein's *Terumat Hadeshen* (§137). This work is considered authoritative by Ashkenazim and Sephardim alike; his decision has been accepted everywhere. On the other hand, *Qiddush* should be recited immediately after nightfall (*Shulḥan 'Arukh Oraḥ Ḥayyim*, §472, #1) for the benefit of the small children. A similar problem with the timing of the *Qiddush* also exists with the other holidays of pilgrimage. Since the second day of any holiday is a rabbinic usage, it cannot intrude on the biblical holiness of the first day, and therefore all observances of the second day must wait until *after* nightfall of the first day. On Tabernacles, the *Qiddush* has to be recited in the *sukkah* with an appropriate benediction; this cannot be done when it is still daylight and there is no obligation to sit in the *sukkah* yet. Similarly, on *Shemini Aẓeret* one has to wait until there no longer is any biblical obligation to sit in the *sukkah*. On Pentecost, it has become customary to wait until nightfall for reasons explained later in the commentary on the counting of the *'Omer*.

The *Qiddush* of the *Seder* night has a triple function. First, it is the sanctification of the day as Holiday; second, it is the benediction over the first of the Four Cups of wine; and third, it is the introductory benediction for the ceremony of remembrance of the Exodus. The formula "a holiday in remembrance of the Exodus," used on all holidays, takes over a special function on Passover. In the Yemenite (and some other North African and Oriental) rites, the third function of the *Qiddush* is emphasized by a poetic amplification authorized by the *siddur*, or order of prayers, of R. Saadia Gaon, head of the *piuṭ*-friendly Babylonian Academy of Sura in the early tenth century. The *Talmud* (*b. Pesaḥim* 106a)[49] notes that Rav Ashi (the first editor of the

---

49 אמר בורא פרי הגפן ואגיד ביה, חזייה להחוא סבא דגחין.

Babylonian *Talmud*, head of the Academy of Sura during much of the fifth century) had no inhibition "to say the benediction over wine and to add poetic amplifications" (for the *Qiddush* on Sabbath morning) but adds that these amplifications were not well received. The addition to the *Qiddush* is never mentioned in European sources.

The first benediction of the *Qiddush*, the blessing of the wine, introduces the material substrate for the sanctification of the holiday and later permits the drinking of the wine. Since (*y. Berakhot* VI,1 9d; cf. *b. Berakhot* 35a)[50] "'the Lord is the owner of the earth and everything in it' (*Ps.* 24:1), anyone who enjoys anything of this world embezzles sacred property unless he redeems it by giving proper praise to its Owner." Since embezzling of sacred property is a serious crime (*Lev.* 5:14-16), a Jew cannot eat or drink any food without reciting the proper benediction. This requirement is much stricter than that of saying Grace; the latter is an explicit biblical commandment (*Deut.* 8:10) but applies only to people who eat more than a minimal amount of food.

One may note that the benediction for table grapes, the original fruit of the vine, is "Creator of the fruit of the tree." The special benediction for wine, "Creator of the fruit of the vine," expresses the importance of wine for human civilization in antiquity and also the principle that God as Creator of the universe is also the origin of human technology. Today, wine is little more than a mild relaxant and a legal drug. In antiquity, adding wine to water was essential to make the water drinkable; the alcohol in the heavy subtropical wines played the role of disinfectant similar to the chlorine used in our drinking water. In the *Talmud*, the term "wine" for human consumption and, in particular, wine used in religious ceremonies never refers to pure wine but always to wine mixed with water. The Hebrew expression מוזג, usually translated as "to pour wine," really means "to mix (with water)." Mixed wine is defined (*Mishnah Niddah* II,7)[51] as "two parts of water and one of wine." There even is a minority opinion that unmixed wine is just fruit juice and requires the benediction over grapes, not wine (*b. Berakhot* 50b; *y.*

---

50 כתיב להי הארץ ומלואה תבל ויושבי בה. הנהנה כלום מן העולם מעל עד שיתירו המצות.

51 וכמזוג שני חלקים מים ואחד יין.

Berakhot VI,1 10a).[52] "Wine" in talmudic and other classical sources therefore is a drink with approximately 4–5% alcohol, based on an estimate of 12–15% alcohol for unimproved subtropical wine. The *Talmudim* also report (*y. Terumot* VIII,5 45c; *b. 'Avodah Zarah* 30a) that Jews for health reasons do not drink or otherwise use wine of questionable sanitary quality, in particular drinks that had been left standing overnight in an open jar or bottle:[53] "Wine that was left standing in an open vessel must be poured down the drain even if it is wine of the heave-offering. A dish cooked with water that was left standing open overnight must be poured down the drain." The celebrant of any *Qiddush* therefore asks the company סַבְרִי *sawrī*, "Is it reasonable [to drink this wine]?" and they answer לְחַיִּים *leḥayyim*, "May it be for life [health]." The question has remained in use in all Jewish groups while the answer for the *Qiddush* is given only in Oriental communities. The formula for the answer but not the question is retained everywhere for social drinking.

Since the drinking of wine for *Qiddush* and the Four Cups is a religious obligation, it requires a certain minimal cup size. The standard cup, a quarter of a *log*, is defined in the Jerusalem *Talmud* (*y. Pesaḥim* X,1 37c) as the volume of $2\times2\times(1+5/6) = 7\ 1/3$ cubic digits and in the Babylonian *Talmud* (*b. Pesaḥim* 109a) as $2\times2\times(2+7/10) =$ 10.8 cubic digits. The actual determination of this volume depends on the size of the cubit of 24 digits. The best approximation of a cubit from archeological data is 1/2,000 of a Roman mile, or 55.5 cm. The corresponding volume of the Babylonian cup would be 134.3 cm^3 or 3.8 fl. oz. This value corresponds well, within the precision of the known archeological evidence, with the statement of *Mishnah Kelim* XVII,11:[54] "Some [authorities] define the small fluid and dry measures as Roman." The Roman *quartarius*, the equivalent of the Hebrew *revi'it*, is best estimated as 133.3 cm^3 or 3.8 fl. oz. For practical

---

52 יין עד שלא נתן לתוכו מים אין מברכין עליו בורא פרי הגפן אלא בורא פרי העץ ונוטלין ממנו לידים משנתן לתוכו מים מברכין עליו בורא פרי הגפן ואין נוטלין ממנו לידים דברי רבי אליעזר.

Wine that does not yet contain any water does not require the benediction "Creator of the fruit of the vine" but "Creator of the fruit of the tree" and it may be used {in place of water} for washing of the hands; after it has been mixed with water one says the benediction "Creator of the fruit of the vine" and one may not use it for washing one's hands; these are the words of R. Eliezer.

53 יין שנתגלה ישפך ואפילו של תרומה. תבשיל שבישלו במים מגולין אפילו של תרומה ישפך.

54 ויש שאמרו מדה דקה מדות הלח והיבש שיעורן כאיטלקי.

purposes, Yemenite Jews follow the tradition of Maimonides (*Hilkhot 'Eruvin* I,12) that the weight of a cup of water is 17.5 dinar or 1,680 grains. This corresponds to 109 cm^3 or 3.1 fl. oz. Sephardic and Ashkenazic Jews used to follow the Gaonic tradition reported by Alfassi and Rashi that the size of a cup is 1.5 standard eggs. Some Gaonic authorities define the size of a standard egg as the volume of water weighing 12 2/3 dinar (*R. Nissim Gaon, 'Eruvin* 82b), corresponding to a cup of 118 cm^3 or 3.3 fl. oz., while other authorities (*Oẓar Hageonim 'Eruvin*, pp. 66–67) let it depend on local conditions. These matters are not mentioned in the *Shulḥan 'Arukh* but the latter's source *Ṭur* (*Oraḥ Ḥayyim* #482) gives the size of the cup as 10 (Parisian) cubic digits or 126 cm^3 and 3.6 fl. oz.; the current Sephardic practice (*Kaf Haḥayyim Oraḥ Ḥayyim* §186 #46) defines a standard egg as a volume of water weighing 18 dirham or 58 g; the resulting cup of 87 cm^3 or 2.5 fl. oz. is also accepted in recent Israeli (*Meqor Ḥayyim Hashalem*) and American (*Ezras Torah Fund, Luaḥ*) compendia[55]. Other American authors measure the cup by the size of average eggs on the market today. The required properties of the vessel containing these amounts is dicussed later in the section "Recital: Mixing the Second Cup."

Since the cup by most determinations is relatively small and should not contain much alcohol, four cups consumed during a long meal is not excessive. The *Talmudim* mention that at the first meal a mourner eats after a funeral, he drinks either two (Israeli tradition, *y. Berakhot* IV,1 6a) or three (Babylonian, *b. Ketubot* 8b) cups before the meal, five or four during the meal, and three afterward. Nevertheless (*b. Pesaḥim* 108b),[56] "the head of the household may give his children and the members of his household to drink from his own cup on condition that he himself drink the greater part of the cup." On the *Seder* night, this does not apply to boys over 13 years of age and girls over 12 years of age since they are required to have their own "Four Cups." One may continue to finish the cup in small sips after one has consumed the larger part of the wine if this was the original intention (*RAVIA Pesaḥim*, p. 155).

---

55 The Talmud works with a much smaller size of eggs. It is stated in *Erubin* 83a that שיגר בוֹניוּס לרבי מוֹדיא דקוּנריס דמן נאוּסא ושיער רבי מאתן וּשבע עשׂרה ביעין , "Bonius sent Rabbi a *modius* (64 *quartarii*, 8.536 liter) of Nausa artichokes and Rabbi estimated them at 217 eggs." This makes 1.5 eggs only 59 cm^3.

56 השקה מהן לבניו ולבני ביתו יצא; אמר רב נחמן בר יצחק והוּא דאשתי רוּבא דכסא.

Today, the vocalized Ashkenazic and Sephardic versions of the Hebrew *Haggadah* differ in many places where the consonantal text is identical. This is a late development caused by the theory advanced by R. Eliahu of Wilna (1722–1797), Isaac Stanow (1732–1804) of the Mendelsohn circle, and the latter's follower R. Wolf Heidenheim (1737–1832), that prayer texts should follow the rules of biblical rather than of rabbinic Hebrew. This attitude has been adopted by all nineteenth-century editors of Ashkenazic prayer texts and resulted, for example, in a general substitution of *qamaẓ* ָ for *segol* ֶ at the end of a clause, leading to the expression הַגָּפֶן for "the vine" in the Ashkenazic text instead of הַגֶּפֶן found in most printed texts through the eighteenth century (similar to the substitution of הַגָּשֶׁם for הַגֶּשֶׁם in the second benediction of the *'Amidah* prayer). In all vocalized Ashkenazic *Haggadah* and prayer texts preceding Heidenheim, the benediction over wine is identical with the Sephardic version. The biblical punctuation of Ashkenazic prayer texts is a regrettable distortion of tradition, as we shall see many times in the course of our study of the *Haggadah* text. Yemenite rabbinic Hebrew is very consistent in its use of pausal forms (e.g., suffix ־ֶךָ for ־ְךָ as second person singular masculine possessive) and in shifting the stress from the final to the penultimate syllable in most words. Historically (i.e., pre-Heidenheim), Ashkenazic and Sephardic rabbinic Hebrew always used pausal forms in a moderate way, a development traced back by Y. Kutscher[57] to late Second Temple times, but only Ashkenazim continued the rabbinic shift of stress parallel to Yemenite practice (usually, in contrast to Yemenites, also in the recitation of biblical passages). In this sense, the introduction of the *meteg* ֽ to indicate stress not on the last syllable is also an unhistoric innovation by Heidenheim, but it has become an accepted standard and, with the acceptance of a modified Sephardic pronunciation of Hebrew in Israel, is now quite necessary.

All Jewish groups start the *Qiddush* on Sabbath with the recitation of the verses *Gen.* 2:1–3; Sephardim in addition recite *Lev.* 23:4 on holidays. The recitation of the verses from Genesis is not mentioned in the *Talmud* but seems to be a very old custom, possibly dating back to the times of the Second Commonwealth. It is mentioned in all sources on the Ten Martyrs who were executed after the two

---

57 *The Language and Linguistic Background of the Isaiah Scroll*, p. 36.

wars with the Romans (*Beth Hamidrasch Jellinek* 6, p. 30, p. 35[58]; *Qinnah Arze Hallevanon*). The twelfth-century authority *Roqeaḥ* (#52)[59] states that the verses are recited before *Qiddush* since they must be recited during the obligatory evening prayers as stated in the *Talmud* (*b. Shabbat* 119b):[60] "Rav, or R. Yehoshua ben Lewy, said: Even a single person (i.e., one not in a congregation) must recite *Gen.* 2:1-3 in his evening prayer"; the verses are repeated at the time of *Qiddush* to help those who for some reason did not have occasion to say their prayers or to recite the verses since (*l.c.*[61]) "everybody who prays on Sabbath Eve and recites *Gen.* 2:1-3, by this act almost becomes a partner of the Lord in the act of Creation." All Jewish groups start the recitation with the last two words of *Gen.* 1:31 since their first letters are YH and together with the first letters of the first two words of *Gen.* 2:1, WH, form the holy Name. The earliest source for this is the sixteenth-century Ashkenazic authority R. Moshe Isserles in his notes on *Tur Oraḥ Ḥayyim* §372. The recitation of the verses emphasizes that the Sabbath is a cosmic day connected with the Creation, whereas the holidays refer to events in Jewish history and their sanctity depends on God's selection of the people of Israel through the Exodus. However, in the *Qiddush* for Sabbath, the Sabbath is also celebrated as "first of the holy seasons" (i.e., first in every biblical list of holidays; *Lev.* 23, 28-29, interpretation of *RAVIA Pesaḥim*, p. 132) and "a remembrance of the Exodus from Egypt" following the second Decalogue (*Deut.* 5:11-15) where the master's obligation to let his slaves rest on Sabbath is presented as a consequence of their redemption from slavery in Egypt. The interpretation of this is that the Sabbath is a cosmic day but its rules depend on the election of Israel. Consequently, the final (Babylonian) doxology for the *Qiddush* of a holiday that falls on Sabbath is (*b. Berakhot* 49a) "Praised are You, o Lord, Who sanctifies the Sabbath, Israel, and the holidays" since the intrinsic sanctity of the Sabbath is independent of the election of Israel.

---

58   כיון שהוֹציאוהו ליהרג התחיל בקדוּש היוֹם, כיון שאמר אשר ברא אלהים לעשוֹת יצתה נשמתו.

When they lead him to execution he started to recite *Qiddush*, by the time he said "from God's act of Creation", he expired.

59   ומה שאוֹמרים ויכוֹלוּ על הכוֹס שאם שכחוֹ בתפילתוֹ בערב שבת לכך תקנוּהוּ לוֹמר על הכוֹס.

60   אמר רב ואיתימא ר' יהוֹשע בן לוי יחיד המתפלל בערב שבת צריך לוֹמר ויכוֹלוּ.

61   כל המתפלל בערב שבת ואוֹמר ויכוֹלוּ מעלה עליו הכתוּב כאילוּ נעשה שוּתף להקב״ה במעשׂה בראשית.

The *Qiddush* texts for all holy days and all Jewish groups follow the Babylonian tradition characterized by the personal statement "Praised are You, o Lord . . . Who chose *us* from all peoples, lifted *us* up from all tongues," in contrast to the impersonal form used in Israel (*Tosefta Berakhot* III,7),[62] "Because of Your love, o Lord, our God, for Your *people Israel* and the mercy You showed *to the people of Your covenant,* You gave us this great and holy day in love." Like most Palestinian prayer texts that contradict Babylonian forms, this version survives only in the Ashkenazic ritual and for a special occasion, in this case the cantor's prayer on the Day of Atonement. In older sources, the main benediction for *Qiddush* on Sabbath is essentially identical in all rites, in particular if one remembers that in manuscript traditions one may never expect completely identical texts from one manuscript to the next. The common text current in the fourteenth century is:

ברו·ך אתה יי אלהינו· מלך העולם אשר קדשנו במצותיו ורצה בנו· ושבת קדשו באהבה (ו·ברצון) הנחילנו· זכרון למעשה בראשית. (כי הוא יום זה) תחילה למקראי קודש זכר ליציאת מצרים. כי בנו· בחרת ואותנו· קדשת מכל העמים ושבת קדשך באהבה ו·ברצון הנחלתנו·. ברו·ך אתה יי מקדש השבת.

"Praised are You o Lord, our God, King of the Universe, Who sanctified us by His commandments, had pleasure in us, and let us inherit His holy Sabbath in love [Ashkenazim and Yemenites add: and goodwill], a remembrance of the work of Creation. [Ashkenazim and Sephardim add: Because this day is] The first of the holy assemblies as remembrance of the Exodus from Egypt. Truly You chose us and sanctified us from all peoples and let us inherit Your holy Sabbath in love and goodwill. Praised are You, o Lord, Who sanctifies the Sabbath."

This text becomes identical to the ninth-century Babylonian texts of R. Saadia Gaon and R. Amram Gaon if the words in parentheses are removed. In this case, the differences between rituals are clearly the result of later additions. The current Ashkenazic and Yemenite texts are still identical to the old traditional text (for Ashkenazim at least for the consonantal text; see the earlier remark on Heidenheim punctuation). The Sephardic text is much changed. The

---

62 ומאהבתך יי אלהינו שאהבת את ישראל עמך ומחמלתך מלכנו שחמלת על בני בריתך נתת לנו יי אלהינו את יום השביעי הגדול והקדוש הזה באהבה.

basis of the changes is a statement of the kabbalistic *midrash Zohar*, a main focus of interest of Sephardic Jewry starting from the fourteenth century. The *Zohar* (*Wayaqhel* 207b)[63] explains that the recitation of *Gen.* 2:1-3 is our testimony to the existence of God and His creating the world and, therefore, "everybody who gives this testimony with both heart and understanding will receive full pardon for all his sins. [Follows an abbreviated quote of the *Qiddush*]. This *Qiddush* is parallel to the previous testimony of faith and contains another 35 words, just as there are 35 words in *Gen.* 2:1-3." The current Sephardic *Qiddush* is therefore shortened to contain exactly 35 words.[64] The reasonable interpretation of the *Zohar* passage is that the *Qiddush* has 35 words dealing specifically with the Sabbath, i.e., after the passage quoted in the text by abbreviations common to many benedictions. [In the opinion of R. Abraham Abele Gumbinner (*Magen Avraham Orah Hayyim* §271, #22) the passage refers to the evening prayer and not to the *Qiddush* at all.] The acceptance of the *Zohar* and other sources of *midrash* character as sources for rabbinic decisions was a radical and revolutionary change introduced by the scholars of the generation of the expulsion of Jews from Spain and disseminated from the kabbalistic center of Safed by the writings of R. Moshe Cordovero and R. Hayyim Vital Calabrese, the latter representing the teachings of R. Isaac Luria (*ARI*). The previous practice was defined by R. Hai Gaon (*Sefer Ha'eshkol, Hilkhot Sefer Torah*, p. 47):[65] "Everything that was accepted into the Talmud is more authentic than what was not accepted; and even so one does not base one's decisions on the homiletic parts (*ăgadah*) of the *Talmud* but one has to explain the difficulties of these parts because they were written for a purpose; if

---

63 וכל מאן דיסהיד דא וישוי לביה ורעותיה לדא מכפר על כל חובוי. בא״י א״מה אק״ב ורצה בנו וכו'. האי קידושא איהו בחד מתקלא לקבל סהדותא דהימנותא ואינון תלתין וחמש תיבין אחרנין כמה דאית בויכולו.

64 ברוך אתה יי אלהינו מלך העולם אשר קדשנו במצותיו ורצה בנו ושבת קדשו באהבה וברצון הנחילנו זכרון למעשה בראשית, תחלה למקראי קדש זכר ליציאת מצרים. ושבת קדשך באהבה וברצון הנחלתנו. ברוך אתה יי מקדש השבת.
"Praised are You o Lord, our God, King of the Universe, Who sanctified us by His commandments, had pleasure in us, and let us inherit His holy Sabbath in love and goodwill, a remembrance of the work of Creation. The first of the holy assemblies as remembrance of the Exodus from Egypt. Truly You let us inherit Your holy Sabbath in love and goodwill. Praised are You, o Lord, Who sanctifies the Sabbath."

65 והשיב: כל הנקבע בתלמוד מחוור הוא ממה שלא נקבע בו, ואף על פי כן אגדות הכתובות בו אם לא יכוונו או ישתבשו אין לסמוך עליהם כי כלל הוא אין סומכין על אגדה; אבל כל הקבוע בתלמוד, שאנו מצווים להסיר שבושו, יש לנו לעשות כן, כי לולי שיש בו מדרש לא נקבע בתלמוד, ואם אין אנו מוצאים להסיר שבושו נעשה כדברים שאין הלכה; אבל מה שלא נקבע בתלמוד אין אנו צריכין לכל כך, אם נכון ויפה הוא דורשין ומלמדין אותו, ואם לאו אין אנו משגיחים בו.

we cannot explain the difficulties they become like other statements that are not binding (*hălakhah*). But what was not accepted into the *Talmud* itself is not so important for us; if it is correct and fine we shall preach and teach it, otherwise we shall disregard it." This is the basis of the statement of the foremost Spanish kabbalist and Talmudic authority Nachmanides on a homily in *Midrash Ekhah Rabbati* (*Milḥamot Hashem* #20): "I do not believe at all the statement of this *ăgadah*" and he explains (*loc. cit.* #39):[66] "We have a third kind of books called *midrash*, meaning sermons. . . . So if you want to believe in it, it is fine, and if you do not want to believe in it, no harm is done." Since Nachmanides was a student of the kabbalistic school of R. Isaac the Blind, the grandson of the author of the *Sefer Ha'eshkol*, he was raised in the tradition of strict adherence to the *Talmud*, to the exclusion of outside sources.

The text of the main benediction of the *Qiddush* appears in two versions already in the oldest sources. The text of R. Amram Gaon (*Seder shel Pesaḥ*) has only "Who chose us from all peoples, lifted us up from all tongues"; this is complemented in the *Siddur* of R. Saadia Gaon (*Haggadah shel Pesaḥ*) by "and sanctified us through His commandments" and in the text of Maimonides (*Hilkhot Shabbat XXIX,19*) by "chose us and made us great, wanted us and gave us splendor." The version of R. Saadia Gaon, a direct adaptation of the corresponding section of the daily prayers for holidays, is the only one found in Ashkenazic sources and the dominant one in Sephardic sources. The version of Maimonides is accepted by Yemenites and was in use in some Spanish congregations through the fourteenth century (*Abudirham*, p. 218). In the middle part of the benediction, we can note a few deviations between the rituals (excluding the poetic inserts of the Yemenite ritual, which are not obligatory and which will be treated separately at the end of this chapter). The Sephardic version that has "in love" both before and after the enumeration of (Sabbath and) holidays is found in most old sources: R. Amram Gaon (*loc. cit.*), Maimonides (*loc. cit.*) and the old Ashkenazic source *Maḥzor Vitry* (p. 294). R. Saadia Gaon (*loc. cit.*) has "in joy" for the second "in love." It seems that this repetition was found unnecessary and so the first "in love" was lost in Yemenite manuscripts and the second (except for the

66 עוד יש לנו ספר שלישי הנקרא מדרש, רוצה לומר שׂרמוני״ש. . . . וזה הספר מי שיאמין בו טוב, ומי שלא יאמין בו לא יזיק.

Sabbath) in almost all German manuscripts; the omission of the second "in love" except on Sabbath is stated as common usage by the fifteenth-century texts *MaHaRIL* (p. 166) for the Western and *Sefer Haminhagim Tyrna* (p. 43) for the Eastern Ashkenazic rituals. In all old texts, irrespective of ritual, the Sabbath is not mentioned by name but circumscribed by *yōm hammanōaḥ*, "day of rest" (or "day that makes one rest"). The European rituals eliminated this expression because it was rejected by Ḥayyim Viṭal Calabrese on the authority of *ARI*, who considered it uneducated just as the biblical Manoaḥ, the father of Samson, was an uneducated person.

The formula of the *Qiddush* expresses the twofold aspect of Jewish holidays. As *mo'ed* or *zĕman*, festive times anchored in the agricultural year, they are celebrated by Jews everywhere: Passover is the beginning of the harvest of barley, Pentecost the general time of First Fruits and the wheat harvest, Tabernacles the fall Thanksgiving. As *ḥag* the holidays had to be celebrated by a pilgrimage to the temple. Therefore, the holidays are mentioned twice in the Sephardic and Yemenite rituals, once as *ḥag* and once as *yōm ṭōv*, a general holiday. This is the version of R. Amram Gaon, Maimonides, and all other ancient Sephardic and Oriental sources except R. Saadia Gaon, who is followed by all Ashkenazic sources in mentioning *ḥag* alone.

If the *Seder* is given on Saturday night, the benedictions over light and *Havdalah* are added. The order of the benedictions in the Babylonian tradition (*b. Pesaḥim* 102b; *y. Berakhot* VIII,1 12a) in that case is יין (wine), קדוש (*Qiddush*), נר (light), הבדלה (*Havdalah*), זמן (festive time), abbreviated into an acronym יקנה"ז, *YQNHZ*, pronounced *yakenhaz* and represented, in German illuminated manuscripts and early prints, by the picture of a hare chase (*jag den haas* "chase the hare"). *Havdalah* is the declaration of the difference between Sabbath and workday or between Sabbath and holiday; since the Sabbath day has to be declared holy, its end also needs a declaration to permit work to be started.

The form of the benediction over fire, "Creator of the illuminating fire," is parallel to the formula for the use of wine, "Creator of the fruit of the vine." Just as "the fruit of the vine" is wine, the product of human technology, so the fire here is man-made fire created for human convenience. In the words of the Babylonian

Talmud (*b. Pesaḥim* 54a):[67] "R. Yossi says: Two things were in the Dinive plan of Creation on Sabbath Eve but were not created until the end of Sabbath. At the end of Sabbath, the Holy One, praised be He, gave knowledge of a heavenly kind to Adam. He took two stones and ground them one on the other to produce light. He also brought two animals and made them mate to produce the mule; according to Rabban Shimon ben Gamliel, the mule was first produced by 'Anah (*Gen.* 36:24)." The Jerusalem *Talmud* makes the connection with the *Havdalah* service more explicit (*y. Berakhot* VIII,6 12b):[68] "R. Lewy in the name of R. Bazira: Thirty-six hours did Man enjoy the light that was created on the First Day of Creation, Twelve on Friday, Twelve in the night of Sabbath, and Twelve during the day of Sabbath; in this light Adam saw from one end of the world to the other. In this unending light, the entire Creation started singing God's praise as it is said (*Job* 37:2), 'All under the heavens sing to Him, His light is on the corners of the world.' When the Sabbath ended, darkness came. Adam was afraid that this was what was said (*Gen.* 3:15): 'You will crush its head and it will crush your heel,' certainly it will crush me, so he said (*Ps.* 139:11), 'But the darkness will crush me.' R. Lewy said: At this moment the Holy One, praised be He, let him find two flintstones that he hit one on the other and made fire; that is what is said (*Ps.* 139:11), 'Now the night is light for me,' and he praised the Creator of the illuminating fire. Samuel says: Therefore we give praise for the [man-made] fire at the end of Sabbath because that was the time of its first production." Psalm 139 is ascribed to David in the Book of Psalms, but in all of talmudic literature it is taken to describe the experiences of Adam. According to one opinion (*b. Berakhot* 61a),[69] Eve was not created out of a rib (צֵלָע *ẓēlā'*) but of a side (צֶלַע *ẓéla'*) of Adam since it says (*Gen.* 1:27), "Male and female He created them," and Adam asserts (*Ps.* 139:5), "You formed me back and front," as a Janus-shaped creature with equal rights for male and female. All these aggadic

67 ר' יוסי אומר: שני דברים עלו במחשבה ליבראות בערב שבת ולא נבראו עד מוצאי שבת; ובמוצאי שבת נתן הקב"ה דעה באדם הראשון דוגמא של מעלה והביא שני אבנים וטחנן זו בזו ויצא מהן אור והביא שתי בהמות והרכיב זו בזו ויצא מהן פרד. רבן שמעון בן גמליאל אומר פרד בימי ענה היה.

68 ר' לוי בשם ר' בזירה שלשים ושש שעות שימשה אותה האורה שנבראת ביום הראשון, שתים עשׂרה בערב שבת ושתים עשׂרה בלילי שבת ושתים עשׂרה בשבת, והיה אדם הראשון מביט בו מסוף העולם ועד סופו. כיון שלא פסקה האורה התחיל כל העולם משורר שנאמר כל השמים ישרהו, למי שאורו על כנפות הארץ. כיון שיצאת שבת התחיל משמש החושך ובא. ונתיירא אדם ואמר אלו הוא שכתוב בו הוא ישופך ראש ואתה תשופנו עקב; שמא בא לנשכני ואמר אך חושך ישופני. אמר רבי לוי, באותה השעה זמן לו הקדוש ברוך הוא שני רעפין והקישן זה לזה ויצא מהן האור. הדא הוא דכתיב ולילה אור בעדני. ובירך עליה בורא מאורי האש. שמואל אמר לפיכך מברכין על האש במוצאי שבתות שהיא תחילת ברייתה.

69 דו פרצופין ברא הקדוש ברוך הוא באדם הראשון שנאמר אחור וקדם צרתני.

stories are not to be taken literally but as an easy vehicle for philosophical aphorisms, since rabbinic Judaism, except for a few medieval aberrations, always avoided systematic philosophy or theology, and this for good reason. Clearly, the passages quoted here and a host of similar and connected statements give a basis for a theology of human technology, research, and development, as part of the fulfillment of the Divine creation of the world.[70] It will also be clear that Jewish "fundamentalist" tradition is never a narrow self-centered interpretation of the text standing alone but must be instructed by tradition, the "oral law." An anti-evolutionist interpretation of Genesis as favored by Christian fundamentalists would be considered a Karaite heresy by Jews strictly adhering to talmudic teachings. The vanishing light referred to in the talmudic passages is the light created during the First Day of Creation which was hidden after Adam's sin (*b. Ḥagigah* 12a),[71] "And is reserved for the Just in the World to Come as it is said (*Gen.* 1:4), 'And God considered the light for the Good ones' and it is said (*Is.* 3:10), 'Call the Just "Good."'"

The *Talmud* points out (*b. Berakhot* 52b)[72] that the formula of the benedictions over wine and fire, "Creator of," is atemporal and therefore implies both past and future, an assertion of continuous Creation. This is the formulation of the school of Hillel, the only surviving school among the diverse movements active toward the end of the Second Commonwealth. An opposing view is given by the school of Shammai, proponents of a static, completed creation and predestined world, whose benediction formula "Who created" is strictly in the past tense.

It will be relevant for our later discussion to note here that the *Talmud* discusses two interpretations of the requirement (*Mishnah Berakhot* VIII,7)[73] "that they may not make the benediction over fire until they enjoy its light." In the Babylonian *Talmud* (*b. Berakhot*

---

70 Cf. the author's 1992 paper given in the bibliography.

71 ולמי גנזו לצדיקים לעתיד לבוא שנאמר וירא אלהים את האור כי טוב ואין טוב אלא צדיק שנאמר אמרו צדיק כי טוב.

72 בברא כוליה עלמא לא פליגי דברא משמע, כי פליגי בבורא. בית שמאי סברי בורא דעתיד למיברא ובית הלל סברי בורא נמי דברא משמע.

73 אין מברכין על הנר עד שיאותו לאורו.

53b),[74] Rav is of the opinion that it is not necessary to directly enjoy the light but only that somebody may enjoy it, whereas Rava requires that one must directly enjoy the light. Rav, one of the fathers of Babylonian *Talmud* study and founder of the Academy of Sura, was educated in Palestine at the academies of R. Yehuda the Prince and his uncle R. Ḥiyya; he represents the Palestinian tradition. Rava, who lived a hundred years later, presents the local Babylonian tradition. The difference between Western (Galilean) and Eastern (Babylonian) traditions is made clear in the Jerusalem *Talmud* (*y. Berakhot* VIII,7 12c), which reports that R. Zĕʿira, a Babylonian known from the Babylonian *Talmud* as R. Zera and who immigrated to Tiberias, wanted to impose the Babylonian rule on his students who complained that this represented an unheard-of new restriction.[75] Since Rava's opinion has to be followed in practice, being the later one, it is customary from Gaonic times (at least if Sunday is not a holiday) to check one's fingernails by the light of the *Havdalah* torch in order to derive some benefit from its light (R. Hai Gaon in *Teshuvot Hageonim Lyck* #49).[76] The light must be started after the end of the Sabbath in imitation of Adam. On weekdays, one lights a *Havdalah* torch especially for this purpose; on a holiday the holiday candles, lit after the end of the Sabbath, also serve for *Havdalah*. The old Ashkenazic custom for *Havdalah* on weekdays is to fill the cup until it overflows, as a sign of overflowing wealth to be acquired during the coming week, and to extinguish the torch in the spilled wine (R. Moshe Isserles, *Oraḥ Ḥayyim* §296, #1). Due to the opposition of R. Isaac Luria (*ARI*), Sephardim and ḥasidic Ashkenazim do not follow this custom (*Kaf Haḥayyim, loc. cit.* #9–13).

The formal requirements for the benediction of *Havdalah* are (*b. Pesaḥim* 103b; *y. Berakhot* V,1 9b)[77] "at least three and at most

74 אמר רב לא יאותו יאותו ממש אלא כל שאילו עומד בקרוב ומשתמש באורו ואפילו ברחוק מקום ורבא אמר יאותו ממש.

75 רבי זעירא מקריב קומי בוצינא. אמרו לו תלמידיו מה את מחמיר עלינו.

76 ועוד מנהגנו להביט בצפרנים ואומרים מפני שהן פרות ורבות לעולם; הלכך מי שרוצה לצאת ידי חובת ברכה זו צריך שיאות לאור הנר כמו שנהגו הראשונים כדי שיתחייב בברכה. In addition, we are used to look at our fingernails; it is said that we do this because nails never stop growing (and this is a good sign for one's money during the week). Therefore, anyone who really wants to fulfill his obligation with this benediction should enjoy the light in this age-old manner so that he should be required to recite the benediction.

77 הפוחת לא יפחות משלוש והמוסיף לא יוסיף על שבע.

seven" of the distinctions mentioned in the Torah. The three distinctions chosen by the *Talmud* (*b. Pesaḥim* 103b) are those between holy and secular (*Lev.* 10:10), between light and darkness (*Gen.* 1:4), and between Israel and the Gentiles (*Lev.* 20:26). The remaining distinctions were introduced to reach the admissible number of seven distinctions as already noted by R. Jacob Tam (*Tosafot Pesaḥim* 104a) and describe the distinction between the Sabbath, when all work is forbidden, and the six days of work, when all kind of work is not only allowed but required, the Sabbath and holidays, when preparation of food is permitted, and between the Sabbath and the weekday portion of the holidays of Passover and Tabernacles, when urgent work only is permitted. The last of these additional distinctions is not found in most Yemenite manuscript prayer texts. The last sentence, "You separated and sanctified Your people Israel" is missing in R. Saadia Gaon's version and is rejected by a number of medieval authors (cf. *Sefer Ha'iṭṭur* 266a) but justified by Rabbenu Tam, who explains it as a reference to the gradation of the people of Israel into levels of holiness of Israelites, Levites, and Aharonide priests. This makes it pertinent to the final doxology praising God "Who separates between several kinds of holiness."

The small differences that exist between the texts of the various rituals are of two different kinds. Some differences can be traced back to variants in talmudic manuscripts and are found in old texts of each ritual; they only became fixed by the choice of the printer of the standard text for each ritual. For example, whether to enumerate the different separations in a simple list as in the Ashkenazic text or to connect them by a *waw* as in the Sephardic and Yemenite texts is a difference found in *Talmud* manuscripts (*Diqduqe Soferim Pesaḥim*, p. 315); different styles were already chosen by different copyists of the *Siddurim* of R. Saadia Gaon and R. Amram Gaon. Ashkenazic and Sephardic texts mention the difference "between Israel and the nations" but the Yemenite text has "between Israel and the Gentiles." Here "nations" is a biblical expression and is found in the Venice edition of the *Talmud*, R. Amram Gaon, and the *Maḥzor Vitry*, which are among our oldest sources. "Gentiles" is an expression of rabbinic Hebrew and is the choice of the Munich manuscript of the *Talmud* (a French source), R. Saadia Gaon, and the Spanish *Tiqqune Zohar* (#69, p. 118). Since the requirement is to quote some of the separations mentioned in Scripture, the choice of a biblical expression in a prayer that otherwise is in rabbinic Hebrew is quite natural. Other differences are due to recent changes. The suffix in the expression בקדשתך "in Your holiness" is ָךְ, *-ākh*, in all sources, being standard rabbinic Hebrew. The Ashkenazic form ְךָ, *-ekhā*, is biblical Hebrew and was introduced as one of the reforms of the Stanow-Heidenheim period. In all current Sephardic texts, derived from the Livorno editions of the early nineteenth century, the *pi'el* form *qiddashta*, "You sanctified," found in all sources of all rituals up to the eighteenth century, is changed to *hiqdashta*, a *hif'il* form that in biblical Hebrew might possibly also have a meaning "You sanctified" but whose standard meaning in Rabbinical Hebrew is "You offered as a vow," following *Lev.* 27:14. The change is not recognized in the recent Sephardic halakhic compendium *Kaf Haḥayyim* (*Oraḥ Ḥayyim* §296). I was unable to determine the origin of this change, which moreover is not supported by the reading of any recorded *Talmud* manuscript (*b. Berakhot* 33b).

The benediction of thanksgiving for reaching the present time is required on all holidays, including New Year's Day and Yom Kippur, and permitted, on a personal basis, for all joyous occasions that happen not more than once a year (*b. 'Eruvin* 40b), or other joyous, extraordinary occasions like building a new house (*Mishnah Berakhot* IX,4), even if they happen repeatedly (*b. Berakhot* 60a).[78]

A benediction has to be recited not only before using any food but also, in general, before any action taken solely for the performance of a Divine commandment. Since the entire celebration of the *Seder* is in fulfillment of a biblical commandment, as will be explained in the chapter on the Recital, one would expect a special benediction at the start of the ceremony, as is done, for example, for the celebrations of Ḥanukkah and Purim. In the case of the *Seder*, the celebration is interrupted by translations, discussions, and explanations, and therefore the benediction is recited after the reading of the relevant portions and not before. A special benediction at the start of the *Seder* would give the celebration the status of a liturgy, where no interruption would be tolerated. The absence of a special benediction at the start of the *Seder* for this reason is an old ruling at least from Gaonic times (*Seder R. Amram Gaon, Seder shel Pesaḥ*). A kind of

78 בנה בית חדש וקנה כלים חדשים אומר ברוך שהגיענו לזמן הזה. ור' יוחנן אמר אפילו קנה וחזר וקנה צריך לברך.

substitute is the poetic insert of the *Qiddush* in the ritual of Yemen and a few other Oriental and North African communities. This insert is expressly authorized as an optional feature by R. Saadia Gaon and, therefore, belongs to the oldest surviving synagogal poetry. The poem follows the general principles of synagogal poetry; it is a web of biblical and talmudic phrases and each quote has to be taken as an allusion needing a commentary.

Line 1: The heave-offering, תְּרוּמָה, consists of the first grains taken from the new harvest. They are given to the priest and acquire holiness similar to a sacrifice. This *tĕrūmāh* is called "beginning" in *Num.* 18:12: "All the best of olive oil, all the best of wine and grain, their *beginnings* which they [i.e., Israel] give to the Lord, I gave them to you [Aaron]." Israel is called holy as a "beginning" of the Lord's harvest in *Jer.* 2:3: "Israel is holy to the Lord as *beginning* of His harvest; all those who shall try to devour them will have sinned; catastrophe will overtake them, says the Lord." This verse is quoted again in line 5. The verse in Jeremiah is taken as proof (*b. Qiddushin* 53a) that *tĕrūmāh* is called "holy to the Lord."
Line 2: The second half is a phrase borrowed from the *Musaf* prayer for holidays in the version adopted by European[79] Jews rather than the Yemenite text.[80]
Line 3: The second half is from *Job* 9:10.
Line 4: *Num.* 16:3; cf. *Ps.* 89:6, 89:8 for different synonyms of "Assembly of Saints." "Desirable vineyard" is a sentence from *Amos* 5:11 but the meaning of "vineyard" here is from *Is.* 5; "Desirable Plantation" is from *Is.* 5:7.
Line 5: "Treasure," *Ex.* 19.5; cf. line 1.
Line 6: Reference to *Gen.* 15:5, 22:17.
Line 7: The first half is from *Deut.* 26:19.
Line 8: This is not a biblical quote. The word used for "splendor" is Aramaic (used in *Dan.* 2:31). The splendor of their faces is like the sun as sons of Jacob whose name is "sun" (*Gen.* 37:9); according to *Midrash Gen. rabbah* (Chap. 84, 10), Jacob asked Joseph from where he knew that Jacob's secret name was "Sun."[81] Their looks are like angels as descendants of Abraham, about whom is it said (*Bereshit rabbah* 59[6][82]) in *Ps.* 45:3: "You are more beautiful than man."

---

79 שובה אלינו בהמון רחמיך בגלל אבות שעשו רצונך.

80 בה עלינו בהמון רחמיך בגלל אבותינו שעשו את רצונך.

81 בשעה שאמר יוסף והנה השמש והירח אמר יעקב מי גילה לו ששמי שמש.

82 יפיפית מבני אדם הוצק חן וגו'. נתיפית בעליונים שנאמר הן אראלם צעקו חוצה.

According to the same *midrash* 8(9),[83] man was created in such splendor that the angels, who do not see God, started to worship him until they saw his frailty. By a Babylonian *ăgadah* (*b. 'Avodah Zarah* 22b),[84] the snake put pollution into Eve when he consorted with her; that pollution still pollutes sex for mankind, except for the Jews, who were cleansed at Mount Sinai, and the converts whose souls were cleansed there (*b. Shabbat* 146a); they are restored to the desirable state of mankind before the Fall.

Lines 9–10: *Is.* 49:7.

Line 11: *Is.* 61:9.

Line 12: The first half is in the language of prayers; for the second part, cf. *Deut.* 28:10, *Jer.* 14:9.

Line 13: Assembly: *Ps.* 82:1; Treasure: *Ex.* 19:5; Inheritance: *Deut.* 9:29; from the Creation: *Deut.* 32:8 and compare the comments on "Prayer."

Line 15: *Deut.* 9:10, 30:20.

Line 17: *Neh.* 9:29. The phrase is also used in the *Havdalah* insert in the holiday prayers.

The Proclamations. This is an elaboration of *Ps.* 145:12, "To proclaim to mankind His strong deeds and the glory of the majesty of His kingdom."

Line 1: *Deut.* 4:20.

Line 2: This line is not based on a biblical quote. The root *šq'* does not appear in the *pi'el* conjugation in biblical Hebrew; it is rabbinic Hebrew and appears also in the litany *Dayyenu*. The Hebrew expression seems to be a translation of the Aramaism *rāmāh* in the Song of Moses, *Ex.* 15:1.

Line 3: This is the interpretation given by the *Mekhilta* (*Bo*, sec. 12) to *Ex.* 12:28:[85] "'The Children of Israel went and did.' They could not perform the commandment right away but since they accepted the obligation wholeheartedly, the Torah recognizes their deed as if it had been done immediately." This explanation of a simple past instead of the future perfect is accepted by Rashi in his commentary *ad loc.*

נתיפית מתחתונים שנא' נשיא אלהים אתה בתוכנו.

83 א"ר הושעיא בשעה שברא הקדוש ברוך הוא אדם הראשון טעו בו מלאכי השרת לומר לפניו קדוש. . . . מה עשה הקדוש ברוך הוא, הפיל עליו תרדמה וידעו הכל שהוא אדם.

84 דאמר מר יוחנן בשעה שבא נחש על חוה הטיל בה זוהמא. . . . ישראל שעמדו על הר סיני פסקה זוהמתן, גוים שלא עמדו על הר סיני לא פסקה זוהמתן. אמר ליה רב אחא בריה דרבא לרב אשי גרים מאי? אמר ליה אף על גב דאינהו לא הוו, מזלייהו הוו כדכתיב את אשר ישנו פה עמנו עומד היום וכו'.

85 ויעשו, וכי כבר עשו? אלא משקבלו עליהם לעשות מעלה עליהם כאלו עשו.

Line 4: God's beloved are Abraham, Isaac, and Jacob. At a circumcision, God is praised as "He who sanctified the beloved from the womb" (*b. Shabbat* 137b). The "beloved" is identified as Isaac by Rashi, Abraham by Rabbenu Tam, and Jacob by R. Sherira Gaon (quoted in *'Arukh*, s.v. ידיד). A different list, not applicable here, is given in *Avot deR. Nathan*, version 2, chap. 43.

After the *Qiddush*, one drinks the cup of wine. A biblical command (*Deut.* 8:10) requires one to praise God after eating. Therefore, it was the Ashkenazic custom (*Sefer Haminhagim R. Avraham Klausner* §106) to insert here the short form of Grace used for wine. This is still a matter of controversy for the students of R. Meir of Rothenburg in the fourteenth century; the usage is accepted by R. Mordokhai bar Hillel (*Mordokhay Pesaḥim* 36a) but rejected by R. Asher ben Yeḥiel (*Teshuvot Harosh*, chap. 14, #6). It is obvious that Sephardim who follow R. Asher and consider the Second Cup as a sequel to the first, with any number of sips admissible if one is thirsty during the recitation of the *Haggadah*, may not recite the short form of Grace at this moment. As a consequence, the recitation becomes questionable also for Ashkenazim. Since Grace does involve an invocation of the Divine Name, a questionable invocation would be a desecration of the Name. Therefore, everybody follows the conclusion of R. Asher ben Yeḥiel that the short form of Grace *may not* be recited here. The same controversy and resolution apply to the Third Cup. There always was unanimity that the Second Cup belongs to the meal and, therefore, is covered by the full Grace recited after the meal.

Washing of the Hands, Celery

A formal dinner in classical antiquity always took place in two steps. First the guests were offered appetizers while sitting on chairs in an anteroom. A Jewish source is *Tosefta Berakhot* IV,8:[86] "What is the order of a dinner? The guests enter and sit on chairs and armchairs until they are all assembled. When they are all assembled, they are given water and everybody washes one hand. Wine is mixed for them and every guest says the benediction for himself. Appetizers are set before them and every guest recites the benediction for himself. Then they go [to the dining hall] and lie down on couches. . . ." The main meal was taken lying on couches in the *triclinium*, Hebrew טרקלין, a hall set with tables. Around each table there were three couches. On each couch there was room for three people. Since the *Seder* is a family affair and the children also participate, the appetizer is taken on the couches in contrast to the usage during the rest of the year. Another reason to start the meal right in the dining room is that nothing can be eaten before the *Qiddush*, and *Qiddush* has to be performed "at the place of the main meal" (*b. Pesaḥim* 101a; *y. Berakhot* VI,6 10d).[87] Usually cakes or other sweets are served before the main meal; this is not possible on Passover and therefore the appetizer is כרפס celery, *karafs* in Persian, Arabic, and Aramaic. In regions where Arabic is unknown, the unvocalized word *krps* is pronounced *karpas;* this is the correct pronunciation of the word כרפס, *krps* in *Esth.* 1:6, meaning "white linen cloth" (کرپاس *karpās* in classical Persian, parallel کرباس *karbās* "canvas" in modern Farsi). The celery is not mentioned in the *Talmud*, which only has "vegetables" in general. Since the *maror* is eaten before the main meal but after the *mazzah*, the benediction for the *mazzah* as bread includes the entire meal and the bitter herbs may receive only a benediction for the fulfillment of a commandment but not one as food. The appetizer in the form of a vegetable therefore gives one the opportunity to say a separate

---

86 כיצד סדר סעודה. אורחין נכנסין ויושבין על ספסלים ועל גבי קתדראות עד שיתכנסו. נתכנסו כולן נתנו להם לידים, כל אחד ואחד נוטל ידו אחת. מזגו להם את הכוס, כל אחד ואחד מברך לעצמו. הביאו לפניהם פרפראות, כל אחד ואחד מברך לעצמו. עלו והסבו. . . .

87 אין קידוש אלא במקום סעודה. The principle is accepted by all Palestinian and most Babylonian authorities.

benediction for all vegetables eaten during the *Seder* ceremony. The Jerusalem *Talmud* (*y. Pesaḥim* X,3 37c)[88] reports that "all Galilean authorities in the name of R. Yoḥanan [require] that one has to dip the bitter herbs two times," meaning once for the appetizer and once for the commandment of *maror*, but it is also noted that in Babylonia one insists on a vegetable that is not a bitter herb since it is the opinion of most Babylonian authorities, in contrast to that of R. Yoḥanan, that a religious obligation is fulfilled when it is performed even if the performer had no intention to fulfill that particular commandment. According to the Babylonian opinion, formally ascribed (*b. Pesaḥim* 115a)[89] to R. Ḥisda, a student and successor of Rav, one may not say *any* benediction for the *maror* eaten with the *mazẓah* if *maror* was eaten as the vegetable. The Babylonian *Talmud* (*loc. cit.*) mentions only that one takes "vegetables other than bitter herbs"; the Jerusalem *Talmud* (*y. Pesaḥim* X,3 37d) notes that Rav insisted on using תרדין, white beets. Celery appears first in the list of acceptable vegetables given by R. Amram Gaon; this was adopted by the eleventh-century French authority and poet R. Yosef Tov Elem (*Seder Shabbat Haggadol*):[90] "One takes garden-rocket or celery or coriander or lettuce." The fifteenth-century text *MaHaRIL* (*Seder Hahaggadah*, p. 96) explains that celery is preferred since the letters of the name כרפס can be rearranged as ס פרך "60 forced" to indicate that 600,000 Israelites did forced labor in Egypt. The text also recommends leeks or parsley (πετροσέλινον "celery of rocks") if celery is not available; any vegetable that usually is eaten raw is also acceptable.

Yemenites and other Oriental groups who follow Maimonides (*Ḥamez̤ Umaz̤z̤ah* VIII,2)[91] "take the vegetable and dip it in *ḥaroset*," which is the only substance mentioned in the *Mishnah* (*Pesaḥim* X,3) for dipping and is a very festive and tasty sauce. The dipping in *ḥaroset* is prescribed in all old sources, from the Babylonian *siddurim* of R. Saadia Gaon and R. Amram Gaon to the French authority Rashi (*Sefer Hapardes*, p. 49) whose student writes,[92] "He dips in *ḥaroset*, eats, and gives to each member of his household an olive-sized piece." The Jewish groups that follow the *Shulḥan 'Arukh* as primary source, i.e., Ashkenazic and Sephardic Jews, dip in vinegar or in saltwater as

---

88 חבריה בשם ר׳ יוחנן צריך לטבל בחזרת שתי פעמים.

89 מתקיף לא ר׳ חסדא לאחר שמילא כריסו הימנו חוזר ומברך עליה?

90 שקל גרגירא או כרפסא או כוסברתא או חסא.

91 לוקח ירק ומטבל אותו בחרוסת.

92 וטובל בחרוסת, אוכל ומאכיל לבני ביתו כזית.

prescribed by Rashi's grandsons Shemuel (Rashbam) and Jacob (Rabbenu Tam). The reason given (*Tosafot Pesaḥim* 114a, s.v. מטבל)[93] is that the arguments given for the use of *ḥaroset*, namely, that it reminds one of the Exodus and that it removes danger from eating the bitter herbs, do not apply to other vegetables eaten before the recitation of the main body of the *Haggadah*. Therefore, the *Shulḥan 'Arukh* follows the opinion of R. Isaac (*RI*), the nephew of Rashbam and Rabbenu Tam (*Sefer Haterumah* #242)[94] that one may not use *ḥaroset* for dipping the vegetables since the *Mishnah* (*Pesaḥim* X.3) calls *ḥaroset* a *mizwah*, a religious obligation, and hence, using the *ḥaroset* before the appointed time would be as bad as using *maror* for the first vegetable. The twelfth-century author Roqeaḥ proposes to use wine if *ḥaroset* is not acceptable, presumably to give the dipping a more festive character (*Roqeaḥ* §283, p. 153).[95]

The *Seder* celebration in Jerusalem during the existence of the Temple centered on the Paschal lamb that had to be eaten in ritual purity. Every member of the *Seder* party had to be ritually pure. The traditional practice of ritual purity recognizes not only the kinds of impurity mentioned in the Torah but also a number of additional stages that would make food unfit for consumption in purity. One important such addition is that the hands of any person, also one otherwise ritually clean, are unclean in a secondary way unless washed with a sufficient amount of water and kept clean by permanent attention to the state of one's hands since (*b. Sukkah* 26b)[96] "hands are always busy" and (*Yadayim* III,2)[97] "everything that makes the heave-offering unfit for consumption makes hands unclean in a secondary way." In addition (*Parah* VIII,7),[98] "everything that makes the heave-offering unfit for consumption makes fluids a primary pollutant." Primary pollutants render all foods they come in contact with unfit for consumption in a state of ritual purity and all sacrifices unfit for any

---

93 היכא שהטיבול ראשון הוי בשאר ירקות אין צריך לטבול בחרוסת אלא או בחומץ או במים ומלח כמו שהיה נוהג ר״ת דהא אמר בגמרא דחרוסת משום קפא וליכא קפא אלא במרור, ומ״ש לר״א בר צדוק דקאמר מצוה זכר לטיט דלא שייך אלא במרור לזכר ד'ומררו את חייהם בחומר' ועוד דלא שייך מצוה דטיבול ראשון אינו אלא להיכירא ודלא כר״ר יוסף שעשה בסידורו 'ויטבול בחרוסת' וכן רבינו שלמה בסידורו וה״ר שמעיה.

94 ופסק הגאון רבנו תם ורבנו יצחק בן אחותו דאסור לעשות טיבול ראשון בחרוסת משום דעיקר טיבול שני הוא מצוה עם המרור וקודם המצוה אין למלאות כריסו מחרוסת אך לתיאבון יאכלנו כמו המצה.

95 ולוקח כרפס הוא אפיא או ירק אחר ומטביל ביין או בחרוסת.

96 ידים עסקניות הן.

97 כל הפוסל את התרומה מטמא את הידים להיות שניות.

98 כל הפוסל את התרומה מטמא את המשקין להיות תחלה.

use. It is therefore essential that the hands should be cleansed with water before the dipping of the celery in any fluid since any drop of fluid on one's unpurified hands renders the person a primary pollutant who is excluded from the *pesaḥ* sacrifice. (As a biblical principle, secondarily unclean matters cannot act on food. However, since certain body fluids [*Lev.* 15] are primary sources of ritual pollution, as a rabbinic ordinance and a precautionary measure, all fluids must be watched closely [*b. Shabbat* 14b]. The ritual pollution transmitted by unwashed hands is of rabbinic character.)

The full ceremony of ritual washing with the corresponding benediction is observed only among Yemenites and a few other groups of Oriental Jews. The benediction is required by Maimonides (*Ḥameẓ Umaẓẓah* VIII,1), Rashi (*Sefer Hapardes*, p. 49), and all Gaonic and early medieval European authorities. [The translation of the benediction, "to lift the hands," follows R. Hai Gaon quoted by Rashi (*Sefer Hapardes*, p. 188; *Siddur Rashi* #102, p. 51), who derives the meaning from the biblical expression (*Is.* 63:9), "He lifted and carried them until eternity." Rashi adds that one uses the rare root *nṭl* instead of the more common *nś'* because the vessel commonly used for washing the hands was called **אנטל** *anṭal*[99] (or **נטלא** *naṭla*).] European Jews (Ashkenazim and Sephardim) follow R. Eliezer of Tuch(heim) (*Tosafot Pesaḥim* 115b) and R. Meir of Rothenburg (*Hagahot Maimuniot Ḥameẓ Umaẓẓah* VIII, #1),[100] who hold that the benediction was required in previous generations, who were careful observers of the laws of purity but, since we do not have the possibility to observe these laws, a benediction at this point would mean pronouncing God's name in vain. As a consequence, in Ashkenazic households only the head of the house washes his hands at this point, without any benediction. This restriction of the action is first reported by the fifteenth-century source *Leqeṭ Yosher* (p. 88) in the name of "old prayer books".[101] While this source, a compilation by a student of R. Israel Isserlein of Wiener Neustadt, disapproves of the usage, his contemporary R. Shalom of Vienna approved of it (*MaHaRIL*, p. 96) against a number of his contemporaries. Of the latter's students, R. Eizik Tyrna seems to approve (*Sefer Haminhagim*, p. 47) since he

---

99 נטילת ידים על שם כלי ששמו אנטל והוא מחזיק רביעית.

100 ואומר הר״מ ז״ל נראה דזהו דוקא בדורות ראשונים שהיו נזהרים בטהרה אבל אנו אין לנו לברך על נטילה זו וכן היה רגיל לעשותן בלי ברכה וכן פירשו התוספות.

101 וראיתי במחזורים ישנים שכתב 'ויטול הבקי את ידיו', כלומר העושה את הסדר.

writes in the singular "*he* washes his hands," but R. Jacob Molin disapproves (*MaHaRIL loc. cit.*). This controversy never spread to Sephardic communities, who continue the old tradition that everyone washes his hands before touching moist vegetables. There is no washing of the hands for *Qiddush* since the wine is in a cup and one assumes, in the tradition of the school of Hillel, that one may pour wine and water without spilling (*y. Berakhot* VII,2 12a; *b. Berakhot* 52a; cf. also later, p. 302).

In a related disagreement, Yemenite and some other Oriental Jews, following Maimonides (*Ḥameẓ Umaẓẓah* VIII,2)[102] and Rashi (*Pardes Hagadol,* #133),[103] require that a minimal amount of vegetable, more than the volume of an average olive, be consumed by each participant since the eating of the vegetable is part of the prescribed ritual but the consumption of a quantity less than the volume of an olive cannot be counted as fulfilling any obligation whatsoever. (The size of an average olive is discussed in the chapter on *Maẓẓah* and *Maror.*) Ashkenazic and Sephardic Jews follow R. Meir of Rothenburg (*Hagahot Maimuniot Ḥameẓ Umaẓẓah,* VIII, #4)[104] and prefer to eat a smaller quantity to avoid the obligation to say the very short form of Grace that must be said after eating food in quantities larger than the volume of an olive. R. Meir of Rothenburg was the supreme rabbinic authority in Germany in the second half of the thirteenth century. After his death, his foremost student Asher ben Yeḥiel, known as *Rosh*, emigrated to escape the fate of his teacher and settled in Toledo, Spain, where he became one of the leading rabbinic authorities. As a consequence, many of R. Meir's opinions have been accepted by both Ashkenazic and Sephardic communities. The preoccupation with quantities is not found in talmudic sources and, therefore, not in Maimonides, since in classical times the appetizer was an integral part of the dinner (cf. p. 228) and, hence, was covered by Grace after the meal, irrespective of the time consumed by discussion before the meal. All Ashkenazic sources before R. Meir require the recitation of the short form of Grace after eating the vegetable. R. Meir of Rothenburg's opinion can be supported by Rashi's view (*b. Pesaḥim* 114a)[105] that *maror*, eaten after

---

102 מתחיל ומברך בורא פרי האדמה ולוקח ירק ומטבל אותו בחרוסת ואוכל כזית הוא וכל המסובין עמו; כל אחד ואחד אין אוכל פחות מכזית.

103 ומברך בפה״א וטובל בחרוסת ואוכל ומאכיל לכל אחד ואחד כזית.

104 ומהר״ם כתב והורה שאין צריך כזית בטיבול זה.

105 וטיבול ראשון כדי שיכיר תינוק וישאל לפי שאין רגילין בני אדם לאכול ירק קודם סעודה.

bread, does not need a benediction as food and that the appetizer is introduced only to make the children ask, "Why is this night different from all other nights?" The Yemenite tradition follows the author of *Sefer Ha'iṭṭur* (*Hilkhot Maẓẓah Umaror* 266b)[106] that the benediction over bread covers only food *usually* eaten during the course of a dinner, exluding bitter herbs eaten separately. This implies that the benediction over celery is an integral part of the ceremony, being needed for the *maror* as food and, therefore, the time spent by the recitation of the *Haggadah* is not an interruption. The same author (*loc. cit.*)[107] is of the opinion that the expression "dipping" used in the *Mishnah* is simply a synonym of "eating," because in antiquity the small table with the *Seder* plate was brought in only after *Qiddush* and vegetable, and the vegetable was eaten without necessarily being dipped. But since today we eat at large tables with a prearranged setup of the *Seder* plate on which the *ḥaroset* is available, there is nothing wrong with dipping. The author who represents the usage of Marseilles in the High Middle Ages knows only the dipping in *ḥaroset*, parallel to today's Yemenite ritual. Since today all groups eat the vegetable as an introduction to the meal, one does not have to recite the short form of Grace even if the quantity is larger than the size of an olive (*Kaf Haḥayyim Oraḥ Ḥayyim* §173 #116).

---

106 ואף על גב דפת פוטר כל מיני מאכל וכיון דברך המוציא פטר דברים הבאים בתוך הסעודה, חזרת אין דרכן ללפת את הפת ולא מחמת סעודה בא וצריך הוא לברך עליו אלא שברכת כרפס פוטרתו וההלילא ואגדתא לאו הפסקה נינהו.

107 טיבול לשון אכילה הוא. . . . ולפי שלא היו מביאין השלחן עד לאחר קידוש לא היו מביאין חרוסת, אבל מפני שמנהגינו לפרוס מפה שיהיה סדור הכל נהגו לטבול בחרוסת והרשות בידו.

Breaking of the Maẓẓah

In Ashkenazic and Sephardic households, the head of the house now breaks the second *maẓẓah* into two parts and puts the larger piece away to be eaten after dinner. In the Yemenite ritual, the *maẓẓah* is broken only before dinner, after the recitation of the *Haggadah*, following Maimonides (*Ḥameẓ Umaẓẓah* VIII,6). In the old Ashkenazic *minhag*, the uppermost *maẓẓah* was broken (*RAVaN*, p. 166a; *Sefer Miẓwot Gadol*, chap. 41; *Ṣefer Minhagim R. Avraham Klausner* §109[108]) in order to perform the commandment at the first possible moment. In that case also, the broken part would be inserted between the two whole *maẓẓot* as prescribed by the *Talmud* (*b. Berakhot* 39b; cf. p. 201). Today's usage follows *RAVIA* (§525), who declares that the breaking itself is not a commandment; so the interpretation of the talmudic statement would be to take the middle *maẓẓah* and put the broken part back at its place. The Provençal *Orḥot Ḥayyim* (p. 80) allows any one of the three *maẓẓot* to be broken; in Southern Europe the *maẓẓot* were never baked with distinguishing signs. The piece that is removed is covered by or wrapped in a napkin so that it should not be eaten accidentally during dinner (*MaHaRIL*, p. 102); the napkin is chosen in remembrance of the verse (*Ex.* 12:34), "The people carried their dough before it became sour, their provisions bundled in their clothes on their backs" (*Sefer Minhagim loc. cit.; Orḥot Ḥayyim*, p. 80 [17]); the breaking also is taken to symbolize the splitting of the Red Sea. The Exodus is enacted at this point in the Tunisian ritual. In many families, the children hide the broken *maẓẓah* during the second washing of the hands; they will demand a reward for producing the *maẓẓah* again for *afiqomen*. This gives them a monetary incentive to stay awake at least until Grace is said. In other families, the father hides the *maẓẓah* and the children hunt for it to claim the reward.

The *maẓẓah* is broken since it is called (*Deut.* 16:3) by an expression that can be translated by "bread of the poor" and (*b. Pesaḥim* 115b/116a)[109] "since a poor man usually has to eat broken

---

108 ויקח מצה העליונה ויבציענה לשנים, וישים חציה תחת המפה לפי שנאמר משארותם צרורות בשמלותם על שכמם.

109 לחם עוני, עני כתיב; מה עני שדרכו בפרוסה אף כאן בפרוסה.

pieces of bread, we use here a broken piece." As a side effect, the piece for the *afiqomen* is now ready. The unbroken top and bottom *maẓẓot* represent the double bread, *leḥem mishneh*, used on all Sabbaths and holidays in remembrance of the Mannah. This is stated explicitly only for the Sabbath (*b. Shabbat* 117b):[110] "R. Abba said: On Sabbath, one is required to break one's bread on two whole loaves since Scripture mentions 'double bread' (*Ex.* 16:22)." One imitates the rituals of Sabbath on holidays in this respect just as one does for the *Qiddush*; in a responsum ascribed to R. Natronai Gaon in *Maḥzor Vitry* (p. 87, #111) and to R. Sherira Gaon in *Pardes* (p. 194), *Pardes Haggadol* (p. 21b, #91), and the collection *Shaare Teshuvah* (#222), it is explained:[111] "You should know that we have to break our bread on two loaves on a holiday just as one has to do on the Sabbath. The reason is that on the Sabbath one has to use two loaves because Mannah did not descend on Sabbath and Israel was forewarned to collect a double portion [on Friday]; as Rava[112] said: One is required to break one's bread on two whole loaves on Sabbath. Since on holidays also the Mannah was not descending, we are required to break our bread on two whole loaves. From where do we know that Mannah did not descend on holidays? The Sages taught (*Mekhilta Beshallaḥ parshah* 4, p. 169): "(*Ex.* 16:26) 'Six days you shall collect it.' R. Yehoshua says: This teaches us that the Mannah did not descend on Sabbath. From where do we know the same for holidays? The same verse says, 'On a day of rest, it will not be there.'" The argument goes as follows. The verse in its Masoretic punctuation reads: "Six days you shall collect it; but on the Seventh day שבת, it will not be there." The problem is how to interpret the word שבת. Does it mean "Sabbath" or "day of rest"? The order to collect only six days of the week implies that on the seventh day one should not collect. The second part of the sentence gives the reason: there will be nothing to collect. But this

---

110 אמר ר' אבא בשבת חייב אדם לבצוע על שתי ככרות דכתיב לחם משנה.

111 הוו ידעין שצריכין אנו לבצוע על שתי ככרות ביום טוב כדרך שצריכין לבצוע עליהם בשבת. מה טעם, מפני שבשבת עצמה לא נתחייבו לבצוע על שתי ככרות אלא משום שלא ירד מן בשבת והוזהרו ישראל ללקוט לחם משנה. ואמר רבא חייב אדם לבצוע על שתי ככרות בשבת. וביום טוב נמי כיון שלא ירד בו מן חייבים אנו לבצוע על שתי ככרות. ומניין שלא ירד מן בימים טובים שכן שנו חכמים ששת ימים תלקטוהו. ר' יהושע אומר למדנו שלא ירד מן בשבת. ביום טוב מניין. ת"ל שבת לא יהיה בו.

112 It is impossible to decide whether Rava mentioned here is R. Abba mentioned in all sources of the *Talmud*, *b. Shabbat* 117b, a Babylonian who emigrated to Galilee during the second half of the third century, or Rav Abba bar Yosef bar Ḥama, usually designated by Rava, a head of the Babylonian Academies in the first half of the fourth century. The name *Rava* substitutes for *R. Abba* in the Munich ms. of the parallel in *b. Berakhot* 39b.

makes the word שבת quite superfluous. Since the Torah is presumed not to contain any superfluous words,[113] *šbt* must here mean "rest," any day of rest, and not specifically the Sabbath. The Gaon presents the later Babylonian practice. In Galilee, only one loaf was used on Sabbath (*RAVaN* 166a)[114] in order "not to take Friday into the Sabbath," since one portion of the Mannah collected on Friday was consumed before the Sabbath. *RAVaN*'s source prescribes two whole loaves only for the Babylonian Sabbath, not the holidays.

In most Jewish groups, the *mazzot* are put between two cloth covers, just as the two loaves of Sabbath and holidays are put between two cloth covers. However, there are some Sephardic groups that cover the entire table setting, plates, cups, and bread, with a second tablecloth before the *Qiddush*. The table has to be covered by a tablecloth in honor of Sabbath and holiday; this is a talmudic requirement (*b. Pesaḥim* 100a):[115] "One spreads a tablecloth and makes *Qiddush*." The reasons for covering either the entire table or putting the bread between two napkins are discussed by the early thirteenth-century Provençal *Sefer Hamikhtam* (*Pesaḥim*, p. 78).[116] The authors of the Provence usually are alert to the opinions of the Sephardic authorities in Spain to their South and those of the Ashkenazic North. "We usually set the table [for Sabbath] on Friday; but in order that it should not look as if we would like to eat now before the Sabbath, and to make it clear that the meal is in honor of the Sabbath, we put another tablecloth over the settings until after *Qiddush*. Some people give as reason that we cover the bread [until we made *Qiddush*] so that the bread should not be offended [when *Qiddush* is made over wine, but bread, more vital as food than wine, should have precedence in the order of benedictions by the principle 'not to bypass an obligation'; cf.

---

113 The principle is already found in Philo, *De fuga et inventione*, 54: σαφῶς εἰδῶς, ὅτι περιττὸν ὄνομα οὐδὲν τίθησιν. . . . "Well knowing that he [Moses] never puts in a superfluous word. . . ." Cf. also H. Guggenheimer, *Logical Problems in Jewish Tradition.*

114 בחלוקת אנשי בבל ואנשי א״י מצאתי אנשי בבל בוצעין על ב׳ ככרות בשבת שלימות לקיים לחם משנה, אנשי א״י על אחת שלימה שלא להכניס של ערב שבת בשבת. אנשי בבל כשחל פסח בשבת מניח פרוסה בין שתי השלימות ובחול על אחת ובוצע מן הפרוסה ומברכין עליה המוציא ועל אכילת מצה, אנשי א״י בין בחול בין בשבת מניח פרוסה על השלימות ובוצע.

115 פורס מפה ומקדש.

116 נהגנו להביאה ולערכה מבעוד יום. וכדי שלא יראה שנרצה לאכול עכשיו קודם שיקדש היום ונאכל לכבוד שבת פורסין עליה מפה עד אחר הקידוש. ויש שנותנים טעם לפריסת המפה, כדי שלא תכלם הפת כשמקדשין על היין ולא עליה, וכן בברכת המזון. ויש שאומרים שפריסת המפה הוא זכר למן שהיה טל למעלה וטל למטה, כמו שאנו עושין לחם משנה גם כן זכר למן. ונהגו לתת שתי ככרות של לחם משנה זו על גב זו בין המפות.

p. 200]. Some people say that the bread should lie between two sheets as a remembrance of the Mannah that was presented between an upper and a lower level of dew just as we use two loaves of bread in remembrance of the Mannah. We also put the two loaves between the sheets one on top of the other."

Maimonides (*Ḥameẓ Umaẓẓah* VIII,6) and some other medieval authorities (*Hagahot Maimuniot, loc. cit.* #6) require only two *maẓẓot* instead of the three in general use. The source is a talmudic statement (*b. Berakhot* 39b):[117] "Everybody agrees that at the *Seder* one puts the broken piece inside (בתוך) the whole *maẓẓah* for the benedictions since it is called 'bread of the poor.'" Maimonides obviously is of the opinion that for the *Seder* one uses only hot, freshly baked *maẓẓah*, which can be bent. *RAVIA* (#525) explains the opinion that one needs only two *maẓẓot* (at least if the *Seder* is not on Sabbath) by vocalizing בתוך not *bĕtōkh* "inside" but *bĕtāwekh* "in the middle," meaning that the broken *maẓẓah* is lying on top of the whole *maẓẓah* and in its middle. This is exactly the practice of Galilean and early Babylonian Jewry as reported by *RAVIA*'s grandfather *RAVaN* (loc. cit.).

---

117 הכל מודים בפסח שמניח פרוסה בתוך שלימה ובוצע, מאי טעמא לחם עני כתיב.

Recital

Mixing the Second Cup

In most Sephardic and Oriental communities, the Second Cup is filled at this moment. This is the opinion of R. Amram Gaon and Maimonides (*Seder Hahaggadah*):[118] "He starts with the Second Cup and recites 'We left Egypt in a hurry.'" Most Ashkenazic communities and some Sephardic ones follow the opinion of R. Saadia Gaon and Rashi in his *Talmud* commentary, who explains the language of the *Mishnah* (*b. Pesahim* 116a): "One mixes him the Second Cup and here the son asks his father" as meaning:[119] here, at the moment that one mixes the Second Cup, the son asks his father, "In what is this night different from all other nights, that one mixes a second cup before the meal?" In these communities, the cup is mixed just before *mah nishtannah.* The practical manuals from Rashi's school, *Maḥzor Vitry, Siddur, Ha-Orah*, and indeed most French sources before the expulsion of Jews from France follow R. Amram Gaon in their instructions. R. Yosef Tov Elem and all medieval German sources follow R. Saadia Gaon. He is followed also by *Shulḥan 'Arukh* (§473, #7). Among the Livorno printers who in the nineteenth century provided most of the Sephardic world with liturgical books, the later leading firm Benamozegh followed Maimonides and the earlier firm Saadun the *Shulḥan 'Arukh.* Since the section *"This is the bread of poverty"* is not mentioned in the *Talmud* and since its recitation is also accompanied by acts that may lead children to ask why this is done, both ways of pouring the cup are in conformity with talmudic instructions. The main difference is the interpretation to give to the next section of the *Haggadah.* The intention of the groups that mix the cup at this moment is described by the old Italian source *Shibbolé Haleqet* (§218, p. צג):[120] "One mixes the Second Cup, everybody takes his cup in his

---

118 מתחיל על כוס שני ואומר בבהילו יצאנו ממצרים.

119 וכאן הבן שואל אביו. כאן במזיגת הכוס שני הבן שואל את אביו מה נשתנה עכשיו שמוזגין כוס שני קודם אכילה.

120 מוזגין כוס שני ונוטל כל אחד ואחד כוסו בימינו והקערה או הסל בשמאלו שבהם

right hand and lifts the *Seder* plate with his left hand; they lift the plate and recite in unison 'This is the bread of poverty . . .' in praise, song, and rhythm, just as we find that our forefathers in Egypt sang in praise when they were eating *mazzah*." The German attitude is explained by R. Ephraim of Bonn (late twelfth century) that the Second Cup is the Cup of Salvation, as expressed by the benediction recited before the meal, and therefore it is inappropriate for a declaration about "bread of poverty." After the expulsion of Jews from France, only the German attitude survived in theoretical Ashkenazic literature, but the contrary opinion is alive and well in practice.

The cup of wine is the vehicle of benediction, as pointed out in the chapter on the *Qiddush*. The paradigm of a cup of benediction, or "Cup of Salvation" (*Ps.* 116:13), is the cup of wine used for Grace. The *Talmud* (*b. Berakhot* 51a; *y. Berakhot* VII,6 11cd) lists a number of requirements for a cup of blessings.[121] There are four essential requirements and six additional features. The four essential ones are that the cup must be "washed" inside and out and "dried" before being used; it must be "fresh" and "full." As a consequence, in the Yemenite ritual all cups are washed and dried for each one of the Four Cups. The other rituals only require a fresh cup for *Qiddush*. They insist that refilling a cup restores its validity; this has talmudic authority (*y. Berakhot loc. cit.*).[122] Today's Yemenite usage is the medieval French one; the procedure followed by the other communities was approved by early medieval German rabbis (*RAVIA* #514).[123] There are some problems with the interpretation of "fresh and full." The Sephardic interpretation is that "fresh" refers to the wine. Therefore, in the Sephardic ritual one fills the cup for Grace two-thirds full for the blessing, and during Grace one mixes the wine with the desirable amount of water at the mention of the Land of Israel. Most other rituals follow the interpretations of either Rashi (*ad loc. Berakhot*

כל הדברים הראוין להיות שם כמו שהזכרנו למעלה ומגביהין את הקערה ואומרים פה אחד בהלל ובשיר ובנחת הא לחמא עניא וכו' שכן מצינו באבותינו במצרים שאמרו שירה והלל על אכילת מצה.

121 עשׂרה דברים נאמרו בכוס של ברכה: טעון הדחה ושטיפה, חי ומלא, עיטור ועיטוף, נוטלו בשתי ידיו ונותנו בימין, ומגביהו מן הקרקע טפח ונותן עיניו בו, ויש אומרים אף משגרו במתנה לאנשי ביתו. אמר ר' יוחנן אנו אין לנו אלא ארבעה בלבד הדחה ושטיפה חי ומלא.

122 ר' יונה טעים אכסא ומתקן ליה. Cf. *Tosafot Berakhot* 52a, s.v. טעמו.

123 יש נוהגין שכל ששתו ממנו מחזיקין אותו לפגום אם לא יערה לחוץ כל מה שבכוס וימזוג יין אחר לקדש, וכן לברכת המזון, וכן נוהגין בצרפת, וכן ראיתי נוהג מורי הרב ממיץ. . . . ובבית אבא מרי ראיתי שלא היה מערה בחוץ, אך כשהיה שותה ממנו היה מוסיף עליו מעט יין או מים, וכן נוהגין בארץ אשכנז.

51a)[124] that the wine should be mixed only in the cup and not be poured already mixed, or of Rosh (R. Asher ben Yeḥiel, *ad loc.*)[125] that "fresh" refers to the cup which should be neither chipped nor dented. "Full" means that the cup should contain at least the minimum volume of wine as discussed under *Qiddush* (*b. Berakhot* 52a) and that it should look full. Eastern Ashkenazic families, following R. Moshe Isserles and R. Jacob ben Asher (*Ṭur Oraḥ Ḥayyim* 183)[126] often insist that a cup of blessing should be filled to its rim. This custom is acknowledged by the modern commentary *Mishnah Berurah* (§183 [9]) even though it is recognized that some spilling of wine is almost inevitable when the cup is lifted and, therefore, in a situation where ritual purity is important, the hands would have to be washed every time before the cup is lifted. Since the *Talmud* is emphatic (*b. Berakhot* 52ab) that one may lift the cup without spilling wine on its outside, the custom of the other Jewish groups has historical validity. If the cup is filled to the rim, one would at least expect the celebrant to wash his right hand, as explained in the *Tosefta* quoted on p. 228 and required explicitly by R. Salomon ben Adrat (*RaSHBA, Responsa ascribed to Nachmanides*, #202; *Sefer Haḥinnukh* #21). The cup has to be washed and dried as a matter of respect for religious ceremonies. The cup has to be full as a sign that we expect God's blessing in its fullness. The wine or cup has to be "fresh" since the Hebrew word for "fresh," חי, primarily means "alive, living."

The additional features are: it should be "crowned," i.e., surrounded either by people or by vessels; "covered," the benedictions should not be said without decent head cover; the cup should be lifted up with both hands and held in the right hand, the lucky side, one hand breadth over the table; one should look at the cup while reciting the benediction to avoid making a mechanical ritual out of the recitation; and after drinking, one may give the blessed cup to one's wife as a fertility rite. Mystical interpretations of the ten conditions are presented in *Zohar III* (p. 245b, 273b) and *Tiqqune Zohar* (#47, end).

---

124   חי. שמוֹזגוֹ במים בכוֹס חי.

125   ויˉˊˊמ דחי אכלי קאי דומיא דאינך ופירושוֹ שלם.

126   מלא כפשטיה שיהא מלא על כל גדוֹתיו.

Showing the *Mazzah*

Before the presentation of the *mazzot*, the egg and bone are removed from the *Seder* plate in Western Ashkenazic families since one does not want to imply that we present the *Pesah* sacrifice together with the *mazzot*. In the Middle Ages, this was the general Ashkenazic custom. However, the fourteenth-century French authority Rabbenu Perez objected to the removal since in his opinion it gave the bone the status of a sacrifice; he prefers the arrangement of Maimonides followed by all other Jewish groups (*Orhot Hayyim* 90a). Already Rashbam (R. Shemuel ben Meir, Rashi's oldest grandson) did note (*loc. cit.*) that the removal was a misinterpretation of the talmudic rule (*b. Pesahim* 116b) that states that the meat should not be lifted; that rule refers to the statement of Rabban Gamliel (cf. p. 309) toward the end of the *Haggadah* recital. In many Jewish groups, the entire plate is lifted and presented. After the presentation, the *mazzot* or the entire *Seder* plate are covered again. Originally, when the guests were lying on couches and the *Seder* plate, the conversation piece, was on a small table in front of the head of the house, the entire table was then removed so that the children would complain that the food was removed after the appetizer only, indicating that there would not be any more food. Only in the absence of such reaction or a reaction to mixing the Second Cup, the head of the house himself would have to point out the special features of the *Seder* celebration in the next piece, the Four Questions (*b. Pesahim* 115b):[127] "Abbai [the orphaned nephew of Rabba bar Nahmani] was sitting before Rabba. When he saw that they were removing the small table, he said to them [the servants]: 'We did not yet eat and you remove the table?' Rabba said to him: 'You freed us from the need to recite *mah nishtannah*.'"

The current form of the declaration that accompanies the presentation of the *mazzot* is a mixture of dialects and styles. This, and the diversity of the different recensions, shows that the declaration is no longer in its original form. The celebration in Jerusalem originally would not begin with the presentation of the *mazzot* but with the introduction of the Paschal Lamb.

Sephardic and Oriental versions of the *Haggadah* start with

---

127 אביי הוה יתיב קמיה דרבה. חזא דקא מדלי תכא מקמיה. אמר להו: עדיין לא קא אכלינן, אתון קא מעקרי תכא מקמן? אמר ליה רבה: פטרתן ממימר מה נשתנה.

the declaration "We left Egypt in a hurry," as noted above (p. 238). This introduction is not part of the declaration for the *mazzot* but an explanation for why we hurry to fill a second cup when the drinking of that cup is a long time off. The declaration therefore is appropriate for those rituals that fill the Second Cup immediately after the vegetable is consumed, following R. Amram Gaon and Maimonides. Since in the Ashkenazic ritual the cup is not filled in a hurry, the Ashkenazic version has no need to explain our hurry with the hurry of our forefathers. The language comes from *Mekhilta deR. Shimon ben Yoḥay* (p. 14)[128] referring to *Ex.* 12:11: "So you shall eat it [i.e., the *Pesaḥ* sacrifice], . . . and you shall eat it in a hurry, it is a *Pesaḥ* for the Lord." The question is, who is in a hurry? In the *Mekhilta deR. Ishmael* (*Bo*, sec. 7, p. 22)[129] there are three opinions given about the meaning of the hurry. The first, anonymous opinion is that the Egyptians were in a hurry to get rid of the Jews; this would refer to the time after midnight when the firstborn were already slain. A second opinion, of R. Joshua ben Qorḥa, is that the Jews were in a hurry to prepare for their departure the next morning; this refers to the entire night and is the opinion adopted by *Mekhilta deR. Shimon ben Yoḥay.* The third opinion, reported in the n. of R. Eliezer, is that the hurry was divine, to slay all firstborn exactly at midnight. He therefore restricts the hurry to the time before midnight. This is in line with the tradition of R. Eliezer that the *Pesaḥ* sacrifice must be eaten before midnight as a biblical commandment (see later in the discussion of "The Sages"). All this discussion uses the original biblical word for hurry, חִפָּזוֹן. The *Mekhilta deR. Shimon ben Yoḥay*, which explains the hurry as the hurry of travelers therefore adopts the opinion, generally ascribed to R. Akiba, that the "hurry" and the *Pesaḥ* meal were extended during the entire night. It is the only source that replaces the classical word חִפָּזוֹן by the later בְּהִילוּת; the root בהל appears in this sense first in Proverbs and Ecclesiastes. It is not clear why the Hebrew abstract noun *bĕhīlūt* lost its final *t* and appears now as Aramaic *bĕhīlū*, in particular since the verb "we left" is still the Hebrew יָצָאנוּ and not the Aramaic נַפְקָן; maybe the change in form is inspired by *Job* 29:3, בְּהִלּוֹ נֵרוֹ *bĕhillō nērō* "His light is a blinding white."

128 וככה תאכלו אתו וג' ואכלתם אותו בחפזון בבהילות יוצאי דרכים.

129 ואכלתם אותו בחפזון זה חפזון מצרים. . . . ר' יהושע בן קרחה אומר ואכלתם אותו בחפזון זה חפזון ישראל. . . . אבא חנן משום רבי אליעזר אומר זה חפזון שכינה.

It would be best not to translate the characterization of the *mazzah* in the declaration, to leave the sentence as "This is the *leḥem 'ōnī*" since the *Talmud* (*b. Pesaḥim* 115b) has too many explanations for that biblical expression (*Deut.* 16:3):[130] "Samuel said: It is written *leḥem 'ōnī*, the bread about one gives answers (*'nh*). There is also a Tannaitic statement: *leḥem 'ōnī*, the bread about which one gives many answers. Another explanation: *leḥem 'ōnī* is spelled *leḥem 'ānī* [i.e., defective; the word could be read as 'poor"]; just as a poor man has to content himself with a broken piece of bread, so we are using now a broken *mazzah*. Another explanation: just as the poor man has to fire the oven by himself while his wife is baking, so the *mazzot* have to be baked with the husband firing the oven while his wife bakes." The last statement is usually taken to mean that the *mazzot* have to be baked quickly to avoid any fermentation of the dough and, therefore, the oven has to be heated up while the dough is kneaded. Some medieval authors (e.g., *Roqeaḥ* #281)[131] require that the *mazzah* for the *Seder* be baked by the husband-and-wife team in the afternoon of the Fourteenth of Nisan; this is said to be the standard of the Jews living along the valley of the Rhine and is based on a statement of the Jerusalem *Talmud* (*y. Pesaḥim* II,4 29b) to the effect that one cannot be sure that for *mazzot* baked earlier the necessary diligence was exerted to make sure that no fermentation did occur. This custom has not survived anywhere.

The sources show that one may translate *leḥem 'ōnī* by "bread of poverty." One might also translate "bread of deprivation" (see the discussion of עניגו, p. 295). The common translation as "bread of distress" or "bread of affliction" cannot be justified; the *mazzah* is the festive bread used in the Temple (*Lev.* 2:11): "No flour offering that you will offer to the Lord shall be processed as *ḥamez*." This is true also in other religions of antiquity; the Roman Flamen Dialis was even forbidden to see sour bread (*Gellius, Noctes Atticae* X,15). R. Yosef Gikatilla points out that later in the *Haggadah* the *mazzah* is shown to be the bread of liberation.

---

130 לחם עוני לחם שעונין עליו דברים הרבה, דבר אחר לחם עוני מה עני שדרכו בפרוסה אף כאן בפרוסה, דבר אחר מה דרכו של עני הוא מסיק ואשתו אופה אף כאן נמי הוא מסיק ואשתו אופה.

131 מנהג לאפות בערב פסח ממנחה גדולה ואילך אף על גב דבירושלמי מצה ישנה בפלוגתא דבית שמאי ובית הילל היא. וכן בתוספתא מכשרת מצה ישנה. מיהו המנהג כתקרובת הפסח דהיינו מז' ולמעלה כדאיתא בריש תמיד נשחט. מצוה לאפות שלוש מצות בלילה ראשונה, ובלילה שנייה של פסח יאפה שלוש מצות, חביבה מצוה בשעתה.
לשון הירושלמי: מצה הישנה תפלוגתא דבית שמאי ובית הלל. אמר רבי יוסה דברי הכל היא מכיון שלא עשאה לשם פסח דבר בריא שלא דיקדק בה.

In all old and most modern versions, the declaration starts with *hā laḥmā*, "this is the bread," except for the standard Eastern European Ashkenazic text, which reads *kĕhā laḥmā* "bread, similar to this [was eaten by our forefathers in Egypt]." This change of the tradition in the interest of accuracy or veracity is approved by R. Eisik Tyrna in his *Sefer Haminhagim*, the basic source of the Eastern European Ashkenazic ritual (p. 49), is opposed as a change of tradition by R. Moshe Isserles (*Darke Moshe Ṭur Oraḥ Ḥayyim* §473 #17), but is accepted by the authoritative commentary *Magen Avraham* (*Oraḥ Ḥayyim* §473 #24). The Western Ashkenazic author *Noheg Kaẓon Yosef* (p. 220), while accepting the change in principle, points out that the correct form would be הא כלחמא עניא "this is like the bread. . . ." R. Ḥayyim Viṭal, in the name of R. Isaac Luria (*Kitve Ha'ari, Sha'ar Hakawwanot, Pesaḥ*, chap. 6, p. 83c), punctuates הֵא *hē*. The oldest Babylonian *Haggadah* fragment known (*Ginze Schechter* 2, p. 259) may read either האי, a form equivalent to הֵא, or מאי לחמא עניא "what was the bread of deprivation."

The only genuine Aramaic punctuation of דאכלו is the Yemenite one, based on *Dan.* 3:8, 6:25. Ashkenazic and Sephardic punctuations are influenced by Hebrew. The form אבהתנא for "our fathers" is Palestinian/Syriac; the corresponding Babylonian form is אבהן (*Ben Yehuda*, s.v. אב).

The sentences after the first one are typical Babylonian-talmudic composition. The original form is best preserved in the Sephardic text, which is given by R. Amram Gaon and the medieval Italian Ashkenazic *Tanya Rabbati* (p. 96). The last sentence indicates that Passover is not only the festival of past liberation but also of future redemption. In that, it is a counterpart to the prayer for redemption in the final benediction of the Recital and follows the talmudic statement (*b. Rosh Hashanah* 11a),[132] "They were liberated during Nisan; they will be redeemed in Nisan in the future." The language and structure of the amplification

> Now we are here.
> The next year in the land of Israel.

---

132 בניסן נגאלו בניסן עתידין ליגאל.

Now we are here slaves.
The next year in the land of Israel free men!

is Babylonian-talmudic and close to the Hebrew introduction to the Babylonian Cosmic Hymn in the morning services for the Sabbath:[133]

Nothing is comparable to You (*Ps.* 40:6).
There is no one but You (*1 Chr.* 17:20).
There is nothing except You (*Is.* 45:14).
Who may compare with You? (*Ps.* 89:7).

Nothing is comparable to You, o Lord our God, in this world,
There is no one but You, our King, for the life of the World to Come,
There is nothing except You, our Redeemer, for the days of the Messiah,
Who may compare with You, our Savior, at the Resurrection of the Dead!

One may speculate that the original Palestinian declaration contained a praise of the Temple; it needed replacing after the destruction of the Temple when everyone could perform the entire *Seder* ritual "here," without a pilgrimage to Jerusalem. "In the Land of Israel" naturally means with a rebuilt Temple and restored Temple service as well as biblical status for all commandments connected with the Land.

The Four Questions

The last of the introductory sections of the *Haggadah* is the catalog of questions. To induce the children to ask, the *Seder* plate is removed. (In Western Ashkenazic families, the *mazzot* are covered.) Not one of the *Haggadot* printed in Germany during the eighteenth and nineteenth centuries mentions the removal of the plate in the Yiddish or German instructions. Heidenheim's original *Haggadot* mention the

---

133 אין ערוך לך   ואין זולתך   אפס בלתך   ואין דומה לך
אין ערוך לך יי אלהינו בעולם הזה
ואין זולתך מלכנו לחיי העולם הבא
אפס בלתך גואלנו לימות המשיח
ואין דומה לך מושיענו לתחית המתים.

removal of the plate and its return after the questions in the Hebrew but not in the German instructions. The seventeenth- and eighteenth-century prints all mention only the uncovering of the *maẓẓot* after the recitation of the questions. This includes even the manuscript *Haggadah* that the chief rabbi of Pressburg Moses Schreiber, known as חת״ם סופר, had caused to be written in 1777 for his wife, the daughter of the great talmudic authority Akiba Eiger. This goes back to Rashi (*Maḥzor Vitry*, pp. 270–271),[134] who requires only that the plate be moved to the end of the table. This procedure is still prescribed in the basic book describing the *minhaĝ* of Frankfurt/Main, *Yosif Omeẓ* (§752), composed before 1637 and distributed in manuscript copies but not printed until 1723, who notes that "one puts the plate at the end of the table even though it would be better to remove the plate altogether."[135] It follows that one never did remove the plate from the table in the Ashkenazic ritual but one moved the plate to the end of the table until the seventeenth century. For a question-and-answer session, one needs at least two participants, one of whom has to be an adult (*RAVIA Pesaḥim*, p. 163)[136]; later on for *Hallel* after Grace three participants are required, one to recite the *Hallel* and two to respond (*Midrash Tehillim* 113:3).[137]

In Ashkenazic families, the questions are recited by a child, usually the youngest child at the table who can read. This usage is neither universal nor original; in the *Mishnah* (*Pesaḥim* X,4) the list of questions is a guide for the head of the household to point out the differences between this dinner and other dinners if the children do not ask spontaneous questions. It is also clear that the questions were not an integral part of the service during the Second Commonwealth since today each group has its own catalog of questions. The genuinely old parts of the *Haggadah* are common to all groups and differ only in minor points of spelling and punctuation. The Ashkenazic usage is explicit in *RAVIA* (*loc. cit.*) and implicit in the commentaries of Rashi and his grandson to the *Mishnah*.

---

134   יש טועים בסדר פסח ומגביהין הקערה עצמה כשמתחילין לומר הא לחמא. ומסלק הבשׂר מתוך הקערה. וראיתי את ר׳ שאינו נוהג כן. אפס מסלק הקערה כמוה שהיא ומניחה על השלחן בקרן זוית, ואם יש שם אז תינוק ישׁאל מה נשתנה הלילה הזה.

135   אחר גמר כהא לחמא ישׁים הקערה עם כל אשר בה בסוף השלחן, אכן יותר טוב להסירה לגמרי מן השלחן דומיא דעקירת השלחן שהיתה בימיהם.

136   ואם אינו יודע הבן לשאול אשתו שואלת או הוא שואל לעצמו. ולכך נהגו שאין אדם קורא לבדו האגדה וקורא תינוק אליו כדי שישׁאל לו.

137   הללו יה הללו עבדי ה׳ הללו את שם ה׳. מכאן אמרו חכמים אין הלל פחות משלשה בני אדם, למי אומר הללו לשנים.

There exist four different groups of recensions of the catalog of questions in the sources.

1. *Mishnah* in the Jerusalem *Talmud*, ms. Munich II of the Babylonian *Talmud*, quotes from the Babylonian *Talmud* by R. Isaac Alfassi (*RYF*) and R. Asher ben Yeḥiel (*ROSH*):

In what is this night different from all other nights?

All other nights we dip once, this night two times.

All other nights we eat *maẓẓah* or bread, this night only *maẓẓah.*

All other nights we eat meat roasted, pickled, and cooked, this night roasted only.

Another manuscript related to this group is Munich I (complete Babylonian *Talmud*); its order is (a) *maẓẓah*, (b) dipping, (c) roast.

2. *Mishnah* in the printed (Venice) version and the Oxford ms. of *b. Pesaḥim.* In the Venice print the order is:

(a) All other nights we eat *maẓẓah* or bread, this night only *maẓẓah.*

(b) All other nights we eat all kinds of vegetables, this night bitter herbs.

(c) All other nights we eat meat roasted, pickled, and cooked, this night roasted only.

(d) All other nights we dip once, this night two times.

In the Oxford ms. the order is (a) (d) (c) (b). Cf. *Diqduqe Soferim Pesaḥim*, pp. 360–361.

3. *Siddur* of R. Saadia Gaon:

(a) dipping, (b) *maẓẓah*, (c) roast, (d) bitter herbs,

(e) All other nights we eat first sitting up and then reclining but this night we are reclining from the start.

4. The fourth group contains the sources for all current versions. The essential features these versions have in common are (i) four questions in the Babylonian tradition represented by group 2 and (ii) the elimination of the question about roast meat since during the night of the *Seder* one never could eat a lamb roasted on a spit outside the sanctified parts of the city of Jerusalem and today, after the destruction of the Temple, even roasted pieces of meat are not allowed except in communities that have an old, fixed tradition in this respect

(*Mishnah Pesaḥim* IV,4; *y. Mo'ed Qaṭan* III,1 81d).[138] Sephardic and Oriental Jews follow the order of R. Amram Gaon and Maimonides:

(a) dipping, (b) *maẓẓah*, (c) bitter herbs, (d) reclining,

while Ashkenazic Jews follow the order of Rashi given in *Maḥzor Vitry*:

(a) *maẓẓah*, (b) bitter herbs, (c) dipping, (d) reclining.

The arrangement of Maimonides is simply that of R. Saadia Gaon when the question about the roast is deleted; the order of Rashi seems to be derived from a text parallel to the Venice print with the roast deleted and the question about reclining added at the end. As R. N. Rabbinowicz points out in his *Diqduqe Soferim* (*loc. cit.*, note ל),[139] all texts add the question about reclining at the end since it is not mentioned in any talmudic source; logically it should belong first. The best surviving witness to Rashi's *Talmud* text is ms. Munich I, which has only three questions; by Rashi's time in the late eleventh century, prayer texts already had several centuries of separate development.

The question about the roasted meat presents a problem even for the *Seder* service in Jerusalem during the time of the Temple. The Paschal Lamb, which could be eaten only by persons who had earlier subscribed to that particular meal, was only one of two sacrifices eaten that night. The main course really was the festive offering (*ḥăgīgāh*) of the Fourteenth of Nisan. The Paschal Lamb was eaten in small portions after the recital of the *Haggadah*, for the benedictions over the special foods required for this night and, again, in portions the size of an olive, after the meal, just before Grace. The *Mishnah* (*Pesaḥim* VI,6) requires the festival offering only when the Paschal Lamb was not sufficient for both the required consumption and a festive meal but, as a matter of fact, both *Talmudim* (*b. Pesaḥim* 70a; *y. Pesaḥim* VI,5 33c) state that[140] "the festival offering that comes with the Paschal Lamb must be eaten first so that the Paschal Lamb can be eaten on a full stomach" and no hungry person will be tempted to break one of its bones. There is an opinion which the Babylonian *Talmud* (*loc. cit.*) ascribes to Yehuda ben Tema, of the generation of R. Akiba, that[141] "the festival offering that is brought with the Paschal

138 מקום שנהגו לאכול צלי בלילי פסחים אוכלין. מקום שנהגו שלא לאכול צלי בלילי פסחים אין אוכלין.

139 ושאלה דכולנו מסובין לפי שלא נזכרה בגמרא קבעוה לבסוף אף שקדמה לכולן.

140 חגיגה הבאה עם הפסח נאכלת תחילה כדי שיהא פסח נאכל על השׂבע.

141 בן תימא אומר חגיגה הבאה עם הפסח הרי היא כפסח ואינה נאכלת אלא ליום ולילה וחגיגת חמשה עשׂר נאכלת לשני ימים ולילה אחד. . . . מאי טעמא דבן תימא, כדמתני רב לחייא

Lamb follows the rules of the Paschal Lamb and may only be eaten during the afternoon of the Fourteenth of Nisan and the following night, but the festival offering of the Fifteenth of Nisan may be eaten two days and one night [like every other festival offering]. What is the reason of Ben Tema? It is what Rav taught his son Ḥiyya: (*Ex.* 34:25): "You may not bring the blood of My sacrifice while you still have leavened matter; neither the festival offering nor the Paschal Lamb shall stay overnight till the morning.'" A Babylonian talmudic authority then declares (*loc. cit.*)[142] that the language of the question "this night roast only" is according to Ben Tema. Those authorities who hold that the festival offering is an absolute requirement of the *Seder* service in Jerusalem explain the verse (*Deut.* 16:2) "You shall sacrifice at *Pesaḥ* [i.e., the Fourteenth of Nisan] from the flock and cattle" to include the cattle for the festival offering and sheep or goats for the Paschal Lamb (*b. Pesaḥim* 70b); the majority holds that the festival offering is voluntary and conditional; the verse is interpreted to mean that the Paschal Lamb must be from sheep or goats but those animals that were bought for *Pesaḥ* but not needed for lack of subscribers may be sacrificed as festival offerings under the rules valid for cattle, to be consumed during two days and one night.[143] The Jerusalem *Talmud* (*y. Pesaḥim* VI,5 33c)[144] declares that as a generally agreed rule, the festival offering of the *Seder* night cannot be eaten anymore the next day, but the reason is not the biblical verse but a practical consideration: since meat or sauce of the *pesaḥ* might have been mixed up with the *ḥagīgah* and other foods present on the table, all leftovers have to be burned together. The Jerusalem *Talmud* does not treat the question of roasted or boiled festival sacrifice. The *Mishnah* (*Pesahim* X,3)[145] requires that the central piece of the *Seder* plate for the celebration at the Temple in Jerusalem should be the Paschal Lamb, instead of the three *maẓẓot* used today. This implies that the festival offering was brought in only during the actual meal and was not visible during the recitation; therefore, it could not be the object of a dissertation before the meal. In any case, there are many good reasons why the question about roasted meat should be dropped.

בריה לא ילין לבוקר זבח חג הפסח. זבח חג זה חגיגה, הפסח כמשמעו.

142 תא שמע הלילה הזה כולו צלי ואומר רב חסדא זו דברי בן תימא.

143 דכתיב וזבחת פסח ליי אלהיך צאן ובקר, והלא אין פסח אלא מן הכשבים ומן העזים, אלא מותר הפסח יהיה לדבר הבא מן הצאן ומן הבקר.

144 תני חגיגה הבאה עם הפסח היתה מתבערת עמו. איתא חמי חגיגה נאכלת לשני ימים ופסח נאכל עד חצות ותימר הכין. בעולה עמו על שלחנו, התבשילין העולין עמו על השלחן צריכין להתבער עמו.

145 ובמקדש היו מביאים לפניו גופו של פסח.

The expression "all other nights we dip once" was changed to "all other nights we do not need to dip even once" by Rava in the first half of the fourth century (*b. Pesaḥim* 116a). This shows that after a century of Sassanid rule, the Greco-Roman symposium dinner was no longer known among Babylonian Jews. This is in contrast to the first generation of Babylonian talmudists, whose leaders Samuel and Rav had studied in Galilean academies in the early third century and who lived under the hellenized Parthians. Since the *ḥaroset* remains on the plate, whether it was used for the first dipping or not, it is clear that it will be used for another dipping.

Most versions of the *Mishnah* have no question for the bitter herbs. It is clear from the language of the *Mishnah* (*Pesaḥim* X,3),[146] "after the table is brought before him, he dips, possibly using bitter lettuce," that in the absence of other vegetables one may use bitter herbs (in *ḥaroset*) for *karpas*, the first vegetable. It was mentioned before (p. 229) that the first dipping is convenient for the later consumption of the bitter herbs as a *mizwah*, a religious commandment. In the interpretation of the Jerusalem *Talmud* and, hence, probably in the opinion of the editor of the *Mishnah*, the question on dipping is identical to the question of the bitter herbs. S. Zeitlin (*JQR* 38) conjectured that the addition of the question on the bitter herbs in Babylonia as against the Galilean version of three questions can be explained as an allusion to the bitterness of the exile. This is more a homiletic embellishment than a serious conjecture since the manuscript evidence shows that the Babylonian *Mishnah* also has only three questions. It seems more likely that the text of the *Haggadah* evolved from three to four questions in Babylonia (the late Palestinian *Haggadah* text reproduced by Goldschmidt as the oldest surviving *Haggadah* manuscript text still has only the three questions of the *Mishnah*) and that then the *Haggadah* text, as the familiar one, crept into some Babylonian *Mishnah* manuscripts. Probably the Four Questions became a counterpart to the Four Cups. Dr. M. Petruck conjectures that the Four Questions won out over the original three, even in Ashkenazic texts otherwise dependent on Palestinian models, in part to exclude any allusion to the Christian "Three" in a ritual of redemption.

The question about lying on couches (really "being assembled

---

146 הביאו לפניו מטבל בחזרת.

in a circle") is not mentioned in any of our talmudic sources. It is found for the first time, in the sources known to us, in the ninth-century *siddur* of R. Saadia Gaon. The question, "All other nights [at formal dinners] we eat first sitting up on chairs [for the appetizer] and then assembled on couches [for the main meal]; this night we start out assembled on couches," refers to the description of a dinner given in a Tannaitic source (cf. p. 228) quoted in both *Talmudim* (*b. Berakhot* 43a; *y. Berakhot* VI,6 10d). It may be that the avoidance of chairs from the start is more than a technical necessity for the *Qiddush*. In Plutarch, *Life of Cato major*, Cato eats his dinner *sitting up* as a sign of mourning. Any sign of mourning would be banned from the *Seder* celebration.

A closer look at the text shows that there is really only one rhetorical question, "In what is this night different from all other nights?" The three or four details are only the points made by the father to his son explaining the outward differences. There remains the explanation of the differences; for the original three points the explanation is given at the end of the recital in the section "Rabban Gamliel," making the entire recital a coherent literary unit bracketed by question and answer.

If any of the participants do not understand Hebrew, the entire *Haggadah* should be translated for them or, today, they may read along in translation. The Four Questions and the main answers *must* be translated for them (R. Natronai Gaon, *Oẓar Hageonim Pesaḥim*, p. 123;[147] Rashi *Maḥzor Vitry*, p. 295). In the Yemenite ritual, a boy therefore recites here a short version of the *Haggadah* in Judeo-Arabic for the benefit of those who do not understand Hebrew. In Djerba, the entire *Haggadah* is translated paragraph by paragraph into Judeo-Arabic by the head of the household. In many Sephardic communities, the *Haggadah* is translated paragraph by paragraph into Judeo-Spanish (Ladino) and a complete German (or, today, English, Spanish, etc.) translation is the standard in many Western Ashkenazic families.

The Ashkenazic and Sephardic form מְסֻבִּין is a passive participle, we are "lying on couches" dinner guests. The Yemenite vocalization מֵסֵבִּין is an active (*pa'il*) participle, "we are going to lie on

---

147 אוֹמר מה נשתנה וּמתרגם לאינשי ביתיה.

couches." Y. Kutscher (*Isaiah Scroll*, p. 41) takes the first form to be an Aramaism and equivalent to the second. The meaning "to lie on couches" is also otherwise attested from the later Second Temple period[148] but the biblical meaning would be "to form a circle, to assemble in a circle." The couches in the classical dining hall were assembled in almost circular form.

נשתנה is the mishnaic equivalent of biblical משתנה, the present participle of the t-passive. Similarly, the plural endings ין- are the mishnaic (Palestinian) Hebrew equivalents of classical ים-, not Aramaic. The relationship between biblical and rabbinic Hebrew will be discussed further in the commentary on the final benediction of the recital.

Disgrace and Praise

The main part of the *Haggadah* is a discussion of the Exodus leading up to an answer to the Four Questions. The structure of the main part is indicated by the *Mishnah* (*Pesaḥim* X,4):[149] "One starts with *gĕnūt* and ends with *shĕvāḥ*." The last expression, *shĕvāḥ*, means "praise." The first expression, *gĕnūt*, usually means "disgrace" in a moral sense. In a different context, the *Talmud* (*b. Soṭah* 32b) notes that *gĕnūt* refers to *Deut.* 26:5, part of the required reading of the *Haggadah*. The core of the *Haggadah* is the recitation and discussion of the description of the Exodus in the "reading for First Fruits," *Deut.* 26:5–9. In the first interpretation of the *Talmud*[150] "one has to declare one's disgrace in a loud voice," since in the reading of the First Fruits it is said: "Proclaim loudly and say: My father [Laban, the father of our mothers Rachel and Leah] is a lost Aramean [a sinner, a lost soul in the World to Come]" and it is a disgrace to have to admit to such an ancestor. However, the majority opinion in the *Talmud* rejects the principle that

---

148 Hebrew Sirach 41:19:

עם בעולה אל טת אציל, ואל תסב עמה למסך שכר

With a married woman do not lie on the elbow, and do not lie on a couch with her mixing drinks.

149 מתחיל בגנות ומסיים בשבח.

150 רבי שמעון בן יוחי אומר אדם אומר שבחו בקול נמוך וגנותו בקול רם . . . גנותו בקול רם ממקרא ביכורים.

one should make a public declaration of a private disgrace and opts for the interpretation[151] that "one should declare one's pain in public so that the public will remember him in their prayers." Here the *Talmud* accepts the interpretation of the *Haggadah* of *Deut.* 26:5: "The Aramean [Laban] destroyed my father [Jacob] who was forced to go into exile in Egypt," but replaces *gĕnūt*, "disgrace," with *ẓa'ar*, "pain." It seems from here that the original *disgrace* was *Deut.* 26:5, that my father was forced to go into exile, and the *praise* was *Deut.* 26:9, that the Lord gave us a land flowing with milk and honey. However, long before talmudic times the terms were applied to the introduction and epilogue of the core of the *Haggadah*, the *midrash* on *Deut.* 26:5–9. In this interpretation, *praise* is the song of praise, the *Hallel* and its introduction, recited after the *Haggadah* proper (this is not identified explicitly in the sources). The Jerusalem *Talmud* (*y. Pesaḥim* X,5 37d)[152] quotes Rav to the effect that *disgrace* is the statement: "Originally, our forefathers were idolators." In the Babylonian *Talmud* (*b. Pesaḥim* 116a), that opinion is contrasted with another, that *disgrace* means "We were slaves to Pharaoh in Egypt." The sources differ widely about the names of the authorities who represent these opinions. We find as authors

Sources	**Idolators**	**Slaves**
Talmud (printed editions of Venice and Basel), Manuscript Munich II, R. Isaiah of Trani	Rav	Rava
Alfassi (and modern *Talmud* editions emended after Alfassi), *Sefer Ha'iṭṭur*	Rav	Samuel
Talmud (Oxford manuscript), Abudirham	Abbai	Rava
Talmud (Munich I, complete *Talmud* manuscript)	anonymous	Rav
Rabbenu Ḥananel	Rava	Rav Yosef

Of these authors, Rav and Samuel lived in the first half of the third century C.E. and are usually quoted as opponents in talmudic

---

151 לא תימא גנותו אלא צערו . . . צריך להודיע צערו לרבים ורבים מבקשים עליו רחמים.

152 רב אמר מתחלה.

discussions. Abbai and Rava similarly form a pair of opponents in the first half of the fourth century; one of their teachers was R. Yosef (bar Ḥiyya). (E. D. Goldschmidt identifies R. Yosef here with a sixth-century scholar, one of the final editors of the *Talmud*, the Savoraë. However, he would not appear in a dispute with older authorities and his name seems to have been Rabba Yosef or Yossi Rabba; cf. R. Sherira Gaon's *Letter*, ed. Neubauer, p. 34.) From the testimony of the *Talmud* of Jerusalem it is clear that Rav identifies *disgrace* with *idolators*. Since one may discard the readings "Samuel" and "Abbai" as being induced by the usual pairing, the majority of sources indicates that the second author is Rava. This is confirmed by the text of R. Isaiah of Trani (Italy, twelfth century), whose readings often are the result of a critical discussion. The reading is also accepted by R. Shelomo Luria (sixteenth century), the first author of a text-critical study of the *Talmud*. While the combination Rav–Rava is not frequent, it is not at all unusual in matters regarding Galilean *versus* Babylonian traditions, as we saw in the discussion of *Havdalah* (chapter on *Qiddush*, p. 222). There we saw that Rava sometimes represents old Babylonian traditions independent of the Galilean traditions of Rav. The interpretation that comes to mind first, one that is adopted by many modern authors, is that our current *Haggadah* is a conglomerate with the introduction composed by Rava prefacing the original text composed or authenticated by Rav in a kind of double start. Such agglomerated texts do exist in the Jewish liturgy but mostly in short pieces (attributed to R. *Papa* in the Babylonian *Talmud* [*b. Megillah* 21b], often based on older traditions [*b. Soṭah* 40a = *y. Berakhot* I,8 3d]). The hypothesis of a double composition can be shown to be false in the case of the *Haggadah*, by internal and external evidence. In all other cases of agglomerated texts it is stated explicitly in the *Talmud* (*loc. cit.*) that in deference to different authors one uses a composite text. No such statement is made about the *Haggadah*. Also, since the opinions belong to authorities who lived a century apart, it seems that Rav and Rava are neither authors nor proponents of a text, but they simply identify the expression of the *Mishnah* with existing passages in the *Haggadah*.

It is known from many sources that after the war of Bar Kokhba, Jewish settlements in the Land of Israel were restricted mainly to Galilee and the Golan heights (except for a small settlement centered at Daroma near Gaza). The Galilean population consisted of small groups of scholars, heirs to the traditions of the Judean academies, on one hand and a great majority of uneducated, but obstinately Jewish, mostly rural population, the Galilean *'Am Ha'areẓ* on the other (cf. *W. Bacher, Der galiläische Am Haaretz*). In order to accommodate the uneducated part of the population, the heads of the Galilean academies instituted or tolerated a number of deviations from traditional practices that were never accepted in the centers of the Diaspora of Babylonia and Europe. For example, the speakers of Galilean Aramaic were frequently so ignorant of Hebrew that a congregation could not find readers for the standard weekly readings of the Torah. This forced a reduction of the length of the weekly portions so that the reading of the entire Pentateuch was completed in a three-year cycle (*b. Megillah* 29b)[153] in contrast to the one-year cycle attested to by all other sources. Also, to accommodate those who were unable to read a Hebrew text in a domestic ceremony, it became the rule in Galilee to recite the "Egyptian *Hallel*," *Ps.* 113–118, in the synagogue service for the *Seder* Night (*y. Pesaḥim* X,1 37c)[154] so that the people could complete their religious obligations that night by simply drinking four cups. There does exist a post-talmudic Palestinian text from the *Genizah* (reproduced in Goldschmidt's *Haggadah*, chap. 2) without the section "we were slaves." If we can show that the section "we were slaves" was part of the original service, the best interpretation of the talmudic text is that the Babylonian *Haggadah* was essentially identical with our contemporary version and the one in use during the time of the Temple, but in Galilee the more literate followed a shortened version that began the discussion with "Originally, our forefathers were idolators," while the illiterate said *Hallel* in the synagogue and at home only recited the benedictions over the Four Cups. Rava therefore requires the Babylonian population to follow the old tradition and does not let them adopt the shortened version. This interpretation can be confirmed by a responsum of R. Natronai Gaon (*Seder R. Amram Gaon*, pp. 37–38), who not only forbids the recitation in Babylonia of the *Qiddush* in the impersonal Galilean form but also requires as absolutely necessary the recitation of the *Haggadah* starting with "We were slaves." The oldest known Babylonian *Haggadah* fragments confirm R. Natronai's ruling. Several medieval authorities (Maimonides, *Commentary to the Mishnah, ad loc.*; *Sefer Miẓwot Gadol*, vol. 2, §41) decided that the minimal obligation is the one spelled out by Rav.

---

153 בני מערבא דמסקי לאורייתא בתלת שנין.

154 מהו לשתותן בכרך אחד. מן מה דאמר רבי יוחנן הלל עם שמען בבית הכנסת יצא. הדא אמרה אפילו שתיין בכרך אחד יצא.

It remains to show that the section "We were slaves" was part of the original *Haggadah.* One source is the Greek Bible translation known as the Septuagint. S. Zeitlin (*loc. cit.*) writes that "the wording of this reply as we have it in the *Haggadah* today is of a later period than the Second Commonwealth, because the name for God, *The Holy One, blessed be He*, was not yet used at the time of the Second Temple." This is a weak argument *e silentio*; the expression *The Holy One, blessed be He* appears in many later *midrashim* whose content is already quoted by Josephus. Zeitlin's arguments are directed against the opinions of L. Finkelstein (*HTR* 36, 1943), whose basically sound observations are marred by historical phantasies. The extant Septuagint texts are edited from Christian manuscripts since, soon after the destruction of the Temple, Jewish congregations rejected the original Greek translation, reputedly done at Alexandria in the third century B.C.E. by either 72 (*b. Megillah* 9a; *Masekhet Soferim* I,8; *Letter of Aristeas*),[155] 70 (*Masekhet Sefer Torah* I,8),[156] or 5 (*Masekhet Soferim* I,7) scholars, in favor of more exact translations by Theodotion (Jonathan), Aquila (Onqelos), and Symmachus (Sumkhus), because the original Septuagint was used by early Christian proselytizers in support of their new faith. It is not clear whether the Septuagint text of the Pentateuch in current use is a uniform text. The most reasonable interpretation of the sources for the story of the Septuagint is that a first translation was made by five translators, maybe one for each book of the Pentateuch, and that this unsatisfactory translation was revised by 72 scholars on the initiative of one of the Ptolemean kings of Egypt. The first translation is characterized as unsatisfactory both in Hebrew (*Masekhet Soferim* I,7) and Greek (*Aristeas to Philocrates* 30) sources. On the basis of Aristeas, one should translate the source of *Masekhet Soferim*[157] by "five elders translated the Torah into Greek for king Ptolemy; that day was as bad for Israel as the day the Golden Calf was made since they were not able to translate the Torah satisfactorily." The Alexandrian Greek Aristeas writes that the librarian of Alexandria notified the king that a translation of the books of the Torah was missing in his

---

155 מעשׂה בתלמי המלך שכינס שבעים ושנים זקנים בשבעים ושנים בתים ולא גילה להם על מה כינסם ונכנס אצל כל אחד ואחד ואמר להם כתבו לי תורת משה רבכם.

156 שבעים זקנים כתבו התורה לתלמי המלך יונית והיה אותו היום קשה לישׂראל כיום שעשׂו את העגל שלא היתה תורה יכולה להתרגם כל צרכה.

157 מעשׂה בה' זקנים שכתבו לתלמי המלך את התורה יונית והיה היום קשה לישׂראל כיום שנעשׂה העגל שלא היתה התורה יכולה להתרגם כל צרכה.

library since[158] "it happens that they are written in Hebrew characters and language, and they have been translated somewhat carelessly and not adequately, according to the testimony of experts." According to Aristeas, a ban was pronounced on anybody who would tamper with the improved Greek text of the Septuagint. It is not likely that Christian editors would have changed the Septuagint text at places not relevant for Christian doctrine. (The later canonical Greek Jewish translation of the Torah "was said by Aquila the proselyte following instructions of R. Eliezer [ben Hyrkanos] and R. Yehoshua [ben Ḥanania]" [*b. Megillah* 3a; *y. Megillah* I,11 71c].[159]) Of importance for us is the text of the Septuagint for *Deut.* 6:20–21:

καὶ ἔσται ὅταν ἐρωτήσῃ σε	כי ישאלך
ὁ υἱός σου αὔριον λέγων	בנך מחר לאמר
Τί ἔστιν τὰ μαρτύρια	מה העדות
καὶ τὰ δικαιώματα καὶ τὰ	והחקים והמשפטים
κρίματα	אשר צוה יי אלהינו
ὅσα ἐνετείλατο κύριος ὁ θεὸς	אתכם.
ἡμῶν	
ἡμῖν.	
καὶ ἐρεῖς τῷ υἱῷ σου	ואמרת לבנך
Οικέται ἦμεν τῷ Φαραω	עבדים היינו לפרעה
ἐν γῇ Αἰγύπτῳ	במצרים
καὶ ἐξήγαγεν ἡμᾶς κύριος	ויוציאנו יי ממצרים
ἐκεῖθεν ἐν χειρὶ κραταιᾷ	ביד חזקה.
καὶ ἐν βραχίονι ὑψηλῷ.	

Translation

And it will be when your son will ask you	When your son will ask you
tomorrow, saying:	tomorrow, saying:
What are the testimonials,	What are the testimonials,
the laws, and the judgments	the laws, and the judgments
that the Lord, our God, has commanded	that the Lord, our God, has commanded
us.	you.

158 τυγχάνει γὰρ Ἑβραϊκοῖς γράμμασι καὶ φωνῇ λεγόμενα, ἀμελέστερον δέ, καὶ οὐχ ὡς ὑπάρχει, σεσήμανται, καθὼς ὑπὸ τῶν εἰδότων προσαυαφέρεται.

159 תרגום של תורה אונקלוס אמרו מפי ר' אליעזר ור' יהושע.

And you shall say to your son: We were slaves to Pharaoh in *the land of* Egypt and the Lord led us out *from there* with a strong hand *and an outstretched arm.*	And you shall say to your son: We were slaves to Pharaoh in Egypt and the Lord took us out from Egypt with a strong hand.

Verse 6:20 refers to the question of the intelligent son later in the *Haggadah* and will be discussed in its proper place. The answer in verse 21 clearly is not a translation of the biblical verse but of the first sentence of the discussion in our *Haggadah* text. This can only mean that the section beginning with "We were slaves" was an integral part of the ritual by the time the current text of the Septuagint received its final Jewish form and the Jewish reader expected to hear the allusion to the *Haggadah* in the paraphrase of the biblical text, which is the basis of our paragraph. Similarly, the Septuagint to *I Sam.* 16:11, although not claimed to be part of the original Alexandrian translation, renders the root נסב as "to recline on couches" as required by the interpretation of this root in the *Haggadah*, but the later Aramaic *Targum Yonathan* has the more appropriate "to assemble [in a circle]." All this points to a formulation of the *Haggadah* early in pre-Maccabean times.

It is a characteristic feature of rabbinic literature that practically no extensive quote from Scripture in the *Talmud* and related works is correct. (This remark does not apply to current printed editions of the Babylonian *Talmud* where the "misquotes" of the manuscripts and early prints, which in reality are paraphrases expressing the desired exegesis or homiletic interpretation by small changes in the text, have been "corrected" by pedantic editors. This happened also in the *Haggadah;* see the section on the Four Sons.) The text of "We were slaves" probably escaped modern editors because they were under the impression that the quote ended with "in Egypt," while the Greek text shows that the entire sentence is a quote-paraphrase of the biblical verse. It is taken as that in the twelfth-century text *Shibbolé Haleqet* (*Seder Pesaḥ* §218, p. 187).[160] In talmudic and older rabbinic texts, the deviations from the Masoretic tradition are systematic and form part of the interpretation, the

160 עבדים היינו לפרעה במצרים. היא תשובת מה נשתנה כמו שפירשנו. והיא תשובת הבן החכם בפרשת ואתחנן.

dĕrash, alluded to be a change of the wording of the verse. In our case, the deviations must be explained by the text of the *Haggadah* itself. Such explanations can only be conjectural. It may be that the substitution of *there* for *Egypt* places the redemption in an indeterminate place, everywhere where the Jewish people is enslaved, in the tenor of the paragraphs discussing the Covenant between the Pieces (p. 282). The main *midrash* in the *Haggadah* cites scriptural verses in support of the interpretation (p. 300) of the *hand* as symbol of wonders performed through human intermediaries, in particular Moses and his staff, whereas the *arm* represents the invisible presence of God's angel wielding the sword of pestilence and performing miracles without human intervention. This fits well with the tendency of the anonymous authors of the *Haggadah* to downplay the human side of the delivery from Egypt and to ascribe it only to direct divine intervention. The addition of the *outstretched arm* in the Greek translation therefore tends to confirm the exclusion of Moses' name from the *Haggadah* as a very old tradition.

Independent of the Greek translation, literary analysis also shows the unity of the Recitation in the *Haggadah* and therefore the inclusion of our paragraph in the original text. The second sentence, that without the deliverance from Egypt we all would still be subservient to Pharaoh in Egypt, is the direct foundation for the requirement, given at the end of the Recital, that everyone has to consider himself as personally having been redeemed from Egypt. This is made clear by R. Saadia Gaon's text of the *Haggadah* discussed below and is already recognized by the fifteenth-century commentator Shimon ben Ẓemaḥ Duran.

We conclude that the paragraph "We were slaves" was part of the *Haggadah* as recited during the Second Commonwealth and probably was part of the original text of the Men of the Great Assembly.

The Ashkenazic and Sephardic texts of the paragraph are that of R. Amram Gaon except for the Ashkenazic substitution of inferential *then* for neutral *still* and Sephardic deletion of "all elders" already noted by Abudirham.[161] The Yemenite text, which differs in two words from the European one, *liberated* for *led out* and *tells at*

---

161 ובסדר רב עמרם גורס כלנו זקנים שכבר שמענו והגדנו זה כמה שנים.

length for *tells much,* is a composition of two versions, that of R. Saadia Gaon for the introductory sentence and of Maimonides for the final one. The text of R. Saadia Gaon is a composite of the first and the last section of the Recital:

עבדים היינו לפרעה במצרים ויוציאני יי אֱהינו משם ביד חזקה ובזרוע נטויה. ואלו לא
גאל המקֹבֹה את אבֹותינו ממצרים כבר אנו ובנינו ובני בנינו משועבדים היינו לפרעה
במצרים. ולא את אבֹותינו בלבד גאל המקֹבֹה אלא אף אֹותנו גאל שנֹא ואוֹתנו הוֹציא
משם.

We were slaves to Pharaoh in Egypt but the Lord, our God, led us out from there with a strong hand and outstretched arm. If the Omnipresent Holy, praise to Him, had not liberated our fathers from Egypt, then already we, our children, and our children's children would be subservient to Pharaoh in Egypt. Not only our fathers did the Omnipresent Holy, praise to Him, liberate, but He liberated us with them as it is said (*Deut.* 6:23), "He took us out from there. . . ."

The expression "The Omnipresent" for God is discussed in the section on the Covenant between the Pieces. The choice of the expression "liberated" probably comes from its use in the final paragraph (text, p. 58) to emphasize the literary unity of the *Haggadah,* as noted above.

The text of Maimonides is identical to that of R. Amram Gaon except for the substitution of "tells at length" for "tells much." The meaning of the last sentence, as explained by Abudirham, is that everybody must recite the story of the Exodus as an explicit biblical commandment so that only he who adds his own words is praiseworthy since he did more than the minimum. The old Ashkenazic text of the *Mahzor Vitry* reads,[162] "He who tells about the Exodus from Egypt is praiseworthy," probably meaning that he who tells in his own words in addition to the required reading is praiseworthy. Since the text is ambiguous, it is not often found in later sources.

The vocalization *měshubbah* in the Livorno Sephardic text seems to be an Italian idiosyncrasy, already found in early Bologna and Venice prints. All Oriental *Haggadah* texts have classical Hebrew *měshubbāh* like all other rituals.

---

162 כל המספר ביציאת מצרים הרי זה משובח.

The Sages

The story of the Sages and the *Mishnah* of R. Eleazar ben Azariah are not from the time of the Temple but from the period between the two wars against the Romans (70–135 B.C.E.). We do not know whether there was a piece connecting the introduction to the story of the Four Children in earlier times. Since the discussion of the Sages contains an element of polemic against Christian ideas, one may assume that originally the introduction was followed immediately by the story of the Four Sons, as in R. Saadia Gaon's text. That text is formulated directly on verses relating to the Intelligent Child.

The overwhelming evidence of manuscripts and prints (excepting the Ashkenazic prints starting with Heidenheim and the *Mahẓor Roma* printed under the direction of a Church censor) is that the title of the teachers is *Ribbī*, not *Rabbī*, probably pronounced *Rĕbbī*. It is true that Greek inscriptions in Bet Shearim and Cyprus have the title spelled PABI or PABBI; the actual pronunciation here also might have been *Revi, Revvi*. In Jewish Latin inscriptions from late antiquity, the title appears as *Rebbi* or *Repi*. As Y. Kutscher points out (*Isaiah Scroll*, p. 382), short Hebrew *i* in a closed syllable is always transcribed in the Septuagint by Greek ε. The underlying sound probably is that of modern Turkish ı close to short *e* in English. This pronunciation is also found, for example, in a poem of R. Samuel Hanagid (eleventh-century Spain, *Divan*, #7) addressed to Rav Nissim, where for reasons of meter it is clear that the vocalization is רְבִי, *Rĕvī*. It is also noteworthy that in the old Babylonian supralinear vocalization the name Ephraim appears as אפר״ים Iphraim (corresponding to אֶפְרַיִם in current Tiberian vocalization), not necessarily with a different pronunciation of the vowel. Therefore, it is best to transcribe the title by *Rebbi*. It may be that *Rabbi* comes from analogy with the Babylonian title *Rab, Rav*, but in European languages it is borrowed from the Greek of the New Testament (*Matth.* 23:7–8), where the title *Rabbi* is clearly an anachronism since no teacher of the Law before the destruction of the Temple had any title except for the last presidents of the Synhedrion, called *Rabban*. The presidents of the Synhedrion were the heads of the unofficial Jewish autonomous administration under Roman rule; their title may have been introduced as an act of defiance. The Jewish pronunciation of the title is also shown by the name of Rabbanite Jews in Cairo *Genizah* documents, אלריבונין *al-ribunīn*, showing clearly the *y*-sound.

The Yemenite vocalization of the plural, *ribbötēnu*, is found in very few European manuscript *Haggadot*. The European form *rabbōtēnu* is an address form that does not necessarily imply a title. (Cf. *Letter of R. Sherira Gaon; 'Arukh, s.v. Abbai*).[163]

The story of the four or five Sages has no source or parallel in rabbinic literature, except for a note that the contemporary Rabban Gamliel celebrated the *Seder* for an entire night at Lod (*Tosefta Pisḥa* X,12).[164] If the story is historical, it cannot be dated before the election of the young R. Eleazar ben Azariah to vice president of the Synhedrion since in the enumeration of the participants R. Eleazar ben Azariah is placed in the middle, at the place of honor at the dinner table. The Yemenite version has no mention of Rebbi Akiba, the student of R. Eliezer and R. Yehoshua and student and colleague of R. Tarfon and the only participant who was neither a Cohen nor a Levite and had not actually served in the Temple. The Yemenite version, therefore, is a "remembrance of the Temple." In the other versions, R. Akiba is mentioned because Bene Berak was his home town (*b. Sanhedrin* 32b) and he appears later in a discussion with R. Eliezer and R. Yossi the Galilean. *Bĕne Beraq* is mentioned (*Jos.* 19:44) as one of the cities allotted to the tribe of Dan; its name was preserved in the name of the Arab village Ibn Ibraq, today absorbed by modern Bene Berak. R. Akiba was said to have been 120 years old when he was executed by the Romans in 138 C.E. and to have been the leader of the Synhedrion during approximately the last forty years of his life (*Sifry Deut.* §357 #7).[165] He could not have reached a leadership position as long as his teachers R. Eliezer and R. Yehoshua were active. If the story is historical, it must be dated in the last twenty years of the first century C.E. when, after the death of Rabban Yoḥanan ben Zakkai, the rich aristocratic priest Rebbi Eliezer ben Hyrkanos and the poor levitic nail-smith Rebbi Yehoshua ben Ḥanania jointly were leading the Synhedrion and its fight for a clear separation between Christians

---

163 ודאי כמו ששמעת כי רבי מחכמי ארץ ישׂראל הסמוּכין שם בסנהדרין שלהם דאמרינן לענין סמיכת זקנים דסמכין ליה וקרו ליה רבי ויהבין ליה רשוּתא למידן דיני קנסות. ורב מחכמי בבל הסמוּכין בישיבות שלהן. והדורות הראשונים שהיו גדולים מאד לא היו צריכים לרברבם לא ברבן ולא ברבי ולא ברב לא לחכמי בבל ולא לחכמי ארץ ישׂראל שהרי הלל עלה מבבל ואין מרברבין אותן עם הזכרת שמותיהן ולא שמענו כי התחילה זו אלא בנשׂיאות מרבן גמליאל הזקן ורבן שמעון בנו הנהרג בחרבן הבית ורבן יוחנן בן זכאי כולן נשׂיאים ואף רבי התחיל סמוּכין מאותה שעה.

164 מעשׂה ברבן גמליאל וזקנים שהיו מסוּבין בבית ביתוס בן זונין בלוד והיו עוסקין בהלכות הפסח כל הלילה עד קרות הגבר הגביהו מלפניהן ונוערו והלכו להן לבית המדרש.

165 רבי עקיבה למד תורה בן ארבעים שנה ושמש את החכמים ארבעים שנה ופירנס את ישׂראל ארבעים שנה.

and Jews. Their celebration must have taken place before the decision, taken to preserve uniformity of practice among different Jewish groups, to enforce the rulings of the majority of the Synhedrion against dissenting, well-founded opinions that led to the excommunication of Rebbi Eliezer, the foremost student of Rabban Yoḥanan ben Zakkai, who would never agree to an opinion or pronounce a statement that he had not heard from his teachers (*b. Bava Meẓi'a* 59b, *Yoma* 66b; *y. Mo'ed Qaṭan* III,1 81c).[166]

The introductory paragraph "We were slaves" makes no specific reference to the Passover celebrations; Passover is not mentioned in *Deut.* 6:20–23. During the *Seder* night, there is a special obligation to explain the Exodus and its implications to one's children. Because of the special duty, one has to go to great lengths to keep the children awake and interested. The *Haggadah* will explain later that these special requirements hold only during the time it is lawful to eat the *Pesaḥ* sacrifice together with *maẓẓah* and bitter herbs. As R. J. Ettlinger points out (*Haggadah Minḥat 'Ani*, p. 27), both Rebbi Eliezer (*y. Berakhot* I,3 3a) and Rebbi Eleazar ben Azariah (*b. Berakhot* 9a; *b. Pesaḥim* 120b) are of the opinion[167] that "one is forbidden to eat the *Pesaḥ* sacrifice after midnight since it is said (*Ex.* 12:8), 'They shall eat the meat during that night,' and also (*Ex.* 12:12), 'I shall cross the land of Egypt during that night.' Since the second expression by its context is defined as 'not after midnight,' the first one also has to mean 'not after midnight.'" One may not perform religious duties outside the appointed times since it is said (*Deut.* 13:1), "You should carefully execute all that I commanded you; do not add to them nor reduce

---

166 ביקשו לנדות את ר' ליעזר אמר אמרין מאן אזל מודע ליה. א״ר עקיבה אנא אזל מודע ליה. אתא לגביה אמר ליה רבי חביריך מנדין לך. נסתיה נפק ליה לברא אמר חרוביתא חרוביתא אין הלכה כדבריהם איתעקרין ולא איתעקרת. אין הלכה כדבריי איתעקרין ואיתעקרת. אין הלכה כדבריהם חוזרין ולא חזרת. אין הלכה כדבריי חוזרין וחזרת. כל הדין שבחא ולית הלכה כר' אליעזר. אמר רבי חנינה משניתנה לא ניתנה אלא אחרי רבים להטות.

They voted to excommunicate Rebbi Eliezer and asked, who will go tell him? R. Akiba said, I will go and tell him. He went to him and said: My teacher, your colleagues excommunicate you. He [R. Eliezer] went to try him [R. Akiba], took him outside and said: "Carob tree, Carob tree, if their decision is correct, be uprooted," it was not uprooted. "If my decision is correct, be uprooted," it was uprooted. "If their decision is correct, go back," it did not go back. "If my decision is correct, go back," it did go back. In spite of all these wonders, the law does not follow R. Eliezer. Rebbi Ḥanina said: When the Torah was given, it was given (*Ex.* 23:2) "to follow [or, to turn aside with] the majority."

167 דתניא ואכלו את הבשׂר בלילה הזה רבי אלעזר בן עזריה אומר נאמר כאן בלילה הזה ונאמר להלן ועברתי בארץ מצרים בלילה הזה מה להלן עד חצות אף כאן עד חצות.

them." Hence, it seems, neither R. Eliezer nor R. Eleazar ben Azariah could have participated in a *Seder* whose ceremonial explications continued during the entire night. The discussions of the Sages during the second half of the night therefore were not in fulfillment of the duties of the *Seder* but of the duties of every day and night of the year. Since the story is an illustration of the maxim expressed in the preceding paragraph that "he who tells much about the Exodus is praiseworthy," that maxim also cannot refer specifically to the *Seder* night. Both sages were able to participate in the entire discussion because they both subscribe to the opinion of Ben Zoma, given in the next paragraph, that there is an obligation from the Torah to remember the Exodus every single night of the year. The students interrupted them at the first signs of dawn, when one may see the difference between white and purple-blue or, according to R. Eliezer, between purple-blue and dark green (*Mishnah Berakhot* I,2).[168] All known manuscripts of the Tannaitic *Mekhilta deR. Ishmael* (*Bo*, p. 74)[169] have a statement of R. Eliezer, who interprets the verse used as question of the "wise son," *Deut.* 6:20, to imply a duty of every scholar to deal with the legal rules of Passover *until midnight*. If our story is historical, R. Eliezer will have continued talking strictly about nonlegal matters.

The Yemenite version of the last clause, קְרִיַת שְׁמַע, is the Galilean Hebrew of *Yerushalmi* sources; the European (Ashkenazic-Sephardic) קְרִיאַת שְׁמַע is normative (biblical and Babylonian) Hebrew.

The statement of Rebbi Eleazar ben Azariah is a *mishnah* (*Berakhot* I,5) and does not deal with the *Seder* at all but with the evening service for every night of the year. The Yemenite text follows the *Talmud* of Jerusalem and Maimonides, the European texts (Ashkenazic and Sephardic) follow the Babylonian *Talmud* and the separate *Mishnah* manuscripts. The *Yerushalmi* text may imply that R. Eleazar's statement was made during the discussion at Bene Berak. The Exodus is remembered every evening in the third section of the *Shema'* (*Num.* 15:37–41) and in the benediction following the *Shema'*. (There is an ancillary question whether the entire third section should be recited in the night or only *Num.* 15:37,41 for the mention of the

---

168 מאימתי קורין את השמע בשחרית? משיכיר בין תכלת ללבן, ר' אליעזר אומר בין תכלת לכרתי.

169 ר' אליעזר אומר מנין אתה אומר שאם היתה חבורה של חכמים או של תלמידים שצריכים לעסוק בהלכות פסח עד חצות לכך נאמר מה העדות וכו'.

Exodus.) As an institution of the Men of the Great Assembly, both the *Shema'* (or the Decalogue) and the benediction must be recited each night. The question is whether this daily remembrance of the Exodus is a biblical commandment or a rabbinic institution. According to Ben Zoma, whose opinion is accepted by R. Eliezer and R. Eleazar, it is a biblical commandment applicable during the entire night.

Simeon Ben Zoma has no title because he lived during the last period of the Temple and died young (*y. Ḥagigah* II,1 77b).[170] According to Rashi (*Rosh Hashanah* 31b), Rabban Yoḥanan ben Zakkai did not survive the fall of Jerusalem for more than two years. The *Tosafot* conjecture (*Shabbat* 54b, *s.v. hawa*), following Rabbenu Tam, that R. Eleazar was elevated to vice president about five years after the fall of Jerusalem. These dates fit together well with R. Eleazar quoting Ben Zoma as a recent opinion. The conjecture of *Tosafot* is based on the premise that R. Eleazar was only 18 years old when he was called to fill the vacuum left by the removal of Rabban Gamliel as head of the Synhedrion (16 years old by the testimony of the Jerusalem *Talmud, y. Berakhot* IV,1 7d). This is the Babylonian *Talmud*'s interpretation of R. Eleazar's saying that he is *like a 70-year-old*, implying that he was in fact very far from being 70 (*b. Berakhot 28a),*[171] but on his elevation, being chosen as a direct descendant of Ezra, eighteen rows of his hair turned white. The Jerusalem *Talmud* takes the statement at face value to mean (*y. Berakhot* I,9 3d)[172] that he lived a long life even though he held high office from young age (*y. Yebamot* I,4 3a/b). Most modern scholars think it unlikely that Rabban Gamliel could have taken over the official presidency of the Synhedrion before the assassination of Domitian in 96 C.E. and, since some time must have passed before his high-handed ways aroused enough resentment to cause his removal, it is then difficult to date the elevation of R. Eleazar in the first century C.E.[173] The elevation of R. Eleazar because of his connection with Ezra can be taken as a sign that the majority of the scholars of the time wanted to rebuild the

---

170 שוב מעשה ברבי יהושע שהיה מהלך בדרך [בבלי חגיגה טו א: שהיה עומד על גב מעלה בהר הבית] ובן זומא בא כנגדו שאל בשלומו ולא השיב. . . . ולא היו ימים קלים עד שנפטר בן זומא.

171 ההוא יומא בר תמני סרי שני הוה איתרחש ליה ניסא ואהדרו ליה תמני סרי דרי חורתא.

172 אע״פ שנכנס לגדולה האריך ימים, הדא אמרה שהגדולה מקצרת ימים.

173 See also the discussion in Louis Ginzberg, *A Commentary on the Palestinian Talmud*, vol. I, p. 206. (The quote in the last line of p. 206 does not prove what is claimed there.)

Jewish community in the Land of Israel as a Torah-centered entity far away from world politics, resembling Ezra's commonwealth under Persian rule. This would correspond to R. Yehoshua's political views as leader of the peace party; his motto was (*Gen. rabbah* 64[8])[174] "let us be happy if in dealing with that people [the Romans] we are not hurt." R. Yehoshua and most likely also R. Eleazar died before the revolt of Bar Kokhba. This makes the interpretation of the Jerusalem *Talmud* questionable unless one assumes with *Tosafot* and Graetz that Rabban Gamliel was granted permission by an emperor of the Flavian dynasty, around 80 C.E., to become president of the Synhedrion in fulfillment of a promise made to Rabban Yoḥanan ben Zakkai, and this even though Rabban Gamliel's father Rabban Shim'on was executed after the fall of Jerusalem as head of the revolutionary government (66–71 C.E.).

The opinion of Ben Zoma is accepted not only by R. Eliezer and R. Eleazar but is supported also by our Masoretic punctuation for which כֹּל in *Deut.* 16:3 is a noun. The Masoretic vocalization requires the translation: "the entirety of the days of your life." The other Sages translate "all days of your life" (or maybe "during the life of anyone of you"); they must read כָּל־יְמֵי with a *maqqef*. One may date this interpretation to the time between the two Jewish wars when the *Shema'* replaced the Decalogue as the centerpiece of Jewish worship and consciousness. The leaders of the people at the time (*b. Berakhot* 12a; *y. Berakhot* I,8 3c)[175] "removed the Decalogue from the liturgy because of the quarrels of the Christians" who restricted universal validity to the Ten Commandments and discarded the other laws of the Pentateuch for a "New Covenant." It is reported that R. Eliezer had a period of sympathy with some Christian interpretations (*b. Avodah Zarah* 16b/17a; *Tosefta Ḥulin* II,6)[176] that even led to his incarceration; it may be assumed that after his bad experiences he joined R. Yehoshua in drawing the line. The argument of the Sages in the *Mishnah* is that the remembrance of the Exodus will never be removed from Jewish worship since there never will be a "New Covenant." This interpretation follows from the discussion reported in

---

174 דיינו שנכנסנו לאומה זו בשלום ויצאנו בשלום.

175 כבר בטלום מפני תרעומת המינין.

176 פעם אחת הייתי מהלך בשוק העליון של ציפורי ומצאתי אחד מתלמידי ישו הנוצרי ויעקב איש כפר סכניא שמו אמר לי כתוב בתורתכם לא תביא אתנן זונה מהו לעשות הימנו בית הכסא לכהן גדול ולא אמרתי לו כלום אמר לי כך לימדני ישו הנוצרי מאתנן זונה קובצה עד אתנן זונה ישוב ממקום הטנופת באו למקום הטנופת ילכו והנאני הדבר ועל ידי זה נתפסתי למינות.

the *Tosefta* (*Berakhot* I,10–15) and both *Talmudim* (*b. Berakhot* 12b; *y. Berakhot* I,9 4a):[177] "Ben Zoma said to the Sages: Will one really have to mention the Exodus from Egypt in the days of the Messiah? Has it not been said (*Jer.* 23:7–8): 'See, days will come, says the Lord, when one no longer will say, the Lord is living Who brought up the Children of Israel from the land of Egypt but only, the Lord is living Who led up and Who brought the descendants of the house of Israel from the land of the North and from all the lands where I had dispersed them there'? They answered him: Not that the Exodus will lose its place in the liturgy but the deliverance from subjection to foreign governments will be the main point and the Exodus a secondary matter."

On a purely formal level, the discussion between Ben Zoma and the other Sages is about the interpretation of the singular "you" in the sentence "so that you should remember the day of your Exodus from Egypt all/the entire days of your life." A Hebrew noun can be in the singular, the plural, in a few cases also the dual, and the collective, which is formally identical with the singular. The collective is used for groups of at least twenty members. One will say תְּשַׁע עֶשְׂרֵה אֲנָשִׁים "nineteen men" but עֶשְׂרִים אִישׁ "twenty man." It is a generally accepted principle of rabbinic interpretation of Scripture that precepts formulated in the plural address every single individual but those in the singular/collective address either the entire Jewish people or a defined group; see also the introductions to the sections on Grace and Counting the *'Omer*. Therefore, the other sages are justified in their reading of the verse in question as referring to the collective life of the Jewish people, including the Messianic Age when nobody will have to worry about anti-Semites anymore.

The "convincing argument" of Ben Zoma that is accepted by R. Eleazar is about the benediction following the *Shema'*, not about the recitation of the *Shema'* itself, since one discusses "speaking about, mentioning," אמר, and not "reciting," קרא, as would be required for a biblical passage.[178] This is also implied by Josephus (*Antiquities*

---

177 אמר להם בן זומא לחכמים וכי מזכירים יציאת מצרים לימות המשיח? והלא כבר נאמר 'הנה ימים באים נאום יי לא יאמר עוד חי יי אשר העלה את בני ישראל מארץ מצרים כי אם חי יי אשר העלה ואשר הביא את זרע בית ישראל מארץ צפון ומכל הארצות אשר הדיחם שם'. אמרו לו לא שתעקר יציאת מצרים ממקומה אלא שתהא שעבוד מלכיות עיקר ויציאת מצרים טפל לו.

178 *Tosefta Kifshutah, Berakhot*, p. 12. According to *Yosif 'Omeẓ* §19, the root קרא used for the recital of the *Shema'* means formal recital, following all Masoretic musical accents.

IV,12)[179] talking of a biblical commandment: "Twice each day, at the dawn thereof and when the hour comes for turning to repose, let all acknowledge before God the bounties which He has bestowed on them through their deliverance from the land of Egypt: Thanksgiving is a natural duty, and is rendered alike in gratitude for past mercies and to incline the giver to others yet to come." This is an exact description of the benedictions following the recitation of the *Shema'* morning and evening (in Josephus' time the benedictions may have followed the recitation of the Decalogue) but fits the remembrance of the Exodus neither in the Decalogue nor in the *Shema'*. It seems that the ruling underlying the statement of Ben Zoma was the generally accepted one in Josephus' time, the middle of the first century C.E. His statement also makes it clear that the Gaonic (Babylonian) opinion (*Siddur R. Amram Gaon* 6b), not to allow any prayer for future redemption to be inserted in the benediction, is true to the ancient practice in the time of the Temple. "Speaking about" is the essence of the *Seder* night, so R. Eleazar and R. Eliezer may well stay until the next morning. The assertion of the eternity of the covenant from Sinai implicit in the statement of the Sages is the basis of the following paragraph.

Older Ashkenazic prints and manuscripts are split about 50-50 in vocalizing שֶׁתֵּאָמֵר or שֶׁתֵּאָמַר. The Yemenite version, להביא את ימות המשיח, is that of the *Talmud* of Jerusalem, *Tosefta* (Erfurt manuscript), and *Halakhot Gedolot* (Warsaw ed.). Most other sources have the Ashkenazic/Sephardic להביא לימות המשיח, formed after *Ps.* 127:18–19 or representing an Aramaism.

The Four Sons

The invocation that precedes the argument regarding the special duty to teach one's children during the *Seder* uses the expression *hammāqōm*, "The Omnipresent," literally "the Place," as a name of God. This has been explained in the chapter on the Prayer (p. 206). The expression is used a few times in the Babylonian *Talmud* (*b. Berakhot* 16b, *'Avodah Zarah* 40b, *Niddah* 49b). The argument of *Pesiqta*

---

179 Δὶς δ'ἑκάτης ἡμέρας ἀρχομένης τε αὐτῆς καὶ ὁπότε πρὸς ὕπνον ὥρα τρέπεσθαι μαρτυρεῖν τῳ θεῷ τὰς δωρέας, ἅς ἀπαλλαγεῖσιν αὐτοῖς ἐκ τῆς Αἰγυπτίων γῆς παρέσχε, δικαίας οὔσης φύσει τής εὐχαριστίας καί γενομένης ἐπ' ἀμοιβῇ μὲν τῶν ἤδη γεγονότων ἐπὶ δὲ προτροπῇ τῶν ἐσομένων.

rabbati (p. 206) is taken up by *Midrash Bereshit rabbah* (chapter 68) who adds to its interpretation of *Gen.* 28:11, "he prayed to the Place" another one:[180] "he prayed at the Temple site." This is also the received interpretation of *hammāqōm* in *Gen.* 22. The talmudic use of the word may be a substitution for עֲבוֹדָה, the Temple service, used by several talmudic sages (R. Akiba *b. Giṭṭin* 58a; R. Ḥiyya *b. Yevamot* 32b; R. Lazar *y. Bava Batra* VIII,5 16b) as an oath, avoiding the Divine Name. We shall see later that in the original version of the *Haggadah* in use during the Second Commonwealth, *hammāqōm* was introduced as the name of the Temple. It is therefore reasonable to assume that originally הַמָּקוֹם stands for God worshiped in the Temple. This corresponds to the second of Philo's interpretations (p. 206). We know from passages in Philo (*De somniis* I,63; *De fuga et inventione* 75) that the talmudic use of "the Place" as a Divine Name is a very old practice. The names appearing in talmudic sources all belong to late authors with the exception of R. Yossi ben Ḥalafta. It is also remarkable that in the *Pesiqta* (*loc. cit.*) he is given his full name; usually he is called simply R. Yossi. The historical setting makes it likely that it was he who, in popular consciousness, changed the meaning of the invocation *hammāqōm* from "God worshiped in the Temple" to "The Omnipresent." The revision of the text of the *Haggadah* that eliminated a mention of the Temple in the recital of the Exodus may also be due to his circle, to discourage attempts to rebuild the Temple by human efforts, after the catastrophe of the war of Bar Kokhba.

In the written and printed Ashkenazic sources predating Heidenheim (except the Sulzbach *Haggadah*, 1755 ff.), the vocalization of the last word in the paragraph is לִשְׁאָל *lish'ol* [but in Middle Ages probably pronounced *lish'al* like the Sephardi/Yemenite text.][181] The current vocalization לִשְׁאוֹל is intended as harmonization with biblical Hebrew; it is, however, found in the the oldest-known Babylonian *Haggadah* text (*Ginze Schechter* II, p. 260) and the traditional text of Maimonides, which otherwise is identical with the modern Yemenite text. The Palestinian talmudic source of R. Ḥiyya has the spelling לשאל. The text of R. Saadia Gaon does not have the invocation of the Omnipresent as giver of the Torah; it may be that R. Saadia does not accept the story of the Four Children as an authoritative interpretation of the relevant biblical verses (see below).

---

180 דבר אחר ויפגע במקום, צלי במקום, צלי בבית המקדש.

181 Cf. Y. F. Gumpertz, *Mivtaë Sefatenu*, chap. I, p. 22.

The questions of the Four Sons are from the Tannaitic *Midrash* to Exodus known as *Mekhilta* (*deR. Yishmael, Bo, Pisqa* 18) and the Jerusalem *Talmud* (*y. Pesaḥim* X,4 37d). The questions are not mentioned in the Babylonian *Talmud*. That *Talmud* as a matter of course does not mention known liturgies; as *Tosafot* (*Shabbat* 9b, *s.v. hā*) point out, the clearest indication of that is in *b. Berakhot* 34a, where the Babylonian Rav Ḥisda explains the Galilean form of the benediction over fruits to his Babylonian students and the Galilean Rebbi Yoḥanan explains the form used in the Diaspora. The *Talmud* of Jerusalem quotes the liturgies and many texts in constant use are based on *Yerushalmi* texts, for example the prayer for the fast of the Ninth of Av (*y. Berakhot* IV,3 8a). It is reasonable to conclude that the section of the Four Sons is one of the standard parts of the ancient *Haggadah* (as we shall confirm from the Septuagint) that was preserved in Babylonia and eliminated in later Galilean observance. The author of the quote in the *Talmud* of Jerusalem is Rebbi Ḥiyya, an immigrant from Babylonia. The questions are identical in the *Mekhilta* (our *Haggadah* text) and the *Talmud* but the answers are different, although of the same meaning.

Mekhilta (*Haggadah*)

The Torah spoke about Four Children, one wise, one wicked, one simple-minded, and one who does not know how to ask. What does the wise one say? "What are the testimonials, the ordinances, and the laws that the Lord, our God, has commanded *us*?"

R. Ḥiyya[182]

The Torah spoke about Four Children, a wise child, a wicked child, a stupid child, and a child who does not know how to ask. What does the wise child say? "What are the testimonials, the ordinances, and the laws that the Lord, our God, has commanded *us*?"

The wise son quotes *Deut*. 6:20. The text reads *us*, not *you*, in the Septuagint (see above, p. 258), the *Mekhilta*, the Jerusalem *Talmud*, Maimonides' autograph codex and all early prints (*Hilkhot Ḥameẓ Umaẓẓah*), and many European manuscripts. Already Rashi (*Siddur*, p.

182 תני ר' חייה כנגד ד' בנים דיברה תורה בן חכם בן רשע בן טיפש בן שאינו יודע לשאל. בן חכם מהו אומר מה העדות והחקים והמשפטים אשר צוה ה' אלהינו אותנו אף אתה אמור לו בחוזק יד הוציאנו ה' ממצרים מבית עבדים. בן רשע מה הוא אומר מה העבודה הזאת לכם. מה הטורח שאתם מטריחים עלינו בכל שנה ושנה. מכיון שהוציא את עצמו מן הכלל אף אתה אמור לו בעבור זה עשה ה' לי. לי עשה לאותו האיש לא עשה. אילו היה אותו האיש במצרים לא היה ראוי להיגאל משם לעולם. טיפש מהו אומר מה זאת ואף אתה למדו הילכות הפסח שאין מפטירין אחר הפסח אפיקומון. שלא יהא עומד מחבורה זו ויכנס לחבורה אחרת. בן שאינו יודע לשאל את פתח לו תחילה.

191; *Maḥzor Vitry*, p. 292) points out that the biblical verse has "you," not "us," but that the child really has no reason to say "us" instead of "you" since presumably he is a minor and not required to perform any religious duty except as a matter of training and, as a child of parents alive when Moses delivered his last speech, he certainly did not leave Egypt.[183] Many Ashkenazic manuscripts and some printed editions (both German and Italian) still read "us" through the eighteenth century. Most printed editions, derived from texts published by responsible editors, have adopted the distortion of *us* into *you*. Sephardic and Oriental texts, based on Babylonian traditions, regularly have *you*. The distortion of the Tannaitic text makes it more difficult to grasp the antiquity of the text that appears even in the Septuagint, and it hides the talmudic usage to slightly misquote the biblical text in order to give more poignancy to the interpretation. In the *Haggadah*, the emphasis is on the distinction between wise and wicked sons; the biblical text itself has no reference to Passover but deals with an everyday question. The addition of "And it will be" in the Septuagint (p. 258) is probably an allusion to the question of the Third Son (*Ex.* 13:14).

There is general agreement among the commentators with the explanation of Nachmanides (*ad loc.*):[184] "The 'testimonials' (in *Deut.* 6:20) are the commandments that are called testimonies because they are remembrances of His miracles and testimonies to them like *maẓẓah*, Tabernacles, Passover, the Sabbath, the phylacteries, and the *mĕzuzah*. The 'ordinances' are those commandments for which no reason is hinted at in the Torah. The 'laws' are the legal instructions of these commandments, e.g., that the court has to stone him who works on the Sabbath, to condemn to the stake him who lies with a woman and her mother, or to condemn to forty lashes him who sows two different kinds together since the laws necessary for an orderly society (called *laws* in *Ex.* 21:1), e.g., the laws on torts and similar civil ordinances, that are contained in the Torah are clearly just and good, everybody will agree to that [so the wise child will not ask about them]."

---

183 ומה אתכם. כלומר אתם שיצאתם ממצרים שהיה הדבר אליכם.

184 מה יעידו אלה המצוות הנקראים עדות בעבור שהם זכר לנפלאותיו ועדות בהם כגון המצה והסוכה והפסח והתפילין והמזוזה. ומה החקים כי נעלם טעמם בתורה. והמשפטים ישאל מה המשפטים שנעשה במצות האלה שנסקל העושה מלאכה בשבת ונשרוף הבא על אשה ואמה ונכה את הארבעים לזורע כלאים כי משפטי ישוב המדינות כדיני השור והבור והשומרים ושאר הדינים שבתורה צדיקים וטובים הן כל רואיהם יכירון.

The wise child gets different answers in the Pentateuch, the *Haggadah*, and the *Yerushalmi*.

Mekhilta (*Haggadah*)	R. Ḥiyya
So you tell him (of) the rules of *Pesaḥ*: The *Pesaḥ* sacrifice may not be followed by *epikōmen*.	So you tell him, "With a strong hand did the Lord lead us out of Egypt, the house of slaves."
What does the bad one say? "What does this service mean to you?" To you, but not to him. And because he excluded himself from the community and therefore negated the principle [of Judaism], dull his teeth and tell him: "Because of this did the Lord do for me when I left Egypt." For me, but not for him. If he had been there, he would not have been redeemed.	What does the bad child say? "What does this service mean to you?" What is this exertion that you impose on us every year? Since he excluded himself from the community, tell him, "Because of this did the Lord do for me when I left Egypt." For me He did it, for that man He did not do it. If that man had been in Egypt, he would not have been worthy ever to be redeemed.
What does the simpleminded say? What is this? So tell him, "With a strong hand did the Lord lead us out of Egypt, the house of slaves."	The stupid child says: "What is this?" Teach him the rules of *Pesaḥ*, that one may not follow the *Pesaḥ* sacrifice *epikōmon*, that he should not get up from the group he is celebrating with and join another group.
As for the one who does not know how to ask, you start with him as it is said: "And you shall tell your child on that day, saying: Because of this the Lord did for me when I left Egypt."	With the child who does not know how to ask, you have to begin and start with him.

As noted before, the question of the wise child is *Deut*. 6:20 and has nothing to do explicitly with Passover. The answer is given in *Deut*. 6:21, but neither of the two texts picks that verse. Similarly, the wicked son does not get the answer (*Ex*. 12:27) prepared for his question (*Ex*. 12:26). The explanation is given by the author of *Orḥot Ḥayyim* (82c), who notes that it would be trivial to give the biblical answers which everybody knows anyhow but that the *Haggadah* is

Midrash Tannaïm and an example of an instructed analysis of the verses that leads to a deeper understanding of the text by oral tradition.[185] It is also true that the compilers of the *Haggadah* did refrain, if at all possible, from using one verse for two different purposes. Since *Deut.* 6:21 was already used for the introduction, the answer to the wise son in the standard *Haggadah* is a paraphrase of *Deut.* 6:25: "It will be a righteous act for us to keep this entire commandment before the Lord, our God, in the way He commanded us." The expression *the way He commanded us* or *the way I commanded you* is always taken to refer to the amplifications of the Oral Law. This is the explicit interpretation of the Tannaitic *Midrash Sifry* (#75) of the statement in *Deut.* 12:21 ". . . and prepare from your cattle and your sheep that the Lord gave you, the way I commanded you . . .":[186] "The way I commanded you, just as ritual slaughter is required for sacrifices (*Lev.* 1:5), so it is required for all animals used for food." Similarly (*Sifry Deut.* #303)[187] about the declaration required by the farmer in *Deut.* 26:13, ". . . I gave it [the tithes] to the Levite, the stranger, and the widow, following all your commandments that You commanded me," the explanation being that nobody can make the declaration if he transgressed the prohibitions enumerated in the Oral Law, e.g., to separate the Second Tithe before the First (*Mishnah Ma'aśer Sheni* II,11). It is therefore appropriate to answer the question of the wise son with a statement of Oral Law (*Mishnah Pesaḥim* X,8). The answer given to the wise child in R. Ḥiyya's text addresses another point discussed later in the treatment of the simple-minded child. Some *Mekhilta* manuscripts and the oldest Babylonian *Haggadah* text (*Ginze Schechter* II, p. 260) do not require the father to tell his son כהלכות הפסח *according to the laws of Pesaḥ*, but **בהלכות** הפסח *all through the laws of Pesaḥ*. In fact, the *Mishnah* in question, "one does not append *epikōmen* after the *Pesaḥ* sacrifice," is the penultimate *Mishnah* in the entire tractate *Pesaḥim*; conceptually, it is the last one since it deals with the situation after the meal when the sacrifice has been consumed. The natural interpretation is that the wise son should be instructed in all details of the law down to the last one.

---

185 וי״ל כי מסדרי ההגדה לא חששו להזכיר הפסוקים הכתובים בתורה על השאלות כי זה דבר פשוט שישיב להם כמו שכתוב אך בא להודיענו היכן דברה כנגד ד' בנים ובחכם ורשע החדוש שאינו כתוב בתורה אך אנו דורשין ממנו תשובה לרשע מייתור לי ולא לו ובאמרו לכם משמע שהוציא את עצמו מן הכלל שלא קיבל מלכות שמים לאמר יי אלהינו גם אין לשון לכם מורה שום שתוף עצמו עמהם.

186 כאשר צותיך, מה קדשים בשחיטה אף חולין בשחיטה.

187 ככל מצותך אשר צויתני. הא אם הקדים מעשר שני לראשון אינו יכול להתודות.

One should explain also what *epikōmen* is. The Sephardic vocalization *ăfiqōmen* is really identical to the Yemenite *ăfiqōman* since in Yemen both ֶ and ָ are pronounced as short Arabic *'a'*. There are old Italian and Oriental vocalizations *ăfiqēmōn, ăfīqīmōn.* The Western Ashkenazic vocalization is identical to the Sephardic one through the middle of the eighteenth century; after that time Western Ashkenazic pronunciation became almost identical with Eastern Ashkenazic, since most Hebrew teachers in the West were imported from the East because intra-Jewish jobs at that time did not need a work permit from Gentile authorities and the movement of impoverished Polish Jews to the West never stopped after the Chmielnicki pogroms. As a consequence, Western Ashkenazic also lost the pronunciation of ח, *ḥ* close to *h* and the soft pronunciation of *g* without *dagesh.* Heidenheim for some unknown reason vocalizes *ăfikoumēn.* The Eastern Ashkenazic pronunciation *ăfiqoumon* is derived from a popular Aramaic etymology of the word, אפיקו מן, "bring something," ascribed to R. Kalonymos of Rome, rabbi of Worms at the end of the eleventh century, and contained in the explanation of the entire passage from Rashi's school, e.g., *Maḥzor Vitry*, p. 292:[188] "The wise one asks as follows: 'What are the testimonials and the ordinances?' Why do we eat the festival offering before the *Pesaḥ* sacrifice when the latter one is the main obligation? So you have to tell him the rules of the *Pesaḥ:* we eat the *Pesaḥ* last because after the *Pesaḥ* one may not have *ăfiqoumon;* after the meal, when one has finished the repast, one eats an olive-sized bite from the meat of *Pesaḥ* so that its taste should linger in one's mouth for the remainder of the night and one cannot say 'bring something!' get and bring desserts, in order not to take away the taste of *Pesaḥ* from his mouth. Today, therefore, we eat a piece of *mazzah* at the end as a remembrance of the Temple. . . . Another explanation: in Greek, *ăfiqouman* means 'something.'" The *Talmudim* report three interpretations of the word אפיקומן. One has to reconstruct a Greek original from the different meanings. This is not an easy task and the results are tentative only, since it is clear from the sources that the *Talmudim* are unsure of meaning and etymology. The first explanation is quoted by R. Ḥiyya in

---

188 וכן החכם שואל. מה העדות והחוקים. כלומר למה אנו אוכלין החגיגה קודם לפסח הלא הפסח עיקר. ואף אתה אמור לו כהילכות הפסח. שלפיכך אנו אוכלין החגיגה קודם לפסח והפסח אחרון לפי שאין מפטירין אחר הפסח אפיקומן. בגמר אכילה כשנפטרים מסעודתם אוכלין כזית מבשׂר הפסח כדי שיהיה הטעם בפיו כל שעה ואחר שיאכל כזית פסח אין מפטירין אפיקומן. כלומר אינו רשאי ליפטר מסעודתו בדבר אחר ולומר אפיקומן, הוציאו והביאו מינין של מאכל בקינוח סעודה, שלא להפקיע טעם פסח מפיו. ולכך אנו אוכלין כזית מצה באחרונה זכר לפסח מקדש . . . ד״א בלשון יווני אפיקומן כלום של דבר.

the answer to the stupid child above; the same explanation is reported in the Babylonian *Talmud* (*b. Pesaḥim* 119b) by Rav, R. Ḥiyya's nephew. They agree that after the meal one may not go ἐπὶ κῶμον, go in revelry from one party to another, often in a disorderly way. The κῶμος, after-dinner revelry, was probably the aspect of Gentile dinners most reprehensible to Jews. The second interpretation, given both in the Babylonian (*loc. cit*) and in the Jerusalem *Talmud* (*y. Pesaḥim* X,8 37d) by Samuel, Rav's contemporary in Babylonia, and the later Galilean teacher Rebbi Yoḥanan, is that of "dessert," either sweets or meat delicacies. The closest Greek word comparing to אפיקומן and giving the sense of "dessert" is ἐπιγεῦμα. This ruling may underlie the description of the *Seder* celebration by Philo (p. 185, note 3). A third meaning, reported in the Jerusalem *Talmud* only (*loc. cit.*), by Galilean teachers with Greek sounding names, is "kinds of song," meaning ἐπικώμιον, drinking songs, also one of the more objectionable aspects of the κῶμος. The second interpretation is the one underlying the commentary of the school of Rashi quoted above; it also is the one chosen by the traditional translations (German/Yiddish, Spanish/Ladino, Arabic) found in current *Haggadot*. The word chosen by the Arabic translation of Djerba, אפפאכי, means "delicious sweet fruits, sweets," following R. Yoḥanan. The other translations mostly explain that all desserts are inadmissible.

The bad child, the presumed interlocutor of *Ex.* 12:26, gets the same treatment by both the *Haggadah* and R. Ḥiyya. The biblical answer is *Ex.* 12:27, "The Lord passed over our houses when He smote the Egyptians but He saved our houses." The verse is used later, in the section *Rabban Gamliel*, so the answer is paraphrased. The texts of the rituals differ in the position of a connective ו:

Ashkenazic (*Mekhilta, Ginze Schechter* II, p. 260) כפר בעקר ואף אתה הקהה
Yemenite (Maimonides) וכפר בעקר אף אתה הקהה

Saadia has both *wawim*; the Sephardic text has neither. In the text of Maimonides, the *waw* must be translated "therefore," it gives a slightly better text. The bad child seems to question why we go to all the trouble and expense connected with the Passover celebration. The costliness of Jewish worship was an item of intense discussion during the Second Commonwealth, as shown by the disgrace of the priestly family Bilgah, a daughter of whom married a Gentile mainly because she objected to the enormous sums expended for the Temple service (*b. Sukkah,* 56b; *y. Sukkah* V,8 55d; *Tosefta* IV,28):[189] "Bilgah always distributes its portion near the South wall [of the Temple, far from the place of sacrifice near the North wall, *Lev.* 1:11] because of Miryam Bilgah who became an apostate and then married an officer of the Hellenistic government. When the Gentiles entered the Temple she came and knocked on the top of the altar [the way one disciplines a child] and said: 'Wolf [λύκος], wolf, you destroyed the property of the Jews and did not help them in the time of their need.'" The standard traditional interpretation (*Mekhilta deR. Ishmael, Bo,* #12, p. 41)[190] of the next verse, *Ex.* 12:27, ". . .the people bowed down and prostrated themselves . . ." is that the people, after hearing the answer to give to the rebellious child, gave thanks not only for the Divine promise of being spared, redeemed, and blessed with children but also for not having died during the days of darkness (three days of foggy darkness, *Ex.* 10:22, and three days during which no Egyptian could get up, *Ex.* 10:23) when those Jews who did not want to leave Egypt died and were buried unnoticed by the Egyptians. The text starts with noting the ambivalence parents generally have toward bad children by explaining that the future implicit in *Ex.* 12:26, "It will be that your children will say to you: 'What does this service mean to you?'" is (a) bad, because it shows there will be children ignorant of and hostile to the teachings of the Torah, and (b) good, because in implies a Divine promise that there always will be children.

The question of the simpleminded child (*Ex.* 13:14) is not about Passover at all but about the sacrifice of firstborn animals and the redemption of firstborn sons. The question is essentially the same as the one asked by the wicked child, only here it is in wonder, not in rebellion. Why does one have to hand over the firstborn of sheep and cattle to the priest as sacrifices and redeem the firstborn of humans and donkeys? The answer is that "the Lord led us out of Egypt with a strong hand," the obligations of a Jew are of a personal nature, a kind

---

189 בלגה לעולם חולקת בדרום מפני מרים בת בלגה שנשתמדה והלכה ונשאת לסרדיוט אחד משל מלכות בית יון. וכשנכנסו גוים להיכל באה וטפחה על גגו של מזבח אמרה לו לוקוס, לוקוס, אתה החרבת נכסיהן של ישראל ולא עמדת להן בשעת דוחקן.

190 והיה כי יאמרו עליכם בניכם. בשורה רעה נתבשרו ישראל באותה שעה שסוף התורה עתידה להשתכח ויש אומרים בשורה טובה נתבשרו ישראל באותה שעה שהן עתידין לראות בנים ובני בנים להם שנאמר ויקוד העם וישתחוו וגו'. למה השתחוו משום שנאמר וחמושים עלו בני ישראל אחד מחמשה ויש אומרים אחד מחמשים ויש אומרים אחד מחמש מאות עלו. ר' נהוראי אומר העבודה ולא אחד מחמש מאות עלו שנאמר רבבה כצמח השדה נתתיך וגו' וכתיב ובני ישראל פרו וישרצו שהיתה אשה אחת יולדת ששה בנים בכרס אחד ואתה אומר אחד מחמש מאות עלו! ואימתי מתו בשלשת ימי אפלה שנאמר לא ראו איש את אחיו שהיו קוברין מיתיהן והודו ושבחו שלא ראו אויבים ושמחו במפלתם.

of payment for services rendered, and not at all representative of universal moral values and obligations; the latter are understood by themselves and do not need any explicit commandments. According to the version of R. Ḥiyya, one has to give the same interpretation also to the question of the wise child, the *testimonials* being the commandments that cost money and appear to have no moral value in the eyes of non-Jews. Therefore, the wise child gets the answer given to the simpleminded in the *Mekhilta* text. Instead of *simpleminded*, R. Ḥiyya has *silly* or *dumb*; that child must be taught what to do before he can start to ask questions. Since compulsory education has been a feature of Judaism since the Second Commonwealth when Shimon ben Shetaḥ (ca. 100 B.C.E.) required instruction for all children (*y. Ketubot* VIII,11 32c)[191] and the High Priest Joshua ben Gamla (ca. 60 C.E.) ordered public schools to start at ages 6 or 7 for all Jewish children (*b. Bava Batra* 21a),[192] there is nothing unusual in teaching Talmudics to a child of less than average intelligence, as implied in R. Ḥiyya's text.

In the *Haggadah*, the story of the Four Children serves as a literary device to introduce the child who does not know how to ask and with it verse *Ex.* 13:8, which contains the obligation to talk about the Exodus in the *Seder* night. The entire introduction from "We were slaves" leads up to the formulation of this obligation in the next paragraph. The obligations stipulated in *Ex.* 13:1-8 refer only to *maẓẓah*, not *Pesaḥ*, in connection with the spring festival. These obligations are therefore independent of the existence of the Temple; sacrifices are not mentioned in this biblical paragraph and the next. The verse is attributed as answer to a child who does not know how to ask because it is not preceded by any question, in contrast to the three verses interpreted up to now. There is disagreement among the Bible commentators as to how to understand the syntax of the second half of the verse, בַּעֲבוּר זֶה עָשָׂה יי לִי בְּצֵאתִי מִמִּצְרָיִם. Rashi and Ibn Ezra follow the *Mekhilta* and take זֶה "this" to refer to the special obligations connected with the festival of Passover; "The Lord did wonders for me at the Exodus in the expectation that I should follow His commandments and perform the required acts [spelled out *Ex.* 13:6–7]." Ibn Janaḥ, Rashbam, and Nachmanides read the verse as if it were בַּעֲבוּר אֲשֶׁר עָשָׂה יי לִי בְּצֵאתִי מִמִּצְרָיִם "[I am performing these acts] because

---

191 התקין שמעון בן שתח ג' דברים . . . ושיהו התינוקות הולכין לבית הספר.

192 עד שבא יהושע בן גמלא ותיקן שיהו מושיבין מלמדי תינוקות בכל מדינה ומדינה ובכל עיר ועיר ומכניסין אותן כבן שש כבן שבע.

of what the Lord did for me at the Exodus from Egypt." The use of *this* as relative pronoun is found, e.g., in *Ps*. 74:2 הַר־צִיּוֹן זֶה שָׁכַנְתָּ בּוֹ "Mount Zion on which You dwelled." In Psalms, זֶה may be a poetic substitute for prosaic אֲשֶׁר. In any case, the *Mekhilta/Haggadah* is firmly committed to a retrospective meaning of "this."

In all *Haggadot* except Heidenheim's, the masculine personal pronoun "you" in this section is spelled אַתְּ instead of the standard אַתָּה. The shortened form is the standard *Yerushalmi* spelling and found in all *Galilean* sources, the *Talmud* of Jerusalem, and the *Mekhilta*; it is not the biblical feminine "you." "You start with him," more exactly "you open up for him," means that you have to be his first teacher. In the sources, the pronoun "you" is taken as a singular: it is the obligation of every Jewish parent to teach his children. The pronoun could also be read as a collective, in form identical to the singular: the Jewish community has a collective responsibility to teach all its children.

The next paragraph gives the logical analysis of the commandment contained in *Ex*. 13:8 as it is applicable to the child who does not know how to ask. Our current Ashkenazic and Sephardic text, which starts with יָכוֹל "one should have thought" should not have a paragraph here but continue the discussion. If one desires to introduce a paragraph, as in the traditional Ashkenazic texts, the better version is the Yemenite *Haggadah*, which copies the *Mekhilta* text (*deR. Ishmael, Bo*, p. 66)[193] by repeating the beginning of the verse but not repeating the second half. The Yemenite text of the *Haggadah* is identical with the *Mekhilta* text of a Yemenite manuscript. The paragraph is in condensed talmudic style; the reasoning goes as follows:
(*Ex*. 13:8) "You are obliged to tell your child" one might have thought [*Mekhilta* text: I could have understood this to mean] that the obligation starts from the day of the New Moon [of Nisan which, according to the traditional interpretation of *Ex*. 12:2 is the anniversary of the original commandment to Moses and Aaron] but Scripture says [Yemenite version: you must learn from the verse which says] "on that day." I could then think that the verse means the Fourteenth of Nisan, the day of the *Pesaḥ* sacrifice. However, the verse also says "because of this." It must refer to something one can

---

193 והגדת לבנך שומע אני מראש חדש ת״ל ביום ההוא. אי ביום ההוא יכול מבעוד יום, ת״ל בעבור זה בשעה שיש מצה ומרור מונחים לפניך על שולחניך.

point to with one's finger, and that is only when *mazzah* and bitter herbs are presented before you.

The root הגד is translated here "to tell," which would make *Haggadah* to mean "tale." The root can also mean "to declare" (this is the meaning of the Eastern Aramaic translation, *Targum Onqelos*, חוי of the verb הגדתי in *Deut.* 26:3, the introduction to the core *Haggadah, Deut.* 26:5-9), or "to praise" (the translation שבח of the same word הגדתי by the Western Aramaic *Targum Yerushalmi* [*Pseudo-Jonathan*] and the Arabic translation שקר by R. Saadia Gaon), and it may be understood in that way by Philo (cf. p. 185).

According to Maimonides (*Hilkhot Ḥamez̦ Umaz̦z̦ah* VII,1)[194] the origin of the obligation to celebrate the *Seder* is not *Ex.* 13:8, which fixes the date, but *Ex.* 13:2, "Remember this day on which you [plural] left Egypt" and one can only fulfill a formal commandment "to remember" by a declaration, in the same way the commandment "to remember the Sabbath day" (*Ex.* 20:8) is fulfilled by recitation of *Qiddush*. This interpretation of *Ex.* 13:2 is from the late Tannaitic source *Mekhilta deR. Shimon bar Yoḥay* (*Midrash Hagadol* II, p. רכז),[195] which takes the plural "you" to indicate a community involvement in teaching and declaration. The older source *Mekhilta deR. Ishmael* (*Bo* 16, p. 60)[196] takes the verse to mean that one has to remember the Exodus in one's morning prayers, parallel to Ben Zoma's derivation for the same obligation in the nightly service. In any case, since no sacrifice in mentioned in *Ex.* 13:1-9, it is clear that the obligation to teach children at the *Seder* is applicable to all Jews, at all times, everywhere, and does not depend on the Temple service.

The text from "We were slaves" up to this point is an introduction. After it has been established that in the *Seder* night there is an obligation to tell about (or declare, or praise) God's wonders that led to the Exodus, the actual declaration now follows.

---

194 מצות עשׂה של תורה לספר בנסים ונפלאות שנעשׂו לאבותינו במצרים בליל חמשה עשׂר בניסן שנאמר זכור את היום הזה אשר יצאתם ממצרים כמו שנאמר זכור את יום השבת. ומנין שבליל חמשה עשׂר תלמוד לומר והגדת לבנך ביום ההוא לאמר בעבור זה בשעה שיש מצה ומרור מונחים לפניך.

195 ויאמר משה אל העם זכור את היום הזה. משום שנאמר והיה כי ישאלך בנך מחר לאמר, יכול אם שאלך אתה מגיד לו ואם לאו אי אתה מגיד לו, ת״ל והגדת לבנך, אע״פ שלא שאלך. אין לי אלא בזמן שיש לו בן, בינו לבין עצמו, בינו לבין אחרים מנין, ת״ל ויאמר משה אל העם זכור את היום הזה אשר יצאתם ממצרים.

196 ויאמר משה אל העם זכור את היום הזה אשר יצאתם ממצרים אין לי אלא שמזכירין יציאת מצרים בימים, בלילות מנין שנא׳ למען תזכר את יום צאתך מארץ מצרים כל ימי חייך.

As mentioned before, the introduction was not required to be recited in Galilee from the third century C.E. on; one is required to do one's duty but no one has to talk about the obligation to do one's duty.

Our Forefathers Were Idolators

The sentence from the Book of Joshua (*Jos.* 24:2-4) that is the core of this paragraph was very relevant for the Jews of the Second Commonwealth. The quote is from Joshua's speech to the people after the distribution of land and leading to a newly sworn *voluntary* Covenant (*Jos.* 24:25) confirming the Covenant *imposed* by God at Sinai. Now most of the particular duties imposed by the Torah on the produce of the Land (the heave for the priests, tithes for the Levites and the poor, the Sabbatical Year, etc.) are imposed as duties on the land distributed as family heritage to all tribes by Moses and Joshua. These commandments became obsolete when the tribes were led into captivity, including the obligations of the remaining Israelite population of Galilee who, according to our sources, were never exiled and who reappear in history at the time of the Hasmonean revolt without any record of resettlement in Galilee. The continued obligation to observe the Laws that depend on the Land therefore is derived only from the voluntary covenant enacted by the people in the time of Ezra and Nehemia (*y. Shevi'it* VI,1 36b):[197] "Rebbi Lezer says: they voluntarily accepted the duties of the tithes. Why do I say this? (*Neh.* 10:1) 'With all this, we enact a written trust and covenant signed by our princes, Levites, and priests.' How does R. Lezer explain the inclusion (*Neh.* 10:37) of 'the firstborn of our cattle and flocks' [an obligation that does not depend on the Land and therefore is universal]? Since they accepted upon themselves the obligations (of heave and tithes) that they could have avoided, Scripture gives them merit for those obligations that they had to fulfill anyhow as if they had accepted these also voluntarily." The same idea is also expressed by an opponent of rabbinic Judaism who is reported (*y. Shevi'it* IX,9 39a) to have said:[198] "*Ḥallah* [the heave to be taken from bread dough]

197 אמר רבי לעזר מאיליהן קיבלו עליהן את המעשׂרות. מה טעם? ובכל זאת אנחנו כורתים אמנה וכותבים ועל החתום שׂרינו לויינו וכהנינו. מה מקיים ר' לעזר ואת בכורות בקרינו וצאננו? מכיון שקיבלו עליהם דברים שלא היו חייבין עליהן, אפילו דברים שהיו חייבין עליהן העלה עליהן כאילו מאיליהן קיבלו עליהן.

198 חלה מדבר תורה שביעית מדרבן גמליאל וחביריו.

is a biblical obligation [*Num.* 15:20] but the Sabbatical year is now an obligation only by the authority of Rabban Gamliel and his colleagues." The Babylonian *Talmud* (*b. Shabbat* 88a)[199] finds the record of the voluntary acceptance of these obligations in the verse (*Esth.* 9:27): "The Jews confirmed and accepted irrevocably upon themselves, their descendants, and prospective converts," which is interpreted to mean that "they confirmed now [with Esther, Mordokhai, Ezra, and Nehemiah] the obligations that they had accepted earlier [under Moses and Joshua]." So the verses from the Book of Joshua are not only an introduction to the recital of the events of the Exodus but also an amplification of the answer given to the simpleminded child: we have to fulfill the Commandments of the Torah, even if they are onerous and costly, not only because of the involuntary obligation imposed upon us by the events of the Exodus and the Covenant of Sinai, but also because of the two voluntary covenants enacted by Joshua and Ezra-Nehemia. The entire paragraph can be viewed as a continuation of the preceding discussion.

The Masoretic text of Joshua has the irregular form ארב for standard ארבה "I increased." As the Jerusalem *Talmud* points out in the discussion of the *Haggadah* (*y. Pesaḥim* X,5 37d),[200] the shortened form could be interpreted as being derived either from ריב "quarrel" (meaning "how many quarrels did I cause him until I gave him Isaac"), or from ארב "ambush" ("I ambushed him, to give him his due either for his sins or his merits"). It is clear from the text of the *Yerushalmi* that old texts of the *Haggadah* had the full, standard spelling at this place. The Masoretic short spelling at this place is found only in *Haggadot* derived from the Heidenheim text. The straightforward meaning seems to be that of all eight of Abraham's children only Isaac counts. In the same way, Esaw got a permanent dwelling place from the start and therefore was excluded from the promise made to Abraham in *Gen.* 15:13-14 and discussed in the next paragraph. The text from Joshua has two parts. The first part (v. 2) refers to the "shame" of being descended from idolators. The second part (v. 3) describes the election of Abraham and the selection of Jacob's descendants as holy people. Therefore, all old *Haggadah* texts make a break in the text and start a new paragraph at verse 3. The run-on of both verses in the Ashkenazic text is also a Heidenheim innovation.

---

199 אמר רבא אעפ״כ הדור קבלוה בימי אחשורוש דכתיב קימו וקבלו היהודים, קיימו מא שקבלו כבר.

200 וארבה. אמר ר׳ אחא וארב כתיב כמה ריבים עשיתי עמו עד שלא נתתי לו את יצחק. דב׳ אחר נעשיתי לו אורב אין חטא מיתן ליה ואין זכה מיתן ליה.

The South Tunisian *Haggadah* has here a lengthy insert in Judeo-Arabic describing the discovery of monotheism by Abraham at the age of 3 by the study of astronomy and his rescue from the fiery oven. Text, translation, and commentary are given in the Appendix. The underlying *midrash* is very old; even Philo (*De mutatione nominum* 66–67, *De Cherub.* 4) declares the name *Avram* to mean "master of the high,"[201] i.e., astronomer (not, as now commonly explained, a theophorous name *The Father is exalted*).

The Covenant between the Pieces

After having excluded the descendants of Abraham other than Isaac and the descendants of Isaac other than Jacob, the compilers of the *Haggadah* in the next paragraph introduce the theme of the current and future redemption and lay the foundation for the final benediction over the *Haggadah*. The *Haggadah*'s interpretation of *Gen.* 15:13–14 is that not only did God lead Israel out of Egypt within the exact time frame specified by the Covenant between the Pieces (*Gen.* 15) but *it*, the Covenant (a feminine noun in Hebrew), is also our current protection. The implication is that one should translate *Gen.* 15:14 as "Also every people whom they will serve I shall judge . . . " (*Gen. rabbah* 44[22]).[202] The problem addressed by the *Midrash* is a seeming inconsistency in the biblical narrative. It is first said that Abram believed implicitly the promise of children and that this was an act of great merit (*Gen.* 15:6), but then he turns around in verse 8 and seems to ask for a sign that he in fact will inherit. The *Midrash* explains that *Gen.* 15:8 is not a complaint but an inquiry (*Gen. rabbah* 44[17]);[203] there is no inconsistency in the biblical narrative. *Genesis* 15:5 contains a Divine promise of posterity for Abraham; in verse 6 he unconditionally accepts that promise, which concerns only himself. Verse 7 contains a new promise, to give the land of Canaan as

---

201 Ἀβραμ γὰρ ἑρμηνεύεται μετέωρος πατήρ.

202 **וגם את הגוי אשר יעבודו דן אנכי.** היה לו לומר גם. מאי וגם. **אלא גם** הוא מצרים, וגם לרבות ארבע מלכיות. **דן אנכי.** ר״א בשם ר׳ יוסי בן זמרא אמר בשתי אותיות הללו הבטיח הקב״ה לא״א שהוא גואל את בניו. ושאם יעשו תשובה גואלן בעב׳ אותיות.

203 **במה אדע.** ר׳ חייא ב״ר חנינא אמר לא כקורא תגר אלא אמר לו באיזה זכות. אמר לו בכפרות שאני נותן לבניך.

inheritance to his descendants. Since all Divine promises are given on condition of good behavior, how can Abraham know that his descendants will inherit the land even if they do not merit it? The answer of the second *midrash* is that Israel will always have means to atone for its sins and therefore the Lord is ready to confirm the promise unconditionally. The first *midrash* extends the unconditional promise for the future and all oppressions but notes that the mode of salvation will depend on the state of Israel's adherence to the Torah. If Israel is in a state of holiness then the future redemptions will be miraculous; otherwise they will be through natural agents. In this sense, the verses have been understood by the commentators through the ages, from Gaonic Babylonia (R. Saadia Gaon, *Beliefs and Convictions* VIII,5) to medieval Spain (Nachmanides *ad. loc.* 15:7).

There are two chronological problems connected with the Covenant between the Pieces (*Gen.* 15:13–16) that are given the same resolution in all rabbinic sources and therefore must be understood as background of the *Haggadah*. It is stated in *Gen.* 15:13 that ". . . your descendants will be strangers . . . four hundred years" but *Ex.* 12:40 reads "the settlement of the Children of Israel, the time they lived in Egypt, was four hundred and thirty years." On the other hand, the chronologies given in Genesis and Exodus do not allow for such a long period. This is one of the recognized changes in which the original Septuagint deviated from the Hebrew (*b. Megillah* 9a; *y. Megillah* I,11 71d); the verse in Exodus is rendered[204] "the time they lived in Egypt and in Canaan." It is the general opinion (*Mekhilta deR. Ishmael*, p. 50; *Mekhilta deR. Shimon ben Yoḥai*, p. 34; *Ex. rabbah Bo* 18[9]; *Tanḥuma Bo* 9; *Targum Yerushalmi Ex.* 12:40[205]) that "the period of settlement of the Children of Israel in Egypt was 30 periods of seven years, i.e., 210 years, and the count of 430 years is from the moment the Lord spoke to Abraham, from the moment He spoke to him on the Fifteenth of Nisan between the Pieces to the day they left Egypt." The 400 years are counted by general agreement from the birth of Isaac. Then it follows that Abraham was 70 years old at the Covenant between the Pieces (*Seder Olam* 1) and, therefore, the covenant reported in *Gen.* 15 must precede Abraham's departure from Ḥaran (*Gen.* 12:4) by five

---

204 ἡ δὲ κατοίκησις τῶν υἱῶν Ισραηλ, ἣν κατῴκησαν ἐν γῇ Αἰγύπτῳ καὶ ἐν γῇ Χανααν, ἔτη τετρακόσια τριάκοντα.

205 וְיוֹמַיָּא דְיָתִיבוּ בְּנֵי יִשְׂרָאֵל בְּמִצְרַיִם תְּלָתִין שְׁמִטִּין דִּשְׁנִין דִּסְכוּמְהוֹן מָאתַן וַעֲשַׂר שְׁנִין וּמִנְיַן אַרְבַּע מְאָה וּתְלָתִין שְׁנִין מִן דְּמַלֵּיל יי לְאַבְרָהָם מִן שַׁעְתָּא דְּמַלֵּיל עִמֵּיהּ בְּחַמִיסַר בְּנִיסָן בֵּינֵי פְּסוּגַיָּיא עַד יוֹמָא דִּנְפָקוּ מִמִּצְרַיִם.

years. The stay of 210 years in Egypt is detailed in *Seder Olam* 3:[206] since Jacob was born when Isaac was 60 (*Gen.* 25:26) and Jacob entered Egypt when he was 130 years old (*Gen.* 47:9), his family stayed in Egypt 400-(60+130) = 210 years. One might think it possible that they really stayed in Egypt 400 years, but Qehat was one of the immigrants into Egypt (*Gen.* 46:11) and lived to be 133 years (*Ex.* 6:18), his son Amram lived 137 years (*Ex.* 6:20), Moses the son of Amram was 80 at the time of the Exodus (*Ex.* 7:7), for a total of 133+137+80 = 350 years. Hence, the meaning of the verse *Gen.* 15:13 must be that Abraham's descendants will be strangers for 400 years. "They will enslave them" refers to the time of servitude, and "and mistreat them" refers to the time of suffering, for a total of 400 years. Joseph died at age 110 (*Gen.* 50:26). We do not find that any of the brothers lived a shorter life and there are no indications that any one of them lived longer than Levi, 137 years (*Ex.* 6:16). Scripture asserts that Israel was not enslaved in Egypt as long as one of the brothers was alive since it is stated first that Joseph and all his brothers died (*Ex.* 1:6) but afterward a new king arose (*Ex.* 1:8). (Jacob was 77 when he came to Ḥaran [*Seder Olam* 2], so he married at 84. Levi was born when he was 87; hence, Levi came to Egypt at 43 and lived there another 94 years.) This leaves a maximum of 116 years for the time of slavery. A lower limit for the time of slavery can be found from the age of Miryam, who was six years older than her brother Moses (this number is purely traditional and not supported by any verse in Scripture) since traditonally her name, meaning "bitterness," refers to the oppression. The scholarly etymology of the name Miryam is unsure; E. Täubler derives the name from Arabic *ra'im* "to love tenderly." Prof. Täubler also notes (in the handwritten notes on the margins of his *Biblia Hebraica*) that the chronology of *Seder Olam* can be sustained quantitatively by the note in *Num.* 13:22 that Ḥebron was founded only seven years before Ẓoan (Tanis) in Egypt. An Egyptian document (ANET, p. 252) asserts that at the start of the Ramesside dynasty, the

---

206 נאמר לאברהם אבינו בין הבתרים ידוע תדע כי גר יהיה זרעך וכו׳ ואי זה זרע זה יצחק שנ׳ כי ביצחק יקרא לך זרע. וביצחק הוא אומר ויצחק בן ששים שנה בלדת אותם. ואבינו יעקב אמר לפרעה ימי שני מגורי שלשים ומאת שנה וגו׳ הרי קצ׳ נשתיירו שם ר״י שנים . . . או יכול כל ד׳ מאות שנה היו ישראל במצרים והלא קהת מיורדי מצרים היה וכתיב ושני חיי קהת קל״ג שנה, ושני חיי עמרם קל״ז שנה ופ׳ שנים של משה הרי ש״נ שנה אלא מה ת״ל ועבדום וענו אותם ד׳ מאות שנה ללמדך שכל זמן שזרעך בארץ לא להם ת׳ שנה. וימת יוסף וכל אחיו. יוסף מת בן ק׳ שנה. אין לך בכל השבטים שקצר ימיו מיוסף ואין לך בכל השבטים שהאריך ימים יותר מלוי וכל זמן שהיה קיים לא נשתעבדו ישראל למצרים שנ׳ וימת יוסף וכל אחיו ויקם מלך חדש על מצרים. נמצא משמת לוי עד שיצאו ישראל ממצרים קי״ו שנה ואין השעבוד יותר על כן ולא פחות מפ״ו שנה כשנותיה של מרים. ולמה נקרא שמה מרים על שם מירור.

probable dynasty of oppression and Exodus, Tanis was just 400 years old. That means that Ḥebron was formed of Qiryat Arba', Mamre, and possibly other places (*Gen.* 13:18, 23:2) just about the time of Abraham's arrival in Canaan.

The Covenant between the Pieces is introduced here because, according to the traditional explanation of *Ex.* 12:41 given above, it happened during the *Seder* night. Then the 400 years mentioned in *Gen.* 15:13 imply that Isaac was born during the same night and the angels visited Abraham on the Fifteenth of Nisan (*Seder Olam* 5).

The Sephardic and Oriental version of the Covenant, that the Lord *is computing* the end, is found in all known sources that predate the European High Middle Ages, both of Babylonian (R. Saadia Gaon, R. Amram Gaon) and Galilean (Cairo *Genizah*) types. The same language is found in a few Ashkenazic manuscripts from the Balkans. The Ashkenazic version, that the Lord *did compute,* is found in Maimonides, *Maḥzor Vitry,* and the Italian Ashkenazic 1609 *Haggadah* from Venice. The present participle used in the Sephardic and Oriental versions is an expression of the belief in the eternity of the Covenant and its unconditional promise. It is understood as such in the thirteenth-century Italian Ashkenazic *Shibbole Haleqet* (§218, p. 190):[207] "My brother Benjamin, may his Lord guard and bless him, explains the clause that 'the Holy, praise to Him, is computing the end' not as referring to the Exodus but to the ultimate redemption in order to strengthen those who recite the *Haggadah* because at the Annoucement between the Pieces did the Holy, praise to Him, show to our father Abraham all exiles, their servitudes, wanderings, and redemptions, and now, when we come to tell about the Exodus from Egypt, their spirit is strengthened by the promise given, they enjoy and console themselves that at the end the promise will be kept to them as it was kept the first time. 'Praise to Him Who keeps His promise to Israel' means, praise to the Omnipresent who will keep the promise of redemption given to us."

According to the Ashkenazic (and Maimonides') version,

---

207 פי' אחי ר' בנימין נר"ו שזה שאמר שהקב"ה מחשב את הקץ לא קאי איציאת מצרים אלא אגאולה אחרונה קאי והוא להחזיק לב אומרי ההגדה לפי שבבשורת בין הבתרים הראה לו הקב"ה לאברהם אבינו כל הגליות ושעבודן וגלותן וגאולתן ועכשיו שבאין לספר ביציאת מצרים לבם מחזק על ההבטחה ומשתעשעין ומתנחמין בה שעתיד לקיימה להן באחרונה כמו שקיים בראשונה וכה פתרונו: ברוך שומר הבטחתו של ישראל, כלומר ברוך המקום שעתיד לשמור לנו ההבטחה של גאולה שהבטיחנו.

preferred by Abudirham, the computation refers only to the Exodus and the substitution of a relatively short span of persecution for the 400 years of the verse. That interpretation does not fit with the next paragraph when we lift the cup to celebrate the eternity of the promise given between the Pieces. In this and the following paragraphs, the Yemenite reading כְּמוֹ is the Babylonian form adopted by Maimonides; the European כַּמָּה is found among early medieval texts only in Palestinian *Genizah* fragments. Saadia's text has here מה and nothing in the later paragraphs. The reading מה has survived here only in the Bombay ritual; it is found also in old Italian sources. The Amsterdam *Haggadah* of 1695 and its many Ashkenazic copies from the eighteenth century have a queer inconsistency, using כמו the first three times and כמה afterward. The Yemenite addition, *His people* Israel, is already found in Maimonides.

It is customary to lift one's cup for the invocation that follows the remembrance of the Covenant. The source of this custom is an imitation of the old tradition to lift one's cup for the invocation at the end of the Recital. The custom is mentioned first in the writings of the Safed kabbalists at the end of the sixteenth century. The reason given is (*Perush al pi hasod, Offenbach Haggadah 1722)*[208] that the numerical value of the Hebrew word for "wine," יין, is 70, and therefore our "cup of salvation," which is lifted (*Ps.* 116:13), is at the same time the cup of destruction for the seventy Gentile nations (enumerated in *Gen.* 10) (cf. p. 186). There is no mention of lifting the cup in the Amsterdam *Haggadah* of 1662, but the Amsterdam *Haggadah* (Ashkenazic and Sephardic) of 1695 has a note,[209] "one must lift the cup, so wrote *ARI* of blessed memory," meaning that a note to this effect is found in the writings of R. Ḥayyim Viṭal Calabrese. All later Ashkenazic *Haggadot* have the same note. Sephardic *Haggadot* do not require the lifting of the cup, since the (Ashkenazic) halakhic authority Magen Avraham (*Oraḥ Ḥayyim* §473, #27) requires only to hold the cup, not to lift it, based on a reference to the kabbalistic work *Shĕne Luḥot Habĕrit.*[210] If one lifts (or holds) the cup, one covers the bread since, in the hierarchy of edibles, wine definitely comes in second behind life-sustaining bread. The bread

208 כאן מגביהין את הכוס, נ״ל משום דיין עולה ע׳ ודומה לכוס של ברכה שכל העכו״ם ישתו הכוס התרעלה לעתיד.

209 צריך להגביה הכוס, כן כתב האר״י ז״ל.

210 The reference probably is to vol. 2, col. 2d, dealing with handling the cup for *Hallel*.

should have our attention not only because of this fact but also since during this night it is the "answer bread" on which the *Haggadah* should be recited. Therefore, when we lift the Cup of Salvation, the bread should not have to compete with wine for attention. Earlier generations who did not lift the cup here certainly were of the opinion that the verse "I shall lift up the Cup of Salvations and invoke the Name of the Lord" can refer only to a situation that leads to an invocation of the Name, i.e., a benediction, as at the end of the *Haggadah* recital and for saying Grace.

The doubling of *to completely destroy us* is found in all old Ashkenazic texts. It is missing in all old Oriental texts, as in today's Yemenite ritual. From the commentary of Abudirham it seems that his Spanish text was identical to today's Yemenite text. The current doubling in Sephardic texts may therefore be borrowed from Ashkenazic *Haggadot*. All old sources have והיא as first word of the paragraph, including Maimonides. The initial ו is dropped in most Oriental texts.

The *Midrash*

Since it was established that there is an obligation, spelled out in the Torah, to explain, or declare, the Exodus, it is clear that one has to look for such a declaration in the Torah itself. There is just one such declaration, *Deut.* 26:5-9, the declaration made when presenting First Fruits in the Temple. The centerpiece of the *Haggadah* is, therefore, based on that declaration. It was also noted before (Disgrace and Praise, p. 253) that *Deut.* 26:9 was the original *praise* concluding the recital. In the words of the *Mishnah* (*Pesaḥim* X,4),[211] "he explains from 'The Aramean is destroying my father' until he finishes the entire section *totally*." The word in italics is characteristic of the Babylonian version of the *Mishnah*. As a matter of fact, it has been pointed out by R. David Hoffmann that no current text has us finish the entire section. The complete text is preserved in the Tannaitic *Midrash* to Deuteronomy, *Sifry*. There we find essentially the current text of the *Haggadah*, but the introduction "Go and Learn" is replaced by a short statement discussed below and verse 9, not commented on in our

---

211 ודורש מארמי אובד אבי עד שיגמור כל הפרשה ***כולה***.

Haggadah texts, appears as: "'And He brought us to this place,' which means the Temple, 'and gave us this Land,' which means the Land of Israel." After the war of Bar Kokhba and the decision by rabbinic authorities to discourage the reestablishment of a Jewish Commonwealth by use of arms, this explanation was no longer desirable. In its place we find a lengthy discussion by later teachers about the number of plagues. As usual, the Babylonian text of the *Mishnah* shows the earlier form; this would date the introduction of the discussion of the number of plagues to after 218 C.E. when Rav brought the first version of the completed *Mishnah* to Babylonia. One might conjecture, although without any proof at all, that the invocation after the declaration of the eternal validity of the Covenant can serve as a counterbalance to the omission of *Deut.* 29:9 and dates to the same period.

In the entire recital, Ashkenazic and Sephardic sources quote each verse before the discussion; all ancient Oriental sources have the discussion only as in the Yemenite text.

Deut. 26:5

The first clause of *Deut.* 26:5 presents some difficulties. The most natural translation of ארמי אבד אבי וירד מצרימה is "My father has been a straying [*Jer.* 50:6; *Ps.* 119:176, or: an unlucky, *Job* 29:13, 31:19; *Prov.* 31:6] Aramean who then descended into Egypt," taking אבי "my father" as the subject, אבד "straying, unlucky" as adjective to ארמי "Aramean" with an implied copula in the past tense followed, as is the rule in biblical narrative, by the next clause in the imperfect, וירד, "he descended," ruled by the subject of the first clause. This is the translation preferred, e.g., by Ibn Ezra, Qimḥi, and S. R. Hirsch. The translation of the Septuagint:[212] "My father abandoned Syria and descended into Egypt" keeps one subject but is very difficult to read into the Hebrew. For the preceding attempts to classify as traditional interpretation, the Masoretic accents would have to be ארמי אבד אבי to be read *arammy ovēd, avy* when in fact they are ארמי אבד אבי *arammy, ovēd avy*. The only possible translation of the sentence with this punctuation is to postulate an otherwise undocumented transitive meaning of the verb stem אבד [parallel Arabic באד "to perish, become extinct," in the 4th (*af'al*) conjugation "to destroy, extirpate"] and to

212 Συρίαν ἀπέβαλεν ὁ πατήρ μου καὶ κατέβη εἰς Αἴγυπτον.

accept the interpretation of the *Haggadah*, *Targum Onqelos*:[213] "Laban the Aramean wanted to destroy my father; he then descended into Egypt" and the Arabic translation of the Torah by R. Saadia Gaon:[214] "Laban the Aramean (Armenian) almost succeeded to destroy my father," which leaves the second clause dangling, "so he descended into Egypt" with a change of subject (my father, object of the first clause, now is the subject of the second clause) and a most unusual imperfect following a present participle. Instead of the introductory clause comparing Laban (the Aramean, *Gen.* 25:20) to Pharaoh, *Sifry* (§301) starts with the explanation:[215] "'The Aramean is destroying my father; this teaches us that Jacob came to Syria to be ruined and Scripture holds Laban culpable as if he had destroyed him." Most medieval commentators agree that the source for the statement about Laban's evil intentions is *Gen.* 31:29, where Laban declares that "I have the power to ruin you." Since for literary reasons the section needs an introduction, the reference to Laban is made to precede the quote rather than follow it in genuine midrashic style. Even though all old Oriental sources (from Babylonia, Galilee, Egypt) follow the Yemenite text in not quoting the verses before the discussion, the style adopted by the *Haggadah* in contrast to its source makes the recitation of the verses natural. The introductory phrase "go [out] and learn" is the *Yerushalmi* equivalent of Babylonian **תא שמע**, "come and hear," which introduces Tannaitic statements in a talmudic discussion. This sentence, therefore, declares the following piece to be of Tannaitic origin. The epithet "the wicked" given Pharaoh in the Yemenite *Haggadah* appears already in R. Saadia Gaon's text.

He descended into Egypt. The author of *Shibbolë Haleqet* (p. 191)[216] points out that the assertion of a forced move is based on *Gen.* 46:3: "Do not be afraid to descend into Egypt"; since Jacob was afraid to go into Egypt he certainly did not go voluntarily. It is not necessary to assume with the author that he was afraid of actual enslavement but the circumstances of his burial (*Gen.* 50) show clearly that nobody could leave Egypt without an exit visum, difficult to obtain. The

---

213 לָבָן אֲרַמָּאָה בְּעָא לְאַבָּדָא יַת אַבָּא. וּנְחַת לְמִצְרַיִם.

214 אן לבן אלארמני כאד אן יביד אבי. . .

215 מלמד שלא ירד אבינו יעקב לארם אלא על מנת לאבד ומעלה עליו הכתוב כאילו ארמי אבד אבי איבדו.

216 ומנין שהיה אנוס שנאמר אל תירא מרדה מצרים, מכלל שהיה מתירא לירד מפני השעבוד.

Sephardic vocalization דִּבֵּר *dibbēr* is Masoretic (*Jer*. 5:13).[217] The unvocalized commentary of *Maḥzor Vitry* also points to *Jer*. 5:13 as the source of the expression in the *Haggadah*, but explains its meaning by דִּיבּוּר *dibbūr*.[218] It is clear then that *dibbēr* was the common text of all Jewish groups and that the reading *dibbūr* is a later adaptation to Ashkenazic rabbinic Hebrew. The paragraph is missing in *Sifry*, an old Gaonic text (*Ginze Schechter* II, p. 260), and Maimonides. It is found in R. Saadia Gaon's text and in a late *Midrash, Pesiqta Zuṭrata.*

He dwelt there temporarily. The verse *Gen*. 47:4 is somewhat ambiguous since it contains both the root גור "to have temporary residence" and ישב "to stay, to reside." E. Täubler notes, on the margin of his *Biblia Hebraica* to *Jud*. 4:2, that ישב mostly means "to have as headquarters, as place of business." This meaning applies well here in view of the need to keep shepherds out of Egypt proper (*Gen*. 46:34). The words added in small print were introduced by Heidenheim; they are not found in any Ashkenazic *Haggadah* printed before 1800 but are in a few manuscripts, mostly from Hamburg. The shorter text is from R. Saadia Gaon and Maimonides; the longer version is found in R. Amram Gaon.

With few men. The 70 souls are enumerated in *Gen*. 46:8-27 (Jacob, 32 descendants of Leah, 16 of Zilpah, 14 of Rachel, 7 of Bilhah). Note that the descendants of a maid are always one-half of those of her mistress.

There he became a people. That the Israelites were distinguished as a people is implied by *Ex*. 1:9 where the king of Egypt is reported to have said to his people, "The nation of the Children of Israel is more numerous than we are." The talmudic tradition (*Mekhilta deR. Ishmael, Bo,* p. 14)[219] asserts that the Israelite people was redeemed from Egypt because they did not assimilate; they changed neither names nor language, nor did they engage in illicit relations (with one exception, *Lev*. 24:10-11), nor did they inform against one another.

---

217 וְהַדִּבֵּר אֵין בָּהֶם, "the [divine] Word is not in them." Cf. also *Ps*. 144:8,11: דִּבֶּר־שָׁוְא "vain proclamations."

218 אנוס היה יעקב אבינו שנאנס על פי הדיבור של הק' שהוא אומר לרדת. וירד משמע על כרחו מדלא כתיב ויצא. הדיבר לשון המקרא הוא, והדבר אין בהם.

219 רבי אליעזר הקפר ברבי אומר וכי לא היה בידם של ישראל ארבע מצות שאין כל העולם כדאי בהם שלא נחשדו על העריות. ולא על לשון הרע. ולא שנו את שמם. ולא שנו את לשונם.

Great. The texts are divided about the position of "great," whether it belongs to "there he became a great people" or to the next clause, "great, strong." The first alternative is found in *Sifry*, the *siddurim* of R. Saadia Gaon and R. Amram Gaon, and most Ashkenazic (Northern and Italian) manuscripts and prints. The second alternative is that of Maimonides and all printed Oriental versions. The Sephardic manuscript and printed versions repeat "great" in both positions. The division of the Masoretic text, לגוי גדול, עצום ורב, as well as the absence of a connective between "great" and "strong," confirm the first alternative as traditional interpretation of the text. The translation should be, "there he became a great people, powerful and numerous." According to Rashi (*Maḥzor Vitry*, p. 293) the expression "great people" has nothing to do with numbers but refers to the Israelites staying together in a well-defined tribal territory.

Strong. According to the Talmud (*b. Berakhot* 7a; cf. *Shĕmot rabbah* 1[7]),[220] "numerous" as in *Ex.* 1:7 means a minumum of 600,000 souls. The standard interpretation of *Ex.* 1:7 (*Mekhilta deR. Ishmael Bo*, p. 42)[221] is that the people grew to be so large because sixtuple births were a common occurrence. This is a figure of speech that must not be taken verbally. Every Israelite family in Egypt was encouraged to have as many children as possible since its state subsidy was given as Aid to Dependent Children (*Gen.* 47:12): "Joseph provided for his father and brothers, and all of his father's family, food according to the children's mouths." If a generation is counted as 30 years, then in order to increase from 70 to 600,000 in seven generations, each male on the average has to have four surviving male children. The interpretation of the Jerusalem *Talmud* in a similar situation is that the women had easy pregnancies and painless births (*y. Yevamot* IV,11 6b; parallel *b. Berakhot* 63b).

And numerous. In all old sources, the reference is exclusively to *Ez.* 16:7. Some Sephardic texts of the fifteenth century already have a reference to verse 6. The inclusion of that verse was made common by the students of R. Isaac Luria (*Eẓ Ḥayyim, Pesaḥ*); the order is inverted in Ashkenazic ḥasidic *Haggadot* since the reference "numerous" obviously refers to verse 7. In the theory of *ARI*, the "bloods" are the ungodly forces that hinder redemption.

---

220 (ד"ה כג יז) ובני רחביה רבו למעלה וכו' ותני ר' יוסף למעלה מששים רבוא אתיא רביה רביה כתיב הכא רבו למעלה וכתיב התם ובני ישראל פרו וישרצו וירבו.

221 וכתיב ובני ישראל פרו וישרצו שהיתה אשה אחת יולדת ששה בנים בכרס אחד.

The chapter in Ezekiel is an allegory in which the Jewish people is depicted first as a growing young girl and then as a woman. On the surface, the reference here is simply to the simile of the grasses on the field, which contain an enormous number of blades. The simple interpretation is that the growth of the people was not interrupted by their enslavement. Such a simple statement cannot account for the rest of the prophet's imagery. The oldest Aramaic paraphrase of the Prophets, the *Targum* of Jonathan ben Uziel, always preferring meaning to plain text, translates *Ez.* 16:6-7 in the spirit of the interpretation implied by the *Haggadah*:[222] (v. 6) "The remembrance of the Covenant of your forefathers rose before Me; I appeared to redeem you since it was clear before Me that you were tortured in your slavery, and I said to you: by the blood of your circumcision I shall have mercy upon you, and I said to you: by the blood of the *Pesaḥ* sacrifice I shall redeem you." (v. 7): "I made you numerous like the grasses of the field, you grew to be many and strong, and you became families and tribes. By the good deeds of your forefathers, the time of the deliverance of your people approached while you were enslaved and tortured." The interpretation of the feeding breast as the good deeds that sustain the world, one of the basic tenets of the Kabbalah firmly rooted in talmudic theology (see the chapter "The Prayer"), has two different interpretations in talmudic tradition.

The first group of interpretations follows the imagery of the Song of Songs. The *Midrash* (*Cant. rabbah* 8[9])[223] interprets the verses (*Cant.* 8:9-10) "We have a small sister (אחות) yet without breasts; what shall we do for our sister on the day she has to be spoken for? If

---

222 וְעַל דִּכְרָן קְיָם אֲבָהָתְכוֹן קֳדָמַי אִתְגְלֵיתִי לְמִפְרַקְכוֹן אֲרֵי גְלֵי קֳדָמַי אֲרֵי אַתּוּן מְעֻנַן בְּשִׁעְבּוּדְכוֹן וַאֲמָרִית לְכוֹן בִּדְמָא דְמְהוּלְתָּא אָחוּס עֲלֵיכוֹן וַאֲמָרִית לְכוֹן בְּדַם פִּסְחָא אֶפְרוֹק יַתְכוֹן. רִבְבַת כְּצִמְחֵי חַקְלָא יְהַבְתִּיכוֹן וּסְגִיתוּן וְתַקִיפְתּוּן וַהֲוֵיתוּן לְזַרְעִין וּלְשִׁבְטִין וּבְעוֹבָדֵי אֲבָהָתְכוֹן תַּקְנַיָא עִידַן פּוּרְקַן כְּנִישְׁתְּכוֹן מְטָא אֲרֵי אַתּוּן מְשַׁעְבְּדִין וּמְעֻנַן.

223 ר' ברכיה פתר קרא באברהם אבינו. אחות לנו קטנה זה אברהם אבינו שנ' אחד היה אברהם ויירש את הארץ. ואיחה כל העולם לפני הקב"ה. בר קפרא אמר כאדם שהוא מאחה הקרע. עד שהוא קטן היה עסוק במצות ומעשים טובים. ושדים אין לה שעדיין לא בא לכלל מצות ומעשים טובים. מה נעשה לאחותינו ביום שידובר בה. ביום שגזר נמרוד הרשע ואמר לירד לכבשן האש. אם חומה היא נבנה עליה טירת כסף. אם חומה היא זה אברהם. אמר הקב"ה אם מעמיד הוא דברים כחומה. נבנה עליה טירת כסף נצילנו ונבנה אותו בעולם. ואם דלת היא נצור עליה לוח ארז. אם דל הוא ממצות וטלטל מעשיו כדלת. נצור עליה לוח ארז. מה צורה זו אינה מתקיימת אלא לשעה אחת. כך איני מתקיים עליו אלא לשעה אחת. אני חומה. אמר אברהם לפני הקב"ה אני חומה ואעמיד מעשים טובים כחומה. ושדי כמגדלות שאני עתיד להעמיד כתים כתים וחבורות של צדיקים כיוצא בי בעולמך. אז הייתי בעיניו כמוצאת שלום. אמר לו הקב"ה כשם שירדת לכבשן האש כך אני מוציאך בשלום הדא הוא דכתיב אני יי אשר הוצאתיך מאור כשדים.

she is a wall, we shall build on her a tower of silver; if she is a door, we shall fix on her a plate of cedar" parallel to the *Targum* to Ezekiel: "We have a small אחות [lexical meaning 'sister' but word taken here as 'unification,' from the root אח, 'to be brotherly,' with ות as suffix of abstraction]; this is Abraham about whom it is said (*Ez.* 33:24): 'Abraham was unique [אחד] and he inherited the Land'; he united [אחה] the earth dwellers before God. Bar Qapara said, like a taylor who mends [אחה, 'reunites'] a torn garment. When he was still small he was occupied with God's commandments and good works. 'Yet without breasts,' he was not commanded yet any commandments or good works. 'What shall we do to our אחות on the day that he will be spoken about,' on the day that Nimrod the wicked gave the order to throw Abraham into the fiery oven. 'If he is a wall, We shall build on him a tower of silver.' God said: if he stands strong like a wall, We shall build the world on him. 'If he is a דלת ["door," but taken here to mean "poor risk" from root דל "meagre, poor," and again ת as suffix forming an abstract notion], we shall fix on him a plate of cedar'; if he is poor [דל] in good works and movable in his behavior like a door, then, just as the wooden plate is good only for a temporary fix, I shall keep him up only temporarily. (*Cant.* 8:11) 'I am a wall.' Abraham said before God: I am a wall and I am preserving the good works like a wall; 'my breasts are like towers'; among my descendants there will be many groups and associations of just people who will be the foundation of the world like me. 'Then I was finding peace in His eyes'; God told him: Just as you went into the fiery oven so I shall lead you out of it in peace as it is said (*Gen.* 15:7), 'I am the Lord who led you out of the fire of the Chaldeans.'" (For the story of Abraham and Nimrod, see the Appendix.)

The second group is based on a talmudic passage (*b. Soṭah* 11b)[224] that explains why Israel is represented as a woman at the Exodus: "R. Akiba preached: Israel was freed from Egypt through the good works of the saintly women of that generation. When they went to draw water, God made small fish swim into their pitchers; they were drawing half water and half fishes. They went and boiled two pots, one of hot water and one of fish, which they brought to their

---

224 דרש ר' עקיבא בשכר נשים צדקניות שבאותו הדור נגאלו ישראל ממצרים. בשעה שהיו הולכות לשאוב מים הקב"ה מזמן להם דגים קטנים בכדיהן ושואבות מחצה מים ומחצה דגים ובאות ושופתות שתי קדירות אחת של חמין ואחת של דגים ומוליכות אצל בעליהן לשדה ומרחיצות אותן וסכות אותן ומאכילות אותן ונזקקות להן בין שפתים שנ' אם תשכבון בין שפתים וגו', בשכר תשכבון בין שפתים זכו ישראל לביזת מצרים שנ' כנפי יונה נחפה בכסף ואברותיה בירקרק חרוץ.

husbands in the fields. There they washed their husbands, rubbed them with oil, fed them and gave them to drink, and slept with them between the hedges as it is written (*Ps.* 68:14), 'If you sleep between the hedges.' As reward for sleeping between the hedges [a secret place, not open to public view; Rashi *ad loc.*] did Israel receive the spoils of Egypt, as it is said (*Ps.* 68:14), 'dove's wings covered with silver and her limbs with fine gold.' The women returned to their homes pregnant; at the time of delivery they went and gave birth on the fields under the apple tree, as it says (*Cant.* 8:5), 'Under the apple tree I woke you up'; God sent an angel from Heaven to clean and straighten the children just as the midwife straightens the child, as it is said (*Ez.* 16:4), 'And your birth, the day you were born, your navel string was not cut and you were not washed in water for smoothness, etc.' Then the angel collected for them two cakes, one of oil and one of honey, as it is said (*Deut.* 32:13), 'He lets him suck honey from the rock and oil from pebbles.'[225] When the Egyptians noticed the babies, they came to kill them; by a miracle they were swallowed up by the ground. The Egyptians then brought oxen and plowed on their backs, as it is said (*Ps.* 16:7), 'The plowers plowed my back.' After the Egyptians went away, the children sprouted like grass on the fields, as it is said (*Ez.* 16:7), 'I made you numerous like the plants of the field,' and after they grew up they came in flocks to their houses, as it is said (*loc. cit.*), 'You did increase and grow, you came with greatest ornaments [עדי עדים].' Do not read here עדי עדים but עדרי עדרים 'in herds, herds.' When God appeared to them on the Red Sea they recognized him first, as it is said (*Ex.* 15:2), 'This is my God and I shall praise Him beautiful.'"[226]

The sermon on *Ps.* 68:14 is the basis of the Yemenite insert to the litany "Dayyenu" later in the *Haggadah*. The Septuagint translation of *Ez.* 16:7 is quite literal except that for עדי עדים they read ערי ערים "in cities,"[227] which by modern scholars has been taken as an

---

225 וכיון שמתעברות באות לבתיהם וכיון שמגיע זמן מולדיהן הולכות ויולדות בשדה תחת התפוח שנ' תחת התפוח עוררתיך וגו', והקב"ה שולח מלאך משמי מרום ומנקר אותן ומשפר אותן כחיה זו שמשפרת את הילד שנ' ומולדותיך ביום הולדת אותך לא כרת שרך ובמים לא רוחצת למשעי וגו', ומלקט להן שני עיגולין אחד של שמן ואחד של דבש שנ' ויניקיהו דבש מסלע ושמן מחלמיש צור.

226 וכיון שמכירין בהן מצרים באין להורגן ונעשה להן נס ונבלעין בקרקע, ומביאין שוורים וחורשין על גבן שנ' על גבי חרשו חורשים וגו'. לאחר שהולכין היו מבצבצין ויוצאין כעשב השדה שנ' רבבה כצמח השדה נתתיך, וכיון שמתגדלין באין עדרים עדרים לבתיהן, שנ' ותרבי ותגדלי ותבואי בעדי עדים, אל תקרי בעדי עדים אלא בעדרי עדרים, וכשנגלה הקב"ה על הים הכירוהו תחלה שנ' זה אלי ואנוהו.

227 πληθύνου. καθὼς ἡ ἀνατολὴ τοῦ ἀγροῦ δέδωκά σε. καὶ ἐπληθύνθης καὶ ἐμεγαλύνθης καὶ εἰσῆλθες εἰς πόλεις πόλεων. οἱ μαστοί σου

example of misreading ר for ד or as a mistake. Since the Septuagint translation of Prophets also may be assumed to have been edited, such a mistake is unlikely. It seems that the Septuagint version is an early example, preceding R. Akiba by centuries, of the interpretation of *Ez.* 16:7 reported in the *Talmud*.

The *Mekhilta* (*deR. Ishmael, Bo,* p. 62)[228] reports first in the name of R. Eleazar ben Azariah the statement from *Midrash Cant. rabbah*, based on *Ps.* 105:42–43, then in the name of R. Shimon ben Yoḥai[229] an interpretation based on *Ez.* 16:5 following R. Akiba, but the *Mekhilta* then adds a third opinion, of Rabbi (Yehuda the Prince),[230] based on *Ez.* 20:7–9, that the Exodus was a pure act of divine grace, not a reward for merit. Rabbi therefore must take the quote from Ezekiel in the *Haggadah* at pure face value without allegorical interpretation.

The meaning of עדי, translated in the text as "ornament," is a matter of controversy among medieval grammarians. There is no doubt that עדי in *Ex.* 33:6 and *Ez.* 23:40 means "ornament." The same meaning is accepted by Yehuda Ḥayuj and David Qimḥi also for *Ez.* 16:7; the last named author (*Mikhlol, s.v. 'dh*) puts in the same category the heading *'ēdūt* for "Psalm of Splendor" (*Ps.* 80:1). Jonah ibn Janaḥ (*Sefer Hashorashim, s.v. 'd,* p.355) derives the word in *Ez.* 16:7 from עד "culmination" and explains that וַתָּבֹאִי בַּעֲדִי עֲדָיִים "you came to the ultimate culmination, meaning the total perfection and absence of blemish in the appearance of a girl."[231] But *s.v. 'dy* (*loc. cit.*, p. 356), he derives it from Arabic عَدْ "to be quick" and explains the verse to mean "you grew quickly."[232]

There is a singular inconsistency in the use of כְּמוֹ or כְּמָה for "as" in the Livorno *mahzor* text which at this point switches from the

---

ἀνωρθώθησαν, καὶ ἡ θρίξ σου ανέτειλεν, σὺ δὲ ἦσθα γυμνὴ καὶ ἀσχημονοῦσα.

228 ר' אלעזר בן עזריה אומר בזכות אברהם אבינו הוציאם ממצרים שנ' כי זכר את דבר קדשו את אברהם עבדו ואומר ויוציא עמו בששון ברנה.

229 ר' שמעון בן יוחי אומר בזכות המילה הוציאם הב"ה שנ' ואעבור עליך ואראך מתבוססת בדמיך וכו'.

230 רבי אומר . . . סוררים היו אלא שנוהג עמהם בכושרות וכן הוא אומר . . . איש שקוצי עיניו לא השליכו ואת גילולי מצרים לא עזבו ואעש למען שמי לבלתי החל לעיני הגוים אשר המה בתוכם אשר נודעתי עליהם לעיניהם להוציאם מארץ מצרים.

231 ותבאי בעדי עדים, הגעת לתכלית התכליות כלומר תכלית השלמות והתמימות ויפעת הבחורות.

232 ותבאי בעדי עדיים אבל ענינו דומה ללשון הערב שהוא ענין המרוצה והמהירות בהליכה כלומר שגדלת והגעת אל הבחרות במהרה ובזמן קרוב.

Galilean to the Babylonian form. This is not found in earlier Italian prints and is similar to the inconsistency noted earlier for the Amsterdam Ashkenazic text.

Deut. 26:6

The Egyptians gave us a bad name, i..e., they invented a pretext for the oppression. It is the characterization of an oppressive regime that nobody can leave the country without a permit, which is given only in cases of national interest. Otherwise, they simply could have expelled the Israelites. Even Joseph needed a special permit from Pharao to leave the country for his father's burial (*Gen.* 50:4–6.)

They mistreated us. The *Midrash* (*Ex. rabbah* 1[15])[233] explains that the policy was to require so much work that the men had to sleep at their workplace; the intention was to prevent them from having children. In the *Midrash*, this piece is the introduction to the sermon of R. Akiba on the essential role of women in the Exodus and the explanation of the large increase in population under duress. "Mistreatment and hard labor" is not only unusual and excessive but also work (*loc. cit.)*[234] for which the workers were neither trained nor fit.

The standard talmudic translation of Pithom and Ra'amses is Tanis (in the Eastern Delta of the Nile) and Pelusium (on the shore of the Meditteranean, near today's Port Said).

Deut. 26:7

We cried to the Lord. The *Midrash (Ex. rabbah* 1[42]) notes that in *Ex.* 2:23 one should not translate "many days," just as in *Lev.* 15:25 "many days" means just three days; it is not reasonable to assume that the king of Egypt was known to be dying for a very long time. A probable interpretation of the verse is that with the continuation of the policy of enslavement under a new ruler, the people realized finally that they were confronted not with the whims of one ruler but

---

233 ד' גזירות גזר פרעה עליהם. בתחלה גזר וצוה לנוגשים שיהיו דוחקין בהן כדי שיהיו עושין הסכום שלהם. ולא יהיו ישנים בבתיהם. והוא חשב למעטן מפריה ורביה אמר מתך שאינן ישנין בבתיהן אינן מולידין. . . . והיו ישנין על הארץ. א״ל הא־להים אני אמרתי לאברהם שאני מרבה בניו ככוכבים . . . ואתם מתחכמים להן שלא ירבו נראה איזה דבר עומד או שלי או שלכם, מיד **וכאשר יענו אותו כן ירבה.**

234 ר' שמואל בר נחמן א״ר יונתן מלמד שהיו מחליפין מלאכת אנשים לנשים ומלאכת נשים לאנשים.

with an unchanging government policy. They turned to God only after their political hopes were dashed permanently.

He saw our deprivation. The *Talmud* takes the biblical עני in the sense of mishnaic intensive (*pi'el*) form עִנּוּי, "deprivation"; otherwise, one would have to translate "poverty." In the discussion of the deprivations that a Jew is required to accept on the Day of Atonement (deprivation from food, drink, washing, ointment, and sex), the *Talmud* (*b. Yoma* 74b)[235] quotes the *Haggadah* as proof that *'innūy* means forced deprivation from sexual fulfillment. In the same discussion, the *Talmud*[236] translates *Gen.* 31:50 by: "If you should deprive my daughters [of their right to sexual fulfillment] by taking additional wives . . ." and *Gen.* 34:2 by "'He took her, slept with her, and then deprived her" by not satisfying the desires Shekhem had awakened in Dinah, or by using her for sexual practices that satisfy the male but not the female. The second interpretation is rejected by Rashi in his commentary on the *Talmud* but accepted in his commentary on the Torah. In any case, the intentional failure of a husband to satisfy the sexual desires of his wife is sinful. The Egyptians' organization of the Hebrews' slave labor was intended to deprive them of family life; this makes the Egyptian organizers guilty of a collective sin. The verse quoted (*Ex.* 2:25) as proof means that God came to know something that only God, but not man, can see, and sex is the prime example of nonpublic activity. The *Targum Yerushalmi* to *Ex.* 2:25[237] takes that verse to mean that everybody had secretly abjured the idolatry and abominations of Egypt without telling anybody (an implicit polemic against the opponents of the opinion of R. Akiba on *Ez.* 16:6 above). (Naḥmanides [*Gen.* 18:21], based on the Gaonic *Sefer Habahir* [§77],[238] declares that God's, the Omniscient's, knowledge referred to in Scripture always means "God's mercy.")

And our oppression, this is the suffering. The *Targumim* use דחק, used in the *Haggadah* to *explain* the expression לחץ in *Deut.* 26:7,

---

235 ונילף מענוי מצרים דכתיב וירא את ענינו ואמרינן זו פרישות דרך ארץ.

236 תשמיש המטה דאיכא ענוי מנא לן דכתיב אם תענה את בנותי ואם תקח נשים, אם תענה מתשמיש ואם תקח מצרות. ואימא אידי ואידי בצרות. מי כתיב אם תקח? ואם תקח כתיב! . . . אמר ליה רב פפא לאביי הא תשמיש גופא איקרי ענוי דכתיב וישכב אותה ויענה, אמר ליה התם שעינה מביאות אחרות.

237 וַחֲמָא יי צַעַר שִׁעֲבוּדְהוֹן דִּבְנֵי יִשְׂרָאֵל וּגְלֵי קֳדָמוֹי יַת תְּיוּבְתָא דְעָבְדוּ בְטוּמְרָא דְּלָא יָדְעוּ אִינַשׁ בְּחַבְרֵיהּ.

238 ומאי תודיע, תרחם. כד״א וירא אלהים את בני ישראל וידע אלהים.

as *translation* of that word. The same root is used in *Ex.* 6:6 as translation of סבל "to bear, endure, suffer." Therefore, the second meaning has to be chosen to give meaning to the interpretation of the Haggadah; otherwise the sentence would be a tautology. The suffering, again, is the forced construction work by people trained in other trades, and the production of adobe bricks without straw (Rashi in *Maḥzor Vitry*, p. 293).[239] The Hebrew sentence וְאֶת לַחֲצֵינוּ זֶה הַדְּחַק is probably inspired by *Jud.* 2:18, כִּי יִנָּחֵם יי מִנַּאֲקָתָם, מִפְּנֵי לֹחֲצֵיהֶם וְדֹחֲקֵיהֶם, "because the Lord showed mercy in view of their prayers, [and saved them] from their oppressors and afflicters." The Aramaic *Targum Yonathan* renders לֹחֲצֵיהֶם וְדֹחֲקֵיהֶם by דַּחֲקֵיהוֹן וּמְשַׁעְבְּדֵיהוֹן, using Aramaic דחק as translation of Hebrew לחץ and משעבד "enslaver" as Aramaic translation of Hebrew דחק. The differences in vocalization of דחק go back to talmudic usage. The Yemenite (and old Italian) vocalization *dōḥaq*, the biblical Hebrew form for the meaning "oppressor," is the preferred talmudic form for the meaning "straits, pressure," if the word appears without definite article (cf. Levy's Dictionary, I 390b). The usual form of the talmudic word with Hebrew definite article is *dĕḥaq*, the standard Aramaic vocalization; this is found in the printed Sephardic and all older Ashkenazic texts. A Hebrew segolate form *daḥaq* appears sporadically, so in the Amsterdam *Haggadah* of 1662, an Ashkenazic print oblivious of *dagesh forte*, and some Oriental manuscripts. The form *dĕḥāq*, correct according to the rules of biblical Hebrew and found in *Haggadot* of Heidenheim and his imitators, is a modern invention. It is clear from the defective spelling in the texts of R. Saadia Gaon and *Maḥzor Vitry* that they read *dĕḥaq* or *daḥaq;* Maimonides has *dōḥaq*. So it seems that all forms except *dĕḥāq* are legitimate dialectal forms of the same word.

Deut. 26:8

The Lord led us out of Egypt. The Septuagint translation of the verse:[240] "The Lord *himself* led us out of Egypt with His great strength and strong hand and *His own* outstretched arm and great apparitions and signs and wonders," shows that the emphasis on God's own action, not through the intermediary of angels or human messengers, is a very old tradition. A number of Oriental (Yemenite and Iraqi) rituals have here an aggadic insert in which God tells the

---

239 הדחק. תוכן לבנים.

240 καὶ ἐξήγαγεν ἡμᾶς κύριος ἐξ Αἰγύπτου αὐτός ἐν ἰσχύι μεγάλῃ καὶ ἐν χειρὶ κραταιᾷ καὶ ἐν βραχίονι αὐτοῦ τῷ ὑψηλῷ καὶ ἐν ὁράμασιν μεγάλοις καὶ ἐν σημείοις καὶ ἐν τέρασιν.

angels not to interfere in Egypt. This insert is not mentioned in our old Oriental sources but it must have been part of most *Haggadot* in the late first millennium C.E. The source of the insert is not the *Sifry* but the *Mekhilta* (*deR. Shimon ben Yoḥai* to *Ex.* 12:2). All rituals depending on the authority of Rashi (i.e., Ashkenazic and Sephardic) have discarded the passage because of Rashi's strong opposition to the anthropomorphisms and the angelology of the insert (*Maḥzor Vitry*, p. 293),[241] which in his opinion diminishes God's glory, and the source is suspect since it is not found in his *Mekhilta* (*deR. Ishmael*). He also reports that in the land of Israel the insert was formally banned but that it was said in Provence. The insert is mentioned with approval by Yehuda Halevi in his *Kuzari* (III,§73) but, not being part of one of the three model texts of R. Amram Gaon, R. Saadia Gaon, and Maimonides, it does not appear in commentaries. The parallel insert of the Ashkenazic and Sephardic rituals is not found in any manuscript of either *Sifry* or *Mekhilta*, nor in any other old Oriental source. It was accepted by almost all Oriental communities when after the expulsion of the Jews from Spain and the rise of the kabbalistic school of Safed, the Sephardic ritual supplanted most local Oriental prayer rituals. The assertion, "I and not an angel" seems to contradict *Ex.* 12:23 where it is asserted that God, seeing the blood of the *Pesaḥ* sacrifice on the doorposts, will not let the destroying angel enter Jewish houses. Rabbi E. R. Dangoor (*Adi Zahav*, *Ex.* 12:12) takes the expression in the *Haggadah* to mean that no angel could act without direct instructions from God, superseding the action of natural law. All Divine action in this world is called "angel." The messenger, with definite article, is probably Moses; cf. *Num.* 20:16. The "judgments" are in plural since they varied to cause their worshipers maximum embarrassment (*Mekhilta deR. Ishmael*, p. 24).[242]

The treatment of the demonstrative pronoun is varied in Ashkenazic texts. The Amsterdam text of 1695 has everywhere feminine זוֹ; eighteenth-century prints vary between זוֹ and זוּ; Heidenheim has systematically a neuter זוּ, in that he is followed by most modern Ashkenazic texts. Sephardic and Oriental texts employ always grammatically correct זוֹ (f.) and זֶה (m.).

---

241 אמרו כשירד. אינו מסדר האגדה ואינו כתוב במכילתי עם שאר דברי אגדה הכתובים על דברי ארמי אובד אבי. ואותו כקל וחומר האמור והלא עבדיו מקיפין אותו כדי שלא ימצא צער בגופו. ואתה מלך. אטו מי איכא צערא קמי קב״ה. והכת' הוד והדר לפניו. לפיכך אינו עיקר ואין ר' רגיל לאומרו. . . . ובארץ ישראל גזרו שלא לאומרו, ובפרוונצא נהגו לאומרו.

242 שפטים משונים זה מזה; של אבן היתה נמסת ושל עץ היתה נרקבת ושל מתכת נעשית חררה.

Outstretched arm. The sword here is God's, bringing a plague over Jerusalem as punishment for David's census. So the *arm* is a plague brought on and halted by the action of God alone (see the inserted *Himself, His own,* in the Septuagint translation), whereas *hand* (a word often meaning "left hand") is the (animal) plague brought on through the announcement of Moses.

Great apparition. The importance of *Deut* 4:34 is explained in the Midrash (*Gen. rabbah* 2[6]; *Cant. rabbah* 44[22]):[243] "Rebbi Yudan said: From 'To come, to take for himself . . .' to '. . . great apparitions' there are 72 letters, and if somebody protests that there are 75 letters, tell him that the second גוי ["people"] is not counted. Rebbi Avin said: He delivered them with His name because the Name of the Holy, praise to Him, is 72 names." The statement of the *Haggadah* therefore means that God revealed Himself in the power of His secret name. The 72 Names are explained by Rashi (*b. Sukkah* 45a) as being contained in the verses *Ex.* 14:19–21, each of which has 72 letters. If the verses are written on top of one another, the first and third in the right order but the second in reverse order, each column of three letters forms one Name.[244] Of these, the first (*wāho*) and the 36th (*any*) are used in the invocation recited during the procession with willow twigs on Tabernacles (*Mishnah Sukkah* IV.4),[245] the 72nd and last (*mōm*) is the Divine Name underlying the Aramaic oath formula, masculine (מומי) in Galilean Aramaic (*y. Nedarim* I,2 37a) and feminine (*mōmĕtā*) in Babylonian (*b. Bava Qama* 114a).

Signs. By the biblical account, the staff was a heavenly instrument. The traditional view of the staff is given in *Targum Yerushalmi, Ex.* 14:21:[246] "Moses lifted his hand over the Sea with the great and precious staff which had been created from the Beginning [i.e., at the end of the Sixth Day of Creation, *Avot* V,9]; carved in it are

---

243 א״ר יודן מלבא לקחת לו גוי ועד מוראים גדולים עֹבֿ אותיות הן ואם יאמר לך אדם עֹהֿ הם אמור לו צא מהן גוי שני שאינו מן המנין. א״ר אבין בשמו גאלן ששמו של הקב״ה עֹבֿ שמות הן.

244 ויסעמלאכהאלהימההלכלפנימחנהישראלוילכמאחריהמויסעעמודהעננמפניהמויעמדמאחריהמ
הלילהלכהזולאהזוברקאלוהלילהתאראיוכשחהוןנעהיהיולארשיהנחמניבומירצמהנחמניבאביו
ויטמשהאתידועלהימויולכיהוהאתהימברוחקדימעזהכלהלילהוישמאתהימלחרבהויבקעוהמים

245 ר׳ יהודה אומר אני והו הושיעה נא.

246 וְאַרְכִין מֹשֶׁה יַת יָדֵיהּ עַל יַמָּא בְּחוּטְרָא רַבָּא וְיַקִּירָא דְאִיתְבְּרִי מִן שֵׁרוּיָא וּבֵיהּ חָקִיק וּמְפָרַשׁ שְׁמָא רַבָּא וְיַקִּירָא וְעֵישַׂרְתֵּי אָתְוָתָא דִי מְחָא יַת מִצְרָאֵי וּתְלַת אַבְהָת עָלְמָא וְשִׁית אִימְהָתָא וּתְרֵיסַר שִׁבְטוֹי דְיַעֲקֹב.

the Great and Explicit Name [of God], the Ten Signs that hit the Egyptians, the three fathers of the world [Abraham, Isaac, Jacob], the six mothers [Sarah, Rebecca, Rachel, Leah, Bilhah, Zilpah], and the twelve tribes of Jacob." The *Targum* implies that "the Ten Plagues" is the valid interpretation of "signs," the staff being the instrument that made the plagues supernatural.

In the *Seder* of all Jewish groups except the Western Ashkenazic, one pours a drop of wine out of one's cup for each of the three expressions "blood, fire, colums of smoke," the Ten Plagues, and the three abbreviations. In most groups, one dips one's finger in the glass and lifts one drop that is dropped onto one's plate; a few, mostly Oriental groups, and the followers of Rabbi A. I. Kook, pour from cup to plate or from cup to another cup. Western Ashkenazic Jews follow the instructions of Heidenheim (older Western *Haggadot* do not mention the dipping); Heidenheim in this follows the marginal glosses to the *Sefer Haminhagim* of R. Eisik Tyrna (p. 50, #98),[247] the main source of the Eastern Ashkenazic *Minhag*; all other groups follow the the main sources of the Western Ashkenazic customs, *MaHaRIL* and *Yosif Omeẓ* (#759). The dipping is first mentioned in the (late-fourteenth-century) Ashkenazic text *Amarkal*, who ascribes the custom to the circle of the German Ḥasidim. A complete explanation is given in *MaHaRIL*, a collection by a student of R. Jacob Segal Molin (p. קז, #27):[248] "R. Jacob Segal said that when during the recitation of the *Haggadah* one comes to 'blood, fire, and columns of smoke,' one should lift with one's finger a drop from one's cup, and later on for the Ten Plagues and the three abbreviations, for a total of 16 drops corresponding to the 16 faces [of the four heavenly animals in the vision of Ezekiel, *Ez.* 1]; [this explanation is from] *Roqeaḥ*, and other reasons are also given there. Similarly, R. Shalom [of Wiener Neustadt, teacher of Eisik Tyrna and Jacob Molin] did pour a drop from his cup for each of the Ten Plagues; he said that that was the *minhag* of *RAVIA*. He gave as reason that with this action we want to ask that we should be saved from all this but it should fall on our enemies since the Four Cups are for the success of Israel." The language of the

---

247 כשמונה י' מכות אז יכניס אצבעו לכוס ויזרוק חוץ על כל מכה ומכה (ראבי״ה) ומצאתי שזורקין באצבע קטנה שנקראת זרת.

248 אמר מהר״י סג״ל כשאומר בהגדה דם ואש ותמרות עשן יטיף באצבעו מכוסו לחוץ באומרו כל תיבה פעם אחת. וכן כשאמר דצ״ך עד״ש באח״ב בין בפרט בין בכלל ס״ה י״ו פעמים נגד י״ו פנים, רוקח. ועוד טעמים יש שם. וכן מהר״ש כשאמר דם צפרדע כו' שוטף בכל תיבה ותיבה פעם אחת מן הכוס לחוץ. ואמר שכן נהג רבי״ה, ונראה לו הטעם דר״ל מכל אלו יצילנו ויבואו על שונאינו דהא הכוסות להצלחה לישראל.

first version of *MaHaRIL* is copied by R. Moshe Isserles in his glosses to the *Shulḥan 'Arukh* (§473, #7); this is the version generally accepted also by non-Ashkenazic groups.

The existing versions of the books *Roqeaḥ* and *RAVIA* fail to mention the lifting or pouring of drops of wine. It can be argued that our versions were edited from defective manuscripts; since Jewish books in Europe were favorite targets of book burnings organized by the Inquisition, such a possibility is always present. However, in the case here the attribution to *Roqeaḥ* and *RAVIA* is unlikely since these authors require a benediction for the washing of the hands before dipping the vegetable. This implies that they require that the *Seder* be conducted in accordance with the rules of ritual purity that were followed in the Temple. These rules exclude touching the wine with one's hands without washing since nobody was watching his hands during the recital of the *Haggadah*. The attribution to *RAVIA* is clearly a misreading of the *Amarkal* text;[249] the reference to *RAVIA* is to his discussion (*RAVIA*, vol. 1, §168) of the old French custom to recite a benediction for both parts of *Hallel* during the *Seder;* according to *Amarkal*, the French custom was still followed in thirteenth-century Germany by many authorities. The reference to *Roqeaḥ* is buttressed by reference to an impressive array of names of the German *Ḥasidim*; the reference seems to be genuine and taken from a text of Eleazar Roqeaḥ other than his main book. Since the mystical *Roqeaḥ* will not exclude that a mystical custom, in this case a reference to God's sword, may override a rule of law, the attribution of the custom to the circle of R. Yehuda the Pious seems genuine. But even in the form of pouring, the usage is questionable since the wine spill on one's plate is a permanent source of pollution. In some Oriental rituals, e.g., Djerba and Bombay, the celebrant only spills wine 16 times from his cup into another cup. This is the Yemenite custom following the *ARI*. In Bombay, the celebrant is then required to wash his hands before he wipes the rim of his cup and refills the cup. This

---

249 מנהג אבותינו כן וכן הנהיג רבי' אליעזר הגדול כל בני ביתו וכן רבי' קלונימוס וכל משפחתו ורבי' אליעזר חזן ורבי' שמואל ובנו ורבי' אברהם כשקורין בהגדה ביד חזקה זו הדבר ובזרוע נטויה זו החרב דם ואש ותמרות עשן דם צפרדע כנים ערב דבר שחין ברד ארבה חשך מכת בכורות דצ״ך עד״ש באח״ב על כל תיבה נותנין אצבע בכוס יין ומטיפין לחוץ וגם אבא מרי הריב״ק עושה כן י״ו פעמים ומטיפין לחוץ כנגד חרבו של הב״ה י״ו פנים ואין לשנות מנהג אבותינו הקדושים, ע״כ לשון הרוקח. כתב ראבי״ה שנראה לי עיקר שאין מברכין על קריאת הלל בליל פסח כמו שפירשו הגאונים הטעם שהרי מפסיקים בסעודה ושתי פעמים אין לברך ברכה אחת וכן פירשו רב צמח גאון ורב האי גאון. ורב יהודה בר יצחק פי' שאין לברך ור״י הבחור והרב ר' יהודה בר יו״ט ומהר״ם מרוטנבורק היו מברכין לקרוא קודם אכילה ולגמור אחר אכילה.

is a legally correct adaptation of the Ashkenazic custom. In Djerba he is only required to wipe the rim and refill the cup. Since a "cup of benediction" should always be full, the failure of the other rituals to refill the cup is another indication that the entire ceremony is of late origin.

Another Interpretation. The standard interpretation of this paragraph is ascribed by Ibn Ezra to the poet and medical doctor Yehuda Halevi (*Ex.* 9:1) who explains that the first two Plagues came from the Nile, the next two, lice and wild animals, from the earth (wild animals being created from the earth, *Gen.* 1:24), the next two, plague and boils, by air-carried infections; the next two, hailstorm and locusts, were weather related, and the last two were absolutely supernatural.

Rebbi Yehuda. R. Yehuda is known also from other sources to construct mnemonic abbreviations (*Menaḥot* 96a) "that one should not err"; it is not clear what error should be avoided here. R. Yehuda may disagree with the previous grouping of the Plagues by twos, or, in an opinion ascribed to Rashi, insist that the correct order of the Plagues is that given in the Pentateuch and not that of Psalm 79. Another frequently asserted grouping, already found in Philo (*Moses* I, 113), is that the first three plagues were produced by Aaron using his staff, the next three either by both Aaron and Moses together or by action of neither of them, the next three by Moses alone, and the last by direct Divine action. It is also asserted (*Ex. rabbah* 5[6]) that the Ten Plagues were written on the staff of Moses only in abbreviation. Another interpretation is that the first three Plagues were directed at the magicians, the next three at Pharaoh's ministers, and the last four at Pharaoh directly, who was the last holdout against recognizing God's power. If one would venture an additional explanation, one may note that the Plagues came in three waves, starting in the countryside and ending on people's bodies: (1) blood in the Nile, frogs in the house, lice on the body; (2) wild animals in the fields, animal plague in the barns, boils on the body; (3) hailstorm on the crops, locusts entered houses, darkness immobilized people; the final plague then resulted in death.

R. Yossi the Galilean

As noted before, the Babylonian *Mishnah* implies that the *Midrash* should explain the entire Declaration for First Fruits, *Deut.* 26:5-9, but our *Haggadah* stops at verse 8. The explanation of verse 9, "He brought us to this place and gave us this land, a land flowing of milk and honey," is (*Sifry* #301):

"He bought us to this Place; this is the Temple. I could think this is the Land of Israel, but since it says 'He gave us this Land,' so the Land is mentioned. Why does it say, 'He brought us to this Place'? As reward for our coming to this Place He gave us this Land.

"'A land flowing of milk and honey.' It says here, 'A land flowing of milk and honey' and it says there (*Ex.* 13:5) 'A land flowing of milk and honey.' Since there it is defined as land of five peoples [Canaanite, Hittite, Emorite, Hiwwite, Yebusite], so here it means the land of the same five peoples. R. Yossi the Galilean says, one may not bring First Fruits from Transjordan since that is not a land flowing of milk and honey."[250]

The addition of R. Yossi the Galilean is from a discussion in *Mishnah Bikkurim* I,10[251] where the majority holds that the land conquered by Moses is "Land that God has given me" (*Deut.* 26:10) and, therefore, only produce of land that is neither within the boundaries of the conquest of Moses in Transjordan nor within the biblical boundaries of Canaan (*Num.* 34:1-15) is excluded from being First Fruits accepted in the Temple. R. Yossi excludes those lands that are not at least in part flowing of milk and honey (*y. Bikkurim* I,10 64b).[252]

---

250 **ויביאנו אל המקום הזה.** זה בית המקדש או יכול זה ארץ ישראל כשהוא אומר **ויתן לנו את הארץ הזאת** הרי ארץ ישראל אמורה ומה תלמוד לומר **ויביאנו אל המקום הזה** בשכר ביאתנו אל המקום הזה נתן לנו את הארץ הזאת.
ארץ זבת חלב ודבש, נאמר כאן **ארץ זבת חלב ודבש** ונאמר להלן **ארץ זבת חלב ודבש** מה **ארץ זבת חלב ודבש** האמורה להלן חמשת עממים אף **ארץ זבת חלב ודבש** האמור כאן ארץ המשת עממים. רבי יוסי הגלילי אומר אין מביאים ביכורים מעבר לירדן שאינו זבת חלב ודבש.

251 ואלו מביאין וקורין: מן העצרת ועד החג, משבעת המינים, מפירות שבהרים מתמרות שבעמקים ומזיתי שמן, ומעבר הירדן. ר' יוסי הגלילי אומר אין מביאין בכורים מעבר הירדן שאינה ארץ זבת חלב ודבש.

252 מה ביניהון? אמר ר' אבין חזי שבט מנשה ביניהון. מאן דאמר אשר נתתי ולא שנטלתי מעצמי חצי שבט מנשה לא נטלו מעצמן. מאן דאמר ארץ זבת חלב ודבש אפילו כן אינה ארץ זבת חלב ודבש.

After the destruction of the Temple and the war of Bar Kokhba, the inclusion of verse 9 and its declaration that the gift of the Land is conditioned on pilgrimage to the Temple would only lead to feelings of sorrow and aggravation, not appropriate for a holiday. Therefore, that section of the *Midrash* was removed and replaced by a discussion between some leading scholars of the period between the two Jewish wars taken from the *Mekhilta* (*deR. Ishmael*, p. 114). R. Saadia Gaon declares this part and the following litany (of which the Yemenite insert is an integral part) as later, optional amplifications. From the language of the later, Galilean version of the *Mishnah*[253] ("he finishes the entire paragraph") as compared to the (older) Babylonian version (p. 288) "he finishes the entire paragraph totally"), one may assume that the discussion of verse 9 was removed from the Haggadah by R. Yehuda the Prince, editor of the *Mishnah*, after the completion of the first version of the *Mishnah*.

In the insert, the argument of R. Yossi is straightforward; the hand has five fingers. However, the basis of the argument is shaky since the "hand" is mentioned also for a single plague (*Ex.* 9:3), as mentioned above in the Recital. Also, the hand is so much more than simply five fingers, as Philo points out on the same subject (*Moses* I, 112);[254] in his opinion, the entire universe would be destroyed by the action of God's hand. R. Yossi the Galilean is mentioned as one of the proponents of homiletic discussion of Scripture (*Agada*); the paragraph inserted in the *Haggadah* also is a homily and not intended as a logical deduction. The basis of the argument disagrees with another tradition, quoted in *Pirqe Avot* (V,4) and given in great detail in *Aboth deR. Nathan* (version 1, chap. 33; version 2, chap. 38):[255] "Corresponding to the ten times our father Abraham was tested by God and found whole, God performed ten miracles for his descendants in Egypt, brought Ten Plagues over Egypt, performed ten miracles for Israel at the Sea, and

---

253 ודורש מארמי אובד אבי עד שהוא גומר כל הפרשה.

254 ἀλλ' ὅμως τοσοῦτον ἴσχυσεν, ὡς ἀπαρογεῦσαι πᾶσαν Αἴγυπτον καὶ ἐκβοᾶν ἀναγκασθῆσαι, ὅτι "δάκτυλος θεοῦ τοῦτ' ἐστί". χεῖρα γὰρ θεοῦ μηδὲ τὴν σύμπασαν οἰκουμένεν ὑποστῆσαι ἂν ἀπὸ περάτων ἐπὶ πέρατα, μᾶλλον δ' οὐδὲ τὸν σύμπαντα κόσμον.
Yet so great was its power that all Egypt lost heart and was forced to cry out, "This is the finger of God"; for as for His hand not all the inhabited world from end to end could stand against it, or rather not even the whole universe.

255 כנגד עשׂרה נסיונות שנתנסה אברהם אבינו ובכולם נמצא שלם. כנגדן עשׂה הקב״ה עשׂרה נסים לבניו במצרים. כנגדן הביא הקב״ה עשׂר מכות על המצרים במצרים. כנגדן נעשׂו לישראל עשׂרה נסים על הים. כנגדן הביא עשׂר מכות על המצריים בים:

brought ten plagues over the Egyptians at the Sea." The ten miracles in Egypt are not specified; according to Maimonides (*Commentary Avot* V,4) the miracles were that the Jews were spared from the Plagues, as is recorded in the Bible explicitly for nine of the ten plagues. For the one exceptional plague, lice, Maimonides is of the opinion that Jewish dwellings were not free of them but the Jews were not hurt by them, which in itself is a medical miracle. The miracles on the Sea are specified; in the count of Maimonides they were: (1) the waters of the Sea were split, (2) the split was not open but as tunnels in the water, (3) the floor of the Sea was dry, (4) but when the Egyptians followed the sea floor became muddy, (5) there were 12 parallel tunnels, one for each tribe, (6) the water froze and became harder than stone, (7) the water froze in separate layers, not as one block, (8) the frozen water was transparent, so the tribes could see one another, (9) there were sweet water fountains on the way in the Sea, and (10) any unused sweet water froze immediately. Only a few of these miracles are reported in the biblical text, but the midrashic text in *Aboth deR. Nathan* finds allusions to the rest in verses of Psalms and Prophets. The ten plagues that descended on the Egyptians at the Sea are not specified in the talmudic sources. According to Maimonides (*loc. cit.*), the plagues at the Sea were of the same kind as the Ten Plagues in Egypt but more diversified, following R. Yossi. Maimonides proves that the plagues at the Sea were more impressive and renowned than those in Egypt proper by the reference in *1 Sam.* 4:8 when the Philistines, apprised of the arrival of the Ark of Covenant at the camp of Israel, exclaim,[256] "This is the God Who smote Egypt with all kinds of plagues in the desert!" The desert here is the desert at the Red Sea (Rashi *ad loc.*).

The discussion between R. Eliezer and R. Akiba is based on R. Yossi's homily. The discussion needs some explanation. The problem is *Ps.* 78:49:

He sends against them the embers of His wrath	יְשַׁלַּח־בָּם חֲרוֹן אַפּוֹ
Anger and rage and trouble	עֶבְרָה וָזַעַם וְצָרָה
A pack of angels of disasters.	מִשְׁלַחַת מַלְאֲכֵי רָעִים

The stanza as written is composed of three lines of eight syllables each. The question is how to make caesuras. The poetic books

---

256 אלה הם האלהים המכים את מצרים בכל מכה במדבר.

(Psalms, Proverbs, Job) have their own system of accents. If a verse has two parts only, the caesura is indicated by *etnaḥta* (֑), as in the prose books. If a verse has three parts then, as in prose books, the second caesura is *etnaḥta.* The first caesura, indicated in prose books by *segolta* (֒), is given in the poetic books in several ways. If the first caesura is definitely stronger than the second one, the first caesura is *'oleh wĕyored* (֥֫); if it is of even strength with the second caesura it usually is indicated by the *major revia'* (֗). (The "*minor revia*" has the same form as the major but is a very weak divider immediately preceding a caesura.) The first accent in the third line is *revia' mugrash*, a secondary divider. The last accent of a stanza is always *sof-pasuq* ׃. The accents show that the stanza is completely balanced, consisting of three lines of equal length and identical pauses. R. Eliezer read the stanza as if the first caesura were an *'oleh wĕyored*, to be translated by a colon: "He sends against them the embers of His wrath: Anger, rage, and trouble, a pack of ministers of disasters." (Compare *Ps. 93* for verses with three caesuras.) R. Akiba, here as elsewhere, considers the Masoretic accents to be musical notes only, independent of meaning. Therefore, he has the freedom to move the colon and look at the verse structure as example of enjambement: "He sends against them: The embers of His wrath, anger, rage, and trouble, a pack of ministers of disasters."

In the last clause of the stanza, משלחת does not mean "mission, legation, embassy" as in modern Hebrew but "pack" (of man-eating animals, *Bava Meẓia* VII,10; *y. Terumot* IX,7 48b; y. *Shevi'it* IV,2 35b). The vocalization *mĕnayin* is attested to by vocalized manuscripts of the *Mishnah* and all printed and manuscript *Haggadot* preceding the Ashkenazic texts of Stanow and Heidenheim, who for some reason punctuate *minnayin*, an unwarranted deviation from common standard rabbinic Aramaic מְנָא "from where?" Another deviation of current Ashkenazic texts from common vocalization is the interpretation of the toponymic "the Galilean," *haggālīlī*, as a construct, *haggĕlīlī*. This appears first in the Amsterdam *Haggadah* of 1695 and, in the eighteenth century, is a charactistic of Ashkenazic *Haggadot* copied from that edition. Those copied from earlier *Haggadot* continue the traditional form, *haggālīlī*.

The meaning of the homiletic excursion is given by *Ex.* 15:26: ". . . every plague that I put on Egypt, I shall not put on you . . .," so the more the Egyptians were smitten, the less the Jews have to fear; cf. the reason given by *MaHaRIL* for spilling wine droplets at the mention of the Ten Plagues.

Dayyenu

The litany and summary following the *midrash*, qualified also as an optional addition to the *Haggadah* text by R. Saadia Gaon, may nevertheless be an old song accompanying the *Haggadah* since both of them end with references to Land and Temple as required by *Deut.* 26:9. As noted by Abudirham, the litany consists of fifteen lines, parallel to the fifteen "sequential songs," *Ps.* 120–134. After the verse about the Egyptians' money, the Yemenite *Haggadah* has preserved another insertion from the *Siddur* of R. Saadia Gaon (it is not in Maimonides). The piece is from the (possibly Babylonian) *Mekhilta deR. Shimon ben Yoḥai* (p. 32); a short version in quoted in the (Galilean) *Mekhilta deR. Ishmael* (p. 47). The main point of the insert is that the booty taken from the Egyptians on the shores of the Red Sea (mentioned only implicitly in *Ex.* 14:30) was much larger than the amounts taken from the Egyptians in Egypt (mentioned explicitly in *Ex.* 12:36). The interpretation of *Ez.* 16:7 contained in the insert is slightly more literal than the one given in the main *Midrash.* The association of *Ps.* 68:14 with the booty in Egypt and on the Sea is an old tradition; see the sources for *Ez.* 16:7 quoted earlier (p. 293). בתי סוֹרָאוֹת is an assimilation to Semitic forms of ב-תיסוֹרָאוֹת, from Greek θησαυρός, treasury.

The litany follows the order of the biblical text: Mannah (*Ex.* 16:4 ff.) - Sabbath (*Ex.* 16:23 ff.) - Election at Mount Sinai (*Ex.* 19:5–6) - Torah (*Ex.* 20). A gloss in *Maḥzor Vitry* points out that the litany implies that the Election at Sinai is distinct from the reception of the Torah and the Ten Commandments. The basis for this is a Babylonian tradition (*b. 'Avodah Zarah* 22b, *Shabbat* 146a, *Yevamot* 103b)[257] that is clearly directed against the Christian doctrine of original sin: "Why are Gentiles dirty in sex? Mar Yoḥanan said: When the Snake slept with Eve (as Rashi points out, *Shabbat* 146a, Mar Yoḥanan reads הִשִּׁיאַנִי

257 מפני מה גוים מזוהמין שלא עמדו על הר סיני שבשעה שבא נחש על חוה הטיל בה זוהמא ישראל שעמדו על הר סיני פסקה זוהמתן גוים שלא עמדו על הר סיני לא פסקה זוהמתן. א״ל רב אחא בריה דרבא לרב אשי גרים מאי? א״ל אע״ג דעינהו לא הוו מזלייהו הוו.

"led me astray" [*Gen.* 2:13] as הִשִּׂיאַנִי "he married me"), it polluted her. The pollution stopped for Israel at Mount Sinai; Gentiles who were not at Mount Sinai are still polluted. Proselytes are also free from pollution since all souls destined to be Jewish were present at Mount Sinai." Similarly, it is pointed our by the early *Midrash, Seder Olam* (Chap. 5),[258] that the people had been reminded of the Seven Noaḥidic Commandments at Marah where, in addition, they received the Sabbath, the duty to honor father and mother, and the principles of civil administration.

The final statement of the summary, "He brought us into the Land of Israel and built for us the Temple to atone for all out transgressions," is a clear reference to the *Midrash* on *Deut.* 26:9 that was eliminated from the *Haggadah*: it means that we obtained the Land permanently because the Temple atones for our sins and, therefore, the people in Zion are not burdened by the sins that would make them unworthy of the Land.

The difference between Ashkenazic and Sephardic texts in the summary, whether to connect the statements by "and" or not, is already present in old manuscripts even though older Ashkenazic sources are not quite consistent in their use of the connective. In this case, the Ashkenazic text conforms to that of the extant copies of R. Saadia Gaon. The difference must express two old scribal traditions. The additional words in the Yemenite tradition also must represent a local development.

Rabban Gamliel

The statement of Rabban Gamliel is a *Mishnah* (*Pesaḥim* X,5); the verses cited from Scripture seem to have come from the *Haggadah* text into our *Talmud* editions. The correct translation seems to be: "Everybody who does not give the etymological explanation of these three words (*Pesaḥ, mazzah, maror*) does not fulfill his duty." The source is *Ex.* 12:27, used earlier as answer to the bad child, where it is stated "you shall say."

---

258 ויבואו מרתה וגו' ואומר שם שם לו חוק ומשפט ושם נסהו. שם נתנו לישראל עשר מצוות, שבע מהן שנצטוו עליהן בני נח . . . , הוסיפו עליהן ישראל באותה שעה שבת ודינים וכיבוד אב ואם.

The explanations of *Pesaḥ* (Passover) and *mārōr* (bitter herbs) are straightforward. The explanation of *maẓẓah* is made difficult since the explanation must be a biblical verse and there is none which contains the etymology of "*maẓẓah*." The verse *Ex.* 12:39 that is used does not even give an adequate explanation of the commandment to eat *maẓẓah* in the *Seder* night. In Egypt, *maẓẓot* were used with the *Pesaḥ* sacrifice; this is the basis of the commandment to eat *maẓẓah* (*Ex.* 12:18), which applies to the *Pesaḥ* ceremony whether it is performed on the Fourteenth of Nisan or the Fourteenth of Iyar (*Num.* 9:9–14) for persons ritually unclean in Nisan; this bread may qualify as the "bread of deprivation," mentioned at the start of the *Haggadah*. Then there was the *maẓẓah* baked during the Exodus, a "bread of freedom"; this may qualify as historical reason for the abstinence from leavened bread during the seven-day holiday (*Ex.* 13:6). The quote of *Ex.* 12:39 seems to refer to a statement of the *Mekhilta deR. Ishmael* (p. 49) that a miracle occurred at the Exodus that will be repeated (on the base of an extremely obscure statement, *Hos.* 7:4–5) at the time of the final redemption. Before the Exodus the Israelites had prepared the dough but they were expelled before they could bake the bread. Earlier in the same *Mekhilta*,[259] *Ex.* 12:34 is interpreted to mean "The people carried its dough that was not yet sour together with the leftovers [*maẓẓah* and *mārōr* from the night before] bundled in their clothes on their shoulders [even though they had many beasts of burden (*Ex.* 12:38)], in order to honor the Divine Commandment," and by the action of the sun, the dough was dried out and did not get sour; it was turned into unleavened bread. The bread of liberation accordingly was made *maẓẓot* not by intentional action but by nature.[260] The expression *'uggōt maẓẓōt* therefore must be translated "dried-out cakes"; the verse contains the etymology מוץ "to squeeze dry"; cf. *Lev.* 1:15, 5:9. (This etymology was taught by the late Rabbi Dr. Arthur Weil of Basel in his classes.)

There are two major differences between the European and

---

259 וישׂא העם את בציקו טרם יחמץ מגיד שלשו את העיסה ולא הספיקו לחמצה עד שנגאלו וכן אתה מוצא לעתיד לבא דכתיב (הושע ז ד-ה) כלם מנאפים כמו תנור בערה מאפה ישבות מעיר מלוש בצק עד חמצתו. יום מלכנו החלו שׂרים חמת מיין. משארותם אלו שיורי מצה ומרור אתה אומר כן או אינו אלא שירי פסחים כשהוא אומר לא תותירו ממנו עד בוקר הרי שירי פסחים אמור ומה אני מקיים משארותם צרורות בשׂמלותם אלו שירי מצה ומרור. צרורות בשׂמלותם על שכמם רבי נתן אומר וכי לא היתה שם בהמה והרי כבר נאמר וגם ערב רב עלה אתם וצאן ובקר ומה ת״ל על שכמם אלא שהיו ישׂראל מחבבין את המצוות.

260 ויאפו את הבצק מגיד שלשו את העיסה ולא הספיקו לחמצה עד שנגאלו וכן אתה מוצא לעתיד לבא מהו אומר ישבות מעיר מלוש בצק עד חמצתו יום מלכנו.

Yemenite texts. The European texts agree with the printed editions of the Babylonian *Talmud* in stating that "Rabban Gamliel used to say" (as an exhortation). Yemenite texts (following Saadia Gaon and Maimonides) state that "Rabban Gamliel said" (stating an obligation). The Yemenite text is that of the *Mishnah* in the Jerusalem *Talmud* and the reading of the (French) Munich manuscript of the *Talmud* as well as a number of Alfassi manuscripts. Also, European *Haggadot* agree with the Babylonian *Talmud*, R. Saadia Gaon, and Maimonides, to read עַל שׁוּם "because of"; Yemenite *Haggadot* follow the Jerusalem *Talmud* in reading עַל שֵׁם "because of which biblical reference" (cf. Levy's Dictionary, s.v. שֵׁם I2). It seems that the biblical verses were introduced explicitly in the talmudic manuscripts from the *Haggadah*; they are missing in the *Mishnah* in the oldest sources.

The differences between Ashkenazic and Sephardic texts are minor points of spelling and vocalization. The vocalization מָה is found before Stanow and Heidenheim only in Italian (local and Sephardic) *Haggadot;* the old Ashkenazic form here also is מַה. The vocalization לְהַחֲמִיץ is old Ashkenazic tradition. The ending ין- for ים is Galilean and standard for Sephardic texts; older Ashkenazic prints and manuscripts vary in their usage. The version that God saved the Israelites *immediately* is the text of Maimonides.

Celebration

We have already noted the tendency of the compilers of the *Haggadah* to use the same verse only once in the course of the discussion. The adherence to this principle seems to be an old Babylonian tradition. The Galilean *Mishnah* (*Pesaḥim* X,5) requires the quote of *Ex.* 13:8, already used as introduction to the Recital and retained in the European *Haggadot*. The proof from *Deut.* 6:23 is required in apodictic form by Rava, the defender of the old exilic custom (*b. Pesaḥim* 116b).[261] Maimonides takes this requirement to supersede that of the *Mishnah* (see the Yemenite text). Saadia Gaon, an Egyptian graduate of the Galilean academies who became Gaon in Babylonia, has no biblical quote here at all. At first glance it seems that the Babylonian quote is the better supporting argument for the

261 אמר רבא צריך שיאמר ואותנו הוציא משם.

requirement that *we* should praise the Lord for the freedom gained by our ancestors since, in that verse, Moses is speaking to the people born or raised in the desert at a time when the adults who had left Egypt were dead except for Moses, Joshua, and Caleb. A similar argument could also be advanced for the wise son whose question in the language of the verse is about "the laws . . . which the Lord has commanded you, the older generation," whereas the bad child asks the question in Egypt. However, the standard talmudic attitude is that the Torah as God's word is timeless and absolute; therefore, any *you* must mean the reader and both verses are equally acceptable.

The absolute interpretation of Scripture is exemplified, e.g., in the discussion (*b. Qiddushin* 68a)[262] of *Deut.* 21:15: "If a man has two wives, one loved and one hated. . . ." Since there is neither love nor hate before God, the verse must mean that one is married in an unobjectionable way and thus loved by God in the fulfillment of His commandment, whereas the other one has contracted a marriage that is forbidden but valid, such as the marriage of a Cohen to a divorcee, and therefore is hated as an offender. The timelessness of Scripture can be seen (*b. Sanhedrin* 91b)[263] from the imperfect (future) without *waw consecutive* in *Ex.* 15:1, which can be translated as "Then Moses and the Children of Israel will sing this song," meaning that not only did Moses sing at the Red Sea but he will sing again at the time of the Resurrection.

All old Babylonian, Galilean, and European sources require that one should *view oneself* as if one was liberated from Egypt. This is also the text of the standard Spanish commentators Abudirham and Abravanel. The oldest documented source speaking about the duty *to conduct oneself*, the reading of medieval and modern Oriental and modern Sephardic texts, seems to be the French *Sefer Mizwot Gadol* (II, #41).

The paragraph under discussion, the conclusion of the Recital, is the direct sequel to the starting paragraph, "*We* were slaves in Egypt." The entire recital is therefore bracketed by paragraphs expressing the same idea. This shows the entire recital, from the start,

---

262 כי תהיין לאיש שתי נשים האחת אהובה והאחת שׂנואה, וכי יש שׂנואה לפני המקום ואהובה לפני המקום? אלא אהובה אהובה בנישׂואיה, שׂנואה שׂנואה בנישׂואיה.

263 א״ר מאיר מניין לתחיית מתים מן התורה שנאמר אז ישיר משה, שר לא נאמר אלא ישיר, מכאן לתחיית המתים מן התורה.

as one literary unit and not an agglomeration of different texts as proposed by text-critical scholars.

The cup is raised for the following song of praise. This is an originally Ashkenazic custom that spread to all other Jewish groups by the influence of *Ṭur* and *Shulḥan 'Arukh* (*Oraḥ Ḥayyim* §473). The custom is based by Rashi (*Pardes*, p. 51)[264] on the talmudic statement (*b. Berakhot* 35a; *'Arakhin* 11a) "from where do we know that a song of praise must be said over a cup of wine? From the verse (*Jud.* 9:13), 'the vine said to them: shall I leave my juice that makes God and man happy.' It makes man happy; how can it possibly make God happy? The verse teaches you that a song of praise must be said over wine." Since the cup is raised, the bread must be covered (cf. p. 286). For some unknown reason, Heidenheim in his *Haggadot* instructs his readers to put down the cup for the *Hallel*, against the explicit text of the *Shulḥan 'Arukh* and all earlier Ashkenazic *Haggadot*.

The first (Jerusalem *Talmud*) recension of the *Mishnah* (*Pesaḥim* X,5 37b) has only the seven expressions of praise found in the Sephardic text. The number seven is preferred for its symbolic value by some Ashkenazic authorities (*Tosafot Pesaḥim* 116a; *Mordokhay Pesahim* 38a); based on *Ps.* 119:164, "Seven times a day I am praising You"; it is a general practice not to increase the number of praises (or *Qaddish* recited by any one person) over seven per day. A student of the fifteenth-century authority R. Israel Isserlein notes that nevertheless the Ashkenazic *Haggadot* all have nine expressions (*Leqet Yosher*, p. 90), following the *Mishnah* (second recension) of the Babylonian *Talmud* (*b. Pesaḥim* 116b) that contains nine expressions of praise. Such an "abundance of praise" is accepted explicitly by *MaHaRIL* (p. קז).[265] The manuscripts vary in the lists of expressions of praise and redemptions. The Yemenite *Haggadah* with eight expressions of praise and a different order of praises and redemptions follows the text of Maimonides. This text is represented among the surviving *Talmud* manuscripts by Munich II. Only European versions have retained the Galilean verb *qallēs*, taken from the Greek κλέος "fame," both in good and evil, used by Aquila in his translation of יִתְקַלָּס (*Hab.* 1:10), and accepted by Rashi (*Ez.* 22:4) as standard meaning of

---

264 וכשיגיע ללפיכך נוטלין כל אחד כוסו בידו מפני שבאים לפתוח בשיר והלל. ומצינו בהגדה מניין שאין אומר שירה אלא על היין שנ' ותאמר להם הגפן החדלתי את תירושי המשמח אלהים ואנשים כו', אם אנשים משמח אלהים במה משמח, אלא מלמד שאין אומרים שירה אלא על היין.

265 בלפיכך מרבינן לישנא דשבח.

the root *qls* in biblical Hebrew. Other commentators, mostly not Ashkenazic, find a pejorative meaning of the root *qls* in biblical Hebrew (*ReDaQ, Sefer Hashorashim,* on *Ez.* 16:31, 22:5, *Jer.* 20:8, *Ps.* 44:14). Some modern lexicographers want to derive the Aramaic root from the Greek acclamation καλῶς, "how beautiful!" In classical Arabic, the root קלס means "to dance while singing, to sing harmoniously" and קלּס, the intensive second conjugation used in the Hebrew forms, "to receive somebody with great pomp; to make bonnets." Any use of the root has disappeared in Oriental prayer texts after its rejection by some Gaonic authorities (*Shibbole Haleqet,* #8); in the *Qaddish* prayer the word has disappeared even in Ashkenazic texts.

In most *Talmud* manuscripts, all non-Ashkenazic and most old German Ashkenazic manuscript *Haggadot*, the introduction to *Hallel* closes with "Let us say before Him: Halleluja!" The discussions of the early Ashkenazic authorities imply that the French tradition was "Let us say before Him a new song [שיר חדש, masculine]: Halleluja!" This reading is not accepted by any rabbinic authority. The new song is actually an old song; the meaning of the clause is "Let us sing before Him the song, newly composed for the Exodus: Halleluja!" The basis for this interpretation is a talmudic statement (*b. Pesaḥim* 117a):[266] "Rav Yehuda said in the name of Samuel: The song recorded in the Torah [*Ex.* 15:1-19] was said by Moses and Israel when they ascended from the Sea but this *Hallel* ['song of praise,' *Ps.* 113-114], who did compose it? The prophets among them [those who left Egypt] instituted it for Israel so that for every deliverance from any persecution, may it not come over them, they should recite it for their freedom upon being delivered." A few lines later, we read:[267] "Who composed this *Hallel*? R. Yossi [the Galilean] said: My son Eleazar asserts that Moses and Israel composed it when they ascended from the Sea, but his colleagues disagree with him and say that David composed it. However, his words are more convincing than theirs: it is impossible to think that Israel shoud celebrate their holidays [from Moses to David] without a song of praise." (It is agreed that the second

---

266 אמר רב יהודה אמר שמואל שיר שבתורה משה וישראל אמרוהו בשעה שעלו מן הים, והלל זה מי אמרו? נביאים שביניהן תקנו להן לישראל שיהיו אומרין אותו על כל פרק ופרק ועל כל צרה וצרה שלא תבוא עליהן ולכשנגאלין אומרים אותו על גאולתן.

267 הלל זה מי אמרו? רבי יוסי אומר: אלעזר בני אומר משה וישראל אמרוהו בשעה שעלו מן הים וחלוקין עליו חביריו לומר שדוד אמרו ונראין דבריו מדבריהן, אפשר ישראל שחטו את פסחיהן ונטלו לולביהן ולא אמרו שירה?

part of the *Hallel*, recited after Grace, is Davidic.) On the basis of this interpretation, all early medieval authorities who do not reject the addition read either "Let us say before Him, וְנֹאמַר לְפָנָיו, a new song, שירה חדשה, (feminine): Halleluja!" (*Tosafot Pesaḥim* 116b) or "There was said before Him, וְנֶאֱמַר לְפָנָיו, a new song, שירה חדשה, (feminine): Halleluja!" (*Mordokhay Pesaḥim* 66a). The latter version is found sporadically in Ashkenazic *Haggadot*. The note in *Mordokhay* could also be interpreted to refer to a reading וַנֹּאמַר, which, however, is not attested. The reason for the change from masculine *shīr* to feminine *shīrāh* is found in a *midrash* (*Mekhilta deR. Ishmael*, p. 118; *Cant. rabbah* I,37)[268] that the nine songs recorded in the Bible as thanksgiving for past deliverance (in Egypt for the *Seder*, *Is*. 30:29; on the Red Sea, *Ex*. 15:1; for the well in the desert, *Num*. 21:17; Joshua in the Valley of Ayalon, *Jos*. 10:12; the song of Deborah, *Jud*. 5:1; the song of David, *2 Sam*. 22:1, the song of Solomon for the dedication of the Temple, *Ps*. 30:1; the song of Josaphat, *2 Chr*. 20:26) are referred to in the feminine but the song that we anticipate for the final redemption in the time of the Messiah will be in the masculine. The idea is best expressed by R. Simon bar Isaac bar Abun, early medieval author of the poem *Ī Patros*, sung in traditional Ashkenazic congregations during the morning service of the last two days of Passover. After describing the Nine Songs, the poet continues:[269]

> These songs were composed in the language of *shīrāh*
> Their deliverance came as to a woman giving birth, with troubles and losses,
> The strength of the last *shīr* is like males that cannot give birth,
> (*Ps*. 149) Sing for the Lord a New Song (שיר), His praise in the assembly of the pious!

---

268 **את השירה הזאת** וכי שירה אחת היא? והלא עשׂר שירות הן! הראשונה שנאמרה במצרים שנ׳ השיר יהיה לכם כליל התקדש חג. השנייה שנאמרה על הים שנ׳ אז ישיר משה. השלישית שנאמרה על הבאר שנ׳ אז ישיר ישׂראל. הרביעית שאמר משה שנ׳ ויהי ככלות משה לכתוב את דברי השירה הזאת. החמישית שאמר יהושע שנ׳ אז ידבר יהושע ליי ביום תת יי וגו׳. הששית שאמרה דבורה וברק שנ׳ ותשר דבורה וברק בן אבינועם. השביעית שאמר דוד שנ׳ וידבר דוד ליי את דברי השירה הזאת. השמינית שאמר שלמה שנ׳ מזמור שיר חנוכת הבית לדוד. התשיעית שאמר יהושפט שנ׳ ויעמד משוררים ליי מהללים בהדרת קדש לפני החלוץ אומר הודו ליי כי לעולם חסדו. העשׂירית לעתיד לבא שנ׳ שירו ליי שיר חדש תהלתו מקצה הארץ. כל השירות שעברו קרואות בלשון נקבה כשם שהנקבה יולדת כך התשועות שעברו היה אחריהם שעבוד אבל התשועה העתידה להיות אין אחריה שעבוד לכך קרואה בלשון זכר . . . שכשם שהזכר אינו יולד כך התשועה העתידה לא יהא אחריה שעבוד שנ׳ ישׂראל נושע ביי תשועת עולמים.

269 שִׁירוֹת אֵלּוּ לְשׁוֹן שִׁירָה מְיוּסָּדִים
כִּי תְשׁוּעָתָם כַּיּוֹלֵדָה לָבֹא צָרוֹת וּמְסְפָּדִים
תּוֹקֶף שִׁיר אַחֲרוֹן כִּזְכָרִים לֹא יוֹלְדִים
שִׁירוּ לַיי שִׁיר חָדָשׁ תְּהִלָּתוֹ בִּקְהַל חֲסִידִים.

As a consequence, all rituals have the masculine form for the song promised for the final redemption in the benediction after the first part of *Hallel*.

Hallel means "song of praise." Three sections of Psalms are used in the synagogue service under that title. The first one, known either as *Hallel* without qualification or as *Egyptian Hallel* is the song recited at the *Seder* and on all joyous holidays as well as on Ḥanukkah, *Ps*. 113–118. The song of praise for rainfall in answer to special prayers for rain in case of draught is *Ps*. 136, the *Great Hallel*. The daily song before the morning prayers, intended as a preparation for the life in the World to Come, is the Daily *Hallel* (*b. Shabbat* 118b),[270] defined in *Masekhet Sofĕrim* (XVII,11) as *Ps*. 145–150; the name is explained by Rashi (*Shabbat ad loc.*) from *Pss*. 148 and 150, which contain many repetitions of the verb "to praise." In all rituals, the Daily *Hallel* is prefaced and followed by a benediction. The *Talmud* (*b. Ta'anit* 6b; *y. Ta'aniot* I,3 64b) requires that the Great *Hallel* be accompanied by a benediction. On days when the Egyptian *Hallel* is recited in its entirety (the first two days of Passover, Pentecost, all days of Tabernacles and *Shemini Aẓeret*, *Ḥanukkah*), *Hallel* is followed by a benediction for all Jewish groups. The same benediction is required by the *Talmud* after the recitation of the entire *Hallel* during the *Seder*; the details of that benediction will be discussed in the chapter "*Hallel*." On these days, *Hallel* is also preceded by a benediction that originally read לגמור את ההלל, usually translated "to finish the *Hallel*" for all Jewish groups. This is R. Saadia Gaon's preferred formula. The text was changed by R. Meir of Rothenburg for Ashkenazim (*Ṭur Oraḥ Ḥayyim* §488) to לקרוא את ההלל "to recite the *Hallel*" (text prescribed by R. Amram Gaon and admitted by R. Saadia Gaon also for the full *Hallel*) for fear that one might inadvertently omit a word in the recitation and then the benediction would sound untrue. Sephardim and Yemenites have retained the original formula. On days when a truncated version of *Hallel* is recited (the later days of Passover and the days of the New Moon), Sephardim and Ashkenazim start with a benediction "to recite the *Hallel*" and end with the unchanged final benediction. A responsum of Rabbenu Tam, a grandson of Rashi, reported in *Maḥzor Vitry* (p. 193), notes that in rabbinic Hebrew the root גמר may mean simply "to recite" and that

---

270 א״ר יוסי יהא חלקי מגומרי הלל בכל יום. והאמר מר הקורא הלל בכל יום הרי זה מחרף ומגדף? כי קאמרינן בפסוקי דזמרא.

therefore there is no difference in meaning between the two formulas. His point of view finds support in R. Saadia Gaon's indifference to the choice of words in the benediction. Yemenites recite the "half-*Hallel*" without an introductory benediction since none is authorized in the code of Maimonides for this occasion.

Today, no Jewish group recites a benediction for *Hallel* before the recitation. This is in accordance with decisions of the Geonim. The reason given by R. Ẓemaḥ Gaon (*Oẓar Hagĕonim Pesaḥim* #346)[271] is that one interrupts the recitation by meal and Grace. This is confirmed by R. Hai Gaon (*loc. cit.* #348), who adds the reason that in the *Seder* ceremony *Hallel* is not "recited" as biblical text but is "sung," as declared in the preceding paragraph. He is quite adamant that this is the custom of all of Israel. Nevertheless, the problem was discussed through most of the Middle Ages, with a number of French Tosafists referring to other (anonymous) Geonic sources and insisting on reciting two benedictions, one after the Recital and another one after Grace (cf. *Or Zarua'* §256, II,60b[272]). The reasons of the French Tosafists are shown to be invalid in a lengthy responsum of the leading German authority of the time, *RAVIA* (#168); an unnecessary benediction amounts to taking God's name in vain. The basis of the discussion in Northern Europe, whose prayer customs were greatly influenced by Palestinian practice, is that the Jerusalem *Talmud* includes the night of *Pesaḥ* in the list of formal recitations of the *Hallel* (*y. Sukkah* IV,5 54c)[273] whereas the Babylonian *Talmud* omits the night in the parallel list (*b. 'Arakhin* 10a).[274] It seems from the Jerusalem *Talmud* (*y. Pesaḥim* X,1 37c)[275] that in those parts of Galilee where people were functionally illiterate, they assembled in

---

271 ואין מברכין בלילי פסחים לגמור את ההלל מפני שחולקין אותו באמצע והכן שדר רב צמח בר רב שלמה.

272 ותקנו לשון גומרים כדי להבחין בימים שגומרימן לימים שמדלגין; לכך תקנו גאונים שאין מברכין לגמור כ״א לקרא כקורא בפסוקי תורה.
They instituted the language "to finish" to distinguish between the days on which one finishes [*Hallel*] and the days on which one skips [part of *Hallel*]; therefore, the Geonim instituted [at this point in the Recital] that one should not recite the benediction "to finish" but "to recite," like any persons who recites scriptural verses.

273 תניא שמונה עשׂר יום ולילה אחד קורין בהן את ההלל בכל שנה. שמונת ימי החג ושמונת ימי חנוכה ויום טוב של עצרת ויום טוב הראשון של פסח ולילו.

274 דאמר רבי יוחנן משום רבי שמעון בן יהוצדק שמונה עשׂר ימים שהיחיד גומר בהן את ההלל שמונה ימי החג ושמונה ימי חנוכה ויום טוב הראשון של פסח ויום טוב של עצרת ובגולה עשׂרים ואחד.

275 דא״ר יוחנן הלל אם שמען בבית הכנסת יצא.

their synagogues to recite *Hallel* under the leadership of a knowledgeable man with the customary benediction since there was no interruption of the recitation. *RAVIA* (*loc. cit.*) even reports a similar custom not only for *Hallel* but also for the Recital in the *Haggadah* in medieval Spain.[276] On the authority of R. Jacob ben Asher of Toledo (*Ṭur Oraḥ Ḥayyim* §473),[277] the recitation of *Hallel* with benedictions in the synagogue in the service of Passover Eve was accepted by all Sephardic congregations and, as a consequence of the acceptance of some features of the Sephardic ritual by the *ḥasidic* sects, also generally by Eastern European Ashkenazic congregations. *Hallel* is not recited in the synagogue in the Western European Ashkenazic ritual and is recited without any benedictions by Yemenites since the recitation is not sanctioned by Maimonides and the custom is a modern development, influenced by the Syrian Sephardic ritual.

The original Babylonian way of reciting the *Hallel*, retained today only in the Yemenite ritual, is for one man to recite each half-verse separately and the listeners to answer "Halleluja" at the end of each verse (*b. Sukkah* 38b).[278] Since *Hallel* starts with the plural imperative *hallĕlū* "praise!" there must be at least one celebrant and two (a plural) of listeners for a total of three (*Midrash Tehillim, Ps.* 113, #3).[279] The Galilean way of reciting *Hallel* was for two people (or chorals) to recite together, each one singing half a verse (*y. Berakhot* VIII,9 12c; *Megillah* I,11 72a).[280] The *Mishnah* (*Pesaḥim* X,6) reports that according to the house of Hillel, the authoritative opinion for current custom, the first two Psalms of *Hallel* have to be recited before the meal; according to the house of Shammai only Psalm 113 is recited before the meal. The reason for the house of Shammai is spelled out in the Jerusalem *Talmud* (*y. Pesaḥim* X,6 37d):[281] *Ps.* 114 starts "When Israel left Egypt" but in the night they did not leave

---

276 ובתשובות ראיתי שעוד בימים האלו המנהג בארץ ספרד ובבבל שהשליח ציבור עושה בפסח הסדר בבית הכנסת מפני עמי הארץ שאין בקיאים בהגדה לאומרה.

277 ויש מקומות שנוהגין לקרות ההלל בבית הכנסת בצבור כדי שלא יצטרכו לברך עליו בשעת ההגדה ומה טוב ומה נעים ההוא מנהגא.

278 הוא אומר הללו עבדי ה' והן אומרים הללויה מכאן שאם היה גדול מקרא אותו עונה אחריו הללויה:

279 מכאן אמרו חכמים אין הלל פחות משלשה בני אדם. למי אומר הללו, שנים.

280 דאנן חמי רבנן ורברבייא קיימין בציבורא אמרין ברוך הבא ואילין אמרין בשם ה' ואילו ואילו יוצאין ידי חובתן.

281 אמרו להן בית שמאי וכי יצאו ישראל ממצרים שהוא מזכיר יציאת מצרים? אמרו להן בית הלל אילו ממתין עד קרות הגבר אדיין לא הגיעו לחצי גאולה היאך מזכירין גאולה ואדיין לא נגאלו; והלא לא יצאו אלא בחצי היום שנ' ויהי בעצם היום הזה הוציא יי את בני ישראל וגו'. אלא מכיון שהתחיל במצוה אומרים לו מרק.

Egypt; they were confined to their houses, so the recitation is inappropriate. The answer of the house of Hillel is that in this case *Ps.* 114 cannot be recited at all at the *Seder* since the actual Exodus took place only the following day (*Ex.* 13:4); therefore, we may as well recite *Ps.* 114 before the meal. The Septuagint and *Midrash Tehillim* combine *Ps.* 114–115 into one psalm; they conform to the opinion of the House of Shammai that appears to represent the original institution. These sources then split *Ps.* 116 into two psalms, the way that they are recited in the synagogue. In any case, it is clear that the generally received opinion is that *Ps.* 113 speaks about events that happened in Egypt during the night of liberation. According to the *Midrash* (*Tehillim Ps.* 113, #2, a *Yerushalmi* source),[282] when Pharaoh called on Moses and Aaron in the night (*Ex.* 12:31), he was forced to issue a formal proclamation that the Israelites were no longer his servants but free men and the servants of the Lord. *Ps.* 113:1 is the end of this formal proclamation; the "servants of the Lord" are not a select group of pious but the entire people of Israel. Psalm 113 is identified as the song mentioned in *Is.* 30:29: "The song [of deliverance] shall be for you as in the night sanctified for the holiday." The idea that Israel is free only as servant of the Lord is explicit in *Lev.* 25:55 (see *Sifra* [*Behar* §9, #4]):[283] (*Lev.* 25:55) "'Because the Children of Israel are My servants, they are My servants whom I brought out of the land of Egypt' with the condition that they should no more be enslaved; 'I am the Lord their God,' this teaches us that everyone who tries to enslave them here on earth is guilty as if he tried to enslave God."

Psalm 113 is notable for the many constructions where a final *yod* is added for reasons of meter. In verse 9, **בית** has been translated as "family" (see *Ex.* 1:21). The barren, עקרה, probably is the old maid who is barren and downtrodden for want of a husband. This makes

---

282 אתה מוצא עשׂרים וששה דורות משברא הקב״ה את עולמו עד שיצאו ישׂראל ממצרים ולא אמרו הלל, עד שיצאו משיעבוד מצרים שהיה של טיט ולבנים אמרו הלל. ואימתי אמרו? בשעת מכת בכורות עמד פרעה והלך אצל משה ואהרן בלילה ואמר להם קומו צאו מתוך עמי, אמרו לו שוטה וכי בלילה אנו עומדין, וכי גנבים אנו שנלך בלילה? בבוקר אנו יוצאין שכך אמר לנו הקב״ה ואתם לא תצאו איש מפתח ביתו עד בוקר. אמר להם הרי כבר מתים כל מצרים שנ׳ כי אמרו כולנו מתים. אמרו לו, מבקש אתה לכלות המכה הזאת? אמור הרי אתם בני חורין, הרי אתם ברשותכם, ואין אתם עבדי אלא עבדי ה׳. התחיל פרעה, צווח ואמר, לשעבר הייתם עבדי אבל עכשיו הרי אתם בני חורין, הרי אתם ברשותכם, הרי אתם עבדי ה׳ וצריכים אתם להללו שאתם עבדיו שנ׳ הללויה הללו עבדי ה׳. וכן הוא אומר כי לי בני ישׂראל עבדים, וכן הוא אומר השיר יהיה לכם כליל התקדש חג.

283 כי לי בני ישׂראל עבדים עבדי הם אשר הוצאתי אותם מארץ מצרים על תנאי שלא ישתעבדו בהם. אני ה׳ אלהיהם מה ת״ל מלמד שכל המשתעבד בהם למטן מעלין עליו כאילו משתעבד למעלן.

verse 9 a perfect parallel to verse 8. A similar motive is found in *Ps.* 68:7: "God introduces singles to a family, He frees the chained at the correct time." The Exodus is the main theme of Psalm 68 (quoted already several times in the commentary on the *Midrash);* the talmudic interpretation of *Ps.* 68:7 is (*b. Sotah* 2a; *y. Beẓah* V,2 63a) that "pairing husband and wife is as wonderful a Divine achievement as the parting of the waters of the Red Sea." Another talmudic tradition (*Gen. rabbah* 71[3])[284] identifies עֲקָרָה with עִקָּרָה "the root, mainstay," translating *Gen.* 29:31 not "Rachel was barren" but "Rachel was the principal wife." This *Midrash* is the origin of the meaning "housewife" for עקרת הבית in modern Hebrew. In Jewish tradition, the five books of Psalms are parallel to the five books of the Torah, and each Psalm has many meanings, just as every verse of the Torah has many meanings. So one has to expect that a Psalm of deliverance that was introduced as a *shīrāh* also alludes to future persecutions just as Moses was sent to the Children of Israel to announce (*Ex. rabbah* 3[7] on *Ex.* 3:14)[285] that the Name of God is "I shall be with you in future sufferings just as I am with you in this suffering." In this third sense does the *Talmud* (*b. Giṭṭin* 57b) explain in a lengthy aggadic piece that the mother of verse 9 who is happy with her children is the mother whose seven children were killed by Antiochus (*2 Macc.* 7) because they refused to worship idols: the mother is barren since her children are dead, but they are happy together in Paradise. A similar thought may underly the prayer of Hannah (*1 Sam.* 2:1–10, in particular, v. 5), which in large part is parallel to Psalm 113.

Psalm 114 starts with the assertion that the Israelites in Egypt had preserved their identity by clinging to their own language: the Egyptians are characterized as the people of foreign tongue (*Midrash Tehillim* 114 #4).[286] The parting of the waters of the Red Sea is ascribed to an earth tremor that shook even the Jordan valley. That description contradicts the details given in *Ex.* 14:21, where the parting is induced by the extraordinary meteorological event of a spring hurricane blowing from the East (implying a cool North

---

284 **ורחל עקרה.** א״ר יצחק רחל היתה עיקרו של בית.

285 **אהיה אשר אהיה.** רבי יעקב ב״ר אבינא בשם ר' הונא דציפורין אמר. אמר הקב״ה למשה אמור להם בשעבוד הזה אהיה עמם ובשעבוד הם הולכים ואהיה עמם.

286 אמר ר' אלעזר הקפר בזכות ארבעה דברים נגאלו ישראל ממצרים, שלא שינו את שמם, ולא שינו את לשונם, ולא גילו את מיסתורין שלהם, ולא היו פרוצים בעריות . . . ולא שינו את לשונם, שהיו מספרים לשון הקודש, שנ' בית יעקב מעם לועז היתה יהודה לקדשו, ללשון הקודש שלו . . .
Cf. p. 290, "There he became a people."

Arabian desert and a hot Northern Sahara) unless the earthquake refers to the return of the waters when (*Ex.* 14:27) "the Lord emptied the Egyptians into the Sea." The word חולי in verse 7 is certainly not an imperative "dance!" since that verse together with verse 8 forms the answer to the preceding question. The final *yod* may be a genitive or a definite article of the construct state, just as in *Ps.* 113. The traditional interpretation (*loc. cit.*)[287] given in the text uses the meaning חול "to work, create, give birth" (*Ps.* 90:2; *Thr.* 4:6), rather than from חול "to dance, blow the flute" or חיל "to tremble." This translation is also common to all Judeo-German translations in eighteenth-century prayer books: פֿר דען הערן דער דיא ערד בשאפֿן האט "before the Lord Who created the earth."

Final Benediction

The formal commandment of the recitation and the explanation of the Exodus has now been fulfilled; the conclusion is marked by the benediction of praise for the deliverance, just as a benediction is recited after the reading of the Torah or the Esther scroll. At the latter occasions one also has a benediction preceding the recitation; by the unanimous vote of the Geonim, the place of an introductory benediction for the *Seder* is taken by *Qiddush* that also mentions the Exodus. On other festivals of liberation, Ḥanukkah and Purim, one adds an introductory benediction in praise of God "Who did miracles for our fathers in those days at this time." This benediction is not recited on Passover because, in a note ascribed to R. Amram Gaon by *Orḥot Ḥayyim* (I, 80b),[288] it is explained that the permanent salvation of the Exodus (and the consequent election at Mount Sinai) are of a much higher level than temporary miracles.

The text of the benediction is given in the *Mishnah* (*Pesaḥim* X,7), shortened in the Babylonian *Talmud* and more detailed in the Jerusalem *Talmud*. The *Mishnah* presents two versions. The short form, according to Maimonides (*Ḥameẓ Umaẓẓah* VIII,5) used during the time of the Temple, is reported in the name of R. Ṭarfon and contains only a praise for the Exodus. The longer form, ascribed to R.

---

287 אלא מלפני אדון חולי ארץ, מלפני אדון שיצר את הארץ, דכתיב ותחולל ארץ ותבל.

288 וכתב ר' עמרם לא ליטעי אינש למימר שעשׂה ניסים דיום ישועה עדיף מנסים.

Akiba and probably his own composition, adds a prayer for the rebuilding of the Temple. General rules of formation of blessings require that the original theme be taken up again at the end; the lengthened form therefore needs a second invocation of the Lord "Who delivered Israel" at the end. This is the current explanation of the explicit requirement of the *Talmud* (*b. Pesaḥim* 117b)[289] and the unvocalized reading of all *Talmud* manuscripts. The Yemenite traditional reading is "Redeemer of Israel," authorized only for the *'Amidah* prayer, possibly derived from a vocalization as participle, גָּאֵל "Who is redeeming," instead of the commonly used past tense, גָּאַל "Who delivered."[290] The Galilean version was in all cases a timeless "King, Rock of Israel and its Redeemer" (*y. Berakhot* I,9 3d)[291]; this did survive in the Ashkenazic ritual for the poetic inserts in the evening prayers for holidays.

The Ashkenazic *Haggadah* texts in current use all follow Heidenheim in expressing "[He] let us come to this night" by והגיענו ללילה הזה. The unanimous reading of all earlier, medieval and modern, Ashkenazic *Haggadot* is והגיענו הלילה הזה, identical with the current reading of Sephardic and Yemenite texts. The only sources constructing "let us come to" with dative ל are R. Saadia Gaon, the Galilean text from the *Genizah*, and Maimonides in his legal code (*loc. cit.*). All other sources, both *Talmudim*, early *Mishnah* prints and manuscripts, Maimonides in his *Haggadah* text, R. Amram Gaon, and all medieval decisors and commentators construct the verb with the accusative of time. This is a good biblical construction (*Esth.* 2:12; cf. also *Gen.* 28:12, *Is.* 30:4, *Esth.* 4:3). Heidenheim, pointing out the contradiction in the two versions of Maimonides, declares the accusative construction as a scribal error. However, the manuscript evidence (not available to Heidenheim) contradicts his statement. In the text given in this *Haggadah*, therefore, the original Ashkenazic version has been restored, leading to a common text for all Jewish

---

289 אמר רבא ק״ש והלל גאל ישראל דצלותא גואל ישראל.

290 Cf. note 21 in Elbogen, *Der jüdische Gottesdienst*, p. 18. D. Goldschmidt, *Passover Haggadah*, p. 58, writes that "doubtless the original wording was גּוֹאֵל יִשְׂרָאֵל 'He Who redeems Israel.'" This assertion is not supported by any source; it contradicts the nature of Rava's statement. We have seen repeatedly before that Rava states the old Babylonian *minhag* in contrast to Galilean usage.

291 וצריך לומר צור ישראל וגואלו.

groups. The best lesson to be learned from this example is, never emend!

The plural "bitter herbs" of the Yemenite text in contrast to "bitter herb" of the European versions is from the text of Maimonides who follows the Galilean version modeled on a biblical expression, *Num.* 9:11. The singular is found in all Babylonian texts. The difference between the indirect address form of Ashkenazic/Yemenite (Amram, Saadia, Maimonides) texts יגיענו "may He let us reach" and the direct Sephardic הגיענו "let us reach" goes back to variants in *Talmud* manuscripts (*Diqduqe Soferim Pesaḥim*, p. 363, note [מ]). The manuscript sources of the *Talmudim* have either "there we shall eat from the *Pesaḥ* sacrifices and the family offerings" or "there we shall eat from the *Pesaḥ* sacrifices." The family offering is the festive sacrifice (חֲגִיגָה) offered on the Fourteenth of Nisan according to the rules of זֶבַח שְׁלָמִים, a sacrifice in redemption of a vow (*Lev.* 3). The order followed today, "there we shall eat from the family offerings and *Pesaḥ* sacrifices," appears in the text of Maimonides and, as an explicit correction of the mishnaic text, in the collection of decisions and rules from the school of R. Meir of Rothenburg known as *Mordokhai* (*Pesaḥim*, p. 66a), with the justification that the *zewaḥ*, the family sacrifice, precedes the *Pesaḥ* in the order of the meal. The family festival offering and the controversy of Ben Tema is discussed in the chapter on the Four Questions, p. 249. In some Ashkenazic circles one follows the rule of R. Jacob Weilla (*Respona MaHaRIW* #193)[292] to recite the benediction in the original order of the *Mishnah*, "from the *Pesaḥ* sacrifices and the family offerings" if the *Seder* is held Saturday night since then it was not possible to slaughter the *ḥăgīgāh* during the Sabbath and only the *Pesaḥ* was offered since its slaughter, by biblical commandment, is required on the Fourteenth of Nisan and therefore overrides the Sabbath prohibition of slaughter in general. The medieval *Sefer Ha'iṭṭūr* (p. 266a)[293] reports that R. Jacob of Orléans (martyred in the pogrom of London, Sept. 3, 1189) for this reason did not put an egg on the *Seder* plate on Saturday night. The author notes that there are other reasons than the Sabbath that also eliminate the obligation to bring a *ḥăgīgāh* and therefore nothing

---

292 כשיבוא פסח במוצאי שבת יאמר מן הפסחים ומן הזבחים דאין חגיגה קריבה בשבת ובליל שני יאמר מן הזבחים ומן הפסחים דחגיגה נאכלת קודם הפסח, והוא הדין בשאר ימות השבוע.

293 ושמעתי על ר' יעקב מאורליינישׂ לא היה עוֹשׂה בפסח שחל להיות במוֹצאי שבת אלא תבשיל אחד לפי שאין חגיגה דוחה כדתנן אימתי מביא עמוֹ חגיגה בזמן שׁבא בטהרה כו' ובחול ובמוֹעד ואל ישנה אדם דא״כ כשבא בחוֹל אין באין בטהרה ואין מביאין עמוֹ חגיגה.

should be changed Saturday night. This is also the opinion of his contemporary, R. Isaac, the nephew of Rabbenu Tam, known as *RI*, the greatest halakhic authority among the Tosafists (*Tosafot Pesaḥim* 114b, s.v. אחד)[294] and, therefore, the generally accepted practice is not to make any changes.

The "new song" that is promised in the benediction naturally is a *shīr*, the masculine form corresponding to the final redemption.

While the current rituals essentially agree on the consonantal text of the benediction, there are differences in vocalization. The prayers were formalized in early talmudic times in the current Hebrew language spoken in educated circles in Israel, known as "language of the Sages" (*b. Ḥullin* 137b, *'Avodah Zarah* 58b). Compared to biblical Hebrew, the language of the Sages shows a preference for certain feminine plural forms but also, as noted in the commentary on *Qiddush*, uses the suffix *-ākh* for the second person singular masculine possessive pronoun and shows other preferences for classical feminine forms used for masculine. Vocalized *Haggadah* texts before the end of the eighteenth century show no difference between Sephardic and Ashkenazic versions in this respect. Current Ashkenazic texts deviate from the historical forms under the influence of R. Eliahu of Wilna in Eastern Europe and Isaac Stanow and Wolf Heidenheim in Western Europe. (Some Ashkenazic authorities have gone to quite absurd lengths in the adaptation of texts to biblical paradigms; se we find versions of the *Qaddish* in which the rabbinic subjunctive *yitgaddal* "may [His great Name] be magnified" is changed into biblical reflexive [t-passive] *yitgaddēl* "[His great Name] will magnify itself.")

It is an old tradition to celebrate the fulfillment of a required reading by an alphabetic poem. One of them, אֲשֶׁר בִּגְלַל אָבוֹת for the completion of the yearly cycle of Torah readings, is preserved by Yemenite and Western Ashkenazic Jews in the service of *Simḥat Torah*. In the *Siddur* of R. Amram Gaon (p. 52a) and in *Maḥzor Vitry* (p. 459), the poem is a benediction containing Name and Kingdom; it must be considered to be of talmudic or pretalmudic origin. The poem after the recitation of the Esther scroll on Purim, אֲשֶׁר הֵנִיא, is preserved

---

294 כשחל י״ד להיות בשבת אין צריך רק בישול אחד דחגיגת י״ד אינה דוחה שבת ומיהו אומר ר״י דמכל מקום אין לחלק דדמי לחובה אם היינו מניחין מלעשות שני תבשילין וגם יש לחוש שמא לא יעשו בשאר פסחים.

in most Ashkenazic rituals. *Mahzor Vitry* (p. 214)[295] declares the poem to be a composition of the Men of the Great Assembly. The poem after the recitation of the *Haggadah*, אַתָּה גָּאַלְתָּ, is found today only in Yemenite texts, incorporated in the final benediction. It is treated as an optional insert by R. Saadia Gaon, on the same level as the insert in *Qiddush* and the section starting *R. Yossi the Galilean*. The poem shows the same signs of high antiquity as the other two alphabetic poems: it is a straightforward recital without any of the involved allusions characterizing synagogal poetry from talmudic times onward.

The word תַּשְׁנִיק in line ו is talmudic meaning "suffocation, choking." The root שנק is used by *Targum Onqelos, Ex.* 14:27, to translate Hebrew נער "to pour out" (into the Sea). Rashi *ad loc.* defines the Aramaic to mean "to tear apart, to drive insane"; R. Saadia Gaon translates שנק by Arabic גׄרק "to drown somebody." God's beloved in line ט is Aaron; this is not a standard appellation since the Bible mentions as God's beloved only Abraham (*Jer.* 11:15), Benjamin (*Deut.* 33:12), Solomon (2 *Sam.* 12:25), the Temple (*Ps.* 84:2), and Israel (*Jer.* 12:7). The last quote is the base for lines ר,מ. Israel's beloved is God (*Is.* 5:1).

The second cup is consumed immediately following the final benediction of the *Haggadah*. The difference between the Ashkenazic-Yemenite procedure, which requires a benediction, and the Sephardic, which does not, have been discussed earlier (pp. 188-189).

---

295 וזה פיוט מיסוד אנשי כנסת הגדולה.

Maẓẓah and Maror

The hands are washed before the bread is broken. It is a characteristic of rabbinic (pharisaic) Judaism that bread is never eaten with unwashed hands. Bread is not only one of the most basic foods; in antiquity it also was used in place of forks and spoons. Therefore, the requirement to wash one's hands before eating bread essentially meant that washing was required for all foods except fruits and some snacks. Since food is the object of many biblical laws, the observant tried to eat everyday (profane, חוּלִּין) food according to the rules of ritual purity that apply to the priests' portion of the harvest (heave-offering, תְּרוּמָה, *Lev.* 22:1–16). The washing of the hands for bread is part of the "discipline of the heave" (*y. Bikkurim* II,1 64d, *Ḥagigah* II,5 78b).[296] The "discipline of the heave" for the priest in addition requires immersion of the entire body in water after any possible contact with unclean matter (*Lev.* 22:6) and waiting until the next sundown (*Lev.* 22:7). This clearly is an impossible requirement for everyday life, so one requires for profane matter only the washing of the hands, sufficient to remove tertiary contamination. It is the mark of the Jew who follows rabbinic discipline not to eat bread until his hands have been washed (with a minimum of a *revi'it* of water; cf. "*Qiddush*," p. 212–213).

In the time of the Temple, the entire company was ritually pure by immersion in water. Nevertheless, the hands have to be washed again for eating the sacrifices since unguarded hands are always unclean in a secondary matter (cf. "Washing of the Hands, Celery," p. 230). The washing of the hands has to be followed immediately by the benediction over the bread (*b. Berakhot*, 42a; *y. Berakhot* I,1 2d).[297] The benediction over the bread that precedes every meal is the act required to let us eat anything without committing larceny (cf. "*Qiddush*," p. 211). For the *Seder*, the *maẓẓah* is eaten not only as introduction to the meal but also to fulfill the obligation to eat *maẓẓah* during the night of the *Seder*. Therefore, one

---

296 אלא משום נטילת סרך.

297 תכף לנטילת ידים ברכה.

recites two benedictions, one for the *mazzah* as food and one for the obligation to eat *mazzah.* As a formal obligation, the *mazzah* must be eaten in a minimal amount, *kĕzayit* כזית, the volume of an average olive used for the production of oil (*Kelim* XVII,8).[298] For practical purposes, *Shulhan 'Arukh (Orah Hayyim §486)*,[299] authoritative for Ashkenazic and Sephardic Jews, follows an interpretation of *Tosafot* (*Yoma* 80b)[300] that an average olive is not more than half a chicken egg. *Tosafot*, writing in a region where olives were not found, and certainly olives used for the production of oil were never seen, note that the *Talmud* asserts that a mouthful is either one egg or two olives. Naturally, because of the ovaloid shape of olives, the volume occupied by two olives packed together contains at least one-third empty space. Therefore, the statement of *Tosafot* does not contradict the opinion of Maimonides mentioned later, that the size of an olive is less than one-third of the size of an egg. Maimonides lived all his life in olive-growing countries. Ashkenazic usage takes the statement of the *Shulhan 'Arukh* to mean that the volume of an average olive is at most one-third of a *rĕvi'it*, determined as 1.5 eggs (see "*Qiddush*," p. 212). To be on the safe side, a *kĕzayit* is measured as one-third of a *rĕvi'it*, meaning between 40 and 45 cm^3 or 1.1 to 1.25 fl. oz. The corresponding measures following Maimonides would be between 26 to 30 cm^3 or 0.74 to 0.84 fl oz.[301] Sephardic tradition determines not volume but weight of water; the Sephardic *kĕzayit* following *Tosafot* and *Shulhan 'Arukh* is the weight of 9 Egyptian *darāhim* or 27.8 gr., 0.98 oz., corresponding to 0.79 fl. oz. The reduction of all measures of volumes to weights (except for the heave, *hallah*, taken from dough) is a tradition that is already established in Maimonides' *Commentary on the Mishnah* (*'Idiut* I,2)[302] (cf. *Kaf Hahayyim* §486). Maimonides himself (*Shabbat* VIII,5)[303] determines the size of a dried fig as a third

---

298 כזית שאמרו לא גדול ולא קטן אלא בינוני, זה אגורי.

299 שיעור כזית יש אומרים דהוי כחצי ביצה.

300 דאין בית הבליעה מחזיק יותר משני זיתים . . . ושיערו חכמים אין בית הבליעה מחזיק יותר מביצת תרנגולת.

301 According to R. Hayim Berlin of Wolozhyn, the size of the olive is that of the average black olive of commercial "large" size or about .1 fl. oz. The size of the olive derived from the Talmudic determination of the egg as one 217-th of a Roman modius gives a standard olive of about .4 fl.oz. The details are discussed in the paper by A.I. Greenfield noted in the Bibliography.

302 ואני עשיתי מדה בתכלית מה שיכולתי מן הדקדוק ומצאתי הרביעית הנזכרת בכל התורה מכיל מן היין קרוב כ״ו כספים הנקראים דרה״ם בערבי ומן המים קרוב כ״ז דרה״ם ומקמח החטה כגון שמונה עשׂר דרה״ם . . . ואלו דרה״ם כולם מצריות. (One Egyptian Derhem = 3.09 grams).

303 וגרוגרת אחת משלושה בביצה.

of an egg and, hence, the size of an average olive as less than a third of an egg of 18 *darāhim*, 18.53 gr. or 0.65 oz. Yemenites in general follow Maimonides; however, for the *mazzah* as biblical commandment they today accept the Sephardic standard (R. I. Subeiri in *Agadta dePisḥa*). A number of Ashkenazic authorities of the eighteenth century (R. Yeḥezq'el Landau of Prague, *Z̤ĕlaḥ Pesaḥim*, p. 109, followed by R. Eliahu of Wilna and R. Shneur Zalman of Lyadi) who take the size of an egg not as a standard but a volume to be determined by actual measurements, identify olive and egg in size. It has been noted (*'Arukh Hashulḥan Oraḥ Ḥayyim* §486) that in Eastern Europe eggs were small all through the middle of the nineteenth century until the local strains of chickens were replaced by others imported from the West; the larger Western strains were the result of breeding efforts. A modern egg cup for boiled eggs has diameter of not less than 1.55 in.; egg cups from the early nineteenth century seldom have diameter of more than 1.25 in. This means that the ratio of volumes of modern to early-nineteenth-century eggs is approximately $(1.55/1.25)^3 = 1.9$ and the volume of one-half of an average late-twentieth-century egg is 0.95 of the volume of an average late-eighteenth-century egg. It is much better to follow Rashi and the Geonim in defining the volume of an egg as a universal standard as explained in the chapter on *Qiddush*.

The language of the benediction, "to produce bread from the earth," is formed after *Ps*. 104:14; the first part of the Psalm describes how the circulation of water in the atmosphere brings the rain necessary for agriculture and the production of bread on planet Earth. Without this reference, one would expect the benediction to be formulated in terms of אדמה *ădāmāh*, "soil" for agriculture, used in the benediction for the vegetable, but not in terms of ארץ, *ereẓ*, meaning mostly "land" in the geographical or "earth" in the astronomical sense.

The second benediction, to be recited over the "guarded *mazzah*," is unique for the *Seder* night; it is not required for eating *mazzah* during the remainder of Passover. The reason is that we find two contradictory Bible verses, *Ex*. 12:15 "Seven days you shall eat *mazzot*" and *Deut*. 16:6 "Six days you shall eat *mazzot*." Since it is clear, e.g., from *Ex*. 13:7, that for seven days no leavened matter can be found in a Jewish household, no leavened bread can be eaten on the Seventh Day of Passover. The verses can be reconciled by one of the exegetical rules of R. Ishmael: "If two verses deal with the same subject matter and one is less stringent than the other, the lesser requirement applies generally" (*Sifra* 1a).[304] In our case, the seventh day is excluded from the obligation of eating *mazzah* in *Deut.* 16:8. It follows that there is no obligation to eat *mazzah* on any day of Passover but there is a prohibition of leavened bread. The only obligation to eat *mazzot* is spelled out in *Ex.* 12:18: "In the First Month, in the night following the Fourteenth of the month, you must eat *mazzot*." Therefore, there is a special obligation, to be celebrated by a special benediction, during the *Seder* night (*Mekhilta deR. Ishmael*, p. 27).[305] All other times during Passover, *mazzah* just happens to be the only bread available. Since now there are two obligations, one to give praise for the *mazzah* as food and the other to give praise for the obligation to eat *mazzah* during the *Seder* night, pieces from two different *mazzot* are eaten together. In order to avoid a long discussion of which one of the two obligations is the more important one, the general custom is for each participant to eat a *kĕzayit* from each one of the two *mazzot* (*Oraḥ Ḥayyim* §475, #1).

Different Jewish groups disagree on the manner in which the *mazzot* are handled for the benedictions. Yemenite followers of the *balādī* ritual follow Maimonides, as always (*Ḥameẓ Umaẓẓah* VIII,6,8). Maimonides requires the *mazzah* for the *afiqōmen* to be broken at this point; this is also required in the *siddur* of R. Amram Gaon and is described as a Babylonian usage in the Provençal *Sefer Ha'iṭṭur* (*Maẓẓah Umaror*, p. 269a).[306] The *mazzot* are held together for the first benediction over bread as food, a prerequisite for the benediction for the *mazzah*. Then each participant receives a part from the upper whole and the middle broken *mazzah* but nobody eats or talks until the celebrant has recited the second benediction. This also is prescribed by R. Amram Gaon[307] and R. Saadia Gaon[308] and is referred to as

---

304 כל דבר שהיה בכלל ויצא מן הכלל ליטעון טוען אחר שהוא כענינו יצא להקל ולא להחמיר.

305 שבעת ימים מצות תאכלו. כתוב אחד אומר שבעת ימים מצות תאכלו וכתוב אחד אומר ששת ימים תאכל מצות. כיצד יתקיימו שני מקראות הללו? השביעי הזה בכלל היה ויצא מן הכלל ללמד על הכלל מה שביעי רשות אף כולן רשות, או מה שביעי רשות אף לילה הראשון רשות, ת״ל בראשון בארבעה עשר יום לחודש, הכתוב קבעו חובה.

306 ומנהג בבלי אחר ששתה כוס שני מנהג להצניע תחת המפה זכר צרורות בשמלותם.

307 (סדור רב עמרם גאון): דהכי אמר מרנא ורבנא משה ריש מתיבתא דמברך ברישא המוציא דלית ברכה דקדימה להמוציא, דאורחא דמלתא לברוכי לקב״ה דאפיק לחמא מן ארעא והדר לברוכי על מצה דמתעביד מנה מצוה, הלכך מברך המוציא לחם ברישא ובוצע ולא אכיל עד דמברך על ההיא אומצא לאכול מצה והדר אכיל, דלא אפשר למיכל מקמי דלבריך עליה לאכול מצה, דאית למימר לאחר שמילא כריסו ממנו חוזר ומברך עליו, אלא מברך המוציא לחם ושקיל פרוסה ומברך עליה לאכול מצה וטמיש בחרוסת והדר אכיל, והכי נהיגינן במתיבתא למיעבד.

308 ויקח בידו ככר וחצי ויברך המוציא, ואם היה ליל שבת יברך על שתי ככרות וחצי, ויחלק להם ולא יאכלו ולא ידברו אלא כל אחד יחזיק הפרוסה בידו עד שיברך המברך אשר קדשנו במצוותיו

Babylonian custom by R. Izḥaq ibn Ghiat in Spain. After the second
benediction, the *mazzah* is dipped in *ḥaroset* and eaten. This,
according to R. Amram Gaon, is the custom of the Babylonian
academies. The rule of the academies and of Maimonides is that
everything eaten before the meal is dipped in *ḥaroset*. The oldest
Ashkenazic authorities note this rule as one of the Geonim (*Hagahot
Maimuniot Ḥameẓ Umazzah* VIII,8[8]).[309] R. Saadia Gaon requires that
the *mazzah* be dipped in salt, the way bread is eaten during the year.
His ruling was accepted by all old Sephardic and Ashkenazic
authorities since *mazzah* is baked without salt and therefore is not
tasty enough to be food for which we praise the Lord (*RAVIA*
§525).[310] This is still the accepted Sephardic rule. Among Ashkenazic
authorities we find in the early fifteenth century R. Israel Isserlein of
Wiener Neustadt, who started out dipping his *mazzah* in salt but then
changed his mind, saying that in this "night of protection" no taste
enhancers are needed,[311] and *MaHaRIL* (p. קי),[312] who declares that
the love of the commandment makes the *mazzah* tasty for everybody.
This is taken up by R. Moshe Isserles (*Oraḥ Ḥayyimı* §475 #1), whose
reasoning is that bread made from very white flour never needs taste
enhancers. His ruling is followed by most Ashkenazic families.

The Sephardic way, to take the uppermost, whole *mazzah* for
the benediction over bread as food and then to add the broken *mazzah*
for the benediction of the obligation to eat *mazzah* during the *Seder* is
implied by Rashi's instructions (*Maḥzor Vitry*, p. 282).[313] This is still
reported as general custom (meaning both Sephardic and French
Ashkenazic) by the thirteenth-century *Sefer Hamanhig* (*Pesaḥ* #77).[314]
The custom is retained in Sephardic communities since it was endorsed
by the leading kabbalistic texts, R. Ḥayyim Viṭal Calabrese's *Pĕri Eẓ
Ḥayyim* (gate 21, chap. 3) and R. Moshe Cordovero's *Sha'ar
Hakawwanot* (p. 83b–c) even though the principal Sephardic authority,

---

וצונו על אכילת מצה ויטבלו במלח ויאכלו.

309   וכן מצאתי בתשובות הגאונים.

310   ויטביל במלח לפי שאינה מלוחה.

311   (לקט יושר ע' 84) ועשה מלח על המצות בליל פסח, לשנה אחרת לא עשה מלח על
המצות ואמר שהוא ליל שמורים.

312   אמר מהר״י סג״ל מצה דברכת המוציא שתי לילות דפסח אין טובלין במלח כמו
בשאר השנה משום חיבת מצה.

313   ונוטל ידיו ומברך על השלימה המוציא. ועל הפרוסה על אכילת מצה. ואוכל
משתיהן יחד. ונוֹתן לכל המסובין.

314   ולוקח המצה השלימה ומברך עליה ברכת הנהנין הקודמת בכל מקום לברכת המצוה
דאסור ליהנות מן העולם הזה בלא ברכה ומברך המוציא ולא יאכל ולא יבצע עד שיברך על המצה הפרוסה
על אכילת מצה ויבצע משתיהן ויאכל בהיסבה דרך חירות.

R. Josef Karo, opts for the way the *mazzot* are currently handled in the Western Ashkenazic ritual, viz., that all benedictions are made over all three *mazzot* together, even if only the first two are eaten at this moment (*Orah Hayyim* 475,1).[315] As an actual custom this is not reported before R. Menahem of Joigny, one of the twelfth-century Tosafists (*Tosafot Pesahim* 116a),[316] based on a reading of the relevant *Talmud* text (*b. Berakhot* 39b) that is slightly different from the manuscript readings known to us: "Everybody agrees that for the *Seder* one puts the broken *mazzah* between the two whole ones for benediction and breaking." This custom has not only the *Talmud* text but also logic to speak for it. On all other festive days, the benediction over bread is made holding two whole loaves even though only one of them is actually broken at the beginning of the meal. Therefore, there is no reason to leave the third *mazzah* out for the first benediction. The current custom of most Ashkenazic families, to take all three *mazzot* for the first benediction but only the upper two for the second one, is attributed by the Western Ashkenazic *MaHaRIL* (p. 109)[317] to his teacher R. Shalom of Wiener Neustadt (*Minhagë R. Shalom* #398 [9]). The reason seems to be that only the first two *mazzot* are used for the actual fulfillment of the biblical requirement at this moment. To be very exact, the benediction for the fulfillment of a commandment should be made עוֹבֵר לַעֲשִׂיָּה, at the moment one starts to act (*b. Pesahim* 119b). Since the *Seder* is usually made for a large company, the distribution of the *mazzah* pieces will take some time. In this respect, the Yemenite custom of distributing the *mazzah* before the recitation of the second benediction conforms best to talmudic requirements and is prescribed by R. Saadia Gaon (p. 145).[318] Other rituals do not follow his custom, probably because it requires the participants to be totally silent throughout the procedure. The basic text of Eastern European customs, *Sefer Haminhagim* of R. Eisik Tyrna (p. 51) still clings to the "Sephardic" way.[319] The procedure of

---

315 ויקח המצות כסדר שהניחם הפרוסה בין שתי השלמות ויאחזם בידו ויברך המוציא ועל אכילת מצה.

316 נראה דגם המוציא צריך לברך על הפרוסה וכן משמע בפ׳ כיצד מברכין דקאמר הכל מודים לענין פסח שמניח פרוסה בתוך השלימות ובוצע.

317 ויתפוס שלושה מצות בידו, העליונה להמוציא והשלישית ללחם משנה והפרוסה על שם לחם עוני. ויברך ברכת המוציא ויניח השלישית להשמט מידו ויברך על הפרוסה עם תפישת העליונה על אכילת מצה. וכן נוהג נמי מהר״ש ויברך שתי הברכות טרם ישברם.

318 ויחלק להם ולא יאכלו ולא ידברו אלא כל אחד מהם יחזיק את הפרוסה בידו עד שיברך המברך אשר קדשנו במצותיו וצונו על אכילת מצה.

319 ויברך המוציא על מצה העליונה שהיא הראשונה ולא יבצענה עד שיקח הפרוסה שבין שתי השלימות ויברך אשר קדשנו במצוותיו וצונו על אכילת מצה על שתיהן.

MaHaRIL was accepted for Eastern European Ashkenazim on the authority of R. Shelomo Luria (*Responsa*, #88), R. Isaiah Horovitz (*Shĕne Luḥot Habbĕrit, Pesaḥim* 2b), and the commentary *Bĕer Heṭev* to *Shulḥan 'Arukh* (*Oraḥ Ḥayyim* 475,1). R. Shelomo Luria and some manuscripts of *MaHaRIL* require that the uppermost *mazzah* be broken into two pieces between the first and second benediction, possibly to start acting at the appropriate time. The language of the benedictions for *mazzah* and *maror*, "Who santified us by His commandments and commanded us concerning the eating of *mazzah* (or *maror*)" follows R. Saadia Gaon. The formulation of R. Amram Gaon, "commanded us to eat *mazzah* (or *maror*)," still used by R. Yosef Tov Elem, more appropriate in its direct form since the fulfillment of the commandment cannot be delegated to another person (cf. p. 194), has not been accepted anywhere. Since the *mazzah* starts the dinner, it has to be consumed reclining on one's couch.

The bitter herbs, *maror*, which are eaten after the bread, do not need any separate benediction as food; that is included in the benediction for bread since this night the consumption of bitter herbs is an act necessary to start the dinner, hence an integral part of the dinner (*Orḥot Ḥayyim* 80d).[320] The bitter herbs do require a benediction for the execution of a religious commandment. The obligation to eat bitter herbs is today only a rabbinic ordinance in remembrance of the Temple since, in contrast to the obligation to eat *mazzah*, all biblical references (e.g., *Ex.* 12:8) mention bitter herbs only as an accessory to the *Pesaḥ* sacrifice (*b. Pesaḥim* 120a).[321] The *Mishnah* (*Pesaḥim* II,5) enumerates the vegetables that qualify as bitter herbs in their order of preference: חֲזֶרֶת, עוּלְשִׁין, תַּמְכָּה, חַרְחֲבִינָא, מָרוֹר. In the Babylonian *Talmud* (*b. Pesaḥim* 39a) the order is: חֲזֶרֶת, תַּמְכָּה, חַרְחֲבִינָה, עוּלְשִׁין, מָרוֹר. According to both *Talmudim*, the preferred חֲזֶרֶת is חסא *ḥassa*, a form of lettuce (Latin *lactuca*) close to the romaine or escarole sold today under the Hebrew name חַסָּה *ḥassah* or the Arabic כּסא *khassa*. For the speaker of Hebrew or Aramaic, the preference comes from the similarity of the name with the root חוס, "to have

320 ואין מברכין על החזרת בפה״א שכבר בירך על הכרפס בטבול ראשון ובאותה ברכה יצא שלא היה הפסק בקריאת ההגדה משום דמיכל ומקרי בהדדי אפשר ויש נותנין טעם אחר מפני מה אין מברכין על החזרת ב״פ האדמה לפי שברכת המוציא פוטרתה מברכת הנהנין שהיא כדברים הבאים בתוך הסעודה מחמת הסעודה אחר שהיא באה לצורך מצוה ואינו רשאי לאכול סעודתו בלתי יאכל מרור אחר מצה.

321 מצה בזמן הזה דאורייתא ומרור דרבנן. ומאי שנא מרור, דכתיב על מצות ומרורים, בזמן דאיכא פסח יש מרור ובזמן דליכא פסח ליכא מרור. מצה נמי הא כתיב על מצות ומרורים, מצה מיהדר הדר ביה קרא בערב תאכלו מצות.

compassion" (*b. Pesaḥim* 39a):[322] "The All-Merciful had compassion for us." The Aramaic and Hebrew sound *ḥ* ח is the confluence of two Arabic sounds, *ḥ* ח and *kh* ֹב. In Arabic, כס means "to be common, base" and חסא "to feel compassion, to bend over somebody." Both verbs also exist in Aramaic, both spelled identically חסא. The name of lettuce, used in antiquity for medicinal purposes and quite different from our mild plants softened by two thousand years of cultivation, is not necessarily derived from the first verb in its Aramaic form, but Pliny (*Natural History* XIX[8]125, XX[7]24) mentions lettuce several times in his catalog of medicinal plants and informs us that the most base variety is called πικρίς "bitter" in Greek. This kind of lettuce may either be our *ḥassa* or the last plant in the list that is sold under the name of "bitter." עֻלְשִׁין *'ulshīn* are identified by both *Talmudim* (*b. Pesaḥim*, 39a; *y. Pesaḥim* II,5 29c) with endives (Pliny *N.H.* XIX[8]129). תַּמְכָּא *tamkā* is identified in the Jerusalem *Talmud* (*y. Pesaḥim* II,5 29c) as *gingidium*, a plant of the family of carrots that grows in Syria and is very bitter (Pliny *N.H.* XX[5]33). Rashi explains *tamkā* as (Latin) *marrubium*, horehound; Alfassi has Arabic שִׁילַם, a Persian word designating *lolium temolentum*, darnel. Later Ashkenazic sources (*Hagahot Maimuniot Ḥameẓ Umaẓẓah* VII,13) identify the word as (Middle High German) *krên*, "horseradish." חַרְחֲבִינָא *ḥarḥavīna* is explained (*b. Pesaḥim* 39a) by Aramaic אצוותא דדיקלא. Rashi explains this as a parasitic plant growing on trees; his Romance translation *voudille* would mean "sweet-scented virgin's bower." Later Ashkenazic sources (*RAVIA* #473) identify the plant as vermouth, Romance *amerfeuille* "bitter leaf." The Jerusalem *Talmud* explains *ḥarḥavīna* as a plant closely related to *'ulshīn*. Alfassi and Maimonides identify the plant as אלקרצעינה *al qirṣa'na*, "eringo." In current practice, the bitter herb used in addition to romaine lettuce is horseradish with green leaves (*Sefer Mizwot Gadol*, II, #41 in the name of R. Jacob Tam; R. Jacob Weilla, *Responsa* 140a).[323] Since it is impossible to eat a full *kĕzayit* of raw horseradish stem, it is recommended to use grated horseradish, which, being exposed to the air during the reading of the *Haggadah*, will get less hot (*Mishnah Berurah* §473, 36).

The bitter herbs are dipped in *ḥaroset* for health reasons, as was noted earlier; the details of *ḥaroset* are in imitation of the mortar

---

322 ואמר רבא מאי חזרת חסא דחס רחמנא עילוון.

323 נראה הא דכתב רבנו תם 'ולא שרשים' היינו השרשים הקטנים המתפצלים לכאן ולכאן אבל השורש הגדול שבו עומד הירק הוי בכלל קלח.

made by the Israelites in their slavery in Egypt. The recipe of R. Isaac Luria (*ARI*), or rather that of his mother, for *ḥaroset* calls for a mixture of three kinds of spices: sweet spikenard, ginger, and cinnamon (sticks), and seven kinds of mashed fruit: grapes, figs, pomegranate kernels, dates, walnuts, apples, and pears (R. Moshe Cordovero, *Sha'ar Hakawwanot* 83d, note 6). R. Moshe Cordovero also reports that in Northern Europe, where only the last three kinds of fruit were available, *ḥaroset* was made from apples (Yiddish **אפפעל**), pears (**בירן**), and walnuts (**נוס**) by re-interpretation of the expression (*Ex.* 35:32) **ובחרוֹשת אבן למלאת** "to artfully set stones" to read **ובחרוֹשת אב״נ למלאת** "to fill up *ḥaroset* with A(ppel), B(irn), N(uss)."

At the celebration of the *Seder* in Jerusalem during the time of the Temple, the eating of bitter herbs was followed by the benediction over the festive offering (*ḥagīgāh*), the "cattle" of *Deut.* 16:2 (*Sifry Deut.* #129), and then the benediction over the *Pesaḥ* sacrifice. According to Maimonides (*Ḥameẓ Umaẓẓah* VIII,8-9),[324] a bite-size portion of the *Pesaḥ* was then eaten, either alone or in the manner of Hillel, followed by the festive meal and, just before Grace was recited, each participant had to eat another small piece of the *Pesaḥ* sacrifice. In the opinion of R. Moses of Coucy (*Sefer Miẓwot Gadol* II #41),[325] the *Pesaḥ* was eaten only once, at the end. The sandwich in Hillel's manner, to eat *maẓẓah* and *maror* together, is only a remembrance today since the verse *Num* 9:11, ". . . on *maẓẓot* and bitter herbs they shall eat it," is about the "Second *Pesaḥ*," the sacrifice of the Fourteenth of Iyar for men who were not ritually clean on the Fourteenth of Nisan; this ceremony cannot be observed outside the Temple precincts. Since the obligation to eat *maẓẓah* on Passover is permanent but the obligation to eat bitter herbs is only a rabbinic requirement as long as the Temple is not rebuilt, one may not eat *maẓẓah* and *maror* together to fulfill the biblical commandment; the sandwich is eaten today as a remembrance of the Temple (*b. Pesaḥim* 115a).[326]

---

324 ומברך אשר קדשנו במצותיו וצונו על אכילת הפסח ואוכל מגופו של פסח. . . . ואחר כך נמשך בסעודה ואוכל כל מה שהוא רוצה לאכול ושותה כל מה שהוא רוצה לשתות. ובאחרונה אוכל מבשׂר הפסח אפילו כזית ואינו טועם אחריו כלל.

325 ואחר כך אוכל מגופו של פסח ומברך אשר קדשנו במצותיו וציונו על אכילת פסח ובזמן הזה במקום הפסח אוכל באחרונה המצה הבצועה.

326 הכי אמר הלל משמיה דגמרא לא ניכרוך איניש מצה ומרור בהדי הדדי וניכול משום דסבירא לן מצה בזמן הזה דאורייתא ומרור דרבנן ואתי מרור דרבנן ומבטיל ליה למצה דאורייתא.

The Sephardic and Oriental custom following Maimonides (*Ḥameẓ Umaẓẓah* VIII,8)[327] and the Provençal authorities (*Orḥot Ḥayyim* 81a [27]) is to dip the sandwich in *ḥaroset* since it is eaten with bitter herbs. The Ashkenazic custom was not fixed from the earliest times. It is impossible to determine the original Babylonian custom in this matter since the texts of both R. Amram Gaon and R. Saadia Gaon are reported with dipping (text of R. Amram Gaon published by R. N. Koronel, quote of R. Saadia Gaon by Abudirham) or without it (quote of R. Amram Gaon in *Sefer Hamanhig, Pesaḥ* #83, published text of R. Saadia Gaon). Since the sandwich contains *maror*, and *maror* requires *ḥaroset*, dipping was required by a number of Ashkenazic authorities, foremost among them R. Meir of Rothenburg (*Hagahot Maimuniot Ḥameẓ Umaẓẓah* VIII [7]);[328] his main argument was that this procedure was required in the Temple. The older Provençal *Sefer Hamanhig* (*Pesaḥ* #83) argues that not dipping will lead people astray when the Temple will suddenly be rebuilt. Rashi (*Maḥzor Vitry*, p. 282)[329] requires that the *maror* be dipped in *ḥaroset* before it is put into the sandwich. However, R. Yosef Tov Elem (Bonfils), a contemporary of Rashi, in his didactic poem on the rules of Passover that in Eastern Europe used to be part of the service of the "great Sabbath" preceding Passover, mentions the sandwich without any dipping,[330] probably as a quote from his copy of R. Amram Gaon. In this he is followed by *RAVIA* (p. 166) who notes that *Mishnah* and *Talmud* mention only two dippings, one before the Recital and one afterward. His ruling was adopted by R. Eisik Tyrna (*Sefer Minhagim*, p. 52),[331] who insists that the main reason for *ḥaroset* is not as a remembrance of slavery in Egypt (*b. Pesaḥim* 115a) but for health reasons (*b. Pesaḥim* 115b), to attenuate potentially damaging bitterness; eating the bitter herbs between two layers of bread has the same

---

327 וחוזר וכורך מצה ומרור ומטבל בחרוסת ואוכלן בלי ברכה זכר למקדש.

328 'ואחר כך כורך מצה ומרור כאחת ומטבל בהרוסת.' וכן נהג מהר״ם וכן מודה רבנו תם בטבול זה שתהא בחרוסת שהרי אנו עושין אותה זכר למקדש כהלל והלל היה מטבל בחרוסת שהרי זו היתה אכילת מרור שלו. . . . אמנם רבי יוסף טוב עלם יסד בסדורו בלא טיבול וכן נראה לרבי״ה וליתר גאוני אשכנז.

329 וחוזר ובוצע ממצה שלישית. ואוכל ממנה ומן המרור הנטבל בחרוסת יחד.

330 לוֹקֵחַ פְּרוּסָה וּמְבָרֵךְ לֶאֱכוֹל מַצָּה בְּמֶלֶל
וּבַהֲדֵי דְהַהִיא דְהַמּוֹצִיא אוֹכֵל וְכוֹלֵל
וּמְבָרֵךְ בַּחֲזֶרֶת לֶאֱכוֹל מָרוֹר וְטוֹבֵל וְכוֹלֵל
וְהָדָר אָכֵל מַצָּה וּמָרוֹר בְּלֹא בְרָכָה וְכוֹרְכָן בְּבַת אַחַת כְּהִלֵּל.

331 ויקח מצה שלישית וכורכה עם לטו״ך או עם קרי״ן ויאכל כזית בהסיבה בלא טיבול ובלא ברכה כהלל[א].

[א] כי מה שצריך טיבול היינו משום סכנתא דקפא, אבל עכשיו שיש מצה עמו אין צריך, ואף על פי שהלל היה טובל בחרוסת משום שהוא לא היה אוכל מרור קודם לכן.

attenuating effect. R. Eliahu of Wilna (commentary to *Oraḥ Ḥayyim* §475,1) finds this argument explicit in the Jerusalem *Talmud* (*y. Pesaḥim* X,3 37d),[332] which states that *maror* is eaten all year long with bread and needs *ḥaroset* for the *Seder* only because it is consumed by itself. R. Shalom of Wiener Neustadt (*Minhagim* #398,400) dipped for himself but did not insist that his students or guests do the same. His student *MaHaRIL* (p. 113, #35-36) acted in the same way. These authorities also leave the question whether to recline as an individual option. Those who insist on dipping because of the precedent for the *Seder* in the rebuilt Temple also must insist on reclining. The question of reclining is not mentioned in Ashkenazic *Haggadot* of the seventeenth and eighteenth centuries; reclining is universally prescribed only starting with the editions of R. Eliahu of Wilna and W. Heidenheim.

The Yemenite version of the introduction to the sandwich is the language of the final instruction of the *Talmud* (*b. Pesaḥim* 115a).[333] This text is in general use among Oriental Jews and was also the text of the autochthonous Italian ritual. The Sephardic text is close to the Talmud text (*b. Pesaḥim* 115a)[334] that introduces the discussion of Hillel's observance. The language of this sentence is attested by both Sephardic and Ashkenazic *Talmud* manuscripts. The Ashkenazic version, which has "together" for talmudic and Sephardic "in one batch" is already found in the *Maḥzor Vitry* (p. 282).[335] The current Ashkenazic text seems to be derived from this French version; from the language of the late-twelfth-century *Ma'asë Roqeaḥ* (#68) and the *Roqeaḥ* of R. Eliezer of Worms (p. 154),[336] it seems that in the twelfth century the text of the German congregations along the Rhine was close to today's Yemenite text but with R. Yosef Bonfils's addition "without blessing and without dipping" probably taken, as mentioned earlier, from the Ashkenazic version of R. Amram Gaon's *siddur*. That addition is not found in the printed Amsterdam *Haggadah* of 1662 but it is printed, for Ashkenazim, in the Amsterdam *Haggadah* of 1695. The addition is found in most Ashkenazic *Haggadot* of the eighteenth

---

332 שבכל הלילות אנו מטבילין אותו עם הפת וכאן אנו מטבילין אותו בפני עצמו.

333 בלא ברכה זכר למקדש כהלל.

334 אמרו עליו על הלל שהיה כורכן בבת אחת ואוכלן שנאמר על מצות ומרורים יאכלוהו.

335 זכר למקדש כהלל. שהיה כורך מצה ומרור ופסח ביחד. משום שנאמר על מצות ומרורים יאכלוהו.

336 בלא טיבול ובלא ברכה ובלא הסיבה זכר כהלל על מצות ומרורים יאכלוהו.

century since most of them are copies of the Amsterdam 1695 edition; it is not found in the few editions based on the Amsterdam 1662 edition. Heidenheim obviously was uncomfortable with the addition, given the number of authorities who require or tolerate dipping. Since he did not want to eliminate any traditional prayer text, he moved the text, in prayer typeface, to the instructions. His text reads (first Hebrew, then German in Hebrew letters, then the first line of his *Haggadah* text):

כּוֹרֵךְ: יקח כזית מן המצה השלישי התחתונה וכזית לאַטוּגאַ או חזרת וכורכו עם המצה ויאכלם
בהסבה **בלא טיבול ובלא ברכה** רק יאמר זה:
מאַן נימט אײן כזית לאַטיק אָדר קרען אונד אײן כזית פֿאָן דער אונטערשטן מצה אונד
איסט בײדע צוזאַממן **בלא טיבול ובלא ברכה** אונד לאַנט:
זֵכֶר לְמִקְדָּשׁ כְּהִלֵּל:

Translation:
One takes a *kĕzayit* from the third *maẓẓah* and a *kĕzayit* lettuce or horseradish, bundles it up with the *maẓẓah* and eats it reclining, **without dipping and without benediction**, only one says the following:
A remembrance of the Temple following Hillel.

It was the standard before 1848 to write Hebrew words in a German text in Rashi script and German words in a Hebrew text in *mashiṭṭa*, script. Because of the huge success of the Heidenheim prints, which quickly became the standard of Ashkenazic non-ḥasidic prayer texts, the history behind this complicated composite text quickly became forgotten and the additional text disappeared from Ashkenazic consciousness. After 1848, J. Lehrberger, the son-in-law and successor of Wolf Heidenheim, changed all German instructions and translations written in Hebrew letters into German texts printed in German characters (Roman alphabet, Gothic typeface). At that occasion, the Hebrew text was eliminated from the German translation. In the early twentieth century, the entire Heidenheim *Haggadah* was revised and newly translated by Rabbi Dr. Selig Bamberger. In his edition, the reference to "without dipping and without benediction" was removed also from the Hebrew text. (The Heidenheim prayer book similarly did not fare well in the hands of a later editor.) The current standard of Ashkenazic Orthodox observance, *Mishnah Berurah* (§475, #19), decides that Jewish groups that do not dip the sandwich have to continue not dipping, but all others, including those without a firm background of family or group customs, should dip the sandwich following the Sephardic custom. Therefore, current Ashkenazic practice has eliminated the addition "without dipping and without benediction."

Many Jewish groups start the festive meal by eating eggs, not only the single egg on the *Seder* plate but one egg for every participant. The reason is explained by R. Israel Isserlein (*Leqet Yosher*, p. 85):[337] According to R. Yehoshua (*b. Rosh Hashanah* 11a; *y. Rosh Hashanah* I,2 56d)[338] our Patriarchs were born and died on Passover (it being the sign of a perfectly just person to die at his birthday, *Ex.* 23:26). Now a hard-boiled egg, being oval and without beginning or end, is the usual symbolic first food presented to a bereaved person after a funeral to show our compassion for his boundless sorrow. Therefore, we eat hard-boiled eggs in remembrance of the Patriarchs.

As explained in the answer to the wise child, the *Pesaḥ* sacrifice had to be eaten as the last morsel so that its taste should linger on and, in the same way, one may not eat any solid food after the *maẓẓah* of remembrance has been consumed (*b. Pesaḥim* 119b).[339] This last piece is called "*afiqomen*" because the *Mishnah* states that one may *not* have *afiqomen* after the consumption of the sacrifice and the name reminds one of this rule (*RAVIA* #525, p. 167) (cf. p. 274). Since the *Pesaḥ* sacrifice **must** be eaten before midnight (it becomes ritually unclean at midnight, *Mishnah Pesaḥim* X,9),[340] the *afiqomen maẓẓah* **should** be eaten before midnight (*loc. cit.*, p. 168).

---

337 וזכורני בב׳ לילות של פסח אכל כל אחד מבני ביתו בתחלת הסעודה ביצה מבושלת קשה, ולפעמים אכל אחד ב׳ ביצות, וכן המנהג באושטריך. ואמר שמת אברהם אבינו בליל פסח.

338 בניסן נברא העולם בניסן נולדו אבות בניסן מתו אבות.

339 אין מפטירין אחר מצה אפיקומן.

340 הפסח אחר חצות מטמא את הידים.

Grace

The obligation to say Grace is derived (*b. Berakhot* 21a; *y. Berakhot* V,7 11a)[341] from *Deut.* 8:10: "When you will eat and be satisfied, then you must praise the Lord your God for the Good Land that He gave you." It is a general principle of talmudic interpretation that a commandment expressed in the singular is directed toward the people as a collective whereas one in the plural imposes an obligation upon every single individual. For example (*b. Menaḥot* 65b; *Tosafot, s.v. usfartem*),[342] the institution of the Jubilee year is the responsibility of the supreme rabbinic authority since it is based on *Lev.* 25:8, "You [sing.] must count for yourself seven weeks of years," whereas the counting of the seven weeks of *'Omer* between Passover and Pentecost is an obligation of the individual based on *Lev.* 23:15: "You [pl.] must count, starting after the holiday, from the day on which you brought the *'Omer* of waving. . . ." Since the individual eats and is satisfied, it is clear that after any meal the individual also has the obligation to give thanks for the food. The meaning of the singular in *Deut.* 8:10 is that there is a special obligation to give thanks as a group if the meal was taken as a group; this is called *zimmūn* "appointment, summons." By rabbinic ordinance, a group consists of at least three adults, so they can have one leader and at least two respondents as required by *Ps.* 34:4: "Praise [pl.] the Lord with me, let us elevate His name together" (*b. Berakhot* 45a; *y. Berakhot* VII,1 11a).[343] Both *Talmudim* (*b. Berakhot* 48b; *y. Berakhot* VII,1 11a)[344] explain the biblical commandment as follows: When you will eat and be satisfied, then *you must praise* that is the *zimmūn* [since "you" is singular], *the Lord your God* that is the first benediction to "Him, Who feeds all," *for the Land* that is the second benediction for the Land of Israel, *the Good one* that is the

---

341 מנין לברכת המזון לאחריה מן התורה? שנאמר ואכלת ושבעת וברכת.

342 וספרתם לכם שתהא ספירה לכל אחד ואחד. גבי יובל כתיב וספרת לך דאבית דין קאמר רחמנא.

343 שלשה שאכלו כאחת חייבין לזמן. מנא הני מילי? אמר רב אסי דאמר קרא גדלו ליי אתי ונרוממה שמו יחדיו.

344 תנו רבנן מנין לברכת המזון מן התורה? שנאמר ואכלת ושבעת וברכת זו ברכת הזימון, את יי אלהיך זו הזן את הכל, על הארץ זו ברכת הארץ, הטובה זו ברכת בונה ירושלים. וכן הוא אומר 'ההר הטוב הזה והלבנון', אשר נתן לך זה הטוב והמטיב.

third benediction for Jerusalem [called Good Mountain, with the Temple called Lebanon, in *Deut.* 3:25], *that He gave you* that is the fourth benediction for "all good things."

The last part of the interpretation seems far-fetched and is not uncontroversial. The majority opinion (*b. Berakhot* 48b; *y. Berakhot* VII,1 11a)[345] holds that the fourth benediction "for all good things" is a later addition, *viz.*, that "the day when the dead of Betar were allowed to be buried, at Yavne they ordered 'all good things' to be said, praise to 'the Good' that the bodies were not decomposed and to 'Him Who does good' that permission was received for the burial." The siege of Betar was the last battle of the war of Bar Kokhba; that war was a rebellion in the eyes of the Roman state, and slain rebels were never allowed to be buried under Roman law (cf. *Suetonius, Tiberius* 61). Since the fourth benediction is held to be a rabbinic requirement only, people who work on hourly wages or otherwise on a time basis were not required to recite this last blessing during the working day. To indicate the break after the third benediction, the last of the first three benedictions end with "Amen" (*b. Berakhot* 45b).[346] For Ashkenazic Jews, this is the only time a person says "Amen" for one of his own benedictions; otherwise "Amen" (considered as abbreviation for **אל מלך נאמן** "God, trustworthy King" [*b. Shabbat* 119b]) may only be said as confirmation of another person's benediction. This is the original Babylonian tradition (*b. Berakhot* 45b)[347] confirmed by R. Hai Gaon (*Sefer Ha'eshkol*, p. 45).[348] The Sephardic tradition here follows an alternate tradition, reported only in the Jerusalem *Talmud* and in the name of the Babylonian Rav Ḥisda (or Ḥasda, *y. Berakhot* V,5 9c) that one may finish one's own benediction with "Amen" at the end of every major section of a prayer service. A third opinion, not followed by any Jewish group today, is that of R. Naḥshon Gaon that one may say "Amen" after one's own benediction only after the third benediction of Grace and in the morning and evening prayers after the doxologies preceding the

---

345 דאמר רב מתנא אותו היום שניתנו הרוגי ביתר לקבורה תקנו ביבנה הטוב והמטיב, הטוב שלא הסריחו והמטיב שניתנו לקבורה.

346 אביי עני ליה בקלא כי היכי דלשמעו פועלים וליקומו, דהטוב והמטיב לאו דאורייתא.

347 תני חדא העונה אחר ברכותיו הרי זה משובח ותניא אידך הרי זה מגונה; לא קשיא הא בבונה ירושלים הא בשאר ברכות.

348 וכתבו רב יהודאי ורב האי בכל ברכה אחרונה שאין אחריה כלום יכול לומר אמן והכי משמע בירושלמי דאמר סתמא מאן דתני הרי זה חכם בעונה לבסוף. ואיכא מרבואתא דאמרי דוקא בבונה ירושלים אתמר דעונה אמן.

recitation of the *Shema'* (*Sefer Ha'eshkol*, p. 9).[349] (The reason for the last ruling is that the *Shema'* contains 245 words so that the three letters of *Amen* together with the *Shema'* give a total of 248, the traditional number of human limbs in talmudic anatomy [*Ahilut* I,8], to fulfill the demand of *Ps.* 35:10: "All my bones shall say, O Lord, who is like You?")

The Jerusalem *Talmud* (p. 339) ascribes the opinion that the benediction "for all good things" is of biblical origin to R. Ishmael, a student of R. Yehoshua who lived before the revolt of Bar Kokhba. Similarly, the Babylonian *Talmud* (*b. Berakhot* 48b)[350] has a statement of Rebbi Eliezer, the colleague of R. Yehoshua and student of Rabban Yoḥanan ben Zakkai before the destruction of the Temple, who like R. Yehoshua died long before the revolt of Bar Kokhba, and who already refers to "the benediction instituted by the Sages" or "the benediction instituted by the Sages at Yavne." Therefore, it seems that the benediction was formulated at the latest at Yavne after the fall of Jerusalem in 70 C.E. to give thanks for the continued existence of the Jewish people but that it gained popular acceptance only after the war of Bar Kokhba when permission was received to bury the dead of Betar. This interpretation is in accordance with other historical information contained in the *Talmud*. It is reported (*b. Rosh Hashanah* 31b)[351] that according to tradition, after the fall of Jerusalem the seat of the Synhedrion was at Yavne (an imperial domain in the Southern plain), Usha (lower Galilee in the North), Yavne, Usha, and then at Shefar'am, Bet Shearim, Sepphoris, and Tiberia, all in Galilee. We also hear (*b. Shabbat* 33b)[352] that Rebbi Yehuda bar Illai, a resident of Usha (*Cant. rabbah* 2,16), was appointed official spokesman of the Synhedrion by the Roman government because he publicly appreciated

---

349 ואמרו משמיה דרב נחשון ריש מתיבתא דסורא בשלושה מקומות יחיד עונה אמן לעצמו: בבונה ירושלים, בבוחר בעמו ישראל, ובאוהב עמו ישראל.

350 ובשבת מתחיל בנחמה ומסיים בנחמה ואומר קדושת היום באמצע. רבי אליעזר אומר רצה לאומרה בנחמה אומרה, בברכת הארץ אומרה, בברכה שתקנו חכמים ביבנה אומרה.
Most Ashkenazic manuscripts do not have the note "in Yavne" but this does not change the meaning of the remark.

351 וכנגדן גלתה סנהדרין מגמרא מלשכת הגזית לחנות ומחנות לירושלים ומירושלים ליבנה ומיבנה לאושא ומאושא ליבנה ומיבנה לאושא ומאושא לשפרעם ומשפרעם לבית שערים ומבית שערים לצפורי ומצפורי לטבריא.

352 נענה רבי יהודה ברבי אלעאי ראש המדברים בכל מקום . . . ואמאי קרו ליה ראש המדברים בכל מקום דיתבי רבי יהודה ורבי יוסי ורבי שמעון ויתיב יהודה בן גרים גבייהו, פתח ר' יהודה ואמר כמה נעים מעשיהן של אומה זו, תקנו שווקים תקנו גשרים תקנו מרחצאות. ר' יוסי שתק. נענה רבי שמעון בר יוחי ואמר כל מה שתקנו לא תקנו אלא לצורך עצמן: תקנו שווקים להושיב בהן זונות, מרחצאות לעדן בהן עצמן, גשרים ליטול מהן מכס. הלך יהודה בן גרים וסיפר דבריהם ונשמעו למלכות, אמרו יהודה שעילה יתעלה, יוסי ששתק יגלה לציפורי, שמעון שגינה יהרג.

their activities. It is also reported (*b. Ketubot* 50a)[353] that the Synhedrion promulgated important decrees at Usha during the time of activity of R. Akiba, i.e., before the outbreak of the revolt of Bar Kokhba. In the aftermath of the revolt, the Synhedrion was abolished and the study of Torah forbidden. When a later emperor revoked the Hadrianic decrees of persecution, the Synhedrion was reconstituted. According to the *Talmud* (*b. Berakhot* 63b)[354] this was at Yavne; the *Midrash* (*Cant. rabbah loc. cit.*)[355] puts it at Usha. Most writers of Jewish history follow the *Midrash*, a Galilean compilation of unknown date and editorship. However, it is difficult to accept this preference against the triple testimony of the *Talmud*, a Babylonian text of known date and editorship, even if its composition was relatively late and took place far away from the areas where the events described took place. There may have been only one meeting at Yavne is desolate Judea for symbolic reasons. That meeting instituted a propaganda campaign for the study of Torah and emphasized the importance of the Fourth Benediction of Grace.[356] The majority who hold that the Fourth Benediction was instituted at Yavne also hold that *Deut.* 8:10 gives only a framework for possible praises of which the one for food for the whole world is attributed to Moses but that for the Land is credited to Joshua, the one for Jerusalem to David and Solomon (*b. Berakhot* 48b).[357]

The Babylonian *Talmud* (*b. Berakhot* 20b) reports an inconclusive discussion over the question of whether men and women are equally obligated to say Grace. This discussion follows another piece[358] in which it is clearly stated that the obligation to say Grace is not bound to any fixed time even though one usually eats full meals

---

353 א״ר אילעא באושא התקינו המבזבז אל יבזבז יותר מחומש. תניא נמי הכי המבזבז אל יבזבז יותר מחומש שמא יצטרך לבריות ומעשה באחד שבקש לבזבז ולא הניח לו חבירו ומנו רבי ישבב ואמרי לה רבי ישבב ולא הניחו חבירו ומנו רבי עקיבא.

354 תנו רבנן כשנכנסו רבותינו לכרם ביבנה היו שם רבי יהודה ורבי יוסי ורבי נחמיה ורבי אליעזר בנו של רבי יוסי הגלילי, פתחו כולם בכבוד אכסניא ודרשו. פתח רבי יהודה ראש המדברים בכל מקום בכבוד התורה.

355 בשלפי השמד נתכנסו רבותינו לאושא ואלו הן: רבי יהודה ורבי נחמיה ורבי מאיר ורבי יוסי ורבי שמעון בן יוחי ורבי אליעזר בנו של רבי יוסי הגלילי ורבי אליעזר בן יעקב.

356 See also H. Albeck, *Die vierte Eulogie des Tischgebets*, MGWJ 73(1934), pp. 430 ff.

357 אמר רב נחמן משה תקן לישׂראל ברכת הזן בשעה שירד להם מן, יהושע תקן להם ברכת הארץ כיון שנכנסו לארץ, דוד ושלמה תקנו להם בונה ירושלים, דוד תקן על ישׂראל עמך ועל ירושלים עירך ושלמה תקן על הבית הגדול והקדוש, הטוב והמטיב ביבנה תקנוה כנגד הרוגי ביתר.

358 נשים חייבות בברכת המזון. פשיטא מהו דתימא הואיל וכתיב 'בתת ה' לכם בערב בשׂר לאכל ובשׂר בבקר לשׂבע' כמצות עשׂה שהזמן גרמא דמי קמ״ל.

mornings and evenings and Scripture explicitly describes the provision of quails and Mannah in terms of "morning and evening" (*Ex.* 16:6–8); hence, the obligation of women is identical to that of men. Therefore, the later discussion can refer only to the obligation of *zimmūn* and the recitation of Grace by a group, as contrasted to separate recitation by each individual. Medieval authorities disagree on the meaning of the discussion. Alfassi and Nachmanides (*RYF Berakhot* 12a) equate men and women in their obligations, Maimonides (*Hilkhot Berakhot* V,1)[359] and *RAVIA* (*Berakhot* #61)[360] declare the question unresolved and therefore women should not recite Grace for men. R. Abraham ben David of Posquières (*RaVaD*) energetically supports Alfassi in his commentary on the latter's compendium but is silent in his notes to Maimonides, meaning that he supports Alfassi's interpretation in theory and Maimonides' in practice. This expresses current practice. Maimonides also requires that women who say *zimmūn* together refrain from adding the invocation "our God" in the presence of ten women. This ruling is repeated in *Shulḥan 'Arukh* (§199) even though it has no basis in the *Talmud*, which requires only ten free adults. It is reported of R. Simḥa of Vitry, a student of Rashi, that he counted women to supply the number of three or ten adults required for *zimmūn* (*Mordokhai Berakhot* #158). Of the Ashkenazic authorities of the late eighteenth century, R. Eliahu of Wilna (*Notes to Shulḥan 'Arukh loc. cit.*) requires three or more women who ate together to recite *zimmūn*, most other authorities only give them the right to do so. R. Shneur Zalman of Lyadi, the founder of Lubavich Ḥasidism, in his *Shulḥan 'Arukh Harav* (*ad loc.*) even gives women who ate together with men the right to hold their own *zimmūn*. This is Sephardic practice (*Kaf Haḥayyim* §199 #23); current Ashkenazic practice is that women always can fulfill their obligations by listening to men's *zimmūn* if the entire Grace is recited aloud. This is true also for men who do not understand Hebrew; otherwise it is preferable for them to recite Grace in the vernacular (*Ṭur, Shulḥan 'Arukh* §199).

It is a general principle that a blessing must have a material substrate for which it is recited, as explained in the secition on *Qiddush*. Now Grace is said for food that is already eaten. If Grace

---

359 נשים ועבדים חייבין בברכת המזון. וספק יש בדבר אם הן חייבין מן התורה לפי שאין קבוע לה זמן או אינם חייבין מן התורה. לפיכך אין מוציאין את הגדולים ידי חובתן. אבל הקטנים חייבין בברכת המזון כדי לחנכן במצות.

360 ולא איפשיטא ליה בגמרא הא דתנן נשים חייבות בברכת המזון אי מדאורייתא אי מדרבנן, ונפקא מניה לאפוקי גברא ידי חובתו, דלא אתי דרבנן ומפיק דאורייתא, ואזלינן לחומרא ולא מפקי.

were just an acknowledgment for bounty received, there would be no question that Grace may be recited for itself. However, Grace is also a prayer for continued, future blessing. In addition, the conditions spelled out by the *Talmud* (*Berakhot;* see p. 239) for a cup of benediction are really presented for the cup over which Grace is recited. This shows that reciting Grace over a full cup of wine is at least a desirable act. The question is whether Grace may be recited without a cup of wine. The *Mishnah* describing the *Seder* (*Pesaḥim* X,7) states[361] that "one mixes the Third Cup and recites Grace over it." According to one opinion in the *Talmud*, this shows that saying Grace over a cup of wine is a general requirement; the contrary opinion is that one uses the occasion to recite Grace over a full cup since one has to formally drink Four Cups anyhow.[362] There are three interpretations found in the literature explaining the meaning of the talmudic discussion in the two tractates mentioned. The tradition of the Geonim, represented by Maimonides (*Berakhot* VII,15) and Alfassi (*Pesakhim* #794) is that the use of a cup of wine is always meritorious but not required except for the *Seder*. The opinion of the later Tosafists (reported *Hagahot Maimuniot Berakhot* VII [ס]) is that the cup is *required* for *zimmūn*. This is also the opinion of the Sephardic *Zohar Ḥadash, Midrash Ruth*.[363] Only a few Ashkenazic authorities, among them R. Meir of Rothenburg, require a cup for every recitation of Grace. The *Zohar* (II, p. 174)[364] requires that at least some food remain on the table since Heavenly blessing does not dwell on an empty table. During the *Seder* night, the celebrant usually is the head of household and he also recites Grace (*Shulḥan 'Arukh Oraḥ Ḥayyim* §479, note of R. Moshe Isserles),[365] even though normally a guest should recite Grace to give him occasion to ask for Divine blessing for his host (*loc. cit.* §201).

It is clear from the great diversity of texts that through most of the talmudic period only the general contents and the final doxologies were fixed, in general agreement with the institutions of the Men of the Great Assembly. This is true for the Israeli tradition

---

361 מזגו לו כוס שלישי מברך על מזונו.

362 א״ל רבינא לרבא שמעת מינה ברכה טעונה כוס א״ל ארבעה כסי תקינו רבנן דרך חירות הואיל ואיכא כל חד וחד נעביד ביה מצוה.

363 ברכת המזון בג׳ צריך כוס שלא בג׳ אין צריך כוס.

364 אסור ליה לבר נש לברכא על פתורא ריקניא. מאי טעמא משום דברכתא דלעילא לא שריא באתר ריקניא.

365 ונהגו שבעל הבית מברך ברכת המזון בליל פסח שנאמר טוב עין הוא יברך והוא מקרי טוב עין שאמר כל דכפין ייתי ויכול.

up to the destruction of the Jewish community in Palestine by the first Crusade in 1099, while in Babylonia there was an early movement toward standardization of the text.[366] It is reported in the Jerusalem *Talmud* (*y. Berakhot* IV,4 8b) as commentary on the statement of Rebbi Eliezer[367] that "he who uses a fixed formula for prayer cannot pray from the heart," that the formula extended as an invitation to lead the congregation in prayer was[368] "come and present a *Qeroba*," a poetic formulation of the prayers (based on the fixed contents and final doxologies),[369] meaning probably: present your own composition for the prayer. In this sense, one finds frequently short poems for Grace in Palestinian texts; all known Palestinian *Haggadah* fragments from the Cairo *Genizah* contain such poetic forms of grace. A typical one is a recently published text:[370]

בָּרוּךְ אַתָּה יי אֱלֹהֵינוּ מֶלֶךְ הָעוֹלָם
אֵל מְהוּלָּל בַּפֶּסַח בְּלֶחֶם אֲכִילַת עוֹנִי
כִּי בוֹ פְּדִיתָנוּ וּנְבָרְכָךְ צוּרֵנוּ
כַּכָּתוּב פּוֹתֵחַ אֶת יָדֶךָ וּמַשְׂבִּיעַ לְכָל חַי רָצוֹן
בָּרוּךְ אַתָּה יי הַזָּן אֶת הַכּוֹל.

בִּמְקוֹם דֶּשֶׁא עַמְּךָ מֵאֶרֶץ אֲרוּרִים גָּאַלְתָּ
בִּזְכוּת דַּם פֶּסַח חוֹק דָּת וּבְרִית
כַּכָּתוּב וְאָכַלְתָּ וְשָׂבָעְתָּ וּבֵרַכְתָּ אֶת יי אֱלֹהֶיךָ עַל הָאָרֶץ הַטּוֹבָה אֲשֶׁר נָתַן לָךְ
בָּרוּךְ אַתָּה יי עַל הָאָרֶץ וְעַל הַמָּזוֹן.

גְּאוּלָּה תָּחִישׁ לְשׁוֹמְרֵי מִצְוֹת
זִיכֵּר לְצִיּוֹן עֲבוֹדַת קָרְבָּן
כַּכָּתוּב בּוֹנֵה יְרוּשָׁלַיִם יי נִדְחֵי יִשְׂרָאֵל יְכַנֵּס
בָּרוּךְ אַתָּה יי בּוֹנֶה יְרוּשָׁלָיִם.

Praised are You o Lord, our God, King of the Universe
The Power, praised on Passover by the bread eaten in deprivation
Truly, on this day You rescued us and we shall praise You, our Rock.

---

366 Many texts of Grace have been collected by L. Finkelstein; see the bibliography. The reconstruction by Finkelstein of an original common text from Hasmonean times contradicts all evidence and tradition.

367 העושה תפלתו קבע אין תפלתו תחנונים.

368 בוא וקרב עשה קרבינו.

369 See L. Ginzburg, *A Commentary on the Palestinian Talmud*, vol. III, pp. 350–351.

370 Y. Razhavi, "New Poetic Texts of Grace," *Sinai* 108 (5752), pp. 193–231.

As it is written, "You open Your hand and satisfy all living beings in pleasure."
Praised are You, o Lord, Who feeds all.

From a grazing place You liberated Your people from the land of the cursed
By their merits of the blood of *pesaḥ*, the proclaimed law and Covenant
As it is written, "You will eat and be satisfied; then you must praise the Lord, your God, for the Good Land that He gave you."
Praised are You, o Lord, for the Land and the food.

Liberation do speed for those who keep the commandments!
He remembers for Zion the Service of the sacrifice
As it is written, "The Lord is builder of Jerusalem, the dispersed of Israel He shall gather in."
Praised are You, o Lord, Who builds Jerusalem.

A similar poetic form was still used for wedding dinners and similar joyous occasions in Provence during the fourteenth century (*Orḥot Ḥayyim*, p. 36d).

As most of these compositions for Grace, the poem is written in a style that is easily understood by everybody. A short commentary may be needed for the second stanza. The Israelites were delivered at Passover in Rameses (*Ex.* 12:37), the new name of the district of Goshen (*Gen.* 47:11) reserved for grazing flocks and herds. The Egyptians are descendants of Ham (*Gen.* 10:6), who is cursed (*Gen.* 9:25). The mention of Torah and Covenant is obligatory in the second benediction; this will be discussed later.

The characteristically Palestinian features of this version of Grace are the poetic form and the use of biblical quotes, *Ps.* 145:16 for the first benediction, *Deut.* 8:10 for the second, and *Ps.* 147:2 for the third. The doxologies are common to all versions except that there exists a second form of the third benediction, "He Who in His mercy builds Jerusalem." The Babylonian versions of Grace have no reference to biblical verses. Today's versions have accepted the Galilean verses into the Babylonian texts of the first two benedictions. The third benediction today is the composition of a Babylonian and a different kind of Galilean text, as will be explained later. It is a principle of composition of benedictions that in longer benedictions the topic of the final doxology should be spelled out at the end of the text. In the *Talmudim* this is spelled out only for *Havdalah* (*b. Pesaḥim* 104a[371]; *y. Berakhot* V,2 9b), but in practice it is accepted for all benedictions. The Provençal *Orḥot Ḥayyim* (35b #49)[372] explains that, therefore, the insertion of biblical verses in the First and Third Benedictions is unnecessary since in both cases the final theme is clearly spelled out in the text. The latter argument underlies the current practice of all rituals for the Third and the normative Ashkenazic ritual for the First Benedictions.

The original Babylonian formula for Grace seems to be close to the text given by R. Saadia Gaon:

The celebrant: Let us praise (our God) of Whose bounty we ate!
Company and celebrant: Praised be (our God) of Whose bounty we ate and from Whose goodness we live!

המברך: נְבָרֵךְ (לֵאלֹהֵינוּ) שֶׁאָכַלְנוּ מִשֶּׁלּוֹ!
מסובין ומברך: בָּרוּךְ (אֱלֹהֵינוּ) שֶׁאָכַלְנוּ מִשֶּׁלּוֹ וּבְטוּבוֹ חָיִינוּ!

Praised are You o Lord, our God, King of the Universe, Who feeds us and the entire world in goodness, grace, kindness, and mercy. Praised are You, o Lord, Who feeds all.

בָּרוּךְ אַתָּה יי אֱלֹהֵינוּ מֶלֶךְ הָעוֹלָם הַזָּן אוֹתָנוּ וְאֶת הָעוֹלָם כֻּלּוֹ בְּטוֹב בְּחֵן בְּחֶסֶד וּבְרַחֲמִים. בָּרוּךְ אַתָּה יי הַזָּן אֶת הַכֹּל.

We thank You o Lord, our God, that You let us inherit a desirable, good, and spacious land, covenant and Torah, life and food. For everything we thank You and praise Your name forever and ever. Praised are You, o Lord, for the Land and for the food.

נוֹדֶה לְּךָ יי אֱלֹהֵינוּ כִּי הִנְחַלְתָּנוּ אֶרֶץ חֶמְדָּה טוֹבָה וּרְחָבָה בְּרִית וְתוֹרָה חַיִּים וּמָזוֹן וְעַל כֻּלָּם אָנוּ מוֹדִים לָךְ וּמְבָרְכִים אֶת שִׁמְךָ לְעוֹלָם וָעֵד. בָּרוּךְ אַתָּה יי עַל הָאָרֶץ וְעַל הַמָּזוֹן.

Have mercy o Lord, our God, on us, on Your people Israel and on

רַחֵם יי אֱלֹהֵינוּ עָלֵינוּ עַל יִשְׂרָאֵל

371 ואמר רב יהודה אמר שמואל המבדיל צריך שיאמר מעין חתימה סמוך לחתימתו.

372 וגם בזו [ברכה ג'] אין אומרים שום פסוק כי יש סמוך לחתימה מעין חתימה בלי הפסוק.

Your city of Jerusalem and on Your Temple, Your abode, Zion the dwelling place of Your glory, on the great and holy house over which Your Name is called. And return the kingdom of the house of David to its place in our days.

עַמֶּךָ וְעַל יְרוּשָׁלַיִם עִירֶךָ וְעַל הֵיכָלֶךָ וְעַל מְעוֹנֶךָ וְעַל צִיּוֹן מִשְׁכַּן כְּבוֹדֶךָ וְעַל הַבַּיִת הַגָּדוֹל וְהַקָּדוֹשׁ אֲשֶׁר אַתָּה שִׁמְךָ נִקְרָא עָלָיו וּמַלְכוּת בֵּית דָּוִד תַּחֲזִיר לִמְקוֹמָהּ בְּיָמֵינוּ.

On Sabbath: Have pleasure and succor us o Lord, our God, with all Your commandments and the commandment of this great and holy Seventh Day since this day is great and holy before You. We shall rest on it according to the commandment of Your pleasure. In Your pleasure let us rest so there may be neither worry nor sorrow on the day of our rest.

בשבת: רְצֵה וְהַחֲלִיצֵנוּ יי אֱלֹהֵינוּ בְּכָל מִצְוֹתֶיךָ וּמִצְוַת יוֹם הַשְּׁבִיעִי הַגָּדוֹל וְהַקָּדוֹשׁ הַזֶּה כִּי יוֹם גָּדוֹל וְקָדוֹשׁ הוּא מִלְּפָנֶיךָ וְנִשְׁבּוֹת בּוֹ כְּמִצְוַת רְצוֹנֶךָ. כִּרְצוֹנְךָ הָנַח לָנוּ וְאַל יְהִי צָרָה וְיָגוֹן בְּיוֹם מְנוּחָתֵינוּ.

Our God and God of our fathers! May there arise, come, arrive, be received, taken notice of, and remembered before You for good we, our fathers, and Jerusalem Your city, and Your people, the entire house of Israel, on this holiday of Passover. Take notice of us on it, o Lord our God, for good things, and remember us for blessing, and help us for life.

אֱלֹהֵינוּ וֵאלֹהֵי אֲבוֹתֵינוּ. יַעֲלֶה וְיָבֹא, יַגִּיעַ וְיֵרָאֶה, יִזָּכֵר וְיִפָּקֵד זִכְרוֹנֵנוּ וְזִכְרוֹן אֲבוֹתֵינוּ וְזִכְרוֹן יְרוּשָׁלַיִם עִירֶךָ וְזִכְרוֹן עַמְּךָ כָּל בֵּית יִשְׂרָאֵל לְפָנֶיךָ לְטוֹבָה בְּיוֹם חַג הַמַּצּוֹת הַזֶּה. זָכְרֵינוּ יי אֱלֹהֵינוּ בּוֹ לְטוֹבָה וּפָקְדֵינוּ בוֹ לִבְרָכָה וְהוֹשִׁיעֵנוּ בוֹ לְחַיִּים.

And build Jerusalem soon. Praised are You, o Lord, Builder of Jerusalem. Amen.

וּבְנֵה אֶת יְרוּשָׁלַיִם בְּקָרוֹב. בָּרוּךְ אַתָּה יי בּוֹנֶה יְרוּשָׁלַיִם אָמֵן.

Praised are You o Lord, our God, King of the Universe, Omnipotent, our Father, our King, our Creator, our Redeemer, the good and beneficent King Who every single day is very benevolent toward us, may He forever give us grace and kindness and comfort and mercy and all good.

בָּרוּךְ אַתָּה יי אֱלֹהֵינוּ מֶלֶךְ הָעוֹלָם הָאֵל אָבִינוּ מַלְכֵּנוּ בּוֹרְאֵנוּ גּוֹאֲלֵנוּ הַמֶּלֶךְ הַטּוֹב וְהַמֵּטִיב אֲשֶׁר בְּכָל יוֹם וָיוֹם הוּא מַרְבֶּה לְהֵיטִיב עִמָּנוּ וְהוּא יִגְמְלֵנוּ לָעַד חֵן וָחֶסֶד וָרֶוַח וְרַחֲמִים וְכָל טוֹב.

The All-Merciful, may He reign forever and ever.
The All-Merciful, may He enlighten our eyes with the light of His Torah, let us succeed on all our ways, put His fear before our eyes, remove illness from our midst, turn against those who plot evil against us, be our help and support, deal with us for the sake of His Name, and spread peace over us. He Who spreads peace in His heights, may He spread peace over Israel.

הָרַחֲמָן יִמְלוֹךְ לְעוֹלָם וָעֶד יִשְׁתַּבַּח נֶצַח סֶלָה.
הָרַחֲמָן יָאִיר עֵינֵינוּ בִּמְאוֹר תּוֹרָה. יַצְלִיחַ לָנוּ בְּכָל דְּרָכֵינוּ, יָשִׂים יִרְאָתוֹ לְנֶגֶד עֵינֵינוּ, יָסִיר מַחֲלָה מִקִּרְבֵּנוּ, יִגְעַר בְּחוֹשְׁבֵי רָעָתֵנוּ, יִהְיֶה עוֹזֵר וְסוֹמֵךְ, יַעֲשֶׂה עִמָּנוּ לְמַעַן שְׁמוֹ, יָשִׂים עָלֵינוּ שָׁלוֹם. עוֹשֶׂה שָׁלוֹם בִּמְרוֹמָיו הוּא יַעֲשֶׂה שָׁלוֹם עַל יִשְׂרָאֵל.

The text of *zimmūn* given by R. Saadia is identical to Maimonides' text, i.e., today's Yemenite text. The addition of "our God" for a company of ten adult males is required by the *Mishnah* (*Berakhot* VII,3). It is necessary for the celebrant to repeat the answer of the company in order not to exclude himself from the praise of the Lord. The addition, in both Ashkenazic and Sephardic rituals, of "Praised be He and praised be His Name" is found in *Maḥzor Vitry* (#83).[373]

The Yemenite (Maimonides) version of the First Benediction is a combination of the original Babylonian (R. Saadia) text and the Palestinian quote of *Ps*. 145:16. The long (Livorno) version of Sephardic Grace is not found in medieval texts; it is the poetically amplified version of the kabbalist school of the followers of R. Isaac Luria, made popular by the editions of R. Ḥayyim Yosef David Azulai in Livorno. The older (Amsterdam) text is identical with the classical Ashkenazic text except for one sentence. This is the text discussed in the sequel.

The many synonyms that appear in the text of Grace are not simply agglomerations of words of praise but allusions to biblical passages (*Maḥzor Vitry, loc. cit*.). In the First Benediction, the goodness of God toward all His creatures and His mercy are quoted from *Ps*.

373 נברך שאכלנו משלו. ועונין ברוך הוא שאכלנו משלו ובטובו חיינו. ברוך משביע רעבים ברוך משקה צמאים. ברוך הוא וברוך שמו.

145:9. The grace of God is bestowed upon whom He chooses (*Ex.*33:19). The kindness of God is constantly referred to in both *Hallels* (*Ps.* 118,136). The sentence "He gives bread to all flesh because His kindness is eternal" is *Ps.* 136:25. It is uncommon that a complete biblical verse should be quoted without an introduction such as "as it is said" or "as it is written." Early Ashkenazic sources (*Maḥzor Vitry, loc. cit.*)[374] show that originally the sentence was not an exact quote but a kind of paraphrase: "*He Himself* gives bread to all flesh because His kindness *with us* is eternal." The introductory *He, Himself* is still retained in Ashkenazic texts. The *with us* was removed by medieval authorities, possibly of the school of Rashi (Yosef Qaro, *Bet Yosef* on *Ṭur Oraḥ Ḥayyim* §187[375]; his quote from *Pardes* of Rashi is not found in the printed editions but is hinted at in *Siddur Rabbenu Shelomo bar Shimshon miGermaiza,* p. 250, a source contemporary with or preceding Rashi). The word is already missing in the text of *Or Zarua'* (I, #199) of R. Isaac of Vienna, the teacher of R. Meir of Rothenburg in the early thirteenth century, and in the Italian *Shibbolé Haleqet* (#157). The omission is confirmed by all students of R. Meir. These authorities omitted to add the usual introduction; the late change accounts for the anomaly in quotation. The *great* goodness of the Lord, not letting us lack food in the desert and giving us the Land of Israel, is a quote from *Neh.* 9:25. The difference in vocalization in the three rites, חָסַר (Ashkenaz, Yemen) *vs.* חִסֵּר (Sepharad) and יֶחְסַר (Ashkenaz, Sepharad) *vs.* יְחַסֵּר (Yemen) are all found as possible versions in early Ashkenazic texts (*Or Zarua'* I,#199, *Mordokhai Berakhot* #217[376]). Depending on the vocalization of the consonantal text, the corresponding passage of the First Benediction either is a declaration of faith that the Lord will not let the deserving go without food (*Is.* 51:14) or a prayer: may the Lord not let us lack food. Since it is a talmudic precept that every prayer wish must be preceded by at least one paragraph of pure praise of the Lord (*b. Berakhot* 32a)[377] and considering that formulated as praise the sentence is borrowed from Isaiah, it follows that the European (Ashkenazic and Sephardic) version is the natural one, based on *Neh.* 9:21, *Deut.* 2:7. This is the conclusion of *Or Zarua'* and *Mordokhai* (*loc. cit.*). The oldest

---

374 הוּא נוֹתֵן לחם לכל בשׂר כי לעוֹלם חסדוֹ עמנוּ.

375 והרא״ש לא היה אומר תיבת עמנו וגם המרדכי כתב בשם ספר הפרדס שאין לאומרו.

376 ובטוּבוֹ הגדוֹל לא חיסר ואל יֶחֱסַר, פירוּש לא חיסר משמע לא מחסר. דבר אחר מגזירת איבר ושיבר ואם כן היה לוֹ לוֹמר אל יְחַסֵּר לנוּ.

377 דרש רבי שׂמלאי לעוֹלם יסדר אדם שבחוֹ של הקב״ה ואחר כך יתפלל.

Ashkenazic sources (*Maḥzor Vitry, loc. cit.*) follow standard Palestinian usage and quote *Ps.* 145:16 at the end of the First Benediction, but already many medieval texts eliminate the quote as an unnecessary reference to a Psalm of David in a text that is ascribed to Moses (*Orḥot Ḥayyim* 35b [49]).[378] The consensus of all (Ashkenazic, Sephardic, and Oriental) sources is that the correct vocalization of "His creatures" in rabbinic Hebrew is בְּרִיּוֹתָיו; the current Ashkenazic spelling בְּרִיּוֹתָיו is unhistorical.

The different versions of the Second Benediction depend on different readings in the Babylonian *Talmud.* There (*b. Berakhot* 48b) one reads, "R. Eliezer says: He who did not mention 'a desirable, good, and spacious land, Covenant and Torah' in the second and the 'Kingdom of David' in the third benediction did not fulfill his obligation" (printed text and ms. Munich; *Maḥzor Vitry* #64; *Pisqe RYD ad loc.*)[379] or "R. Eliezer says: He who did not mention 'a desirable, good, and spacious land, Covenant and Torah, life and food' in the second benediction . . ." (*Siddur Rashi* #98, *Sefer Sedarim Rashi* #85).[380] The first, shorter list is supported by the parallel of the Jerusalem *Talmud* (*y. Berakhot* I,9 3d), but the second one underlies Ashkenazic and Sephardic versions, both of which originally had the typical talmudic style of a list followed by an elaboration (cf. "Showing the Maẓẓah," pp. 244-245). Maimonides and the Yemenite text follow the first version of the Babylonian text or the Jerusalem *Talmud.* The addition "life and food" is not discussed in the *Talmud*; this supports the first version as authentic Babylonian. The source of the addition is not known. *Maḥzor Vitry* (*loc. cit.*)[381] still has the list:

Covenant, Torah, Food, and Life
The Covenant that You did seal in our flesh
The Torah that You taught us
Life that You graced us with in grace and kindness
Food to eat that You feed and provide us with permanently.

---

378 ראשונה ברכת הזן ומשה רבינו תקנה בשעה שירד המן ולכך י״א שאין לומר בה פסוק פותח את ידיך רק חותמין בא״י הזן את הכל בלי פסוק וטעמא דמסתבר הוא כי איך נאמר פסוק שאמרו דוד לדברי משה רבינו ע״ה.

379 תניא ר' אליעזר אומר כל שלא אמר ארץ חמדה טובה ורחבה ברית ותורה בברכת הארץ ומלכות דוד בבונה ירושלים לא יצא ידי חובתו.

380 תניא ר' אליעזר אומר כל שלא אמר ארץ חמדה טובה ורחבה ברית ותורה חיים ומזון בברכת הארץ ומלכות דוד בבונה ירושלים לא יצא ידי חובתו.

381 נודך ה' אלהינו על שהנחלת לאבותינו ארץ חמדה טובה ורחבה ברית ותורה חיים ומזון, על שהוצאתנו מארץ מצרים. . . .

The list is omitted as redundant in the Ashkenazic text following a decision of an early Tosafist (*Tosafot Berakhot* 48b, *s.v.* בְּרִית; *Or Zarua' loc. cit.*),[382] who maintains that the list was mentioned in the *Talmud* only as mnemotechnic device. A comparison with other Babylonian synagogal poetry makes this argument unconvincing The items on the list follow a logical sequence. The Land is given on condition that the Torah be kept (*Ps.* 105:44; *y. Berakhot* I,9 3d)[383]; the Torah was given by a triple Covenant (*Ex.* 34:10; *Lev.* 33:10; *Deut.* 29:8) based on the earlier Covenant of circumcision (*Gen.* 17:7, mentioned thirteeen times in the Pentateuch). Therefore, the mention of the Covenant precedes that of Torah. The Land of Israel is called desirable (*Jer.* 3:19), good, and spacious (*Ex.* 3:17).

In the early European Middle Ages, the question was discussed whether women should mention the Covenant of circumcision and the Torah when saying Grace. Ashkenazic tradition follows Rashi (*Sefer Hasedarim* #86),[384] who argues that women should recite the entire text since circumcision performed by a woman is acceptable in talmudic law (*b. 'Avodah Zarah* 27a)[385] and women, while not required to study Torah, are responsible to make sure that their sons are taught to read and memorize rules of Law (*b. Soṭah* 21a).[386] The Sephardic tradition follows *RaVaD* (R. Abraham ben David of Posquières, quoted in *Kol Bo,* p. 23a)[387] in excluding women since they are not circumcised and slaves since they may not study Torah. The Yemenite tradition here is identical with the Ashkenazic one since the Yemenite authority, Maimonides, does not mention the problem at all. In the Yemenite and Western Ashkenazic rituals the husband is supposed to recite Grace aloud so that his wife and daughters satisfy their obligation by listening attentively to his prayer and answering "Amen." In this setting, the problem does not arise.

---

382 אין צריך להזכיר ברית ותורה וחיים ומזון דדי להזכיר על בריתך שחתמת בבשׂרנו ועל תורתך שלמדתנו וכו׳ דהיינו ברית ותורה והגמרא לסימנא בעלמא נקטיה.

383 ר׳ סימון בשם ר׳ יהושע בן לוי אמר לא הזכיר תורה בארץ מחזירין אותו. מה טעם ויתן להם ארצות גוים מפני מה בעבור ישמרו חוקיו ותורותיו ינצרו:

384 ואף נשים ראויות לומר על בריתך שחתמת בבשׂרנו, שלפיכך נתקן בלשון רבים לכלול כל ישׂראל. דמשמע ישׂראל מוהלין, ל״מ נשי ל״מ גברי, מדנקט הכתוב המול ימול לומר על אשה שכשרה במילה.

385 דאשה כמאן דמהילא דמיא.

386 נהי דפקודי לא מפקדא באגרא דמקרין ומתניין בנייהו.

387 וכתב הראב״ד ז״ל דנשים ועבדים לא אמרו להו דנשים לאו בני ברית ועבדים לאו בני תורה.

The current Yemenite text of the third benediction reproduces the original Babylonian text. The Babylonian sources (*b. Berakhot* 48b–49a) do not mention any prayer for sustenance in this section, but only a prayer for the kingdom of David and the rebuilding of Jerusalem; see the text of R. Saadia Gaon given above. The prayer for sustenance is of *Yerushalmi* origin (*y. Shabbat* XV,3 15b).[388] The current texts all start by asking for *mercy* for the city of Jerusalem and the dynasty of David. The original Sephardic tradition was to start on the Sabbath with a plea for *consolation* instead, following *Halakhot Gedolot, R. Ḥananel*[389] (quoted by *Or Zarua'*) and Alfassi on *b. Berakhot* 48b:[390] "On Sabbath one starts and finishes with consolation and mentions the holiness of the day in the middle." They also require the Sabbath doxology to read "Who consoles Israel and builds Jerusalem." The text change is approved by the German Ashkenazic *RAVIA* (#129), who points out that the language is appropriate since one of the fundamental *midrashim* for prayer texts, *Pirkē Rebbi Eliezer* (chap. 20), uses that language to explain that the Sabbath did *console* Adam after his expulsion from Paradise. The Italian Ashkenazic authority *RYD* (*Berakhot* #143) notes that the Third Benediction is never called "benediction of consolation" and, therefore, the language used by the *Talmud* must mean a change from weekday practice.[391] Current texts follow Rashi (*Talmud* commentary *ad loc.*), who rejects a text change and notes that a plea for mercy is also a plea for consolation and that both texts, רַחֵם "have mercy" and נַחֲמֵנוּ "console us," are equally acceptable.[392] Rashi's opinion was accepted by both Ashkenazic and Sephardic authorities on the authority of R. Asher ben Yeḥiel and R. Yosef Qaro (*Bet Yosef, Oraḥ Ḥayyim* §188).[393] Since the root *nḥm* נחם means not only "to console" but can

---

388 ר' זעירה שאל לר' חייה בר בא מהו מימר רעינו פרנסנו. אמר ליה טופס ברכות כך הן.

R. Zeïra (a Babylonian immigrant to Galilee) asked R. Ḥiyya bar Abba (a Galilean authority): "May one say 'shepherd us, provide for us' [on the Sabbath and in general]?" He answered him: "This is the form [τύπος] of [our] benedictions."

389 ופי' ר״ח בשבת בונה ירושלים בנחמה ואומר נחמנו ה' אלהינו ומסיים בנחמה ונחמנו בתוכה כי אתה בעל הנחמות ברוך א'ה מנחם ציון ובונה ירושלים.

390 ובשבת מתחיל בנחמה ומסיים בנחמה ואומר קדושת היום באמצע.

391 בעל הלכות גדולות ורבינו חננאל ורבינו יצחק פאסי זצ״ל מפרשים שמתחיל בנחמינו ומסיים מנחם ישראל ובונה ירושלים. אבל המורה פירש בניין ירושלים קרי נחמה כל היכי דמתחיל בין רחם בין נחמנו. ואינו נראה לי דהא זימני טובא מדכר בונה ירושלים בהילכתין ואינו קורא לה ברכת נחמה, שמע מינה דהכא דווקא קאמר שיזכיר נחמה בשבשת.

392 ובשבת מתחיל בנחמה. כלומר אינו צריך לא לסיים ולא להתחיל בשבת אלא מתחיל ומסיים בנחמה; בנין ירושלים קרי נחמה כל היכי דמתחיל בין רחם בין נחמנו.

393 וגם הרא״ש כתב דלא נהירא ליה המחלקים בין נחם לרחם ולזה נוטה דעת הר' יונה וכן דעת הרמב״ם שא״צ לשנות ברכה של חול.

serve as a synonym of *rḥm* רחם "to have mercy" by a substitution of liquids (see *Hos.* 11:8), Rashi is right from a linguistic point of view. By his silence about a special Sabbath text, Maimonides endorses Rashi's position.

For the multiple expressions used in the first paragraph of the Third Benediction, biblical sources show that God has mercy on Israel (*Ez.* 39:25), Jerusalem (*Zach.* 1:12), Zion (*Ps.* 102:14), His dwelling (*Joel* 4:17), and the throne of His glory (*Jer.* 17:12). God is the shepherd of Israel (*Ps.* 80:2). The use of *zūn* זון in the sense "to feed" is an Aramaism in talmudic Hebrew; similarly, *parnes* פרנס "to provide (nonfood items)" is a Greek loan word frequent in talmudic Hebrew. The biblical equivalent of both expressions is *kalkel* כלכל "to sustain." The prayer for independence from charity of flesh and blood is a prayer for life since he who hates gifts will live (*Prov.* 15:27). The longer Sephardic version derives from a Palestinian original; it is modeled after a morning prayer current in the circle of the third-century teacher R. Yannai (*y. Berakhot* IV,2 7d)[394] and accepted in Babylonia as a supplication after the daily prayer (*Siddur R. Amram Gaon* 12a).

By rabbinic interpretation, the "day of joy" mentioned in *Num.* 10:10 is the Sabbath (*Sifry* #77).[395] Since Jerusalem must be remembered on all happy occasions (*Ps.* 137:6), it is appropriate to insert the Sabbath prayer into the benediction for Jerusalem (*Maḥzor Vitry*, p. 54). The same argument applies to holidays. The basic text of the insert, both from Babylonian and Palestinian sources, is well

---

394 רבוֹני חטאתי לך יהי רצוֹן לפניך יי אלהי שתתן לי לב טוֹב חלק טוֹב יצר טוֹב סבר (חבר) טוֹב שם טוֹב עין טוֹבה ונפש טוֹב ונפש שפלה ורוח נמוכה. אל יתחלל שמך בנו ואל תעשׂינו שׂיחה בפי כל הבריוֹת ואל תהי אחריתנו להכרית ולא תקוותנו למפח נפש. ואל תצריכנו לידי מתנת בשׂר ודם ואל תמסוֹר מזוֹנוֹתינו בידי בשׂר ודם שמתנתם מעוּטה וחרפתם מרוּבה. ותן חלקינו בתוֹרתך עם עוֹשׂי רצוֹנך בנה ביתך היכלך עירך ומקדשך במהרה בימינו.

My Master! I have sinned before You! May it be Your pleasure, o Lord my God, that You may give me a good heart, a good portion, good inclinations, a good mind (or: a good companion), a good reputation, a benevolent eye, a good and lowly soul, and a meek spirit. May Your name not be desecrated by us and do not let us be the talk of all creatures. May our end not be to be destroyed nor our hope turned to destruction of our soul. And do not let us need the gifts of flesh and blood; do not deliver our sustenance into the hands of flesh and blood whose gifts are small and the shame of which is big. And let our lot be in Your Torah with those who do Your will; build Your House, Your Hall, Your City, and Your Temple soon, in our days.

395 וּביוֹם שׂמחתכם אלוּ שבתוֹת, ר' נתן אוֹמר אלוּ תמידים.

represented by the Maimonides text of the Yemenite ritual. The current Ashkenazic and Sephardic versions are extensions of the common text. The Ashkenazic text is already complete in *Maḥzor Vitry.* The Sephardic text of Abudirham in the fourteenth century is still identical with the Ashkenazic text; the later elaboration dates from the kabbalistic circles of Safed in the sixteenth century. *Genizah* texts show that the verse from Scripture before the final doxology in Palestinian texts was *Ps.* 147:2 for weekdays and holidays but on Sabbath was replaced by several others such as *2 Chr.* 23:25 (in a *Genizah* text) or *Is.* 66:13 (*Maḥzor Vitry).* The language of the Ashkenazic insert is explained in a *Yerushalmi* source, *Lev. rabbah* 34 (15).[396] The expression וְהַחֲלִיצֵנוּ, translated by "give us ease," was chosen in reference to the Sabbath from *Is.* 58:11-13 because of its many possible meanings: "to remove" (*Deut.* 25:9), "to arm" (*Deut.* 3:18), "to save, extricate" (*Ps.* 140:2), and, principally for use here, "to make rest, give ease" (*Is.* 58:11). The unusual, and possibly ungrammatical, form הָנִיחַ "let us rest" in the Ashkenazic version is well documented already in *Maḥzor Vitry* and is a reference to the form יָנִיחַ "to make rest" used in the *Midrash.* All other (Babylonian) versions have הַנַּח, correct in normative grammar.

The insertion for the holiday (*Masekhet Soferim* XIX,7)[397] is originally a prayer for remembrance in the middle section (*zikhronot*) of the *Musaf* prayer of New Year's Day (*Rav Paltoy Gaon, Teshuvot Ḥemda Genuza* #99).[398] It is used for holidays and the days of the New Moon because every single one of them is, like New Year's day, a day of remembrance and forgiveness, as stated in *Num.* 28:22,30, 29:16,19,22,25,28,31,34,38. For the same reason, the beginning words of the insert "may there arise, come, arrive" are the theme of the very old poem that starts the penitential service on the Eve of the Day of Atonement. All current rites have the same eight biblical expressions of God's remembrance; some slight deviations are found in old manuscripts. According to *Maḥzor Vitry* (p. 196, #231), the expressions of remembrance are connected with the subjects of

---

396 ועצמותיך יחליץ. ישמוט ישזיב ויניח. ישמוט כד״א וחלצה נעלו מעל רגלו. יזיין כד״א חלוצים תעברו. ישזיב כד״א חלצני ה׳ מאדם רע. ויניח מכאן קבעו חכמים לומר רצה והחליצנו בשבת.

397 וכשם שמקלסין יום ראשון וחולו של מועד כך מקלסין ימים טובים בתפילה ביוצר במנחה בערבית והיכן קילוסו אלהינו ואלהי אבותינו גלה כבוד מלכותך עלינו ואחריו אנא אלהינו שם יעלה ויבוא כו׳.

398 בראש השנה אומר יעלה ויבא ויגיע כשאר מועדים או אינו צריך . . . מנהג הוא זה המקום שנהגו לומר אומרים ואם אי אתם רגילין לומר אין אתם צריכין לומר שכבר שליח ציבור יורד לפני התיבה והרי הוא אומרה בזכרונות.

remembrance. Our remembrance shall *arise* before God since we lift (in Hebrew, "make arise") Jerusalem to the top of our joy (*Ps*. 137:6); therefore, the expression "to arise" refers to Jerusalem. Similarly, the cry of the children of Israel did *come* before God (*Ex*. 3:9); this refers to the remembrance before God of the entire people of Israel in any future distress and in *Num*. 10:9, God's remembrance and help is promised in case of calamities that *come*. The third expression, *to arrive*, refers to the remembrance of the Messiah since the Just expect and will *arrive* at the Day of Salvation (*Dan*. 12:12). To *be accepted* refers to the remembrance of our fathers Abraham and Isaac: Abraham called Mount Moriah the "mountain of which the Lord *will be accepting*" our prayers (*Gen*. 22:14). Since the offering of Isaac on Mount Moriah is one of the central themes of the service of New Year's Day, the Day of Remembrance, this last expression introduces a series of expressions connected directly to the prayers of New Year's Day. They are first "to be received with pleasure" (*Ps*. 106:4); the verse contains both the roots זכר "to remember" giving the biblical name Day of Remembrance of New Year's Day and פקד "to take notice of" appearing later in the list as the expression used for Isaac's miraculous birth celebrated on this day (*Gen*. 21:1). The next expression, "to be heard," refers to *Mal*. 3:16, one of the verses of remembrance recited in the old Palestinian service of the Day of Remembrance and preserved in the poem (probably dating to the talmudic period) of Yossi ben Yossi for the Service of Remembrance, זכרונות, on that day. The last expression, "to be remembered," refers to *Jer*. 2:2, used in the same service. The request for remembrance in a good way is an adaptation of a verse of Nehemiah (*Neh*. 5:19). The final sentence of the original Ashkenazic version of the insert (*Mahzor Vitry*, p. 68, #93)[399] asked for help *in a good way* similar to the current Sephardic text and included a prayer for survival analogous to the current Yemenite text. This shows that the different versions all follow ancient paradigms. An enlargement of R. Saadia Gaon's short version is already found in R. Amram Gaon's *siddur*.

Since the Third Benediction contains a prayer for the kingdom of David but any human kingdom is infinitely less than the Kingdom of Heaven, the *Talmud* (*b. Berakhot* 49a)[400] requires that in this

---

399 זכרינו ה״א בו לטובה ופקדינו בו לברכה והושיענו בו לחיים טובים בדבר ישועה ורחמים חוס וחננו וחמול ורחם עלינו ומלטינו מכל צרה ויגון כי אל מלך חנון ורחום אתה.

400 איידי דאמר מלכות בית דוד לאו אורח ארעא דלא אמר מלכות שמים.

section one should not mention any title of King for God. Therefore, the final clause in the insertion for the holiday should be ". . . because You are a gracious and merciful God" (*Jonah* 4:2) (*Abudirham*, p. 323).[401] However, the mention of God as King is required for the Day of Remembrance and appropriate for the daily *'Amidah* prayer on all special days; by analogy and habitude the invocation of God as King has slipped into the text of Grace at an inappropriate place except in the Western Ashkenazic ritual (R. Yospe Shammes, *Minhagim Warmaisha* 2, p. 233:[402] R. Moses Isserles, *Darke Moshe* #3 to *Ṭur Oraḥ Ḥayyim* §188). The modification of the verse *Jonah* 4:2 to include the mention of God as King is another indication that the prayer originated in the Service of the New Year; which is a celebration of God as King.

The original final doxology of the Third Benediction in Babylonian and Palestinian, Ashkenazic and Sephardic rites was either "He Who builds Jerusalem" or "He Who consoles Israel by building Jerusalem" (cf. p. 353*)*. The currently accepted form, "He Who in His mercy builds Jerusalem," is the Oriental version of Maimonides that was accepted by R. Meir of Rothenburg and his students (*Mordokhai Berakhot* #217).[403] Some authorities (*Orḥot Ḥayyim* 35a)[404] objected to this text since the rebuilding of Jerusalem will take place not through mercy but as of right (*Is*. 1:27). The final approval of the enlarged version as against the short biblical form of *Ps*. 147:2 was helped by the authority of R. Yosef Karo (*Bet Yosef*, *Ṭur Oraḥ Ḥayyim* §188),[405] who pointed out that, according to *Zach*. 1:16, the Temple will be rebuilt when God returns to Jerusalem in mercy and that, therefore, the enlarged formula is not unacceptable. As mentioned before, "Amen" is said at this point to mark the end of the three biblical benedictions. Rav Ashi, the main editor and paramount authority of the Babylonian *Talmud*, requires that this "Amen" should be said in an undertone so that people would not be led to believe that

---

401 וכתב הראב״ד כי מזה הטעם כשאומר כאן יעלה ויבא ביום טוב ובראש חודש אין לומר בסופו כי אל מלך חנון ורחום אתה.

402 אף ביעלה ויבא לא יסיים כי אל מלך רחום אתה רק כי אל רחום וחנון אתה, ודלג מלת מלך.

403 ב״א ה׳ בונה ירושלים. ומהר״ם היה אומר בונה ברחמיו.

404 שלישית בונה ירושלים ודוד ושלמה תקנוה וחותמין בה בא״י בונה ירושלים ואין אומרים בה ברחמיו לפי שלא יבנה ירושלים כי אם במשפט שנא׳ ציון במשפט תפדה.

405 ואם אמר ברחמיו נראה לי שאין מחזירין אותו שכבר מצינו על בנין הבית רחמים בזכריה ׳שבתי לירושלים ברחמים ביתי יבנה בה׳.

the Fourth Benediction was superfluous (*b. Berakhot* 45b).[406] This is the traditional usage and is followed also in the *Seder* night except that in those Ashkenazic families where the entire family sings Grace in the traditional melody, "Amen" may be sung at normal voice level (*Ṭur Oraḥ Ḥayyim* §188, *Darke Moshe* #2).

The Fourth Benediction is referred to in the *Talmud* as הטוב והמטיב "He Who is good and does good." Now there exists another benediction going under the same name and whose text is simply

בָּרוּךְ אַתָּה יי אֱלֹהֵינוּ מֶלֶךְ הָעוֹלָם הַטּוֹב וְהַמֵּטִיב.
Praised are You o Lord, our God, King of the Universe, Who is good and does good.

This benediction is to be recited in case of extraordinary events that are lucky for more than one person, in contrast to the benediction "Who kept us alive and upright and let us reach this time" which is appropriate not only for public holidays but also for private events benefitting only one person (*b. Berakhot* 59b).[407] It is difficult to see how this benediction could respond to a biblical injunction; it is however to be recited upon entering into an inheritance shared by several persons (*b. Berakhot* 59b;[408] *y. Berakhot* IX,3 14a) and might apply to the sovereign gift of the Land. Since the repeal of the decrees of persecution promulgated after the revolt of Bar Kokhba (or the establishment of the Synhedrion at Yavne after the destruction of the Temple) was a public good benefitting many, it was appropriate to decree that this benediction should be added to Grace (*Talmid Rabbenu Yona, Alfassi Berakhot* 36a).[409] In talmudic Babylonia, the requirement was added to mention the Kingdom of Heaven three times in this benediction to balance the omission in the Third Benediction (*b. Berakhot* 49a).[410] The result is represented by R. Saadia Gaon's and today's Yemenite texts. Since this resulted in differentiating the general formula "Who is good and does good" from the particular one used for Grace, the way was open for further elaborations of the

---

406 רב אשי עני ליה בלחישא כי היכי דלא נזלזלו בהטוב והמטיב.

407 הא דאית ליה שותפות הא דלית ליה שותפות.

408 מת אביו והוא יורשו בתחלה אומר ברוך דיין האמת ולבסוף הוא אומר ברוך הטוב והמטיב, התם נמי דאיכא אחי דקא ירתי בהדיה.

409 מתחלה כשתקנו הטוב והמטיב לא תקנו בה כל זה הנוסח אלא הטוב והמטיב בלבד ואחר כך הוסיפו בה כל אלו הדברים.

410 רב פפא אמר הכי קאמר צריכה שתי מלכיות לבר מדידה.

benediction. Early in European tradition this resulted in the addition of the triple mention of God's being good and kind to us in past, present, and future tenses. This development explains the deviation of the formula of the Fourth Benediction from standard talmudic rules, which admit only benedictions that either are a short statement of thanks, like the benedictions over bread, wine, vegetables, and "Who is good and does good," or a prayer formula like *Qiddush*, *Havdalah*, and the first three benedictions of Grace. A prayer formula can either be long or short (*Mishnah Berakhot* I,4). A "long" formula starts with the full introduction "Praised are You o Lord, our God, King of the Universe" and ends with a final "Praised are You, o Lord. . . ." A "short" formula starts immediately with the topic of prayer and ends with "Praised are You, o Lord. . . ." A "long" benediction either starts a prayer, as in Grace, or stands alone, as in *Qiddush* and *Havdalah*. A "short" benediction is one that follows another benediction in the same prayer; the Second and Third Benedictions of Grace are "short." If the Fourth Benediction has biblical character, it should be "short"; if it is purely rabbinic, it should be "long." But it is neither long nor short since it starts out like a "long" benediction but fails to have a final doxology. Historically, this is explained by the origin of the Benediction from a short statement of thanks. Theoretically (Rashi *Berakhot* 49a)[411] we accommodate the opinion that the Fourth Benediction is a rabbinic institution by ending the Third by "Amen" and the opinion that the Fourth is a response to a biblical injunction by having only one expression of Praise.

The invocations of God as the All-Merciful after the four formal benedictions have no direct talmudic source. For a long time, they were considered a private matter not to be fixed by a formula. In the early fifteenth century we still find that the leading teacher of the time, R. Israel Isserlein of Wiener Neustadt, on the request of his students did spell out for them the exact text of the Four Benedictions but refused to indicate any text for the final invocations since they should not be standardized (*Leqet Yosher*, p. 37).[412] The final fixation came only by the printed editions that presented a uniform text for large geographic areas. Even there, we find that through the end of

---

411 ומאן דאמר אינה צריכה מלכות קסבר דאורייתא. ומברכת הארץ היא כדאמרינן לעיל 'אשר נתן לך זה הטוב והמטיב' והויא לא ברכה הסמוכה לחברתה ומיהו פותח בה בברוך לפי שפתיחתה היא חתימתה שכולה הודאה אחת היא ואינה הפסקה ודומה לברכת הפירות והמצות.

412 זה הסדר הגיה בכתב ידו הגאון ריש גלותא מוהר״ר איסרליין זצ״ל אבל מכאן והלאה לא רצא להגיה כי אמר אין נפקותא בדבר.

the eighteenth century the Western Ashkenazic text of the invocation preceding the prayer for the host was[413] "The All-Merciful, may He send us the prophet Elijah of blessed memory and bless every single one of us by name." The current Ashkenazic text is the Eastern European one that was accepted by Heidenheim from the (Eastern European) *siddur* of Isaac Stanow. The prayer for the appearence of Elijah is a prayer for the coming of the Messiah since Elijah must precede the Messiah (*Mal.* 3:23).[414] Similarly, eighteenth-century Ashkenazic texts request that God may break either "the yoke of the Diaspora" or "the yoke of the Gentiles" from our necks as in the Sephardic version; the unspecific "our yoke" is also a Stanow-Heidenheim revision for political reasons.

The centerpiece and justification of this section is the prayer of the guest for his host. This is required by the *Talmud* (*b. Berakhot* 46a)[415] and all rabbinic authorities down to the *Shulḥan 'Arukh* (*Oraḥ Ḥayyim* §201). The Sephardic version of Grace reproduces exactly the talmudic text preceded by an enlarged version of a prayer for blessing of the table on which the dinner was served. The Yemenite text is a much-enlarged version of the talmudic text. The prayer has all but vanished from the Ashkenazic version without approval of any rabbinic authority (YomTov Lipman Heller, *Ma'adané Yomtov, Rosh Berakhot,* chap. 7, #11, note 9).[416] What happened is that the talmudic middle part of the old Ashkenazic prayer was lost and only the non-talmudic beginning and end are retained. The original version reported by *Maḥzor Vitry* (#83) reads:

The All-Merciful, may He bless the master of this house, him, his house [i.e., his wife], his children and all his property, his dependents, his supporters, and those who wish him well, with sons, daughters, riches and property like our fathers Abraham,	הרחמן הוּא יברך בעל הבית הזה אוֹתוֹ ואת ביתוֹ ואת בניו ואת כל אשר לוֹ ואת עמדיו ואת סוֹמכיו ואת דוֹרשיו ואת דוֹרשי שלוֹמוֹ וטוֹבתוֹ בבנים וּבבנוֹת בעוֹשר וּבנכסים כמוֹ שנתברכוּ אבוֹתינוּ אברהם יצחק ויעקב בכל מכל כל כן

413 הָרַחֲמָן הוּא יִשְׁלַח לָנוּ אֶת אֵלִיָּהוּ הַנָּבִיא זָכוּר לַטּוֹב וִיבָרֵךְ אוֹתָנוּ כָּל אֶחָד וְאֶחָד מִמֶּנּוּ בִּשְׁמוֹ.

414 "Correct" (Stanow-Heidenheim) Ashkenazic text have here the name of the prophet spelled *Elijah* as in the biblical reference, not the traditional *Eliyahu* as in the preceding footnote.

415 מאי מברך? יהי רצוֹן שלא יבוֹש בעל הבית בעוֹלם הזה ולא יכלם לעוֹלם הבא. ורבי מוֹסיף בה דברים: ויצלח מאוֹד בכל נכסיו ויהיוּ נכסיו מוּצלחים קרוֹבים לעיר ואל ישלוֹט שׂטן לא במעשׂה ידיו ולא במעשׂה ידינוּ ואל יזדקק לא לפניו ולא לפנינוּ שוּם דבר הרהוּר חטא ועבירה ועוֹן מעתה ועד עוֹלם.

416 מימי תמהתי על שמשנין הנוּסח בענין אחר.

יתברכו יחד בברכה שלימה ונאמר אמן:

Isaac, and Jacob who were blessed with everything, of everything, everything, so may they all be blessed together in perfect blessing, and let us say "Amen."

יהי רצון מלפני אלהי השמים שלא יבוש בעולם הזה ולא יכלם לעולם הבא. ויצליח מאד בכל נכסיו ויהיו נכסיו ונכסינו מצליחין וקרובין לעיר ואל ישלוט שטן במעשה ידיו ואל יזדקק לא לפניו ולא לפנינו שום דבר הרהור חטא ועבירה ועון מעתה ועד עולם:

May it please the God of Heaven that he should not be ashamed in this world nor disgraced in the World to Come. May he prosper in all his possessions and may his and our possessions be prosperous and close to the city; let Satan be given power neither over his nor over our work, may there occur neither before him nor before us any thought of sin or transgression or guilt from now to eternity.

ממרום ילמדו עליו ועלינו זכות שתהא למשמרת שלום ישא ברכה מאת יי וצדקה מאלהי ישענו ונמצא חן ושכל טוב בעיני אלהים ואדם:

High up may they credit him and us with keeping the peace; (*Ps.* 24:5) "may he be deemed worthy of blessing from the Lord and justice from God of our salvation," and may we find grace and good understanding in the eyes of God and man.

One sees that in the current version the first paragraph is shortened, the second is eliminated, and the third, which should be part of the prayer of the guest for his host, has become part of Grace recited by everybody. This probably is a consequence of the expression "and let us say 'Amen'" that usually concludes a section of prayers. Since the main part has dropped out, the prayer of the guest was reduced to one line in a longer paragraph recited by everybody, including the host. The reference to Abraham, Isaac, and Jacob who were blessed, Abraham with everything (*Gen.* 24:1), Isaac of everything (*Gen.* 27:33), and Jacob [had] everything (*Gen.* 33:11), is from the *Talmud* (*b. Bava Batra* 16b–17a),[417] which infers from these verses that the patriarchs tasted the Future World in this world, they were free from evil inclinations, and the Angel of Death had no power over them. In the Sephardic text, this reference is part of a general invocation that includes the Western Ashkenazic prayer for individual blessing referred to above and which makes perfect sense in the Sephardic context, given the talmudic interpretation. The Western

---

417 שלשה הטעימן הקדוש ברוך הוא בעולם הזה מעין העולם הבא אלו הן אברהם יצחק ויעקב. אברהם דכתיב ביה בכל, יצחק דכתיב ביה מכל, יעקב דכתיב ביה כל. שלשה לא שלט בהן יצר הרע, אלו הן אברהם יצחק ויעקב דכתיב בהו בכל מכל כל.

Ashkenazic practice of including the request in a prayer for the appearance of the prophet Elijah seems predicated on an identification of the Days of the Messiah with the World to Come; this is not standard doctrine in theoretical texts. Excluding the prayer for the host, the text of *Maḥzor Vitry* has 13 invocations of the All-Merciful, equal in number to the attributes of Divine mercy (*Pesiqta Rabbati*, chap. 16)[418] compared to nine in the current Ashkenazic and 17 in the Sephardic text. The Ashkenazic addition, enlarging the prayer for part of the genuinely Good Day, i.e., the End of Days, appears only in the nineteenth century.

The structure of these invocations in all rituals follows the talmudic rule (*b. Berakhot* 32a; cf. p. 350) that one always should start with praise of the Lord before asking for favors. Therefore, at least the first three invocations (five in the Sephardic text) are praise; the rest are supplications. The Yemenite ritual does not have any supplications since Grace is also recited on the Sabbath when supplications for personal needs are inappropriate. In the Ashkenazic version, the first invocation is modeled on *Ex.* 15:18; the third is partially inspired by *Is.* 49:3. In all rituals, the invocations are followed by *Ps.* 18:51 on weekdays and *2 Sam.* 22:51 on Sabbath and holidays. According to Abudirham (p. 326),[419] *Ps.* 18:51 is the original verse but *2 Sam.* 22:51 is the more majestic verse and more appropriate to the majesty of Sabbath. This is a tradition of R. Asher ben Yeḥiel and R. Meir of Rothenburg. *Maḥzor Vitry* has *2 Sam.* 22:51 everyday. The final paragraph of Grace, "He Who makes peace in His heights, may He make peace for us and all of Israel," appears at the end of the prayer of the guest for his host in R. Saadia Gaon's text. The sentence is used not only as conclusion of Grace but also of the *'Amidah* prayer. Here the Yemenite text follows the *Zohar* (II, 169a),[420] which restricts the use of that sentence to the *'Amidah* prayer as expression of the true faith of David (*Is.* 55:3). After this official close of Grace, *Maḥzor Vitry* requires the celebrant to recite silently *Ps.* 34:10–11, the first two of the verses currently in use in the

---

418 אמר רבי סימון י״ג מידות רחמים כתובים בהקב״ה.

419 וקבלתי מרבותי כי בשבת יש לומר מגדול ישועות בוא״ו ובחול מגדיל ביו״ד ונראה לי הטעם מפני שהשבת הוא מלך גדול כנגד החול ומגדול הוא מלא וא״ו וחולם בוא״ו הוא מלך גדול, ומגדיל הוא חסר יו״ד והירק בלא יו״ד הוא מלך קטן. ועוד מגדיל הוא בתילים ועדיין לא היה דוד מלך. ומגדול הוא בנביאים וכבר היה מלך.

420 ובשבת דלא אשתכח דינא למהוי נצח והוד כלל חסדים אומר רצה והחליצנו למהוי תרוייהו חסדי דוד הנאמנים וע״ד אל תהי צרה ויגון וכו׳ דהא רצה ומודים אינון חסדי דוד ושים שלום דקאמרן בצלותא בברכת עושה שלום במרומיו הוא ברחמיו יעשה שלום עלינו.

Ashkenazic text of Grace, followed, as introduction to the benediction over wine, by *Ps.* 116:13, referring to the Cup of Salvation which the *Talmud* (*b. Pesaḥim* 119b; *Abudirham,* p. 327) identifies as the cup over which King David will say Grace after the meal of the Just at the End of Days. Abudirham (*loc. cit.*) requires five verses before the invocation of the Cup of Salvation. Additional verses have been introduced to the Ashkenazic and Sephardic texts starting in the eighteenth century by various editors. In Western Ashkenazic and some Italian localities, the recitation of these verses has disappeared.

As stated before, the Cup of Grace is the Third Cup of the four required at the *Seder*.

Hallel

The second part of *Hallel* celebrates the final redemption in the time of the Messiah and the reestablishment of the Temple service. In the Babylonian tradition (*b. Pesaḥim* 118a),[421] *Ps.* 115:1 "Not to us, not to us" refers to the sufferings preceding the arrival of the Messiah, and *Ps.* 116:9 "I shall walk before the Lord in the Lands of the Living" refers to Resurrection, the Living being those who participate in Eternal Life. In the Galilean tradition (*y. Megillah* II,1 73a),[422] *Ps.* 115:1 refers to the present, *Ps.* 116.1 to the Age of the Messiah, *Ps.* 118:27 to the wars of Gog and Magog (*Ez.* 38-39), *Ps.* 118:28 to the World to Come. In any case, it is appropriate to preface the recitation of *Hallel* with scriptural verses that invite the Day of Judgment, which must precede the final redemption. These verses assume the role of an introduction in the absence of a formal benediction. The two verses recited in all rites already occur in the *siddur* of R. Amram Gaon (Koronel ed.); they are not mentioned by either R. Saadia Gaon or Maimonides. The longer Ashkenazic version is really an abbreviation of the introduction in *Maḥzor Vitry* (p. 196), which also contains

Ps. 69:26:	May their strongholds be desolate, their tents be without dweller!

Ps. 35:5-6:	May they be like chaff in the wind,
	  with an angel of the Lord pushing!
	May their way be dark and slippery,
	  with an angel of the Lord pursuing!

Ps. 28:4:	Give them commensurate with their deeds and
	    evil intentions
	  According to their handiwork give to them,
	  Return to them what they deserve!

Ps. 5:11:	Declare them guilty, o Lord,

---

421 וכי מאחר דאיכא הלל הגדול מאי טעמא אמרינן האי? משום שיש בו ה׳ דברים האלו: יציאת מצרים וקריאת ים סוף ומתן תורה ותחיית המתים וחבלו של משיח. יציאת מצרים דכתיב בצאת ישראל ממצרים, וקריעת ים סוף דכתיב הים ראה וינס, מתן תורה דכתיב ההרים רקדו כאלים, תחיית המתים דכתיב אתהלך לפני ה׳, חבלו של משיח דכתיב לא לנו ה׳ לא לנו.

422 א״ר אבון עוד היא אמורה על הסדר. בצאת ישראל ממצרים לשעבר. לא לנו ה׳ לא לנו לדורות הללו. אהבתי כי ישמע ה׳ לימות המשיח. אסרו חג בעבותים לימות גוג ומגוג. אלי אתה ואודך לעתיד לבא:

Let them fall by their own counsels,
Push them off by their crimes
Because they rebelled against You!

R. Samuel of Falaise (*Or Zarua'* II,119b),[423] who belongs to the minority of authorities who require a benediction for the part of *Hallel* recited before the meal, now requires a second benediction "to finish the *Hallel*" (*loc. cit.* 120b)[424] because of the interruption by celebration and meal. He nevertheless requires the recitation of the verses before restarting *Hallel* but, because of the benediction, his interpretation of the verses is retrospective, not prospective: in the Recital we mentioned the Egyptians many times and he who mentions the evildoer must deny him part in the World to Come. According to R. Zeraḥya, reported in *Orḥot Ḥayyim* (p. 81c), the verses underscore the derivation of the Four Cups from the four cups of doom the Gentiles will drink at the End of Days (cf. p. 186).

Since, for the majority opinion, the recitation of *Ps.* 69:6-7 is the introduction to *Hallel*, the celebration of the Fourth Cup, it is appropriate to fill the cup before the verses are read. This is the way the cup is handled today in non-Ashkenazic rituals and it also was formerly the Ashkenazic *minhag* (*Ma'asé Roqeaḥ, Seder Leyl Pesaḥ* #68).[425] In time, the recitation of these verses has turned into an Ashkenazic ceremony of anticipation of the Messiah and, therefore, the Fourth Cup is poured only after that ceremony. The basic sources of the Ashkenazic *minhag*, *MaHaRIL* and Isaac Tyrna, still consider *Ps.* 69:6-7 as introduction to *Hallel* and require that the cup be filled immediately after the Third Cup is emptied. It is customary in Ashkenazic families to prepare a Fifth Cup for Elijah, the precursor of the Messiah (*Mal.* 3:33) and the future redemption. The Fifth Cup is poured in a separate cup, either (in most Western Ashkenazic families) before *Qiddush* or (in most Eastern Ashkenazic families) at this point before the recitation of "Pour out your anger. . . ." The ceremony (in its Western Ashkenazic form) is first reported by R. Zelikman Bingo (a

---

423 וקורא עד חלמיש למעינו מים ומברך לקרא ההלל ולא לגמור לפי שמפסיקין אותו בסעודה.

424 צריך לפתוח בשפוך והטעם לפי שהזכרנו מצרים פעמים רבות והמזכיר רשע צריך לקללו לפיכך אנו פותחים בשפוך. ובלא לנו צריך לברך לגמור את ההלל לפי שהאכילה היתה הפסק בין הברכה הראשונה.

425 ולאחר ברכת המזון מוזגין כוס רביעי ואומרים עליו שפוך חמתך.

student of *MaHaRIL*, p. 195).[426] He gives as possible reason that we expect Elijah to appear during the *Seder* and if no cup were prepared for him, the necessary interruption would disturb our celebration. The connection with a Fifth Cup mentioned as optional in some readings of the Babylonian *Talmud* (*b. Pesaḥim* 118a; see below) and the delay of pouring the cup until after Grace is attributed to R. Yehuda Leway ben Beẓalel, "the High Rabbi Loeb" of Prague in the early seventeenth century. However, this attribution is in late sources of questionable correctness.[427] The first mention of the Cup of Elijah in a legal work is *Ḥoq Ya'aqob* (§480)[428] by R. Jacob Rischer, an eighteenth-century Lithuanian scholar who became rabbi of Metz in Lorraine. It seems from his language, "in these lands one pours an extra cup," that he learned of the custom in the West and does not know yet of a connection with the talmudic Fifth Cup. The first homiletic connection of the Cup of Elijah with the recitation of the verses before the second part of *Hallel* seems to be by Moses Ḥagiz (*Shte Haleḥem*, end; early eighteenth century) who notes that the four expressions of deliverance in *Ex.* 6:6–7 given as basis for the institution of Four Cups (p. 185) are followed in verse 8 by a fifth expression, "*I shall bring* you to the Land." Since the entry into the Land under Joshua turned out to be temporary, we still expect God to fulfill the fifth redemption in the days of the Messiah and therefore prepare a cup which after the final redemption will be turned into a regular obligation. In all Ashkenazic families, the verses before *Hallel* are recited while the door is opened. R. Moshe Isserles (*Oraḥ Ḥayyim* §480)[429] attributes the origin of this custom to R. Israel Bruna (middle of the fifteenth century) and explains: "One opens the door to remind oneself that this is the 'Night of Preservation' (*Ex.* 12:42) and that as reward for this belief the Messiah will come and pour out his wrath over the heathen; this is what we do." There is no reason to doubt the attribution since R. Jacob Weilla, the slightly older contemporary of R.

---

426 והנה ראיתי יש בני אדם בלילי פסח שמוזגין כוס מיוחד ומעמידין על השלחן ואומרים שזה הכוס לאליהו הנביא, ולא ידעתי מאין זה הטעם. ונראה דהטעם יוצא מהכא, שאם יבא אליהו הנביא בליל פסח כאשר אנו מקוים ומחקים לו זה הלילה וצריך גם הוא לכוס, דאפילו עני מישראל לא יפתחו לו מד' כוסות, ואי לא הוי כוס מוכן לשם א"כ צריכים אנו להתעסק לו בכוס ודילמא ימנע מסדר של פסח.

427 Cf. *Hagada shel Pesaḥ* in "All books of *MaHaRaL* of Prague," Judaica Press, New York, 1969.

428 ונוהגין באלו המדינות למזוג כוס אחד יותר מהמסובין וקורין אותו כוס של אליהו הנביא.

429 ויש אומרים שיש לומר שפוך חמתך וכו' קודם לא לנו (ר"ן פרק ערבי פסחים) ולפתוח הפתח כדי לזכור שהוא ליל שמורים ובזכות אמונה זו יבא משיח וישפוך חמתו על הגוים (מהרי"ב) וכן נוהגים.

Israel Bruna, writes simply (*MaHaRYW* 193),[430] "One pours the Fourth Cup and starts 'Pour out Your wrath.'"

The current *Talmud* text (*b. Pesaḥim* 118a)[431] reads: "Our teachers taught: The Fourth [cup], one finishes *Hallel* over it and says the Great *Hallel*." This is the reading insisted on by Rashi. The text of Rabbenu Ḥananel and Alfassi is "Fifth" in place of "Fourth." In the opinion of R. Rabinowicz (*Diqduqé Soferim Pesaḥim*, p. 186a, note ב), the *Talmud* text has simply been emended by Rashi. However, it seems that Rashi did not emend it but preferred the text of the Academy of Pumbedita that admitted only four cups, over that of Sura, where an optional fifth cup was allowed (*Oẓar Hageonim Pesaḥim*, p. 126, note ב). From the silence of *Yerushalmi* sources, it seems that Galilean practice also admitted only four cups; no surviving ritual admits a fifth cup.

The translation of *Hallel* given in the text follows the interpretation of Rashi and Ibn Ezra with two exceptions. In *Ps.* 118:10–12, אֲמִילַם *'amīlam* is derived from *mūl* "to circumcise," following the *Targum* of Rav Yosef and R. David Qimḥi, as regular *hiph'il* and not as irregular form from *mll* "to wither" (Rashi) since the latter derivation cannot be reconciled with Masoretic punctuation (one would expect short "i" and double "l"). One must assume that for metric reasons the word is not in pausal form *'amīlēm*. The translation of דעך "to be destructive" (*Ps.* 118:12) follows R. Yeḥiel Hillel (*Meẓudat Ẓiyyon ad loc.*), Jastrow's Dictionary, and the meaning "to crush, squash, crumple" of the root in Arabic. *Ps.* 118:12 may either refer to *Deut.* 1:44 speaking of the Emorite or, more likely, to Phoenician cults connected with human sacrifices: "The heathen jump around me [in expectation of a human sacrifice] and prepare the fire of thorns."

The sequence *Ps.* 115:17–18 shows that the dead and those who are descending into silence are those who have no part in Eternal Life.

---

430 וימזוג כוס ד׳ ויתחיל שפוך.

431 Reading of *Halakhot Gedolot*, R. Amram Gaon, R. Saadia Gaon, R. Cohen Ẓedeq Gaon, Rabbenu Ḥananel, RYF, Maimonides, ROSH, and some *Talmud* mss.: ת״ר חמישי גומר עליו את ההלל ואומר הלל הגדול, דברי ר׳ טרפון.

Reading of Rashi, RaSHBaM, ms. Munich I, printed (Venice) *Talmud*: ת״ר רביעי גומר עליו את ההלל ואומר הלל הגדול, דברי ר׳ טרפון.

It is a very old tradition to repeat verses *Ps.* 118:21–29 (*Mishnah Sukkah* III,11). The original meaning probably is that the verses were sung by the choir of Levites in the Temple and then repeated by the people (*Midrash Shoḥer Ṭov* 118 #22).[432] Verses *Ps.* 118:1–4 are in the form of an address to several people requiring an answer; therefore, it is traditional that the *Seder* should not be recited but in groups of at least three people so that one may address the other two and they answer. Traditionally, *Ps.* 118:21–29 either represents a quartet sung by the prophet Samuel, Isay, and David and his brothers (*b. Pesaḥim* 119a)[433] or a composition sung by many voices; the architects (being blamed for lack of imagination or foresight in *Ps.* 118:22), Isay and his wife, their sons, the tribe of Juda, and Samuel (*Targum Ps.* 118:23-27)[434]; we repeat the verses in their honor (*Rashbam Pesaḥim* 119b).[435] The punctuation of the last two words of the Hebrew text of *Ps.* 118:25 is subject to some controversy. The Aleppo (Ben Asher) codex of the Bible and the Yemenite prayer book have הוֹשִׁיעָה נָּא, הַצְלִיחָה נָּא, following the Masoretic rule of דְּחִיק, that an unstressed final *qāmaẓ* induces a doubling of the following consonant. No Ashkenazic prayer book manuscript can be trusted in these grammatical niceties, neither can the Sephardic *siddur*. The Venice Rabbinical Bible has the self-contradictory punctuation הוֹשִׁ֫יעָה נָּא, הַצְלִ֫יחָה נָא Recent Masoretic texts follow R. Y. S. R. Norzi (*Minḥat Shay ad loc.*), who reluctantly opts for הוֹשִׁ֫יעָה נָּא, הַצְלִ֫יחָה נָא. This is grammatically correct and represents a dissimilation of parallel expressions that occurs sporadically in the Hebrew Bible. The Hebrew text of this *Haggadah* follows the Yemenite *tiqlāl* and popular pronunciation.

The *Mishnah* (*Pesaḥim* X,8) requires that the recitation of

---

432 אנשי ירושלים אומרים מבפנים אנא ה׳ הושיעה נא ואנשי יהודה אומרים מבחוץ אנא ה׳ הצליחה נא.

433 א״ר שמואל בר נחמני א״ר יונתן אודך כי עניתני אמר דוד, אבן מאסו הבונים אמר ישי, מאת ה׳ היתה זאת אמרו אחיו, זה היום עשה ה׳ אמר שמואל, אנא ה׳ הושיעה נא אמרו אחיו, אנא ה׳ הצליחה נא אמר דוד, ברוך הבא בשם ה׳ אמר ישי, ברכנוכם מבית ה׳ אמר שמואל, אל ה׳ ויאר לנו אמרו כולן, אסרו חג בעבותים אמר שמואל, אלי אתה ואודך אמר דוד, אלהי וארוממך אמרו כולן.

434 מן קדם ה׳ הות דא אמרו ארדיכליא, היא פרישא קדמנא אמרו בנוי דישי.
דין יומא עבד ה׳ אמרו ארדיכליא, נדוץ ונחדי ביה אמרו בנוי דישי.
בעו מנך ה׳ כדון אמרו ארדיכליא, בבעו מנך ה׳ אצלח אמרו אמרו ישי ואינתתיה.
בריך דאתי בשום מימרא דה׳ אמרו ארדיכליא, יברכון יתכון מן בית מקדשא דה׳ אמר דוד.
אלהנא ה׳ אנהר לנו אמרו שבטיא דבית יהודה, כפיתו טליא לנכסת חגא בשלשלון עד די תקרבוניה ותשדון אדמיה בקרנת מדבחא אמר שמואל נביא.

435 משום כבוד ישי ושמואל ודוד ואחיו שאמרוהו מאודך ולמטה כדאמרן לעיל כופלין אותו.

Hallel (or of *Hallel* followed either by the "Great *Hallel*" [*Ps*. 136 or *Ps*. 23; cf. *b. Pesaḥim* 118a]) be concluded with the "Praise for the Song." *Maḥzor Vitry* has *Hallel* followed by *Ps*. 136 and *Ps*. 23; this has not survived in any rite. However, through the sixteenth century we find Ashkenazic texts with additional Psalms or verses recited after the Great *Hallel*, e.g., *Ps*. 135 after *Ps*. 136 in the Amsterdam *Haggadah* of 1662 or the first verse of *Ps. 33* in the *Haggadot* of Prague (1526), Mantua (1561). According to the Babylonian authority Rav Yehuda bar Yeḥesq'el, the "Praise for the Song" is the benediction reserved for the ordinary recitation of *Hallel*, "*yĕhallĕlūkhā*" (*b. Pesaḥim* 118a)[436] but the Galilean Rebbi Yoḥanan identifies the benediction with *"nishmat kol ḥai,"* the benediction appropriate for the recitation of the Great *Hallel*, originally reserved for thanksgiving services in the night following rainfall that ended a drought (*b. Ta'anit* 6b; *y. Ta'aniot* I,3 64b).[437] Since fasting for a drought was not regularly practiced in Babylonia where agriculture depended on irrigation canals drawing water from Euphrates and Tigris, the difference between Babylonian and Galilean authorities can be explained simply on basis of practice: in Babylonia, *Hallel* was the only song of praise; in Galilee, the Great *Hallel* was the most impressive and regularly recited in the night. All extant Babylonian prayer texts (R. Saadia Gaon and R. Amram Gaon) follow Rav Yehuda and require only *yĕhallĕlūkhā*, either after *Hallel* or after Great *Hallel*. Rav Amram Gaon is quite emphatic that this is the only correct way of interpretation of the *Talmud* text,[438] but he is not followed by any authority outside of Babylonia. Since one does not recite any benediction at the start of the two parts of *Hallel*, a final benediction is not logically required. The final benediction must therefore be one of the original institutions of the *Seder* night.

Of the multitude of medieval arrangements, only two have survived. The Ashkenazic non-ḥasidic ritual follows R. Ḥayyim Cohen, the grandfather of R. Moses of Coucy, the thirteenth-century author of the "Great Book of Commandments" (*Sefer Mizwot Gadol, 'Asé* 14;[439]

---

436 מאי ברכת השיר? רב יהודה אמר יהללוך ה' אלהינו; ור' יוחנן אמר נשמת כל חי.

437 ור' יוחנן מסיים בה הכי אילו פינו מלא שירה כים ולשוננו רנה כהמון גליו עד אל יעזבונו רחמיך ה' אלהינו.

438 חלוקין רב יהודה ורבי יוחנן, דקא אמרינן מאי ברכת השיר רב יהודה אמר יהללוך, ר' יוחנן אמר נשמת כל חי, והלכה כרב יהודה וכן מנהג בשתי ישיבות.

439 ורבינו חיים כהן לא היה חותם ביהללוך כי אם בנשמת לבדו משום דלישנא דברכת השיר משמע חדא ברכה.

Tosafot Pesaḥim 118a, *s.v. R. Yoḥanan*) in reciting *yĕhallĕlūkhā* after *Hallel* without the concluding doxology, followed by Great *Hallel*, "*nishmat*," and the benediction for the Daily *Hallel*. This was accepted north of the Pyrenees on the authority of R. Meir of Rothenburg (*Orḥot Ḥayyim* 81c).[440] All other rituals follow R. Yosef Karo (*Bet Yosef, Oraḥ Ḥayyim* §486),[441] who adopted the ruling of R. Meir 'Arama, an exile from Saragossa in Spain who settled in Saloniki, to have the Great *Hallel* immediately follow the Egyptian *Hallel*, and to conclude with *nishmat* and the addition to *nishmat* from the Sabbath service but without the final doxology, followed by the full text of *yĕhallĕlūkhā* including the final benediction. This ruling accommodates the traditional inclusion of *nishmat* with adherence to the basic Babylonian decisions but is not based on earlier authorities. R. Yosef Karo states that he could not find any old authority for the arrangement of R. Meir 'Arama but a Gaonic responsum quoted in *Sefer Ha'iṭṭur* (II, p. 270a)[442] describes its procedure as current in the Academies of Sura and Pumbedita; the author of *Sefer Ha'iṭṭur* for himself prefers the Ashkenazic (Palestinian?) arrangement.

The lengthy prayer text of *nishmat*, "The souls of all living shall praise Your name," has been analyzed by several modern authors, among them I. Elbogen and E. D. Goldschmidt; their analyses and dissections of the text are unsatisfactory. Since we are talking about a prayer text, it is clear from the institutions of the Men of the Great Assembly that only outline and general structure were fixed in ancient times but the details of the text were left to the individual. Even the standardization of the text in Gaonic times and even more in the German Middle Ages did not lead to a fixed text. Nevertheless, we can easily identify two main recensions. The Babylonian text, represented by R. Saadia Gaon, R. Amram Gaon, and Maimonides, differs from today's Yemenite text only in minor points. The longer European text, exemplified by Ashkenazic and Sephardic versions, may derive from Galilean practice. The earliest Ashkenazic version available, that of *Maḥzor Vitry*, is rather closer to both Sephardic and

---

440 הר״מ נ״ע היה נוהג שלא לחתום הברכה בברכת השיר אלא כשמגיע כי מעולם ועד עולם אתה אל פותח הלל הגדול ונשמת כל חי וחותם בישתבח אבל ביהללוך לא היה חותם.

441 שמעתי בשם מהר״ר מאיר בן ערמאה ז״ל שגומר את ההלל ואינו אומר יהללוך כלל ואחר גמר הלל אומר הלל הגדול ונשמת כל חי וישתבח עד ומעולם עד עולם אתה אל ואז יאמר יהללוך עד מלך מהולל בתשבחות ויטבו בעיני דבריו לצאת ידי ספק ואף על פי שאינו ממש כמו שכתבו הפוסקים מכל מקום כיון דנפקי בהכי מידי ספיקא שפיר דמי.

442 וכרב יהודה נהגו בשתי ישיבות וחוזר וחותם יהללוך, וכן שדר ממתיבתא. ויפה הוא לחתום בישתבח עד מלך מהולל בתשבחות.

Yemenite versions than today's text, which underwent some changes even after the introduction of standard printed texts.

The first paragraph has few variants in the versions and in older texts. In the second paragraph, *all* older texts have תּוּשְׁבָּחוֹת, rabbinic Hebrew vocalization in contrast for biblical תִּשְׁבָּחוֹת propagated by R. David Qimḥi[443] and elevated to standard use by the authority of *ARI*. The Ashkenazic text here was identical to today's Yemenite version, that God's praise "is sung in hymns" without qualification. The current Ashkenazic version is rejected in a similar case by the *Talmud* (*b. Taanit* 6b),[444] when a formula of praise of God by "*many songs of thanksgiving*" is rejected because the Hebrew could be interpreted to mean "by *most, but not all,* songs of thanksgiving." The fourteenth-century Ashkenazic *Hagahot Maimuniot* (*Seder Tefillah* #2) still requires to silence the reader if he uses the text "sung in *many* hymns"; nevertheless, this is the formula of all printed German and Italian Ashkenazic texts. The vocalization of "creature" is בְּרִיָּה, as was noted in the section on Grace, p. 351. In the second sentence of the second paragraph, the old Ashkenazic version is "The Lord is awake, He does neither slumber nor sleep," as in the Sephardic text. The introductory phrase was eliminated because it does not fit the biblical source, *Ps.* 124:4, "Behold, the Guardian of Israel does neither slumber nor sleep." This process of adaptation to biblical quotes has already been noted in the discussion of Ashkenazic Grace. The text of "He awakens the sleeping" was המקיץ רְדוּמִים in all rituals (but not in the printed version of Maimonides). *Orḥot Ḥayyim* (p. 64c) already notes a polemic of R. Asher ben Yeḥiel against those who change the word into (the now current Ashkenazic and Sephardic) נִרְדָּמִים. In the third paragraph, the old Ashkenazic text was equal to the other versions in reading ואלו "and even if [our mouths were full of song]," referring to the preceding paragraphs of praise. The connecting *waw* was already lost in the first prints. The multiplication of the number of benefits in the Ashkenazic text is already reported as Rashi's text in *Maḥzor Vitry* (p. 148). While all current texts read רִבֵּי רְבָבוֹת "myriads of myriads," there is another reading in both Ashkenazic and Sephardic sources, רַבֵּי רְבָבוֹת, "lots of myriads." The one difference between the texts that can be traced back to the earliest Ashkenazic sources is about the bad

---

443 Quoted in Elijah Baḥur's (Elijah Levita) notes to Qimḥi's *Sefer Hashorashim*, s.v. שבח.

444 ברוך רוב ההודאות. רוב ההודאות ולא כל ההודאות? אמר רבא אימא אל ההודאות.

sicknesses from which the Lord has saved us. All Oriental and Mediterranean sources have רַבִּים "many, frequent," but all Northern sources have נֶאֱמָנִים, taken from *Deut.* 28:59, even if they also add רַבִּים. The word נֶאֱמָן means either "trustworthy," meaning that the illness will resist medical efforts until the time decreed by the Lord has passed (*b. 'Avodah Zarah* 55a; *Rashi Deut.* 28:59) or "long-lasting," as in *1 Sam.* 25:28 where Abigail wishes David a "long-lasting dynasty" (R. Saadia Gaon and Rashbam on *Deut.* 26:59).

The quote from *Ps.* 35:10, "All my bones shall say, o Lord, who is like You?" in Sephardic pronunciation reads *kāl aẓmōtay*. *Ps.* 35:10 and *Prov.* 19:7 are the only two occurrences in the Bible where Hebrew כָּל "all" is read *kāl* and not *kŏl*. In Ashkenazic tradition, the verse is taken as an exhortation to move one's body while reciting Psalms. The final sentence for the Sephardic ritual is a combination of several biblical themes; it is already found in R. Saadia's text.

The insert for the Ashkenazic ritual has undergone a rearrangement in the later Middle Ages. The original arrangement as given in *Mahẓor Vitry* was

Who can be compared to You, who may be equal to You, who can be valued like You, the great, strong, awesome God (*Deut.* 10:17), the Highest Power, Owner of Heaven and earth?	מִי יִדְמֶה־לָּךְ וּמִי יִשְׁוֶה־לָּךְ וּמִי יַעֲרָךְ־לָךְ, הָאֵל הַגָּדוֹל הַגִּבּוֹר וְהַנּוֹרָא, אֵל עֶלְיוֹן, קֹנֵה שָׁמַיִם וָאָרֶץ.
God in the power of Your strength, Great in the glory of Your Name, Eternal Power and Awesome in Your awesomeness, He Who reigns forever, Exalted and Holy is His Name.	הָאֵל בְּתַעֲצוּמוֹת עֻזֶּךָ הַגָּדוֹל בִּכְבוֹד שְׁמֶךָ הַגִּבּוֹר לָנֶצַח וְהַנּוֹרָא בְּנוֹרְאוֹתֶיךָ, הַמֶּלֶךְ הַיּוֹשֵׁב עַל כִּסֵּא רָם וְנִשָּׂא. שׁוֹכֵן עַד, מָרוֹם וְקָדוֹשׁ שְׁמוֹ.
We shall sing Your praise, laud and glorify You, and praise Your holy Name, as it is said (*Ps.* 103:1) "For David. My soul, praise the Lord, and all my innards His holy Name." And it is written (*Ps.* 33:1): "Sing, o just, in the Lord; praise becomes the straightforward."	נְהַלֶּלְךָ וּנְשַׁבֵּחֲךָ וּנְפָאֶרְךָ וּנְבָרֵךְ אֶת־שֵׁם קָדְשֶׁךָ, כָּאָמוּר 'לְדָוִד, בָּרְכִי נַפְשִׁי אֶת־יי, וְכָל־קְרָבַי אֶת־שֵׁם קָדְשׁוֹ.' וְכָתוּב 'רַנְּנוּ צַדִּיקִים בַּיי, לַיְשָׁרִים נָאוָה תְהִלָּה.'

In this version, we have typically a verse, *Deut.* 10:17, mentioning, in the Hebrew word order: God, great, strong, awesome, followed by an amplification in Babylonian style (cf. pp. 246-247). After this, the statement that we shall sing God's praise is based on two statements, first *Ps.* 103:1, giving David as an example, followed by *Ps.* 33:1, showing that David's example should be imitated by all who aspire to the title of just and straightforward. This combination of Babylonian composition with talmudic-type reasoning based on a chain of biblical verses makes it likely that the Ashkenazic version preserves an otherwise lost Babylonian enlargement of the basic Galilean text. It is qualified as a later addition to the standard text by *Maḥzor Vitry* (p. 150).[445]

Already *Maḥzor Vitry* notes that some people change the order of the addition to that current today. The explanation for the changed order is explained by *Kol Bo* (sec. 37) in the name of R. Meir of Rothenburg.[446] The reader is supposed to begin the special holiday melodies in the morning service on Pentecost, the anniversary of the Decalogue from Mount Sinai, with "God in the power of Your strength" since the Torah, God's gift to His people, is called "strength" in *Ps.* 29:11: "The Lord gave strength to His people." The next line, "Great in the glory of Your name," is the start of the song for the festivals of Tabernacles and the Eighth Day of Assembly. This is justified by an involved homiletic derivation. In the Temple service, the festival of Tabernacles was characterized by the great number of sacrifices required (*Num.* 29:12–34), among them seventy bulls. On the other hand, the Eighth Day of Assembly following the seven days of Tabernacles requires only single sacrifices like the solemn Days of Awe, New Year and the Day of Atonement (and the New Moon). According to the talmudic count (*b. Sanhedrin* 17a), the number of nations on earth descended from Noah is seventy (*Gen.* 10). The bulls sacrificed during the festival of Tabernacles are brought in behalf of the seventy nations of Gentiles but the single bull of the Eighth Day is brought for Israel, who in importance outweighs the seventy nations. Tabernacles, therefore, is only the introduction to the Eighth Day and, in the oldest existing collection of homilies (*Pesiqta deRav Kahana*, chap. 30), the lesson in Prophets for the Eighth Day is *Is.* 26:15: "You added to this people, o Lord, You added glory to this people but You pushed away the rest of the earth." This is the meaning of the

445 בסדר רב עמרם רננו צדיקים וכל עצמותי תאמרנה. ואין כתוב בו אריכות זה.

446 כתב ה״ר מאיר בשבועות מתחיל החזן האל בתעצומות עוזך בשביל מתן תורה שהתורה נקראת עוז שנ׳ ה׳ עוז לעמו יתן. ובסוכות ובשמיני עצרת ובשמחת תורה מתחיל הגדול בכבוד שמך לפי שנ׳ יספת לגוי נכבדת ונדרש בפסיקתא על האבות ושמיני עצרת ושמחת תורה. ובפסח מתחיל הגבור לנצח לפי שהקב״ה נראה כגבור על הים ובראש השנה ויום הכפורים מתחיל המלך היושב לפי שהקב״ה יושב בדין.

reference to "glory" in the phrase for Tabernacles. On Passover God is addressed as Eternal Power for His exercise of power at the Red Sea, and during the High Holidays He is addressed as King, as is required generally during the Days of Awe. The phrase used for God on His throne is *Is.* 6:1. On the Sabbath, God is addressed as "He Who reigns forever" (*Ps.* 29:10), since the Sabbath is the completion of Creation and, therefore, the crowning ceremony of God as Master of the Universe. This order is still the Western Ashkenazic tradition; in Eastern Ashkenazic usage the different beginnings for the three festivals of pilgrimage have disappeared together with their separate melodies, and the reader starts with the first line.

In all three rituals the four lines following *Ps.* 33:1 contain the acrostic יצחק, Isaac. This may be (*Kol Bo, loc. cit.*)[447] because a talmudic source (lost, but quoted in *Yalqut Shim'oni Ps.* 33)[448] connects *Ps.* 33:18–19 to the experiences of Isaac, who prayed for God's grace and therefore was saved from death at the hands of Ishmael (*Gen. rabbah* 53[15] on *Gen.* 21:9 explains that Sarah noticed Ishmael shooting arrows at Isaac "in jest" [*Gen.* 21:9][449] and from famine in the land of the Philistines (*Gen.* 26:12). It seems that the original text was close to the Ashkenazic version since the verb הלל appearing in the first line of that version takes up the introductory theme תהלה of the introductory verse *Ps.* 33:1 and, also, the first two lines of R. Saadia Gaon's text are identical with the Ashkenazic one. The Sephardic and Oriental versions result from a rearrangement in order to obtain the accompanying acrostic רבקה *Rebecca.*

The current final section of the "Blessing for the Song" begins with "And in the choirs of the myriads. . . ." In the thanksgiving service for rain after a drought the final doxology was (*b. Ta'anit* 6b)[450] "Praised are You, o Lord, God of praises." The difference in vocalization of the Hebrew word for "choirs" seems to reflect old differences. The current Ashkenazic version, *maqhēlōt*, appears in all old reliable Ashkenazic (German and Italian) sources and also in the

---

447 ונראה לי משום המדרש דעל רננו צדיקים שהוא על יצחק נחתו בו.

448 **אל יראיו** זה יצחק, **למיחלים לחסדו** שהיה מיחל להקב״ה, **להציל ממות נפשם** שבקש ישמעאל להרגו שנ׳ ותרא שׂרה את בן הגר גו׳, **ולחיותם ברעב** שנ׳ וימצא בשנה ההיא מאה שערים.

449 ר׳עזריה משום ר׳ לוי אמר: אמר לו ישמעאל ליצחק נלך ונראה חלקנו בשדה. והיה ישמעאל נוטל קשת וחצים ומורה כלפי יצחק ועושׂה עצמו כאילו מצחק.

450 ברוך רוב ההודאות. רוב ההודאות ולא כל ההודאות? אמר רבא אימא אל ההודאות. . . .

Iraqi tradition; the Sephardic spelling *miqhălōt* is prevalent in eighteenth-century Ashkenazic *Haggadot* as reading of the German *Ḥasidim* (*Siddur Ḥaside Ashkenaz*, p. קנה). The construct form *maqhălōt* found in current Ashkenazic *Haggadot* and prayer books is a Heidenheim invention. The meaning of the introductory sentence is: "May our praise of the Lord be as acceptable as if recited in an assembly of ten thousand [a myriad]." This refers to a statement of R. Yossi the Galilean (*Mishnah Berakhot* VII,3)[451] that "the language of a benediction has to change according to the number of people assembled, as it is said (*Ps.* 68:27): 'In assemblies of those of Israelite origins praise God, the Lord!'" and in his interpretation an "assembly" is one of 10,000 people at least. The other sages take the verse to mean that any congregation, of at least ten adults, is as good as any other to sing the praise of the Lord (*y. Berakhot* VII,3 11c).[452]

The final section, containing the doxology for the Ashkenazic ritual, is not connected with the "Blessing for the Song" but is the final benediction recited at the close of the Daily *Hallel* and as such is the conclusion of the introductory service also on Sabbath and holidays. The number of expressions of praise is fifteen in the European rituals (*Ṭur Oraḥ Ḥayyim* §51)[453] based on a Babylonian Gaonic ordinance. The number was fixed at fifteen at the same time that *1 Chr.* 29:10–14, *Neh.* 9:6–11, and *Ex.* 14:30–15:19 were added to the Daily *Hallel*, since the fifteen expressions of praise are contained in these additional verses. Fifteen is also the number of benefits enumerated in the litany **דיינו** at the end of the Recital. The Yemenite text has only thirteen expressions, corresponding to the number of attributes of Divine Grace (*Zohar Ex.* 132a).[454] The *Zohar* also requires not to interrupt the recitation of these "vessels of grace"; they should be recited in one breath. R. Saadia Gaon's text has only eleven expressions; R. Amram

---

451 ר' יוסי הגלילי אומר לפי רוב הקהל מברכין שנ' במקהלות ברכו אלהים ה' ממקור ישראל.

452 מה מקיימין רבנן טעמא דרבי יוסי הגלילי במקהלות בכל קהילה וקהילה.

453 ובתקון הגאונים יש נוהגין לומר ויברך דויד את ה' לעיני כל הקהל עד ומהללים לשם תפארתך כאשר הוא בספר דברי הימים ויברכו שם כבודך עד שירת הים כאשר הוא בספר עזרא ושירת הים, והטעם לפי שכל אותם ט״ו לשונות של שבח הסדורים בברכת ישתבח דורש במכילתין מתוך שירת הים ומתוך אותן פסוקים של ויברך דויד.

454 כיון דמטי בר נש לישתבח נטל קב״ה ההוא כתרא ושוי לה קמיה וכנסת ישראל שריאת לאתתקנא למיתי קמי מלכא עלאה. ואצטריך לאכללא לה בתליסר מכילן דרחמי עלאי דמנהון אתברכת. ואינון תליסר בוסמין עלאין כד'א נרד וכרכום קנה וקנמון וגו' והכא אינון: שיר ושבחה הלל וזמרה עוז וממשלה נצח גדולה וגבורה תהלה ותפארת קדושה, הא תריסר, ולבתר לחברא לה בהדייהו ולומר ומלכות והוו תליסר בגין דאיהי מתברכא מנייהו. ועל דא אצטריך בשעתא דאתכלילת בינייהו לשוואה לבא ורעותא בהאי ולא לישתעי כלל דלא לפסוק בינייהו.

Gaon's text is identical with the current European text. The Ashkenazic text ends here with the final benediction for the Daily *Hallel*. In practically all texts preceding Stanow-Heidenheim, the benediction ends חַי הָעוֹלָמִים "life of the universe," not חֵי הָעוֹלָמִים "eternally living" as in current texts. The older spelling is required by Maimonides (*Yesodé Hatorah* II,10) for reasons of doctrine since the reading חֵי gives God's existence an adjectival and temporal, i.e., ephemeral, dimension. Older European authorities, if they discuss the problem at all, mention חַי as the standard version and חֵי as the reading of some people (*RAVaN* 166a). The first to prefer the modern reading is R. Yomtov Lipman Heller (*Tosafot Yomtov, Tamid*, last note) based on the biblical expression חֵי הָעוֹלָם "the Eternal," *Dan.* 12:7. The modern reading was still rejected in the eighteenth century by Eliahu Tiktin in his notes to *Levush*, §52 but it was accepted by Eliahu of Wilna in his *siddur*, based on an interpretation "giving life to (both) worlds."

Sephardic and Oriental rituals end the recitation of *Hallel* with the final benediction of the Egyptian *Hallel*, as mentioned earlier. The text of this benediction is uniform in all rituals except for the final doxology, which is short in the European and long in the Yemenite ritual. However, there also did exist a long Ashkenazic form: "Praised are You o Lord, our God, King of the Universe, Who is glorified by Psalms in the mouths of His people, lauded and extolled by the songs of Your servant David. Praised are You, o Lord, Who is glorified by Psalms," used by Rashi and his teacher R. Jacob ben Yaqar on the days of the New Moon (*Rashi Responsa* #56, *Mahzor Vitry* #226, p. 193)[455] as initial benediction. It is remarkable that in all three rituals these declarations and benedictions are vocalized by the rules of biblical Hebrew.

---

455 לפיכך איני מברך עליו אשר קדשנו במצותיו וצונו. אבל אני מברך עליו ברוך אתה ה' א"מה המהולל בפי עמו משובח ומפואר בשירי דוד עבדך ברוך אתה ה' מהולל בתשבחות. ולאחריו יהללוך כדרכה. ולא שמעתי יותר כי לא דקדקתי מרבותיי. שלמה בר' יצחק (ובתשובות: וכן מנהג רבי יעקב בן יקר).

Conclusion

Sephardic (not Italian) and Oriental *Haggadot* end the *Seder* with the Fourth Cup and the short form of Grace after the recitation of *Hallel*. In some Yemenite families one sings informally of the songs of Mori Shalom Shabazi (Salim Shebezi); these are given after the Ashkenazic *Haggadah* text. In kabbalistic circles, the men recite the Song of Songs after the conclusion of the *Seder*. The old Ashkenazic way described in *Maḥzor Vitry* also was to end the *Seder* at this point. Later on, several poems and songs were added. In the times of R. Meir of Rothenburg, the first three poems already were added as standard, and he used to drink the Fourth Cup after all these additions (*Magen Avraham, Oraḥ Ḥayyim* 480, #2),[456] since he also held that after the Fourth Cup one may not drink any more. In order not to be thirsty when he went to bed, he moved the Fourth Cup to the latest possible moment. In the Western Ashkenazic ritual, one still follows the order of R. Meir to drink the cup after the first three additions, even though in the meantime another three songs became standard and R. Meir's original reasoning would require one to move the Fourth Cup to the end of the last song. Eastern Ashkenazic usage follows R. Shelomo Luria and R. Joel Sirkes (*Baḥ* on *Ṭur Oraḥ Ḥayyim* §480, end),[457] who insist to finish the required service before later additions are recited.

The short form of Grace, known as "one benediction incorporating three" (*Mishnah Berakhot* VI,8),[458] is required after the consumption of anything for which the Land of Israel is praised in *Deut.* 8:8 and which is not eaten with bread (since bread requires the long form of Grace): cakes of wheat and barley, grapes and wine, figs, pomegranates, olives, dates, and date-honey. The benediction follows *Deut.* 8:10 and in one sentence includes praise and thanks for food, the Land, and Jerusalem. The Yemenite (Maimonides) text represents the

---

456 מהר״ם היה שותה אחר הפיוטים ואחר כי לו נאה כדי שלא יהא צמא כשישכב.

457 כתב מהרש״ל דמה שכתוב בטופסי המחזורים ברכת בורא פרי הגפן אכוס ד׳ אחר אז רוב ניסים ואומץ גבורותיך אינו מן הראוי אלא בסוף חתימת ישתבח מיד יברך בורא פרי הגפן והכי משמע בשאלה ששאלו לר׳ האי גאון על דברי ר׳ סעדיא בסימן שאחר זה ואחר כך יתחיל אז רוב ניסים כו׳ ואומץ גבורותיך ושאר פיוטים וכן עיקר.

458 אכל תאנים ענבים ורימונים מברך אחריהן שלש ברכות דברי רבן גמליאל. וחכמים אומרים ברכה אחת מעין שלש.

text of the *Talmud* (*b. Berakhot* 44a); the European versions also include an allusion to the later Fourth Benediction of Grace. The closing formula, "for the Land and the fruit of the vine," is mentioned in all post-talmudic Babylonian sources but not in the *Talmud* itself. Maimonides, the source of the Yemenite ritual, is the only early authority sticking to the formula "for the Land and the fruit of the tree" mentioned in the *Talmud* for grapes and the other fruits requiring the short form of Grace. After eating any food that does not require either the long or the short form of Grace, one has to recite the formula (*b. Berakhot* 37a; *y. Berakhot* VI,1 10b)[459]: "Praised are You o Lord, our God, King of the Universe, Creator of many living creatures, and the needs of all that You have created to keep all living alive. Praised are You, life of the Universe."

All rituals follow the decision of R. Sherira Gaon (*Oẓar Hageonim, Pesaḥim* #208)[460] that the short form of Grace is needed only after the Fourth Cup because nobody may stop drinking before the Fourth Cup is consumed. That ruling was always followed by Oriental and Sephardic Jews; it is implicit in the rules of Maimonides, authoritative in the Orient, and R. Iẓḥaq ibn Ghiat, main authority in Spain. A dissenting opinion, maybe of Ashkenazic students of the Babylonian academies, held that all cups except the Second need the short form of Grace (*loc. cit.* #355).[461] This was the practice of Ashkenazic Jews on the authority of Rashi (*Sefer Ha'orah*, p. 100),[462] who argues that, since the Four Cups are four separate obligations and therefore do not fall under the category of even numbers (cf. p. 188), they could not be considered continuations of one another; this argument does not apply to the Second Cup, which is the introduction to the meal. The Oriental-Sephardic ruling was accepted in the Ashkenazic ritual by R. Shalom of Austria and made to prevail by his students *MaHaRIL* (p. 99)[463] in the West and R. Eisik Tyrna

---

459 בָּרוּךְ אַתָּה יי אֱלֹהֵינוּ מֶלֶךְ הָעוֹלָם בּוֹרֵא נְפָשׁוֹת רַבּוֹת וְחֶסְרוֹנָן עַל כָּל מַה שֶּׁבָּרָאתָ לְהַחֲיוֹת בָּהֶם נֶפֶשׁ כָּל חַי. בָּרוּךְ חַי הָעוֹלָמִים.

460 אלא לאחריו אמאי מחייב על כל חד וחד הא יתיב ודעתיה אשאר כוסות הללו הלכך מברך ברכה אחרונה ודיו.

461 ועכשיו באו תלמידים לקמן ואמרו כי על כל כוס וכוס צריך ברכה לאחריו כמו שצריך לפניו.

462 ובעי ברוכי על הגפן ועל פרי הגפן בתר כוס ראשון ושלישי ורביעי אבל בתר שני לא, והיינו טעמא דשלשתן הללו כל אחד מצוה באנפי נפשיה הוא ואין דעתו לאכול, אבל כוס שני היכי אפשר לברך בתריה שהוא כוס של תחילת אכילה ויש לו לאכול ולשתות כל סעודתו ואין בו שום הפסקה.

463 ברכה אחרונה דכוסות איתא בה פלוגתא דרבוותא. ואמר מהר״ש דנראה לו מן הרא״ש דפסק דאין לברך ברכה אחרונה על שום כוס עד אחר כוס רביעי והממעט בברכות לא הפסיד וטוב יותר מלברך ברכה לבטלה. וכן דרש מהר״י סג״ל ברבים לנהוג כדברי הרא״ש.

(*Minhagim*, p. 47) in the East. His position, following that of R. Asher ben Yeḥiel (cf. p. 188) is, that one may not recite a benediction not universally recognized as necessary.

The poem recited after the short form of Grace, חסל, really does not belong to the *Haggadah* at all but is the conclusion of the *Seder*, the recitation of the laws of the preparation for Passover on the Fourteenth of Nisan and the rules for celebrating during the night of the Fifteenth, recited by observant Ashkenazic congregations during services of the "Great Sabbath" preceding Passover. The best known of these compositions, retained in the Eastern European Ashkenazic ritual, was composed by R. Yosef Tov Elem (Bonfils), an eleventh-century authority and the author of חסל. The original meaning of the second stanza is: "As we were able to recite all laws pertaining to Passover, may we be worthy to execute them." In the *Seder* night, the stanza is taken to express a wish to participate in the Temple service for Passover. The people, "who can count them?" are the descendants of Jacob (*Num.* 23:10). The "firm saplings" represent Israel (*Ps.* 80:16). The paragraph was introduced into the *Haggadah* by R. Shalom of Austria and accepted by both *MaHaRIL* (p. 123) and R. Eisik Tyrna (p. 54). The latter authority is the first one to mention the recitation of "Next year in Jerusalem!"

The next two compositions are taken from synagogal poetry. The first one, "It happened at midnight," is an alphabetic litany from one of the first Hebrew liturgical poets, Yannai, who may tentatively be dated to the sixth century C.E. The litany is incorporated in the Ashkenazic *Qerova*, the poetic development of the *'Amidah* prayer, for the "Great Sabbath," the Sabbath preceding Passover, major parts of which were composed by R. Yosef Tov Elem as mentioned above. The second litany, "And you shall say, a sacrifice of *Pesaḥ*," is part of the *Qerova* for the day of Passover by Eleazar Qalir (Qilir, perhaps Cyrillus, probably eighth century C.E.), the most prolific of Palestinian liturgical poets. His composition, based on *Lev.* 22:26–23:44, became the Ashkenazic service for the morning of the Second Day of Passover. The reading from *Leviticus* is the reading for the Second Day in the Diaspora; it was the reading for the unique Passover day in Galilee (*Mishnah Megillah* III,5). In the early eighteenth century, it was the *minhag* of Frankfurt/Main and most of Poland to recite the first composition during the first *Seder* night and the second composition during the second night (*Magen Avraham* §480). In Mayence, Metz, Prague, and Italy, both compositions were recited during both nights

(*Ḥoq Ya'aqov* §480). In most Ashkenazic *Haggadot*, the instructions follow *Magen Avraham.*

The two alphabetic litanies are typical medieval synagogal compositions, combinations of biblical and midrashic allusions. They need a line-by-line commentary.

It Happened at Midnight

א The slaying of the firstborn in Egypt (*Ex.* 12:29) happened at midnight. The poem contains the thought developed in *Pirqe R. Eliezer,* chap. 37, where it is asserted that all miraculous salvation that is reported of the Patriarchs and the Jewish people happened in the *Seder* night. The same thought appears also *Ex. rabbah* 18, end; *Num. rabbah* 20 contains a homily on the subject that most instances of salvation reported in the Bible happened during the night. Since the times of composition of these *midrashim* cannot be determined relative to the time of Yannai's activity, it is difficult to determine who is dependent on whom.

ב The night is divided not into hours but three or four watches (*b. Berakhot* 3b; *y. Berakhot* I,1 2c).

ג The pious wanderer is Abraham; the reference is to *Gen.* 14:15 where we are told of Abraham, pursuing the four kings from Mesopotamia, "the night was split over them, he and his servants smote them." The passive construction here is an echo of the passive imperfect of the biblical verse, which implies that an unmentioned (divine) power divided the night for Abraham, a parallel to the Exodus (*Gen. rabbah* 43[3]; *Pirqe R. Eliezer* 37).

ד The king of Gerar is Abimelech (*Gen.* 20:3). *Targum I Esther* 6:1 states that Abimelech's dream was in the night of the Fifteenth of Nisan.

ה Laban the Aramean (*Gen.* 31:29); the appearance was in the night preceding Laban's encounter with Jacob. The expression "preceding night" is from *Gen.* 31:42.

ו *Gen.* 32:25; the language is from *Hos.* 12:5. According to *Gen. rabbah* (§77, 2) the superior being was the angel of Esaw; according to *Targum Yerushalmi* he was the Archangel Michael and the tribe of

Levi was selected for priestly service in that night. The language of Hosea, וישׂראל ישׁר, is in a minority of sources; the inverted וישׁר ישׂראל is found more frequently.

ז ח Patros is an Egyptian tribe, *Gen.* 10:13.

ט Sisera is the commander of *Ḥaroshet Haggoyim* (*Jud.* 4:2); the stars of the night fought against Sisera (*Jud.* 5:20). According to the *Talmud* (*b. Pesaḥim* 118b), the victory over Sisera with his 900 chariots was greater than the victory over Pharaoh with his 600 chariots on the shores of the Red Sea. The stars are said to have heated the iron of the chariots and put them out of combat. There is no reference to Sisera flying.

י The reference is to *Is.* 10:32, the *hafṭarah* of the Eighth Day of Passover. By tradition, Isaiah refers to Sennaherib (*2 Kings* 19:35). Jerusalem was saved from Sennaherib because *Hallel* was recited in the Night of Preservation (Rashi on *Is.* 30:29).

כ *Is.* 46:1; probably also a reference to the apocryphal *Bel and Draco* in the Septuagint.

ל The secret of Nebuchadneẓẓar's dream was revealed to Daniel, the "desirable man" (*Dan.* 10:11), in the night (*Dan.* 2:19).

מ Belshaẓẓar used the holy vessels (*Dan.* 5:3, 5:30). According to R. Saadia Gaon, Belshaẓẓar decided to use the Temple vessels since the Jews had not been redeemed in the seventieth *Seder* night after the fall of Jerusalem.

נ Daniel in the lions' den (*Dan.* 5:18–28). Here the text follows most manuscripts and all eighteenth-century prints in reading בְּעִתּוֹתֵי, "in the time of." A few prints and manuscripts have בְּעַתּוּתֵי, a scribal error resulting in a reading בִּעֲתוֹתֵי, frequent in modern Eastern Ashkenazic *Haggadot* and conjectured to mean "in the terrors of."

ס Haman is the Agagite (*Esth.* 3:1); source of "in the night" unknown.

ע *Esther* 6:1; king Ahasuerus could not sleep in the third night after the Thirteenth of Nisan (*Esth.* 3:12), which would make it the night of the second *Seder*; it is moved to the first *Seder* night in *Targum I*.

פ The winepress as simile for the wars preceding the final redemption is from *Is*. 63:3. According to *Yalquṭ Shim'oni* (*Is*. #407) and Rashi (*Is*. 63:5),[464] this redemption is independent of Israel's worthiness but is the consequence of the Gentiles' anti-Semitism.

צ The simile of the watchman (*Is*. 21:11–12).

ק The Day of the Lord is neither day nor night (*Zach*. 14:7).

ר *Ps*. 74:16; cf. also the song "For Him it is right."

ש *Is*. 62:6; the watchmen will never stop invoking the Lord until He turns Jerusalem into the praise of Earth.

ת Darkness symbolizes the Diaspora; the language is taken from *Ps*. 139:12.

And You Shall Say: A Sacrifice of *Pesaḥ*

The refrain is *Ex*. 12:27, cf. the section "Rabban Gamliel."

א Passover is always first in any list of holidays (*Lev*. 23:4, *Num*. 28:16, *Deut*. 16:1); cf. also *Ex*. 12:2 where Nisan is instituted as first month.

ב Ethan the native-born, author of *Ps*. 89:1, is identified as the patriarch Abraham in *b. Bava Batra* 15a,[465] based on *Is*. 41:2, where Abraham is described to have awakened from the East.[466] The reference is to the Covenant between the Pieces, which took place during *Seder* night according to an opinion attributed to R. Yehuda in

---

464 וחמתי היא סמכתני. חמתי שיש לי על האומות אשר אני קצפתי מעט על עמי והמה עזרו לרעה היא סמכתני חיזקה ידי ועוררה את לבי ליפרע מהם ואף על פי שאין ישראל ראוין והגונים לגאולה.

465 אמר רב איתן האזרחי זה הוא אברהם, כתיב הכא איתן האזרחי וכתיב התם מי האיר ממזרח.

466 Ethan is called הָאֶזְרָחִי. This can either be a gentilic, "descendant of Zeraḥ," or it can mean "native-born," from זרח (II, Arabic צרח) "to be of pure race," or "coming from sun-rise," from זרח (I, Arabic דרח) "to rise, shine (said of the sun)." In the *Torah*, אזרח consistently means "native-born."

Pirqe R. Eliezer, chap. 28.[467]

ד,ה,ו The visit of the angels with Abraham is told *Gen.*, chap. 18. In verse 7, Abraham is described to have taken a "young cattle" to slaughter for his guests. The poem is a composition of Qalir for the service of the first day of Passover in Israel where the Torah reading was *Lev.* 22:26 ff. (*Mishnah Megillah* III,5). (In the Babylonian ritual, followed today, both the reading and the poem are used for the second day.) The reading starts (v. 27): "When a bull, a sheep, or a goat is born. . . ." It is explained in *Lev. rabbah*, chap. 27, that "bull," not "calf," is used in order not to mention the sin of the Golden Calf; this is explained at length in the composition of Qalir introducing our litany. The "cattle" or calf of Passover (*Deut.* 16:2) is the *ḥagīgah* sacrifice.

ז,ח The visit of the angels to Sodom, the destruction of Sodom, and the rescue of Lot are told in *Gen.*, chap. 19. The episode is traditionally dated at Passover since Lot baked *mazzot* (*Gen.* 19:3).

ט Moph (*Hos.* 9:6) is Noph (*Is.* 19:13), Egyptian Mennufe, Memphis near old Cairo; the name of the capital serves as designation of the country. The image of God sweeping Egypt out as with a broom is from *Is.* 14:23. The pre-Heidenheim vocalization of בעברך is בְּעֶבְרָךְ

י "Firstborn," literally "head of virility," a biblical expression (*Gen.* 49:3). The language of the line imitates *Ps.* 78:51.

כ,ל *Ex.* 4:22-23.

מ The encircled city was Jericho (*Jos.* 6:1).

נ The reference is to the victory of Gideon over the Midianites (*Jud.* 7:13), based on the dream of a Midianite who saw a "roast cake of barley"[468] in the interpretation of *Targum Jonathan*.[469] The written text (*Qetib*) has צלול "clear" instead of the vocalized צְלִיל "roast." According to Rashi (*ad loc.*, from an unidentified source),[470] the generation was "cleared of" just men. (R. David Qimḥi declares צלול as dialectal variant of צליל.) The identification of the nocturnal victory of Gideon as happening in the second night of Passover is quoted in

467 ר' יהודה אומר אותו הלילה שנגלה הקב״ה על אברהם אבינו הוא ליל פסח.

468 וְהִנֵּה צְלוּל לֶחֶם שְׂעֹרִים מִתְהַפֵּךְ בְּמַחֲנֵה מִדְיָן.

469 וְהָא חֲרַר דִּלְחֵם שְׂעוֹרִין מִתְהַפִּיךְ בְּמַשְׁרְיַת מִדְיָנָאֵי.

470 צליל. צלול כתיב שהיה הדור צלול מן הצדיקים.

Yalquṭ Shim'oni Jud. #62 from a lost old *Midrash* source. The second day of Passover, "the day following the day of rest," was the day of the ceremony of the *'Omer* (*Lev.* 23:9–15).

ס The reference is to Sennaherib (*2 Kings* 19). Pul is the name of an Assyrian king (*2 Kings* 15:19), identified with Tiglat Pileser and Sennaherib (*b. Sanhedrin* 94a). Lud (*Gen.* 10:22) is probably Lydia in Asia Minor or the people of the Lubdi, mentioned in cuneiform inscriptions as dwelling near the sources of Euphrates and Tigris. "Conflagration" is from *Is.* 10:16.

ע *Is.* 10:32, still speaking of Sennaherib.

פ The handwriting on the wall (*Dan.* 5:5). The lower parts of Babylonia, the alluvial marshes, are called צוּל, "drowning country," in *Is.* 44:27.

צ The language is from *Is.* 21:5, a vision about Medes and Elamites destroying an unnamed country, possibly Babylonia, here taken to refer to *Dan.* 5.

ק The reference is to *Esth.* 4:17. The decree for the extermination of the Jews was given on the Thirteenth of Nisan (*Esth.* 3:12); therefore the three days of fasting decreed by Esther were the 14th (*Pesaḥ*), 15th, and 16th of Nisan (Passover). *Targum I* to *Esth.* 4:17 starts: "And Mordokhai transgressed and did not keep the joy of the holiday of *Pesaḥ.*"

ר *Esth.* 7:10; by the preceding data, Haman, the head of the criminal house, was executed in the night of the 18th of Nisan.

ש *Is.* 47:9. "These two," widowhood and the loss of all children, are brought on the female representative of *'Uz, Oz*, the land of Edom (*Thr.* 4:21), traditionally identified with Rome. This tradition is explained by Ibn Ezra on *Gen.* 27:40:[471] "The Edomites were converted to Judaism by Hyrkanus I (about 120 B.C.E.) and they became the backbone of the Jewish army. But the Romans who destroyed the

---

471 גם בימי הורקנס הזקן שׁמם שׁומרי ירושׁלים והכניסם לברית מילה. גם בימי אגריפס כאשׁר נלכדה ירושׁלים באו גדודי אדום לעזור ליהודה, ורוֹמא שׁהגלתנו הוא מזרע כתים וכן אמר המתרגם וצים מיד כתים (במדבר כד כד: וְסִיעָן מִצְטָרְכָן מֵרוֹמָאֵי), והיא מלכות יון בעצמה כאשׁר פירש בספר דניאל (ז,ג-ו). והיו אנשׁים מתי מספר שׁהאמינו באישׁ שׁשׁמוֹהוּ אלוֹה. וכאשׁר האמינה רוֹמי בימי קוֹנסטנטין שׁחדשׁ כל הדת ושׂם על דגלוֹ צוּרת האישׁ ההוא ולא היו בעולם שׁישׁמרו התוֹרה החדשׁה חוּץ מן האדוֹמיים. על כן נקראה רוֹמא מלכות אדום. ג׳כ נקראו היום אנשׁי מצרים ושׁבא וארץ עילם ישׁמעאלים ואין בהם מי שׁהוא מזרע ישׁמעאלים כי אם מתי מספר.

Temple are from Cretan/Greek stock, and also the Aramaic *Targum Onqelos* translates ‘fleets from the direction of Crete’ (*Num*. 24:24) by ‘and fleets are called from Rome’; Rome is identified as Greece in *Daniel*, chap. 7. But the first few people who believed in the deity of Jesus were (Jewish) Edomites, and when Constantine converted the Roman Empire to Christianity, it took the name of ‘Edom’ from these few Edomites. In the same way, we call today Egyptians and (Moslem) Yemenites ‘Ismaelites’ even though almost no descendants of Ismaelite Arabs live among them."

ח *Is*. 30:29: "The song of ultimate redemption will be for you like the song (the *Egyptian Hallel*) when you first started to celebrate the holiday in the night (in Egypt)," midrashic interpretation of Rashi. The talmudic interpretation (*b. Pesaḥim* 94b[472]; *y. Pesaḥim* IV,3 36d) is that the "song," *Hallel*, is required only if the night is that of a holiday; it follows that *Hallel* is not required for the celebration of the "Second *Pesaḥ*," held in the night of the Fifteenth of the Second Month, Iyyar, for people who could not be ritually clean for the slaughter of the *Pesaḥ* sacrifice on the Fourteenth of Nisan (*Num*. 9:9-12).

The third song, "For Him it is right, it is His due," is of unknown authorship and date. We know that the song was not used in the eleventh century but was well established by the end of the thirteenth century. The song is not found in any prayer service. In its form, it is the description of a choir of angels singing the praises of the Lord. This kind of composition is characteristic of the (Palestinian/Ashkenazic) *Hekhalot* literature. A characteristic song of angels, "Nobility and faith are the Eternal Living's,"[473] from *Hekhalot Rabbati*, "the great book of the Heavenly halls," is a central song of praise in the Ashkenazic morning service of the Day of Atonement, and the prologue of the book, telling of the ascent of the High Priest R. Ishmael to Heaven, to try to save the lives of his colleagues about to be martyred by the Romans, is an integral part of the Ashkenazic penitential service of the High Holidays. The central theme of the *Hekhalot* literature is God’s granting of forgiveness to the Jewish people as a consequence of the Jews’ and the angels’ singing of God’s praises. As such it is appropriate to the High Holidays. The

---

472 א״ר יוחנן משום ר׳ שמעון בן יהוצדק אמר קרא השיר יהיה לכם כליל התחדש חג, לילה המקודש לחג טעון הלל, לילה שאין מקודש לחג אין טעון הלל.

473 האדרת והאמונה לחי עולמים.

expression with which the poem starts, אַדִּיר בִּמְלוּכָה "Noble in Kingdom," is mentioned in the Jerusalem *Talmud* (*y. Rosh Hashanah* IV,6 59c)[474] as a possible substitution in the doxology "Praised are You, Holy King" of the *musaf* service for New Year's Day. The expression is used by Yannai in his *seder* for that service; Yannai there also uses כַּבִּיר הַמְּלוּכָה, which our author quotes for the letter ב. A connection with the Day of Atonement can be found in the prayer of the angels for the Jewish people (*Pirqe Hekhalot Rabbati* [*Wertheimer*], chap. 14):[475] "Free, free, o Creator; forgive, forgive, o Strong of Jacob; erase their sin, erase their sin, because You are the *Noble of kings*." The *Hekhalot* literature was the inspiration of the circle of "German *ḥasidim*," the circle of R. Yehuda Heḥasid, at the end of the twelfth century. The German sages of that period were also students of the Jerusalem *Talmud*. It is most likely that the composition stems from the circle of the German *ḥasidim* and may have originally been composed for the High Holidays, in particular the Morning Service of the Day of Atonement, which contains a number of similar poems, or, as can be seen from the detailed discussion of the refrain, it may have been composed directly for the *Seder* night. It is less likely to be an older Palestinian *Hekhalot* composition for the High Holidays.

In the litany, the angels give references to three biblical passages. לְךָ וּלְךָ "Yours, only Yours," refers to the speech of David in handing to Solomon the blueprint of the Temple (*1 Chr.* 29:11–16): "*Yours*, o Lord, is magnificence, power, splendor, glory, and majesty, as well as everything in Heaven and on earth; Yours, o Lord, is the Kingdom and being elevated over anyone who acts as head man. Also riches and honor are before You, You rule over everything, in Your hand are force and power, it is in Your hand to increase and fortify all. And now, our God, we thank You, and we praise the Name of Your splendor. And who am I, and who are my people, that we should find force to donate all this [i.e., the gifts for the Temple enumerated chap. 29:2–7]! Because strangers we are before You and sojourners like all our forefathers; our days on earth are only a hopeless shadow. O Lord, our God, all that huge amount that I did prepare in order to build a House to Your holy name, it is from You, *and only Yours is all*." The first three verses of this quote are recited every day in the

---

474 ר' אבהו בשם ר' לעזר בכל מקום עבר והזכיר אדיר המלוכה לא יצא חוץ מן האל הקדוש של ראש השנה ובלבד במוסף.

475 התר התר יוצר בראשית, סלח סלח אביר יעקב, מחול מחול קדוש ישראל, כי אדיר מלכים אתה.

morning prayers as introduction to the recitation of the Song at the Red Sea. This may justify the inclusion of the litany in the Passover service, based on a *midrash* (*b. Berakhot* 58a)[476]: "*Yours, o Lord, is magnificence* refers to the Exodus [variant reading: to Creation], *power* refers to the splitting of the Red Sea, *splendor* to sun and moon that stood still for Joshua, *glory* to the fall of Rome, *majesty* to the war of the valleys of Arnon (*Num.* 21:13–20), *as well as everything in Heaven and on earth* to the war of Sisera (*Jud.* 5:20), *Yours, o Lord, is the Kingdom* to the war of Amaleq (*Ex.* 17:8–16), *and being elevated* that is the [future] war of Gog from Magog (*Ez.* 38); *over anyone who acts as head man* is commented by R. Naḥman bar Abba as meaning that not even the head of a water district is elected unless he is appointed first by Heaven. In the name of R. Akiba we have taught: *Yours, o Lord, is magnificence,* that is the splitting of the Red Sea, *power* refers to the slaying of the firstborn, *splendor* to the theophany on Mount Sinai, *glory* to Jerusalem, *majesty* to the Temple."

The second expression, לְךָ כִּי לְךָ "Yours, truly Yours," refers to a verse in a hymn of Jeremiah (*Jer.* 10:7): "Who would not fear You, King of the Gentiles, *truly Yours is due*, because among all the sages of the Gentiles and their governments there is nothing like You!" The same reference explains the somewhat strange refrain "it is His due." The verse is the basis of a thirteen- (or fourteen-) part composition for the Day of Atonement, in the older Ashkenazic morning service. In the interpretation of *Midrash Psalms* (93), what is truly due to the Lord are His garments described in *Ps.* 93: majesty and strength, a fitting companion to the first reference.

The last expression, לְךָ אַף לְךָ "Yours, surely Yours" is from *Ps.* 74:16: "*Yours* is day, *surely Yours* is night, You prepared light and sun!" The connection with the *Seder* is given in *Gen. rabbah* 6(3):[477] "Yours

---

476 דרש רבי שילא לך ה׳ הגדולה זו יציאת מצרים שנאמר וירא ישראל את היד הגדולה. והגבורה זו קריעת ים סוף שנאמר ויבואו בני ישראל בתוך הים. והתפארת זו חמה ולבנה שעמדו ליהושע שנאמר וידום השמש וירח עמד. והנצח זו מפלתה של רומי וכן הוא אומר ויז נצחם על בגדי. וההוד זו מלחמת נחלי ארנון שנאמר על כן יאמר בספר מלחמות ה׳. כי כל בשמים ובארץ זו מלחמת סיסרא שנאמר מן השמים נלחמו. לך ה׳ הממלכה זו מלחמת עמלק וכה״א ויאמר כי יד על כס יה. והמתנשא זו מלחמת גוג ומגוג וכן הוא אומר הנני אליך נשיא ראש משך ותובל. לכל לראש אפילו ריש גרגותא מן שמיא מנו ליה. במתניתא תנא משמיה דר׳ עקיבא לך ה׳ הגדולה זו קריאת ים סוף, והגבורה זו מכת בכורות, והתפארת זו מתן תורה, והנצח זו ירושלים, וההוד זה בית המקדש.

477 לך יום אף לך לילה לך יום מקלס ולך לילה מקלס. מה היום ברשותך, אף הלילה ברשותך. בשעה שאתה עושה לנו נסים ביום לך יום, ובשעה שאתה עושה לנו נסים בלילה אף לך לילה. בשעה שאתה עושה לנו נסים ביום אנו אומרים לפניך שירה ביום, ובשעה שאתה עושה לנו נסים בלילה אנו אומרים לפניך שירה בלילה. עשית לנו נסים ביום ואמרנו לפניך שירה ביום: ׳ותשר דבורה וברק בן אבינועם

is day when You perform miracles for us during daytime and we acclaim You and sing to You during daytime as in the Song of Deborah (*Jud. 5);* Yours is night when You perform miracles for us during nighttime and we acclaim You and sing to You during nighttime as in the *Hallel* of the Egyptian *Seder*; for You *it is right* that we sing, since You prepared light and sun!" This *midrash* is, therefore, also the source of the refrain "for Him it is right."

One may be astonished to see God being addressed as "humble." This refers to a talmudic statement (*b. Megillah* 31a)[478] attributed to R. Yoḥanan: "Every time Scripture mentions the power of God, it mentions His care for the humble. This is written in the Torah, repeated in the Prophets and the Hagiographs. It is written in the Torah (*Deut.* 10:17–18): 'Truly, the Lord, Your God, is the Supreme Power and the Master of masters, the great, strong, and awesome God, Who will show no favor and not take bribes, Who provides justice for the orphan and the widow and loves the stranger to give him bread and clothing.' It is repeated in the Prophets (*Is.* 57:15): 'Truly, so says He Who is exalted and elevated, eternally reigning, and Whose name is Holy: high up and in holiness I am enthroned but I am with the pounded and the meek of spirit, to enliven the spirit of the downtrodden and to revive the heart of the pounded.' It is tripled in Hagiographs, as it it written (*Ps.* 58:5–6): 'Make a path for Him Who rides the clouds, YH is His name, rejoice before Him! The father of the orphans and judge of widows, God in His holy abode!'"

The translation of the biblical *hapax* **שנען** as "angel" follows the *Targum* to *Ps.* 68:18.

The last three songs are of unknown composition and authorship. They appear first in the Prague *Haggadah*, printed from woodcuts in 1526, and have been repeated in all Ashkenazic *Haggadot* and most Italian *Haggadot* ever since. Until the end of the eighteenth century, the Ashkenazic *Haggadot* also included the Judeo-German versions; these versions still survive in some German Jewish families.

ביום'; עשית לנו נסים בלילה ואמרנו לפניך שירה בלילה 'השיר יהיה לכם כליל התקדש חג'. לך נאה לומר שירה ביום, לך נאה לומר שירה בלילה, למה, שאתה הכינות מאור ושמש.

478 א"ר יוחנן כל מקום שאתה מוצא גבורתו של הקב"ה אתה מוצא אנוותנותו. דבר זה כתוב בתורה ושנוי בנביאים ומשולש בכתובים. כתוב בתורה 'כי ה' אלהיכם הוא אלהי האלהים ואדוני האדונים' וכתיב בתריה 'עושה משפט יתום ואלמנה', שנוי בנביאים 'כה אמר ה' רם ונשא שוכן עד וקדוש וגו' וכתיב בתריה 'ואת דכא ושפל רוח', משולש בכתובים דכתיב 'סולו לרוכב בערבות ביה שמו' וכתיב בתריה 'אבי יתומים ודיין אלמנות'.

The Hebrew text was imported into Italy at the latest by the Mantua *Haggadah* of 1561, which in most respects is a copy of the Prague *Haggadah*. The Ashkenazic Jewish community of Italy, before the mass immigration of Sephardic Jews to the Apennine peninsula and even more so afterward, was in close contact with Austrian Jewry and, through the latter's mediation, with Bohemian and Moravian Jewry. The later (Sephardic) Livorno printers adopted the final songs from the Mantua *Haggadah*. These Livorno printers became the providers for Sephardic prayer books for all places settled by the refugees from Spain in the Mediterranean basin and, under the spreading influence of the kabbalistic circles of Safed, for all Oriental communities (Syrian, Iraqi, Persian) that adopted the Sephardic ritual instead of their own. Under their influence, some of the final songs were adopted by Oriental communities; still today an Arabic version of the final "song of the kid goat" is part of the Syrian/Iraqi *Seder*. There even exist Yemenite manuscript *Haggadot* containing the last two songs.

It is probable that the final three songs were first in Judeo-German (Western Yiddish) and only later translated into Hebrew or Aramaic. Both the Hebrew and Judeo-German texts and their translations are found in the *Haggadah*. The first song is an alphabetic prayer for the rebuilding of the Temple, well in accordance with the general theme of the second part of the *Seder* and a fitting introduction to the *'Omer* ceremony noted for the Second Night in most Ashkenazic *Haggadot* (see below). The second song, a numerical riddle, ends with the lucky number 13, in Judaism the symbol of God's attributes of mercy (*Ex.* 34:6-7); they are, in the interpretation of Rashi *ad loc.*:

Lord, merciful before man sins,
Lord, merciful after man sins,
Power, able to help,
Merciful
and Gracious,
Long Forbearing, waiting for man to repent,
Full of Kindness, to people not quite measuring up to standards of conduct,
and Truth, to reward those who do His will.
He preserves Kindness to Thousands (of generations), for the descendants of His pious,
He forgives acts of criminality,
rebellion, acts done to show defiance of God's will,

and sin, negligent and inadvertent sin,
and He cleanses the penitent.

The remaining attributes quoted in verse 6 are attributes of justice, not of mercy: *He does not cleanse* the unrepentant, *He investigates the sins of the fathers in their* (unrepentant) *sons for three or four generations*, to apportion guilt between the sinning parent-educator and the unrepentant independent son.

The diabolization of the number 13 in Christian beliefs may be connected with the Christian rejection of the Jewish doctrine of God's universal kindness and its replacement by a doctrine of salvation of only a small, select group saved by a particular faith. The eleven stars are those of Joseph's dream (*Gen.* 37:9). The connection of the numbers 3 and 4 with Fathers (Abraham, Isaac, Jacob) and Mothers (Sarah. Rebecca, Rachel, Leah) is given by the *Talmudim* (*b. Berakhot* 16b; *Semaḥot* I,14),[479] which insist that "our father" and "our mother" as titles of honor may be applied only to these, but neither to the surrogate mothers Bilhah and Zilpah, because of their servile status, nor to the fathers of the Twelve Tribes, whose importance in biblical history does not compare with that of the Fathers.

The last song, an allegory of the automatic justice in God's creation, is almost certainly an adaptation from Judeo-German into questionable Aramaic. The original Judeo-German speaks of a goat kid דאַס דאָ האַט געקויפט דאַס פּעטערליין "that Daddy bought," but the original Aramaic reads דְּזַבִּין אַבָּא "that my father sold." If the allegory describes God as the father and the Jewish people as the kid, the question might be whether it is intended to represent Israel as bought by God at the Exodus or as sold in the Diaspora by the destruction of the Temple. The Aramaic was corrected by Stanow and Heidenheim to read דְּזַבַּן אַבָּא "that my father bought"; this form is today the accepted Western Ashkenazic text. It is safe to say that this meaning was the original intention of the Aramaic poet who lost his way in the several conjugations of the verbal stem *zbn;* it is also the interpretation of the Arabic version. The proof that Judeo-German was the original language comes from the Aramaic passage on the cat which in all pre-Heidenheim sources reads וְאָתָא שׁוּנְרָא וְאָכְלָה "there

479 אין קורין לאבות אבינו אלא לשלשה האבות ולא לאימהות אמנו אלא לארבע האימהות.

came the cat (*m.*) and ate (*f.*)"; Heidenheim was the first to change the verb into the correct masculine form וְאָכַל. The feminine form is quite natural in German where *Katze* is feminine and remains sentimentally a feminine even in the neuter diminutive קעצליין, *Kätzlein.* (The Arabic translates "the she-cat ate [*f.*].") The vocalization of the last two songs in the present *Haggadah* follows the consensus of all sixteenth/eighteenth-century sources in the few instances where it deviates from the Heidenheim text. The money paid for the kid goat is 2 pennies in the German, 2 Abbaside (full weight gold) coins in the Arabic, and 2 *zuz* in the Aramaic. A *zuz* is equated by *Targum 1 Sam.* 9:8 to a quarter *sheqel*; in the *Talmud*, a *zuz* usually is a Roman imperial silver *denar*. Both determinations are about 0.11 Troy ozs., or between 3.4 and 3.5 grams of silver coin; a silver penny in the coinage of Charlemagne was 1/240 of a pound of sterling silver or 1.9 grams. In the Talmud, the expected yield of a business capital of 50 *zuz* brings a person above the poverty line (*Mishnah Peah* VIII,9), so the Arabic translation seems to be more appropriate.

The Yemenite songs, from the pen of the most prolific of Yemenite song writers, the sixteenth-century author and holy man Mori Selim Shebezi, are written in very easily understood Hebrew. The first two are in Spanish style, counting short (-̆) and full (-) syllables following the scheme

---̆ ----̆ ----̆   --̆ ----̆ ----̆

The last song is written in Ashkenazic style, with four lines of four full syllables each per stanza. In the second song, the "noble daughter" is the Jewish people; the last stanza is an allusion to *Ps.* 113:9. In the last song, the friend is Abraham, in Arabic כ̇ליל אללה *khalīl Allah*, "God's friend." The three crowns of the Jews are the crown of Torah, the crown of Kingdom, and the crown of a good reputation (*Abot* IV,17).

Counting the *'Omer*

Most *Haggadot* of Ashkenazic type require the counting of the *'Omer* after the recitation of the *Haggadah*, just before the last two songs. The biblical decree (*Lev.* 23:15) requires that "you [plural, referring to the duty of each individual; cf. p. 338] should count for yourselves from the day after the *shabbāt*, from the day on which you bring the *'Omer* of weaving; there should be seven complete weeks (*shabbāttōt*)." The *'Omer* is the measure of the sacrifice of new barley described in *Lev.* 23:9-14; no grain from the new harvest may be consumed before that sacrifice. The Fiftieth Day (Pentecost in Greek) is the festival of *Shāvuōt* on which a sacrifice of two wheat breads signals the start of the wheat harvest. The use of the word *shabbāt* in *Lev.* 23:11,15 is ambiguous; in verse 15 it means both day and week at different places in the same sentence. The rabbinic interpretation of *shabbāt* here is "holiday" (of Passover). During the later Second Commonwealth, the barley for the *'Omer* was cut with great ceremony as a demonstration against earlier Sadducees who did require that the *'Omer* was to be brought on the first Sunday following Passover (*Mishnah Menaḥot* X,3).[480] In rabbinic tradition, the Fiftieth Day after the *'Omer* is always the Sixth of Sivan, the traditional anniversary of the theophany of Mount Sinai and the proclamation of the Ten Commandments. In Sadducee tradition, Pentecost is purely an agricultural and Temple festival. As such it is described by Philo (*Special Laws, II*) and treated as an appendix to the *'Omer* ceremony. (Christian practice manages to combine the Sadducee date of Pentecost, the seventh Sunday after Passover, with its rabbinic interpretation, the elevation of the entire Jewish nation to prophetic status.) The connection of counting with the Temple ceremony is explained by the *Talmud* (*b. Menaḥot* 66a)[481] in the following way. Two verses deal with the count, *Lev.* 25:15: "You shall count for yourselves from the day after the *shabbāt*, from the *day* on which you bring the *'Omer* of weaving; there should be seven complete weeks"; and *Deut.*17:9: "Seven weeks you shall count for yourself; from the moment the sickle starts at the standing grain you shall start to count seven weeks." It is clear from the second verse that counting has to start at the time of cutting. The first verse requires that seven *complete* weeks elapse between Passover and Pentecost; the weeks cannot be complete unless they start immediately after the Passover holiday, just after nightfall of the Sixteenth of Nisan. On the other hand, the presentation of the *'Omer* in the Temple is a day ceremony, it happens during daytime of the Sixteenth of Nisan. Since the *'Omer* cannot be brought after the destruction of the Temple, the counting today is not a biblical obligation but a remembrance of the Temple

---

480 וכל כך למה. מפני הבייתוסים. שהיו אומרים. אין קצירת העומר במוצאי יו״ט.

481 מיום הביאכם תספרו חמשים יום יכול יקצור ויביא ואימתי שירצה יספור ת״ל מהחל חרמש בקמה תחל לספור. אי מהחל חרמש תחל לספור יכול יקצור ויספור ואימתי שירצה יביא ת״ל מיום הביאכם. אי מיום הביאכם יכול יקצור ויספור ויביא ת״ל שבע שבתות תמימות תהיינה, אימתי אתה מוצא שבע שבתות תמימות בזמן שאתה מתחיל לימנות מבערב. יכול יקצור ויביא ויספור בלילה, ת״ל מיום הביאכם, הא כיצד קצירה וספירה בלילה והבאה ביום.

(*loc. cit.*).[482] This explains the short prayer for the restoration of the Temple service that is recited after the counting (*Mahzor Vitry*, p. 301). Since an old tradition, discussed in the section on the Prayer (p. 207), connects the counting of the *'Omer* with the harmony of the heavenly spheres, the importance of the count is not diminished by it being in remembrance only, and it still takes an important place in the Jewish year. The days of the *'Omer* after Passover represent a period of danger in general, for crops in particular (*Lev. rabbah* 28[3])[483] since the grain harvest depends greatly on the weather during these weeks. Therefore, it is an old and generally observed custom not to marry in this period since that would represent a risky beginning. In addition, for European Jewry it is a period of mourning since, in the Middle Ages, most pogroms were incited by the Christian clergy in its sermons between Easter and Pentecost. These aspects should not diminish the joy of the holiday.

The biblical text requires only one day, the Fifteenth of Nisan, to be kept as a holiday. The celebration in the Diaspora of a second day for each biblical holiday is a tradition of very high antiquity; originally the second day was necessitated by the uncertainties of a lunar calendar determined by observation in Jerusalem when communication with the Diaspora was slow and unsafe. The celebration of the second has been continued as an institution after the publication of fixed calendar rules (*b. Bezah* 4b; *y. Eruvin* III,10 21c)[484] since in times of persecution the dissemination of knowledge needed to compute the correct calendar may be impossible. The night of the second *Seder* in the Diaspora therefore requires two contradictory ceremonies: the *Seder* as the ceremony of a night that might be that of the Fifteenth of Nisan, and the counting of the *'Omer* in the night of the Sixteenth of Nisan. For the reasons explained above, the recital of the benediction and the counting should take place at the earliest possible time. All early authorities and the *Shulhan 'Arukh* (§489.1) require the counting to take place at the end of evening services of the Sixteenth of Nisan. This is also the position of all Sephardic and Oriental kabbalists (*Nahar Shalom*, p. 133).

---

482 זכר למקדש הוא.

483 א״ר אלעזר כתיב ולא אמרו בלבבם נירא נא את ה׳ אלהינו יהיב לכון כולא ולית אתון צריכין ליה מן הדין שבועֹת חקות קציר ישמר לנו, ישמור לנו מרוחות רעות ומטללים רעים, ואימתי, באלו שבע שבועות שבין פסח לעצרת.

484 רבי יוסי מישלח כתיב להון אע״פ שכתבו לכם סדרי מועדות אל תשנו מנהג אבותיכם נוחי נפש.

All through the Middle Ages, it was the practice of Ashkenazic communities to follow the Galilean order of prayers in combining afternoon and evening prayers held at the end of the day when (inconvenient and expensive) artificial illumination was not yet needed (*Rashi Berakhot* 2a).[485] Today, even Western Ashkenazic communities that follow the old custom during the year do postpone evening prayers during the *'Omer* period until after nightfall in order to recite the count at its appropriate time. This was not the medieval practice. The twelfth-century author of the glosses to *Maḥzor Vitry* (pp. 301-302)[486] reports that his teacher used to count with the congregation in the synagogue, but without a benediction, during the early evening service and then repeat the counting with benediction at home after nightfall. The fifteenth-century West German *MaHaRIL* (pp. 150–151)[487] still requires everybody to count (with benediction) in the synagogue but then requires a second count (without benediction) at home after the meal. The slightly older Austrian *Leqet Yosher* (p. 97)[488] notes this practice only for Friday evening, when everybody wanted to start his Sabbath meal during daylight. In the eighteenth century, artificial illumination was already more convenient to use and less expensive; the eighteenth-century manual of practice from Frankfurt am Main, *Noheg Kaẓon Yosef* (p. 225),[489] notes for the second *Seder* that women and children, who did not attend synagogue services, count the *'Omer* at the table, to the exclusion of the men who were in the synagogue. This is the only source that ever mentions a practice of women to count the *'Omer*; since the counting is a prescribed action at a fixed time, it cannot be obligatory for women (cf. p. 190). Ashkenazic and Italian later kabbalists, following R. Moses Azariah da Fano, insist that the correct procedure is to finish first the *Seder* and then count at the end[490]; since the *'Omer* has cosmic implication (cf. p. 207), a mixing of holiday and weekday cosmic influences would have destructive consequences. Since this kabbalistic interpretation clearly contradicts the talmudic

---

485 למה קורין אותה בבית הכנסת כדי לעמוד בתפילה מתוך דברי תורה והכי תניא בברייתא בברכות ירושלמי.

486 רבי התפלל ערבית ביום ולא רצה לברך על ספירת העומר עם אחרים כי היה דואג שמא יעשה ברכה לבטלה. וספר עם האחרים ולו בירך. והיינו תמיהים ספירה זו למה ואמר שמא אשכח ונמצאתי קרח מיכן ומכן.

487 ספירת העומר מתחילין אחר תפילת ערבית יום שני דפסח . . . וכל בעלי בתים חוזרין ומספרים אחר הסעודה בביתם.

488 בליל שבת סופרים בבית הכנסת אע״פ שעוד היום גדול.

489 והנשים והטף שלא היו בבה״כ סופרים בבתיהם.

490 The abundant literature is surveyed in *Minḥat 'Omer*.

determination of the meaning of "complete weeks" as explained earlier, the kabbalists then shift the emphasis to the completion of the Seven Weeks by prohibiting the evening prayers of Pentecost to start before nightfall of the Fiftieth Day of *'Omer*. This kabbalistic influence is the main root of the appearance of the Count of *'Omer* in Ashkenazic and Italian *Haggadot*.

Appendix

The Judeo-Arabic story of the election of Abraham and his rescue from the fiery oven is a rendition of the Hebrew text of the old *Midrash* source *Sefer Hayashar* (pp. 18a-20b). The only substantial deviation of the tale of *Utqul Djerba* from the printed text of *Sefer Hayashar* is that in the latter source the shooting star that announces the birth of Abraham devours four other stars, not three. The rhymed *Utqul Gafṣa* is a later elaboration of the story, including an exposition of the main teachings of Judaism connected with the story of Creation.

Abraham's age when he recognized the existence and unity of God is the subject of much midrashic speculation; that age is variously given as 3,[491] 13,[492] 40,[493] or 48 years.[494] Maimonides emphasizes the direct connection between Abraham's rejection of idolatry and the Exodus. In his *Laws concerning Idolatry* (*Hilkhot 'Avodah Zarah* I,3),[495] after explaining the story of Abraham similar to that in our text, he notes the direct transmission of Abraham's theology to Isaac, Jacob, and the latter's sons. He states that in Egypt all tribes except Levy were in danger of reverting to idolatry under the influence of the surrounding culture when God appointed Moses to save them from idolatry and, incidental to that main task, to lead the tribes of Israel out of Egypt.

The story of Abraham being thrown in a fiery oven comes from reading *Gen.* 11:31 (with *Targum Yerushalmi*) as: "Teraḥ took his son Abram, his grandson Lot the son of Haran, and his daughter-in-law

---

491 *b. Nedarim* 32a, *Gen. rabbah* 64(4).

492 *Pirqē R. Eliezer*, chap. 26.

493 Maimonides, *Hilkhot 'Avodah Zarah* I,3.

494 *Gen. rabbah* 64 (4), in the name of R. Yoḥanan and R. Ḥanina, the main Galilean authorities.

495 ויעקב אבינו למד בניו כולם והבדיל לוי ומנהו ראש והושיבו בישיבה ללמד דרך השם ולשמור מצות אברהם. וצוה את בניו שלא יפסיקו מבני לוי ממונה אחר ממונה כדי שלא תשכח הלימוד. והיה הדבר הולך ומתגבר בבני יעקב ובנלוים עליהם ונעשית בעולם אומה שהיא יודעת את ה'. עד שארכו הימים לישראל במצרים וחזרו ללמוד מעשיהן ולעבוד כוכבים כמותן חוץ משבט לוי שעמד במצות אבות. ומעולם לא עבד שבט לוי עבודה זרה. וכמעט קט היה העיקר ששתל אברהם נעקר וחוזרין בני יעקב לטעות העולם ותעיותן. ומאהבת ה' אותנו ומשמרו את השבועה לאברהם אבינו עשה משה רבינו רבן של כל הנביאים ושלחו.

Sarai, the wife of his son Abram, and went with them *out of the flames of the Chaldeans* in order to travel to the land of Canaan," translating אור "flame," not "place" like the Septuagint and Ibn Ezra (who compares *Is.* 31:9, ". . . so says the Lord, Who owns a place in Zion . . ."), or valley (Menaḥem ben Saruq), or "city of Uru" (modern translators).

The detail mentioned in *Utqul Djerba* that idolatry started with Enosh, the grandson of Adam, is the rabbinic interpretation of *Gen.* 4:26: אָז הוּחַל לִקְרֹא בְּשֵׁם יי. The root *ḥll* of the *pu'al* form הוּחַל can mean both "to desecrate, to profane" and "to start." The meaning of the same root in Arabic is "to loosen, to untie" which similarly has the dual meaning of either to remove a religious prohibition (for food this makes *ḥallāl*, "not forbidden," the Arabic equivalent of Hebrew *kasher* "fit [for consumption]") or to loosen a knot or fetters that impede movement. The translation of the Septuagint and most moderns of the verse is "then the invocation of the Lord's name was started" but all rabbinic sources (*Mekhilta Jithro sec.* 6; *Sifry Eqeb* #43; *Targum Onqelos, Targum Yerushalmi, Gen. rabbah* 23[7], 26[4]) understand the verse to mean "then the invocation of the Lord's name was profaned."

"The Good that no one's eye has seen" referred to in the rhymed Gafṣa version is the Future World, mentioned in *Is.* 63:3: "No eye has ever seen, o God, except You, what He will do for him who trusts in Him."

Bibliography

Biblical Literature

A quote from the Bible is given by book (abbreviated title) chapter:verse. The standard commentaries are quoted from the rabbinic Bible *Miqraöt Gedolot* מקראות גדולות. The best edition for Pentateuch is תורת חיים, 7 vols. (Jerusalem: Mossad Harav Kook, 1986–1993), and for Prophets and Hagiographs is מקראות גדולות (Vienna 1875; reprinted Tel Aviv: Schocken, 1959).

Talmudic and Midrashic Literature

The *Mishnah* and minor tractates (*Masekhet Soferim*) are quoted by tractate, chapter (roman numeral), *mishnah*.

The *Talmud of Jerusalem* is quoted by a prefix *y.*, name of tractate, chapter (roman numeral), *halakhah*, followed by folio and column of the Venice/Krotoszyn editions.

The *Babylonian Talmud* is quoted by a prefix *b.*, folio and page of the Wilna edition.

The other works of the talmudic period and the *midrashim* are quoted from the following editions:

Aboth deRabbi Nathan, ed. S. Schechter, Wien 1887.

Aristeas to Philocrates (Letter of Aristeas), edited and translated by Moses Hadas, Harper, New York 1951.

Die Texte aus Qumran, ed. E. Lohse, Darmstadt 1971.

Geschichte der zehn Märtyrer מעשׂה עשׂרה הרוגי מלכות, in: *Bet ha-Midrasch*, ed. A. Jellinek, vol. 6, reprint Jerusalem 1967.

Josephus Flavius, *Jewish Antiquities*, Loeb edition, London/Cambridge, Mass. 1957–1981.

Massekhet Hēkhalot מסכת היכלות, in: *Bet ha-Midrasch* ed. A. Jellinek vol. 2, reprint Jerusalem 1967.

Mechilta d'Rabbi Ismael מכילתא דרבי ישמעאל, ed. H. S. Horovitz, I. A. Rabin, reprint Jerusalem 1960.

Mekhilta d'Rabbi Šim'on b. Jochai מכילתא דרבי שמעון בר יוחאי, ed. J. N. Epstein, E. Z. Melamed; Jerusalem 1955.

Midrash (Gen., Ex., Lev., Num., Deut., Cant., Ruth, Threni, Esther) Rabbah מדרש רבה, reprint Jerusalem 1952.

Midrash Tanḥuma מדרש תנחומא, ed. H. Z. Schrentzel, Stettin 1865.

Midrash Tehillim מדרש תהלים המכונה שוחר טוב, ed. S. Bóber, Wilna 1891.

Midrash Zuta מדרש זוטא, ed. S. Bóber, Berlin 1894.

Pesiqta d'Rav Kahana פסיקתא והיא אגדת ארץ ישׂראל מיוחסת לרב כהנא, ed. S. Bóber, Lyck 1868.

Pesiqta Rabbati פסיקתא רבתי, ed. M. Friedmann, Vienna 1880.

Philo Judaeus, *Works*, Loeb edition, London/Cambridge, Mass. 1929-1941.

Pirqē Hēkhalot rabbati פרקי הכלות רבתי, in: *Battē Midrashot*, ed. S. A. Wertheimer, vol. 1, Jerusalem 1980.

Pirqē Rebbi Eliezer פרקי דרבי אליעזר, Warszawa 1879.

Seder 'Olam rabbah מדרש סדר עולם רבה, Jerusalem 1971.

Sefer Hayashar ספר הישר, Prague 1840.

Sifra d'be Rav ספרא דבי רב, ed. Schlossberg, Vienna 1862.

Sifry d'be Rav ספרי דבי רב, ed. M. Friedmann, Vienna 1864.

Sifry Deuteronomy ספרי דברים, ed. L. Finkelstein, New York 1969.

Targum (*Onqelos, Yerushalmi* on the Pentateuch, *Jonathan* on Prophets, *Targum Psalms, Song of Songs, Targum Esther I*) in rabbinic Bible *Miqraöt Gedolot.*

Gentile Classical Literature

Aulus Gellius, *Noctium Atticarum libri xx*, Leipzig 1886.

C. Plinius Secundus, *Naturalis Historiae libri xxxvii*, Stuttgart 1967.

Plutarch, *Vitae Parallelae*, Leipzig 1888–1896.

Suetonius, *De vita Caesarum*, Leipzig 1907.

Vergil, *Opera*, Oxford 1900.

Rabinnic Literature

Ninth and Tenth Centuries

Differences between Eastern and Western practices, החלוקים בין אנשי מזרח ובני א"י, ed. Margaliuth, Jerusalem 1938.

Gaonic Responsa, תשובות הגאונים, Lyck 1864.

Gaonic Responsa, תשובות הגאונים חמדה גנוזה, Jerusalem 1863.

Gaonic Responsa, תשובות הגאונים שערי תשובה, Leipzig 1880.

Halakhot Gedolot הלכות גדולות, Warszawa 1874.

Halakhot Gedolot (Spain) ספר הלכות גדולות, ed. E. Hildesheimer, Jerusalem 1972.

R. Amram Gaon, *Seder* סדר רב עמרם גאון ed. N. Koronel, Warszawa 1865; ed. Frumkin, Jerusalem 1912.

R. Ḥananel, *Commentary on the Talmud*, on the margin of the Wilna Talmud.

R. Nissim, *Commentary on the Talmud*, on the margin of the Wilna Talmud.

R. Saadia Gaon, *Commentary on Sefer Yeẓirah*, כתאב אלמבאדי, ed. and transl. R. Y. Qafeḥ, Jerusalem 1972.

R. Saadia Gaon, *Beliefs and Convictions*, ספר הנבחר באמונות ובדעות, ed. and transl. R. Y. Qafeḥ, Jerusalem 1970.

R. Saadia Gaon, *Siddur* סדור, ed. Davidson, Asaph, Joel, Jerusalem 1961.

R. Saadia Gaon, *Arabic Translation of the Pentateuch*, in *Taj*, Jerusalem, n.d.

R. Sherira Gaon, *Letter*, אגרת ר' שרירא גאון, in A. Neubauer, *Medieval Jewish Chronicles*, vol. 1, Oxford 1888.

Sefer Habahir or *Midrash R. Neḥonia ben Haqanah*, ed. R. Margaliuth, Jerusalem 1978.

Eleventh Century

R. Izḥaq ben Ya‘aqov, *Alfassi (RYF)* הלכות רב אלפס, in Wilna Talmud.

R. Izḥaq ibn Ghiat, *Halakhot* הלכות ר' יצחק ן' גיאת, Fürth 1862.

R. Natan ben Yeḥiel, *Dictionary 'Arukh*, ערוך, in: *'Arukh hashalem*, ed. A. Kohut, 1875-1888.

Rashi, R. Shelomo Izḥaqi, *Commentary on the Bible*, in *Miqraöt Gedolot*.

Rashi, R. Shelomo Izḥaqi, *Commentary on the Talmud*, in all Talmud editions.

Rashi, R. Shelomo Izḥaqi, *Pardes* ספר הפרדס, ed. Ehrenreich, Budapest 1924.

Rashi, R. Shelomo Izḥaqi, *Pardes hagadol* פרדס הגדול, ed. M. L. Frumkin, Warszawa 1870.

Rashi, R. Shelomo Izḥaqi, *Ha-Orah* ספר האורה, ed. S. Bóber, Lemberg 1905.

Rashi, R. Shelomo Izḥaqi, *Sefer Hasedarim* ספר הסדרים, ed. Elfenbein, New York 1951.

Rashi, R. Shelomo Izḥaqi, *Siddur* סדור רש"י, ed. J. Freimann, Berlin 1911.

Rashi, R. Shelomo Izḥaqi, *Responsa* תשובות רש"י, ed. Elfenbein, New York 1941.

R. Shemuel Hanagid, *Introduction to the Talmud*, מבוא התלמוד, appendix to Wilna Talmud tractate *Berakhot*.

R. Shemuel Hanagid, *Diwan*, ed. D. S. Sassoon, Oxford 1934.

R. Yehuda Halevi, *Kuzari*, ספר הכוזרי, Jerusalem 1946.

R. Yonah ibn Janaḥ, *Book of Roots*, ספר השרשים, ed. W. Bacher, Berlin 1896.

R. Yosef Tov Elem, *Composition for the Great Sabbath*, סדר לשבת הגדול, in S. Baer, *Seder 'Avodat Israel* (Eastern European ed.), Rödelheim 1868.

Sefer Ma'aśe Hageonim ספר מעשׂה הגאונים, ed. A. Epstein, J. Freimann, Berlin 1910.

Twelfth Century

R. Abraham ben Iẓḥaq of Narbonne, *Sefer Haëshkol* ספר האשכול, ed. Z. B. Auerbach, Halberstadt 1868.

R. Abraham ben Meïr ibn Ezra, *Commentary on the Pentateuch*, ed. C. D. Chavel, Jerusalem 1973.

R. Eleazar ben Yehuda of Worms, *Roqeaḥ* ספר רוקח, Jerusalem 1960.

R. Eleazar ben Yehuda, *Maäseh Roqeaḥ* ספר מעשׂה רוקח, Sanok 1872.

R. Eliezer ben Natan, *RAVaN* ספר ראב"ן, ed. S. Albeck, Warszawa 1904.

R. Eliezer ben Natan, *Commentary to the Haggadah*, Bene Berak 1985.

R. Eliezer of Metz, *Sefer Yereïm* ספר יראים השלם, ed. A. A. Schiff, Wilna 1891.

R. Ephraim of Bonn, *Commentary to the Haggadah*, ed. R. S. E. Stern, *Moriah* 15, fasc. 9–10, pp. 17-24, 1990.

R. Iẓḥaq of Marseilles, *Sefer Haïṭṭur* ספר העיטור, Warszawa 1883.

R. Moshe ben Maimun, Maimonides, *Mishneh Torah* ספר משנה תורה לרמב"ם, Wilna ed.

R. Moshe ben Maimun, Maimonides, *Commentary on the Mishnah*, in all *Talmud* editions.

R. Shemuel ben Meïr, *RaSHBaM*, *Commentary*, in all editions of the Babylonian *Talmud Pesaḥim.*

R. Shim'on of Frankfurt, *Yalqut Shim'oni* ילקוט שמעוני, New York 1944.

R. Simḥa of Vitry, *Maḥzor Vitry* מחזור ויטרי, ed. S. Horovitz, Nürnberg 1923.

R. Zeraḥya ben Iẓḥaq Halevi, *Sefer Hamaör* המאור הקטן, in all *Alfassi* editions.

Thirteenth Century

Minhagé R. Ḥayyim Palṭiel, cf. D. Goldschmidt, *Researches*, under Modern Scholarship.

R. Abraham ben Natan of Lunel, *Sefer Hamanhig* ספר המנהיג, ed. I. Raphael, Mosad Harav Kook, Jerusalem, 2nd printing 1994.

R. Asher ben Yeḥiël, *ROSH* רבינו אשר, in all editions of the Babylonian *Talmud*.

R. Asher ben Yeḥiel, *Teshuvot HaROSH* שו״ת הרא״ש, reprint Jerusalem, n.d.

R. Baruch of Worms, *Sefer Haterumah* ספר התרומה, Warszawa 1917.

R. David ben Levi of Narbonne, *Sefer Hamikhtam* ספר המכתם, ed. M. Y. Blau, New York 1955.

R. David Qimḥi, *ReDaQ, Sefer Hashorashim* ספר השרשים, ed. J. H. R. Biesenthal, F. Lebrecht, Berlin 1847.

R. David Qimḥi, *ReDaQ, Commentary on Psalms*, ed. M. Kamelhar, Jerusalem 1967.

R. Eliezer ben Yoël Halevi, *RAVIA Berakhot, Pesaḥim*, ספר ראבי״ה, ed. A. Aptowitzer, reprint New York 1983.

R. Izḥaq ben Moshe of Vienna, *Or Zarua'* אור זרוע, Zhitomir 1862.

Levite of Barcelona, *Sefer Haḥinnukh* ספר החינוך, Jerusalem 1992.

R. Menaḥem Hameïri, *Bet Habeḥirah Berakhot* בית הבחירה ברכות, ed. S. Dickmann, Jerusalem 1965.

R. Menaḥem Hameïri, *Bet Habeḥirah Pesaḥim* בית הבחירה פסחים, ed. Y. Klein, Jerusalem 1964.

R. Menaḥem Hameïri, *Magen Avot* מגן אבות, ed. Last, London 1869.

R. Moshe of Coucy, *Sefer Mizwot Gadol* ספר מצות גדול, Venezia 1547.

R. Moshe ben Naḥman, Nachmanides, *Commentary on the Pentateuch*, in *Miqraöt Gedolot*.

R. Moshe ben Naḥman, Nachmanides, *Milḥamot Hashem* מלחמות השם, in all *Alfassi* editions.

R. Moshe ben Naḥman, Nachmanides, *Sefer Hawiquaḥ* ספר הויקוח, in C. D. Chavel, *The Writings of Nachmanides* כתבי רבנו משה בן נחמן, vol. 1, Jerusalem 1963.

R. Moshe ben Naḥman, Nachmanides, *Commentary to Sefer Yeẓirah* פרוש ספר יצירה, in C. D. Chavel, *The Writings of Nachmanides* כתבי רבנו משה בן נחמן, vol. 2, Jerusalem 1964.

R. Shelomo ben Adrat (RaSHBA), *Responsa*, שאלות ותשובות הרשב״א, תשובות האלף, Wien 1812.

R. Shelomo ben Adrat (RaSHBA), *Responsa Ascribed to Nachmanides*, תשובות הרשב״א המיוחסות להרמב״ן, Wien 1898.

R. Shelomo ben Shimshon of Worms, *Siddur* סדור רבנו שלמה מגרמייזא, ed. M. Herschler, Jerusalem 1972.

R. Shimshon bar Ẓadoq, *Tashbets* תשב״ץ, Cremona 1706.

R. Yeshaya I of Trani, *Pisqé RYD Berakhot* פסקי רי״ד ברכות, ed. Wertheimer-Lyss, Jerusalem 1964.

R. Yeshaya I of Trani, *Pisqé RYD Pesaḥim* פוקי רי״ד פסחים, ed. A. J. Wertheimer, A. Lyss, D. Krausar, Jerusalem 1966.

R. Yeshaya I of Trani, *Sefer Hamakhria'* ספר המכריע, Livorno 1779.

R. Yeshaya II, *Pisqé RIAZ* פסקי ריא״ז, printed with *Pisqé RYD*.

R. Yona Gerondi, *Commentary on Pirqe Abot*, in the Wilna *Talmud* edition.

R. Yosef Gicatilla, *Commentary on the Haggadah*, also attributed to R. Shelomo ben Adrat, Jerusalem 1967.

R. Ẓidqiah ben Abraham Harofe, *Shibbolé Haleqeṭ* שבלי הלקט, ed. S. Bóber, Wilna 1887.

Sefer Hazohar ספר הזהר, Wilna (Mantua) ed., reprint Jerusalem 1970.

Talmid R. Yonah Gerondi תלמיד רבנו יונה, in all editions of *Alfassi Berakhot*.

Tanya Rabbati תניא רבתי, ed. S. Horovitz, Warszawa 1869.

Tiqquné Zohar תקוני זהר, ed. R. Margaliut, 2nd ed., Jerusalem 1978.

Fourteenth Century

R. Abraham Hacohen of Lunel, *Orḥot Ḥayyim* ספר ארחות חיים, Firenze 1754.

R. Abraham Hacohen of Lunel, *Kol Bo* כל בו, reprint Tel Aviv, n.d.

R. David ben Yosef Abudirham, *Abudirham Hashalem* ספר אבודרהם השלם, Jerusalem 1980.

R. Meïr Hacohen, *Hagahot Maimuniot* הגהות מיימוניות, in most editions of Maimonides, *Mishneh Torah*.

R. Mordokhai ben Hillel, *Sefer Mordokhai* ספר המרדכי, in most editions of *Alfassi*.

R. Shalom of Wiener Neustadt, *Hilkhot MaHaRaSH* הלכות מהר״ש, Jerusalem 1980.

R. Ya'aqov ben Asher, *Ṭur* טור, Wilna ed., reprint Jerusalem 1960.

Sefer Amarkal ליקוטים מהלכות מועדים מספר אמרכל, ed. J. Freimann, reprint Jerusalem 1976.

Fifteenth Century

R. Abraham Klausner, *Minhagim* ספר מנהגים, ed. Y. Y. Dissin, Jerusalem 1978.

R. Eisik Tyrna, *Sefer Haminhagim* ספר המנהגים, ed. S. Y. Spitzer, Jerusalem 1979.

R. Israel Isserlein, *Terumat Hadeshen* ספר תרומת הדשן, Bene Berak 1971.

R. Shimon ben Ẓemaḥ Duran, *Commentary on the Haggadah*, in Passover *Haggadah*, Rödelheim 1822.

R. Ya'aqov Molin Segal, *Sefer MaHaRIL* ספר מהרי״ל, collected by Zalman of St. Goar; ed. S. Y. Spitzer, Jerusalem 1989.

R. Ya'aqov Weilla, *Sheëlot uTeshuvot MaHaRIW* שו״ת מהרי״ו, Jerusalem 1959.

R. Yosef ben Ḥabiba, *Nimmuqe Yosef Pesaḥim* נמוקי יוסף פסחים, ed. M. Y. Blau, New York 1960.

R. Yosef ben Moshe, *Leqet Yosher* לקט יושר, ed. J. Freimann, Berlin 1903.

R. Zeliqman Bingo, *MaHaRaZ Bingo* חידושי מהר״ז בינגא, ed. B. Z. Neusatz, M. H. Neyman, I. M. Fels, Jerusalem 1985.

Sixteenth Century

Elias Levita, Notes to *Sefer Hashorashim*, printed with *Sefer Hashorashim.*

Rabbinic Bible מקראות גדולות, Venice 1547,1568.

R. Ḥayyim Viṭal Calabrese, *Oẓrot Ḥayyim* אוצרות חיים, Frankfurt am Main 1772.

R. Ḥayyim Viṭal Calabrese, *Peri Eẓ Ḥayyim* פרי עץ חיים, in *Writings of ARI*, vols. 13–14, Jerusalem 1987.

R. Izḥaq Abarbanel, *Commentary on the Haggadah*, in Passover *Haggadah*, Amsterdam 1695.

R. Mordokhai Yaffe, *Levush Mordokhai* לבוש מרדכי, Prague 1623.

R. Moshe Isserles, *Darke Moshe* דרכי משה, in all editions of *Ṭur*.

R. Shelomo ben Yeḥiel Lurie, *Amudé Shelomo (Notes to Sefer Miẓwot Gadol)* ספר עמודי שלמה, Jerusalem 1962.

R. Shelomo ben Yeḥiel Lurie, *Responsa MaHaRSHaL* שו״ת מהרש״ל, Lemberg 1859.

R. Yosef Karo, *Bet Yosef* בית יוסף, in all editions of *Ṭur*.

R. Yosef Karo, *Shulḥan 'Arukh* שלחן ערוך, Wilna ed., reprint Jerusalem 1954.

Seventeenth Century

R. Abraham Gumbinner, *Magen Avraham* מגן אברהם, in *Shulḥan 'Arukh.*

R. Eliahu Tiktin, *Notes to Levush Mordokhai*, Prague 1623.

R. Joel Sirkes, *Bayit Ḥadash, BaḤ* בית חדש, in all editions of *Ṭur*.

R. Yedidya Shelomo Rafaël Norzi, *Minḥat Shai* מנחת שי, in *Miqraöt Gedolot.*

R. Yeḥiel Hillėl Altshuler, *Meẓudat Ẓiyon (Lexical notes on Prophets and Hagiographs)* מצודת ציון, in *Miqraöt Gedolot.*

R. Yehushua Falk Katz, *Perisha* פרישה, in all editions of *Ṭur*.

R. Yehuda Löw ben Beẓalel, MaHaRaL of Prague, *Gevurot Hashem* גבורות השם, Commentary on the *Haggadah* collected from his writings, Judaica Press, New York 1969.

R. Yeshaya ben Abraham Horovitz, *Shene Luḥot Haberit, SheLaH* שני לוחות הברית, reprint, n. d.

R. YomTov Lipman Heller Wallerstein, *Ma'adané YomTov* מעדני יום טוב, printed with *ROSH Berakhot.*

R. Yosef Yospe Hahn Nörlingen, *Yosif 'Omeẓ* יוסיף עומץ, Frankfurt am Main 1928.

Yospe Shammes, *Minhagé Warmaisha* מנהגים דק״ק וורמי״שא, Jerusalem 1992.

Eighteenth Century

R. Eliahu of Wilna, *Commentary on the Haggadah*, reprint, n. d.

R. Eliahu of Wilna, *Notes on the Shulḥan 'Arukh* ביאורי הגאון ר״א ז״ל, printed with *Shulḥan Arukh.*

R. Moshe Ḥagiz, *Shte Haleḥem* שתי הלחם, Wandsbeck 1726.

R. Shalom Mizraḥi Didia' Shar'abi, *Nahar Shalom* נהר שלום, Jerusalem 1988.

R. Ya'akov Rischer, *Ḥoq Ya'aqov* חק יעקב, in Wilna ed. of *Shulḥan 'Arukh.*

R. Yeḥezq'el Landau, *Ẓiyyun Lenefesh Ḥayyah, ZeLaḤ* צל״ח, Prague 1767.

R. Yehuda Ashkenazi, *Beër Hetev* באר היטב, in most eds. of *Shulḥan 'Arukh.*

R. Yehuda Leib of Horodec, *Kabbalistic Commentary on the Haggadah* פירוש א״פ הסוד, in Passover *Haggadah*, Offenbach 1722.

R. Yosef Yospe Koschmann, *Noheg Kaẓon Yosef* נוהג כצאן יוסף, Frankfurt am Main 1718.

Nineteenth Century

R. Yeḥiel Michel Halevi Epstein, *'Arukh Hashulḥan* ערוך השלחן, Warszawa 1883 ff.

R. Jacob Jokeb Ettlinger, *Passover Haggadah Minḥat 'Ani* הגדת מנחת עני, Jerusalem 1973.

R. Meïr Friedmann, *Meïr 'Ayyin* מאיר עין, Wien 1895.

R. Israel Meïr Kagan, *Mishnah Berurah* משנה ברורה, Warszawa 1883.

R. Meïr Lebush Malbim, *Commentary on the Haggadah*, reprint Tel Aviv 1967.

R. Rafael N. Rabbinovicz, *Diqduqé Soferim* דקדוקי סופרים, München 1867–1886.

R. Shneur Zalman of Lyadi, *Shulḥan 'Arukh Harav*, שולחן ערוך מכבוד הרב שניאור זלמן, Warsaw 1840.

Twentieth Century

R. Abraham Bornstein, Responsa *Avne Nezer*, שו״ת אבני נזר, Piotrkow 1912.

R. Ezra Reuben Dangoor, *'Adi Zahav* עדי זהב, Jerusalem 1987.

R. David Feinstein, *Kol Dodi Haggadah*, Brooklyn 1990.

R. Z. D. Hoffmann, *Responsa* שו"ת מלמד להועיל, vol. 3, Berlin 1930.

R. A. I. Hakohen Kook, *Siddur 'Olat RAIAH* סדור עולת ראי"ה, Jerusalem 1925.

R. H. D. Levi, *Meqor Ḥayyim Hashalem* מקור חיים השלם, Jerusalem, n. d.

R. Y. Y. Neuwirth, *On the Laws of Passover* בהלכות פסח, Moriah 18, 1992/3, fasc. 5/6, pp. 91-94.

R. H. Y. Scheftel, *Glossary of Talmudic Coins, Measures, Weights, and Times*, ערך מילין למטבעות, מדות, משקלות, וזמנים, Berdichev 1907.

R. I. Schepensky, *Ordinances in Israel* התקנות בישראל, New York-Jerusalem 1991.

R. Jacob Ḥayyim Soffer, *Kaf Haḥayyim* כף החיים, 8 vols., Jerusalem, n. d.

Modern Scholarship

Albeck, H., "Die vierte Eulogie des Tischgebets," *Monatsschrift für Geschichte und Wissenschaft des Judentums* 73 (1934): 430 ff.

ANET, *Ancient Near Eastern Texts Relating to the Old Testament*, ed. J. B. Pritchard, 2nd ed., Princeton 1955.

Bacher, W., *Der galiläische Am-Haarez*. Hebrew translation עם הארץ הגלילי. Jerusalem 1966.

Ben-Iehuda, Eliezer, *Thesaurus totius Hebraitatis*, 2nd ed., Jerusalem 1935 ff.

Elbogen, Ismar, *Der jüdische Gottesdienst in seiner geschichtlichen Entwicklung*. Hebrew translation התפילה בישראל בהתפתחותה ההיסטורית, notes by J. Heinemann, Tel Aviv 1972.

Finkelstein, Louis, "The Oldest Midrash: Pre-rabbinic Ideals and Teachings in the Passover *Haggadah*," *Harvard Theological Review* 31 (1938): 291–317.

Finkelstein, Louis. "Pre-Maccabean Documents in the Passover *Haggadah*," *Harvard Theological Review* 38 (1943): 1–21.

Finkelstein, Louis, "The Birkat Hamazon," *Jewish Quarterly Review*, *N.S.* 19 (1927): 211-261.

Gesenius, W., *Hebräisches und Aramäisches Handwörterbuch über das alte Testament*, ed. F. Buhl, 14th ed., Leipzig 1905.

Gil, M., *Palestine During the First Muslim Period*, Tel Aviv 1983.

Ginzberg, Louis, *Genizah Studies in Memory of Doctor Solomon Schechter* גנזי שכטר, New York 1929.

Ginzberg, Louis, *A Commentary on the Palestinian* Talmud, פירושים וחדושים בירושלמי, New York 1941-1961.

Goldschmidt, Daniel, *Passover* Haggadah, הגדה של פסח, Jerusalem 1969.

Goldschmidt, Daniel, *Researches about Prayer and Synagogal Poetry* מחקרי תפילה ופיוט, Jerusalem 1979.

Greenfield, A. Y., "The Connection Between the Measures of Olive and Egg," הקשר בין שיעור כזית וכביצה. תחומין 14 (5754,1994): 396–411.

Guggenheimer, H., "Logical Problems in Jewish Tradition," in: *Confrontations with Judaism*, ed. P. Longworth. London 1967, pp. 171–196.

Guggenheimer, H., *Seder 'Olam* סדר עולם, New York 1987.

Guggenheimer, H., "A Jewish Fundamentalist Philosophy of Science and Development," *Association F. Gonseth, Institut de la Méthode, Bulletin* 63 (1992): 9–20.

Gumpertz, Y. F., *Studies in Historical Phonetics of the Hebrew Language* מבטאי שׂפתינו, Jerusalem 1953.

Heinemann, J., *Prayer in the Talmudic Period* התפילה בתקופת התנאים והאמוראים, 2nd ed., Jerusalem 1966.

Heinemann, J., *Studies in Prayer* עיוני תפילה, Jerusalem 1981.

Haberman, A. M., "Poetic Forms of Grace." ידיעות המכון לחקר השירה העברית, vol. 5, 1939, pp. 43–105.

Jastrow, M., *A Dictionary of the* Targumim, *the* Talmud Babli *and* Yerushalmi, *and the Midrashic Literature*, reprint New York 1950.

Kahle, P., *Masoreten des Ostens*, Leipzig 1913.

Kasher, M. M., *Complete Haggadah* הגדה שלמה, Jerusalem 1967.

Krauss, S., *Griechische und lateinische Lehnwörter in* Talmud, Midrasch *and* Targum, Berlin 1899.

Kutscher, Y. E., *The Language and Linguistic Background of the Isaiah Scroll*, Jerusalem 1959.

Levin, B. M., *Ozar Hageönim* אוצר הגאונים, Haifa 1928–Jerusalem 1943.

Levy, J., *Wörterbuch über die* Talmudim *und* Midraschim, 2nd ed., reprint Darmstadt 1963.

Lewy, Israel., "Ein Vortrag über das Ritual des Pessachabends." *Jahresbericht des jüdisch-theologischen Seminars Fraenckel'scher Stiftung*, Breslau 1907.

Lieberman, S., *Tosefta kifshutah* תוספתא כפשוטה, New York 1955-1988.

Liebreich, L J., "Aspects of the New Year Liturgy," *HUCA* XXIV (1943): 125–176.

Lifschitz, B., *Donateurs et fondateurs dans les synagogues juives*, Cahiers revue biblique 7, 1967.

Pope, M., *Song of Songs*, Anchor Bible, Garden City 1977.

Razhavi, Y., "New poetic versions of Grace, ברכות-המזון מפוייטות חדשות," *Sinai* 108 (1991): 193–231.

Sperber, H., "Hebrew based upon Greek and Latin transliterations," *HUCA* XII-XIII (1937–38): 238.

Zeitlin, S., "The Liturgy of the First Night of Passover," *Jewish Quarterly Review N.S.* 38 (1948): 431-460.

Haggadot

The text of the *Haggadah* has been established from the following *Haggadot*:

Ashkenazic version

Printed *Haggadot* from Prague 1526, Mantua 1561, Amsterdam 1662, 1695, Frankfurt 1710, Offenbach 1722, Fuerth 1741, Sulzbach 1755, Berlin 1795, Rödelheim 1822, Halberstadt 1878.

Italian version

Maḥzor Roma, Bologna 1540, and Venice 1609.

Sephardic versions

Printed editions Venice 1716, Livorno 1825 (Saadun), Livorno *Maḥzor* (Benamozegh), Bombay 1846, Livorno (Baghdad ritual) 1867, Djerba 1938, Jerusalem (Kurdistan ritual) 1986.

Yemenite version

Printed *Tiqlāl* Jerusalem 1959, several manuscript *Haggadot*; *Agadta dePisḥa* ed J. Hasid, Jerusalem 1967; *Haggadah* ed. Jacob Qirwani, Rosh-Ha'ayin 1984.

Index of Biblical and Talmudic Sources

Talmud

General Index

Heinrich Guggenheimer

Heinrich W. Guggenheimer is professor emeritus of Polytechnic University (formerly Polytechnic Institute of Brooklyn), where he taught mathematics and also Jewish studies in the Department of Humanities. He received his M.S. and Sc.D. degrees from the Swiss Federal Institute of Technology in Zurich and his Jewish training at the Bet Hamidrash of Basel, Switzerland. He also taught at Hebrew University, Bar-Ilan University, Washington State University, and the University of Minnesota. He has published over 150 research papers in mathematics and Talmud and is the author of *Differential Geometry* (1963, 1977), *Plane Geometry and Its Groups* (1967), *Mathematics for Scientists and Engineers* (1976), *Applicable Geometry* (1977), *BASIC Mathematical Programs for Engineers and Scientists* (1987), *Seder Olam* (1987, in Hebrew), and, together with his wife, Dr. Eva H. Guggenheimer, *Jewish Family Names and Their Origins: An Etymological Dictionary* (1992). He currently teaches a daily class in Talmud at Congregation Anshei Shalom, West Hempstead, New York.